IFIP Advances in Information and Communication Technology

657

Editor-in-Chief

Kai Rannenberg, Goethe University Frankfurt, Germany

IFIP – The International Federation for Information Processing

IFIP was founded in 1960 under the auspices of UNESCO, following the first World Computer Congress held in Paris the previous year. A federation for societies working in information processing, IFIP's aim is two-fold: to support information processing in the countries of its members and to encourage technology transfer to developing nations. As its mission statement clearly states:

IFIP is the global non-profit federation of societies of ICT professionals that aims at achieving a worldwide professional and socially responsible development and application of information and communication technologies.

IFIP is a non-profit-making organization, run almost solely by 2500 volunteers. It operates through a number of technical committees and working groups, which organize events and publications. IFIP's events range from large international open conferences to working conferences and local seminars.

The flagship event is the IFIP World Computer Congress, at which both invited and contributed papers are presented. Contributed papers are rigorously refereed and the rejection rate is high.

As with the Congress, participation in the open conferences is open to all and papers may be invited or submitted. Again, submitted papers are stringently refereed.

The working conferences are structured differently. They are usually run by a working group and attendance is generally smaller and occasionally by invitation only. Their purpose is to create an atmosphere conducive to innovation and development. Refereeing is also rigorous and papers are subjected to extensive group discussion.

Publications arising from IFIP events vary. The papers presented at the IFIP World Computer Congress and at open conferences are published as conference proceedings, while the results of the working conferences are often published as collections of selected and edited papers.

IFIP distinguishes three types of institutional membership: Country Representative Members, Members at Large, and Associate Members. The type of organization that can apply for membership is a wide variety and includes national or international societies of individual computer scientists/ICT professionals, associations or federations of such societies, government institutions/government related organizations, national or international research institutes or consortia, universities, academies of sciences, companies, national or international associations or federations of companies.

More information about this series at https://link.springer.com/bookseries/6102

Yingqin Zheng · Pamela Abbott ·
Jose Antonio Robles-Flores (Eds.)

Freedom and Social Inclusion in a Connected World

17th IFIP WG 9.4 International Conference on
Implications of Information and Digital
Technologies for Development, ICT4D 2022
Lima, Peru, May 25–27, 2022
Proceedings

 Springer

Editors
Yingqin Zheng 🆔
Royal Holloway University of London
Egham, UK

Pamela Abbott 🆔
The University of Sheffield
Sheffield, UK

Jose Antonio Robles-Flores 🆔
ESAN University
Lima, Peru

ISSN 1868-4238   ISSN 1868-422X (electronic)
IFIP Advances in Information and Communication Technology
ISBN 978-3-031-19431-3   ISBN 978-3-031-19429-0 (eBook)
https://doi.org/10.1007/978-3-031-19429-0

This Springer imprint is published by the registered company Springer Nature Switzerland AG
The registered company address is: Gewerbestrasse 11, 6330 Cham, Switzerland

Preface

This book consists of the 17th IFIP WG 9.4 conference proceedings (ICT4D 2022). The theme of the conference was "Freedom and Social Inclusion in a Connected World". The conference was originally scheduled to take place in May 2021 in Lima, Peru. Due to the COVID-19 pandemic that started in 2020, with Peru being one of the worst affected countries, the conference had to be held online, despite having been postponed by one year.

The pandemic is not only a public health crisis. Deep-seated inequalities and tensions have been unveiled and magnified under COVID-19 across different social, institutional, and cultural contexts, including in the most advanced economies. Digital connection has never been more profoundly implicated in the freedom and wellbeing of individuals as societies face the challenge of a severe pandemic. New theories, concepts, and philosophical perspectives are needed to shed light on the digital challenges in an increasingly complex and precarious world.

It was at this disruptive, historical moment that the call for papers for ICT4D 2022 was issued. Authors were invited to examine the role of digital technology in relation to diverse forms of exclusion, marginalization, and vulnerabilities, and to investigate the intersections between technology and various systems of power in the uneven landscape of development.

The virtual conference consisted of 13 tracks as listed below, including two foreign language tracks in Spanish and Portuguese respectively, and a track dedicated to Research in Progress papers.

1. Digital Platforms
2. Government Corruption, ICTs, and the Quest for Inclusion
3. Human-Computer Interaction for Ethical Value Exchange and Social Inclusion
4. Digital Entrepreneurship for Development
5. Digital Resilience in Adversity
6. Artificial Intelligence, Inequalities, and Human Rights
7. Pushing Boundaries - New and Innovative Philosophical, Theoretical and Methodological Approaches to Researching ICT4D
8. Reimagining Digital Technology for the "New Normal": A Feminist Approach to Freedom and Social Inclusion
9. Digital Rights and Activism
10. ICT in Displacement and Conflict Zones: Ideas, Disconnects, and Innovations
11. Research in Spanish
12. Research in Portuguese
13. Research in Progress

It was encouraging to see some topic areas developing in this year's IFIP WG 9.4 conference, such as the tracks on feminist approaches, artificial intelligence, and digital rights and activism. In total, 58 papers were submitted, 41 were accepted and presented at the conference, and 40 papers were included in this published version of the proceedings.

Out of the 40 papers accepted in this volume, 3 are short papers. Each paper was reviewed in a double-blind process by at least 2 reviewers.

The keynote speaker of the conference was Tim Unwin, UNESCO Chair in ICT4D, who gave a talk on "Freedom, enslavement and the digital barons: A thought experiment". It is also important to mention the thought-provoking discussions led by the five very interesting panels, all of which were closely linked to the conference theme although not included in the proceedings:

- Freedom and Social Inclusion in a Connected World
  Panelists: Dorothea Kleine, Yingqin Zheng, Kirstin Krauss, Sundeep Sahay

  Moderator: Pamela Abbott
- Differential Privileges Shaping ICT4D: Intersectional Analysis of Implications for Theory, Policy, and Practice
  Panelists: Tony Sandset, Susan Scott, Pitso Tsibolane, Tendani Chimboza

  Moderator: Arunima Sehgal Mukherjee
- Artificial Intelligence for Freedom and Social Inclusion? Limits and Possibilities in the Global South
  Panelists: Carla Bonina, Fabrizio Scrollini, Maria Esther Cervantes, Javiera Atenas, Renata Avila

  Moderator: Carla Bonina
- Mediated Activism: Clicks for Justice and Freedom
  Panelists: Paridhi Gupta, Ashique Ali T, Çağdaş Dedeoğlu

  Moderator: Priyank Chandra
- Feminist and Queer Approaches to Technological Resistance in the Global South
  Panelists: Azadeh Akbari, Margaret Cheesman, Silvia Masiero, Ayushi Tandon, Katherine Wyers

  Moderators: Azadeh Akbari, Margaret Cheesman

We are grateful for the insightful contributions of the panelists as much as the presented papers. We hope to see the perspectives and exchanges from the conference papers and panels, as well as those taking place in virtual roundtables and meetup groups, further developed and fed into a more open, vibrant, and critical discourse of ICT4D.

Yingqin Zheng
Pamela Abbott
Jose-Antonio Robles-Flores

Organization

Conference Chairs

Antonio Diaz-Andrade   Auckland University of Technology, New Zealand
Martin Santana   Universidad ESAN, Peru

Program Chairs

Yingqin Zheng   Royal Holloway, University of London, UK
Pamela Abbott   University of Sheffield, UK
Jose-Antonio Robles-Flores   Universidad ESAN, Peru

Program Committee

Jose Abdelnour Nocera   University of West London, UK
Atta Addo   University of Surrey, UK
Evronia Azer   Coventry University, UK
Rehema Baguma   Makerere University, Uganda
Tanja Bosch   University of Cape Town, South Africa
Suzana Brown   SUNY Korea, South Korea
Alexandre R. Graeml   Federal University of Technology - Paraná, Brazil
Anita Gurumurthy   IT for Change, India
Richard Heeks   University of Manchester, UK
Faheem Hussain   Arizona State University, USA
Vigneswara Ilavarasan   IIT Delhi, India
Andrea Jimenez   University of Sheffield, UK
Caroline Khene   De Montfort University, UK
Endrit Kromidha   University of Birmingham, UK
David Lamas   Tallinn University, Estonia
Silvia Masiero   Loughborough University, UK
Brian Nicholson   University of Manchester, UK
Petter Nielsen   University of Oslo, Norway
Adebowale Owoseni   De Montfort University, UK
Tony Roberts   Institute of Development Studies, UK
Guillermo Rodriguez-Abitia   College of William and Mary, USA
P. K. Senyo   University of Southampton, UK
Tenace Setor   University of Omaha, USA
John Shawe-Taylor   University College London, UK
Matthew Smith   International Development Research Centre, Canada
Aurora Sánchez   Universidad Católica del Norte, Chile
Johan Sæbø   University of Oslo, Norway

Angsana Techatassanasoontorn	Auckland University of Technology, New Zealand
Devinder Thapa	University of Agder, Norway
Mamello Thinyane	United Nations University Institute in Macau, Macao, China
Michaelanne Thomas	University of Michigan, USA
Sara Vannini	University of Sheffield, UK
Kutoma Wakunuma	De Montfort University, UK
P. J. Wall	Trinity College Dublin, Ireland
Marisol Wong-Villacres	Escuela Superior Politecnica del Litoral, Ecuador

Contents

Artificial Intelligence, Inequalities, and Human Rights

**Pushing Boundaries - New and Innovative Philosophical,
Theoretical and Methodological Approaches to Researching ICT4D**

Reimagining Digital Technology for the "New Normal": A Feminist Approach to Freedom and Social Inclusion

Digital Rights and Activism

ICT in Displacement and Conflict Zones: Ideas, Disconnects, and Innovations

Research in Progress

Digital Platforms

Leveraging Government Digital Platforms in Resource-Constrained Countries: Micro-foundations of Woredas in Ethiopia

Debas Senshaw[✉] [iD]

ICT 4D Research Center, Bahir Dar Institute of Technology, Bahir Dar University, Bahir Dar, Ethiopia
debassenshaw@gmail.com

Abstract. The purpose of this paper is to identify the micro-foundations of Woredas in Ethiopia that digitally innovate on the existing government digital platform. The study used a qualitative interpretive case study strategy with three government administrative regions in Ethiopia (called Woredas) that innovate digitally using the government digital platform. To collect data, a structured interview protocol was used. From each of the Woredas (districts), five respondents were chosen to represent users, ICT staff, and management, making a total of 15 respondents. The findings show that the digital platform governance model plays the most important role in digital government innovation. Woredas demonstrate sensing capabilities by learning from the affordances provided by the digital platform. Furthermore, despite the joint nature of their seizing capabilities, no clear organizational structures exist to manifest these capabilities. The governance model, which is centralized in one ICT unit, limits the reconfiguring capabilities.

Keywords: Government digital platforms · Digital platforms · Micro-foundations

1 Introduction

Digital platforms play a significant role in facilitating social networking and creating economic values [1, 2]. Many citizen-government collaboration activities such as voting and participatory policymaking are encouraged by digital platforms [3–6]. The majority of digital platforms share several key features [7]. First, they are technologically mediated. Second, they allow users to communicate with one another. Third, users of digital platforms can perform specific activities. As such, the services provided by digital platforms allow interaction among service consumers and producers [1, 7]. Many low-income countries' digital platforms have lately been enhanced [8].

Improvements in digital platforms that use digital innovation have been shown to notably improve the socio-economic activities of low-income countries [9–11]. Digital innovation in a low-income country may be deemed commonplace in a high-income

Y. Zheng et al. (Eds.): ICT4D 2022, IFIP AICT 657, pp. 3–23, 2022.
https://doi.org/10.1007/978-3-031-19429-0_1

country. Nonetheless, the fundamental thesis of digital innovation remains the development of new products, services, or organizational models through the use of digital platforms [12–14]. In this study, digital innovation refers to the use of the government's digital platform to improve government service delivery. The government of Ethiopia uses the digital platform to provide civil servants with access to government-restricted information and access to content available on the Internet in different sectors such as education, health, agriculture, and governance.

Despite the improvement of digital platforms in resource-constrained countries, the digital development index remains stumpy mainly in Africa [15–18]. The existence of a well-defined digital platform does not ensure its utilization or innovation [19, 20]. Unreliable Internet access, digital illiteracy, a digital divide among users, and the use of the platform by individuals with impairments have all been mentioned as barriers to digital adoption [4, 6, 19–21].

Government digital platform is expected to enhance government performance by lowering costs, increasing revenue, and lowering transaction costs [18, 22]. It is considered a way to improve government and public administration performance, as well as a requirement for economic and social growth, particularly for resource-constrained countries. Social and economic growth are particularly crucial in low-income countries like Ethiopia, where governmental administration is defined by incompetence, limited capacity, and inadequately trained personnel [23, 24]. For instance, Digital platforms based on the local context, such as m-pesa, have been found to have a higher rate of acceptance in resource-constrained countries than platforms taken from other settings [25].

The focus of this study is to understand how Woredas in Ethiopia are using existing digital platforms innovatively. Ethiopia's government created a digital platform that allows various government agencies to integrate data transfers and receive government services. Ethiopia established the government digital platform in 2007. This digital platform is a transaction platform [26] that was designed for the exchange of digital data among government organizations and was mainly created to provide government services to the lowest administrative regions called Woredas. "Woreda" is an Amharic term that refers to an administrative region consisting of about 100,000 people. It's meaning is similar to that of a district. Ethiopia is Africa's second-largest country, with 112,078,730 people [27] and Africa's tenth-largest country with 1,104,300 km^2. 976 (93%) of the 1,050 Woredas have access to the government digital platform. Despite significant investments, only a few Woredas are using the digital platform to innovate government services [28].

The micro-foundations of dynamic capacities (DCs) include cognitive abilities to scan opportunities or uncover prospects, grab chances and/or minimize risks, and restructure or reshuffle the internal resources of government agencies [29]. When government organizations constantly sense and seize opportunities, and reallocate or realign their internal resource to adapt to the agile environment, they generate DCs [30]. The repetitive action of sensing, seizing, and reconfiguring capabilities enable government organizations to transform their business model to be efficient and effective in their routine activities.

Although dynamic capabilities framework (DCF) initially emerged from the perspective of strategic management to make private organizations more competitive, government organizations have also begun to consider the framework as a means to create new government services driven by digital technology. This is because both government and private organizations have similar organizational features such as resources, routines, and capabilities but with different purposes [31–33]. The following are some of the rationale why dynamic capability theory was selected for this research: first, dynamic capability theory considers digital platforms as a central constituent of innovative use of resources, and second, dynamic capability theory switches the focus from resource holdings to resource creativity, which is critical in resource-strapped low-income countries. Additionally, the dynamic capability theory has also been adopted to make sense of resource-constrained countries' digital innovation [34–36]. However, little research has been carried out on the micro-foundations of dynamic capabilities that support digital platforms in resource-constrained countries [37].

The study's goal was to learn about the micro-foundations of local government administrative areas, known as Woredas in Ethiopia, and how these Woredas innovate using the existing government digital platform. Therefore, this research work thought answer the following research question: *How can micro-foundations of dynamic capabilities of government organizations that can leverage the usage of government digital platforms be identified?*

The following is how the rest of the paper is structured: A review of the literature on digital platforms and micro-foundations of dynamic capabilities is provided in the next section. Following this, a description of the government digital platform, and materials and method section are explained. The data analysis and results are then provided, accompanied by a discussion of the findings. Finally, the conclusion, limitations, and future research directions are discussed.

2 Literature Review

2.1 Digital Platforms

The concept of digital platforms is continuously growing, and it's often described in terms of context [1, 38]. Digital platforms are socio-technical frameworks that integrate data, services, technologies, and users to impact community interests [39, 40].

The most significant variations among digital platforms are their market capitalization, sector of operation, and governance methods [7]. The governance technique identifies who is in charge of making platform decisions. The sector in which the platform is created has an impact on the platform's design and administration. Market capitalization is influenced by the ownership structure in which the platform should aim for profit or welfare maximization.

Digital platforms are useful since they lower expenses such as distribution, searching, contracting, and monitoring [4, 40, 41]. Aggregation platforms, such as TripAdvisor and Expedia, compile travel data from a variety of sources into a single platform, reducing the cost of finding information. Online platforms also offer a technical development environment [42–44].

Another quality of digital platforms is their ability to generate innovative ideas [44, 45] and also cross-side network effects [46, 47]. Generativity refers to a platform's potential to produce novel outcomes as a result of big and diversified users [48, 49]. By harnessing the contributions of a large group of people, crowd sourcing, for example, leads to the creation of innovative approaches to solving complex problems. Cross-side network effects show how a user's worth rises as the number of users on the opposite side rises. For instance, when there are more buyers on the other side of eBay or Amazon transactions, the usefulness of the digital platform for the seller grows, and conversely.

However, to implement digital platforms in low-income countries, organizational, cultural, and administrative factors must be taken into account [50]. Due to differences in administrative and cultural aspects, a mere transfer of digital platform ideas does not work in low-income countries[51]. This is because there is a possibility that the solutions would be abused by bureaucratic elites. This could result in corruption, centralism, and inefficiency. To put it another way, a context-based strategy is a more practical method for implementing digital platforms in low-income nations[25, 52].

In addition to being addressed as products, digital platforms are also regarded as ecosystems. Digital platforms, according to the product-oriented approach, are physical goods developed via the engineering of architectural designs, in which economies of scale and scope can be realized through the reuse of components [44, 53–55]. From an ecosystem viewpoint, platforms are considered as a system of business centers that manage and organize interactions across enterprises [42, 44, 56]. This study considers an ecosystem approach, where a government digital platform is used to provide government services and enable an exchange of data and information among government organizations.

2.2 Micro-foundations of Organization's Dynamic Capabilities

Dynamic capabilities are an organization's ability to reconfigure and recombine its internal resources to improve organizational performance [56–59]. In unexpected and dynamic situations, the DCF emphasizes the effective and strategic use of available organizational resources, both physical and nonphysical, to achieve an organizational purpose [59, 60].

Dynamic capabilities enable an organization to implement plans and strategies in novel ways that improve its effectiveness and efficiency [61, 62]. The primary concern in dynamic capability theory is the utilization of existing and available internal resources rather than the acquisition of additional resources [63, 64]. Dynamic capabilities aid in the investigation of not only the non-infrastructural resources required, but also how internal resources are constantly restructured and reused for organizational effectiveness and efficiency [59, 60, 65]. Dynamic capabilities are characterized by the ability to adapt to changing external environments and reinvent existing routines [59, 66, 67]. Dynamic capabilities can lead to greater social and economic progress in low-income countries by allowing them to make better use of their limited resources [68, 69].

Micro-foundations are associated with tacit knowledge and are inbuilt organizational intangible elements. These intangible aspects such as processes, procedures, managerial cognition, and knowledge are known as the micro-foundations of dynamic capabilities [70]. Organizational structures, distinctive competences, decision rules, and disciplines are also micro-foundations of dynamic capabilities, and these micro-foundations can be divided into three interconnected concepts: sensing, seizing and reconfiguring [70]. The micro-foundations of an organization are facilitators of dynamic capabilities and are discussed in the following section.

2.2.1 Sensing

Sensing activity is the primary and fundamental activity to which organizations should pay close attention to discover new opportunities and be aware of unexpected threats. Sensing activity can be defined as scanning the condition or tendency of the environment in search of information from stakeholders and customers. Sensing is accomplished by learning or interpreting available information and new data [71]. This activity allows not only to discover existing opportunities but also to create new ones. Organizations need to implement this opportunity systematically. According to the literature, it is the management body's responsibility to carry out this activity by filtering the important and relevant information [72].

SQ1: How do Woredas that digitally innovate using government digital platform manifest their sensing capabilities?

2.2.2 Seizing

The seizing activity follows the sensing activity. Developing a business model, recognizing resource needs, making proper decisions about technology and resource investments, and lastly guiding and leading people to implement the required changes are all part of seizing activities. Making a significant change in decision making, as well as formulating and designing a new business model, are examples of seizing activity. According to research works, organizational decision-making is a complex process that requires several steps to be functional [72]. This is owing to the fact that numerous functional areas are involved in decision-making. To make decision-making easier, these cross-functional areas should be emphasized [58].

SQ2: How do Woredas that digitally innovate using government digital platform manifest their seizing capabilities?

2.2.3 Reconfiguring

After seizing an opportunity, an organization's resources should be constantly reconfigured. The reconfiguring activity entails rearranging, reallocating, and realigning resources to increase the organization's value. The reconfiguring activity enables the organization to respond to changing circumstances. To complete this activity, it is essential to change the structure of an organization, manage strategy fit, and ensure incentive alignments. To put it another way, organizations should have a loosely coupled structure to foster innovation. A strategic fit necessitates the allocation of assets and other resources to increase or improve the organization's value. Incentives should be set up in such a way that the organization's performance or improvement is guaranteed.

Managerial and organizational processes can both benefit from restructuring activity. Reconfiguring the managerial process entails activities such as improving communication between managers, whereas reconfiguring the organizational process entails activities such as reallocating resources to maintain effectiveness and efficiency.

SQ3: How do Woredas that digitally innovate using government digital platform manifest their reconfiguring capabilities?

3 The Government Digital Platform in Ethiopia

As any of digital platforms it is essential to describe the purpose, governance arrangement and geographical location of the government digital platform in Ethiopia [7]. Regarding its purpose, the government digital platform is an Ethiopian district-based government digital platform. Broadband, terrestrial, and satellite networks connect the lowest levels of government [73–75]. Federal, regional, and Woreda-level government entities across the country use the government digital platform to access government services including video conferencing, directory services, mail services, and Internet connectivity [74, 76].

On the other hand, the digital platform is governed by the former Ethiopian ICT Development Agency (EICTDA), now known as the Ministry of Science and Technology (MST). MST is responsible for developing rules and regulations governing how Woredas use the government digital platform. The government digital platform consists of three-tier architecture, namely, the national data centre, regional data centres, and Woreda data centres. The national data centre (NDC) is in charge of centrally managing the government's digital platform, as well as controlling and maintaining infrastructure, organizing the activities of regional and Woreda data centers, and providing support and training. The regional data centers are in charge of managing and controlling services given to government entities in their respective regions, in addition to serving Woreda centers inside their regions. At the most basic level, each Woreda has Woreda centers that provide direct services to Woreda government offices. Each Woreda centre has at least two ICT Staff who are assigned to manage services and provide ICT training to Woreda-level government offices.

Regarding the geographical location of the platform, the National Data Centre (NDC) is in Addis Ababa, Ethiopia's capital, while regional data centers are in each regional state's capital cities; Woreda centers are in each Woreda's main towns. VSAT connects the majority of Woreda's data centers to the national data center. The NDC is the hub of the government's digital platform, which provides all the services.

4 Materials and Method

This study used a qualitative-interpretive research paradigm, which allowed the researchers to investigate digital innovation based on the government digital platform in its natural environment [36, 77, 78]. Qualitative-interpretivism allows for more freedom in conducting in-depth investigations into patterns [79], using inductive reasoning to pay close attention to process, context, interpretation, meaning, or understanding [80]. This method captures the effects of respondents' actions and experiences on a phenomenon of interest without the use of standardized and predetermined response categories [80, 81].

4.1 Data Collection

The data was acquired utilizing a structured interview instrument and a case study research technique.

4.1.1 Interview Selection

Three process owners (those in government agencies who oversee similar processes), one from each government agency, one from ICT support, and a district administrator (or a representative) from each of the three Woredas were selected. There were 15 respondents in total.

4.1.2 Interview Design

The interview questions were developed based on studies on eliciting sensing, seizing, and reconfiguring capabilities [65]. To analyze Woredas' micro-foundations of dynamic capabilities, theoretical notions such as micro-foundations of dynamic capability theory were operationalized into interview questions. Appendix A contains the interview protocol.

4.1.3 Reliability and Validity

Qualitative research's trustworthiness, rigor, and quality are used to describe its reliability and validity [36, 82]. Qualitative research's quality is determined by its credibility, dependability, confirmability, transferability, and authenticity [83]. Credibility refers to the belief in the study's truth and, as a result, the study's findings. The researcher performed in-depth interviews with open-ended inquiries to establish trustworthiness. This method of interviewing enables researchers to gain a deeper grasp of respondents' real-life experiences. The interview protocol was maintained uniformly for all interviews in similar situations. Dependability refers to the data's consistency across the course of the study. The researcher collected data under similar conditions for all interviews. Audio recordings of the interviews were made, and field notes were gathered throughout the procedure. Confirmability refers to the degree to which the results are consistent. The recorded interviews were transcribed into text and returned back to the respondents to confirm that the transcription reflected what they said. Atlas.ti8 was used to collect extensive notes during the analysis. Transferability describes the degree to which findings can be used in different contexts. The research was conducted in three Woredas with similar socio-economic and political environments. Authenticity refers to how accurately and completely researchers depict a variety of various realities and appropriate study participants. The appropriate government entity in the Amhara Regional State selected the sample Woredas. Furthermore, the respondents included a diverse group of civil workers from various levels of management, as well as users and ICT professionals.

4.2 Case Design

Ethiopia has 1,050 Woredas, 976 of which (93%) have access to the government digital platform. Six Woredas were chosen for the study: three that digitally innovate with the government digital platform (the Amhara Regional State, Dangila town, and Woreta town) and three that do not (Bahir Dar town, Bahir Dar Zuria district and Farta). The Amhara Regional State Science, Technology, and Information Communication Commission's ICT management chose the Woredas (STICC). Due to length constraints, this paper examines only the micro-foundations of dynamic capabilities of the three Woredas that digitally innovate with the government digital platform.

Three ICT sample systems of the government digital platform supporting three different government agencies were chosen from each of the Woredas understudies: the judiciary system, human resources (HR) system, and the finance system.

4.2.1 Judiciary (Court) System

Computer-based information and database technologies enhance the court process. At the federal, regional, and Woreda levels, this system hosts court activities such as cases, records, sessions, charges, verdicts, and penalties. Online court services are provided using video conferencing technology. This technology is important primarily in geographically remote districts or locations where citizens with court cases may find it difficult to travel to the judge's residence.

4.2.2 Human Resource Management System

Video conferencing technology is used in the human resource management process to provide employees with timely information and training, particularly in remote areas. This technology saves time that would otherwise be spent traveling from the workplace to the training facility and vice versa. This also lowers training-related travel and administrative expenses.

4.2.3 Finance Management System

The finance management system uses the government digital platform infrastructure to allocate and distribute and process budgets for government organizations at various levels such as federal, regional, and district. For recording, processing, and reporting financial data, the process employs the Integrated Budget and Expenditure (IBEX) system.

5 Data Analysis and Results

Thematic content analysis methods were used in Atlas. ti8 to analyze the interview data.

5.1 Content Analysis Strategy

Thematic analysis is a method of recognizing themes in qualitative data. A sequence of steps is taken into account in the thematic analysis of unstructured data [84]. To elicit the codes and generate categories (themes) from the data content, an inductive approach was used (see Appendices B-D and Appendices E–G). Process coding was chosen because it corresponds to the study's interpretive nature. Because words that end in "ing" frequently indicate actions in data, process coding enabled the identification of action statements in those words. Furthermore, process coding aided in identifying continuous actions or interactions engaged in response to problems [85, 86].

5.2 Results

This section summarizes the findings of the analysis based on the research questions:

5.2.1 Sensing Capabilities

11 unique codes were elicited with a total count of 59. Four themes were further elicited from codes (Table 1).

Table 1. Sensing capabilities of Woredas (from fieldwork)

Sensing capability themes	Sensing capability codes	Frequency
Using email and messaging services (22)	Using multicast video conferencing	4
	Using messaging services	7
	Using email services	11
Using customer online report and customer feedback (18)	Using customer online report	6
	Using feedback of reports	9
	Understanding customer needs	3
Using telephone and fax (14)	Using telephone	8
	Using fax	2
	Using dedicated call centre	4
Using web site and compliant management system (5)	Using complaint management system	1
	Using web site	4
Total		59

According to the themes, Woredas obtain new information from customers and stakeholders via email and messaging services, followed by customer online reports and customer feedback. The use of a website and a compliant management system is less preferred. Several quotes from the interviews show how some Woredas use their sensing capabilities.

"We usually identify threats and opportunities after we collect feedbacks from our customers using our website."(Male, Court service process owner)

"We use email to collect new information from our customers and identify opportunities." (Male, ICT support)

"We are always searching for opportunities while we communicate with our customers via video conferencing."(Male, Human resource management process owner)

5.2.2 Seizing Capabilities

10 Unique codes were elicited with a total count of 28. Four themes were further elicited from codes (Table 2).

Table 2. Seizing capabilities of Woredas (from fieldwork)

Seizing capability themes	Seizing capability codes	Frequency
Learning from experience sharing and research works (12)	Attending online free tutorials	3
	Looking through research works of others	3
	Sharing experience	6
Conducting panel discussion (7)	Inviting external experts	2
	Discussing on new technologies	5
Analysing customer needs and encouraging employees with new ideas (6)	Analysing customer entire business processes	1
	Using feedback of reports	3
	Encouraging employees with new ideas	2
Analysing the appropriateness of technologies(3)	Evaluating the specification of new technologies	2
	Checking the appropriateness of technologies	1
Total		28

Concerning seizing capabilities, the themes suggest that Woredas shape and interpret new information by learning from experience sharing and looking through research works, closely followed by a panel discussion of new technologies, analyzing customer needs, and encouraging employees to come up with new ideas. This procedure is carried out by enlisting the assistance of external experts from companies and universities. The quotations below illustrate the interviewees' seizing capability codes and themes:

"We use online training to interpret and understand new information obtained from stakeholders and customers."(Male, Court service process owner)

"We use the Internet to make decisions on the specifications of new technologies to invest in them." (Female, Finance process owner)

"We use video conferencing to help our branch offices implement new ideas as fast as possible to seize opportunities." (Male, Human resource management process owner)

"We analyze threats associated with new opportunities after we collect information using compliant management system." (Male, ICT support)

5.2.3 Reconfiguring Capabilities

Nine unique codes were elicited with a total count of 38. Five themes were further elicited from codes (Table 3).

Table 3. Reconfiguring capability of Woredas (from fieldwork)

Reconfiguring capability categories	Reconfiguring capability codes	Frequency
Providing incentives (21)	Providing short term training	7
	Applying better salary package	14
Ensuring appropriate use of technologies (6)	Upgrading service bandwidth	4
	Ensuring alignment of technologies	2
Using better performance technologies (6)	Using better performance hard wares	2
	Using latest version soft wares	4
Using intranet communication(3)	Using intranet communication	3
Improving infrastructure and managing external factors (2)	Improving infrastructure	1
	Managing external factors	1
Total		38

The themes reveal that providing incentives to IT skills in the form of short-term training and a better salary package is critical to retaining IT experts in their work. Ensuring appropriate technology use, as well as using higher-performance technologies, increases the value of the government digital platform services significantly. The interview excerpts below describe how Woredas that digitally innovate using the government digital platform practice reconfiguring capabilities:

"We provide short term training and special salary package for IT experts to sustain the effectiveness of the government digital platform in our Woreda."(Male, Woreda administrator)

"In our organization, effective voice communication and file exchange among the top management body is undertaken by using IP messenger." (Female, Finance process owner)

"We improve the value of our services to our customers by upgrading the service bandwidth of the court case management system." (Male, Court service process owner)

6 Discussion of Findings

The findings indicate that Woredas have sensing capabilities via the government digital platform. The Woredas understand changes in their agile environment to identify and mitigate any threats. Similarly, Owoseni and Twinomurinzi [36] discovered that small and medium enterprises (SMEs) in Lagos, Nigeria use capabilities such as feedback, social media, and Internet-based technologies, among other things, to identify emerging market opportunities in their research. The comparison holds because organizational elements such as resources, routines, and capabilities that enable improved performance can be found in both government and private organizations using the same logic [31–33].

The attempt to translate and exploit these opportunities (the seizing capability) is primarily driven by self-motivated efforts such as learning from experience sharing and looking through research works, analyzing customer needs, and encouraging employees with new ideas. Furthermore, the seizing capabilities of Woredas (Table 2) were related to learning from others' innovations. This could show that learning from the innovation of others rather than investing in innovation is regarded as important for deploying the micro-foundations of Woredas as it is cost-effective [32, 33, 87]. However, there are no apparent Woreda structures in place that outline how to take advantage of identified opportunities. Self-driven efforts that are not part of an organizational structure, such as those in government, tend to be frustrating in large organizational structures. This has resulted from path dependencies that are built up in the past [88]. Other organizations demonstrate their seizing capabilities through organizational learning, in which individual agents in the organization use the organization's structure to gain knowledge from the environment and then communicate among members and subunits to incorporate the shared knowledge into the organization's working procedures [89, 90].

The same capability codes overlap between different capabilities with different contexts, as shown in Tables 1 and 2 of the results section. Government organizations in the Woredas, for example, use feedback of reports as both sensing and seizing capabilities. They use these capabilities in a variety of contexts. They use these sensing capabilities to examine the environment for opportunities and manage threats. However, as seizing capabilities, they also use the same capabilities to shape new information or ideas based on knowledge obtained from feedback report. This exhibits that the micro-foundations are conceptually different but correlated [65].

In terms of the ability to rearrange, reallocate, and realign resources to increase the value of the existing digital platform by capitalizing on identified opportunities (the reconfiguring capabilities), Woredas rely primarily on technical ICT that depends on an external competence that may not be readily available in the Woredas. Moreover, the traditional or centralized (not being decentralized) governance model of the government digital platform contributed to restraining the development of reconfiguring capabilities that could be made by government organizations.

While the role of the government digital platform is to create opportunities for Woredas to provide government services effectively and efficiently, Woredas that perform the repetitive activities of micro-foundations (sensing, seizing, and reconfiguring capabilities) are found to modify their business models that enable them to make sense of digital innovation.

6.1 Implications for Research, Practice, and Policy

The findings have practical and policy implications, particularly for resource-constrained countries like Ethiopia, where the micro-foundations of the dynamic capabilities framework are concerned with making the best use of limited resources already available. In practice, policymakers and practitioners can use the micro-foundations of dynamic capabilities to better understand crucial factors when creating government digital platforms to encourage digital innovation in a quickly changing environment. The micro-foundations uncovered can subsequently be taught to other Woredas who aren't already using the platform. Furthermore, the findings have research implications and can be used as a foundation for researchers to further investigate the design and implementation of government digital platforms in low-income countries from the service innovation perspective of micro-foundations.

The findings are also consistent with the governance model of the government digital platform, which is overseen by a centralized ICT unit. The central unit creates the rules and regulations that govern how Woredas interact with the government digital platform. Local digital innovation is hampered by such a governance model. Many other organizations are increasingly decentralizing digital innovation from a traditional central ICT department to within each department by utilizing more ICT-savvy business users rather than ICT technical experts [12, 91]. Constrained generativity and cross-side effects are also reflected in the governance model. The following section concludes with a reflection on the preceding findings as well as policy and practice recommendations.

7   Conclusion

The study's goal was to identify, using qualitative-interpretive methods, the micro-foundations of Woredas that digitally innovate using Ethiopia's existing government digital platform.

The Woredas demonstrated sensing capabilities by leveraging the digital platform to understand their environment and identify opportunities, but the organizational structures to translate those opportunities into potential digital innovations were lacking.

The governance structures surrounding digital platforms continue to be traditional and centralized to an ICT unit. This governance framework holds back digital innovation.

The preference for self-learning and collaborative partnerships with external experts as a means of capitalizing on identified opportunities and integrating them into new learnings from the external environment is a strength. However, the reliance on an external reconfiguring capability limits the potential digital innovations.

As a result, the research suggests that policy regarding the governance model of government digital platforms be reconsidered to allow for a more distributed model that emphasizes greater collaboration with non-technical personnel supported by technical ICT. The study recommends that sensible efforts be made to incentivize the self-learning and collaborative approach in practice.

7.1 Limitations and Future Research

The study's focus on Woredas of Amhara Regional States was one of its limitations. Future research should look into increasing the number of the Regional States and stakeholders across Woredas.

Funding. No funding was provided for the research.

Appendices

See Table 4, Figs. 1, 2, 3, 4, 5 and 6.

Table 4. Appendix A: Interview schedulef

Sub-research question	Interview questions		
	Process owner	ICT Support	District administrator (or representative)
SRQ1: How do Woredas that digitally innovate using government digital platform manifest their sensing capabilities?	1. From your experience, how do you use the government digital platform to systematically capture new information from stakeholders and customers?	1. From your experience, how do you use ICT to support admin processes to systematically capture new information from stakeholders and customers in your Woreda/zone?	1. From your experience, how is the government digital platform used to help public agencies systematically capture new information from stakeholders and customers?

(*continued*)

Table 4. (*continued*)

Sub-research question	Interview questions		
	Process owner	ICT Support	District administrator (or representative)
SRQ2: How do Woredas that digitally innovate using government digital platform manifest their seizing capabilities?	1. From your experience, how do you use the government digital platform to shape or interpret the new information obtained from customers? 2. From your experience, how do you use the government digital platform to manage new ways of doing things? 3. From your experience, how do you use the government digital platform to make decisions to invest on technologies and resources?	1. From your experience, how do you use ICT to support admin processes to shape or interpret the new information obtained from customers in your Woreda/zone? 2. From your experience, how do you use the government digital platform to upgrade your skills to shape new techniques in your Woreda/zone? 3. From your experience, how do you use ICT to adopt new technologies on the government digital platform?	1. From your experience, how is the government digital platform used to help public agencies shape or interpret the new information obtained from customers and stakeholders? 2. From your experience, how is the government digital platform used to support public agencies to identify new ways of doing things? 3. From your experience, how do you use the government digital platform to help public agencies make decisions to invest on technologies?
SRQ3: How do Woredas that digitally innovate using government digital platform manifest their reconfiguring capabilities?	1. From your experience, how do you use the government digital platform to rearrange or reallocate or realign resources? 2. From your experience, how do you manage incentive alignments to sustain the effectiveness of the government digital platform in your Woreda? 3. From your experience, how do you use the government digital platform to communicate between top-level management bodies?	1. From your experience, how do you use ICT to improve the value of the government digital platform in your Woreda/zone? 2. From your experience, what form of incentive is best to sustain the effectiveness of the government digital platform in your Woreda? 3. From your experience, how do you use ICT to communicate to admin processes so that the government digital platform will assist better?	1. From your experience, how is the government digital platform used to support public agencies to improve the value of their services? 2. From your experience, how do you perform incentive alignments to sustain the effectiveness of the government digital platform in your Woreda? 3. From your experience, how do you use the government digital platform to communicate between top-level management bodies?

Code Groups	Name	▲ Grounded	Density	Groups
◇ Using customer online report and customer feedback (3)	◇ Understanding custjomer needs	3	0	[Using customer online report and customer feedback]
◇ Using telephone and fax (3)	◇ Using compliant management system	1	0	[Using web site and compliant management system]
◇ Using web site and compliant management system (2)	◇ Using customer online report	6	0	[Using customer online report and customer feedback]
◇ Using email and messaging services (3)	◇ Using dedicated call center	4	0	[Using telephone and fax]
	◇ Using email services	11	0	[Using email and messaging services]
	◇ Using fax	2	0	[Using telephone and fax]
	◇ Using feedbacks	9	0	[Using customer online report and customer feedback]
	◇ Using messaging services	7	0	[Using email and messaging services]
	◇ Using multicast vedio conferencing	4	0	[Using email and messaging services]
	◇ Using telephone	8	0	[Using telephone and fax]
	◇ Usingweb site	4	0	[Using web site and compliant management system]

Fig. 1. Appendix B: Sensing capability coding regime

Code Groups	Name	▲ Grounded	Density	Groups
◇ Analyzing customer needs and encouraging employees with new ideas (3)	◇ Analyzing customer entire bussiness processes	1	0	[Analyzing customer needs and encouraging employees with new ideas]
◇ Analyzing the appropreiateness of technologies (2)	◇ Using feedback of reports	3	0	[Analyzing customer needs and encouraging employees with new ideas]
◇ Conducting panel discussion (2)	◇ Attending online free tutorials	3	0	[Learning from exprience sharing and research works]
◇ Learning from exprience sharing and research works (3)	◇ Checking the appropriateness of technologies	1	0	[Analyzing the appropreiateness of technologies]
	◇ Discussing on new technologies	5	0	[Conducting panel discussion]
	◇ Encouraging employees with new ideas	2	0	[Analyzing customer needs and encouraging employees with new ideas]
	◇ Evaluating specification of new technologies	2	0	[Analyzing the appropreiateness of technologies]
	◇ Inviting external experts	2	0	[Conducting panel discussion]
	◇ Looking through research works of others	3	0	[Learning from exprience sharing and research works]
	◇ Sharing expriences	6	0	[Learning from exprience sharing and research works]

Fig. 2. Appendix C: Seizing capability coding regime

Code Groups	Name	▲ Grounded	Density	Groups
◇ Ensuring appropriate use of technologies (2)	◇ Ensuring allignment of technologies	2	0	[Ensuring appropriate use of technologies]
◇ Improving infrastructure and managing external 1	◇ Improving infrastructure	1	0	[Improving infrastructure and managing external factors]
◇ Providing incentives (2)	◇ Managing external factors	1	0	[Improving infrastructure and managing external factors]
◇ Using intranet communication (1)	◇ Preparing better sallary package	14	0	[Providing incentives]
◇ Using better performance technologgies (2)	◇ Providing short term training	7	0	[Providing incentives]
	◇ Upgrading service band width	4	0	[Ensuring appropriate use of technologies]
	◇ Using intranet communication	3	0	[Using intranet communication]
	◇ Using latest version soft wares	4	0	[Using better performance technologgies]
	◇ Using better performance hard wares	2	0	[Using better performance technologgies]

Fig. 3. Appendix D: Reconfiguring capability coding regime

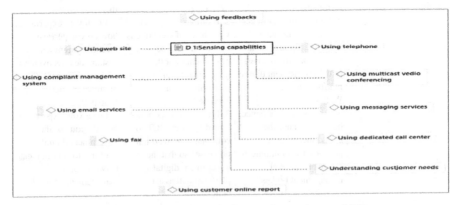

Fig. 4. Appendix E: Network diagram for sensing capabilities

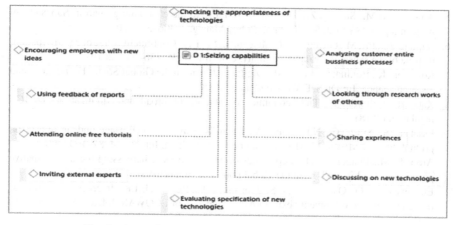

Fig. 5. Appendix F: Network diagram for seizing capabilities

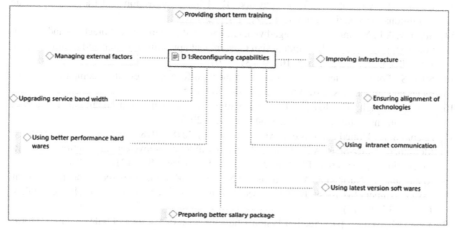

Fig. 6. Appendix G: Network diagram for reconfiguring capabilities

References

1. Constantinides, P., Henfridsson, O., Parker, G.G.: Introduction-platforms and infrastructures in the digital age. Inf. Syst. Res. **29**, 381–400 (2018)
2. Gertjan van Stam, M.: Access to digital platforms: Can mobile networks coverage reports be relied upon? Observations from rural Zambia. In: Proceedings of the 1st Virtual Conference on Implications of Information and Digital Technologies for Development, pp. 177–185 (2021).
3. Nugroho, R.P., Zuiderwijk, A., Janssen, M., de Jong, M.: A comparison of national open data policies: Lessons learned. Transforming Gov.: People, Process Policy **9**(3), 286–308 (2015). https://doi.org/10.1108/TG-03-2014-0008
4. Waller, L., Genius, A.: Barriers to transforming government in Jamaica: Challenges to implementing initiatives to enhance the efficiency, effectiveness and service delivery of government through ICTs (e-Government). Transforming Gov.: People, Process Policy **9**(4), 480–497 (2015). https://doi.org/10.1108/TG-12-2014-0067

5. Albiman, M.M., Sulong, Z.: The role of ICT use to the economic growth in Sub Saharan African region (SSA). J. Sci. Technol. Policy Manag. **7**, 306–332 (2016)
6. Naranjo-zolotov, M., Oliveira, T., Casteleyn, S., Irani, Z.: Continuous usage of e-participation: the role of the sense of virtual community. Gov. Inf. Q. **36**, 536–545 (2019)
7. Koskinen, K., Bonina, C., Eaton, B.: Digital platforms in the Global South: Foundations and research agenda. In: DIODE Working Paper (2018)
8. Katz, R., Callorda, F.: The economic contribution of broadband, digitization and ICT regulation (2018)
9. Esselaar, S., Stork, C., Ndiwalana, A., Deen-Swarray, M.: ICT usage and its impact on profitability of SMEs in 13 African countries. Inf. Technol. Int. Dev. **4**, 87–100 (2007)
10. Aron, J., Muellbauer, J.: The Economics of Mobile Money: harnessing the transformative power of technology to benefit the global poor, England (2019)
11. Ejemeyovwi, J.O., Osabuohien, E.S., Johnson, O.D., Bowale, E.I.K.: Internet usage, innovation and human development nexus in Africa: the case of ECOWAS. J. Econ. Struct. **8**, 1–16 (2019)
12. Nambisan, S., Lyytinen, K., Majchrzak, A., Song, M.: Digital innovation management: reinventing innovation management research in a digital world. MIS Q. **41**, 223–238 (2017)
13. Hinings, B., Gegenhuber, T., Greenwood, R.: Digital innovation and transformation: an institutional perspective. Inf. Organ. **28**, 52–61 (2018)
14. Susanty, A.I., Yuningsih, Y., Anggadwita, G.: Knowledge management practices and innovation performance: a study at Indonesian Government apparatus research and training center. J. Sci. Technol. Policy Manag. **10**, 301–318 (2018)
15. Stier, S.: Political determinants of e-government performance revisited: comparing democracies and autocracies. Gov. Inf. Q. **32**, 270–278 (2015)
16. Das, A., Singh, H., Joseph, D.: Information & management a longitudinal study of e-government maturity. Inf. Manag. **54**, 415–426 (2017)
17. Zhenmin, L.: United Nations e-grovernment survey 2018 (2018)
18. Mensah, R., Cater-Steel, A., Toleman, M.: Factors affecting e-government adoption in Liberia: a practitioner perspective. Electron. J. Inf. Syst. Dev. Ctries. **87**, e12161 (2020)
19. Roengtam, S., Nurmandi, A., Almarez, D.N.: Anwar Kholid: Does social media transform city government? a case study of three ASEAN cities. Transform. Gov. People, Process Policy. **11**, 343–376 (2017)
20. Toots, M.: Why E-participation systems fail: the case of Estonia's Osale.ee. Gov. Inform. Quart. **36**(3), 546–559 (2019). https://doi.org/10.1016/j.giq.2019.02.002
21. Danneels, L., Viaene, S., Van den Bergh, J.: Open data platforms: discussing alternative knowledge epistemologies. Gov. Inf. Q. **34**, 365–378 (2017)
22. Mawela, T., Twinomurinzi, H., Ochara, N.M.: Exploring public sector planning for transformational government. J. Sci. Technol. Policy Manag. **8**, 352–374 (2017)
23. Abu-Shanab, E., Shehabat, I.: The influence of knowledge management practices on e-government success: a proposed framework tested. Transform. Gov.: People, Process Policy **12**(3/4), 286–308 (2018). https://doi.org/10.1108/TG-02-2018-0016
24. Twizeyimana, J.D., Andersson, A.: The public value of E-Government–a literature review. Gov. Inf. Q. **36**, 167–178 (2019)
25. Senshaw, D., Twinomurinzi, H.: Designing for digital government innovation in resource constrained countries : the case of Woredas in Ethiopia. In: 15th International Conference on Design Science Research in Information Systems and Technology. Springer, Kristiansand, Norway (2020).
26. Koskinen, K., Bonina, C., Eaton, B.: Digital Platforms in the Global South : Foundations and Research Agenda. Springer International Publishing (2019).
27. Mettler, T.: World Countries by GDP -TOBI 2020 underserve regions (2019).

28. Miruts, G., Asfaw, M.: The implementation of civil service reforms in Ethiopia: the WoredaNet as a sole promoter to implement civil service reform of Tigray national regional state. Civ. Environ. Res. **4**, 95–102 (2014)

29. Teece, D.J., Pisano, G., Shuen, A.: Dynamic capabilities and strategic management. Strateg. Manag. J. **18**, 509–533 (1997)

30. Cristina, C., Oliveira, F., Junior, W., Clarissa, A., Kunzel, E.: The extended dynamic capabilities model: a meta-analysis. Eur. Manag. J. **38**, 108–120 (2019)

31. Klein, P.G., Mahoney, J.T., Mcgahan, A.M., Pitelis, C.N.: Capabilities and strategic entrepreneurship in public organizations. Strateg. Entrep. J. **7**, 70–91 (2013)

32. Pablo, A.L., Reay, T., Dewald, J.R., Casebeer, A.L.: Identifying, enabling and managing dynamic capabilities in the public sector. J. Manag. Stud. **44**, 687–708 (2007)

33. De Vries, H., Bekkers, V., Tummers, L.: Innovation in the public sector: a systematic review and future research agenda. Public Adm. **94**, 146–166 (2016)

34. Xiao, L., Dasgupta, S.: Dynamic IT capability: an instrument development study. In: Amcis (2009)

35. Sharma, R., Shanks, G.: The role of dynamic capabilities in creating business value from IS assets. In: AISeL, pp. 1–7 (2011).

36. Owoseni, A., Twinomurinzi, H.: Mobile apps usage and dynamic capabilities: a structural equation model of SMEs in Lagos, Nigeria. Telemat. Informatics. **35**, 2067–2081 (2018)

37. Senshaw, D., Twinomurinzi, H.: Reflecting on the role of dynamic capabilities in digital government with a focus on developing countries. In: Proceedings of the 11th Annual Pre-ICIS SIG GlobDev Workshop. AIS eLibrary, San Francisco, USA (2018)

38. Pereira, G.V., Parycek, P., Falco, E., Kleinhans, R.: Smart governance in the context of smart cities: a literature review. Inf. Polity **23**(2), 143–162 (2018). https://doi.org/10.3233/IP-170067

39. Berto, J., Estevez, E., Janowski, T.: Universal and contextualized public services: digital public service innovation framework. Gov. Inf. Q. **33**, 211–222 (2016)

40. Gawer, A.: Digital platforms' boundaries: The interplay of firm scope, platform sides, and digital interfaces. Long Range Plann. **54**, 102045 (2020)

41. Ariana, S., Azim, C., Antoni, D.: Clustering of ICT human resources capacity in the implementation of E-government in expansion area: a case study from pali regency. Cogent Bus. Manag. **7**, 1754103 (2020)

42. Parker, G., Van Alstyne, M.W., Jiang, X.: Platform Ecosystems: How Developers Invert the Firm. MIS Q. **41** (2016)

43. Salge, T.: Don't get caught on the wrong foot: a resource-based perspective on imitation threats in innovation partnerships. Int. J. Innov. Manag. **21**, 1750023 (2017)

44. Reuver, M., Sørensen, C., Basole, R.C.: The digital platform: a research agenda. J. Inf. Technol. **33**, 124–135 (2018)

45. Sedera, D., Lokuge, S., Grover, V., Sarker, S., Sarker, S.: Innovating with enterprise systems and digital platforms: a contingent resource-based theory view. Inf. Manag. **53**, 366–379 (2016)

46. Janowski, T.: Digital government evolution: from transformation to contextualization. Gov. Inf. Q. **32**, 221–236 (2015)

47. Kenney, M., Rouvinen, P., Seppälä, T., Zysman, J.: Platforms and industrial change. Ind. Innov. **26**, 871–879 (2019)

48. Fielt, E., Gregor, S.: What's new about digital innovation ? In: 9th Information Systems Foundations Workshop (ISF 2016). pp. 1–14. Canberra, Australia (2016)

49. Hein, A., et al.: Digital platform ecosystems. Electron. Mark. **30**, 87–98 (2019)

50. Gil-Garcia, J.R., Flores-Zúñiga, M.: Towards a comprehensive understanding of digital government success: integrating implementation and adoption factors. Gov. Inf. Q. **37**, 1010518 (2020)

51. Seshaw, D., Twinomurinzi, H.: The moderating effect of gender on adopting digital government innovations in Ethiopia. In: Proceedings of the 1st Virtual Conference on Implications of Information and Digital Technologies for Development, 2021, pp. 325–341 (2021)

52. Senshaw, D., Twinomurinzi, H.: Innovating with government digital platforms in low-income countries: the dynamic capabilities of Woredas in Ethiopia. J. Sci. Technol. Policy Manag. (2021)

53. Zahra, S.A., Nambisan, S.: Entrepreneurship in global innovation ecosystems. Acad. Mark. Sci. Rev. **1**, 4–17 (2011)

54. Wareham, J., Fox, P.B., Ginner, J.L.C.: Technology ecosystem governance. Organ. Sci. **25**, 1195–1215 (2014)

55. Skog, D., Wimelius, H., Sandberg, J.: Digital Service Platform Evolution: How Spotify Leveraged Boundary Resources to Become a Global Leader in Music Streaming. In: Proceedings of the 51st Hawaii International Conference on System Sciences. pp. 4564–4573, Hawaii (2018).

56. Ghazawneh, A., Henfridsson, O.: Balancing platform control and external contribution in third-party development: the boundary resources model. Inf. Syst. J. **23**, 173–192 (2013)

57. Collis, D.J.: Research note: how valuable are organizational capabilities? Strateg. Manag. J. **15**, 143–152 (1994)

58. Hristov, K.: Internet plus policy: A study on how China can achieve economic growth through the internet of things. J. Sci. Technol. Policy Manag. **8**, 375–386 (2017)

59. Augier, M., Teece, D.J. (eds.): The Palgrave Encyclopedia of Strategic Management. Palgrave Macmillan UK, London (2018). https://doi.org/10.1057/978-1-137-00772-8

60. Chong, M., Habib, A., Evangelopoulos, N., Woo, H.: Dynamic capabilities of a smart city: An innovative approach to discovering urban problems and solutions. Gov. Inf. Q. **35**, 682–692 (2018)

61. Kankanhalli, A., Charalabidis, Y., Mellouli, S.: IoT and ai for smart government: a research agenda. Gov. Inf. Q. **36**, 304–309 (2019)

62. Kankanhalli, A., Zuiderwijk, A., Tayi, G.K.: Open innovation in the public sector: A research agenda. Gov. Inform. Quart. **34**(1), 84–89 (2017). https://doi.org/10.1016/j.giq.2016.12.002

63. Nason, R.S., Wiklund, J.: An assessment of resource-based theorizing on firm growth and suggestions for the future. J. Manage. **44**, 32–60 (2018)

64. Lawson, B., Samson, D.A.: Developing innovation capability in organisations: a dynamic capabilities approach. Int. J. Innov. Manag. **5**, 377–400 (2001)

65. Hossan Chowdhury, M.M., Quaddus, M.A.: Supply chain sustainability practices and governance for mitigating sustainability risk and improving market performance: a dynamic capability perspective. J. Clean. Prod. **278**, 123521 (2021)

66. Wang, C.L., Ahmed, P.K.: Dynamic capabilities: a review and research agenda. Int. J. Manag. Rev. **9**, 31–51 (2007)

67. Hu, G., Shi, J., Pan, W., Wang, J.: A hierarchical model of e-government service capability: an empirical analysis. Gov. Inf. Q. **29**, 564–572 (2012)

68. Janssen, M., van der Voort, H.: Adaptive governance: towards a stable, accountable and responsive government. Gov. Inform. Quart. **33**, 1–5 (2016). https://doi.org/10.1016/j.giq. 2016.02.003

69. Mohammed, M.A., et al.: E-government and its challenges in developing countries: case study Iraqi e-government. Soc. Sci. **11**, 4310–4319 (2016)

70. Irani, Z., Kamal, M.: Editorial. Transform. Gov. People, Process Policy **10**, 354–358 (2016)

71. Foss, N.J., Lindenberg, S.: Micro-foundations for strategy: a goal-framing perspective on the drivers of value creation. Acad. Manag. J. **27**, 85–102 (2013)

72. Wilden, R., Gudergan, S.P.: The impact of dynamic capabilities on operational marketing and technological capabilities: investigating the role of environmental turbulence. J. Acad. Mark. Sci. **43**, 181–199 (2015)

73. Hambrick, D.C., Crossland, C.: A strategy for behavioral strategy: appraisal of small, midsize, and large tentconceptions of this embryonic community. Behav. Strateg. Perspect. **39**, 23–39 (2018)
74. Hare, H.: Survey of ICT and education in Africa: Ethiopia Country Report (2007)
75. Lessa, L., Belachew, M., Anteneh, S.: Sustainability of e-government project success: Cases from Ethiopia. In: 17th Americas Conference on Information Systems. Detroit, Michigan, 4th–7th Aug 2011
76. Lessa, L., Anteneh, S., Klischewski, R., Belachew, M.: Towards a conceptual framework for pledging sustainable e-government success: the case of G2G in Ethiopia. In: Africon 2015 (2015)
77. Madebo, A.N.: Technology and politics in the horn of africa. Int. J. Commun. **13**(2019), 3042–3048 (2019)
78. Dubé, L., Paré, G.: Rigor in information systems positivist case research: current practices, trends and recommendations. MIS Q. **27**, 597 (2003)
79. Yin, R.K.: Case Study Reseach: Design and Methods, 4th edn. Sage Publications, California, USA (2009)
80. Thanh, N.C., Than, T.T.: The interconnection between interpretivist paradigm and qualitative methods in education. Am. J. Educ. Sci. **1**, 24–27 (2015)
81. Eyisi, D.: The usefulness of qualitative and quantitative approaches and methods in researching problem-solving ability in science education curriculum. J. Educ. Pract. **7**, 91–100 (2016)
82. Yilmaz, K.: Comparison of quantitative and qualitative research traditions: epistemological, theoretical and methodological differences. Eur. J. Educ. **48**, 311–325 (2013)
83. Golafshani, N.: Understanding reliability and validity in qualitative research. Qual. Rep. **8**, 597–607 (2003)
84. Connelly, L.M.: Trustworthiness in qualitative research. MEDSURG Nurs. **25**, 435–436 (2016)
85. Braun, V., Clarke, V.: Thematic analysis. In: APA handbooks in psychology®. APA handbook of research methods in psychology, vol. 2. Research designs: Quantitative, qualitative, neuropsychological, and biological, pp. 57–71. American Psychological Association, Washington, DC (2012)
86. Cooper, R.: Decoding coding via the coding manual for qualitative researchers by Johnny Saldaña. The Qual. Rep. **14**, 245–248 (2009)
87. Stuckey, H.L.: Methodological issues in social health and diabetes research. The second step in data analysis: coding qualitative research data. J. Soc. Heal. Diabetes. **3**, 7–10 (2015)
88. Moussa, M., McMurray, A., Muenjohn, N.: A conceptual framework of the factors influencing innovation in public sector organizations. The J. Developing Areas **52**(3), 231–240 (2018). https://doi.org/10.1353/jda.2018.0048
89. Teece, D.: Explicating dynamic capabilities: the nature and microfoundations of (sustainable) enterprise performance. Strateg. Manag. J. **28**, 1319–1350 (2007)
90. Roberts, N., Galluch, P.S., Dinger, M., Grover, V.: Absorptive capacity and information systems research: review, synthesis, and directions for future research. MIS Q. **36**, 625–648 (2012)
91. Sharma, J.K., Singh, A.K.: Absorptive capability and competitive advantage: some insights from indian pharmaceutical industry. Int. J. Manag. Bus. Res. **2**, 175–192 (2012)
92. Gomez, G., Manser, M., Webster, J., Sanchez, J.: Top 5 Challenges of Digital Transformation (2018)

Socioetechnical Factors that Shape E-Government Payment Portal Development in Ghana

Winfred Ofoe Larkotey[1](✉) ⓘ and Princely Ifinedo[2] ⓘ

[1] Valley View University, Accra, Oyibi, Ghana
larkotey@vvu.edu.gh
[2] Brock University, St. Catharines, ON, Canada
pifinedo@brocku.ca

Abstract. The purpose of this study is to understand how sociotechnical factors shape the development of electronic government payment portal in developing countries. E-Government research on payment has focused more on post development phases such as adoption, implementation and use. As a result, little is known about the development phases. To address this research gap, this study focuses on the design and development of an electronic government payment portal in a developing economy. The study employs dialectic process theory as an analytical lens and qualitative interpretive case study as methodology. Findings show that social challenges such as a contradictory requirements of stakeholders, frequent interferences with the development process and technical challenges such as lack of consensus on development tools, lack of relevant ICT skills in the public sector and the use of a rigid software development methodology influenced the development process. The conclusion offers implication for research, practice and policy as well as recommendations for future research.

Keywords: E-Government · E-Payment portal · Developing economies · Dialetic process theory

1 Introduction

The purpose of this study is to understand the social and technical factors that influence the design and development of e-government payment portals in a developing economy and how they are addressed or not. E-Government refers to the interaction and delivery of information and services to citizens as well as other relevant stakeholders through the use of information and communication technologies [1]. E-payment refers to all the automated processes in the exchange and transmission of monetary values over the information and communication technology networks among various stakeholders (for example, government-to- citizens and government-to business) in a business transaction [2]. A portal is a web-based application which generally provides its users the benefit of personalization, single sign-on to all applications, improved content management

© IFIP International Federation for Information Processing 2022
Published by Springer Nature Switzerland AG 2022
Y. Zheng et al. (Eds.): ICT4D 2022, IFIP AICT 657, pp. 24–40, 2022.
https://doi.org/10.1007/978-3-031-19429-0_2

ability from different sources [3]. Traditional online payment systems have been adapted to the virtual environment and new payment systems have been developed to meet electronic transactions requirement needs [4]. All these payment systems have led to making electronic transactions easier and fully automated.

In general, developed country e-government payment research has focused more on adoption and post-adoption issues with less emphasis on the design and development of the portal. Other studies [2, 5] on e-payment have focused more on business-to-consumer (B2C) and business-to-business (B2B) platforms where the payment is embedded in the transaction. However, in relation to government, there could be several payment transactions which involve different stakeholders from different public institutions and therefore, being more complex.

The research question motivating this study is: How do sociotechnical factors influence the development of e-government payment portals in a developing economy and how are such challenges addressed or not. To address this question, the study uses the interpretive case study approach as methodology [6, 7] and the dialectic process theory [4] as a theoretical lens to understand a Ghana's experience in the development of e-government portal for payment, the challenges encountered and attempts to address such challenges. This study is novel due to the fact that it is the first paper to discuss significantly government e-payment portal in Ghana and it also seeks to bring out the peculiar challenges developing economies face and their solutions thereof. No significant study has been done to understand the sociotechnical factors with the development of the government e-payment portal given its numerous sociopolitical and technical issues.

The rest of the study is structured as follows. Section 2 reviews the literature on e-payment in the public sector and developing countries. Section 3 explains the dialectic process theory as the analytical lens for the study. The research setting and methodology are discussed in Sect. 4. This is followed by Sect. 5 which presents the case study and findings followed by analysis and discussion of the findings in the Sects. 6 and 7. Final, Sect. 8 concludes the paper, outlines its contribution, implications and suggestions for further research.

2   E-Payment and Developing Economies

E-Payment systems ensure speed and accuracy of transactions [8, 61]. E-Payments between governments and other stakeholders are seen to be the logical consequence in the growth of Internet payment systems. Common examples of e-payment systems cited in the literature are the payment cards (debit and credit) [9]; point of sales (POS), automated clearing house (ACH), direct debit/deposit, real time gross settlement (RTGS) systems [10] and mobile payments [11, 60]. Pousttchi [12] describes mobile payment as the use of communication techniques with mobile devices for initiation, authorization or completion of payment. With the ubiquitous features of mobile devices [11], Kushchu and Kuscu [13] suggests that most developing economy governments will adopt mobile payment options. However, 13 years after, most governments in developing countries are still struggling with the introduction of e-payment platforms as part of their broader e-government initiatives. While literature [11, 14, 15] on e-government payment have generally focused more on the adoption and post adoption issues (for example implementation, use, benefits) little is known about the pre-adoption issues (design and development). Specifically, there is less focus on the e-government payment portal development with single sign-on capabilities. Furthermore, current research on e-government payment has centered around e-tax (online tax) payments [15]–[18] to the neglect of all other government transactions. Expanding government e-payment transactions to the registration of businesses, licenses, building permits payment of fine fees of transactions and much more will require major rethinking [6]. However, studies on e-government payment have concentrated on specific payment platforms, therefore, neglecting the complex sociotechnical interactions involved with the pre-adoption stages. In an attempt to address this challenge, Csáki et al. [14] discussed how the behavior of citizens and other stakeholders are influenced by the governmental use of payment methods and related policies. However, this research fails to look holistically at all governmental services.

A number of reasons for adoption of e-payment systems of governments are cited in literature. For example, it is noted that e-government payment systems are adopted due to the speed and accuracy of electronic transactions [8]; to avoid the unnecessary media breaks [11]; to empower and provide web-based [19] public services to all citizens as well as other stakeholders through the use of information technology and the presence of a network [20, 21] which could either be wired or wireless [22]. On the part of citizens, use of websites in carrying out financial transactions with government is dependent on issues such as efficiency, security, cost and usability [23]; frictionless use which is impacted by past experience and trust in security [14]; multi-channel payment services, a common archive for all services obtained to specifically keep track of transactions independently and the ability to begin a complex transaction in a channel and complete it in another channel [24], the possibility to interact with an authority to provide clear instructions as well as the availability of clear and unambiguous information in the channel. However, these goals have not been achieved by developing economy governments due to the complex socio-technical challenges faced by most countries. Information on how to go about payments on some government websites are scanty and do not provide much directions to users. Reaching out to authorities concerned in most cases could be a daunting task and almost impossible. Perceived usefulness, ease of use, perceived risk, trust, compatibility, external and interpersonal influences, self-efficacy and facilitation condition [25] are reasons why citizens adopt online tax filing and payment systems.

Literature on e-government payment systems therefore, show that whereas adoption and post- adoption issues [11, 19, 24, 26] have been discussed, there is less focus on the design and development of such applications. Specifically, most discussions on e-government payment view the phenomena as a logical continuation of e-government but not from the viewpoint of a portal.

3   The Dialetic Process Theory

The theoretical foundation for this study is the dialectic process theory [4]. The Dialectic Process Theory developed by Van de Ven and Poole uses the assumption that complex social interactions create confrontations leading to conflicts that bring about change in an organization [27]. The theory is made up of the following concepts: thesis, antithesis and synthesis. Thesis is the original intention of an idea to be achieved by an individual, group or an institution. It could be referred to as the expected outcome of an event. In this study, thesis is the original intention for the development of e-government payment portal. An antithesis is an opposition to the thesis leading to a conflict. These are forces, vents or values that prevent the realization of the thesis. The antithesis of this study refer to all the factors that led to the non-achievement of the thesis. The synthesis is the combination of the best portions of the thesis and antithesis [28]. It refers to the actual outcome. In this study, the synthesis refers to the outcome of the development of the e-payment portal. Figure 1 below presents a diagrammatic view of the theory.

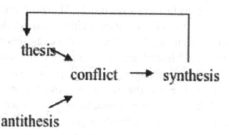

Fig. 1. The concept of dialectics. Source [4]

The theory is based on three principles: Pluralism, Confrontation and Conflict. Pluralism suggests that a phenomenon exists in a world which is made up of either internal or external contradictory forces and colliding events that are always competing for domination and control.

There are inadequacies that are revealed by questioning certain views of the thesis, which eventually lead to confrontations. Conflicts are generated as a result of the confrontations to finally shape the actual outcome of the event. The dialectic process theory has been used to explain enterprise resource planning conflicts [29, 30], in various private organizations as well as knowledge management paradoxes [31]. Other studies used the dialectic process theory to study organizational consequences [15] and to examine the dynamic actions involved with systems development and implementation [32, 33]. For the purposes of this study, the theory helps us to explain the sociotechnical challenges with the e-government payment portal development and how they were addressed or not.

4   Research Setting and Methodology

This study forms part of a broader research into challenges with design and development of e- government portals in a developing economy context and how they are addressed or not.

4.1   Research Setting

This study was conducted in Ghana, a developing economy found on the west coast of Africa and bounded by the Atlantic ocean. Ghana is a developing economy with about

30 million citizens. It recently attained a lower middle income status. According to the International Telecommunication Union (ITU), the percentage of individual using the internet grew from 0.15 in the early 2000's to 23.48% by 2015. This suggests that in recent years, internet penetration is on the increase. In terms of technology infrastructure, Ghana has according to the ITU 2015 report, 4.0 fixed telephone subscriptions, 87.1 mobile-cellular telephone subscriptions, 2.4 fixed broadband subscription (all per 100 people), with 17% and 18.3% of households with a computer and internet access respectively. Hence there is still much to be desired. With a large part of its population (61%) in the rural areas where there are general difficulties such as lack of electricity, difficulty in getting mobile phone reception to make a call let alone assess the internet, payments have generally been through face-to-face cash payments. This requires the physical presence of the individual or business to make payments either through the bank or physically. In recent times, electronic payments have been on the rise. This started from the ATM cards, eZwich card, VISA and MasterCard and currently various mobile payments. With this in mind, the government has changed its way of payments to its citizens and other stakeholders and vice versa. The introduction of the government of Ghana's e-payment portal allows all stakeholders to pay their taxes, make general payments and even allow other businesses to use that same portal for their private businesses.

This portal integrates with the other systems in order to provide a complete transaction. Through this, Ghana is striving to reach the transactional stage [34] for e-government implementation.

4.2 Methodology

The qualitative interpretive case study approach [6, 14, 35] was used to explain the sociotechnical factors that influenced the development of the e-government payment portal. The Case study approach, which provides empirical evidence [36] was used to understand and describe the sociotechnical factors influencing the development of the e-government payment portal in Ghana. The qualitative case study research was chosen to help gather rich data on the phenomenon as well as provide context sensitive insights [16].

This study uses interpretive paradigm [17] as its Philosophical stance and therefore describes its ontology and epistemology from the perspective that both the research phenomenon and the resultant knowledge are socially constructed between the researcher and the participants [17, 18]. Therefore, rather than seeking objectivity, as in the case of a positivist research, this case study seeks to understand how sense is made out of the real-life context within which the e-government payment portal exists [37].

4.3 Data Gathering and Analysis

Data was collected from the National Information Technology Agency (NITA). NITA is responsible for the development and design of e-government portals, therefore, making them directly responsible and involved with the e-government payment portal development process. Fieldwork for data collection occurred between September 2015 and April 2016. We gained access to NITA through our personal contacts and gathered data through multiple sources, including interviews, informal discussions, document and artifact analysis as suggested by Myers [38]. Semi-structured interviews were conducted with 18 participants, including directors and employees from application and business divisions of NITA. The participants for the interviews were selected through purposeful and snowball sampling [39] by identifying employees who participated in the development and/or had knowledge about the e-government payment portal development. The average time for each interview was 58 min. Depending on the consent of the participants, we recorded most of the interviews and later transcribed while others were based solely on note taking. Informal discussions and clarifications through personal visits provided additional data. Further data were gathered through documents analysis which were either through physical (minutes of meetings, reports from developers, technical documentations, manuals, brochures, flyers) or electronic means (the internet, institutional website).

The data collection and analysis were done concurrently [20, 40, 41] as this is in line with interpretive case study principles. The aim of the analysis was to identify the sociotechnical factors that led to the final outcome of the e-payment portal development process. We drew on concepts of the dialectic process theory as the analytical lens and followed the interpretive mode of analysis [18]. This was done inductively by continuously reading the data and reviewing documents on issues relating to thesis (what they wanted to do), antithesis (what were the challenges) and synthesis (what was the final outcome). We individually analyzed the data separately, but frequently met to discuss emerging issues and findings until an agreement was established. There were follow-up interviews in cases where necessary for further insight. Feedback from these sessions was used to improve the analysis and findings.

5   Case Description

Payment of public services in Ghana could be a daunting task. Previously, there were multiple offices, each of which one had to go through for government payments. This led to frustrations such as spending the whole day outside the office for workers and not meeting those to offer the services because they were not around. However, the current e-government payment portal serves as a one stop point for all payments leading to convenience for both citizens and government workers. The idea of the e-payment portal came to being when an e-payment steering team visited Canada to have a firsthand information on how the e-government portal is working. With that in mind, the decision was taken to develop an e-payment portal for government operations, which allows citizens and other stakeholders to conveniently pay their taxes, fees, tangible goods and other services online. The public sector in Ghana does not have persons with the relevant IT skills to develop these applications. To solve this, the government decided to collaborate with the private sector, which has many skilled IT staff as well as a permanent consultant to develop and oversee to the e-government payment portal. Finally, one company was selected through a bidding process. Therefore, as stated by an officer of the National Information Technology Agency (NITA): "the bidding process was competitive, but in the end, we had the company with all the needed skills and resources."

The aim of the Ghana E-Government Payment Platform (GEPP) is to broaden the scope of payment options, streamline payment processes and improve efficiency specifically relating to payments and generally in the service provisioning for all Government Ministries, Departments and Agencies (MDAs). "We had various interest groups who had different interests and expectations. Choosing the options of one over the other opened up for more controversies" a Director said. The application development tool used for the payment portal was Magento. Magento is an Open Source e-commerce application development platform which comes in many versions. MySQL was the database and the web server was Apache all of which are Open Source platforms. All these are Open Source software development tools. The selection of the development platforms was based on three reasons: 1) the evidence provided by the contracted company on how secured the platform was, 2) the procurement issues involved with acquiring such development tools and 3) the conviction of the government institution that this platform was good. The systems development methodology used was the waterfall model. With the waterfall model all data required for the development was completed before the actual portal development. "This methodology was used because most of the payment processes were not streamlined" an Officer said. The contracted company went through lots of pain gathering the needed data from all stakeholders (e.g. Controller and Accountant General, Bank of Ghana and Ministry of Finance and Economic Planning) and went through the business requirements analysis process. According to an officer, "the various interest groups had entrenched positions on what to expect. Once they were neglected, communication stalled, it was difficult coordinating all these processes and groups, especially because of their different shared interest". Based on the requirements gathered from stakeholders, Magento was used to design the features of the e-government payment portal.

The portal was built to integrate with the public e-services portals as well as other portals and payment gateways from stakeholders such as Ghana Revenue Authority (GRA), VISA, MasterCard Payall (cash and cheque), MTN and Airtel Mobile Money Transfers, the various Bank Transfers and eTranzact. This was done through the installation of an Application Programming Interface (API) on the e-payment portal which was supposed to link to the other payment gateways. "In the end, we had to use an unconventional approach which had been suggested not to be helpful to complete the development. This was because, we had to force our way through to agree on the outcomes of the various functional processes. Upon achieving these, we didn't want the situation whereby another group comes to compel us to change the decision. We, therefore, had to make it difficult for this to happen, hence the use of the waterfall model. This worked best to our amazement. Even though the project delayed, we realized that without that approach, we may not have completed by now" a developer narrated. One major challenge faced was that most of these organizations were initially a bit skeptical about the open source development platform used in developing the portal. Hence lots of security concerns were raised by the stakeholders. To address this, the government subscribed to the enterprise edition of Magento which came with extra features and support as well as licensing features that made it more trustworthy and secure. Aside this, the platform was customized to suit the Ghanaian environment.

Another aim, which was integration with other payment gateways was achieved when the Application Programming Interfaces (APIs) of these payment gateways were installed on the e-government payment portal. This was to provide connections to their payment portals to enhance smooth transaction. The e-government payment portal was developed to keep only the addresses of individuals or businesses for shipment or courier purposes. All other details such as the card details, and transaction details are kept on the payment platforms of the other stakeholders. Hence, the e-payment portal serves as a link to these other platforms by bringing the different gateways together on the same platform. As described by one of the developers: "there were various contradictions with user requirement leading to a general delay in the project." There were frequent interruptions due to changes in government workers as well as disagreements on the part of developers and stakeholders. Finally, the GEPP portal was developed. Testing has been done and platform is currently being used by many stakeholders.

6 Analysis of Findings

This section focuses on the analysis of the case study based on the thesis, antithesis and synthesis of the dialectic theory.

6.1 Thesis

The thesis for the e-government payment portal was to serve as a payment platform for paying taxes, fees, bills and other government transactions. Hence, transactions made through this portal were supposed to be saved in a database for a while until the transaction was fully backed-up. There were, however, various issues for and against this which led to the development of the current portal.

6.2 Antithesis

The antitheses were some sociotechnical challenges which created confrontations and finally led to conflicts. These antitheses affected the final outcome of the e-government payment portal.

6.2.1 Social Antithesis

First, there were contradictory requirements from various stakeholders. Over the years, different individuals and groups had processes which were not standardized, however, such processes made their work easier. Although not illegal and not streamlined, these procedures and processes appeared to work well for such MDAs. These norms had become the accepted behavior. Over the years, other workers who joined the institutions applied them in their work. As a result, such practices had become engraved in the work practices of the various MDAs. The difficulty here was that, the various stakeholders upheld their practices so much that they wanted them maintained. Choosing one procedure over the other was not easy since stakeholders did not want to compromise. Gathering data from these institutions was a daunting task.

Second, there were frequent interferences in the development process. There were too many interferences from stakeholders during the design and development. The company at a point in time was asked to hold on with the development because the various stakeholders had to iron out certain differences. All these delayed the completion time. One major interruption to the development process was the frequent changes made to the officials of NITA. In most cases, individuals who were supposed to interact with the third party were transferred. During this period, development process had to be halted. This is because in most situations, these people were the key contacts in the development process and their absence led to a halt in the process. The new people who took over had to be abreast with the current activities before development could continue. This led to the delay of delivery of the finished product.

6.3 Technical Antithesis

Lack of Relevant ICT Skills in the Public Sector led to human resource challenges. The public agencies in Ghana lack qualified and highly skilled IT personnel who could have developed this application. This is due to the unattractive nature of the remunerations and the work environment. Quite a number of them also lack systems analysis techniques, programming skills, database development techniques and many more. In other words, most of the IT employees in the public sector lacked the analysis and design skills of the particular tools used for the e-payment portal development. To address this challenge, the government used the highly skilled IT staff in the private sector to achieve its aim of developing the e-government payment portal. Here, a third party company was contracted and provided with all the funds to develop the portal. Hence, a partnership with the private sector made the government succeed in the development of the e-government payment portal.

The use of a rigid software development methodology was an approach to handle multiple change requests. Challenges arising from the entrenched positions of the various stakeholders led to the usage of the waterfall model. The developers did not want frequent changes even after there had been an agreement. Developers believed using this methodology will make them complete on time. Developers also took the decision to use this rigid methodology in order not to allow the frequent leadership changes of NITA to affect design decisions which had already been made.

There was also a difficulty of Integration with Third Party Applications. There were instances where it was difficult to integrate with other platforms. Compatibility issues, security and privacy issues as well as many more were raised. In the end, it was decided that the e-government payment portal was not going to keep records of transaction details except for the shipping address. However, integration with the e-services portal was easier because the API's were already available.

Lack of Consensus on Development Tools was another technical challenge. It was discovered that most public sector workers, as well as other stakeholders, were a bit skeptical about the use of open source applications due to security reasons. Aside security issues, the compatibility of Magento with other platforms was raised. Another concern stems from the fact that there is no one to call or ask when you have issues with the use or development of the application. To settle this, developers had to go in for the enterprise edition of Magento which could be supported in times of need.

Finally, use of Open Source development platforms to promote Open Governments encouraged interoperability. Open source platforms were used as this will provide collaboration and interoperability among various countries especially among member states of the West African region and to a larger extent, the African Union.

6.3.1 Synthesis-E-Payment Portal

The collision of the thesis to various antithesis led to confrontations, conflicts and finally a synthesis. The first thesis was to develop a payment portal which could eventually keep records of transactions of the various government institutions as this will curb corruption and instant information generation. This was not achieved because the portal only keeps records of the billing or shipping address. Ghana does not have any policies governing the use of open source application tools and how well to protect such users. The solution was therefore to develop a portal which was supposed to serve as a means to communicate with the other payment gateways. Hence, no payment transactions are kept on the e-payment portal.

The synthesis was therefore an e-government payment portal which integrates with the government e-services portal and other payment gateways but keeps only the billing and shipping address of the user.

7 Discussion of Findings

This study groups the antithesis into two categories. The social and technical challenges. This is because the researchers view information technology as the ensemble of equipment, techniques, applications and people that define a social context which includes infrastructure for development and use and the social relations that make up the context [42]. This study, therefore, discusses the antithesis in light of these two groups. The following issues emerged while attempting to address the research question which was to understand the sociotechnical challenges that influence the development of e-government payment portals and how they are addressed or not.

7.1 Social Challenges

Social challenges led to conflicts and finally frequent interferences with the development process. The research findings show that there was difficulty in gathering all the requirements needed for the development of the e-government payment portal. Generally, requirements gathering process which is one of the first activities in software development [43, 61] appears to be a major challenge in the design and development of information systems [7, 44]. There are three processes involved: 1) discovering how an information system should behave and address the problems it intends to within a context, 2) serving as a guide on how the software should be built by describing these findings in a way that can be understood by software developers and 3) managing frequent changes from stakeholders [45]. These processes are critical for success in the software development process [29]. One of the difficulties stems from the fact that there are a large number of participants involved, which extend the length of time for the whole process to be done [30]. This is buttressed by Ross & Schoman Jr [46] who suggest that the results of paying less attention to requirements gathering at the early stages of software development are extremely high costs, leading to missed deadlines, wastages, duplications, disgruntled end users and a repeated cycle of changes. These projects, mostly have so much data to the extent that they lead to difficulty in objectively determining causes for the observed trends in data [30]. These difficulties are broadly grouped into individual cognitive, interpersonal processes and complex challenges [7]. Individual cognitive refers to the inability of stakeholders to explicitly express their needs, imagine beyond the current environmental needs and be able to picture how information technology solves their challenges. Interpersonal processes such as business-IT relationship issues, managing expectations, conflict resolution and negotiation as well as communication skills are some of the social issues with the requirements gathering. Complexity challenges involve prioritization, managing the diversity of inputs, defining interaction and assessing outcomes among others. A solution to these challenges by Damian et al., [47] suggest that stakeholders should be separated from each other and collocated with a system analyst in order to get the best outcome. However, this solution was meant for a small business, therefore, does not solve the challenges faced with large user participants in the design and development of e-government portals. The findings from this study show that contradictory requirements were a major hindrance to the successful design and development of the e-government payment portal. This generally led to the frequent changes in the development process.

7.1.1 Interaction and Coordination Bottlenecks Due to Entrenched User-Group Positions

Findings suggest that there were interaction and coordination challenges that led to the final outcome of the portal. While some of these were external to the case organizations, others were internal. Some studies [48, 49] suggest that situations, where employees communicate and relate to complete tasks is one way of achieving the desired results. In other words, workers combine resources for the purposes of achieving a task in most cases when they perceive external threats. To this end, even though stakeholders may not be friendly to each other, they are bonded by the common tasks they set out to achieve. This is effective within a small group. The difficulty arises, however within and between large varying groups with different interests and expectations [50, 61]. This leads to entrenched user group positions in some situations. Therefore, as a result of different interpretations, the selection of one group's development approach over the other leads to entrenched positions.

7.1.2 Impact of Sociopolitical Values

Development processes are shaped by sociopolitical values [51]. As a result, there are both external and internal controversies leading to various degrees of conflicts and making the process uncertain. The development process is therefore not autonomous. In other words, the process cannot be taken as rational [51]. The development process was characterized by such sociopolitical issues, leading to the final outcome. Frequent change in leadership of the case institutions; lack of autonomy in taking and implementing decisions; perceived power issues due to political affiliation and many more sociopolitical challenges led to the development challenges and the final outcome.

7.2 Technical Challenges

Lack of consensus on development tools leading to integration difficulties and resistance. Various governments across the globe have either adopted or are in the process of adopting open source applications because of the convergence to open standards [32]. Open source software is a term used to describe applications/platforms which are developed, made available to the public including the source codes and open for contributions through the modification of such software [33]. This is due to the following reasons: 1) the success of such products in gaining shares in their markets, 2) the uneasy calm about proprietary software and 3) the general opinion that the old ways of software development are failing to answer questions regarding the demand for effective and efficient software applications [34]. Interest groups involve a community of large users who promote these platforms, increase in the number of organizations using open source platforms and the increasing interest by governments, especially in Europe to use open source software for e-government purposes. Whereas most developed country governments are either using or adapting open source applications [34], it appears that developing economy governments still prefer proprietary software [33]. However, developing economy governments are increasingly using open source platforms as web servers. For example, various ATMs in Ghana use the Linux operating system as against the windows platform. Open source platforms have benefits such as increasing interoperability, reducing the challenges that come with vendor lock-in, providing more flexibility, reducing costs involved with the development of software [32]. Open source is viewed as a new way and innovative approach to developing government software which is flexible, democratic, creative and involves a large number of people as well as more reliable due to the extreme scrutiny by the open source community [34].

Therefore, it is suggested that dwelling on the strengths of open source platforms allows governments to open up its closed-ended processes to a broader input and innovation [52]. However, the research findings suggested that most of the third party institutions were skeptical in connecting to an open source application which led to the current e-government payment platform. Whereas research, in general, is discussing the possibility of open source platforms in developing e-government portals, developing economy literature has focused less on this phenomenon. In general, the findings thus show that the thesis of being able to store transactions was not achieved due to security concerns of the open platform.

7.2.1 Lack of Relevant ICT Skills in the Public Sector

Findings show that developing economy public sector lacks personnel with the needed skill in programming and databases to develop the portal. In an attempt to address this situation, the development of the e-government payment portal was outsourced to a third party private company. Debates on outsourcing issues and problems arose in the public sector at the latter part of the 90's [36] due to the increasing trend with government agencies outsourcing their IT needs [53]. Recent studies have revealed that outsourcing within the public sector has become an increasing trend and is becoming a widely accepted management practice within governments [35]. According to Chen & Perry [54], outsourcing could be a way by which governments get access to skilled IT staff with another benefit such as the economy of scale in order to provide quality e-government applications. On the other hand, outsourcing could also have some major disadvantages such as loss of managerial control over outsourced projects, threat to security and confidentiality, quality problems, hidden costs and reallocation of existing teams [55]. Whereas lack of staffing could be a major hindrance to the development of the e-government portal the findings thus show that lack of relevant ICT skills in the public sector of a developing economy should not be a hindrance to the development of an e-government portal.

7.2.2   Use of Rigid Software Development Methodologies to Achieve Development Goals

The research findings showed that a rigid software methodology, the waterfall model was used for the development of the e-government payment portal. An appropriate lifecycle selection is crucial to success in the development of software [56]. Various studies [57–59] identify the features of the software development process as crucial to the success or failure of software developments. In a situation where many processes were not streamlined, where it was difficult to gather user requirement and there were opposing views on the use of open source platforms, this methodology was not the best approach to use. However, to defy all odds, this approach was deliberately used to force the users to objectively go beyond their differences so that the development could take place. Thus the findings from this study show that even though studies support iterative methods, certain instances such as where processes are not streamlined and individuals deliberately frustrating the process could call for a combination of flexible and rigid methodologies leading to success and development within the time.

7.2.3   The Involvement of a Skilled and Permanent Consultant Who Served as an Intermediary Between and Within the Stakeholders

One major contribution to the development of the e-government payment portal was the employment of a permanent and skilled IT personnel who once worked in the private sector as a consultant on the project. This consultant was employed and paid an equivalent rate of what pertains in the private sector with other benefits. There was, therefore, a thorough scrutiny of the system whenever deliverables were made to ascertain whether they met international standards or not. Serving as the project coordinator, the consultant provided direction to the development. This took away the perennial challenge where third party private organizations who won bids to develop systems for governments did not undergo proper scrutiny from government through an independent consultant.

8   Conclusion

The study used a case study of e-government payment portal development to answer the research question that sought to identify the sociotechnical challenges that influence the development of e-government web portals in developing countries and how they are addressed or not. We identified that one of the challenges which was common is the lack of consensus on a common development platform. Other social challenges such as contradictory user requirements from stakeholders and frequent interruptions with the portal development due to the interferences hindered the general development of the e-government payment portal.

Technical issues that were identified were the use of rigid software development techniques such as the waterfall model in a society where most of the processes were not streamlined with different users giving different narratives of the same processes, the lack of relevant ICT skills in the public sector also led to outsourcing the project to a third party. The study is the second attempt by the authors to investigate challenges with the development of e-government web portals (e-payment) in a developing economy context and how they are addressed. By this, the paper extends the existing e-government literature on developing economy on web-portal development. The originality of the paper, therefore, stems from its application of the dialectic process theory to investigate the sociotechnical challenges influencing e-government portal development in a developing economy context.

In terms of implications for research, the paper demonstrates the applicability of the dialectic process theory to the domain of e-government portal development. With regards to practice, this study provides a clear understanding about the sociotechnical challenges faced during the development of e-government portals in developing countries. It is suggested that developing countries which have similar situations such as lack of relevant ICT skills in the public sector will use the Public Private-Partnership model. In addition, the use of rigid or iterative models should depend on the terrain and which is most pragmatic and not just discard the concept of the waterfall model due to its general weaknesses. Furthermore, to promote open governments, which will allow collaboration and interoperability among various countries, open standards which promote open source applications should be explored. This will help provide flexibility, security, interoperability and cost reduction among e-government portals. In relation to policy, it is suggested that governments enact policies which will educate and promote the use of open standards and open source applications, streamline government processes and encourage interoperability amongst e-government portals at various levels and from different government institutions. Therefore, there is the need for future studies to discuss how open standards and open source platforms could be used by developing economy governments to reduce the rate of failure in the development of e-government web portals. There is also the need to develop theories that are context-based sensitive to determine the individual sociotechnical challenges of a country that influence e-government web portal development. Also, other studies may compare findings from developing economy to those in developed country context to identify and address the unique challenges.

References

1. Cupido, K., Ophoff, J.: A conceptual model of critical success factors for an e government crowdsourcing solution. In: Proceedings of the 14th European Conference on eGovernment (ECEG 2014), pp. 77–84 (2014)

2. Ayo, C., Ukpere, W.: Design of a secure unified e-payment system in Nigeria: a case study. African J. Bus. Manag. **4**(9), 1753–1760 (2010)
3. Gmelch, O., Pernul, G.: A portal-based approach for user-centric legacy application integration in collaborative environments. In: International Conference on Wirtschaftsinformatik, pp. 693–703. Zurich, Swtizerland (2011).
4. Van De Ven, A.H., Poole, M.S.: Explaining development and change in organizations. Acad. Manag. Rev. **20**(3), 510–540 (1995). https://doi.org/10.5465/amr.1995.9508080329
5. Persson, U.M., Alpízar, F.: Conditional cash transfers and payments for environmental services—a conceptual framework for explaining and judging differences in outcomes. World Dev. **43**, 124–137 (2013)
6. Boone, M.: E-Government and Citizen Adoption of Innovations: Factors Underlying Citizen Use of the Internet for State Tax Filing. North Carolina State University (2012)
7. Hansen, S., Lyytinen, K.: Challenges in contemporary requirements practice. In: Proceedings of the Annual Hawaii International Conference System Science, pp. 1–11 (2010)
8. Singh, M.: E-Services and their role in B2C ECommerce. Manag. Serv. Qual. **12**, 434–445 (2002)
9. Rocheleau, B., Wu, L.: e-Government and financial transactions: potential versus reality. Electron. J. e-Government **3**(4), 219–230 (2005)
10. Nnaka, P.: The Nigeria e-payment system. Niger. Mon. **4**(8), 25–27 (2009)
11. Treiblmaier, H., Pinterits, A., Floh, A.: Antecedents of the adoption of e-payment services in the public sector. In: International Conference on Information Systems, pp. 65–75 (2004)
12. Pousttchi, K.: A modelling approach and reference models for analysis of mobile payment use cases. Electron. Commer. Res. Appl. **7**(2), 182–201 (2008)
13. Kushchu, I., Kuscu, H.: From e-government to m-government: facing the inevitable. In: European Conference on E-Government (ECEG 2003) (2003)
14. Csáki, C., O'Brien, L., Giller, K., McCarthy, J.B., Tan, K.-T., Adam, F.: The use of E-payment in the distribution of social welfare in Ireland: charting the daily experience of recipients. Transform. Gov.: People, Process Policy **7**(1), 6–26 (2013)
15. Deluca, D.: Furthering information systems action research: a post-positivist synthesis of four dialectics. J. Assoc. Inf. Syst. **9**(2), 48–72 (2008)
16. Conboy, K., Fitzgerald, G., Mathiassen, L.: Qualitative methods research in information systems: motivations, themes, and contributions. Eur. J. Inf. Syst. **21**, 113–118 (2012)
17. Walsham, G.: Doing interpretive research. Eur. J. Inf. Syst. **15**, 320–330 (2006)
18. Klein, H.K., Myers, M.D.: A set of principles for conducting and evaluating interpretive field studies in information systems. MIS Q. **23**, 67–94 (1999)
19. Treiblmaier, H., Pinterits, A., Floh, A.: Success factors of internet payment systems. Int. J. Electron. Bus. **6**(4), 369–385 (2008)
20. Myers, M.D.: Qualitative Research in Business & Management, 2nd edn. Sage Publications (2013)
21. Orlikowski, W.J., Baroudi, J.J.: Studying information technology in organizations: research approaches and assumptions. Inf. Syst. Res. **2**(1), 1–27 (1991)
22. Nah, F., Siau, K., Sheng, H.: The value of mobile applications: a utility company study. Commun. ACM **48**(2), 85–90 (2005)
23. Wright, D.: Comparative evaluation of electronic payment systems. Inform. Syst. Oper. Res. **40**(1), 71–85 (2002)
24. Russo, C., Ghezzi, C.M., Fiamengo, G., Benedetti, M.: Benefits sought by citizens in multichannel e-government payment services: evidence from Italy. Procedia - Soc. Behav. Sci. **109**, 1261–1276 (2014)
25. Hung, S.-Y., Chang, C.-M., Yu, T.-J.: Determinants of user acceptance of the e-Government services: the case of online tax filing and payment system. Gov. Inf. Q. **23**(1), 97–122 (2006)

26. Alshehri, M., Drew, S.: Challenges of e-government services adoption in Saudi Arabia from an e-ready citizen perspective. World Acad. Sci. Eng. Technol. **4**(6), 881–887 (2010)

27. Benson, J.K.: Organizations: a dialectical view. Adm. Sci. Q. **22**(1), 1–21 (1977)

28. Jarupathirun, S., Zahedi, F.M.: Dialectic decision support systems: system design and empirical evaluation. Am. Conf. Inform. Syst. **10**, 2032–2041 (2004)

29. Videira, C., Ferreira, D., Silva, A.: Patterns and parsing techniques for requirements specification. In: Proceedings of the 1st Iberian Conference Information Systems and Technologies (CISTI 2006), vol. 2, pp. 375–390. Ofir, Portugal (2006). https://www.researchgate.net/pro file/Alberto-Silva-20/publication/228620188_Patterns_and_parsing_techniques_for_requir ements_specification/links/0c9605242d2bde6618000000/Patterns-and-parsing-techniques-for-requirements-specification.pdf

30. Bell, T.E.., Thayer, T.A.: Software requirements : are they really a problem? In: International Conference on Software Engineering, pp. 61–68 (1976)

31. Chae, B., Bloodgood, J.: Paradoxes in knowledge management: a dialectical perspective. In: AMCIS 2004 Proc. (2004)

32. Simon, K.D.: The value of open standards and open-source software in government environments. IBM Syst. J. **44**(2), 227–238 (2005)

33. Amega-Selorm, C., Awotwi, J.: Free and Open Source Software (FOSS): it's significance or otherwise to the e-governance process in Ghana. In: Proceedings of the 4th International Conference Theory Practice Electron. Government, pp. 91–95 (2010)

34. Fuggetta, A.: Open source software - an evaluation. J. Syst. Softw. **66**(1), 77–90 (2003)

35. Moon, J., Choe, Y.C., Chung, M., Jung, G.H., Swar, B.: IT outsourcing success in the public sector: lessons from e-government practices in Korea. Inf. Dev. **32**(2), 142–160 (2014)

36. Parker, D., Hartley, K.: Transaction costs, relational contracting and public private partnerships: a case study of UK defense. J. Purch. Supply Manag. **9**(3), 97–108 (2003)

37. Barrett, M., Walsham, G.: Making contributions from interpretive case studies: examining processes of construction and use. In: Kaplan, B., Truex, D.P., Wastell, D., Wood-Harper, A.T., DeGross, J.I. (eds.) Information Systems Research. IFIP International Federation for Information Processing, vol. 143. Springer, Boston, MA (2004)

38. Myers, M.D.: Qualitative research in information systems. MIS Q. **21**(2), 241 (1997)

39. Patton, M.Q.: Qualitative Evaluation and Research Methods. Sage, Newbury Park (1990)

40. Orlikowski, W.J., Baroudi, J.J.: Studying information technology in organizations: research approaches and assumptions. Inform. Syst. Res. **2**(1), 1–28 (1991)

41. Walsham, G.: Interpretive case studies in IS research: nature and method. Eur. J. Inf. Syst. **4**, 74–81 (1995)

42. Orlikowski, W.J., Barley, S.: Technology and institutions: what can research on Information Technology and research on organizations learn from each other. MIS Q. **25**(2), 145–165 (2001)

43. Bubenko, J.J.: Challenges in requirements engineering. In: Proceedings of the 1995 IEEE International Symposium Requirement Engineering, pp. 160–162 (1995)

44. van Lamsweerde, A.: Requirements engineering in the year 00: a research perspective. In: ACM, pp. 5–19, (2000)

45. Cobleigh, R.L.: Propel: An approach supporting user guidance in developing precise and understandable property specifications. (Doctoral dissertation, University of Massachusetts Amherst). (2008). https://www.researchgate.net/profile/Rachel-Cobleigh/public ation/229422382_PROPEL_An_Approach_Supporting_User_Guidance_In_Developing_P recise_and_Understandable_Property_Specifications/links/0912f5009609a9e098000000/ PROPEL-An-Approach-Supporting-User-Guidance-In-Developing-Precise-and-Understan dable-Property-Specifications.pdf

46. Ross, D., Schoman, K.E., Jr.: Structured analysis for requirements definition. IEEE Trans. Softw. Eng. **3**, 6–15 (1977)

47. Gaines, B.R., Shaw, M.L.G., Eberlein, A., Damian, D.E.H.: Using different communication media in requirements negotiation. IEEE Softw. **17**(3), 28–36 (2000)
48. Gittell, J.H.: Relationships and resilience: care provider responses to pressures from managed care. J. Appl. Behav. Sci. **44**(1), 25–47 (2008)
49. Gittell, J.H.: Coordinating mechanisms in care provider groups: relational coordination as a mediator and input uncertainty as a moderator of performance effects. Manage. Sci. **48**(11), 1408–1426 (2002)
50. Orlikowski, W.J., Gash, D.: Technological frames: making sense of information technology in organizations. ACM Trans. Inf. Syst. **12**(2), 174–207 (1994)
51. Howcroft, D., Light, B.: The social shaping of packaged software selection. J. Assoc. Inf. Syst. **1**(3), 122–148 (2010)
52. O'Reilly, T.: Government as a platform. In: Lathrop, D., Ruma, L. (eds.) Open government: Collaboration, transparency and participation in practice. O'Reilly Media (2010)
53. Gordon, M., Walsh, T.: Outsourcing technology in government: owned, controlled, or regulated institutions. J. Gov. Inf. **24**(4), 267–283 (1997)
54. Chen, Y., Perry, J.: Outsourcing e-government: managing for success. Public Perform. Manag. Rev. **26**(4), 404–421 (2012)
55. Tayauova, G.: Advantages and disadvantages of outsourcing: analysis of outsourcing practices of Kazakhstan banks. Procedia Soc. Behav. Sci. **41**, 188–195 (2012)
56. Gordon, V.S., Bieman, J.M.: Rapid prototyping: lessons learned. IEEE Softw. **12**(1), 85–95 (1995)
57. Lyytinen, K.: Different perspectives on information systems: problems and solutions. ACM Comput. Surv. **19**(1), 5–46 (1987)
58. Butler, T., Fitzgerald, B.: The relationship between user participation and the management of change surrounding the development of information systems: a European perspective. J. End User Comput. **13**(1), 12–25 (2001)
59. Scott, J.E., Vessey, I.: Managing risks in enterprise systems implementations. Commun. ACM **45**(4), 74–81 (2002)
60. Ifinedo, P.: Factors affecting e-business adoption by SMEs in sub-Saharan africa: an exploratory study from Nigeria. In: Al-Qirim, N. (ed.) Global Electronic Business Research: Opportunities and Directions, pp. 319–347. IGI Global (2006)
61. Larkotey, W.O., Effah, J., Boateng, R.: Development of e-government payment portal: A case study from a developing country. In: UK academy for information systems conference proceedings (2017)

Role of Social Media Digital Platforms in Empowering and Establishing Digital Enterprises for Women

Sana Hafeez Shah$^{(\boxtimes)}$ ⓘ and Fareesa Malik ⓘ

NUST, Islamabad, Pakistan
`Sana.msie19nbs@student.nust.edu.pk`,
`fareesa.malik@nbs.nust.edu.pk`

Abstract. This research investigates how the role of social media digital platforms in enabling female digital entrepreneurship in the context of Pakistan. It explores the cultural and social factors that enable or disable women digital entrepreneurs and how digital platforms can facilitate women digital entrepreneurs by addressing these challenges. A qualitative interpretive approach has been used for this research. Extensive interviews with female digital entrepreneurs from Pakistan have been conducted. This article aims to extend prior knowledge of female digital entrepreneurship and interaction with social networking digital platforms since there is limited research. The findings propose two themes out of the research, the first being digital platforms addressing the challenges of time, location, and process of doing business for women, and the second is digital platforms breaking cultural barriers and empowering women. The findings concluded that digital platforms such as social networking sites are enabling more female entrepreneurs overall. Therefore, this paper contributes to the empirical studies on this subject and caters to a contextual research question that will make it original and resourceful.

Keywords: Women digital entrepreneurship · Digital platforms social networking digital platforms · Women entrepreneurship · Social media entrepreneurship · Digital entrepreneurship

1 Introduction

Female entrepreneurship was established as a respected field by the end of the 1990s, and a distinct area of academic research [1]. Since then the inclination towards the concept of women entrepreneurship has gone upwards in developing countries as well as compared to previous times, with reasons being first, the general inclination towards the role of entrepreneurship to boost economic development and secondly the increase in the interest of women in starting their businesses is owed to the fast rise in the female-led entrepreneurial ventures across developing countries [2]. The number of female entrepreneurs has exponentially hiked upwards throughout the world, where women are expected to fill a gap in developed nations whereas in developing countries it is observed

© IFIP International Federation for Information Processing 2022
Published by Springer Nature Switzerland AG 2022
Y. Zheng et al. (Eds.): ICT4D 2022, IFIP AICT 657, pp. 41–54, 2022.
https://doi.org/10.1007/978-3-031-19429-0_3

that most women become entrepreneurs out of necessity [3]. Popular studies depict the internet as a facilitator of entrepreneurial activity potential as it possesses the feature of accessibility as a digital entrepreneurial platform [1, 2]. Women are one of those groups that are facilitated by low barriers of entry for entrepreneurship [3]. This study will focus on the role of digital platforms in empowering and establishing digital enterprises for women, particularly in developing nations.

Previous studies that have studied the relationship between digital technology and women under the domain of cyberfeminism have determined the important potential of digital platforms for the empowerment and emancipation of women. Although, the effect of social and cultural norms on entrepreneurship stays underexplored yet [6]. Digitalization provides a safe space for women unlike offline concerns for a woman which makes their initiation towards entrepreneurship easier. Previous studies especially in social and cultural contexts have assessed the potential for digital entrepreneurship to provide an impartial and meritocratic platform for women that empowers them [7]. There is a realization that the way women interact on social media is not just because them being women but also because the online audience is mostly women which are intertwined deeply [8]. The stats showing that women have predominance in personal selling through social media depicts the innate trustworthiness and communicating brand advocative nature of women. Social media digital platforms have become an enabler of voice for women who had been previously not recognized and marginalized and they can reach a wider audience that is also concentrated on women [9]. Although, these platforms are also criticized for their negative elements as well, such as online female sexual harassment [10].

Digital transformation giants such as Google, Microsoft, Facebook, and Apple not only entirely transformed the business environment, but also changed the way we interact in daily life with each other. Digital entrepreneurship now leads the world in a revolutionary manner and is one of the most important economic development after the industrial revolution [11]. This article will study digital entrepreneurship and its role in creating women digital entrepreneurs in Pakistan and empowering them.

2 Literature Review

2.1 Women Entrepreneurship

Female entrepreneurship was established as a respected field by the end of the 1990s, and a distinct area of academic research. By that time female entrepreneurship had become part of a famous argument for the media outlets and was politically debated for labor markets and employment [12]. Consequently, women's entrepreneurship has gone upwards in developing countries as well, with reasons being first, the general inclination towards the role of entrepreneurship to boost economic development and secondly the increase in the interest of women in starting their businesses are owed to the fast rise in the female-led entrepreneurial ventures across developing countries. Women not only then support economic well-being but also lend a hand to supporting their households by investing in better education, nutrition, and health than men. Also, female entrepreneurs comparatively employ more women employees than male-led businesses. This not only empowers women but also improves the living standards of families. Due to these reasons, women's entrepreneurship is a goal to increase economic activity and alleviate poverty in developing countries [12].

In recent times, the digital space is widely used media and is a platform that is a new space for entrepreneurial activity. In digital entrepreneurship, barriers to entry are rather less as the digital businesses do not require any physical office or expensive equipment and the flexible nature of operations allows to easily access the expertise of technology which is readily available without an enormous amount of effort [7]. Due to convention related to digital entrepreneurship that it is impartial and has a merit-based approach suggests that regardless of the extensive set of assets, some with just a secure internet connection, a laptop/PC, something to offer, and creativity can establish their business [5]. Digitalization provides a safe space for women unlike offline concerns for a woman which makes their initiation towards entrepreneurship easier. Earlier studies especially in social and cultural contexts have assessed the potential for digital entrepreneurship to provide an impartial and meritocratic platform for women that empowers them [7]. There are studies like Dy [13] that add to the literature by examining inequalities resulting from digital entrepreneurship that cater to, especially the marginalized people who are less represented in entrepreneurship, and one of them is women.

The abundant availability of information communication technologies (ICTs) is one of the main underlying pragmatic reasons behind women's entrepreneurship, especially digital entrepreneurship which is prevalent at times when laptops, mobile phones, and emerging digital platforms are readily available to every person [14]. ICTs have eliminated the liabilities attached to being a small business by linking them with large companies where they can combine their flexibility and independence with vastness and access to bigger companies. Mobile technology and other new technologies have provided the opportunity for single-person businesses and small ventures to coordinate, collaborate and cooperate with individuals working independently and foreign companies that are far away [12, 13].

In a study conducted by Fairlie [14], there was more likelihood of starting a business discovered when correlated with the ownership of a personal computer. This was especially in the case of women, who had the liberty to experiment with the presence of their computers to make business plans, study legal terms, research tax codes, and apparent competition in the field. This helped women is getting prepared to be an entrepreneur by learning about specific industries and lowering the costs of operations and marketing. It was additionally concluded by Fairlie [14] that age, education level, and marital status generally increased female entrepreneurship whereas the decreasing factor resulted in the number of children for women.

Females, migrants, and people of color stay marginalized in the domain of entrepreneurship, despite the surge in their entrepreneurial ventures. This phenomenon of an easy means of generating income is beneficial for the rather sidelined members of the society who bear greater hurdles in getting employed and for entrepreneurial aims they consider it to be superior and out of reach [7]. Thus, the literature suggests that women who meet challenges in a conventional type of entrepreneurship can easily find major challenges diminished while going for digital entrepreneurship. Women feel more comfortable in digital space and are regarded more than the cultural and social restraints attached to them for centuries. This concept is also engraved in the term cyberfeminism, in this it is mostly argued in the literature that the offline environment is mirrored in the online environment for women [3]. There is a realization that the way women interact on social media is not just because them being women but also because the online audience is mostly women which are intertwined deeply [8].

In developing countries, like Pakistan is the context of this study, the major reason there is the limited economic development of women is the various patriarchal conceptions in the society where women hold an inferior status and have been ascribed roles with inferior status such as just housewives [17]. These patriarchal notions in society impede the evolution of women's entrepreneurship at least in three means. Firstly, the economic need for survival is one of the main motivations for social media digital platforms [15, 16]. Moreover, in the case of women, balancing their family life is also of great motivation [19]. Whereas the concepts that patriarchy brings let perceive women to be less deserving of economic prosperity and have low self-efficacy which reduces their potential to have entrepreneurial motivations and recognize the business opportunities [20]. Nevertheless, there has been evidence gathered in recent studies about the motivations for women's entrepreneurship in developing nations which include an increased desire for independence, autonomy, and achievement [18–20]. Secondly, the lack of economic capital to initiate a venture is balanced by social capital for subsistence entrepreneurs. The resources gathered by these entrepreneurs are mostly from their internal connections [22]. There is gender restraint faced by women which pose difficulty when finance acquisition is required in the appropriate amount as compared to the male members of the society [5, 21].

2.2 Digital Platforms Female Entrepreneurship

It was argued by McAdam that digital networking platforms such as social media play a powerful role in establishing female entrepreneurship. Digital entrepreneurship has been deemed as a means of overcoming the limitations that are present in the institutional environment, which also include the cultural practices which are unsupportive and have lower barriers to entry which enables the democratization of entrepreneurship [23]. This was established due to three benefits derived from social media tools which are; self-expression, connection with business partners, and customer interaction [3]. Media outlets have become a business platform where you engage with consumers and other stakeholders as well. Customers are contacted either through direct communication or with the help of influencers on social media who are regarded as credible and affordable. Women in Saudi Arabia accepted that this platform has empowered them and reduced their segregation walls. One of the very significant features of social media networking sites is sharing a connection online by finding a person online [24], and users of these sites focused routinely on the cultivation and maintaining personal relations through Twitter, Facebook, LinkedIn, and Instagram [24].

Literature has shown that most of the incentives related to female entrepreneurship have a goal to encourage self-employment and creating small ventures, actively making use of social media networks to advertise services and goods, and using the technology of mobile phones that are proved to be beneficial for women entrepreneurship development [25]. There are computer-mediated tools provided by social media platforms that help share, and create exchange information, ideas, career interests, and videos and pictures in the virtual networks and communities networks [26]. The main obstacle observed for women entrepreneurs is the struggle to balance their private and professional life, and gain financial resources [27], and social media is considered to be an aiding factor in enhancing female entrepreneurship. Social media can encourage establishing new businesses by women because of its flexible nature, nil or low investment, and operating costs for social media usage. There is the ease of collaborating, communicating with new people, gathering relevant information, and keeping in contact with others at a very low cost [28]. It is easy to find supplier and customer contacts through networking, social media also locates where the funding is, promotes innovation, and is a great platform to cultivate strategic partnerships [29]. Social media platforms are deemed to change the course of communication dynamics among businesses and individuals by expanding their networking circle [30]. And due to this very reason, many businesses have resorted to social media platforms for using it as a reliable and worthwhile communication tool [28]. Social media has a significant role in retailing, as it influences the buying decisions of the customers [31], depending highly on the customer reviews and promotions done through social media platforms. There are very few authors exploring the social media influence on the female entrepreneurs [25, 27, 31], even though there has been rising evidence on social media platforms giving rise to female entrepreneurship, in augmentation of the current businesses and providing services and interaction with customers [32]. Moreover, there is no academically proven evidence on social media accelerating the retailing entrepreneurship for women.

Some studies have explored the ultimate facilitating role of ICT in being a potential source for increasing economic activities for women, which applies to both developed and developing countries [33]. The gender gap has reduced when it comes to technology usage [34], women now use ICT to assist their entrepreneurial activities [35]. Previous research has concluded a gender difference when it comes to user behavior (e.g., mostly women use social media for socializing and maintaining relationships [35, 36]. Moreover, most works cited excluded the inclusivity of elder women and women from lower-class for which further research can be conducted to add to the literature.

People regard social media presence as a prerequisite for success as the most customer base is generated through social media and it is an efficient way of gathering feedback [9]. Both positive and negative feedback is regarded as beneficial. Digital social media platforms have transformed the communication possibilities for humans all over the world. There is an abundant number of options for digital social media presence, such as networking platforms (Facebook, Instagram), weblogs, wikis, and e-commerce sites which facilitate entrepreneurs to carry out their business in several ways. Social media platforms are considered not only marketing tools but also regarded as a mode of connection for women's communities. This also took into account the economic benefits and implications of women's online community building [9]. In the socially networked digital age, women are regarded as good transmitters of word-of-mouth, multi-level marketers, and brand advocates given the common assumption about women that they are naturally more expressive and social [37].

There are not only the social benefits women can derive from using social media platforms but also, they can use them to their advantage for starting their businesses and meanwhile balancing their personal everyday lives. Social commerce is understood as an entrepreneurial activity that uses social media to its advantage [38]. To derive favorable results from social commerce it is necessary to understand the use of platform features for women. Therefore, as put forward earlier it is important to recognize the progressing interaction with the social media platforms [39]. In the era of social networking digital platforms, various forms of self-enterprise have come up that facilitate women to financially support themselves. Women can earn through their creative skills such as mommy blogging, blogging about lifestyle, and skill micro-economies [9]. This research also supported the notion that for middle-class women who are at the stage of childbearing, this micro enterprising such as Etsy is a life-modifying solution that extends an arrangement between financially sustaining work and non-paid home chores.

Where social media offers freedom of expression and speech, it is also prevalent that online sexual harassment takes place here [40]. There are different types of harassment including, blackmailing by using a person's private pictures, sending messages that are sexually explicit without consent, being condescending to people due to their gender, publicly attacking someone with explicit language, etc. [41]. Even though sexual harassment takes place with both genders but it is observed through research that women become the main target in online presence, also this kind of sexual harassment is one of the most common types of online harassment against women [3, 4].

3 Methodology

A qualitative interpretive approach was adopted to assess the enabling forces by social media platforms for women digital entrepreneurs through their lived experiences. [3, 5]. The data was collected through semi-structured interviews with female digital entrepreneurs. The interviews were conducted through online means except for one interview that was conducted face to face. The interviews were taken in English and Urdu. Urdu interviews were first translated into English and then transcribed for analysis. The sample consisted of women in the age bracket of 23–40. Most of them are students in universities or housewives. The interviews lasted from 20 to 50 min. The interviews were translated and then transcribed to identify themes and a thematic analysis was conducted. This approach focuses on the participants' understanding of their practical experiences and the way this affected their choice to pursue digital entrepreneurship [3]. A sample of 18 women dealing in their digital ventures was taken. Most of the interviewees were part-time entrepreneurs. They had their entrepreneurial ventures started from 1 year to a 5-year range. These respondents were approached through contacts. A purposive sampling strategy was applied to find women entrepreneurs on digital platforms [6].

Like every other study, the limitations of this study are acknowledged. Despite empirical contribution and significant implications, this research can be further improved for future researchers to study. Firstly, the sample size for this research was small and can be increased to gather more substantial insights for research. This research mainly targeted women having product selling business, but further research can incorporate bloggers, content creators, influencers, and service providers to cover all categories of women digital entrepreneurs. Also, this research mainly takes sample size from urban cities of the country, further research can include the excluded women from rural areas as well. Another limitation of this study is that almost all interviewees had rather successful businesses, few failures can also be incorporated into the next studies for a balanced study. Furthermore, the sample size was mainly from Instagram and Facebook users, this can also be widened to incorporate other social media platforms.

The profiles of the interviewed women are mentioned in the below table, to maintain privacy the names of businesses and places are not revealed, women belong to urban cities of Pakistan (Table 1).

Table 1. Participant identifier

Interview profile data

Participant's identifier	Age	Type of business	Business age	Social media platform
Mischele	40	Bedding	4	Instagram, Facebook
Iqra	22	Design clothing	2	Instagram
Humna	25	Baking	1.5	Instagram
Zara	23	Design clothing	2	Instagram, Facebook
Maria	25	Graphic design	1.5	Instagram
Zenab	28	Retail	1	Facebook
Ubaida	24	Hand painted clothing	2.5	Instagram
Adila	38	Hand painted clothing	5	Instagram, Facebook, Twitter
Shanza	29	Clothing retail	3	Instagram
Zahra	24	Clothing	1	Instagam
Sana	26	Makeup retail	1	Facebook
Rida	26	Statonary	1.5	Instagram, Facebook
Sidra	24	Cooking	1.5	Instagram, Facebook
Maham	27	Cooking	2	Instagram
Rahma	25	Accessories	2	Instagram, Facebook
Saba	26	Doctor accessories	3	Instagram, Facebook
Khair-Un-Nisa	32	Paintings	1.5	Instagram
Nishat	23	Statonary	1	Instagram

4 Findings

The following section summarizes the findings of research on two themes identifying the role of digital platforms in aiding and empowering women entrepreneurs.

4.1 Digital Platforms Address Challenges of Place, Time, and Ease of Doing Business

Female entrepreneurs face difficulty when going out for business, as mostly the industries or markets are male-dominated. It is yet not completely normal for women to roam around freely in male-dominated markets. This creates the challenge of place, as women going out and owning their shop would be highly challenging due to several reasons. Digital platforms have eliminated these concerns for women who become digital entrepreneurs, by the convenience of their homes they can conduct their business. Almost all the respondents of this research agreed to this challenge was solved by digital platforms. When asked why they chose the digital space to start their entrepreneurial venture, one of the interviewees responded as follows:

"It is easier to start as you just have to create an account and there it goes. I had seen a couple of people who inspired me as there is no cost involved the way you have to establish a proper setup to do it physically. There is no need for that here (in digital space), you just have to gain more views and your customers keep coming. These days youngsters are mostly on these platforms. My father is extremely satisfied as if I have to pursue a job in my field, I will have to get ready in the morning and go as we have 9 to 5 jobs these days. But this is according to my convenience. I get up and sleep the way I want to; it is safe and very flexible." (Hamna)

As mentioned above, it solves the concerns of parents and guardians who are worried about women's safety knowing the conditions outside. Another respondent mentioned:

"What makes digital entrepreneurship acceptable in the culture is you don't need to go outside for doing a job. You can earn by sitting at home, especially for women. This makes women's life easier who want to contribute to the house budget and at the same time, their family doesn't allow them to work outside." (Maria)

Digital platforms such as social media networks that are mostly used for business are Instagram and Facebook. Women found it quite easier to start a business on these platforms. As these platforms require not much assistance or any starting costs are involved. Therefore, most women prefer a business with an online presence rather than a physical store for their business.

"I am a huge advocate when it comes to social media's benefits. I do understand the negative side of it as well because I have been in this business from the very beginning since my graduation, but I am a huge advocate of it. Because it gives you a lot of chances to experiment to reach out to a much larger audience, especially for small businesses and people with less money and less investment. They can have the comfort of their home as well without having to rely on other people. There are a lot of benefits when it comes to e-commerce businesses. You don't have to pay the rent; you don't have to cater for the maintenance, and you get a lot of chances to experiment. Physical businesses have limited audiences and a lot of hassle. E-commerce business is a lot easier and that is why I chose e-commerce business rather than physical space." (Rida)

Since online shopping and social media presence is rising at phenomenal levels, digital platforms are considered to reach the maximum audience. As most of the respondents replied for choosing Instagram or Facebook was their obvious choice as they believe and according to their knowledge, these platforms would reach more audiences than any physical store. Also, they think that everyone uses these platforms for starting their ventures as it is easy to reach and increase their audience. Similar responses shared by the respondents are as follows:

"It was because most of the startups are initiated there. One gets a chance to increase one's followers too." (Maham)

"It is extremely easy on Instagram as people just tag me on the picture of a cake made by me in their story or they share my post on their profile and their followers automatically are driven towards me and follow me. Initially, I used my account, so my reach was increased through my friends and family circle through a snowball effect." (Hamna)

"I use Instagram more than Facebook or any other social app. I have more friends and followers on Instagram. This helps me in spreading my business more rapidly. My friends and followers started to like my work and share it in their stories. Social media helped me a lot in this whole process." (by Maria)

The ease of doing business from the convenience of home through digital platforms provides women with a lot of opportunities. Women who are housewives and have the responsibility of children and chores that they can not go out looking for work, use the flexibility offered through digital platforms and not only contribute financially but can feel accomplished as well.

"I think social media platforms are perfect for women, they can be doing a job and well as manage housework also. She can sell what she is doing for a house by sharing cooking recipes, selling homemade food, etc. Social media platform creates many opportunities for especially household women." (Maria)

"Women are not just restricted to selling things online. There are plenty of other platforms to earn, like freelancing, digital marketing, and others. Digital platforms are like the rods provided to fishermen. They are tools to catch fish in the sea. They connect women with the world and let them compete on an equal level, making them feel confident." (Sidra)

4.2 Digital Platforms Breaking Cultural Barriers and Empowering Women

Women meet with several hurdles when they decide to do something on their own, owing to the patriarchal nature of society and culture that is more prevalent in the developing nations. Women in countries like Pakistan have to comply with cultural and religious factors when taking any major decision in their life. Interaction in male-dominated markets is the main concern, as not only does this make women uncomfortable, but it is also not allowed in many households. So digital platforms have provided women a tool to see and experience the outside world, break cultural barriers by having their earning medium despite cultural restrictions, and making them feel empowered. Not all interviewees were facing any problems due to the culture but knew at least someone who did, and also what most women around could face. They had the idea of what more opportunities these platforms hold for the women, thus empowering them.

"I have not faced any issue but there are girls who cannot directly interact openly in a different society. Even from a religious point of view, many girls here do a veil (do not show their face to the public) so they can carry out digital entrepreneurship easily without showing their face and interacting with people, and they can freely develop their personality and job. Many families are unsupportive, and one finds it difficult to go outside in many areas. So, these things become easy digitally." (Hamna)

Rida who runs her stationery business online, explains that she met with a lot of backlashes and that her parents were not supported due to culture, as women are expected to pursue careers such as being a doctor or a teacher as they are regarded as respectful career choices in Pakistan.

"Let me start with my family. I have seen many people who look back and say that their families were very supportive but that has not been the case with me. When you live in a patriarchal society, having an over-ambitious daughter is not a good thing and that is a challenge even for parents. That is the thing that scares my parents because I am very career-oriented, and like to work. I am very passionate about working. They wanted me to take a teaching job where I get free at 2 in the noon and get back home early. But I am not that kind of person. Throughout my working career, my parents have opposed my job. Even now, I did not tell anyone in my family that I was going to start this business. I didn't even tell my closest friends. The reason was that I wanted to test it first and then launch it into the market. Even if my family would not have supported me then my friends would have. So, I wanted to test whether people buy things from me even with a small following. I had twenty planners in the initial batch, and it was sold out in a week. So, I did my testing and then told my mother. She said "Rida, do people buy such things?". So, she asked me whether someone buys such things or not, so I told her that there are people like me who do buy such things. So, I kept telling her repeatedly that people do buy them. People love stationery. I show her all the things and she appreciates them. It has gotten better but not so much that she will assist me in my work." (Rida)

Every woman interviewed positively responded when asked if the venture has empowered them. Being independent gives them a sense of accomplishment which eventually empowers them in face of all the cultural or societal restrictions they have to face in a developing country like Pakistan.

"I can raise my voice so there is empowerment. If I had to sit at home for one and a half years, and I did not have a job concerning my field, I would have been left behind. But now I am interacting with everyone through social media, so it does empower me." (Hamna)

Women despite facing the challenges that come with online presence were observed to be quite satisfied by their experiences, as the price paid for being online and vulnerable to online world is quite less than the benefits, they reap from being a digital entrepreneur. Also, the hassle of online business is quite minimal when compared to conducting business offline. Although working online ensures work-life balance by providing the opportunity to work from home, but one of the responded Mischele, pointed out a very important drawback of being in online business:

"There is no 9-5 timing for me. I am answering to queries, receiving orders around the clock. These cellphones are all the time buzzing with work related stuff. So its like I am all the time working. Sometimes it gets too much, but again I am allowing this by not keeping a work phone separate." (Mischele)

5   Discussion and Conclusion

This article contributes to the literature on women's digital entrepreneurship. It highlights the contributing factors of social networking digital platforms to enable women's digital entrepreneurship. The questions answered in this article are mainly that how social networking digital platforms facilitate the entrepreneurial capability of women. As answered by most respondents that social media has given the freedom to women to start their ventures amidst social and cultural constraints. Given the social and cultural restrictions related to gender segregation, the social media digital platforms have the potential to improve the lived experiences of women [3], which was also confirmed by this study. It was also assessed that most women start their business because of becoming financially independent, which eventually benefits the economy and also their living standard. This research also confirmed through interviews that social media platforms play an important role in women's entrepreneurship [7]. They aid in developing networking with partners and customers.

The findings identified two main themes addressing the role of digital platforms such as social networking sites (e.g., Instagram, Facebook) aiding in women's digital entrepreneurship and empowering women in the society that are marginalized part of the culture and face many restrictions when it comes to nearly competing men. This study focused on the context of the developing country Pakistan. The research built upon the literature focusing on women's entrepreneurship in developing countries amidst patriarchal and culture-bound societies.

The findings identified two main themes generated through the interaction with women digital entrepreneurs. The first one is the digital social networking platforms addressing the challenges of time, location, and the ease of doing business for women. Enabling factors for women digital entrepreneurs are saving time, which women dealing with other home duties or studies regard as an important factor. Another main enabler is the ease of operating a business regardless of any place you are. Digital platforms such as Social Networks are regarded as an easy medium for doing business as it is very handy and with the help of a phone, you can conduct many operations regarding online business. Also, these networking platforms are already being used for entertainment and networking purposes by women which makes it easier. Interviewed respondents found this medium most preferred. Instagram was the most favored social media network as they were already using that platform for networking with friends and family. Mostly mentioned that their target market was already on the market so marketing and selling products through social media were easier.

Social media platforms have an immense role in creating female digital entrepreneurs. These platforms are mostly thrived by women and thus have more space for products targeting women. These platforms such as Facebook and Instagram have greeted a high number of entrepreneurs and influencers in recent times. The Covid quarantine emerged at a time when a huge number of women starting their ventures or blogs emerged. As they had more time on their hand and they were bound to their homes so decided to be more productive. Especially students with various talents were seen most for taking advantage of social networking sites for their ventures.

The second theme identified is digital platforms breaking cultural barriers and empowering women. Women are from a group of marginalized people who have been kept away from entrepreneurship, especially in developing countries due to cultural and social constraints. With the advent of digitalization, the inclination toward entrepreneurship has rocketed upward by women. It has given the flexibility and safe space to conduct business by using their creative skills such as content creation, craft, cooking, retailing, and services. In developing countries such as Pakistan, women are not encouraged to go out and conduct business or even do jobs. Women are mostly responsible to handle home affairs. Also, their safety is preferred by male members of the family therefore they are mostly restricted to their home. Digital platforms have made the lives of women easier by reducing socially created barriers in society. Women now feel empowered that they can run their ventures even while being at the ease staying at any location they prefer. The enabling factor for women in a developing country for entrepreneurship is most importantly safety. And it was established that social media platforms are a safe space for conducting business for women.

Social Networking Digital Platforms come with lots of facilitating factors for digital entrepreneurs, but no place can be completely free from challenges [42]. There are several digital-related challenges faced by women operating online. Women interviewed mostly mentioned scams, harassing, not paying, or returning packages while selling their products online. These challenges can demotivate women who have a lesser budget for investment. Also, as there is no restriction on expressing themselves, people become so much demotivating and criticize unnecessarily. Online sexual harassment is also one of the main concerns for women operating online [10]. Still, as observed, the risk of going out as compared to operating from home are very less.

Through this article, the importance of social media platforms is focused on creating more female digital entrepreneurs. It adds to the literature on female digital entrepreneurship. These platforms bring marginalized people into the face of the world. This article will make the enablers of female entrepreneurial culture focus more on digital networking sites as spaces for generating more female digital entrepreneurs.

References

1. Minniti, M., Naudé, W.: What do we know about the patterns and determinants of female entrepreneurship across countries? Eur. J. Dev. Res. **22**(3), 277–293 (2010). https://doi.org/10.1057/ejdr.2010.17

2. Chakraborty, T., Ganguly, M., Natarajan, A.: Predicting entrepreneurial satisfaction: the role of non-financial incentive factors and quality of life among women digital entrepreneurs. J. Glob. Bus. Adv. **12**(3), 328–355 (2019)
3. McAdam, M.: Digital girl: cyberfeminism and the emancipatory potential of digital entrepreneurship in emerging economies, p. 14 (2020)
4. Accenture: The promise of digital entrepreneurs: creating 10 million youth jobs in the G20 countries (2014)
5. LeBlanc, C.: Why the rise of DIY business tools is good for women business owners. Huffington Post **29** (2015)
6. McAdam, M., Crowley, C., Harrison, R.T.: 'To boldly go where no [man] has gone before' – institutional voids and the development of women's digital entrepreneurship. Technol. Forecast. Soc. Change **146**, 912–922 (2019). https://doi.org/10.1016/j.techfore.2018.07.051
7. Dy, A.M., Marlow, S., Martin, L.: A Web of opportunity or the same old story? Women digital entrepreneurs and intersectionality theory. Hum. Relat. **70**(3), 286–311 (2017). https://doi.org/10.1177/0018726716650730
8. Litt, E.: Knock, knock. Who's there? The imagined audience. J. Broadcast. Electron. Media **56**(3), 330–345 (2012)
9. Duffy, B.E., Pruchniewska, U.: Gender and self-enterprise in the social media age: a digital double bind. Inf. Commun. Soc. **20**(6), 843–859 (2017). https://doi.org/10.1080/1369118X.2017.1291703
10. Nova, F.F., Rifat, M.R., Saha, P., Ahmed, S.I., Guha, S.: Online sexual harassment over anonymous social media in Bangladesh. In: Proceedings of the Tenth International Conference on Information and Communication Technologies and Development, pp. 1–12 (2019)
11. Zaheer, H., Breyer, Y., Dumay, J.: Digital entrepreneurship: an interdisciplinary structured literature review and research agenda. Technol. Forecast. Soc. Change **148**, 119735 (2019). https://doi.org/10.1016/j.techfore.2019.119735
12. Minniti, M.: Female entrepreneurship and economic activity. Eur. J. Dev. Res. **22**, 294–312 (2010)
13. Dy, A.M.: Levelling the playing field? Towards a critical-social perspective on digital entrepreneurship. Futures 102438 (2019)
14. Fairlie, R.W.: The personal computer and entrepreneurship. Manag. Sci. **52**(2), 187–203 (2006)
15. Fuller, T.: Capturing the Dynamics of Co-Production and Collaboration in the Digital Economy (2010)
16. Matlay, H., Westhead, P.: Virtual teams and the rise of e-entrepreneurship in Europe. Int. Small Bus. J. **23**(3), 279–302 (2005)
17. Hanson, S.: Changing places through women's entrepreneurship. Econ. Geogr. **85**(3), 245–267 (2009)
18. Holmén, M., Min, T.T., Saarelainen, E.: Female entrepreneurship in Afghanistan. J. Dev. Entrep. **16**(03), 307–331 (2011)
19. Cromie, S.: Motivations of aspiring male and female entrepreneurs. J. Organ. Behav. **8**(3), 251–261 (1987)
20. Poggesi, S., Mari, M., De Vita, L.: What's new in female entrepreneurship research? Answers from the literature. Int. Entrep. Manag. J. **12**(3), 735–764 (2015). https://doi.org/10.1007/s11365-015-0364-5
21. Naser, K., Mohammed, W.R., Nuseibeh, R.: Factors that affect women entrepreneurs: evidence from an emerging economy. Int. J. Organ. Anal. **17**, 225–247 (2009)
22. Barrios, A., Blocker, C.P.: The contextual value of social capital for subsistence entrepreneur mobility. J. Public Policy Mark. **34**(2), 272–286 (2015)

23. McAdam, M., Crowley, C., Harrison, R.T.: The emancipatory potential of female digital entrepreneurship: institutional voids in Saudi Arabia. Acad. Manag. Proc. **2018**(1), 10255 (2018). https://doi.org/10.5465/AMBPP.2018.58

24. Boyd, D.M., Ellison, N.B.: Social network sites: definition, history, and scholarship. J. Comput. Mediat. Commun. **13**(1), 210–230 (2007)

25. Ukpere, C.L., Slabbert, A.D., Ukpere, W.I.: Rising trend in social media usage by women entrepreneurs across the globe to unlock their potentials for business success. Mediterr. J. Soc. Sci. **5**(10), 551 (2014)

26. Cesaroni, F.M., Demartini, P., Paoloni, P.: Women in business and social media: implications for female entrepreneurship in emerging countries. Afr. J. Bus. Manag. **11**(14), 316–326 (2017)

27. Plazibat, I., Renko, S.: Social media as a channel for boosting female entrepreneurship in retailing. AD Plast. Group **84** (2020)

28. Mukolwe, E., Korir, J.: Social media and entrepreneurship: tools, benefits, and challenges. A Case study of women online entrepreneurs on Kilimani Mums marketplace on Facebook. Int. J. Humanit. Soc. Sci. **6**(8), 248–256 (2016)

29. Zontanos, G., Anderson, A.R.: Relationships, marketing and small business: an exploration of links in theory and practice. Qual. Mark. Res. Int. J. **7**, 228–236 (2004)

30. Judie, C.: An exploratory study on the use of social media as a business networking tool: the case of four female-owned fashion retail businesses in the Stellenbosch area, Cape Town (2015)

31. Ramanathan, U., Subramanian, N., Parrott, G.: Role of social media in retail network operations and marketing to enhance customer satisfaction. Int. J. Oper. Prod. Manag. **37**, 105–123 (2017)

32. Fischer, E., Reuber, A.R.: Social interaction via new social media: how can interactions on Twitter affect effectual thinking and behavior? J. Bus. Ventur. **26**(1), 1–18 (2011)

33. Oreglia, E., Srinivasan, J.: ICT, intermediaries, and the transformation of gendered power structures. MIS Q. **40**(2), 501–510 (2015)

34. Rainer, R.K., Jr., Laosethakul, K., Astone, M.K.: Are gender perceptions of computing changing over time? J. Comput. Inf. Syst. **43**(4), 108–114 (2003)

35. Crittenden, V.L., Crittenden, W.F., Ajjan, H.: Empowering women micro-entrepreneurs in emerging economies: the role of information communications technology. J. Bus. Res. **98**, 191–203 (2019)

36. Hosseini, M., Tammimy, Z.: Recognizing users gender in social media using linguistic features. Comput. Hum. Behav. **56**, 192–197 (2016)

37. Shellnuitt, K.: Why your Facebook feed is filled with women selling essential oils and press-on nails. Libr. Cat. Www Vox Com (2016)

38. Constantinidis, C.: How do women entrepreneurs use the virtual network Facebook? The impact of gender. Int. J. Entrep. Innov. **12**(4), 257–269 (2011)

39. Camacho, S., Barrios, A.: Social commerce affordances for female entrepreneurship: the case of Facebook. Electron. Mark. (2021).https://doi.org/10.1007/s12525-021-00487-y

40. Megarry, J.: Online incivility or sexual harassment? Conceptualising women's experiences in the digital age. Women's Stud. Int. Forum **47**, 46–55 (2014)

41. Biber, J.K., Doverspike, D., Baznik, D., Cober, A., Ritter, B.A.: Sexual harassment in online communications: effects of gender and discourse medium. Cyberpsychol. Behav. **5**(1), 33–42 (2002)

42. Morais, E.P., Pires, J.A., Gonçalves, R.M.: E-business maturity: constraints associated with their evolution. J. Organ. Comput. Electron. Commer. **22**(3), 280–300 (2012). https://doi.org/10.1080/10919392.2012.696952

Gendered Inequality on Digital Labour Platforms in the Global South: Towards a Freedom-Based Inclusion

Rufaro Chibanda[1] , Pitso Tsibolane[1(✉)] , and Thando Nkohla-Ramunenyiwa[2]

[1] University of Cape Town, Cape Town, South Africa
chbruf001@myuct.ac.za, pitso.tsibolane@uct.ac.za
[2] University of Pretoria, Pretoria, South Africa
nkohla-ramunenyiwa.t@up.ac.za

Abstract. The gig economy promises flexible work arrangements and decent income, but it currently maintains a gender gap in employment. This paper analyses how gig platform work exacerbates gender inequalities experienced by women gig workers in the global South. The paper argues that the digital nature of these platforms not only accelerates the already existing inequalities outside of digital platforms, but also compromises the freedom of women on these platforms. Through the lens intersectionality, the paper contributes a philosophical lens on the notions of freedom through an empirical study. Fifteen (n = 15) female gig workers who use a digital cleaning gig platform were interviewed in Cape Town, South Africa. The main research question is: How does the intersectionality of race, gender and class for black female gig workers affect their freedom and compromise human dignity. The paper proposes a freedom-based inclusion for human dignity in digital platform-driven gig economy.

Keywords: Gig economy · Gender · Intersectionality · Exclusion · Freedom

1 Introduction

Digital labour platforms promise to profoundly disrupt normal labour relations, providing platform workers greater agency, dignity, and autonomy over their work lives. While scholars have challenged this promise and its fundamental claims, the critique is largely Euro-American in its nature. Perspectives from the global South, where digital labour platform are rising in popularity, tend to be missing. Despite this dearth of critical perspectives grounded in the social, economic, and historical realities of the global South, digital labour platforms continue to informalize and precarize labour conditions particularly for women who work in highly feminized economic sectors such as domestic cleaning services.

The global South has become one of the most used terms in contemporary academic discourse and has been more popularly used than its so-called predecessor's terms, namely "Third World" and "Developing Countries". What all three terms share is that

Y. Zheng et al. (Eds.): ICT4D 2022, IFIP AICT 657, pp. 55–68, 2022.
https://doi.org/10.1007/978-3-031-19429-0_4

they have never been used to refer to European or North America economies but have rather been used as political labels for countries linked with historical, colonial exploits. Sajed [1] sheds light into this conceptual endeavor of the terms by arguing that the global South is in fact not about a Southern geographical location, it is about any country on the globe (whether it is North, South, West or East) that has experienced the misfortunes of colonialization. In addition, it involves countries which have or are fighting against the compromise of the human dignity of their populations and the compromise of democracy in the nations. The compromise of human dignity and democracies has a become a struggle for centuries and has further become a fight for the attainment of freedom [1].

This attainment of freedom is pertinent in the global South countries, such as South Africa and Brazil. Both countries have sustained the reputation of being two of the most unequal societies in the world. Both countries have been ranked as "mostly unfree", which is the second lowest category for economic freedom ranking in the world, [2]. Moreover, in terms of democracy index, South Africa is ranked 45, Brazil: 49, placing both countries in the category of flawed democracies. The importance of outlining the freedom and democratic indexes serves as foundation for context of the discussion about freedom later in the paper.

Given the above, the inequality in South Africa and Brazil could permeate into the digital gig economy when it comes to technology and access. The gig economy (as a by-product of technological development) has ushered in labour-market activities that connect supply and demand through digital platforms [3]. Gig work can be classified as on-demand-work, or crowdwork. On-demand-work refers to services that are provided physically, with the provider and purchaser in close geographic proximity [4]. Whereas crowdwork are gig tasks that are conducted online [3]. These gig tasks mentioned are organised on digital gig platforms, by companies that set out the platforms' terms of service [5]. The companies act as intermediaries between the gig workers and those that purchase their services. The gig economy has helped give people more flexibility during work, because the work has no fixed hours [6]. Consumers have been provided with access to different services by the click of a button. However, even though the click of a button seems to be easy access, the gap between the rich and the poor even in digital space narrows down access to the gig economy only to those who have the technology [and literacy] to do so, speaking to the [gender] inequalities within the traditional labour market [7].

African women are 15% less likely to own a mobile phone than men are, and 41% less likely to have access and use of the internet [8], this is solely based on their gender. These gendered social norms that disadvantage and constrain women's entry and movement within the labour market may also be experienced digitally, where male relatives restrict women from using any digital technology [4, 9]. Restriction from technology use towards women results in them being disadvantaged by being excluded, because technology tools need an individual to use them practically to gain expertise and understand them better [4, 9].

Even though this study is focused on the population of black women, as they are the ones in this study who largely use the digital cleaning gig platform to get employment, there too lies further exclusions, as not all of them have access to the technology and digital literacy they need to get employment to supply cleaning services. On the one hand, with the demand side, it is a particular class of families who also have the access to technology and digital literacy to demand the service. On the other hand, there is also the exclusion of families who could benefit from such a service for their household but are excluded from demanding such a service because they cannot afford it.

The severity of South Africa's inequality is such that even the women who have the technology to access the digital gig economy to offer their cleaning services for instance, still experience exclusion, human indignity and unfreedoms. Hunt and Samman [10] establish that because women have other responsibilities such as childcare, even though they can access digital gig economy to supply services they are not able to work as many hours as their male counter parts who access digital gig platforms and get paid less. In addition, Hunt and Samman [10] states that men are able to offer services even in areas that would be considered a high crime area for women, which also narrows places where women can offer their cleaning services, as in the case for a cleaning digital gig economy which has a large number of women suppliers. Thus, women workers are excluded from opportunities that men receive in the digital gig economy. Ultimately, the research aims to propose an inclusion in the digital gig economy platform for women which will assist them to embrace the freedoms that will honor their right to human dignity. In fact, this will make their inclusion both on digital and societal platforms worthwhile as it will embrace the intersection of their gendered and racial discrimination.

2 Theoretical Framing – Intersectionality

The theoretical lens for this research is intersectionality, a feministic concept used to expose the marginalization of black women under sexism and racism [11]. It focuses on how wide a spectrum of human identities (such as gender, race, class, ability, sexual orientation, religion, and more) interact on simultaneous levels [12]. Zheng and Walsham [13] have made a call for the adoption of intersectionality as it sensitizes digital researchers to incorporate in their analysis the social positioning of actors within multiple hegemonies, hierarchies, and systems of power, and to problematize taken-for-granted boundaries in designing research questions and research approach. Intersectionality is therefore an important theoretical lens for this research as black women gig workers have been placed within a global South context. South African feminist Hassim [14] reveals that historically, South African women of color have experiences within the intersection of race, gender and class, creating three layers of discrimination. All of which, according to American feminist Hirschmann [15] have been built upon masculine understandings of social construction. In addition, Hirschmann [15] emphasizes that historical male domination, which is part and parcel of social construction, is the space where a woman is expected to create her reality. Her reality exists and is built upon a dominating masculine construction.

With the introduction of the digital gig economy as a platform of employment for black women, the three layers of discrimination as mentioned by Hirschmann [15] are evident, as this third dimension of class is portrayed through the dimension of digital access or lack thereof. It is class that provides or denies digital access, hence, it can be an inclusion or exclusion to the digital. In the midst of this three-layered intersection, what continues to persist is the fact that for inclusion to occur, women need to attain freedom(s).

Therefore, what value does inclusion have if it does not enhance freedom(s)? Satlaelo [16] quotes the Women Empowerment and Gender Equality Bill [17], which states the following "Equality includes the full and equal enjoyment of all rights and freedoms. To promote the achievement of equality, legislative and other measures designed to protect or advance persons, or categories of persons, disadvantaged by unfair discrimination may be taken". The South African Constitution echoes the same sentiments regarding rights and freedoms, in addition, the rights of human dignity for all. As a result, constitutionally, South Africa illustrates the image of a freedom-based inclusion. Nevertheless, this needs to be implemented and not remain as an idea.

3 The Gig Economy and Notions of Freedom

In South Africa, women experience high levels of segregation in the gig economy and most of the negative experiences they face are because they are black, and they are female [10]. These experiences of women in the digital gig platform will be discussed within the following areas specifically, gendered pay gap, insecurity, and recognition. Further, these themes will also be looked at through the lens of negative and positive freedoms.

3.1 Gendered Pay Gap

Gender pay gap can be defined as working-class women being paid less than working-class men in the Labourmarket [18, 19]. Different researchers have shown several figures to define gender pay gaps between men and women [19]. Previous studies done in the United States highlighted men earn 7% more per hour than women on average [18], this is in-line with gender earning gaps within defined jobs [20, 21]. The Census Bureau shows the annual pay of full-time workers, where women earn 80 cents for every dollar man are paid [19]. Another statistic looks at hourly pay and does not exclude part-time workers. It finds that relative to men, women are typically paid 83 cents on the dollar [18, 19]. Different researchers have shown several figures to define gender pay gaps between men and women [19]. Previous studies done in the United States highlighted men earn 7% more per hour than women on average [18], this is in-line with gender earning gaps within defined jobs [20, 21].

The gender pay gap mentioned above can be explained by a couple of varied factors [18]. Firstly, it can be explained by racial discrimination, relative to white male wages, black and Hispanic women are the most disadvantaged [19]. Asian and white women are paid less than their male counterparts are, but they earn better than black and Hispanic women do. This is a representation of the feministic theory of intersectionality, where those with more intersectionality are at a greater disadvantage [11]. There is an overlap of disadvantages for black women because they are disadvantaged by being black and by virtue of being a woman [11].

Secondly, women tend to take jobs that require a lower cadre of skills due to less experience in jobs requiring higher skill levels, so they earn less per hour than their male counterparts [10] do. In many developing countries, social norms have disadvantaged women because they are still beliefs that women should stay home, and men should go to school and later work in the Labour market [22]. According to studies done in the

United States men tend to have more experience especially when it comes to driving because they drive for longer hours each week and conduct more trips than a typical female and so they tend to earn more per hour as this lends them higher on the learning curve [18].

3.2 Insecurity

Insecurity is a feeling of inadequacy and uncertainty; it produces anxiety to handle certain situations [23]. Studies show women normally experience more insecurity than men do [5]. In gig work women experience insecurity in many different forms. Women are normally harassed by passengers while they work [24]. A survey from International Finance Corporation [25] stated that a percentage 64% of females from six different countries complained of not joining the ride-hailing sector in the gig economy for fear of exacerbated harassment induced by passengers [7]. This shows that women experience more vulnerabilities and they make them reluctant to work certain jobs that men work.

In Indonesia, some digital platforms had policy makers make regulation adjustments to their digital platforms against women being harassed at work [7]. These policies were adjusted to ensure the security of women while they work in digital platforms. Women in Indonesia feel safer to work after the regulations were adjusted than they did before [7]. The introduction of the National Commission of Violence Act against Women as the digital platforms code of conduct has lessened the level of harassment during work. This is because perpetrators fear the implications of being reported if they harass women while they work [7].

Studies show women believe digital gig platforms have a responsibility to ensure there is economic security of gig workers in all digital gig platforms, and they should give gig workers more flexibility over their work schedules [4, 7, 10]. If this is improved, women believe they will feel more secure and safe at work [7]. Some digital gig platform's actions to give a scored based feature on the application has improved the harassment levels at work because customers can be rated after each piece of work has been completed [7].

3.3 Recognition

Women are generally less recognized than men within digital platforms [26]. This is because women are perceived to be less educated than men, thus have less skill and experience [22]. Studies have highlighted that woman that drive or take part in parcel and food deliveries experience a higher cancellation rate from customers than their male counterparts [24]. Customers do most of these cancellations because they perceive women will not be competent enough to carry out the expected task for the customer. This lack of recognition demoralizes women and results in them choosing jobs that require less skill i.e., domestic work because those are the types of jobs women are expected to do; even though they will earn less. Women have been segregated for a long time in society and this has caused them to be a vulnerable group that is afraid of challenging the status quo, because they perceive they will not be heard due to experiences and still present experiences, which have normalized discrimination towards women.

Gendered pay gap, insecurity and recognition are themes which come from the challenges black women experience in the digital gig economy. The notion of freedom is not always the easiest concept to define, because with cultural and moral relativism, the term can have a different meaning in different contexts. Thus, this calls for a fitting starting point that would at least embrace diverse contexts to some common ground. It is through Berlin's [27] articulation of his "Two Concepts of Liberty [freedom]" that this can be achieved. These two concepts of freedom (liberty) are negative and positive freedom.

3.4 Gig Economy Platforms and Freedoms

3.4.1 Negative Freedom

The word "negative" in this case does not denote a freedom that is harmful, bad, undesirable, but denotes a negation, a so-called required absence for this freedom to be attained. Berlin [27] illustrates that this is in fact a freedom attained from the absence of an external source, such as coercion, as coercion can be an external hindrance that interferes with one's ability to execute [an act] in a situation where they could have executed that act. Essentially for Berlin [27], this external coercion disarms the ability to execute, hence infringing on one's freedom.

The gendered pay gap, insecurity and [lack of] recognition are all evidence of the ongoing presence of masculine socialization as mentioned by Hirschmann [15] earlier on in the paper. It serves as an external system that infringes on the freedom of the female worker, enforcing patriarchal stereotypes which discourage women to work outside of the home. The insecurity they experience is because of feeling unsafe because of the harassment cases some of them experience. Moreover, the lack of recognition is a lack of the acknowledgment of their capabilities. All of which not only infringe on the freedom of women but further exclude them from their right to human dignity. Also situated in the global South is the narrative of Malaysia, which also sees its women workers negotiating their agency in a society that has been built upon masculine, Muslin, social construction. Ong [28] illustrates that women were historically forbidden from working outside the home space "where they belong", they belong within the authority and protection of the husband which is in the home. Outside the home women were seen as been outside the protection and authority of their husband, and that could place them in positions of vulnerability. Similarly, the negative freedom of the women in Malaysia is disregarded in this case, excluding them from their right to human dignity.

It follows that the digital gig platform escalates the compromise of women's negative freedom because is it built upon the existing patriarchal social construction in society. The challenge with contemporary workspaces such as the digital gig economy is that with the rapid development of technology comes with the pressure to prioritize technological competency. To illustrate this, Wood et al. [29] mention how the function of digital work platforms could easily fall into the trap of promoting bad working conditions because not enough is known regarding its complex disembodied platform which work with embodied human beings. Wood et al. [29] lists the bad working conditions as "low pay, social isolation, working unsocial and irregular hours, overwork, sleep deprivation and exhaustion, [29, p. 937], all of which are the products of oppressive work systems for women, whether they are physical social spaces or digital, virtual platforms.

3.4.2 Positive Freedom

The second notion of freedom as mentioned by Berlin is a pro-active freedom, the freedom to self-actualize, to be one's own master [27]. Further, this kind of freedom is heavily laden on the foundations of subjectivity, not objectivity, a moral agency that is necessary to navigate through society. It is a freedom which stems from one's inner being, drive, motivation, and mindset. This freedom could shed some light going forward, when it comes to the experiences of women in the digital gig economy. However, the findings of the study will determine how this freedom can be applied.

4 Findings

The findings of this paper will be organised according to the previously discussed three themes of the challenges experienced by women in digital gig economy, namely, gendered pay gap, insecurity, and recognition. The data collection was conducted in 2021 (June to September). NVivo 11 was used to facilitated thematic analysis was used [32]. The purposively selected sample of 15 African women was analysed and data saturation was reached at 15th interview beyond which, no further data collection took place.

4.1 Demographics

The responses provided by the women gig works will be presented with ID numbers S01 to S15 to represents all the 15 interviewed respondents. The ID numbers provided serve as a protection of the identity of the respondents. All interviewed women were African (black), working on a single gig work platform living in the Western Cape Province of South Africa (Table 1).

Table 1. Demographics of the participants

ID	Age	Marital status	Experience on platform (years)
S01	40	Married	2
S02	38	Single	3
S03	30	Married	2
S04	27	Divorced	3
S05	40	Married	5
S06	38	Single	3
S07	26	Single	3
S08	36	Single	7

(continued)

Table 1. (*continued*)

ID	Age	Marital status	Experience on platform (years)
S09	35	Single	2,5
S10	32	Married	2
S11	25	Single	1
S12	42	Single	3
S13	36	Divorced	2
S14	31	Single	3
S15	35	Single	3

4.2 Gendered Pay Gap

When it came to gendered pay gap as a challenge for black women in digital gig economies, this is what the findings were as given by the respondents. In this section of the theme unequal pay for equal work presented that most women feel they get less pay compared to men despite of doing the same level of work. Men are given priority for jobs that require a higher calibre of skills and pays higher. This can be confirmed by the response given by S13 below:

> "*I feel as a female we get less pay than men despite of sometimes doing the same level of work. That is why I ended up in the digital cleaning gig platform and not like Uber, I wanted to work with Uber because I feel they earn more. Even at office job you notice men will have higher position than lady not because the lady is not competent but because she is female. It is a society issue but it's unfair to us ladies.*" – S13

In fact, most respondents feel that when it comes to their pay in general, their income is not enough to cater for their expenses especially those related to transport costs, rentals and child-care support. This was seen from responses given by S01, S03, S05 and S08.

> "*It is never enough but I try to find work each week so that I provide for my family. It also depends on how much I made the previous week. I also feel money we get is not enough for us to cater for childcare expenses.*" – S01

> "*It is not really enough; you know there is always so much needed in the home and the money we get is truly regarded as a fair wage but with the responsibilities I have it seems like it never fits.*" – S03

> "*Money is a problem as you know honestly speaking it is never enough for me. I would need more to balance things.*" – S05

> "*I do think the pay rates could be increased I guess as humans we base all this on our own expenses especially things like rentals.*" – S08

> "*Income is never enough rentals here in Cape Town are very expensive which just makes it the more difficult to cater for the family.*" – S14

Other respondents showed that the income is not enough, but it is better than what they received in full-time employment because they can earn money each week. They also mention that digital gig platforms are more flexible and allow one to work when they are free. This can be confirmed by the response given by S08.

"The income I get is really not enough for me I do wish I could receive more. At some point, I had an office job, it provided very good money, and now people thought I was crazy to join the gig world, but I honestly had no choice times have been rough lately. I still feel if compared to my monthly salary that I used to get I earn more now though it is not enough but its more and the work is flexible." – S08

4.3 Insecurity

As per the literature review, harassment is one of the challenges which even with the respondents' highlight was creating an insecurity in their work. Most respondents stated that they had experienced harassment due to the colour of their skin and the mere fact that they were female. Below the aforementioned can be seen by the responses given by S03 and S05.

"Well, it depends what type of harassment. If it is sexually no I have not but something like verbal harassment, I have, and it felt quite uncomfortable to keep working. The lady was white, and I honestly feel most of it was because of the colour of my skin because I am black. I don't know why they request us if they want to be that rude. I did something in a way she did not like, and she was generally in a bad mood on the day. So, the white lady was quite rude about the whole situation, and I had to eventually cancel the booking and reported to the digital cleaning gig platform because I no longer felt safe." – S03

"Well, I cannot really call it harassment but once I went to work for this white man and he said things that made me feel uncomfortable. He reminded me of Apartheid and how they were more superior to me that's why I do their dirty jobs. Maybe, it was harassment, but I told him I did not like the way he was addressing me. He was saying white will always be better, I don't really know what harassing that's maybe why I just thought it's rude and not like harassing." – S05

On the other hand, some respondents categorize themselves as being either lucky or blessed because they have never experienced any form of harassment at work. They have worked for good and polite people. This can be confirmed by S06 response below:

"No, I have been lucky enough to be safe each time I worked. I have never experienced harassment of any kind while working. I have met the most amazing people during the time I clean homes. One time a lady gave me a carton of muffins and beans with transport money to carry back home. Honestly, they are still good people out there. I think sometimes someone will be harassed because of their dressing or conduct in that home." – S06

The safety of the respondents provides more insight regarding their feelings of insecurities when it comes to their experiences on digital gig economy platforms. Most respondents feel scared to go to homes to clean especially for the first time, because they do not know if they will meet someone who may harm them at that household. They feel that because they cannot perform a background check on their clients they are at risk. This can be seen by the response given by S01 and S04.

"It is scary to go to homes when you do not know the people there, but you just must go, so you can survive. So far, I'm glad I have been safe. I wish we could background check the clients we do services for beforehand as well." – S01

"Most times, it is quite scary especially considering how far I have to travel to get work. Most houses I go to I have no idea who I am going to meet until I get there. I feel If they gave us an opportunity to background check the clients it would really be helpful." – S04

Some respondents feel the digital cleaning gig platform could do more to ensure their safety while they work. Yes, they confirm that there is something being done but it is not enough for them they feel vulnerable and want more to be done. Respondents feel the level of safety at work impacts the efficiency they will have at finishing the tasks assigned to them. If they feel unsafe, they will be less efficient at performing their duties. This can be seen in the responses given by S12, S02 and S05.

"I feel the digital cleaning gig platforms could really do more to ensure we benefit, and we are safe at work. Things like introducing panic buttons would help us because in the case that I am not safe it automatically means I don't work as efficiently as expected." – S12

"I do not think I can say they can ever do enough to ensure we are safe. We are mostly females working in a very scary environment so they should keep doing more for us." – S02

"They say they ensure where we go will be safe and we can call if we feel otherwise. But I don't think this is enough they could really do more." – S05

Respondents confirmed that they still travel to work even when they are afraid because they need the money to take care of their families. This can be seen by the response by S15 below

"I still go to work even when I feel unsafe because I need the money to take care of my family. I always have my mobile phone with me in case of emergency I will call my relatives to help me." – S15

4.4 Recognition

Findings presented by the theme of recognition showed that because of how society visualize women, most women have lost opportunities to work due to their gender, race and or background. Their work experience or skills becomes overlooked, leading to them not being recognized as capable for the job. It also showed that some experiences black female gig workers experience is not because they have done something wrong while working but due to stereotyping, they may be expected to fail and so the slightest mistake will cause them harm. This can be confirmed by responses given by S01 and S03.

"I feel that as a female we earn less than men despite of sometimes doing the same level of work. That is why I ended up in digital cleaning gig platform and not like the digital driving platform, I wanted that platform, but I could not get it because I do not have money to get me a driver's license, I grew up in the rural areas all I have ever know is household work because I'm female driving is for men. So, the digital cleaning gig platform became all I could go for. All the boys in my family went to school and now can drive but as girls we were disadvantaged." – S01

"The lady was white, and I honestly feel most of her attitude was because of the color of my skin because I am black and not because I did something wrong." – S03

Findings showed that women feel the way jobs are allocated is unfair because more females are working in domestic work than males. They think it's because domestic work is considered a job for the unskilled, thus it is predominantly female dominated. This can be seen by the response given by S15.

"I feel there is a level of unfairness in the way things are in the way jobs are given. If we look at Sweep South, they are so many black and female ladies. Very few males work in domestic work, and it's characterized with being unskilled. If we want to work in higher skilled jobs, we not given such opportunities which is not fair." – S15

5   Freedom as the Basis of Inclusivity

The concept of freedom in the global South countries, first as a democracy and then as the type of economy the country has is quite telling of the kind of freedom the country would embrace on an individual level for its citizens. With such a flawed democracy (as shown earlier by the Economic Index), South Africa has a lot to grapple with regarding its colonial past, and hence as a nation has a lesson of freedom to transfer to the South African citizen, both male and female. As things stand, the South African constitution [30] is a symbol of hope for the nation, the fact that is has been so well articulated, it used to be an idea, but this idea is now shared in a physical and electronic document for every South African to see. In its inclusive nature it represents the promise that an inclusive society can be imagined, and hence can be realized. Even as technological development has thrown in complexities such as the digital divide and challenges that black women face in digital gig economies, a way forward is possible. Berlin's concepts of freedom are valuable in that they set the bases of freedom, from then on what is added or removed will be what is best suitable for the human subject it is designed for. In this case, these concepts of freedom (liberty) require both an African and a feminist perspective, customizing the freedom accordingly to pertain to black South African women in the digital gig economy.

Siame's [31] rendition of positive and negative freedom is written from the African context and affirms that the freedom of a nation is the freedom for the individual citizen. He illustrates that with a colonial past, the emancipation of Zambia is the emancipation of the Zambian individual. The independence of the nation is the independence of the individual. Conversely, Isaiah Berlin, who is of the view that national freedom is separate from individual freedom, reveals by this standpoint that his take on freedom is not custom made for the African government and its citizens. Likewise, it follows that until South Africa is fully free from the colonial, masculine construction of society on the physical front, this will permeate in the digital front as well. It follows that Hirschmann [15] mention of women to socially construct themselves from the vantage point of postcolonial feminism [15, p. 140] is quite important, as this will allow women to distance themselves from colonial ideals which still fester in African communities. The negative and positive freedom still have an important place, because together, they affirm the statement "I am not restricted by anyone, I am my own master." To have both the "freedom from" and "freedom to" is an essential position for South African women in digital gig spaces. To avoid the criticism that Berlin's freedom receives, which is that it is a binary kind of freedom. This binary nature can be broken by the feature of the African and feminine perspectives into the freedom of black South African women. It is this kind of freedom needed by the black South African woman to be included in the physical or digital spaces she enters. It is a freedom which connects her to her right to human dignity.

6   Conclusion

This paper critically analyses how digital labour platforms, particularly domestic cleaning gig platforms, tend to worsen gender inequalities in the global South for women gig workers. Our in-depth interviews with black women domestic cleaning gig workers provide further empirical evidence of technologically aided structural unfairness that society and policymakers should seek to transform to secure decency in platform labour platforms. This research also illustrates intersectionality as an important analytical lens to visibilize multi-layered and interconnected struggles of the marginalised particularly in contexts where inequality is pervasive. While digital labour platforms have the potential to contribute positively to the livelihoods of marginalized women, there is a need for a sustained global South-based critical analysis to shine the light on the negative consequences of new technologies. This critical analysis reflects and focusses on the extent to which positive and negative freedoms of the vulnerable women are impacted by technology, interlaced with African-centred feminine perspectives of decency and dignity to recentre a holistic view humanness in the future of work. A major limitation to this study is that it considered the views of purposively selected women based in a narrow geographical location (Western Cape, South Africa) working on the same platform. Future studies should consider a more heterogenous sample across a various regions of the country.

References

1. Sajed, A.: From the Third world to the Global South. E-International Relations (2020)
2. Index for Economic Freedom. The Heritage Foundation (2021)

3. Hunt, A., Samman, E.: Gender and the Gig Economy: Critical Steps for Evidence-Based Policy. ODI (2019)
4. Hunt, A., Machingura, F.: A Good Gig? The Rise of On-Demand Domestic Work. ODI (2016)
5. De Stefano, V.: The Rise of the "Just In-Time Workforce": on demand work, crowd work and labour protection in the "gig-economy." Sociol. Comp. Labor Law Policy J. **37**(471), 471–504 (2015)
6. EY Global: How the gig economy is changing the workforce (2018)
7. Putri, T.E., Kusumaningtyas, A.P., Darmawan, P., Simanjuntak, R.T.: #ChoosetoChallenge Unfair Gig Work: Indonesian Women Driver Experience in Ojek Online Industry. Center for Digital Society (2021)
8. Rowntree, O.: Bridging the Gender Gap: Mobile Access and Usage in Low-and Middle-Income Countries. GSMA Connected Women Programme, London (2019)
9. Hunt, A., Samman, E., Mansour-llle, D.: Syrian women refugees in Jordan: opportunity in the gig economy (2017)
10. Hunt, A., Samman, E.: Women in the Gig Economy: Paid Work, Care and Flexibility in Kenya and South Africa. ODI (2019)
11. Crenshaw, K.: Demarginalizing the intersection of race and sex: a black feminist critique of antidiscrimination doctrine, feminist theory and antiracist politics (1989)
12. Crenshaw, K.: Race, gender, and sexual harassment. South. Calif. Law Rev. **65**(1467), 1467–1476 (1992)
13. Walsham, G., Yingqin, Z.: Inequality of what? An intersectional approach to digital inequality under COVID-19. Inf. Org. **31**(1) (2021)
14. Hassim, S.: Critical thoughts on keywords in gender and history: an introduction. Gender Hist. **28**(2), 299–306 (2016)
15. Hirschmann, N.J.: Toward a feminist theory of freedom. Polit. Theory **24**(1), 46–67 (1996)
16. Setlaelo, S.: Conceptions of Freedom in South African Feminisms. Masters Dissertation. University of Johannesburg (2021)
17. South African Government. Women Empowerment and Gender Equality Bill. Ministry of Women and Youth with Disabilities (2013)
18. Cook, C., Diamond, R., Hall, J., List, J.A., Oyer, P.: The Gender Earnings Gap in the Gig Economy: Evidence from Over a Million Rideshare Drivers. NBER Working Paper Series (2018)
19. Gould, E., Schieder, J., Geier, K.: What is the Gender Pay Gap and Is It Real? The Complete Guide to How Women Are Paid Less Than Men and Why It Can't Be Explained Away. Economic Policy Institute (2016)
20. Forsman, A.J., Barth, J.M.: The effect of occupational gender stereotypes on men's interest in female dominated occupations. Sex Roles **76**(7–8) (2017)
21. Bayard, K., Hellerstein, J., Neumark, D., Troske, K.: New evidence on sex segregation and sex differences in wages from matched employee-employer data. J. Law Econ. **21**(4), 887–922 (2003)
22. Pope, D.G., Syndor, J.R.: Geographic variation in the gender differences in test scores. J. Econ. Perspect. **24**(2), 95–108 (2010)
23. Brennan, D.: Signs of Insecurity. WebMD (2020)
24. Setyowati, D.: Go-Jek's female driver orders are often canceled compared to men. Katadata (2018)
25. International Finance Corporation. Driving Toward Equality: Women, Ride-Hailing, and the Sharing Economy. Gender Links Opinion and Commentary Service (2018)
26. OECD. Empowering women in the digital age. Where do we stay? (2018)
27. Berlin, I.: Two Concepts of Liberty. Four Essays on Liberty, England, pp. 118–172. Oxford University Press (1969)

28. Ong, A.: Spirits of resistance and capitalist discipline: factory women in Malaysia. Bull. Sci. Technol. Soc. **8**(4), 448 (1987)
29. Wood, A.J., Lehdonvirta, V., Hjorth, I., Graham, M.: Networked but commodified: the (dis) embeddedness of digital labour in the gig economy. Sociology **53**(5), 931–950 (2019)
30. South African Government. The Constitution of the Republic of South Africa Act 108. The President's Office (1996)
31. Siame, C.N.: Two concepts of liberty through African eyes. J. Polit. Philosophy **8**(1), 53–67 (2000)
32. Braun, V., Clarke, V.: Using thematic analysis in psychology. Qual. Res. Psychol. **3**(2), 77–101 (2006)

Factors Affecting Citizens' Use of e-Participation Platforms: A Case of GovChat Platform in Cape Town Municipality

Aiden Katzef, Nozibele Gcora Vumazonke(ID), Wallace Chigona(ID),
Teofelus Tonateni Tuyeni(ID), and Chimwemwe Queen Mtegha(✉)(ID)

University of Cape Town, Rondebosch, Cape Town, South Africa
{ktzaid001,gcrnoz001,tnyteo002,mtgchi003}@myuct.ac.za,
wallace.chigona@uct.ac.za

Abstract. Citizen participation is critical to a democratic government as it allows the public to be involved in the decision-making process. e-Participation platforms enable the citizens to participate and voice their concerns. However, there is generally a low usage of e-Participation platforms by the citizens. This paper examines the factors affecting citizens' use of e-Participation platforms in facilitating citizen participation. The study employed a case study approach using the GovChat platform in Cape Town municipality. The study used a qualitative research method and a deductive approach to theory. The Capability Approach theory was used to investigate the phenomenon of interest. We used the purposive sampling technique to select the 30 participants in the study. In addition, semi-structured interviews were used to collect data from the selected participants. Our results suggest that personal, environmental and social factors affect the effective use of the GovChat platform by citizens in Cape Town municipality.

Keywords: GovChat · Citizen participation · e-Participation platforms · Government · Municipality · Capability approach

1 Introduction

Citizen participation is integral to the democratic decision-making process as it allows citizens to influence public decisions [1]. The primary goal of citizen participation is to ensure that citizens have a voice in public decisions. Citizen participation legitimises government decisions and ensures that the citizens' interests are reflected in the public choices [2]. Consequently, countries worldwide are implementing various measures to encourage citizen participation in critical public decisions. Participatory Budgeting (PB) is one of the standard measures of involving citizens in budget allocation decision-making. PB is widely considered worldwide as a novel approach to policymaking that permits ordinary citizens to have a say in public budgeting. However, citizen participation is still a challenge in developing countries due to a lack of awareness among decision-makers and officials on its benefits to community transformation [3].

© IFIP International Federation for Information Processing 2022
Published by Springer Nature Switzerland AG 2022
Y. Zheng et al. (Eds.): ICT4D 2022, IFIP AICT 657, pp. 69–88, 2022.
https://doi.org/10.1007/978-3-031-19429-0_5

South Africa experiences a high number of citizen protests due to poor service delivery by local governments and a lack of alignment between the vision and goals of the government and the wants and needs of the citizens [4, 5]. Citizens complain that their voices are only heard leading up to and during the governmental elections when political parties have become notorious for making empty promises [6]. South Africa's history of apartheid continues to affect the nation. Although the country holds regular democratic elections, many citizens still believe that they have no voice [6]. The traditional way of participation is through local government structures, i.e., ward councillors. Ward councillors represent the public voice and ensure accountability in the government [7]. However, many South Africans do not know their respective local ward councillors [8].

Currently, South Africa is beginning to reassess its citizen engagement strategy by looking toward current and future technological trends to connect with the citizens [9]. In 2018, the government launched the GovChat platform to facilitate citizen participation and improve transparency. Despite the launch of the GovChat, service delivery protests are at an all-time high in South Africa, and citizen participation is still low [10]. The GovChat has limited success, with only a fraction of the population adopting the GovChat platform [11].

Studies have shown several factors that impede the use of e-participation platforms. These factors relate to citizens' satisfaction with e-participation platforms and government responsiveness towards e-participation. These factors include the quality of participation, citizens' level of education, trust and responsiveness, perceived benefits, and the ability to interact with the government [12] actively. In addition, other factors such as citizens' community commitment, subjective norms, and strength of offline social ties influence citizens' e-participation [12].

This exploratory study describes factors affecting e-participation using a case of GovChat in Cape Town municipalities. The study provides new insights into the potential uses of GovChat for citizen participation. By asking questions about the application of the GovChat platform and assessing the phenomena in a new light. The study intends to achieve its primary goal of exploring the possible ways in which GovChat can facilitate citizen participation at a local municipal level in the city of Cape Town by answering the following research questions:

- *What factors affect the use of the GovChat platform in Cape Town municipality?*

This study employed the Capability Approach (CA) as the theoretical framework to assess the use of the GovChat platform for citizen participation. The study further adopted an interpretivism research paradigm and used semi-structured interviews as the primary source of data collection. Purposive sampling was employed to select appropriate participants, which constituted ordinary citizens and ward councillors. The study will inform government officials on improving citizen participation through ICT and developing e-participation platforms that the citizens can adopt.

2 Literature Review

2.1 Citizen Participation Process

Citizen participation is a process that allows individuals to influence public decisions and is an integral component of the democratic decision-making process [13]. The terms "citizen participation" and "citizen involvement" are used interchangeably to depict the same meaning. However, these terms are different. Citizen 'involvement' is likened to the top-down approach, while 'participation' is prompted by the citizens [14]. The fundamental question in participation that needs to be scrutinised is 'who is entitled to participate?' [15]. The entitlements to participation are categorised as follows: rights (citizens), spatial location (residents), knowledge (experts), share (owners), stake (beneficiaries/victims), interests (spokespersons) and status (representatives) [15]. The advantages of citizen participation include avoiding conflicts between citizens and government, trust and confidence between the citizens and the agency, and citizens feeling part of the community [16]. Despite the positive attributes of citizen participation, it is very costly and time-consuming [14].

There are distinct levels of citizen participation that can lead to different outcomes, and Arnstein [17] discussed the typology of citizen participation into eight rungs on the ladder. The ladder of citizen participation in Table 1 depicts the degrees of involvement and power struggle by mare citizens trying to gain control in participation [17].

Table 1. Arnstein's ladder of citizen participation [18, 19]

Ladder of citizen participation		
8	Citizen control	Citizen power
7	Delegated power	
6	Partnership	
5	Placation	Tokenism
4	Consultation	
3	Information	
2	Therapy	Nonparticipation
1	Manipulation	

Manipulation and therapy are categorised as nonparticipation and are the lowest rank on the ladder to depict 'no power' [17]. The second category is tokenism which includes informing, consultation, and placation. Informing is distributed top-down from the powerholders to citizens, and there is no room for feedback or power negotiations. This information is spread using means of media news, posters etc. In the consultation stage, information flow is simultaneous; however, the information obtained through consultation is not considered. Lastly, placation citizens can advise, but decision making is left to the powerholders. Citizen power is comprised of partnership, delegated authority, and citizen control. There are arrangements in which both citizens and powerholders can make decisions and delegate responsibilities. It enables citizens to feel accountable for their choices for the community's betterment.

The drawback of the ladder of participation is that it is regarded as 'goal-oriented', meaning citizen participation should attain the highest rank. If not achieved, it means failure in citizen participation [20]. Secondly, the roles and responsibilities change as you move in the ranking. However, this is not always the case because responsibilities might shift during the participatory process [17]. In light of citizen participation in most developing countries, citizens cannot fully participate in developmental discussions due to the economic, political, and social environment; as a result, many fall in the lower rank of the Arnstein ladder of citizen participation [21]. Nevertheless, my scholars have argued that citizens need to participate in the country's decisions [21, 22].

2.1.1 Benefits and Challenges of Citizen Participation

Citizen participation plays a vital role in democracy and creates multiple other benefits for society. Citizen participation aids in informing and educating the public. Active citizens are more knowledgeable and have better access to government decisions [20]. It further helps build and strengthen democracy at the local level [13]. On top of this, government decision-making is maintained as the communities contribute to decision making.

Citizen participation is often bedevilled by several challenges, such as:

- Low citizen knowledge, citizen participation is futile if the public cannot make informed decisions;
- The public belief that their participation is not valued or wanted;
- Lack of public trust or legitimacy;
- Citizen apathy, as all citizens have an opinion about decisions concerning their community, but many lack the drive to participate actively;
- Time constraints restrict citizen participation most current avenues of public participation are time-consuming; and
- Fear that self-interest will conflict with the interests of society restricts citizen participation.

2.2 Citizen Participation in Africa

For democracy to be realised, ordinary citizens need to be involved in the country's decision-making processes. Many African countries are in a transitional phase of democracy, as most countries have had to undergo political transformation [23]. However, through technology platforms, many citizens in the African continent are voicing their concerns. Despite the myriad opportunities that technology provides for ordinary citizens to engage and discuss the decisions in the country, consequences have followed for many citizens [24]. The political landscape for many African nations does not provide the platforms where citizens can loudly and freely engage with the governments to harness democracy. Therefore, many citizens in the continent are not actively involved in decision-making processes [25, 26]. However, some countries in the continent are now beginning to realise that for Africa to transform, and citizens need to be fully engaged.

Scholars have also questioned citizen participation, as many follow the "top-down" approach to development [27]. These approaches have limited both rural and urban development [27]. In addition, literature has also shown that the disadvantaged are usually not included in developmental discussions resulting in poor outcomes that do not serve the needs of the people, which has been a growing concern [25]. In addition, it has also resulted in a lack of trust and confidence in governance [28]. Entities, for instance, civil society organisations, have been able to participate to some extent [19]; however, as already mentioned, these entities' social and political environment has been a challenge to the African continent [5].

2.2.1 Citizen Participation in South Africa

On a national level, the ruling African National Congress (ANC) adopted a centralised technocratic approach to decision-making concerning public spending. Experts in specific fields are elected to decide public expenditures on behalf of the citizens [1]. Citizen participation, however, is best implemented at a local level as these programs are more effective when targeting the grassroots of individual communities [1]. Furthermore, South Africa's local municipalities are autonomous, governing themselves and controlling their affairs, making citizen participation feasible at a local level [1]. However, South Africa still lags in its citizen participation programs but has the potential for growth [29].

Section 214 of the South African Constitution states that South Africa's revenue is to be shared among national, provincial, and local levels of government in a process called fiscal decentralisation [29]. Accordingly, it is the responsibility of these spheres of government to allocate their provisioned cut of the budget to areas and projects they deem appropriate.

The apartheid era in South Africa resulted in the planning of cities and towns with racially divided business and residential areas, with poor areas having far less access to services and far higher population density than affluent areas. In addition, the structure of South Africa's poor areas makes service delivery a challenge, resulting in rural areas being underserviced and underdeveloped. As a result, municipalities have adopted an Integrated Development Planning (IDP) method at a local level to plan future development in these disadvantaged communities [30].

IDP is a citizen participation program that aims to involve citizens within the municipality to find solutions for long-term development [31]. The municipal IDP Committee has community representatives within these municipalities known as wards. Community representation is crucial for the department of provisional and local government in South Africa, but the current representation does not reflect the community accurately. For example, representatives in these committee meetings are often members of a higher income bracket within the community and do not represent the lower-income groups [32].

Department of Provincial and Local Government [31] developed a 5-phase process to develop the IDP. Firstly, an analysis is conducted to collect information on the current conditions in the municipality. Problems faced by people in the municipality and the cause of these problems are identified and prioritised as well as identifying the allocated resources for solving these problems. Secondly, strategies are developed to find solutions to these problems by developing a vision, defining the objectives and identifying the best methods for achieving these objectives. Thirdly, municipalities design projects based on the methods obtained from the strategy phase. Finally, targets and Key Performance Indicators (KPIs) are established for each project to monitor its success. In the fourth phase, all projects and development plans are integrated as these projects cover a broad spectrum of issues from poverty alleviation to healthcare. Finally, the IDP needs to be approved by the council for adoption. The council can also publish a draft IDP for public comment, but the council does not commit to acting on the public's comments.

Although local municipalities have fiscal decentralisation, where different levels of the government have mobility from one another, the autonomy and financial freedom of local government are still limited [29]. This is especially true in poorer communities, as donors are more interested in investing in affluent areas, and the communities are too poor to collect their own revenue through taxes.

Current participatory processes are facilitated at the mayor's office, exposing the processes to possible political interference. Participatory processes can be structured to exclude certain people from actively engaging [33], and it poses a high risk in South Africa, where there are 11 official languages. The participatory processes can exclude people by hosting public deliberations in selected languages. Leduka [34] highlighted the risk that contracting companies might manipulate participatory processes to favour their business interests and disregard the actual needs of the communities.

South Africa's high level of inequality has resulted in many citizens lacking the education necessary to understand how they can engage with the government [35]. Access to this information is also limited, preventing the empowerment of citizens [29]. In addition to this, most of South Africa's ward councillors lack the knowledge and means to inform their citizens of citizen participation processes. According to ward councillors' statistics, South Africa has four hundred and sixty-seven ward councillors [36].

Citizen participation does not end once budgeting decisions have been made; municipal representatives oversee these projects or risk not meeting requirements. Unfortunately, municipal representatives often lack accountability and tend to disregard the oversight of community projects. Issues are only discovered once these projects have been implemented, leading to a waste of limited resources [29].

2.3   Challenges of Citizen Participation in South Africa

South Africa is no exception, and given its economic and political history, it has its challenges regarding citizen participation implementation [1]. Although local municipalities have fiscal decentralisation, the financial freedom of local governments is still limited. This is especially true in poorer communities, as donors are more interested in investing their money into affluent areas, and the communities are too poor to collect their revenue through taxes.

Current participatory processes are facilitated at the mayor's office, exposing the processes to possible political interference. Participatory processes can be structured to exclude certain people from actively engaging in them [33]. This poses a high risk in South Africa, where there are 11 official languages, and participatory processes can exclude a group of people by hosting public deliberations in select languages.

Leduka [34] highlighted the risk that contracting companies might manipulate participatory processes to favour their business interests and disregard the actual needs of the communities.

South Africa's high level of inequality has resulted in many citizens lacking the education necessary to understand how they can engage with the government. Access to this information is also limited, preventing the empowerment of citizens [29]. In addition to this, most of South Africa's ward councillors lack the knowledge and means to inform their citizens of citizen participation processes.

Citizen participation does not end once budgeting decisions have been made; they require municipal representatives to oversee the implementation of these projects, or else they risk not meeting requirements. Unfortunately, municipal representatives often lack accountability and tend to disregard the oversight of community projects. As a result, issues are only discovered once these projects have been implemented, leading to a waste of limited resources [29].

2.4 e-Participation Platforms for Citizen Participation

Digital or e-Platforms for citizen participation are recognised as essential tools that enable citizens to participate in decision-making processes [37]. About 51 e-participation platforms were in use in January 2020, and participatory budgeting is the most utilised in the e-platform [38]. These platforms allow citizens to have a voice in the service delivery and reach a wider audience, providing broader opportunities for engagement and collaboration [39, 40]. There are distinct types and categories of e-participation platforms, formal and informal. The focus of the study is on the platforms developed by the government to engage with the citizens to influence policies at the national and local levels, referred to as formal e-participation platforms. Over the years, e-participation platforms have transformed how citizens interact with private and public organisations [41]. The GovChat platform is an example of a formal e-participation platform, an initiative of the government of South Africa. Although some of the e-participation platforms have been a success, others have failed. Some of the reasons for the failure of e-platforms include stakeholders' dissatisfaction and lack of innovation and support [42].

e-Participation platforms for citizen participation can serve as both Citizen-to-Government (C2G) and Government-to-Citizen (G2C). C2G e-platforms aim to provide citizens with a platform to share, collaborate and disseminate information [43, 44]. A C2G e-platform further allows citizens to engage with public administrators by sending direct messages and discussing public initiatives [42]. G2C e-platforms, on the other hand, offer the citizens diversity of information and services online and enhance the relationship between government and citizens. These services include payments of city utilities and applications for grants and facilities [42]. Table 2 shows some e-participation platforms for citizen participation and governance.

The city of Jakarta, for instance, uses the Olue MyCity to identify issues and problems the city is facing. This mobile application allows citizens to report, among other things, clogged drains, waste disposal issues, damaged streetlights and roads and floods. The government then responds to the problems reported [39]. City-as-a-Platform (CaaP) is considered an emerging form of open governance for urban areas that facilitate collaboration between different actors in society [44]. They proposed four main categories

Table 2. List of some of the e-participation platforms, types, and the countries of origin [39, 43, 45]

Country	e-Participation platform	Platform type
City of Reykjavík, Iceland	Better Reikjavik	C2G, G2C
UK	Fix My Street	C2G, G2C
France, Paris	Madame la Maire, J´ai un idée	C2G, G2C
USA, Boston	New Urban Mechanics	C2G, G2C
Kenya	Ushahidi	C2G
South Africa	GovChat	C2G, G2C
Indonesia, Jakarta city	Qlue MyCity	C2G, G2C

of CaaP, 1) Low G2C–low C2G, where the government's role is limited to providing and making information available to the citizen online. 2) Average G2C–average C2G. In this category, the platform serves to consult and aid the government in decision-making. There is a high level of interaction in this category. 3) Medium G2C–high C2G; these platforms have a high level of interaction and allow for the organisation of virtual events such as workshops. 4) High G2C—high C2G allows high-level interaction and software applications with Application Programming Interface [44].

2.5 GovChat Platform

The GovChat is a Citizen-Government engagement platform to improve governance, transparency, and accountability by providing a platform for citizens to assess service levels. The platform was launched in October 2018. The primary focus of the GovChat is on local government engagement [46]. The platform empowers South Africans to participate in the betterment of the lives of all citizens. The platform allows citizens to rate and report government facilities and services [47]. Citizens can also apply for social grants and log a service delivery request using the GovChat, allowing responsible ward councillors to get involved quickly.

Citizens can use WhatsApp, Messenger, or desktop applications to select services or rate services experienced and facilities. The location functionality on the platform allows citizens to choose the address where the issue to be addressed is located. However, the platform requires users to have the basic computer knowledge to navigate through. For Citizens to use the platform, they need to have access to the internet. Citizens with feature phones can submit service requests through an Unstructured Supplementary Service Data (USSD) code. Currently, the GovChat platform offers three features for the users: Rating and reporting facilities, submitting service requests, and making donations to the community [45]. These features are still relatively limited but appear to be the start of what GovChat has planned for the citizens of South Africa [45]. The GovChat has the potential to play a vital intermediary between the municipality and the citizens and mitigate challenges to citizen participation. In addition, it has the potential to increase citizens' knowledge of current information in the municipality. Furthermore, it also has the potential to increase public trust through the transparency of information. Figure 1 shows a sample of the GovChat application.

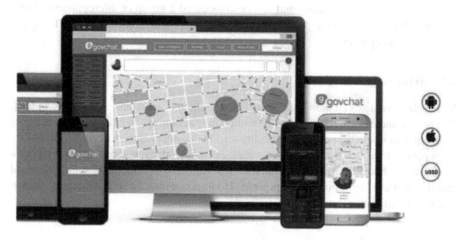

Fig. 1. The GovChat platform [45]

3 Theoretical Framework

The limited use of e-Participation platforms provides the basis for the study. Subsequently, we employed the Capability Approach (CA) to investigate the phenomenon. The CA was developed by an economist Amartya Sen in the 1980s. The theory is prominently used in developmental studies, political science, and philosophy and has gained popularity in Information Systems and Information and Communication Technology for Development (ICT4D) studies [48, 49]. CA is a normative framework that is used to conceptualise notions of inequality, poverty, and well-being. The theory focuses on what people are capable of (capability) and can be (freedom) based on the resources available [49]. The central concept of the framework is its ability to determine what people are effectively able to do and be, taking into account the goods and resources they have access to achieve the life they value. According to the approach, having goods or resources is not enough to imply well-being; rather, it is how people effectively use the goods and resources to achieve the life they value. In our study, the GovChat platform is said to improve citizen participation to enhance their capability by engaging with the government authorities to lead the life they value through means of development and improved service delivery. The theory allows us to understand the factors that affect the use of the commodity; in this case, we imply the commodity as a GovChat platform.

3.1 Capabilities and Functionings

Capabilities and functionings are at the center of the CA. Although the two concepts are related, they have different meanings. An individual's capability can be compared to opportunities open to an individual [51]. The Capability set is made up of potential functionings and opportunity freedom. Functionings, in contrast, refer to potential or attainment [51, 52] and are associated with various aspects of lifestyle. Functionings consist of "beings and doings" and can be considered a group of interconnected functionings. These can include people's well-being, happiness, a decent job, self-respect, safety, and being calm.

3.2 Well-Being and Agency

Well-being evaluates an individual's 'wellness', which is a persons' state of being [53]. The achievements of well-being are measured in functionings, whiles the well-being of freedom is shown in the person's capability set. On the other hand, an agency is the ability for a person to act on the things they value. Personal values and circumstances play a vital role in choosing from their available opportunities. Whether or not an individual can choose from the opportunities presented to improve their value is usually tied down to their circumstances and their values.

3.3 Conversion Factors

Goods and resources are referred to as a commodity. In this study, the GovChat is the commodity that enables citizen participation to achieve the landscape they desire. Freedom is defined as opportunities that people have to live a life of value to them [54, 55]. Freedoms are the actual possibilities for citizens who utilise the GovChat to participate in decision making. However, conversion factors influence individuals in generating the capabilities of the commodities. The conversion factors refer to factors that affect individuals expanding their capability [48]. The conversion factors can be categorised as personal, social, and environmental. Personal factors (such as gender and age) can influence whether and how an individual utilises the commodity to achieve functionings. For example, the level of education may affect how an individual uses a mobile phone to engage with the government. The social factors may include:

– Social institutions (power relations, public policies, institutions). For instance, social arrangements within developing countries of having more citizens in the urban area owning more mobile phones than in rural areas create consequences for e-participation in a democratic setting [56].
– Social norms (rules, behaviours and values). South Africa has a history of apartheid which may still be embedded in their values and norms; for instance, participation in government decisions may not be actively participated due to the apartheid era [57, 58].

Environmental factors such as technical support, infrastructures, electricity, telecommunications, and resources can also influence converting commodities into functionings. For instance, network coverage or electricity supply [59] may pose a challenge for citizens to use e-participation platforms in developing countries.

3.4 Operationalising Capability Approach in the Study

Table 3 depicts the Capability Approach concepts and their relationship in the use of GovChat to influence citizen participation.

Table 3. Capability approach concepts

Concept	Description
Commodity	GovChat and its relevance to Citizen Participation
Conversion Factors	Personal factors e.g., Information and Communication Technology (ICT) literacy and skills affordability Environmental factors e.g., Affordability of ICT and ICT infrastructure Social factors e.g., social institutions, social norms, and public policies
Agents	Citizens
Capabilities	Citizens' capabilities to use the GovChat are influenced by their well-being, such as training and skills, technology, etc

4 Research Methodology

This study adopted an interpretivism research philosophy that has integrated human interest in the study [60]. The study required user experiences and sought to understand the fundamental meanings that underlie the social world by analysing the data obtained through interviews and observations. Interpretivism research philosophy requires data to be collected through a naturalistic approach where interviews and observations are the primary sources of data [60]. This has led to meanings and themes emerging from the study towards the end of the data analysis process. A qualitative research approach was employed for this study because it provides a deeper understanding of the phenomenon. The purpose of the study is exploratory in nature, as the aim of this study is to not just describe and portray GovChat's current role in municipal government but rather seek factors affecting the use of the GovChat platform for citizen participation. The approach to theory in this study was deductive.

The study focused on service delivery in the context of Cape Town, South Africa, through citizen participation at the local municipal level. The city of Cape Town was selected because it is the first city in South Africa to launch the GovChat. For this reason, the target population was Cape Town citizens. There are 30 local councils in the Western Cape, including Cape Town. The city of Cape Town constitutes a hundred and sixteen ward councillors [36]. We drew a sample of 30 respondents consisting of five ward councillors representing the municipality and 25 ordinary citizens. The ordinary citizens were coded as'Citizen Participant X' and'Ward X', representing ward councillors. The ordinary citizens were youth aged 16 to 35. This age group are more inclined to use a mobile device for citizen participation than the older generation [61] and mobile applications such as Whatsapp and messenger. The sample was limited to those who spoke either English or Afrikaans. The reasons for limiting the selection to English and Afrikaans speaking groups is because it is the most spoken language by the selected age group.

Furthermore, the researcher also considered the convenience of conducting the interviews since the researcher was fluent in these two languages. The citizens selected for the investigation are those currently active and those not active in the decision-making processes at Cape Town municipality. The study commenced on March 28, 2019 and ended on September 20, 2019. Table 4 summarises the criterion we used to select the participants in the study.

Table 4. Summary of the criterion used to select the participants

Criteria	Description
Citizens	Ordinary citizens that reside in Cape Town municipality
Ward Councillors	Local councillors in Western Cape
Age	Ordinary citizens aged 16–35
Gender	Male and Female
Language	Those fluent in English or Afrikaans
Digital Skills	None required

The case study on the GovChat platform for citizens draws on primary data collected through semi-structured interviews and document analysis. We conducted semi-structured interviews with ward councillors and ordinary citizens. A range of documents and literature on e-platforms for citizen participation and the GovChat website were reviewed to understand the platforms better. The data collected was then analysed using thematic analysis, where themes from the data were identified, analysed and documented. We highlighted differences and similarities across the data and gained insights into the phenomenon. The first approach was to identify themes. We followed D'Andrade's technique of highlighting repeated words which was achieved by running NVivo's built-in word frequency query. We also applied the constant comparison method, where a line-by-line analysis was conducted to understand each line of the transcribed interviews within the context of the study and compare each line to other lines in the data.

Participation was voluntary, and all participants' identities were kept confidential. Interviews were voice recorded after gaining verbal consent from participants. The recordings are stored in a safe location for transcription purposes. Ethical clearance and approval to conduct the study was granted by the University of Cape Town's Ethics Committee to ensure that the research complies with the code of ethics prescribed by the university.

5   Analysis and Findings

The citizens were aware of the GovChat platform on its benefits to facilitate citizen participation. However, despite the citizens using the GovChat platform, it has contributed to low uptake due to inadequate service delivery. In addition, the analysis conducted showed that several factors also contribute to the low usage of the GovChat platform, and these factors have been grouped into personal, environmental, and social factors. Despite several factors affecting the use of the GovChat platform, the platform also provided capabilities that the citizens could achieve participation, which has been categorised in the capabilities and the functionings section. Table 5 summarises the conversation factors affecting the use of the GovChat platform and its related capabilities and functionings.

Table 5. Conversion factors and capabilities of the GovChat platform

Commodity	Agent	Conversion factor	Capabilities and functionings
GovChat platform	Citizens	Personal Factors – Limited technical skills from the citizens – Limited to citizens with reading and writing skills – Social inequalities	– Provides citizens access to essential information – Allows citizens to access social grant services, municipality services, gender-based violence services, corruption services, etc – Accessible at the citizens' convenience
		Environmental Factors – Affordability of ICT e.g., Mobile phones, connectivity and personal computers – Electricity supply	
		Social Factors – Mobile victimisation when using the platform – Preference to verbal communication	

5.1   Capabilities and Functionings

Our analysis identified the capabilities and functionings the GovChat platform provided for the citizens. First, the GovChat provides essential information to the citizens on services offered by the government, such as social grants, municipality, gender-based violence, school and corruption, which would have been far-fetched to access by ordinary citizens. The platform was convenient as the citizens would voice their concerns at any place and time using either their mobile phones or computers since they do not have to travel long distances to access these services but only had to log into the platform and participate. However, connectivity remains expensive for many citizens in Cape Town due to the high unemployment rate. The affordability of mobile connectivity in South Africa was 51.72% as of January 2021, according to the Digital 2021 report for South Africa. An indication that many South African can hardly afford the connectivity devices and services necessary to use the GovChat platform.

> *GovChat creates an effortless way for citizens to interact, as you can use it whenever and wherever you want, being that it's on a mobile device. Less effort is required to access the GovChat platform. Therefore, we as citizens should be able to contribute to the development of our communities. Before the GovChat platform was created, we never felt as though we mattered, but now we feel like part of our community.* [Citizen Participant 7]

The second factor was the potential for the citizens to voice their concerns. This finding is on par with Danielle and Masilela [47] as they stated that the platform allowed the government to obtain citizen feedback on problems, alternatives, and decisions. Citizens can track their reported requests and rate government facilities. Citizens can log requests for municipal services and report corruption activities, gender-based violence and bullying in schools. This provides the city of Cape Town with critical information on the needs and services required by the citizens. At the same time, the GovChat platform empowers and improves the lives of the citizens of Cape Town [47]. One of the citizens also highlighted that they feel their voice is being heard and their grievances attended to.

> *This GovChat platform works perfectly. That seems to be the purpose of GovChat; you log a problem, and you get your concerns resolved without having to stand in long queues. Now I can even book my medical assessment using the GovChat.* [Ward 2]

In as much as the GovChat platform provided citizens with the voice to air out their concerns, 12 out of 25 ordinary citizens interviewed highlighted a lack of trust in the information they provided to the platform. They cited that some of the information is sensitive and could end up in the wrong hands. For instance, personal data and information on corruption activities, e.g., the contact details of the citizen requesting a service, are shared with the municipal department. As such, many citizens withheld their concerns.

> *It's great to have a platform where people can ask for assistance, seek services, and vent. But what happens with this information? For instance, if I am to report on corruption in my area, I do not know whether the information that I have provided will also implicate me.* [Citizen Participant 14]

In addition, another participant also stated that:

> *Since we are voicing our concerns to government officials, some may take it personally, and consequences may follow. Therefore, we are constrained on what to share because we are unsure how these officials will react, especially when the GovChat gets your details from WhatsApp or Facebook platform when using the tool.* [Citizen Participant 17]

5.2 Personal Factors

Statistics have shown growth in the Mobile uptake in Cape Town and the entire country. It is estimated that 25.5 million internet users in South Africa use smartphones. However, this is less than half of the population [62]. Statista [62] projected that the number of smartphone users in South Africa will reach 26.3 million by 2023. This means that users of the GovChat platform will increase, but at the same time, it will widen the digital divide gap.

The use of the GovChat requires citizens to have some basic technical skills in software applications. These would allow them to download the application on their mobile devices and update it when needed. Also, to be able to navigate and actively participate, e.g., logging a service delivery request and completing a report form. However, a portion of the total population of Cape Town that lacks basic computer skills will be unable to utilise the GovChat platform fully. This contributes to the digital divide and a lack of inclusivity among those with no technical skills or computer literacy.

> Not everyone has the technical skills to navigate the platform. Especially for the elderly who might have problems navigating through the GovChat platform and need assistance in navigating through the platform compared to the youths but there is support available [Ward 5]

While technical skill is essential for citizens to use the GovChat platform, many participants felt that the GovChat platform was mainly for those who knew how to read and write English. The majority of the citizens in South Africa speaks indigenous languages. IsiXhosa, Afrikaans and Setswana are the most spoken languages in the Eastern, Northern and Western Cape. In the Western Cape, 49.7% speak Afrikaans, 24.7% isiXhosa, and 20.3% speak English, respectively [63]. The developers assumed that all citizens were fluent in English when creating the platform. Therefore, it limited the participation of all citizens from all classes of society.

> It was easier for me to navigate the platform and read all the information, but it was challenging for someone who did not read and write. They need to create a platform that includes all languages; otherwise, only a few of us will participate. [Citizen Participant 22]

5.3 Environmental Factors

Like in many developing countries, affordability of ICT such as mobile phones, personal computers and connectivity is still a challenge. Many citizens cannot afford to own a mobile phone, personal computer and internet. The finding is on par with Bisimwa, Brown and Johnson's [64] study that found that the cost of purchase of mobile phones, airtime, internet bandwidth, and repair hindered the use of mobile phones in South Africa.

> An economic barrier would be the fact that you need to have a cellphone to use GovChat and would require data to use WhatsApp. The challenge is that not everyone in cape town can afford to buy a mobile phone to use the platform. As

for me, I can afford to buy a mobile phone, and I also use my personal laptop. The concern is that not every citizen in Cape Town municipality has the same economic standing, making it challenging to harness the platform. [Ward 3]

South Africa has been experiencing loadsheddings or power cuts over the past years. The city of Cape Town was no exception. This has contributed to the disruption of economic activities, leaving many citizens frustrated. The power cuts are attributed to the increasing demand and dilapidated infrastructure which often needs repair. This has negatively affected the use of electronic devices and the use of e-participation platforms such as the GovChat due to the frequent power outage.

Loadshedding is a huge concern in Cape Town and the entire South Africa. It has affected how, and when to use our gadgets. When there is power outage, we use our mobile phones sparingly and avoid using applications that consume a lot of power on our phones. During that time, there is limitation on the activities performed on our phone such as sending a request or reporting a problem on the GovChat platform. [Citizen Participant 25]

5.4 Social Factors

GovChat platform creates room for victimisation, whereby councillors and colleagues can easily identify and victimise citizens that frequently complain about poor service delivery. Additionally, citizens have a negative attitude towards the use of GovChat as they feel that their complaints, contributions and requests are often not attended to or taken into consideration. Thus, they perceive the platform as of less value to them.

I have a concern that our requests are not being taken into account. You don't know where your information is going. There is a grey area between making a service request and seeing the results of this request. [Citizen Participant 4]

Most citizens prefer verbal communication as they feel their concerns are being heard rather than communicating on a platform where they are unsure whether the officials read their request. In addition, the citizens uphold their cultural norms and values as they are accustomed to dialogue. Although the citizens preferred verbal communication, they felt that the platform allowed them to speak out without fear of being criticised by the officials.

Through the lens of Hofstede's cultural dimensions, South Africa, as a collectivist society, requires a platform and instruments to express their opinions, feelings, and concerns using online platforms [65]. Also, to offer them opportunities to interact. Therefore, the GovChat lacks interactive functionalities and does not optimally fulfil a collectivist society's needs.

6   Conclusion

More studies are examining how ICTs can facilitate citizen participation to respond to citizens' demands through e-participation platforms. Our study contributes to e-Participation platforms' literature by seeking to understand factors affecting the use of e-participation platforms by the citizen. The context of the study is the use of the GovChat platform by citizens of Cape Town. Although existing literature discusses the importance of citizen participation, there is paucity of literature that focuses on e-Platforms for citizen participation, specifically in developing countries. e-Participation platforms lay a significant role in the decision-making process at all levels of the government, national and local. Thereby enhancing the living standards of the citizens through better service delivery.

The study contributes to theory by utilising the Capability Approach framework to understand the factors that affect the citizens in using the e-participation platforms. The theory showed that personal, social, and environmental factors affect the citizens of Cape Town municipality use of the GovChat platform. Our study demonstrated that personal factors such as basic technical skills, language and support negatively affect citizens' use of the e-participation platforms. Availability of support to citizens during the use of the GovChat platforms can help encourage citizens to continue using the platform. Additionally, including a functionality that allows users to translate or change to other widely spoken local languages promotes inclusivity.

The study also points to environmental factors such as affordability of ICT devices such as mobile phones and personal computers and connectivity. These devices are enablers of e-participation and until most of the citizens can afford them, they will not be able to participate in decision-making processes. South Africa is one of the countries with high unemployment rates in the world. This means that fewer people can afford communication devices such as mobile phones, personal computers and internet to use the GovChat platform.

On social factors, the study observed that e-participation platforms such as the GovChat may lead to victimisation of the users. The GovChat requires the contact number of the user when logging in and the address or location when reporting cyberbullying or corruption activities. This information is shared with the municipal department and as such, the user can be easily identified which can put the life of the user at risk. The lack of anonymity of the users can adversely affect the use of the GovChat platform because of trust and confidentiality issues. Furthermore, although citizens can track their reported requests, they do not receive feedback from the municipality. This discourages the use of the GovChat platform as citizens feel that their grievances are not attended to. Designing the GovChat in such a way that it is interactive would instill users' confidence.

This study contributes to practice by understanding how and what affects the use of e-platforms for citizen participation. Knowledge and understanding on the use of e-participation platforms would aid developers to develop better e-platforms that are inclusive and that encourage citizens participation.

Lastly, we acknowledged that the study has limitations as the sample was drawn from the population of the city of Cape Town which may have influenced the findings. We suggest that future studies be conducted using a sample from another city or municipality and compare the findings.

References

1. Bassett, C.: An alternative to democratic exclusion? The case for participatory local budgeting in South Africa. J. Contemp. Afr. Stud. **34**(2), 282–299 (2016)

2. Gordon, V., Osgood, J.L., Jr., Boden, D.: The role of citizen participation and the use of social media platforms in the participatory budgeting process. Int. J. Public Adm. **40**(1), 65–76 (2017)

3. Denhardt, J., Terry, L., Delacruz, E.R., Andonoska, L.: Barriers to citizen engagement in developing countries. Int. J. Public Adm. **32**(14), 1268–1288 (2009)

4. Mathekga, R., Buccus, I.: The challenge of local government structures in South Africa: securing community participation. Crit. Dialogue Public Participation Rev. **2**(1), 11–17 (2006)

5. Plessing, J.: Challenging elite understandings of citizen participation in South Africa. Politikon **44**(1), 73–91 (2017)

6. Cornwall, A., Coelho, V.S. (eds.) Spaces for Change? The Politics of Citizen Participation in New Democratic Arenas, vol. 4. Zed Books (2007)

7. Piper, L., Deacon, R.: Too dependent to participate: ward committees and local democratisation in South Africa. Local Gov. Stud. **35**(4), 415–433 (2009)

8. Cherry, J., Jones, K., Seekings, J.: Democratization and politics in South African townships. Int. J. Urban Reg. Res. **24**(4), 889–905 (2000)

9. Moloi, E.N.: Assessing of community involvement in strengthening road safety strategies within Umhlathuze Municipality. Doctoral dissertation (2018)

10. Stoffels, M., Du Plessis, A.: Piloting a legal perspective on community protests and the pursuit of safe(r) cities in South Africa. South. Afr. Public Law **34**(2), 26 (2019)

11. Seekings, J.: Bold promises, constrained capacity, stumbling delivery: the expansion of social protection in response to the Covid-19 lockdown in South Africa. In: CSSR Working Paper, p. 456 (2020)

12. Choi, J.C., Song, C.: Factors explaining why some citizens engage in E-participation, while others do not. Gov. Inf. Q. **37**(4), 101524 (2020)

13. Cuthill, M., Fien, J.: Capacity building: facilitating citizen participation in local governance. Aust. J. Public Adm. **64**(4), 63–80 (2005)

14. Molokwane, T.: Citizen involvement in the formulation of public policy. In: International Conference on Public Administration and Development Alternatives (IPADA) (2018)

15. Pellizzoni, L.: Uncertainty and participatory democracy. Environ. Values **12**(2), 195–224 (2003). https://doi.org/10.3197/096327103129341298

16. Michels, A., De Graaf, L.: Examining citizen participation: local participatory policy making and democracy. Local Gov. Stud. **36**(4), 477–491 (2010). https://doi.org/10.1080/03003930.2010.494101

17. Collins, K., Ison, R.: Dare we jump off Arnstein's ladder? Social learning as a new policy paradigm. In: Proceedings PATH (Participatory Approaches in Science & Technology) (2006)

18. Arnstein, S.R.: A ladder of citizen participation. J. Am. Inst. Plann. **35**(4), 216–224 (1969)

19. Corrigan, T.: South african institute of international affairs democratic devolution: structuring citizen participation in sub-national governance (2017)

20. Carpentier, N.: Beyond the ladder of participation: an analytical toolkit for the critical analysis of participatory media processes. Javnost-The Public **23**(1), 70–88 (2016). https://doi.org/10.1080/13183222.2016.1149760

21. Gaber, J.: Building "a ladder of citizen participation": sherry arnstein, citizen participation, and model cities. J. Am. Plann. Assoc. **85**(3), 188–201 (2019). https://doi.org/10.1080/01944363.2019.1612267

22. Jang, S.G., Gim, T.H.T.: Considerations for encouraging citizen participation by information-disadvantaged groups in smart cities. Sustain. Cities Soc. **76**, 103437 (2022). https://doi.org/10.1016/j.scs.2021.103437

23. Neupert-Wentz, C., Kromrey, D., Bayer, A.: The democraticness of traditional political systems in Africa. Democratization **29**(2), 296–319 (2022). https://doi.org/10.1080/13510347.2021.1953476

24. Oginni, S.O., Moitui, J.N.: Social media and public policy process in africa: enhanced policy process in digital age. Consilience **14**, 158–172 (2015)
25. Kravchenko, S.: The myth of public participation in a world of poverty. Tul. Env. Law J. **23**, 33–55 (2009)
26. Nkohkwo, Q.N.A., Islam, M.S.: Challenges to the successful implementation of e-government initiatives in Sub-Saharan Africa: a literature review. Electron. J. e-Government **11**(1), 252–266 (2001)
27. Mpolokeng, P.G.: People's participation in rural development: the examples from Mafikeng. Afr. J. Polit. Sci. **8**(2), 55–86 (2003)
28. Arkorful, V.E., Lugu, B.K., Hammond, A., Basiru, I.: Decentralization and citizens' participation in local governance: does trust and transparency matter?–an empirical study. Forum Devel. Stud. **48**(2), 199–223 (2021). https://doi.org/10.1080/08039410.2021.1872698
29. Matsiliza, N.S.: Participatory budgeting for sustainable local governance in South Africa. J. Pub. Adm. **47**(2), 443–452 (2012)
30. Gueli, R., Liebenberg, S., Van Huyssteen, E.: Integrated development planning in South Africa: lessons for international peacebuilding? Afr. J. Confl. Resolut. **7**(1), 89–112 (2007)
31. Binns, T., Nel, E.: Devolving development: integrated development planning and developmental local government in post-apartheid South Africa. Reg. Stud. **36**(8), 921–932 (2002)
32. Nabatchi, T.: The (re) discovery of the public in public administration. Public Adm. Rev. **70**, S309–S311 (2010)
33. Shah, A. (ed.): Participatory Budgeting. The World Bank (2007)
34. Leduka, M.: Participatory budgeting in the South African local government context: The case of the Mantsopa local municipality, Free State province. Doctoral dissertation, University of Stellenbosch, Stellenbosch (2009)
35. David, A., Guilbert, N., Hamaguchi, N., Higashi, Y., Hino, H., Leibbrandt, M.: Spatial poverty and inequality in South Africa: a municipality level analysis (2018)
36. Electroral Commision of South Africa: Ward councillors statistics. https://www.elections.org.za/pw/StatsData/List-Of-Current-Ward-Councillors (2022). Retrieved 22 Jan 2022
37. Secinaro, S., Brescia, V., Iannaci, D., Jonathan, G.M.: Does citizen involvement feed on digital platforms? Int. J. Public Adm. **45**, 708–725 (2021). https://doi.org/10.1080/01900692.2021.1887216
38. Royo, S., Pina, V., Garcia-Rayado, J.: Decide madrid: a critical analysis of an award-winning e-participation initiative. Sustainability **12**(4), 1674 (2020). https://doi.org/10.3390/su12041674
39. Allen, B., Tamindael, L.E., Bickerton, S.H., Cho, W.: Does citizen coproduction lead to better urban services in smart cities projects? an empirical study on e-participation in a mobile big data platform. Gov. Inf. Q. **37**(1), 101412 (2020). https://doi.org/10.1016/j.giq.2019.101412
40. Coelho, T.R., Pozzebon, M., Cunha, M.A.: Citizens influencing public policy-making: resourcing as source of relational power in e-participation platforms. Inf. Syst. J. **32**(2), 344–376 (2022). https://doi.org/10.1111/isj.12359
41. Sharma, G., Kharel, P.: E-Participation concept and web 2.0 in E-government. Gen. Sci. Res. **3**(1), 1–4 (2015)
42. Toots, M.: Why E-participation systems fail: the case of Estonia's Osale.ee. Gov. Inf. Quart. **36**(3), 546–559 (2019). https://doi.org/10.1016/j.giq.2019.02.002
43. Gil, O., Cortés-Cediel, M.E., Cantador, I.: Citizen participation and the rise of digital media platforms in smart governance and smart cities. Int. J. E-Plann. Res. **8**(1), 19–34 (2019). https://doi.org/10.4018/IJEPR.2019010102
44. Repette, P., Sabatini-Marques, J., Yigitcanlar, T., Sell, D., Costa, E.: The evolution of city-as-a-platform: smart urban development governance with collective knowledge-based platform urbanism. Land **10**(1), 33 (2021). https://doi.org/10.3390/land10010033

45. GovChat: One platform connecting citizens and government. https://www.govchat.org/ (2021). Retrieved 22 Jan 2022
46. Plantinga, P., Adams, R., Parker, S.: AI technologies for responsive local government in South Africa. In: Global Information Society Watch Artificial intelligence: human rights, social justice and development. Association for Progressive Communications (APC), New York, pp. 215–220 (2019)
47. Danielle, N.E.L., Masilela, L.: Open governance for improved service delivery innovation in South Africa. Int. J. EBusiness eGovernment Stud. 12(1), 33–47 (2020)
48. Zheng, Y., Walsham, G.: Inequality of what? Social exclusion in the e-society as capability deprivation. Inform. Technol. People 21, 222–243 (2008)
49. Morris, C.: Measuring participation in childhood disability: how does the capability approach improve our understanding? Dev. Med. Child Neurol. 51(2), 92 (2009)
50. Chigona A., Chigona, W.: An investigation of factors affecting the use of ICT for teaching in the Western Cape schools. In: ECIS 2010 Proceedings, p. 61 (2010)
51. Robeyns, I.: The capability approach: a theoretical survey. J. Hum. Dev. 6(1), 93–117 (2005). https://doi.org/10.1080/146498805200034266
52. Burger, R., McAravey, C., Van der Berg, S.: The capability threshold: re-examining the definition of the middle class in an unequal developing country. J. Hum. Dev. Capabilities 18(1), 89–106 (2017)
53. Gasper, D.: Is Sen's capability approach an adequate basis for considering human development? Rev. Polit. Econ. 14(4), 435–461 (2002)
54. Chrysostome, E. (ed.): Capacity Building in Developing and Emerging Countries: From Mindset Transformation to Promoting Entrepreneurship and Diaspora Involvement. Springer International Publishing, Cham (2019)
55. Bass, J.M., Nicholson, B., Subhramanian, E.: A framework using institutional analysis and the capability approach in ICT4D. Inf. Technol. Int. Dev. 9(1), 19 (2013)
56. Dalvit, L., Kromberg, S., Miya, M.: The data divide in a South African rural community: a survey of mobile phone use in Keiskammahoek. In: Proceedings of the e-Skills for knowledge production and innovation conference, pp. 87–100 (2014)
57. Enslin, P.: Citizenship education in post-apartheid South Africa. Camb. J. Educ. 33(1), 73–83 (2003)
58. Mattes, R.: The 'Born Frees': the prospects for generational change in post-apartheid South Africa. Aust. J. Polit. Sci. 47(1), 133–153 (2012)
59. Jamasb, T., Thakur, T., Bag, B.: Smart electricity distribution networks, business models, and application for developing countries. Energy Policy 114, 22–29 (2018)
60. Myers, M.D.: Coming of age. In: Galliers, R.D., Stein, M.-K. (eds.) The Routledge Companion to Management Information Systems, pp. 83–93. Routledge, Abingdon, Oxon; New York, NY: Routledge, 2017. (2017)
61. Ochara, N.M., Mawela, T.: Enabling social sustainability of e-participation through mobile technology. Inf. Technol. Dev. 21(2), 205–228 (2015)
62. Statista: Number of smartphone users in South Africa from 2014 to 2023. https://www.statista.com/statistics/488376/forecast-of-smartphone-users-in-south-africa/ (2020). Retrieved 22 Jan 2022
63. South Africa Gateway: What languages are spoken in South Africa's provinces? https://southafrica-info.com/infographics/animation-languages-south-africas-provinces/ (2018). 22 Jan 2022
64. Bisimwa, K., Brown, I., Johnston, K.: Mobile phones use by urban refugees in South Africa: Opportunities and challenges. In: Hawaii International Conference on System Sciences (2018)
65. Vollero, A., Siano, A., Palazzo, M., Amabile, S.: Hoftsede's cultural dimensions and corporate social responsibility in online communication: are they independent constructs? Corp. Soc. Responsib. Environ. Manag. 27(1), 53–64 (2020)

Institutional Work to Routinize the Use of a Digital AMR Monitoring System

Yogita Thakral[1,2](✉) ⓘ, Sundeep Sahay[1,2] ⓘ, and Arunima Mukherjee[1,2] ⓘ

[1] HISP Centre and Department of Informatics, University of Oslo, Oslo, Norway
{yogitat,sundeeps,arunimam}@ifi.uio.no
[2] HISP India, New Delhi, India

Abstract. Antimicrobial resistance is described as a "slow-moving Tsunami" and a top global health threat, particularly affecting low and middle-income countries. A key strategic tool to engage with this challenge is effective monitoring to improve knowledge and awareness and support evidence-based interventions. However, LMICs have an inadequate capacity, resources, infrastructure, and culture to implement digital interventions. To engage with this challenge within the context of a public hospital in India, a global AMR hotspot, empirical work is carried out in studying the design and implementation of an AMR monitoring system and in understanding the process of antibiotics use and associated challenges in their digitization. A practice-based perspective informs understanding of these empirical problems, and how practices evolve into institutional work. This paper contributes to understanding the challenges and approaches to implementing AMR digital monitoring systems.

Keywords: AMR · Information systems · Digital AMR monitoring · Practices · Institutional work · Actors

1 Introduction

This paper seeks to understand the link between information practices and institutional work and how these can be best linked to create enabling structures to strengthen the implementation and use of *digital monitoring systems for Antimicrobial Resistance (AMR) within public hospitals in India.*

Antimicrobial Resistance (AMR) occurs when bacteria, viruses, fungi, and parasites change over time and no longer respond to medicines making infections harder to treat and increasing the risk of disease spread [1]. The World Health Organization (WHO) has described AMR as 'a global crisis' and the perfect example of the complex, multi-sectoral, multi-stakeholder challenges increasingly facing the world [1]. AMR is endangering the future of societies [2], including the achievement of all Sustainable Development Goals (SDGs) [3]. AMR is a lifestyle disease [4] impacting the world inequitably, with Low- and Middle-Income Countries (LMICs) amongst the worst hit, due to the high prevalence of infectious diseases, overcrowding, poor sanitation, weak

© IFIP International Federation for Information Processing 2022
Published by Springer Nature Switzerland AG 2022
Y. Zheng et al. (Eds.): ICT4D 2022, IFIP AICT 657, pp. 89–106, 2022.
https://doi.org/10.1007/978-3-031-19429-0_6

access to diagnostics, inadequate monitoring, indiscriminate antibiotic use, and weak regulations. India is the world's AMR capital [5] reporting an annual AMR attributed mortality of 700,000, estimated to reach 10 million by 2050 globally [2]. India is the biggest producer [6] and consumer of antibiotics globally, reflected in the more than 100% increase in antibiotic use between 2000 to 2015 [7]. Compounding this problem is the relative lack of effective monitoring systems, and while 163 countries have developed National Action Plans (NAPs) to combat AMR, very few have materialized them in practice. A mere 2.3% of monitoring systems globally are in LMICs [7] contributing to the vicious cycle of poor information and evidence base about the AMR problem which limits focused interventions that magnify its spread and associated social inequities.

A strategic priority of the NAPs is to **strengthen the knowledge and evidence base through surveillance**. This is easier said than done because it involves systematic information on various complex and inter-connected parameters, such as i) antimicrobial susceptibility testing (AST); ii) monitoring of resistance; iii) monitoring of consumption and use of antibiotics; and iv) specific skills on areas such as medicines management, hospital-acquired infections, and infection prevention and control. All these represent new forms of knowledge and require specific skills, capacities, and infrastructure, currently largely unavailable in the public sector of most LMICs. This paper argues that trying to build these new forms of knowledge and skills, to enable digital AMR monitoring, will need understanding both at a micro-level of what new or redefined information practices should become part of everyday institutional work, and how these institutional work arrangements could contribute towards systematic and continued monitoring of AMR. Given this background of the research and practice-related challenges, this paper addresses this research question: **What is the institutional work required to routinize the use of a digital AMR monitoring application at the facility level?**

The empirical base for analyzing these research questions is a public hospital in India, which has limited resources and capacities to absorb new initiatives like that required for AMR monitoring. The rest of the paper is organized as follows. In the next section, we discuss institutional practices and institutional work, and their relevance in guiding the analysis. In Sect. 3 we describe the research methods followed by the case study in Sect. 4. Section 5 presents the case analysis and discussion. Conclusions are presented in Sect. 6.

2   Information Practices and Institutional Work

Practices represent *"shared routines"* [8] or *"recognized forms of activity"* [9] that guide behavior. All institutions have a set of practices and organizing principles that provide the logic of the actions of actors as they respond to their work demands [10] that reproduce institutions [11]. The practice lens is oriented towards understanding the recursive interaction between people and technologies within a situated context [12], implying that technology is not treated primarily as an artifact but as an integral element of people's routine work and the lived character of the everyday world, which serves as the object of analysis [13]. Orlikowski [14] writes:

> *"while users can and do use technologies as they were designed, they also can and do circumvent inscribed ways of using the technologies - either ignoring certain*

properties of the technology, working around them, or inventing new ones that may go beyond or even contradict designers' expectations and inscriptions."

A practice-based approach to IS research provides a strong tool to understand how change happens after the introduction of technology, often after the fact. Concepts of situated action [15] and tinkering [16] are relevant to understanding the nature of these information practices, how they occur, what breakdowns happen, and how are they dealt with. This helps to understand what kinds of contingencies emerge in the course of everyday work and how actors deal with them. For example, Mosse and Sahay [17] in their study of communication practices of health workers in Mozambique, described how they needed to send reports every month to their superiors. They deal with breakdowns, such as the printer not working, by going to the nearby church to take their printouts. Such practices help to find better and improved ways to mitigate uncertainties and install more stability into dealing with emerging work contingencies [18, 19].

A practice lens becomes relevant to study a complex societal issue of AMR, which concerns a lifestyle disease and involves multiple actors, artifacts, practices, and structures. Digital AMR monitoring, which is the focus of this paper, represents a novel intervention in the context of a public hospital in India, that requires the development of new practices, which have to also engage with the legacy of existing practices related to manual monitoring. Digital monitoring of AMR to capture, analyze and report data are central to the global response to AMR and is essential for standardized data collection to inform strategies which is unfeasible with the traditional and manual methods of monitoring [4]. Monitoring antimicrobial resistance (AMR) is fundamental to developing strategies and policies to contain the spread of AMR at local, national, and global levels. A digital AMR monitoring system can potentially provide information and evidence to guide clinical decision making; provide information on the effect of antimicrobial resistance and the burden of infectious diseases in the community and guide the stewardship program and infection control strategies.

Institutional work describes *"the purposive action of individuals and organizations aimed at creating, maintaining and disrupting institutions"* [20]. Institutions are 'an organized, established procedure' that reflects a set of 'standardized interaction sequences [21] arising from the interplay between actors and institutional structures influencing institutional change, innovation, and deinstitutionalization processes [22]. There is an ongoing *"duality of work"* representing the interconnected and mutual interconnections between practices and institutions [23], which are both visible and invisible, leading to *creating, maintaining, or disrupting* forms of institutional work [24].

Lawrence and Suddaby [20] identified different types of institutional work that emerge from varying types of practices. *Creating* work describes how new institutions emerge and get established, while *maintaining* is concerned with how institutions are actively produced and reproduced through everyday practices and *disrupting* focuses on the practices that disrupt existing institutions when new interests are not met, contributing to forms of institutional change [25]. The framework of Lawrence and Suddaby [20] is summarized in Table 1:

Institutional work has been extensively used in IS research as a framework to analyze processes of institutionalization, institutional change, and sustainability [26, 27]. For example, Sahay et al. [28] studied the new forms of institutional work required to support

Table 1. Institutional work for creating, maintaining, and disrupting institutions

Forms of Institutional work	Types of Institutional work
Creating	Advocacy; Defining; Vesting; Constructing identities; Changing normative associations; Constructing normative networks; Mimicry; Theorizing; Educating
Maintaining	Enabling work; Policing; Deterrence; Valorizing and demonizing; Mythologizing; Embedding and Routinizing
Disrupting	Disconnecting sanctions; Disassociating moral foundations; Undermining assumptions and beliefs

the introduction of information support for achieving the reform goals of Universal Health Coverage (UHC). They argued that the systems required, such as the focus on integrated individual-level data, represented new forms of institutions such as to enable data sharing, requiring different kinds of institutional work than what existed before [29] examined the relationship between design decisions taken and intended changes in the practices of diabetes care.

In the context of digital AMR monitoring, similar to the study on UHC [28], represents the need to create new forms of institutional work, which however is inter-connected with existing manual processes and the situated context of capacities [30], infrastructures [31], workloads [32] and policy responsiveness [33]. Institutional work helps to understand how information practices need to navigate between the old and new to highlight new or redefined forms of institutional structures. *In this paper, we draw on institutional work as the framework to analyze the information practices of actors around digital AMR monitoring. We study how these practices create, maintain, and disrupt institutions to enable the use of a digital AMR monitoring system.*

3   Research Methods

This was a longitudinal study being conducted since 2019 in the northern state, Himachal Pradesh to understand the practices of different actors around digital AMR monitoring and identify the institutional work done and needed to routinize digital AMR monitoring system in a public hospital. This study was part of a larger initiative under the long-standing ongoing efforts of a national NGO called HISP India in strengthening public health information systems in India.

3.1   Research Site

This study is based in a tertiary hospital setting in Himachal Pradesh in northern India. The state has microbiology testing facilities only in 4 tertiary hospitals, of which we focused on one located in the foothills of the Himalayan Mountain ranges. The hilly geographic terrain makes access to health care services a challenge for its about 7 million citizens [34], 90% of whom are residents in rural areas. With nearly 80% + of the population reliant on the public health system [35], the introduction of the digital monitoring of the AMR project is reflective of this proactive mindset and policies of the government. The tertiary teaching hospital is using an application to monitor the Antimicrobial Susceptibility Test (AST) results at their microbiology lab developed on an open-source platform. This hospital, typical of most public hospitals, suffers from constraints of weak diagnostics, limited capacity, manpower, and infrastructure at the hospital [32], with information on antibiotics currently invisible in the monitoring system.

3.2 Data Collection

The process of data collection was started in March 2020 to July 2021 after the implementation of the application at the microbiology lab in the hospital in November 2019. The major timelines are shown in Fig. 1

Fig. 1. Project timeline

The data collection process included a study of the practices around digital AMR monitoring at the hospital which currently uses the application to manage AST test results at the microbiology lab. This included understanding the practices of actors in the processes that are related to using the digital monitoring system starting from the arrival of the patient, the physician ordering for the AST, sample collection, sample transfer, testing at the lab, documentation, dissemination, and data use. The data collection methods are summarized in Table 2.

Semi-structured, open-ended guides were used to conduct in-depth interviews with physicians, pharmacists, microbiologists, lab technicians, and data entry operators. Questions to understand the workflow at the billing and registration departments, and sample collection unit at the hospital. Discussions were held with staff at the microbiology lab to better understand how information around antibiotics was represented in the AST sample recording, testing processes, data collection, analysis, and use. Discussions were also held with the principal of the hospital to understand the antibiotic policies, guidelines, and the hospital's visions to tackle AMR. Policy documents, both national, state-specific, and hospital-specific were important secondary sources to understand the gap between policy and practice observed, for example, the process of prescription audit as suggested by the state vs how it is done at the hospital. A workshop was held in July 2021 to discuss the implementation process, issues faced by the stakeholders, and to identify the approach to address them.

3.3 Data Analysis

Data analysis was conducted in multiple sequential steps, described below.

Table 2. Data collection methods

Data collection methods	Details
Interviews	Staff at registration and billing counter – 2; Staff at sample collection unit responsible for collection and transfer – 2; Physicians – 7; Pharmacists – 4;10; Microbiologists – 5; Lab technicians- 3; Data entry operator (DEO) at the lab – 1; Principal of Hospital
Observations	Physicians while prescribing; pharmacists while dispensing; DEO while entering data in the application; data management process at microbiology lab; billing and sample collection processes
Discussions	With physicians, microbiologists, staff at the microbiology department, and Principal
Study of policies and documents	National/State-specific policies and guidelines
AMR monitoring application design and development	Engaged in the design, development, and implementation of the AMR monitoring system
Workshop	Microbiologists, hospital management, and microbiologists from the 2 other public hospitals in the state

Step 1: Data collation and organization**:** All data collected including interview notes, observations, and study of documents studied were organized and collated to facilitate analysis. ***Step 2: Transcriptions***: All primary data was transcribed and translated from Hindi to English wherever needed, and digitized. ***Step 3: Thematic analysis***: First, responses were grouped by different stakeholders, and practices, were identified around AMR monitoring. ***Step 4: Identification of the institutional work done by actors:*** The day-to-day work of the stakeholders was analyzed to identify the creating, maintaining, and disrupting work done. ***Step 5: Identification of the work needed to routinize digital AMR monitoring:*** Based on the analysis, we identify the work needed to routinize the information practices that support digital AMR monitoring.

4 Case Study

In this section, we describe the information flow in the facility around antimicrobial susceptibility testing (AST). It is a test done at the microbiology lab that provides information about the resistance profile after registration of the patient, consultation, sample collection, etc. The information flows around the AST process are presented in Fig. 2, starting soon after the patient visits either OPD, IPD, or Emergency Departments. Patient registration is the first step at the hospital. Post-registration, the patient consults the physician, or the physician visits the patient in case he/she is admitted at the IPD.

Doctor orders drugs or an AST. This is followed by sample collection, testing at the lab, documentation of results in the register, sharing of results with the patient/attendant.

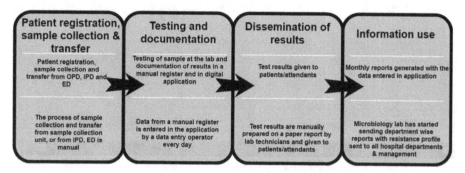

Fig. 2. Information flow around AMR monitoring

The process of data entry by the data entry operator (DEO) takes place with details transferred from the register to the digital application. The data entered in the application is aggregated and the dashboard is updated with the latest resistance figures. Figure 3 shows a section of the data entry application and the dashboard updated automatically based on the data entered daily.

Identifying Information Practices

We identified four key sets of practices to comprise digital AMR monitoring in the hospital: i) patient registration and sample collection at OPD, IPD, and Emergency (EPD); ii) testing of samples at the Microbiology laboratory and the documentation of test results (manual and digital); iii) sharing of test results by the lab to the doctor requesting the test and also to the patients; and, iv) the use of data for providing clinical care to the patients, and for other administrative purposes of reporting. These practices are described below:

4.1 Practice of Sample Collection, Indexing, and Transfer to Microbiology Lab

Upon arrival at the hospital, the patient goes to the registration counter in the main hospital building. The demographic details of the patient and the name of consulting physician are entered into a computerized hospital information system. The patient is given a unique hospital/patient ID that is printed on the Registration form given to the patient. Carrying this slip, the patient then goes to the respective department for consultation with the physician who makes inquiries about the patient's symptoms, orders the sample testing, and maybe prescribes medicines. An AST is generally ordered by the physician only if the patient presents severe symptoms, as described by a physician at the OPD:

An AST is generally prescribed to patients who come with severe symptoms/infections. Some of these patients have consulted many physicians earlier so a

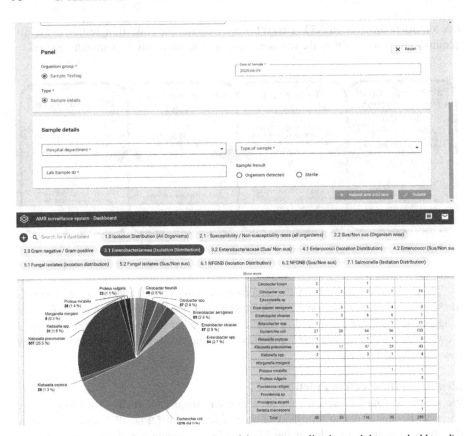

Fig. 3. AMR monitoring system (A snapshot of data entry application and dummy dashboard)

broad-spectrum antibiotic is prescribed, and an AST is ordered. These patients with severe infections are in many cases admitted to the hospital for further treatment.

Some patients come with severe infections, and they need to be admitted to the hospital and an AST is ordered for them. Antibiotics are prescribed to the patient till the time the resistance profile of the patient is received.

The patient comes back to the registration counter to pay for the test after consultation and if an AST is prescribed. He gets an invoice with the test details that he takes to the sample collection unit with him. This process takes place in the wards and the emergency departments for inpatients in the hospital. At the sample collection unit, each sample is given a unique code based on the type of sample and the lab it is to be sent to. For example, a sample sent to the microbiology lab has a code for the lab, the patient's Lab ID, and the sample name. The microbiology as separate registers for different sample types, such as blood and urine. The lab technicians at the Microbiology lab often complain about the quality of data and the sample details received from the sample collection unit from the different departments in the "requisition form" accompanied with all the samples. However, other details like the department where the patient is admitted, his/her diagnosis, and other related fields are often blank because of which the Microbiology lab has incomplete details of the patient and the sample. The manual register with the data entry fields and an incomplete requisition form can be seen in Fig. 4 and Fig. 5.

DEPARTMENT OF MICROBIOLOGY
DR. RAJENDRA PRASAD GOVT. MEDICAL COLLEGE, KANGRA AT TANDA

YEARLY NO.	MONTHLY NO.	DAILY NO.	NAME OF THE PATIENT	AGE	SEX	INVESTIGATION REQUIRED	REPORT
1996	35	8	▇▇▇▇▇	15d	ncl	β clr	Sterile
			R - 1584641				
1997	39	9	▇▇▇▇▇	24	Fn	β elr	MRSA - 2-15 R, 10-210, 40-23-6R,
			R - 1584321	JCU3			21-23 ③, 29-32⑤, 54-12⑧
			1(06-11-21) Saturday				
1998	40	1	▇▇▇▇▇	85	Fp	β clr	MRSA 2-14R ⑤ 10-25⑤ 40-6⑤ 21-2
				mia			23-3K③ 29-36 ⑥ 54-14⑧
1999	41	2	▇▇▇▇▇	Sml	Fcm	β cL	Sterile
			D- 1585136	n			
2000	42	3	▇▇▇▇▇	28	na	β Clr	Acinetobacter baumonii 6-19①
			C- 7641-0	ASU:			11-16(5)46-3① 50-6① 55-84①
							7050a-16⑤ 7-2②
2001	43	4	▇▇▇▇▇	87y	MA	B/C	CONS 2-3② 10-2③ 40-85④ 21-26
			R - 158538	600U			23-27③ 29-3③ 59-28③
2002	44	5	▇▇▇▇▇	D3y	MCl	Blood C/s	MSSA:- 2-2aR, 10-2③, 40-17,2H
			R - 158755	NICU-6			29-36(3), 9 2-6a... a5...

Fig. 4. Register for data entry at microbiology lab (incomplete information maintained and sometimes illegible)

An analysis of monthly data revealed that even the patient's identifiers like patient's CR number and age are missing from 2% records and crucial details to see department wise resistance pattern like the name of hospital department and location are missing from around 35% records. To promote data quality, a full-time resource is hired who checks the manual as well as digital data quality and reports to the in-charge microbiologist. A data quality report with details of missing fields in a month is shown in Table 3:

4.2 The Practice of AST Testing and Documentation of Results

The testing of the samples starts after they are received at the lab and the details are noted in the register by Lab technicians. The testing starts the same day the samples are received, and the process was explained by one of the lab assistants:

Once we receive samples at the lab, a standardized technique is followed for AST testing. The samples are put on a culture medium on Agar. These agar plates are then inoculated overnight. During the night, the organisms grow on the agar place inoculated with test organism and filter paper disc with a specific concentration of antibiotics. The growth is then checked for resistance patterns on the next day. There are specific incubation time ranges for the bacterial colonies as specified by the Clinical and Laboratory Standards Institute (CLSI) which is followed to identify the susceptibility and resistance.

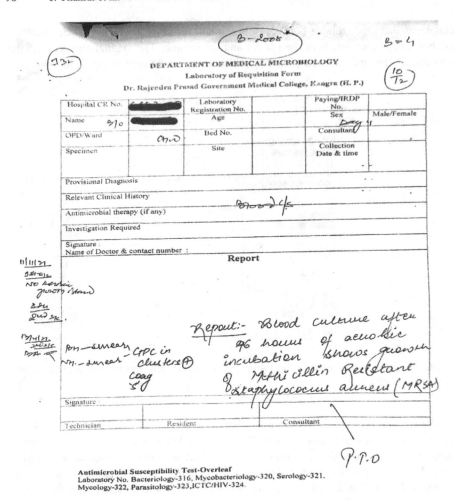

Fig. 5. Requisition form received at the lab with each sample (Incomplete and sometimes illegible)

Once testing is done, the test results are entered on a test result form with the details of the susceptibility and resistance patterns with specific antibiotics. Lab technicians also enter these test results in the register where they entered patient and sample details on the receipt. Once the documentation of the test results is completed in both the test result sheet and the register, the results are ready to be shared with the patients and/or the indenting physician.

The data entered in the registers by 2 PM is entered in the application by a DEO who comes to the microbiology lab for a couple of hours every day. The microbiology department had a manpower crunch, so a DEO was assigned by the hospital administration to enter all data from the registers to the application after he gets free from the Registration Desk, which is his primary appointment. A desktop with an internet connection has been set up on a table in the microbiology lab next to a table where the registers are kept. The DEO has no experience working in the Microbiology department and is new to the

Table 3. Record of missing fields in a month

Data fields missing/incorrect	Blood register		Urine register		General register		Overall %
	Number	%	Number	%	Number	%	
Hospital department	68	25	105	21	260	52	34
Location	50	18	95	19	258	51	32
Computer registration number	1	0.4	0	0	0	0	0.1
Age	1	0.4	9	1.8	1	0.2	0.9
Wrong computer registration number	10	3.7	14	2.8	0	0	1.9
Total number of records	273		501		502		

terms used, and often needs to take help in understanding them from the lab assistants. The DEO told us:

> *I come to Microbiology Department every day after getting free from the Registration Desk. I pick up registers for one sample type at a time, copy and enter the details written in the application. Earlier, I did not understand the terms used in the register and asked the lab assistant for their help. Now, I need less help after entering data for more than one year.*

Some problems have been experienced with the regularity of the DEO work since no dedicated staff could be hired for the same. The DEO was mandated by the hospital principal to come to the lab once he was free from his work at the registration desk in the afternoon. Since the DEO is unaware of the terminology and codes used, he takes help from the lab assistants, who sometimes are not free to answer the queries leading to delays or even incorrect information being entered. To help the DEO, the lab has prepared a sheet with codes and names of the antibiotics, which has been pasted on the wall next to his desk shown in Fig. 6.

Post data entry, the lab staff generates the test results and required reports. All patient details added to the application are aggregated and automated data analysis is done by the monitoring application, providing details of Isolation numbers, rates, resistance profiles, sample type, and location type of the patients i.e., OPD, IPD, ICU, etc.

4.3 Practice of Sharing Test Results

Test results are ready to be shared on the third day after the sample had been submitted to the lab. The lab assistant documents the test results in the lab register and on the test result form, after which it is approved and signed by the doctors at the Microbiology lab. Test results are shared once the resulting form is approved and signed by the resident doctor. Outpatients or their attendants come to the lab, show the form/receipt received from the

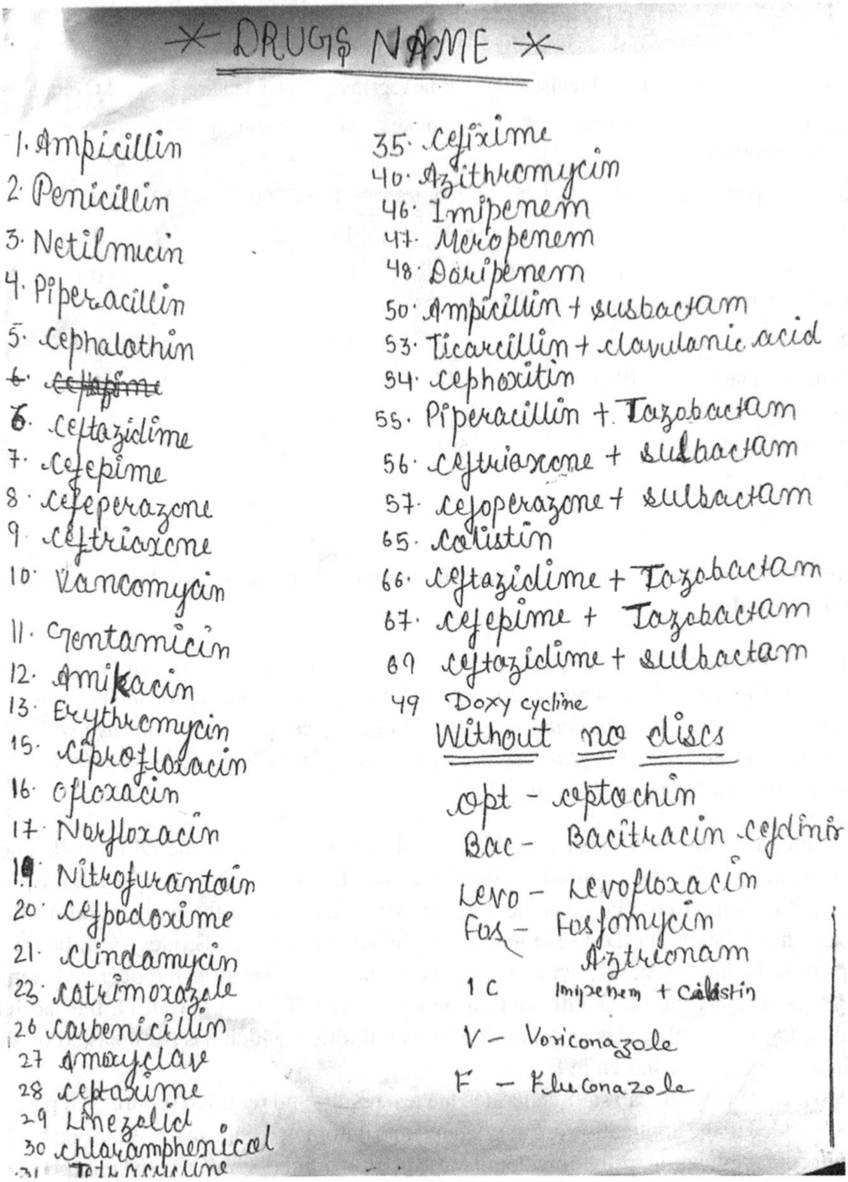

* DRUGS NAME *

1. Ampicillin
2. Penicillin
3. Netilmicin
4. Piperacillin
5. Cephalothin
~~6. cefepime~~
6. Ceftazidime
7. Cefepime
8. Cefeperazone
9. Ceftriaxone
10. Vancomycin
11. Gentamicin
12. Amikacin
13. Erythromycin
15. Ciprofloxacin
16. Ofloxacin
17. Norfloxacin
19. Nitrofurantoin
20. Cefpodoxime
21. Clindamycin
23. Cotrimoxazole
26. Carbenicillin
27. Amoxyclav
28. Ceftazime
29. Linezolid
30. Chloramphenicol
31. Tetracycline

35. Cefixime
40. Azithromycin
46. Imipenem
47. Meropenem
48. Doripenem
50. Ampicillin + sulbactam
53. Ticarcillin + clavulanic acid
54. Cephoxitin
55. Piperacillin + Tazobactam
56. Ceftriaxone + sulbactam
57. Cefoperazone + sulbactam
65. Colistin
66. Ceftazidime + Tazobactam
67. Cefepime + Tazobactam
69 Ceftazidime + sulbactam
49 Doxy cycline

Without no discs

Opt - Optochin
Bac - Bacitracin cefdinir
Levo - Levofloxacin
Fos - Fosfomycin
Aztreonam
I C Imipenem + Colistin
V - Voriconazole
F - Fluconazole

Fig. 6. Antibiotics with codes for DEO (These are written by a lab technician and given to DEO)

registration counter that has the Patient's ID, and get the test results. The attendants of the Inpatients come with the patient's form to collect the test results. These results are added to the patient's file with all the other details. The treating physician has access to the test results via the patient. In the case of Outpatients, the patients visit the physician again with their test results. Based on the AST test results, the physician gives/modifies the antibiotic or line of treatment. In the case of Inpatients, the test results are added to the patient's file once they are collected by the patient's attendant. Physicians look at the test results when they come for daily rounds and take necessary actions such as modifying the line of treatment, or the antibiotics given earlier. A department-wise monthly aggregated report generated by the data quality analyst at the hospital is sent to each department to promote evidence-based prescription of antibiotics.

4.4 Practice of Information Use

A bi-monthly report with details of the isolation patterns of organism groups and some specific organisms, their resistance profiles based on the sample type received, and the antibiotics are prepared by the Microbiology department. The AMR in charge of the department who is a senior consultant with help of resident doctors and post-graduate students prepares this report. This report was earlier prepared manually based on the patient data entered in registers every day. The AMR monitoring application has helped the department to prepare its reports easily. The case-based data entered in the application is aggregated automatically and presented on the dashboards, prepared based on the reporting requirements of the Microbiology Department. A sample dashboard is given in Fig. 7 below.

		Department - Other departments									
		Sample - Urine (Attribute)									
		Escherichia coli									
S.No	Most Resistant/Sensitive	Antibiotics Name	OPD	ICU	NICU	Ward	CCU	Burn Unit	PICU	Unknown	Total
1	Most Resistant	Cefuroxim				29					30
2	Most Resistant	Trimethoprim/Sulfamethoxazole				15					15
3	Most Resistant	Norfloxacin				13					13
1	Most Sensitive	Fosfomycin				27					27
2	Most Sensitive	Nitrofurantoin				25					25
3	Most Sensitive	Trimethoprim/Sulfamethoxazole				14					14

Fig. 7. A sample of data analysis done using the digital AMR monitoring application

The consultant in charge of AMR at the hospital mentioned:

It took a week to prepare the bi-monthly report with the data from registers. The data was aggregated manually by the post-graduate student who helped in making reports and putting them in formats we have the share the report in. With the AMR monitoring application, it takes lesser time to prepare the reports. We need to go and print the individual report and pin them together and share them with the Hospital Management. However, it would be easier to get a summary report from the application that can fit on 2–3 pages and would be easier for the management to comprehend as the current report has around 50 pages. It is difficult to get a full picture of the AMR with several segregated reports.

A monthly report prepared by the Microbiology department is shared with the hospital management and a copy of the report is sent to the state secretariat. This information is currently not actively utilized by the hospital to potentially inform them of the resistance profile of the hospital and prepare an infection control and hospital antibiotics policy. All departments in the hospital receive an aggregated report about the resistance profiles of the patients in their department. However, because of data quality challenges, the report cannot present an accurate picture right now. The reports are currently not shared with the Infection Control Committee at the hospital or the state authorities who are responsible for designing interventions to mitigate the threat of infections.

5   Case analysis and Discussion

5.1   Institutional Work Done

In this section, we discuss information practices within an institutional work framework to understand how these practices lead to *creating*, *maintaining*, and *disrupting* institutions.

In the early phases of this process of implementation of the digital system, the practices of sample collection and testing have not been in focus, but potentially can be with the expanding of the scope of digitization. A summary of the institutional work done by actors that are affected by the introduction of digital AMR monitoring is summarized in Table 4.

Table 4. Institutional work done by the stakeholders

Information practices	Creating	Maintaining	Disrupting
Documentation (Manual and Digital) of test results at the microbiology Lab	(**Defining**) Allocating responsibility to DEO (**Mimicry**) Data entry app interface similar to manual register (**Educating**) the DEO and microbiology team to generate reports	(**Deterring**) Authoritative measures to deal with the resistance of the DEO to come to the lab for data entry (**Routinizing**) Making the process of data entry easier for DEO by providing him a sheet with a list of antibiotics codes	(**Disassociating moral foundations**) Provision of daily reports as a motivation to use the application
Information Use by Microbiology Department/Hospital departments/management	(**Educating**) development of automated reports based on the microbiology team to generate reports in their required formats	(**Routinizing**) The hiring of a new resource to enhance the data quality, active contact through weekly calls (**Policing**) Regular audit and monitoring of the quality (**Valorizing**) Recognition of the work done by the microbiology lab at the workshop	

In the information practice of **sample collection, indexing, and its transfer from OPDs, IPDs, and ED,** there was *maintaining or enabling work* taking place of the existing manual work before the digital intervention was initiated. Similar was the case with the practices around the testing practice, which largely remained untouched.

Within the practice of **documentation (manual and digital) of test results at the microbiology lab,** there was *creating* work done by *defining* roles and allocation of responsibilities for the DEO at the microbiology lab to initiate data entry work. The technical team was engaged with *educating* him regularly to carry out the task of data entry seamlessly, which was designed with *mimicry* as a guideline by designing the data entry screens like the manual registers. *Maintaining* work was done through authoritative measures of *deterring* the DEO from not coming for work every day. *Routinizing* of the practice was done through providing job aids such as sticking a sheet with antibiotic codes and names on the wall next to DEO's desk. *Disrupting* work included *disassociating moral foundations* by replacing the DEO by hiring a new operator directly by the technical team to have greater control over his everyday work. This strengthened the motivation of the microbiologists to use the digital application. The manual work of entering the test results in the registers continued as before in parallel.

While the practice of **sharing test results with patients and physicians** is currently carried out as before, a new potential is being created to do so. This would represent a disruption of existing practices where these results currently don't return to patients, and not always to the physicians. Within the practice of **information used by the microbiology department, hospital departments, and management**, *creating* work is being done by the technical team through *educating* the microbiology team who have now started to demand new reports. *Maintaining* work was done by the technical team keeping regular contact with the microbiology team through WhatsApp and weekly calls that helped in faster resolution of issues encountered. *Disrupting* work was through the new data entry operator who initiated a new practice of checking the quality of the digital data by identifying the missing fields in the indent form, such as the name of antibiotics prescribed or the patient diagnosis. **Disassociation of moral boundaries is taking place** is taking place with the data quality gaps being made visible to the microbiologists, something which was invisible earlier. *Maintaining* work by *routinizing* this practice was done by keeping daily data quality checks on the data entry done by DEO. The microbiology staff was continuously motivated by *valorizing* and recognizing the work done with their contribution to the development of the digital application for AMR monitoring, exemplified by the presentation made by the microbiologists in a workshop where they proudly described their achievements to other nearby hospitals, who were also motivated to introduce a similar application in their labs.

5.2 Institutional Work Needed to Routinize Digital AMR Monitoring

Advocacy and *defining* of budgets, resources & responsibilities to establish the practice of using the digital AMR monitoring application. As the system expands and more data needs to be entered, the data entry support needs to be necessarily strengthened. Furthermore, the data entry person can play an enhanced role in not only doing data entry but in improving data quality and expanding the circulation of data within the hospital. *Enabling work, defining* rules, and regular *policing* to legitimize the technology in the norms and belief system of the stakeholders. New systems need to be developed to extend the technology beyond the microbiology lab such as in the sample collection unit etc. by improving the process of sample indexing and transfer and improving coordination between the sample collection and testing functions [36]. *Disassociating moral foundations* to institutionalize the use of the digital system and the reports by the physicians to make treatment plans for patients, the state, and hospital management to make policy decisions to fight AMR.

In summary, we have described institutional work to enable practices of data entry and information use, which are fundamental to the operations of the digital AMR monitoring application. While some of the measures can be seen to support existing work currently touched by the digital intervention, others are needed to enable the expansion of the interventions in terms of other facilities and the functionalities of the applications.

6   Conclusion

The paper has emphasized the important responsibility of IS research to engage with the expanding and urgent challenge of AMR facing the world, particularly in the context of LMICs. A key role of IS research is in guiding the implementation of AMR digital interventions, drawing upon learnings from other implementation studies, but adapting and expanding to the specific context of AMR in public settings in an LMIC context. Key learning which we have drawn upon is the practice-based approach, which we have supplemented with an understanding of how these contribute to the construction of institutional work.

References

1. Organization, W.H.: Appendix 2: WHO Tools to Facilitate Surveillance of Antibacterial Resistance. World Health Organization (2014)
2. O'Neill, J.: Tackling Drug-Resistant Infections Globally: Final Report and Recommendations. Government of the United Kingdom (2016)
3. Cars, O., Jasovsky, D.: Antibiotic Resistance (ABR) - No Sustainability without Antibiotics (2015)
4. Target: Global Database for the Tripartite Antimicrobial Resistance (AMR) Country Self-assessment Survey (TrACSS). http://amrcountryprogress.org/ (2021). Last accessed 6 Jan 2022
5. Chaudhry, D., Tomar, P.: Antimicrobial resistance: the next BIG pandemic. Int. J. Community Med. Public Health. **4**, 2632–2636 (2017). https://doi.org/10.18203/2394-6040.ijcmph201 73306
6. Pharmaceutical industry in India: Invest in Pharma Sector, https://www.investindia.gov.in/sec tor/pharmaceuticals (2021). Last accessed 8 Nov 2021
7. Klein, E.Y., Tseng, K.K., Pant, S., Laxminarayan, R.: Tracking global trends in the effectiveness of antibiotic therapy using the Drug Resistance Index. BMJ Glob. Health. **4**, e001315 (2019). https://doi.org/10.1136/bmjgh-2018-001315
8. Whittington, R.: Completing the practice turn in strategy research. Organ. Stud. **27**, 613–634 (2006). https://doi.org/10.1177/0170840606064101
9. Barnes, B.: Practice as collective action. In: Schatzki, T.R., Knorr-Cetina, K., Savigny, E. von (eds.) The Practice Turn in Contemporary Theory, pp. 17–28. Routledge (2001)
10. de Certeau, M.: The Practice of Everyday Life. Translated by Steven F. Rendall, 3rd edn. University of California Press (2011)
11. Suddaby, R., Greenwood, R.: Rhetorical strategies of legitimacy. Adm. Sci. Q. **50**, 35–67 (2005). https://doi.org/10.2189/asqu.2005.50.1.35

12. Orlikowski, W.J.: Practice in research: phenomenon, perspective and philosophy. In: Golsorkhi, D., Rouleau, L., Seidl, D., Vaara, E. (eds.) Cambridge Handbook of Strategy as Practice, pp. 23–33. Cambridge University Press (2010). https://doi.org/10.1017/CBO9780511777882.002

13. Lave, J.: Cognition in Practice: Mind, Mathematics and Culture in Everyday Life. Cambridge University Press (1988). https://doi.org/10.1017/CBO9780511609268

14. Orlikowski, W.J.: Using technology and constituting structures: a practice lens for studying technology in organizations. Organ. Sci. **11**, 404–428 (2000). https://doi.org/10.1287/orsc.11.4.404.14600

15. Suchman, L.A.: Plans and Situated Actions: The Problem of Human-Machine Communication. Cambridge University Press (1987)

16. Ciborra, C.U.: From thinking to tinkering: the grassroots of strategic information systems. Inf. Soc. **8**, 297–309 (1992). https://doi.org/10.1080/01972243.1992.9960124

17. Mosse, E.L., Sahay, S.: The role of communication practices in the strengthening of counter networks: case experiences from the health care sector of Mozambique. Inf. Technol. Dev. **11**, 207–225 (2005). https://doi.org/10.1002/itdj.20017

18. Orlikowski, W.J.: Improvising organizational transformation over time: a situated change perspective. Inf. Syst. Res. **7**, 63–92 (1996). https://doi.org/10.1287/isre.7.1.63

19. Timmermans, S., Berg, M.: Standardization in action: achieving local universality through medical protocols. Soc. Stud. Sci. **27**, 273–305 (1997). https://doi.org/10.1177/030631297027002003

20. Lawrence, T.B., Suddaby, R.: Institutions and institutional work. In: Clegg, S., Hardy, C., Lawrence, T., Nord, W. (eds.) The SAGE Handbook of Organization Studies, pp. 215–254. SAGE Publications Ltd, 1 Oliver's Yard, 55 City Road, London EC1Y 1SP United Kingdom (2006). https://doi.org/10.4135/9781848608030.n7

21. Jepperson, R.: Institutions, Institutional Effects, and Institutionalism. New Institutionalism Organ. Anal. 143–163 (1991)

22. Giddens, A.: The Constitution of Society: Outline of the Theory of Structuration. University of California Press (1984)

23. Battilana, J., D'Aunno, T.: Institutional work and the paradox of embedded agency. In: Lawrence, T.B., Suddaby, R., Leca, B. (eds.) Institutional Work: Actors and Agency in Institutional Studies of Organizations, pp. 31–58. Cambridge University Press (2009). https://doi.org/10.1017/CBO9780511596605.002

24. Lawrence, T.B., Suddaby, R., Leca, B.: Introduction: theorizing and studying institutional work. In: Lawrence, T.B., Suddaby, R., Leca, B. (eds.) Institutional Work: Actors and Agency in Institutional Studies of Organizations, pp. 1–28. Cambridge University Press (2009). https://doi.org/10.1017/CBO9780511596605.001

25. Greenwood, R., Suddaby, R., Hinings, C.R.: Theorizing change: the role of professional associations in the transformation of institutionalized fields. Acad. Manage. J. **45**, 58–80 (2002). https://doi.org/10.5465/3069285

26. Beunen, R., Patterson, J.J.: Analysing institutional change in environmental governance: exploring the concept of 'institutional work.' J. Environ. Plan. Manag. **62**, 12–29 (2019). https://doi.org/10.1080/09640568.2016.1257423

27. Närvänen, E., Mattila, M., Mesiranta, N.: Institutional work in food waste reduction: Startups' role in moving towards a circular economy. Ind. Mark. Manag. **93**, 605–616 (2021). https://doi.org/10.1016/j.indmarman.2020.08.009

28. Sundeep, S., Nielsen, P., Aanestad, M.: Institutionalizing Information Systems for Universal Health Coverage in Primary Healthcare and the Need for New Forms of Institutional Work. Commun. Assoc. Inform. Syst. **44**, 62–80 (2019). https://doi.org/10.17705/1CAIS.04403

29. Thorseng, A.A., Grisot, M.: Digitalization as institutional work: a case of designing a tool for changing diabetes care. Inf. Technol. People. **30**, 227–243 (2017). https://doi.org/10.1108/ITP-07-2015-0155

30. Rao, M., Rao, K.D., Kumar, A.S., Chatterjee, M., Sundararaman, T.: Human resources for health in India. The Lancet **377**, 587–598 (2011). https://doi.org/10.1016/S0140-6736(10)61888-0

31. Vong, S., et al.: Using information technology to improve surveillance of antimicrobial resistance in South East Asia. BMJ **358**, j3781 (2017). https://doi.org/10.1136/bmj.j3781

32. Sahay, S., Arora, G., Thakral, Y., Rødland, E.K., Mukherjee, A.S.: Designing for scale: strengthening surveillance of antimicrobial resistance in low resource settings. In: Bandi, R.K., Ranjini, C.R., Klein, S., Madon, S., Monteiro, E. (eds.) The Future of Digital Work: The Challenge of Inequality: IFIP WG 8.2, 9.1, 9.4 Joint Working Conference, IFIPJWC 2020, Hyderabad, India, December 10–11, 2020, Proceedings, pp. 251–264. Springer International Publishing, Cham (2020). https://doi.org/10.1007/978-3-030-64697-4_19

33. Walia, K., Ohri, V.: Strengthening surveillance key to addressing antimicrobial resistance. Indian J. Med. Microbiol. **34**, 413–415 (2016). https://doi.org/10.4103/0255-0857.195378

34. General, R.: Census Commissioner. Census of India, 2011. https://www.google.com/search?q=General%2C+R.+(2011).+Census+Commissioner.+Census+of+India%2C+2011.&rlz=1C1CHBH_enIN804IN805&oq=General%2C+R.+(2011).+Census+Commissioner.+Census+of+India%2C+2011.&aqs=chrome..69i57.269j0j9&sourceid=chrome&ie=UTF-8 (2011). Last accessed 8 Nov 2021

35. NSS 75th Round, (2017–2018). Government of India, Ministry of Statistics and Program Implementation, National Statistical Office, India. http://164.100.161.63/announcements/executive-summary-report-health-india-nss-75th-round

36. Msendma, M.B., Chigona, W., Kumwenda, B., Kaasbøll, J., Kanjo, C.: Legitimization of Data Quality Practices in Health Management Information Systems Using DHIS2. Case of Malawi. ArXiv210809942 Cs. (2021)

The Role of Digital Platforms in Managing Institutional Logics: Case from DHIS2 in Ethiopia

Abyot Asalefew Gizaw[1]([⊠]), Selamawit Molla Fossum[2],
and Birkinesh Woldeyohannes Lagebo[3]

[1] Univesity of Oslo, Oslo, Norway
abyotag@ifi.uio.no
[2] University of Manchester, Manchester, UK
[3] Addis Ababa University, Addis Ababa, Ethiopia

Abstract. Digital platforms are vehicles to transform socio-economic activities leading to growth, innovation, interconnectedness and collaboration. Such platforms are keenly needed in low resource setting countries where developmental agenda is at the forefront of institutions. Often, such platforms originate in the global north and travel to south facing heterogeneous contexts and institutional logics which at times are conflicting. As a result, literature advises for context aware and homegrown solutions to fit into local realities. However, this paper documents how homegrown solutions also face conflicting institutional logics and their inability to adapt leads to failures. Emphasizing on global digital platforms, the paper investigates how they navigate conflicting institutional logics and realize their developmental potential. The paper argues digital platform's inherent constraint and affordance plays a central role in inscribing and accommodating multiple institutional logics. The paper is based on a case study of DHIS2 used as health management information system in Ethiopia.

Keywords: DHIS2 · Digital platforms · Health information system · Institutional logics · Ethiopia

1 Introduction

Digital platforms are strongly regarded as vehicles to transform socio-economic activities leading to growth, innovation, interconnectedness and collaboration [1–3]. However, despite such a promising potential for the global south, focus has been more on the global north leading to a dearth of research on the global south [4]. Recognizing the shortage, research makes an explicit call for IS research that contributes to the developmental potential of digital platforms in the global south [5]. This paper attempts to respond to this call by exploring the link between platforms and institutional logics drawing from empirical material observed in global south health management information system (HMIS) digital platform implementation initiative.

© IFIP International Federation for Information Processing 2022
Published by Springer Nature Switzerland AG 2022
Y. Zheng et al. (Eds.): ICT4D 2022, IFIP AICT 657, pp. 107–119, 2022.
https://doi.org/10.1007/978-3-031-19429-0_7

Investigating digital platforms goes beyond the classic case of information system study in an organization. Digital platforms operate beyond the boundary of a single organization as they are inherently dynamic and transcend heterogeneous institutional logic. Various IS researchers showed how multiple stakeholders' institutional logics within a platform ecosystem compete, dominant or co-exist [6, 7].

Masiero and Nicholson [4] identify market-centered and human-centered competing logics that underpin digital platforms. They further emphasize prioritizing human-centered logics to realize the developmental potential of digital platforms. However, despite a focus on human-centered logics, the reality that most of the platforms prominent in the ICT4D discourse originate from the North and continue to travel across many countries in the south brings a challenge of navigating multiple logics of these countries, including the platform creator ones. This paper aims to discuss how digital platforms play a role in managing completing logics through time.

There are two types of digital platforms – transactional platforms mostly focused on market-oriented exchange business logic and innovation platforms that provide boundary resources for others to innovate apps [5, 8]. In this paper we focus on innovation type digital platforms with developmental impact. These are platforms designed to facilitate locally situated value creation by third party actors. The innovation platform provides stable core functionalities and associated boundary resources such as APIs and technical documentations that local users, governments, development partners and other institutions can consume to rapidly develop and deploy locally relevant context aware apps [9, 10]. The advantage with innovation platforms is that they have done the heavy lifting by providing ready to consume boundary resources where local actors are relieved from dealing with complex technical materiality [11].

However, materializing the developmental impact of innovation digital platforms in the global south is met with locally situated institutional logics that need to be inscribed in the platform to ensure platform sustainability across time and space. Acknowledging the inherent nature of platforms to live through heterogeneous institutions, the paper aims to answer the following research question: how do innovation digital platforms navigate competing institutional logics and sustain through time? Answering this research question, arguably, provides a significant contribution to our understanding on the developmental role of digital platforms in the global south to navigate and inscribe multiple institutional logics in systems.

The empirical material informing this paper is a longitudinal study of a particular digital platform called DHIS2. DHIS2 is a web-based free and open-source health management information system developed by the University of Oslo (UiO), Norway. It is considered as a global public good digital platform currently in use by more than 70 countries in the global south including by the Government of Ethiopia. Before the empirical material, a discussion of foundational theoretical framework is presented. Following the theoretical framework, methodology, case description and analysis are presented. Finally, a concluding section, containing discussions of theoretical and practical contributions, is presented.

2 Theoretical Framework: Institutional Logic

Institutional logic is a perspective that has received much attention in IS to analyze the interrelationships among institutions, individuals, and organizations in social systems [12]. Friedland and Alford [13] discuss the presence of multiple institutional orders in a society with a certain logic. Institutional logic refers to a set of material practices and symbolic constructions which constitutes its organizing principles, assumptions, identities, and domain dimensions which is available to organizations and individuals to elaborate on [6]. Field actors then use institutional logic as the organizing principles to select technologies, authorize actors and specify criteria for effectiveness and efficiency [14, 15].

Institutional logics are never homogeneous in an organization where multiple logics can be found in play simultaneously [13]. Institutionally pluralistic organizations are not passive agents but navigate and maintain contradictory logics. Thus, heterogeneous actors may draw on different logics and exercise their power to influence decision making processes [16]. Logics can complement and compete [17]. Cooperative logics support each other either through facilitative or additive [17] whereas competitive logics contribute to institutional contradictions which result in change or new account of activities in the organization field [12]. Institutional change is often associated with a change of the dominant institutional logic for the field [18, 19]. Once institutional logic becomes dominant, its solutions and issues get the managers attention to influence organizational decisions [20].

Scholars put forward different mechanisms of consolidating divergent institutional logic to bring about institutional change thereby facilitating institutionalization of new logics. For example [12, 21] point out structural overlap, event or temporal sequencing, institutional entrepreneurs and competing institutional logic as mechanisms of institutionalization. Scott [22] on the other hand, outlines three mechanisms– increasing returns, objectification and commitments. While increasing returns emphasizes reinforcement of existing institutions and benefits of economies of scale, increasing objectification accounts for the social construction of reality in objectifying and habituating shared beliefs. The main point in objectification is the interplay of actors. Actors interacting together form mental representations of each other's actions that are represented in the form of routines, documents, software tools and best practices. Mechanism of commitment distances itself from the economic gains, for example incentives, and investigates logics that provide commitments. This mechanism emphasizes the role of identity (who am I?) and appropriateness (what is the appropriate way to behave in this situation?).

Thus, the institutional logic concept enables us to understand aspects of complexity such as multiplicity, heterogeneity, coexistence of different logics [12, 14, 23]. Scott [19] identifies three major elements of institutions, where logics are drawn from- regulative, normative, cultural cognitive. Regulative institutions emphasize explicit regulatory processes (e.g. laws, rules and sanctions) that constrain or enable human behavior. Normative institutions refer to organizational or societal norms and values that are seen appropriate for a certain social order and they are invisible. The cultural-cognitive refers to the frames through which individuals perceive objects and activities and how those cultural-cognitive elements shape decisions that bring about institutional change. When applied to technological studies, there is a technological element [24] that creates institutional contradictions and breaks down persistent institutions incrementally or sustains the already existing institutions. Particularly, the inherent nature of digital platforms to live through heterogeneous institutions suits to apply the concept of institutional logic for the case.

However, most of the information systems literature rarely addresses the material dimensions of institutional logics by emphasizing on how various institutional logics influence human attitudes and engage human behavior [25, 26]. Technology's inherent affordances and constraints can give the agentic behavior for technology [27]. In the institutional logics perspective, material agency can be expressed through the inscription of institutional logics into technological artifacts serving as carriers for these logics. The role of technology in institutional logic studies is often passive, and scantily addresses the material agency of the technology [28]. More specifically, there is a lack of an explicit study that shows how digital platforms navigate competing institutional logics and sustain themselves through time. This paper is aimed at filling this knowledge gap by analyzing how the affordances and constraints of digital platforms accommodate multiple institutional logics underlying the DHIS2 implementation. It also shows the tradeoff that is made and technical debt this approach incurred.

3   Research Approach

This paper is developed as part of the Health Information System Program (HISP) longitudinal action research on HMIS in developing countries [29]. It is an interpretive case study of 'involved researchers' [30] that explores the history of DHIS implementation in Ethiopia.

The authors have played a central role in the development, customization, and implementation since 2003 in various capacities. While two of the authors were active participants in the customization, implementation and research as full-time employees and master students in the period 2003–2007, one of the authors has been working as a core developer and researcher since 2007. Two of the authors participated in reintroducing DHIS2 to MOH in 2015. Since 2015, the core developer has been working in close collaboration with Ethiopia's Federal Ministry of Health (FMoH) to incorporate their requirements technically and organizationally.

Data for this paper were chiefly generated as part of our action research engagement, which was complemented by few interviews and document reviews. Particularly, the period 2007–2015 was covered using data from interviews and document reviews. We used 6 interviews that were collected prior to this study, and we conducted one more with a key informant during the write up of this paper. Documents that were reviewed include strategy documents, assessment results, and PhD and Master theses.

Data were analyzed deductively [31] by applying the institutional logic concept on the case description. To do that we first identified opposing logics throughout the history of DHIS2 in Ethiopia. We then discussed the implication to institutional change (institutionalization).

4 Case Description: DHIS2 Navigating Conflicting Logics in Ethiopia

DHIS2 is a free and open-source Health Management Information System (HMIS) platform first released in 2006 by UiO. However, its earlier versions of 1.3 and 1.4 were operational since 1994. These earlier versions - collectively referred as DHIS - were first introduced to Ethiopia in 2003. Following its Scandinavian tradition of participatory design, UiO established a local in-country team called HISP-Ethiopia. The primary task of the team was to support local customizations, implementations, training, and related capacity building activities. To conduct these activities, HISP-Ethiopia signed a memorandum of understanding (MoU) with five Regional Health Bureaus of Ethiopia and one administration city (i.e., Oromia, Amhara, Tigray, Benishangul-Gumuz, and Addis Ababa) from 2003–2004. These five regions became DHIS pilot sites from 2004–2007.

Ultimately, the HMIS software was implemented in all public health institutions of the Addis Ababa Health Bureau to capture and report routine health information to a higher level. The remaining four regions were at different stages of customization and implementation activities. However, the FMoH criticized fragmented regional efforts and launched a national harmonized HMIS activity following a principle called "One Plan, One Report and One Budget" [32]. The ministry invited development partners to realize the centralized national endeavor. Three major systems used at that time, Tigray e-HMIS, SNNPR (Southern Nations Nationalities and People Region) e-HMIS and DHIS were evaluated by the National Advisory Committee (NAC) of FMoH. Towards the end of 2007, the NAC announced the rejection of DHIS due to lack of local capacity, mismatch between functionalities and needs as well as technical failures.

After DHIS was abandoned in 2007, the FMoH mandated John Snow, Inc., (JSI) and Tulane University Technical Assistant Project in Ethiopia (TUTAPE) to review, design and implement a new HMIS system. In the end both JSI and TUTAPE developed and rolled out their own brand-new local systems. JSI took the SNNPR while TUTAPE took the rest of the country. These two systems were in use in their respective regions till the end of 2017.

For about a decade, both systems have had the chance to roll out their organizational structures, human resources, work practices and system functionalities. However, for several reasons these systems were far from perfect in the eyes of FMoH users. Some of the problems raised were the FMoH never achieved a harmonized HMIS that it requested back in 2007 when DHIS was abandoned. The FMoH also couldn't achieve the local capacity to own the systems as they were reliant on JSI and TUTAPE staff. There were several complaints how the FMoH was sidelined when it comes to the technical matters – for example FMoH users asking for JSI and TUTAPE staff to provide them username and password to access the systems; Health Information Technology Directorate (HITD) staff not getting access to the source codes to make minor adjustments to mention a few. In addition, the standalone nature of the e-HMIS systems was not appreciated by FMoH. An informant pointed out these issues as:

"One of the criteria was, web-based and the systems we had were desktop based. That was the biggest gap between the criteria and the implemented systems......based on the criteria the systems lost big scores as they were not web based.

The health workers need to transfer files using flash. When the frequency of data exchange is often, for example for PHEM data, it means exchange of flash weekly. The situation was not forward looking we identified this as the biggest gap at that point"

These and other problems pushed the FMoH to evaluate existing systems and look for solutions or alternatives. One solution tried was acquiring a third integrator system that can generate national level reports from the two systems. However, this also became problematic – first it was expensive and cumbersome to maintain the system, second it forced FMoH users to rely on others to generate reports out of the data they collected.

While both systems were in use, FMoH showed interest in DHIS2 and contacted HISP UiO. HISP UiO was happy to see the interest after a decade and quickly assigned two of its staff – both Ethiopians but based in Oslo – to follow the matter. These individuals traveled to Addis to meet FMoH officials and discuss the way forward including establishing a local team and MoU based collaborations like it was before pre-2007. The FMoH rejected the idea saying we want to evaluate DHIS2 and try it for ourselves first without any bias from external stakeholders. The Ministry used JSI and TUTAPE experience as a reference. One of our informants described the extent of the partner organization dominance as:

"In previous e-HMIS let alone the source code, even the IT department does not have a password to change the username...." Former directorate, MOH.

The other informants echoed the partner organization dominance as follows

"...We asked the partner organizations to hand over the source code...one delivered after the deadline...the other didn't ..."

These excerpts revealed how much managers were frustrated with the dominance of partner organizations in previous e-HMIS implementations.

However, the problem with this was, the FMoH has no local capacity to do the assessment on DHIS2. Though not an ideal scenario, HISP UiO accepted the FMoH's request and even hired one more local staff to assist on the configuration, testing, training and piloting activities needed for the evaluation. The UiO-hired staff became part of the FMoH team. The team then made the assessment across a number of categories and presented a thorough report to the NAC. The final assessment report ranked DHIS2 with a weighted score of 96.4, JSI's system 72.7 and TUTAPE's 62.3 out of 100.

Once the assessment report was reviewed by the NAC and high-level decision makers of the FMoH, a decision was made for TUTAPE's and JSI's systems to be replaced by DHIS2 throughout the entire country. To facilitate the transition to DHIS2, the FMoH management established three committees – Steering Committee (SC), Core Customization Team (CCT) and Technical Working Group (TWG). The SC was chaired by the state minister which showed the emphasis and urgency given to the task.

Though DHIS2 was given a high score during the evaluation, there was some resistance from users especially on features that they found useful in the old systems but not available in DHIS2. From a usability perspective, features available in DHIS2 were ranked higher. However, because of the tendency to resist changes and the level of learning effort needed on the new system users brought strong resistance. For example, one of the requests was:

"... we used to see target data sets separately during data entry. Now both target and routine data sets come in the same app. These shouldn't be mixed as they are used by different users and departments"

The CCT and TWG tried to clarify by saying,

"... yes they appear on the same app because both are about data entry. You can also select whether to enter for targets or routines. It is also possible to control which user can see and enter which of the data sets".

This, however, was not a satisfactory answer to users. Another request asked by users was "in the old system we used to generate reports in the same format as data entry". The CCT and TWG tried to clarify by saying "data in should not be the same as data out. Once data is captured, you can use DHIS2's pivot table to generate reports in the format you want". This too was not convincing to the users. Several such demands put a strong pressure on the CCT and TWG teams that they needed to find a solution before the SC was swayed back to the old systems.

These demands required a considerable amount of extension to DHIS2 through system design and development. For fear of lack of capacity, the local team again requested the FMoH to contact UiO for official support and get into some form of MoU but again rejected. The team even got an ultimatum that they need to support the ministry as Ethiopian and technical individuals, not as a UiO staff. The team understood FMoH's position that given the amount of influence of the old systems for so many years, it won't be easy for FMoH to be seen siding with UiO.

However, despite the rejection the local team convinced UiO to hire additional staff arguing there is a good potential for DHIS2 to be adopted as a national system. UiO agreed and hired the fourth team member to work on the technical tasks. One of the HISP Ethiopia members, also part of DHIS2's global core team, got heavily involved in the required design and development tasks. This helped the team to develop all features requested by users – for example creating three data entry apps dedicated for target setting, routine reporting and disaggregated disease reporting; creating a report app based on data entry template; extending DHIS2 for Ethiopian calendar; and supporting on-the-fly data validation to mention a few. These extensions were made possible because of DHIS2's core platform, web API and pluggable web app design logic.

The team was also able to extend DHIS2 for practices that are in complete opposite to established practices of UiO and HISP – especially on the need to collect minimum vs maximum data sets. For example, one of the monthly excel templates has about 800 rows to be filled. At the time of converting the template to DHIS2 form, HISP UiO experts advised for revising the form and focus only on minimum actionable data points. But the FMoH rejected the advice and ordered for all the data points to be included and made mandatory so that the form won't be considered complete and acceptable if a single data point is left blank. The technical team went outside their established logic and redesigned DHIS2 as per the FMoH needs. However, soon after users started data entry, the mandatory logic created a problem - because users have no data on many of the rows, but the form asks them to put something. Instead of reducing the form to only available dataset, the Ministry asked for a solution of bulk inserting zero values for those data points users have no information. With no way out of the disagreement, the team implemented the solution as per the request but tried to argue using some statistics where more than 70% of the collected data has zero values. But the ministry insisted on collecting maximum data despite being zero.

These developments were big achievements that convinced users that DHIS2 is a good system for them. Users also took this opportunity to ask the local team to develop additional features that were not part of TUTAPE's and JSI's systems. The team developed as requested. Some of them – for example aggregation type and data set report – were even found to be useful for other countries and adopted into the global DHIS2 nu HISP UiO.

Equally important to the development task was metadata configuration and training that were again spearheaded by the local team. The training and hands-on metadata configuration enabled FMoH users to make configurations as they see fit, decide what to collect and generate reports as per their needs. Finally, DHIS2 was adopted as a national HMIS by the end of 2017. It got rolled out across the country both as an online (where there is internet connectivity) and offline (where there is no connectivity) system. Since then, more than 6000 users were trained, close to 300 million records of data were collected by more than 35,000 organizations throughout the country. It was a big success to see such figures. For FMoH, it gave an opportunity to give official recognition and legitimacy to UiO, HISP Ethiopia team and the DHIS2 platform. For UiO, seeing DHIS2 as a national system was a big success and motivation to support the FMoH more. In 2019, two FMoH staff were invited to Oslo to attend the annual DHIS2 conference where users are allowed to gather and establish a network, share experience, present their achievements and challenges as well as vote on features that need to be included in the upcoming DHIS2 milestones and releases.

The 2020 COVID crisis was also another opportunity for the FMoH to give more recognition to the HISP Ethiopia team and UiO. When the crisis hit, few at the Ministry had the idea of how to manage data collection, notification, tracking and reporting challenges needed to contain the outbreak. Many DHIS2 using countries were able to respond quickly by using the DHIS2 tracker module and COVID-19 surveillance packages developed by HISP UiO. The HISP Ethiopia team adopted the packages by making the necessary localizations. The team even developed four additional apps that assist on bulk importing, SMS notification, certificate generation and validation. FMoH wouldn't have been able to achieve these without the support of UiO and its HISP team in Ethiopia. This convinced FMoH to get into official recognition by signing the long-resisted MoU. The MoU was signed by the state minister on March 09, 2021. Currently the FMoH and UiO are in conversation to develop a joint project by outlining a scope of work that needs to be conducted for the FMoH to upgrade its DHIS2 to the latest versions. The following table summarizes the major events and key stakeholders involved in the HMIS digitization of Ethiopia (Table 1).

Table 1. Major events and stakeholders in digitizing the HMIS of Ethiopia

Period	2003–2007	2008–2014	2015–
Stakeholder	HISP/UiO, JSI	TUTAPE, JSI	HISP/UiO, JSI
Major events	Customization and implementation of DHIS 1.3 & 1.4 in five regions DHIS2 presented as a national solution JSI had own system in one region	e-HMIS was developed locally and implemented at a national level JSI had own system in one region	DHIS2 customized and implemented nationally in collaboration with JSI

5 Analysis and Discussion

Institutional logics are rarely homogeneous; within an organization, multiple logics may be simultaneously in play, contributing to institutional contradictions that bring change in the field [13]. Similarly, the story of DHIS2 in Ethiopia shows several conflicts that the local team, FMoH decision makers, HISP UiO management and DHIS2's material affordance were able to collectively navigate for a successful outcome. It shows the importance of overcoming "design-reality gap" and skillfully accommodating what is required in specific local situations even if what is needed is outside one's established logic.

Throughout the history of DHIS2 implementation, heterogeneous institutional logics were found to compete and at times collaborate [17]. Of these, the policy plan logic based on the one plan, one report and one budget principle was the dominant one.

From the early story of DHIS2 – versions 1.3 and 1.4 – it was evident how its materiality and flexibility were relatively weaker to accommodate the needs of the FMoH. There was a gap along the technical, managerial and policy level, especially with regards to the one plan, one report and one budget institutional logic. Being a system developed in the North and taken to the South, one would also expect a mismatch and conflict of institutional logics [33]. Failure to accommodate the dominant institutional logic led to outright rejection.

JSI and TUTAPE systems, though developed in-house from scratch, were also rejected for their failure to accommodate emerging logics. This shows, the issue is not really whether a system goes from North to South, rather flexibility and material affordance to accommodate emerging logics. These logics are not just technical, but also organizational. For example, not granting FMoH user's full access to the national HMIS system is not technical but managerial that gave TUTAPE more control. System administrators from TUTAPE, not FMoH, had full control on who could use and operate the system. There were also other situations, for example FMoH users not able to generate their own reports but rely on others and HITD technical staff not getting access to the source code to make some adjustments as seen fit by the FMoH. These instances show the temporal nature of institutional logic and that once dominant logic could be secondary or unimportant at other times.

To overcome dominance of partner organizations experienced in the locally developed e-HMIS solutions, the policy plan logic emphasized on "use in-house IT capacity" to DHIS2 customization. This "use in-house IT capacity" for design aimed to put FMoH on the driver's seat. On the other hand, the decision didn't allow for having formal relations with HISP through establishing the HISP-Ethiopia team. This has limited the number of HISP staff required to support the implementation. From the HISP perspective, this was not about dominating but following the Scandinavian tradition of participatory design. Here the policy plan logic clashes with DHIS2 logic which often uses global-local DHIS2 experts' collaboration to satisfy the countries' local requirement.

Institutional logic contradiction is not always resolved but sometimes it needs to be acknowledged [34]. HISP didn't argue but quickly recognized the position of FMoH and accommodated the ministry's logic and went ahead without establishing local HISP Ethiopia team and MoU. As a result, the technical team with limited local HISP staff had been soon challenged by the lack of DHIS2 competence mainly regarding code level customization that directed to include few more HISP members informally that enabled them to address the ministry's unique. With these informal relations with HISP enabled to address the current need of DHIS2 competence to implement DHIS2 and alleviated the MOH dominance concern. On the same vein, HISP has got an opportunity to implement DHIS2 in Ethiopia and gained recognition from the sector.

Another important aspect of DHIS2's materiality was its affordance to inscribe conflicting logics. DHIS2 is designed along the assumption of minimum dataset and single flexible app per functionality. However, for the system to be acceptable by FMoH users and be useful in their work practice, the local team had to go outside the DHIS2 logic and redesign DHIS2 based on the maximum dataset and multiple distinct apps for a single functionality as seen for target setting, routine reporting and disaggregated disease registration. Here, HISP accommodated the policy plan logic, maximum data set, and inscribed in DHIS2 to satisfy users that contradicted with DHIS2 logic assumption.

Following the widely use of the routine DHIS2 which was configured according to the logic of policy and plan, health experts had begun complaining for the inadequacy of DHIS2 to address their specific and detailed information needs. Health experts required, health program specific detailed and/or case-based information to monitor, plan and evaluate the performance of the health service for their respective health programs. Thus, they forwarded their information need to CCT as well as to the HISP staff to be inscribed in DHIS2. Given to DHIS2's flexibility and affordance feature, the CCT team, who were convinced with the importance of health expert information needs, enacted the health expert logic. The health experts' information needs such as PHEM and covid19 were addressed in DHIS2.

Furthermore, DHIS2 has given users absolute control of what to collect and report in the format they needed without relying on other actors. Health experts appreciated the fact that they could generate their own reports and perform analysis in DHIS2 without needing assistance from external stakeholders. Thus, DHIS2 became the collaboration logic to bring both the health experts and the policy experts into one to produce standardized program specific DHIS2.

In addition to this, partner organizations, who often worked in specific health programs expressed their interest to develop data quality apps. Accordingly, various data quality apps such as score card, bottle neck analysis had been developed and deployed with DHIS2 platform. Exploiting the affordability of DHIS2 and the commitment of HISP staff, several apps were developed and deployed in the sector. Ultimately, addressing the major actors' logics underpinned in DHIS2 implementation due to the affordability and flexible feature of DHIS2 and HISP staff commitment. This has convinced MOH to establish formal relations with HISP UiO to be able to address the emergent health sector needs.

In general, the study revealed how DHIS2's material and organizational affordance has facilitated institutions to navigate and enact multiple logics through time. This was observed during the (re)design, customization and implementation of DHIS2 as well as its sustainability in the country. The case analysis shows how different mechanisms were used to bring about the sought institutional change in the e-HMIS landscape of the country. Particularly, mechanisms of commitment [22] and managing competing institutional logics through time [12, 21] were heavily drawn upon to reintroduce and sustain DHIS2 in Ethiopia. However, these mechanisms would not be sufficient without a flexible platform.

Institutional change is often associated with a change of the dominant institutional logic in the organizational field [35, 36]. On the contrary, our analysis shows how institutional change happened, while the dominant logic remains stable, experiencing minor adjustments to accommodate health experts and DHIS2 logics.

6 Conclusions

There has been sufficient IS research that uses institutional logic as a concept to explore the embedded exogenic forces that influence the implementation and use of IT based innovations. However, there has been little focus on the role the platform plays to navigate through heterogenous institutional logics. This paper shows how the flexibility of a platform helps converge divergent logics through time and commitment. It contributes to the little discussed fourth institutional element – IT as an institution.

The paper challenges the taken-for-granted assumption that institutional logic clashes are particularly pertinent when technological innovations are translated from North to South. It shows how a home-grown software that is coded from scratch, in the hope of addressing contextual needs, failed for an innovation platform that is robust enough to accommodate embedded and emerging logics. If innovation platforms are to achieve their developmental goals, they need to acknowledge the presence of heterogeneous institutional logics in the platform ecosystem and platforms need to be designed enabling navigation through these logics.

While our study provided empirical and theoretical understanding on the role of the platform in managing heterogeneous institutional logics, we noticed accommodating institutional logic comes with an opportunity cost of accumulated digital debt. Further research might be required to understand the link between institutional logic and digital debt.

This study is limited to identifying the institutional logics of HIS implementation in Ethiopia at macro level. Thus, the findings may not adequately reflect each case's micro level institutional logics contradictions. A more detailed longitudinal study of both cases would be relevant to unravel implementations' challenges at various stages of implementations due to the dynamic and complex nature of the health sector.

References

1. Heeks, R.: ICT4D 3.0? Part 1—The components of an emerging "digital-for-development" paradigm. Electronic J. Inf. Syst. Dev. Ctries. **86**(3), 1–15 (2020)
2. van Biljon, J., Marais, M., Platz, M.: Digital platforms for research collaboration: using design science in developing a South African open knowledge repository. Inf. Technol. Dev. **23**(3), 463–485 (2017)
3. Walsham, G.: South-South and triangular cooperation in ICT4D. Electron. J. Inf. Syst. Dev. Ctries. **86**(4), 2–7 (2020)
4. Masiero, S., Nicholson, B.: Competing logics: towards a theory of digital platforms for socio-economic development. In: International Conference on Social Implications of Computers in Developing Countries, pp. 3–13. Springer, Cham (2020)
5. Bonina, C., Koskinen, K., Eaton, B., Gawer, A.: Digital platforms for development: foundations and research agenda. Inf. Syst. J. **31**(6), 869–902 (2021)
6. Berente, N., Yoo, Y.: Institutional contradictions and loose coupling: post implementation of NASA's enterprise information system. Inf. Syst. Res. **23**(2), 376–396 (2012)
7. Boonstra, U.A., Eseryel, Y., van Offenbeek, M.A.G.: Stakeholders' enactment of competing logics in IT governance: polarization, compromise or synthesis? Eur. J. Inf. Syst. **27**(4), 415–433 (2017). https://doi.org/10.1057/s41303-017-0055-0
8. Koskinen, K., Bonina, C., Eaton, B.: Digital platforms in the global south: foundations and research agenda. In: International Conference on Social Implications of Computers in Developing Countries, pp. 319–330. Springer, Cham (2019 May)
9. Familia, B.: Bolsa Familia CAIXA (Version 2.4.0) [Mobile application software]. Retrieved from https://apps.apple.com/br/app/bolsa-fam%C3%ADlia-caixa/id1036174679 (2020)
10. Bright, J.: Diving deep into Africa's blossoming tech scene. Retrieved from https://social.tec hcrunch.com/2019/05/31/diving-deep-into-africas-blossoming-tech-scene/ (2022 Apr 15)
11. Ghazawneh, A., Henfridsson, O.: Balancing platform control and external contribution in third-party development: the boundary resources model. Inf. Syst. J. **23**(2), 173–192 (2013)
12. Thornton, P.H., Ocasio, W., Lounsbury, M.: The Institutional Logics Perspective: A New Approach to Culture, Structure and Process. Oxford University Press (2012). https://doi.org/10.1093/acprof:oso/9780199601936.001.0001
13. Friedland, R., Alford, R.: Bringing society back. in: symbols, practices, and institutional contradictions. In: Powell, W.W., Paul, J.D. (eds.) The New Institutionalism in Organizational Analysis, 232–263. University of Chicago Press, Chicago (1991)
14. Greenwood, R., Raynard, M., Kodeih, F., Micelotta, E.R., Lounsbury, M.: Institutional complexity and organizational responses. Acad. Manag. Ann. **5**(1), 317–371 (2011)
15. Lounsbury, M.: Institutional transformation and status mobility: the professionalization of the field of finance. Acad. Manag. J. **45**(1), 255–266 (2002)
16. Gregory, R.W., Keil, M., Muntermann, J., Mähring, M.: Paradoxes and the nature of ambidexterity in IT transformation programs. Inf. Syst. Res. **26**(1), 57–80 (2015)
17. Goodrick, E., Reay, T.: Constellations of institutional logics: changes in the professional work of pharmacists. Work. Occup. **38**(3), 372–416 (2011)
18. Greenwood, R., Suddaby, R., Hinings, C.: Theorizing change: The role of professional associations in the transformation of institutionalized fields. Acad. Manag. J. **45**(1), 58–80 (2002)

19. Scott, R.: Institutional change and healthcare organizations: From professional dominance to managed care. In: Institutions and organizations, 2nd ed. Sage Publication (2001)
20. Thornton, P.H.: Markets from Culture: Institutional Logics and Organizational Decisions in Higher Education Publishing. Stanford University Press, Stanford (2004)
21. Jepperson, R.L.: Institutions, institutional effects and institutionalism. In: Powell, W.W., DiMaggio, P.J. (eds.) The New Institutionalism in Organizational Analysis, 143–63. University of Chicago Press, Chicago (1991)
22. Scott, R.: Approaching adulthood: the maturing of institutional theory. Theory Soc. **37**(5), 427–442 (2008)
23. Grisot, M., Vassilakopoulou, P.: Infrastructures in healthcare: the interplay between generativity and standardization. Int. J. Med. Informatics **82**(5), e170–e179 (2013)
24. Fossum, S.: An Institutional Perspective on Health Information Systems' Standardization: Multiple Case Studies. University of Oslo, Norway (2016)
25. Raaijmakers, A., Vermeulen, P.A.M., Meeus, M.T.H.: Children without bruised knees: responding to material and ideational (Mis)alignments. Organ. Stud. **39**(5–6), 811–830 (2018). https://doi.org/10.1177/0170840617743298
26. Reay, T., Jones, C.: Qualitatively capturing institutional logics. Strateg. Organ. 1–14 (2015)
27. Leonardi, P.M.: When flexible routines meet flexible technologies: affordance, constraint, and the imbrication of human and material agencies. MIS Q. **35**(1), 147–167 (2011)
28. Avgerou, C.: IT as an institutional actor in developing countries. The digital challenge: Information technology in the development context **1**, 46–63 (2003)
29. Braa, J., Monteiro, E., Sahay, S.: Networks of action: sustainable health information systems across developing countries. MIS Q. **28**(3), 337–362 (2004)
30. Sahay, S., Walsham, G.: Information technology in developing countries: a need for theory building. Inf. Technol. Dev. **6**(3–4), 111–124 (1995)
31. Burnard, P., Gill, P., Stewart, K., Treasure, E., Chadwick, B.: Analysing and presenting qualitative data. Br. Dent. J. **204**(8), 429–432 (2008)
32. FMoH: Health sector development program: 2010/11–2014/15, vol. IV. Federal Democratic Republic of Ethiopia Ministry of Health, Addis Ababa, Ethiopia (2010)
33. Masiero, S.: The origins of failure: seeking the causes of design–reality gaps. Inf. Technol. Dev. **22**(3), 487–502 (2016)
34. Hanseth, O., Bygstad, B.: Flexible generification: ICT standardization strategies and service innovation in health care. Eur. J. Inf. Syst. **24**(6), 645–663 (2015)
35. Scott, W.R., Ruef, M., Mendel, P.J., Caronn, C.A.: Institutional change and healthcare organizations: from professional dominance to managed care. Adm. Sci. Q. **427**, 384–387 (2000)
36. Suddaby, R., Greenwood, R.: Rhetorical strategies of legitimacy. Adm. Sci. Q. **50**(1), 35–67 (2005)

Introducing Digital Health in Post Conflict Mozambique: A Historical Perspective

Nilza Collinson[1,2(✉)] and Sundeep Sahay[1]

[1] Department of Informatics, University of Oslo, Oslo, Norway
{nilzac,sundeeps}@ifi.uio.no
[2] Faculty of Sciences, University Eduardo Mondlane, Maputo City, Mozambique

Abstract. Implementation of digital health in low- and middle-income countries is susceptible to influences of several institutional dynamics, through interactions of technological artefacts, political and other environmental conditions. These dynamics may lead to contradictions, not always obvious nor easily acknowledgeable. History can be valuable to understand and pursue explanations around why and how a technology gets adopted and institutionalized or not in particular settings. This study is part of a project focusing on a longitudinal case, where history is reconstructed over twenty years, in three phases: introducing digital health in post conflict Mozambique (2000–2007), disruption of initial efforts to introduce District Health Information Systems (DHIS) platform (2008–2014) and, adoption and scaling up of DHIS2 nationally (2015–2021). For the purposes of this paper, we conduct analysis to the initial period, with institutionalist lenses, aiming to identify the set of contradictions raised within the context of study and discuss implications for the future.

Keywords: Historical reconstruction · Institutional dynamics · Institutional change · Institutional contradictions

1 Introduction

Studies around the implementation of Information Systems (IS) continue to gain interest, with several authors focusing on IS in low- and middle-income countries (LMICs) [30, 49], including stories of failures [22, 64] and successes [2, 31, 49]. While most studies have focused on stories over the short term [2, 31, 63], a limited number of them have focused on long term implementations, spanning more than thirty years [5, 59, 62]. A common analytical focus is on the implementation dynamics and their ongoing implications. In turn, a historical analysis provides the potential to investigate large amounts of existing data, to discern underlying patterns and how they change over time [12].

History provides a valuable tool to reconstruct processes, which helps to explain contemporary occurrences [12] and "allows one to look to the past as a source of alternatives for the future" [23]. Such an analysis helps "provide answers to institutional questions" [23], drawing upon the lens of institutional theory. Several concepts and methods inherited by this theory have been developed along the years and are increasingly being used

© IFIP International Federation for Information Processing 2022
Published by Springer Nature Switzerland AG 2022
Y. Zheng et al. (Eds.): ICT4D 2022, IFIP AICT 657, pp. 120–143, 2022.
https://doi.org/10.1007/978-3-031-19429-0_8

in research. Concepts such path dependency and historical frameworks have been used to explore evolutionary trajectories and unveil patterns embedded in institutional change phenomena [58].

In this paper, we pursue building a historical understanding of the processes of change around the introduction of digital health systems in post conflict Mozambique. We reconstruct the history around the introduction of the technological artefact DHIS (District Health Information Software) around its initial implementation over the period 2000–2007, within the framework of a global Health Information System Programme (HISP) R&D initiative, coordinated by the University of Oslo (UiO) in Norway. The specific research question to address is: *"how institutional dynamics raise contradictions during IS implementation and what are the unfolding implications?"*. In the next section we introduce some related literature, followed by the methods section. The case study and analysis are presented in Sects. 4 and 5 respectively. Finally, we discuss key contributions and conclusions.

2   Related Works

Institutional theory has its origins from the 1950s, and has drawn from multiple disciplines of economics, political science, sociology, and organization theory [26, 48, 53, 60]. The more recent history includes the development of a new institutionalism, and the emergence of other debates focusing on *institutional change, institutional logics* and *contradictions* [26, 60, 65], which provides the basis for the theoretical approach adopted in this paper.

Studies using Institutional theory has been applied in a multidisciplinary basis across domains of such education, health, commerce, markets, among others, either in commercial or public domains, [5, 34, 51, 61]. Within IS, scholars have used this theory to examine several phenomena around the processes of adoption and institutionalization [57], institutional change [5, 46, 47, 49, 62], institutional logics [4, 17, 50], institutional contradictions [44, 52, 56], institutional work [51]. Various concepts have guided these analysis including *institutions, institutionalization, actor, social action, processes, time, context, behavior, patterns, values, meanings, logics, culture, power, political* and *economic situations, conflicts* [23, 26, 43, 54, 65], among others. These are perceived, interpreted, and defined differently in accordance with the perspective adopted.

The concept *institution* is central, representing a *social order* or *pattern* that has attained a certain state or property; and *institutionalization* "denotes the *process* of such attainment" [26]. In the literature this concept has been used interchangeably with the term 'organization', which despite being related are different. The concept of organization refers to a group of individuals, gathered under the same designation and with same purposes [32]. Whereas the concept of institution reaches a broader scope. Thornton and Ocasio [60] describe institutions as *"supraorganizational patterns* of activity" that *follow a specific order within the society,* viewed as an *"inter-institutional system"* [60]. Avgerou [5] suggests that information technology innovations and organizational practices may be considered institutions, as both possess own mechanisms and legitimate elements, although at different institutionalization stages.

Thornton et al. [61] presents the concept of *institutional logic* as "the socially constructed, historical patterns of cultural symbols and material practices, including assumptions, values, and beliefs, by which individuals and organizations provide meaning to their daily activity, organize time and space, and reproduce their lives and experiences". This brings together three complementary and essential dimensions of institutions, namely: structural (coercive), normative and symbolic (cognitive), which enable further understanding on how their logics operate [60].

According to Thornton and Ocasio [60], a better understanding of the societal phenomena is attained by exploring the interrelations between its different constituents. They conceptualize *society as a multilevel inter-institutional system* based in three interconnected levels: "*individuals* competing and negotiating, *organizations* in conflict and coordination, and *institutions* in contradiction and interdependency" [60]. Suggesting that, while individual behavior and organizational dynamics are influenced by specific logics inherited by the institutions in place, the latter is social constructed by the interplay of actions from the first two levels. Furthermore, within this process, institutional logics in contradiction may *resist to change* or *cause institutional changes* to occur [55].

In turn, Schreyögg and Sydow [52] highlights the importance of looking to the overall phenomena over time. These authors refer to the concept of path dependency and the argument behind it, which states that past events exert significant influence on future actions and decision-making. And, considering the hard nature of the institutions, this also applies to explain why and how institutions resist or even change, in specific conditions [52].

Although existing institutions may change over time [33] it does not occur in only one direction [65]. Jepperson [26] presents four distinct types of institutional change. He posits these types of changes in terms of transitions in between stages, triggered by particular conditioning designated as *contradictions*. Suggesting that these conditions can be raised by the *environment* where these institutions play a role, result from the *interplay of different institutions* or even arise after basic *social actions*. In this sense, according to [26]:

- "*Institutional formation* (or establishment) is an exit from social entropy, from nonreproductive behavioural patterns, or from reproductive patterns based upon 'action'";
- "*Institutional development* (or elaboration) represents institutional continuation rather than an exit – a change within an institutional form";
- "*Deinstitutionalization* represents an exit from institutionalization, toward reproduction through recurrent action, or nonreproductive patterns, or social entropy";
- "*Reinstitutionalization* represents an exit from one institutionalization, and entry into another institutional form, organized around different principles or rules".

For long, several scholars have been discussing the complexities around social embeddedness [15, 26, 60]. To better understand this, Seo and Creed [55] proposes the adoption of a dialectical perspective. They suggest a view of these interplay as non-regular cycles, where multilevel institutionalization processes evolve over time, when institutional arrangements in place are challenged, creating a historical context for institutional change.

Seo and Creed [55] conceptualize *institutional contradictions* as "various *ruptures* and *inconsistencies within and among* institutionalized systems of meaning, forms of organization, and logics of action". They suggest that the rise and development of this results from the *"ongoing social construction of institutional arrangements"* and the challenges ascending from their legitimization processes, from internal and external sources [38]. Some *external factors* include: introduction of new technologies, management innovations, changes in political policies, major political disturbances, social reforms, economic crises or dislocations, and shifts in cultural beliefs and practices; while *internal factors* are related with specific features defining the organization ("such as organizational mission, structure, resources, operations, and social relations") or arguments and motives for "change/stability" within the organization [38], *macro* and *micro interdependencies*, and the existence of multi-institutional systems that intersect and overlap [53].

In turn, the interplay of *multiple actors* carrying own interests and objectives may result in *conflicts*, interfering with the interventions in place [65]. Scholars also refer to the potential intervention of individuals (*institutional entrepreneurs*) with both access to resources and the intention to assemble collective actions enabling institutional change [60]. This collective action, also designated as *"praxis"*, is considered an *"essential mediating mechanism"* linking *"institutional embeddedness, contradictions, and change"* [55].

Some scholars associate the sources of contradictions with *legitimacy, adaptation, intrainstitutional conformity*, and *isomorphism* [15, 44, 55, 56]. Seo and Creed [55] argues that this happens when "legitimacy undermines *functional inefficiency*", "adaptation undermines *adaptability*, "intrainstitutional conformity creates *interinstitutional incompatibilities*", and "isomorphism conflicts with *divergent interests*". While in the midst of this challenges, Novalia et al. [44], suggest strategies and mechanisms to attempt a mediation through interventions like: *"short-term fixes, elimination, decoupling, moderation*, and *forging durable identities* and *finding complementarities"*.

Examples of these debates in the context of Low- and Middle-Income Countries (LMICs) are described next from the perspective of six cases, from Africa, Latin America and Asia.

Piotti et al. [46] discusses institutional change in the context of ongoing reforms in Mozambique. They argue that inflexibility in adaptations of formal rules to accommodate informal constraints from the setting may limit the intended outcomes. In addition, limited overlap between formal and informal dimensions of institutions in place may suggest a need to enhance and enforce the mechanisms to enable changes in future implementations.

While Hayes and Rajão [21] discuss the concept of contradictions, looking in particular to how **competing institutional logics,** emerging along the process of introducing a GIS system in Brazil's Amazon region over time, contribute or not to achieve a particular developmental goal. They establish a relation between design and use of ICTs and emergence of conflicting logics, arguing that future implementations need to consider historical events and context to anticipate and enable the potential of digital solutions. Wanderley and Soeiro [64] describe an unsuccessful implementation of a Balanced Scorecard (BSC) system in an electricity company in Brazil, to explore the role of **praxis** in the processes of change. In turn, Volkow [62] uses a framework of institutionalism to pursue understanding of institutional dynamics through a **multilevel approach**. Suggesting that the social context may be better "visualized at a macro level" by observing the interplay of "social institutions" and "at a micro level" through "human actions", where both levels are intrinsically connected.

Sahay et al. [49] uses the theory to explore institutional pressures constraining or enabling the introduction of technological innovations, suggesting that values and meanings underpinning the IT innovation "can influence its adoption and implementation contributing to organizational change (or not)". Nawab et al. [37], exploring their case in the context of Pakistan, brings out the dilemma of the culture of silence, where people do not engage on challenging or disagreement of others point of view. They suggest that this context is not favourable to identify and resolve contradictions, and, while contradictions may trigger "opportunities for organizational renewal", they argue that "unrecognized contradictions are opportunities lost".

In the current study, we find support in these debates for several reasons. First, we perceive the setting as an inter-institutional system, influenced by several institutional orders. Secondly, we understand the importance to discuss these influences from different perspectives in a multilevel context. Thirdly, we understand that historical development of events and processes over the years create opportunities to explore institutional dynamics, different contradictions in place and pursue insights around their implications to the setting.

Along the study we also investigate the phenomena from the perspective of technology as an institution. One of the examples we take as a refence is a study conducted in Mozambique by Nhampossa [42]. This author explores the concepts of technology transfer and translation and draws his arguments around the pilot of DHIS within the setting. Other studies taken, that explore the influences of technology to the emerging institutional dynamics in the same setting, include Chilundo [13], Mosse [35] and Muquingue [36].

To conduct our study, we followed a methodology, as we describe in the next section, and build our analysis around the concepts described previously. In our framework of analysis, we consider: three *historical contexts* (moments), the *processes* and *institutional arrangements* in place and the *contradictions* that emerged around them. Having the *institutionalization processes* in mind, we attempt to explain how these institutional contradictions arise during the period in study.

3   Methods

3.1   Data Collection

The current study is part of a longer-term research initiative of a process spanning 20 years concerning Mozambique's engagement with the introduction and implementation of digital health systems. This study focuses on the first phase. This 20-year history is interpretively reconstructed over 3 phases summarized in the Table 1 below.

Table 1. Timeline of the Historical Reconstruction project

Digital health implementation in Mozambique: historical phases (2000–2021)				
Phase 1: initiation (2000–2007)	Phase 2: disruption (2008–2014)	Phase 3: establishing continuity (2015–2021)		
Health Information Systems Project (HISP) initiation	Disruption of HISP	Adoption	Scaling up	Institutionalization process

Data collection was done primarily between 2019–2021 to understand events that had taken place during 1999 until 2007. Multiple sources of data were used, summarized in the Table 2 below.

Table 2. Data collection sources

Research methods	Data sources
Secondary data	Research articles, 7 PhD and 4 Master thesis Documentation from the MoH website and government archives
Interviews	1 Project Manager (HISP) 2 Former Project Manager (UEM and WCU) 7 Former PhD Students (UEM) 6 Former International Master Students (UiO-UEM) 1 Former consultant (MoH) 3 Former and 1 actual Executive staff (MoH) 2 Data Officers (DIS – MoH) 2 members from the external support team 1 Executive staff and 1 Data Manager from Provincial level 1 Medical Doctor from the setting
Field visit	Selected districts in 5 provinces: Gaza, Inhambane, Niassa, Maputo province and Maputo City
Observations	Headquarters of the MoH (DIS) 3 Provincial Directorate of Health
	1 Health facility at Provincial level 5 Health facilities at District level (near and distant from Districts headquarters) 1 Program Officers Meeting (Province level) 1 Validation and 1 Statistical Meeting (District level)
Survey	20 Statisticians from the Nucleus of Statistics from District and Province

3.2 Data Analysis Process

Data analysis followed a sequential process involving the following steps:

1. **Transcribing and organizing data collected:** All data gathered was collated, translated (from Portuguese to English), transcribed and a **data corpus** [11] was developed to enable analysis.
2. **Data analysis through building themes:** Both authors independently read the transcribed data and identified themes [14]. These were then jointly discussed to develop consensus around relevant themes for further analysis, which included: *processes, context, time, actors, social action, political and economic situations, conflicts, power, values and meanings.*
3. **Relating themes to theoretical concepts:** The identified themes were then related to relevant themes drawn from Institutional theory context [5, 65]. Using these concepts, a narrative of the case study is developed, at both the macro (donors, ministry) and micro (districts and health facilities) and their inter-linkages [62].

4   Case Study

We start by presenting the political-institutional context of Mozambique, including events leading to its independence from Portugal, the subsequent civil war until the peace agreement in 1992, and the early efforts to introduce computers in the health sector. These events had a significant bearing on the initiation of the HISP initiative in 2000.

4.1   The Political-Institutional Context of Mozambique (1975–2000)

Mozambique represents a post-conflict setting scarred by colonial rule and civil war, with key events depicted in the Fig. 1 below.

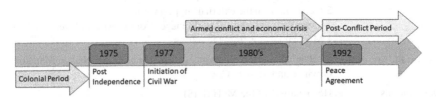

Fig. 1. Timeline between independence and peace agreement: 1975–1992

Events in this period had three key implications on digital health systems, which we now discuss.

Disruption of Health Personnel Post-independence:
The year 1975 was significant when Mozambique achieved independence from Portugal, with citizens given the option to stay in the country or leave for Portugal. This led to a massive drain of skilled people, and the health sector was particularly badly affected. In 1974, the country had around 550 doctors [36], a doctor-citizen ration of 1 to 17349 habitants, with more than half of the health workers concentrated in the capital [7], which dwindled by 85% following 1975 [20, 36]. Less than two years post-independence sparked a bitter armed 16-year long civil war involving rival groups with

different political interests, which led to death of hundreds of health care workers [19]. To address this huge void, the government sought to establish agreements to receive health personnel from foreign countries, such as Cuba, China, former East Germany, the Soviet Union and from several African countries. In addition, around 10,000 people received training from 1975 to 1990 [36].

Destruction of Health Infrastructure with the Civil War:
Mozambique was one of the poorest countries in the world, contributed to by the post-independence brain drain and the destruction and death caused by the civil war which ended in 1992 [19]. During civil war, existing infrastructure, including industries, health facilities, schools and others were vandalized, destroyed, and even abandoned. The existing 113 Hospitals in 1975, were reduced to 39 in 1977, and only 43 functional hospitals remained in 1997 [24]. The civil war led to large-scale loss of life and economic instability contributing to an increasing level of donor dependency [18, 25, 39] and the consequent loss of sovereignty. The increasing attention of the International Monetary Fund (IMF) and the World Bank on Mozambique opened space for external aid [18, 19], particularly in health and education sectors, a trend which continues today.

These contextual influences shaped the initiation of digital initiatives in the country.

4.2   Initiating Digital Health in Post-conflict Mozambique

Despite early adhoc efforts by the Ministry of Health post-independence, it was only in 1992 that the first computerized system designated SIS-Prog was introduced, limited to the central and provincial levels [3]. The Fig. 2 provides a chronology of the different systems introduced in the country during this period.

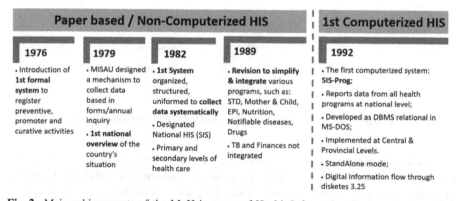

Fig. 2. Main achievements of the MoH in terms of Health Information Systems in the period 1976–1992

The obvious limitations of SIS-Prog opened space for new developments, including the introduction of the HISP initiative and their software called DHIS 1.3 (District Health Information Software, Version 1.3). Key events around this initiation are now described.

Building Relationships and Partnerships: 1998–1999

The HISP project in Mozambique initiated in 1998 within an academic setting, providing opportunities to strengthen the tertiary education capacities in conjunction with HIS building efforts. HISP's entry in Mozambique was built upon a decade of high political visibility and success in post-apartheid South Africa [49], where the DHIS software attained the status of a national standard and attracted the attention of other African countries. The Norwegian pioneers of HISP in South Africa met some officials and researchers in Mozambique, and slowly started to build a network of partnerships, as depicted below in Fig. 3.

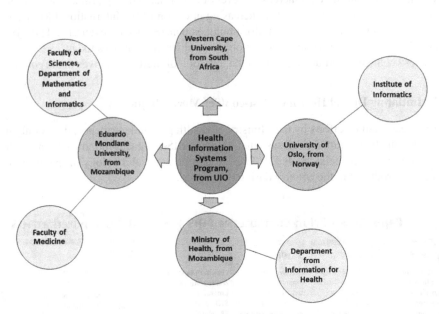

Fig. 3. Organizations involved in the first phase of DHIS implementation in Mozambique

Initial conversations were established between the **HISP** coordinator and a local national university **UEM**, through the **Faculties of Medicine** and **Sciences**. Together, this team commenced conversations with the MoH, which at the time was very receptive to the ideas presented, given their engagement in various health sector reforms [13, 36]. These conversations led to the inclusion of other researchers from UEM and members from the Department of Information for Health (DIS) at the MoH, financially supported by the Norwegian Government [9].

A first step in the growing network was the conduct of **an assessment of the current situation** starting with selected districts in three provinces. This assessment contributed for the MoH in developing its **first strategic plan for the sector** and for HISP to develop a more operational project plan for the HIS implementation. This was submitted, approved and a Memorandum of Understanding (**MoU**) was signed between Oslo, UEM and the MoH in 1998, which envisaged a pilot of DHIS in selected sites across three provinces (Gaza, Inhambane and Niassa) [42]. Selected districts were existing training sites for medical students from UEM [13]. The results of the assessment were presented as research in progress in a meeting in Zimbabwe by 1999, and as a complete research paper published in 2001.

> "*We embarked on this assessment... It was important... the country was coming out of the post-war and emergency phase... entering a much more planned phase... which was expressed in the year 2000 with the elaboration of the first strategic plan for the health sector... which came out the following year...*" *(A former foreign consultant from MoH)*

> "*We did not have trained and specialized personnel, the base was the health workers themselves... doctorates, masters, licentiates, they were a drop of water.*" *(A former local senior manager from the MoH)*

> "*The first step was the introduction of a master course in Mozambique... and enrol PhD students...*" *(A former project coordinator from HISP)*

The HISP planned to take the DHIS application developed in South Africa, and through a process of "technology transfer" customize and adapt it to Mozambique's needs using the capacities of the identified UEM researchers. The capacity building of these researchers was inspired by the Scandinavian tradition of action research [10]. Simultaneously, a multi-disciplinary International Masters program in Health Informatics at UEM, and students from informatics and community health, from both Mozambique and other countries (Ethiopia, Malawi, Tanzania and India) were enrolled during the early years.

Capacity Building Strategies and Interventions: 2000–2007

In 2000, professors from HISP-UiO and another from Western Cape University (WCU) came together and created a **multidisciplinary task force**, including the local researchers to design the **International Master program** [8, 28] to help strengthen HIS capacity in the country. This program included two core components (1) the health information systems as part of the academic course work; and (2) a research component with mandatory fieldwork and thesis in the same area. This structure promoted a form of action research, where students were encouraged to address existing priorities of the MoH, while learning from this experience to write their thesis. The projects worked on included the pilot implementations identified in the MoU and were supported also by the enrolled PhD students. During the period, a significant number of professionals, from the Health Sector and Academy, enrolled to the International Master Program, and by 2007 already 38 master students had been graduated. The program in Mozambique ran for three editions (2001, 2003 and 2005) before the split into 2 new Master Programs in 2006, in Informatics and Public Health [16, 27]. This Masters programmes can be seen as a success, as it continues till today, although in a modified form.

In 2000, as part of the MoU, six UEM faculty members, 3 each from medicine and informatics, enrolled for the UiO doctoral program, of which 5 ultimately graduated.

These students received training on DHIS in South Africa and jointly participated in the customization of the DHIS for the Mozambique context. With the start of the formal studies at UiO, the students were expected to both provide practical implementation support to the projects in the districts, while also doing their course work in Oslo. They were thus operating in split locations, following different objectives, which proved to be a source of contradictions for them, with adverse implications on project outcomes.

> "...we were supposed to do the PhD program in a sandwich mode... but it was not doable... The same people had so many responsibilities, as lecturers, students and implementers... And then, we disappeared and when we came back with our PhD we were seen as strangers..." (A former PhD student)

However, the ultimate completion of 5 PhDs, in a country where no informatics PhDs existed by 2000, can be seen as a huge success towards building tertiary education capacity.

In-service Training Efforts

Both masters and doctoral students were involved with in-service training activities in the selected provinces for the pilot. During this period, MoH introduced two new institutional entities called Nucleus of Statistics, at provincial and district levels, responsible for supporting all the data management functions. However, on the ground, the health workers, with very limited skills and capacities, were responsible for conducting the everyday work, including training other staff. In 2001, the first 10-day course on the technical aspects of DHIS directed to the health workers was launched in Gaza province, including 20 staff drawn from the three pilot provinces.

The quality of training was however constrained by the relative inexperience of the trainers, particularly in understanding diverse information needs of medical doctors, nurses and other technicians. Often, the dominant technical focus of the trainings, failed to develop a sound social-systems perspective to understand the HIS related challenges.

> "...the training to use data entry and analysis began. That's where we began to face difficulties..." (A former local project coordinator)

However, these initial efforts helped create a favourable environment to initiate HISP in Mozambique, with opportunities for MoH to get tools and resources for supporting their health sector reforms, and for UEM to build their tertiary and education capacity within a multidisciplinary framework.

We next describe how the project implementation process developed and the underlying contradictions experienced, which impeded project progress ultimately leadings to its closure.

4.3 The Project Implementation Process

The introduction of DHIS (version 1.3) commenced in 2000, amidst excitement and expectancy, which slowly dwindled over time because of various implementation challenges, which we related to the process of initiation of the pilots, which led to different contradictions.

The Process of Initiation of the Pilots

The piloting interventions were organized mainly by the local HISP coordinator, with support from the technical team from South Africa and the UiO faculty. The baseline software used had been developed in and with South African requirements, in Microsoft Access. As a first step, the application needed to be translated to Portuguese. The PhD and Masters students, all Portuguese speaking, were responsible for this process. However, this was extremely tedious and problematic. Although the team knew Portuguese language, they lack on translation expertise and, while also, often unfamiliar about specific technical terms used, required clarifications from other sources, including South Africa. Many issues and concepts got lost in translation,

*"Terms like **backup, zoom**, and **data mart** do **not have direct translation in Portuguese**... the team was forced to perform a partial or intermediate translation, **mixing English and Portuguese text**. This hybridization of terms often created **problems of interpretation** for the users." Else ... "in order to keep the 'correct' translation, the buttons... had to be enlarged and located in different positions. Or the long strings had to be simplified in order to keep a reasonable layout and distributions of the buttons"* [40]

This process of getting the software ready to initiate pilot implementation was fraught with delays, contributed also by the part time nature of involvement of the PhD students, which dampened some of the initial expectancy. The MoH and the HISP team tended to blame each other for the delays:

Contradictory Objectives of Project "Resource Persons"

The MoU promised full commitment from all parties involved in the project, which however unfolded differently during implementation. While agreeing in principle, in practice MoH never gave explicit instructions to the changeover from SIS-Prog to DHIS. At same time, HISP team could not dedicate full time to the implementation work, because of their simultaneous study commitments. This led to long project delays, with both sides blaming each other for the same. These delays opened the space for other HIS applications to be introduced. The MoH opted to select a tool developed by one of the resident consultants, designated SIMP (*Sistema Integrado de Monitoria e Planificação*) from 2002 onwards, in parallel to DHIS. The HISP team opposed this choice, feeling that the MoH was indifferent and uninterested in the pilot project. This led to further delays and the escalation of the blame game.

Afterwards, unhappy with the progress of the pilots, the MoH hired in 2004 an external consultant from South Africa to evaluate the situation. His report came with several recommendations both to MoH and HISP team, suggesting that their demands were possible to attain and could be included shortly in an improved version of the software. However, in response, a foreign consultant working in the MoH responded extremely critically to this report. For example, he wrote in this response:

"My overall impression of the report is similar to my impression of the consultancy done... A lot of statements, theories... suggestions and recommendations. All with the overall aim of selling the Hisp product... nothing seems to be a problem... everything seems to be relatively easy. But what certainly lack's in the consultant's approach is rapid response and practical solutions... At this moment it is crucial for Sisd to survive to apply the required changes to the software and try to make the pilot provinces a success in the shortest time span possible... Too much credibility has already been lost. We have to solve our urgent problems first." (Excerpt from a letter with comments on the consultancy report)

The HISP team addressed their protests, including other interpretations from the occurrences at the time. In parallel, attempted to initiate developments towards introduction of a GIS application [1]. Despite that, simultaneously the foreign consultant initiated own development of another application, designated Módulo Básico, which afterwards was implemented by the MoH, later in the same year.

"DHIS 1.3 was not adapted to Mozambique... Politics, donors, and the Ministry behind with the ambiguity to decide what system to use... Process of change of DHIS2 started from there, but in 2006-2007 was terminated in Mozambique. (A former project coordinator from HISP)

Technological Contradictions in the Process of DHIS "Technology Transfer"
DHIS was developed in South Africa, with both code and interfaces presented in English, requiring extensive translation work to Portuguese. In addition, as Nhampossa [42] describes, the database was initially designed to respond specific purposes of South Africa and were conflicting with expected outcomes in Mozambique. These contradictions came to the fore when the HISP team were entrusted the task of integrating DHIS with the existing SIS-Prog. Some of the key problems included,

*(1) "**ambiguous data elements**" in SIS-Prog ... e.g., "categories of Children 0–11 months and also 0-4 years, which created an overlap" .... (2) "**organizational structure**" ... "South African health structure... consisted of five levels, while we had four" ... (3) "**fundamental differences between English and Portuguese languages**" ... e.g., "longer words to express concepts" in Portuguese... "which had implications on the user interface design and the use of icons" [41]*

*"... Many of the **functions of DHIS were not yet in Portuguese language**... a person had to adapt based on the English words, which caused disturbances" (A former foreign consultant from MoH)*

Despite these technical disturbances, affecting mostly the ones in the data collection and use of the system, the managers at the district level were satisfied with the outcomes on the reporting side. But because there was not a notification to stop the other systems in place, the work load come from the health workers responsible for the data management was increased and contributed to an increased dissatisfaction among them [35]. This had implications on the commitment to use the new system, and in some cases, they did not engage in quality control assuming that it would be a responsibility to the upper levels in the HIS.

Inadequate Infrastructure and Capacity to Support Digital Health

In general, the existing infrastructural conditions, such as power restrictions, electricity outages, communication limitations, poor transport and road networks, were all not conducive to enable effective implementation of digital systems and their scaling [35, 42].

> *"The available **resources from the project were to pilot** DHIS and **not to implement** it on a national scale... we did not have that time to pilot, improve and return with human and financial resources. This also affected the success of an appreciated project." (a former PhD student)*

> *"...In terms of technological support, there were Health Units that did **not have the resources to buy toner and paper**... we arrived and the PC was there, with the system installed but not working because the **computer broke down**. The support should be given ... But they said they went a long time without receiving visits from MISAU..." (A former local master student).*

The ministry relied on several sources or funding by external aid. This enabled opportunities for systems development, but also created fragmentation, with different donors supporting specific systems for particular health programs, such Malaria, HIV and TB. Overall, the country lacked adequate human resources capacity and expertise to provide dedicated technical support in rural settings, with the bulk of capacity concentrated in the country capital [9]. When DHIS was introduced, the MoH had limited in-house capacity, and relied on donor support which often came with divergent agendas from theirs. There was potential to get support from the researchers, but this also was limited.

5 Analysis

In our case study, we described from an historical perspective, the introduction of digital health in a post conflict Mozambique. The MoH is the central institution in the country responsible for the functioning of the health system. Through our case study, we identified three key moments that were responsible for the implementation trajectory of digital health in the period 2000–2007. This is summarized in Table 3.

Key Moment 1: Post-conflict Conditions Shaping Health System's Context

The setting inherited social constraints from the previous armed and political conflicts, that culminated in 1992 with the peace treatment, and the interventions that were attempted to revert the situation. These, where mainly influenced from political and economic situation in place. While the country is adjusting to the new constitution, a Democratic model, where the government is selected by elections, there is a pressure to

Table 3. Summary of the contradictions identified

Historical moments (before and during phase 1)	Contradictions
Moment 1 (1992–1998): Post-conflict conditions shaping the health systems context	– Compromised financial, human, technical resources leads to high levels of external dependencies – Weak institutions to govern digital health, which require new and more proactive institutions
Moment 2 (1998–2003): Historically existing inefficiencies in the HIS and supporting institutional arrangements	– High levels of fragmented legacy systems driving the need for reform in digital health systems – Demands of new digital health initiatives don't find support from existing context – Divergent interests and power asymmetries, further constrain digital health initiative
Moment 3 (2003–2007): Political-institutional context enabling and constraining the DHIS implementation	– Multiple stakeholders with poorly aligned and often contradictory interests – MoH provides ambiguous support to DHIS, without clear directives to the sites of pilot implementation – Ambiguity leads to proliferation of multiple systems, heightened the already high workload to field level workers – Contradictions arising from project management, technical and capacity building conditions contribute to the halt of the project – Growth of the doctoral and Masters study programmes

implement a five-year governance strategic plan. Although, the country is still resenting from the economic crisis that arose in the 80s. The existent limited budget does not provide much space of manoeuvres to advance with new plans before compensating the massive losses in infrastructure and skilled human resources, while at same provide quality services. There was a need to increase partnerships and with that more compromises with the international donors and request for additional aid programs.

In the Health sector in particular, policies and budgets in place did not allow massive hiring for the state. Budgets were mostly directed to support logistic operations and maintain salaries for existing personnel. Although they were facing a shortage in health personnel, for curative interventions and data management, and the dilemma on hiring technical personnel to help with the introduction of new digital systems instead of doctors.

Health programs begun to receive funds from international agencies. With each of these, introducing different systems and employing foreign consultants familiar with them to support local interventions on the setting. While some were integrated in the Departments of the MoH others went to work in implementations at Provincial and District levels. Some local health personnel were also employed at different levels though this partnerships and projects supporting the health programs. This contributed to higher levels of external dependencies.

Moreover, while the MoH was working to produce strategic and fundamental documents for the sector, policies for information systems were not a priority. Therefore, they had limited formal instruments to regulate the interventions and institutional arrangements around the introduction of digital health.

Some institutional arrangements in place, like for instance the introduction of training facilities for nurses and health technicians, engagement with the training of medical doctors by local universities, were established and developed, and are still in place nowadays. Others, like the development of the HIS resulted in undesired outcomes, with multiple and rigid vertical Health Programs; fragmentation of systems and centralized use of information.

Key Moment 2: Historically Existing Inefficiencies in HIS and Institutional Context
Along the years, the accumulation of several contradictions called for urgent action and need for alternative interventions. Although the previous institutional arrangements were still in place, the existing contradictions open space for an opportunity to introduce changes in the setting. The country was in the midst of a transformational period, where the global interventions were converging to common Agendas of Development, and the collaboration South-South was gaining momentum [6, 29]. A new opportunity came with the interest of HISP in introducing a new digital solution in the HIS of the country.

The project designed meet the criteria of the movements at the time, coming as an alternative solution to resolve the inefficiencies and inconsistencies accumulated from the institutional arrangements in place. This initiative included new institutional arrangements: Introduction of capacity building programs reinforced with research; alternative perspectives for collaborative work and mobilization of resources; and a new system with some resources to support it. In addition, it also aimed at developing some existing process and deinstitutionalize others. There were opportunities to standardize and improve data management processes, decentralize managerial functions to Province and District levels, while at same promote empowerment of users of the digital system, empower managers at data use, and appropriation of the system by the MoH.

Despite that, although there were ongoing projects at national level to improve the communication systems (transports and roads), telecommunication and data services, it was still insufficient to extend these resources to provide a significant coverage, they did not reach all the existing districts. The scenario was similar in relation with the introduction of new technologies.

With the initiation of DHIS pilot, new tasks were introduced to a group of health worker that had no experience with computers, had limited data management skills, and were involved also in reporting activities using other systems from different health programs. With the shortages of health workers, the same group of professionals that had been previously trained as nurses and other health technicians, they were assigned other tasks accordingly. They were overload, and it certainly influenced their motivation to learn and to use the new system. Although, there was a partial acceptance of the new digital solution, within the MoH, Provinces and Districts.

Even though, the assumptions of the responsibilities of each intervenient and expectations were not properly aligned. The set of unresolved contradictions was significant, the presence of the multiple actors involved in the process was more visible. The breach between the team was eminent.

Key Moment 3: Political-Institutional Context Enabling and Constraining DHIS Implementation

During the period, the shifts in the government affected the health sector at large extent. There was a new order inside the Health Sector, still aligned with the Developmental Agendas, but with slight shifts in the power structures. These shifts also affected the implementation team, were some members from the MoH were substituted by others that were not involved directly in the previous processes.

The MoH were involved in the pilots, there was an interest to implement the new system to support the implementation of the first strategic plan that was developed after the assessment conducted in 1999. But no formal directive was emitted to stop the existing systems and only focus attention to DHIS. The strategic plan was ready in 2001 and the pressure increased. While the development of the pilots was in place, another system was under development (SIMP) by a foreign consultant and came to be implemented by the MoH in 2002.

Managers at Provincial level, where the pilot was implemented were interested in the new reporting systems, but nor them or the project did not have resources to scale the system to other districts. In addition, the information flow was still the same, the pressure to send the information from the multiple health programs to the upper levels was enormous.

With the introduction of this new system, the already overloaded Health workers experienced increased difficulties to operate with multiple systems at same time, while also experiencing the problems arising from the scarcity of resources to maintain the existing equipment and continue to use the systems.

The software being transferred was in English and the user's working language was Portuguese. There was a pressure to translate, both in terms of configuration and language. The structural differences of the languages raised challenges to adapt the software to the new setting. Also, there was a recommendation from the MoH to integrate this new solution to one that was already in place (SIS-Prog). DHIS database was not adapted to the setting needs at the begging of the pilot and the requirements were difficult to incorporate. The software that was designed with different logics, associated with the translation issues, both in customization and language (English to Portuguese), generated interface and functionalities constraints. All this contributed to delays, disturbances in the use of the system, contributing to the accumulation of contradictions.

The MoH-DIS-Partners requests were not completely reflected in the software, requested an assessment, and demanded faster corrective actions. At the time, another development (Módulo Básico) was initiated lead by the foreigner consultant that vocalized the inconsistencies of the new solution, and it was placed to use by the MoH-DIS, despite the ongoing developments in the pilots. The HISP-UEM, had their Action-Research activities ongoing, with some periods of field work in the districts and others associated with the academic programs, they were expecting more involvement from the MoH teams to appropriate the system and compensate their absences in the field, while also expecting a recognition of the research results, but this was not visible.

The Inadequate infrastructure and capacity to support the digital health, resulted in an accumulation of social constraints from the setting that were present since the first historical context. The conditions did not improve significantly, neither to support the ongoing processes nor the scaling intents of the team. The Provinces and Districts, left with the system stopped in the midst of any difficulty, pressure to use several systems and other activities, expecting a support that did not come with the desired frequency, with the absence of formal directives to use on instead of the other, saw their motivation diminished over time.

Despite the scenario described and analysed in this section, it is worth mentioning some of the significant outcomes resulting from phase 1, occurring during the period corresponding to our phase 2 and 3, from 2008 until 2021. Along the following years, the establishment and development of the capacity building initiatives satisfied the correspondent goals of the project. The graduation of 38 master students from Africa and Asia, trained on the International Master offered by UEM-UiO, and the completion of the PhD programs by the Mozambican researchers, was considered a success. These results were also significant to the development and continuity of all the capacity building initiatives established during phase 1.

Furthermore, these graduates played a significant and valuable role in the further development of DHIS to the actual DHIS2, which is currently being used globally and in Mozambique. From 2004 the developments on top of DHIS continued outside Mozambique. The nodes created abroad, in some African and Asian countries, contributed significantly for the changes in the technological artefact. A new version with a significant change, designated DHIS2 was released in 2006, shifting from a standalone to an online operating mode. The potential of this technological artefact as a health information system platform increased and attracted the attention of several countries, including Mozambique.

6 Discussion

First, conceptualizing the setting as an inter-institutional system, influenced by several institutional orders, we noted a set of new orders that we perceive as being common to the setting of LMICs, such as External Aid Policies, Developmental Agenda, Technology innovations but also others that are implicit to the underdevelopment conditionings (like Corruption and Poverty, for instance). We would tag this a note to further investigations on the institutional orders influencing these settings as way to further explore the implications deriving from this.

Secondly, we understand the importance to discuss the different influences from the perspectives of the existing multilevel context, where we identify a multiplicity of actors and organizations at play and being influenced by multisource institutions. As we saw from the analysis, the establishment of new process (institutionalization of the education/training initiatives) in our case succeeded and prevailed in the entire phase 1. Although the social constraints were also present, they did not influence conflicting results sufficient to undermine their continuity.

Thirdly, because we understand that the historical development of the events and processes over the years created opportunities for different types of responses in terms of institutional changes, motivated by different contradictions in place in different moments. Although, the other processes suffered from the accumulation of several contradictions, as we could see emerging from the environment (mostly in moment 1); but also, because of the conflicting interplay between the interconnected levels of the inter-institutional system (mostly in moment 2) and the differences in the logics of actions (mostly in moment 3).

Lastly, because engaging within these debates creates opportunities to explore whether these institutional dynamics contributed or not to changes, and the subsequent implications of the outcomes to the setting. We perceived that the contradictions not well mediated accumulate and may indeed contribute to resist to change (overall implementation of DHIS was not successful), create opportunities to change (as with the establishment of the training initiatives), generate unintended results (as happened in the case of the institutionalized processes in moment 1).

7 Conclusion

The current study is part of an ongoing project that intends to conduct a research based in a longitudinal case study of the reconstruction of the institutional history of the HIS in Mozambique, over the last twenty years, based in the implementation of a technological artefact designated DHIS2 (District Health Information System version 2). This, to support the analysis of the interplay between technical, institutional, and human factors involved in the process, and its evolution over time. We attempt such an analysis around the efforts to adopt the DHIS2 software by the Ministry of Health in Mozambique since 2000, and subsequent action toward its institutionalization. At this point, we were able to identify four types of institutional pressures playing determinant roles in the implementation of a technological artefact: conflicts, power relations, social actions, and resources. Thus, playing different roles along the time and contributing for changes within the HIS. We believe that a deeper analysis on their institutional dynamics can provide good insights to future implementation processes and help to further understand how they support initiatives while building ownership, self-reliance, and sustainability of implemented technological artefacts, within the LMICs context.

We perceived from the current study that certain interventions may trigger different outcomes and influence the institutional dynamics that take place during an implementation process. These influence both the technological artefact and the setting where the implementation take place, promoting development of technology and practices around the processes of adoption and institutionalization of technological artefacts within an established HIS.

Although an initial contribution lies in the reconstruction of DHIS2 piece of history, helping to build awareness of the evolution of this technological artefact in a specific setting, it generates important insights to a broader spectrum of technological artefacts as well. This is, because we acknowledge the importance of long-term evaluations to gather an overall picture of the different factors triggering processes of change, spanning from user experiences, implications to organizations where they are being implemented and the practices arising around the implementation of the artefact itself. The case shows clearly how certain levels of pressure, arise from different sources within the setting, generating conditions and influencing the processes of adoption and institutionalization of DHIS. It allows us to see how it creates space and provides insights for further developments and adaptation to a multiple settings context. In turn, to enable this continuity of changes over the time, alongside the process a compromise of different interests coming from the field, donors and owners is needed and denoted to be critical.

The current study contributes both with theoretical and practical insights. The theoretical contributions include the discussion of the institutional orders influencing the LMICs analysis and discussions. In practice, we present a rich case study from the introduction of digital health in a post conflict period within a LMIC country. In addition, from this historical analysis and discussion, we contribute with several insights from the perspective of the contradictions, which may emerge triggering opportunities to either change or resist to changes.

References

1. Aanestad, M., et al.: Strategies for development and integration of health information systems: coping with historicity and heterogeneity. Working paper from the Information Systems Group, University of Oslo, 5, p. 51 (2005)
2. Aanestad, M., Jolliffe, B., Mukherjee, A., Sahay, S.: Infrastructuring work: building a statewide hospital information infrastructure in India. Inf. Syst. Res. 25(4), 834–845 (2014). https://doi.org/10.1287/isre.2014.0557
3. Almeida, E.: Relatório sobre as Boas Prácticas do SIS Moçambique. Ministério da Saúde de Moçambique (2007). [Online] available at https://www.afro.who.int/files/moz-sis_bestpractices.pdf. Accessed on 30 Feb 2019
4. Asah, F., Nielsen, P.: An Integrated Health Management Information System a Missing block in achieving universal health coverage in Cameroon? Selected Papers of the Information System Research Seminar in Scandinavia (IRIS) 2016, 7(6) (2016). [Online] Available in http://aisel.aisnet.org/iris2016/6. Accessed on 6 Jan 2022
5. Avgerou, C.: IT and organizational change: an institutionalist perspective. Inf. Technol. People 13(4), 234–262 (2000)
6. Birn, A.E., Muntaner, C., Afzal, Z.: South-South cooperation in health: bringing in theory, politics, history, and social justice. Cad. Saude Publica 33(2), S37–S52 (2017)
7. Bouene, F.: Moçambique: 30 anos de independência. In Africana Studia, 8, Edição da Faculdade de Letras da Universidade do Porto, pp. 68–84 (2005)
8. Braa, J., Muquingue, H.: Health information systems and open source software development: need for cross-country collaboration in Africa – experiences from the HISP/BEANISH network. In: IST-Africa 2007 Conference Proceedings, pp. 1–7 (2007)
9. Braa, J., et al.: A study of the actual and potential usage of information and communication technology at district and provincial levels in Mozambique with a focus on the health sector. Electron. J. Inf. Syst. Dev. Ctries. 5(1), 1–29 (2001)
10. Braa, J., Monteiro, E., Sahay, S.: Networks of action: sustainable health information systems across developing countries. MIS Q. 28(3), 337–362 (2004)
11. Braun, V., Clarke, V.: Using thematic analysis in psychology. Qual. Res. Psychol. 3, 77–101 (2006). https://doi.org/10.1191/1478088706qp063oa
12. Bryant, A., Black, A., Land, F., Porra, J.: Information systems history: what is history? what is IS history? What IS history? ... and why even bother with history? J. Inf. Technol. 28,

1–17 (2013). https://doi.org/10.1057/jit.2013.3. [Online] available at https://www.researchg ate.net/publication/256051208. Accessed on 9 Nov 2018

13. Chilundo, B.: Integrating Information Systems of Disease-Specific Health Programmes in Low Income Countries: The Case Study of Mozambique, pp. 1–121. Thesis University of Oslo, Oslo (2004)

14. Clarke, V., Braun, V.: Thematic analysis. J. Posit. Psychol. **12**(3), 297–298 (2017). https:// doi.org/10.1080/17439760.2016.1262613

15. Clemens, E.S., Cook, J.M.: Politics and institutionalism: explaining durability and change. Ann. Rev. Sociol. **25**, 441–466 (1999)

16. Department of Mathematics and Informatics – DMI: Currículo de Mestrado em Infor- mática (2011). Available in http://dmi.uem.mz/images/pdfs/curriculo_informatica_2011.pdf. Accessed on 15 Dec 2021

17. Dobson, J., Nicholson, B.: Exploring the dialectics underlying institutionalization of IT artifacts. J. Assoc. Inf. Syst. **18**(12), 848–871 (2018)

18. Funada-Classen, S.: The Origins of War in Mozambique: A History of Unity and Division. In African Minds, pp. 1–56 (2013)

19. Garrido, P.I.: Saúde, desenvolvimento e factores institucionais: O caso de Moçam- bique. WIDER Working Paper No. 2020/131. The United Nations University World Institute for Development Economics Research (UNU-WIDER), Helsinki (2020). Avail- able in https://www.wider.unu.edu/sites/default/files/Publications/Working-paper/PDF/wp2 020-131-PT.pdf. Accessed on 18 Dec 2021

20. Gilio, A., Freitas, G.: A closer look at the Mozambique reality: nursing and health. In Revista Brasileira de Enfermagem, Brasília **61**(1), 98–102 (2007)

21. Hayes, N., Rajão, R.: Competing institutional logics and sustainable development: the case of geographic information systems in Brazil's Amazon region. Inf. Technol. Dev. **17**(1), 4–23 (2011). https://doi.org/10.1080/02681102.2010.511701

22. Heeks, R.: Information Systems and Developing Countries: Failure, Success, and Local Improvisations. The Information Society, ISSN: 0197-2243 (Print) 1087-6537 (2002). [Online] available at the Journal homepage: http://www.tandfonline.com/loi/utis20. Accessed on 29 Nov 2018

23. Immergut, E.M.: The theoretical core of the new institutionalism. Polit. Soc. **26**(1), 5–34 (1998)

24. Instituto Nacional de Estatística – INE: Infra-estruturas Hospitalares 1975–2009 (2011). [Online] Available in http://web.archive.org/web/20111114221033/http:/www.ine.gov.mz/ sectorias_dir/saude_dir/Document.2010-06-22.0502160683. Accessed on 3 Dec 2021

25. Jafar, J.S.: Análise Sócio-Histórica sobre a Guerra Civil em Moçambique, 1976–1992. In Revista Kulambela, **2**(2), 38–53 (2021). Available in https://www.ceadur.ac.mz/kulambela/ index.php/RKCD/article/view/10. Accessed on 3 Dec 2021

26. Jepperson, R.L.: Institutions, institutional effects, and institutionalism. In: Chapter 3, Insti- tutional Theory: Its Role in Modern Social Analysis, pp. 37–66 (1991). In: Jepperson, R.L., Meyer, J.W. (eds.) Institutional Theory: The Cultural Construction of Organizations, States, and Identities, p. 322, 1st edn., Cambridge University Press, New York (2021)

27. Kaasbøll, J., Kanjo, C., Kimaro, H.: Sustainable health informatics master programmes in low and middle income countries. In: Proceedings from the Annual NOKOBIT Conference, (26:1), (eds.) Svalbard (2018)

28. Kaasbøll, J., Macome, E.: Developing sustainable research education in Sub-Saharan Africa. In: Informatics Curricula, Teaching Methods and Best Practice, IFIP Working Group 3.2 Working Conference, pp. 1–9 (2002)

29. Kaasbøll, J., Nhampossa, J.L.: Transfer of public sector information systems between devel- oping countries: south-south cooperation. Presented at "Social Implications of Computers in Developing Countries", Bangalore, India (2002)

30. Khubone, T., Tlou, B., Mashamba-Thompson, T.P.: Electronic health information systems to improve disease diagnosis and management at point-of-care in low and middle income countries: a narrative review. Diagnostics **10**(327), 1–10 (2020)
31. Krishna, S., Walsham, G.: Implementing public information systems in developing countries: learning from a success story. Inf. Technol. Dev. **11**(2), 123–140 (2005)
32. Lune, H.: Understanding Organizations. Polity Press, pp. 216 (2010). [Online] available in https://books.google.co.mz/books?id=T8RqT3CueSEC&printsec=frontcover&dq=concept+of+organization&hl=pt-PT&sa=X&redir_esc=y#v=onepage&q=concept%20of%20organiz ation&f=false. Accessed on 18 Apr 2022
33. Mahoney, J., Thelen, K.: Explaining Institutional Change: Ambiguity, Agency, and Power. Cambridge University Press, p. 236 (2010). [Online] available in https://books.google.no/books?id=PACmgwrYeRMC&printsec=frontcover&source=gbs_ge_summary_r&cad=0#v=onepage&q&f=false. Accessed on 9 Dec 2018
34. Mignerat, M., Rivard, S.: Positioning the institutional perspective in information systems research. J. Inf. Technol. **24**(4), 369–391 (2009)
35. Mosse, E.: Understanding the Introduction of Computer-Based Health Information Systems in Developing Countries: Counter Networks, Communication Practices, and Social Identity: A Case study from Mozambique, p. 144. Thesis University of Oslo, Oslo (2005)
36. Muquingue, H.: Understanding and Improving Medical Students' Exposure to Health Management in Rural Settings of Mozambique. Thesis University of Oslo, p. 289 (2009)
37. Nawab, A., Kumari, R., Babur, M.: Unrecognized contradictions are opportunities lost: refocusing attention for learning. Learn. Cult. Soc. Interact. **31**, 1–9 (2021). https://doi.org/10.1016/j.lcsi.2021.100563
38. Nedović-Budić, Z., Godschalk, D.R.: Human factors in adoption of geographic information systems: a local government case study. Public Adm. Rev. **56**(6), 554–567 (1996)
39. Newitt, M.: A History of Mozambique, p. 706. Indiana University Press, Bloomington and Indianapolis (1995)
40. Nhampossa, J.L.: The challenge of "translating" health information systems from one developing country context to another: a case study from Mozambique. In: ECIS 2004 Proceedings, vol. 130, pp. 1–15 (2004). http://aisel.aisnet.org/ecis2004/130
41. Nhampossa, J.L., Sahay, S.: Social construction of software customization: the case of health information systems from Mozambique and India. In: Bada, A., Adelakun, O. (eds.) Enhancing Human Resource Development through ICT, pp. 339–347. IFIP, Abuja, Nigeria (2005)
42. Nhampossa, J.L.: Re-Thinking Technology Transfer as Technology Translation: A Case Study of Health Information Systems in Mozambique. Thesis University of Oslo, p. 198 (2006)
43. North, D.: Institutions. J. Econ. Perspect. **5**(1), 97–112 (1991)
44. Novalia, W., Rogers, B.C., Bos, J.J.: Incumbency and political compromises: opportunity or threat to sustainability transitions? Environ. Innov. Soc. Trans. **40**, 680–698 (2021). https://doi.org/10.1016/j.eist.2021.05.002
45. Oliver, C.: The antecedents of deinstitutionalization. Org. Stud. **13**(4), 563–588 (1992). [Online] available at https://journals-sagepub-com.ezproxy.uio.no/doi/https://doi.org/10.1177/017084069201300403. Accessed on 28 Nov 2018
46. Piotti, B., Chilundo, B., Sahay, S.: An institutional perspective on health sector reforms and the process of reframing health information systems: case study from Mozambique. J. Appl. Behav. Sci. **42**(1), 91–109 (2006). https://doi.org/10.1177/0021886305285127
47. Piotti, B., Macome, E.: Public healthcare in Mozambique: strategic issues in the ICT development during managerial changes and public reforms. Int. J. Med. Inf. **76**, S184–S195 (2007). https://doi.org/10.1016/j.ijmedinf.2006.05.020

48. Powell, W., DiMaggio, P.: The New Institutionalism in Organizational Analysis, p. 478. University of Chicago Press, Chicago and London (1991). [Online] available in https://books.google.no/books?id=jbTbAgAAQBAJ&printsec=frontcover&source=gbs_ge_summary_r&cad=0#v=onepage&q&f=false. Accessed on 9 Dec 2018

49. Sahay, S., Sundararaman, T., Braa, J.: Public Health Informatics: Designing For Change – A Developing Country Perspective, p. 261. Oxford (2017)

50. Sahay, S., Sæbø, J.I, Mekonnen, S.M. and Gizaw, A.A.: Interplay of institutional logics and implications for deinstitutionalization: a case study of HMIS implementation in Tajikistan. J. Inf. Technol. Int. Dev., 6(3), 19–32, (2010)

51. Sahay, S., Nielsen, P., Aanestad, M.: Institutionalizing Information Systems for Universal Health Coverage in Primary Health Care and the Need for New Forms of Institutional Work, p. 44. Communications of the Association for Information Systems (2019)

52. Schreyögg, G., Sydow, J.: Understanding institutional and organizational path dependencies. In: Schreyögg, G., Sydow, J. (eds.) The Hidden Dynamics of Path Dependence Institutions and Organizations, pp. 3–12. Palgrave Macmillan UK, London (2010). https://doi.org/10.1057/9780230274075_1

53. Scott, W.R.: Institutions and Organizations, 2nd edn., p. 255. Sage Publications, London (2001)

54. Scott, W.R.: Crafting an analytic framework I: three pillars of institutions, chapter 3. In: Institutions and Organizations: Ideas Interests and Identities, 4th edn, p. 360. Sage, Thousand Oaks (2013)

55. Seo, M., Creed, W.E.D.: Institutional contradictions, praxis, and institutional change: a dialectical perspective. Acad. Manag. Rev. 27(2), 222–247 (2002)

56. Sharma, U., Lawrence, S., Lowe, A.: Institutional contradiction and management control innovation: a field study of total quality management practices in a privatized telecommunication company. Manag. Account. Res. 21, 251–264 (2010). https://doi.org/10.1016/j.mar.2010.03.005

57. Sheikh, Y.: Health Information Systems Integration as Institutionalisation: The Case of Zanzibar, p. 266. Thesis from University of Oslo, Oslo (2015)

58. Sorensen, A.: Taking path dependence seriously: an historical institutionalist research agenda in planning history. Plan. Perspect. 30(1), 17–38 (2015). https://doi.org/10.1080/02665433.2013.874299

59. Süli, K.M.: The Port of Rotterdam and the Maritime Container: The Rise and Fall of Rotterdam's Hinterland (1966–2010). Erasmus Universiteit Rotterdam, 290 pp (2014)

60. Thornton, P.H., Ocasio, W.: Institutional logics, Chap. 3. In: Greenwood, R., Oliver, C., Suddaby, R., Sahlin, K. (eds.) The SAGE Handbook of Organizational Institutionalism, pp. 99–129. SAGE Publications (2008) [Online]. Available in https://sk-sagepub-com.ezproxy.uio.no/reference/hdbk_orginstitution. Accessed on 7 Jan 2022

61. Thornton, P., Ocasio, W., Lounsbury, M.: The Institutional Logics Perspective: A New Approach to Culture, Structure and Process. Print ISBN-13: 9780199601936 (2012). Published by Oxford Scholarship [Online] available in www.oxfordscholarship.com. Accessed on 8 Nov 2018

62. Volkow, N.: Interaction between information systems and organizational change: case study of Petroleos Mexicanos. London School of Economics and Political Science, p. 271 (2003)

63. Walsham, G., Sahay, S.: GIS for district-level administration in India: problems and opportunities. MIS Q. 23(1), 39–65 (1999)

64. Wanderley, C.A., Soeiro, T.M.: Contradição Institucional e o Balanced Scorecard: Um caso de mudança sem sucesso. Revista Universo Contábil **12**(1), 45–65 (2016). Available in: https://proxy.furb.br/ojs/index.php/universocontabil/article/view/5206. Accessed on 9 Jan 2022
65. Wendt, C.: Introduction to Lepsius' concept of Institutional Theory. In: Wendt, C. (ed.) Max Weber and Institutional Theory, pp. 1–21. Springer International Publishing, Switzerland (2017). https://doi.org/10.1007/978-3-319-44708-7_1

Journey on Flattening the Curve: The Actors and Networks of Indonesian Contact Tracing System

Taufiq Sitompul[1]([✉]) [iD], Popy Meilani[2] [iD], Syefira Salsabila[3] [iD], Raja Fathurrahim[4] [iD], Ratnasari Wahono[4] [iD], and Jørn A. Braa[1] [iD]

[1] Department of Informatic Faculty of Mathematics and Sciences, University of Oslo, Oslo, Norway
{taufiqhs,jbraa}@ifi.uio.no
[2] Health Information Management, Faculty of Health, Esa Unggul University, Jakarta, Indonesia
popy.meilani@esaunggul.ac.id
[3] Faculty of Public Health, University Halu Oleo, Kendari, Indonesia
syefira.salsabila@uho.ac.id
[4] Castellum Digital Indonesia, Jakarta, Indonesia

Abstract. The contact tracing system implemented in Indonesia is called SILA-CAK, a modified version of DHIS2. SILACAK as a contact tracing system platform created a dashboard following national guidelines, which is a tool to monitor the COVID-19 cases in Indonesia and support decision making. The role of SILA-CAK has throughout several journeys and some changes that can be implemented by several actors involved such as the developer team, government, health workers, and also society. To analyze the connection between all aspects that affect the SILACAK system, A framework is needed to deeply review which can be a historical artifact on the system. Actor- network theory (ANT) is the best practice to know about how networks come into being, to trace what associations exist, how they move, how actors are enrolled into a network, how parts of a network form a whole network and how networks achieve temporary stability.

Keywords: Actor-network theory · Contact tracing · Networks

1 Introduction

The pandemic has been affecting not only the health care system but also the Socio-economic sector that was built by overall county will be disfunction for a while because of Lock-down and other terms that limited socio-economic activities [1]. Hospitals and clinics will be overcrowded caused by patients that lack facilities and limited of health workers that support the patient. All the problem affects developing countries including Indonesia that have not responded well to the crisis because of COVID-19 in healthcare and socio-economic system [2]. After more than 18 months the COVID-19 was first declared in Indonesia, the country had reported more than 4 million confirmed cases of

© IFIP International Federation for Information Processing 2022
Published by Springer Nature Switzerland AG 2022
Y. Zheng et al. (Eds.): ICT4D 2022, IFIP AICT 657, pp. 144–155, 2022.
https://doi.org/10.1007/978-3-031-19429-0_9

COVID-19 and more than 140.000 patients died [3]. The period of June to September 2021 is the worst situation in Indonesia that the confirmed cases reach the peak on more than 50.000 confirmed cases in one day,[1] but COVID vaccines have been given since January 2021 and reached 73,04% for the first dose and 51,52% for the second dose by the period of December 2021.[2]

In response to the COVID-19 pandemic in the beginning period, Indonesia government has signed and ratified regulations and decree to limit mobility of people to prevent other transmissions of the virus such as apply quarantine of international travel, Social restriction, form a task force for COVID-19. While implementing social restrictions, the government of Indonesia also issued regulations about contact tracing to detect the close contact of the confirmed-case patients. The contact tracing is important because the virus carrier who tests in positive results may have already spread the virus to the person who contracts with them, then this strategy will reduce the virus transmission [5, 6].

The contact tracing system implemented in Indonesia is called SILACAK, basically an modified version of DHIS2 COVID-19). The Indonesian government has confirmed SILACAK as the only official contact tracing tool in Indonesia in the Ministry of Health Decree Number HK.01.07/MENKES/4641/2021 on the Guidance on Testing, Tracing, Quarantine, and Isolation on Preventing COVID-19. SILACAK as a contact tracing system platform created a dashboard following national guidelines, which is a tool to monitor the COVID-19 cases in Indonesia and support decision making for stakeholders [7].

As the important system in again COVID-19 in Indonesia, the role of SILACAK has throughout several journeys and some changes in the system. The adaptation of the SILACAK system for Indonesia condition on the pandemic situation as an example the task force recruited more than 80.000 tracers to fulfil the target while the pandemic hit Indonesia in the worst situation, so the registration of the tracer will be exploded and the SILACAK development team innovate with the self-registration tool of WhatsApp chatbot and Web-App. The integration of SILACAK, NAR (National All Record), and Peduli Lindungin App is the other adaptation of SILACAK to simplify the record of the contact tracing [8].

The various changes and adaptation processes on the SILACAK system can be implemented by several actors involved in the process such as the developer team, government, health workers, and also society [9, 10].

To analyze the connection of all aspects that affect the SILACAK, A framework is needed to review which can be a historical artifact. Actor-network theory (ANT) is the best practice to know how networks come to trace what associations exist, how they move, how actors are enrolled into a network, how parts of a network form a whole network, and how networks achieve temporary stability. Actors are human or non-human entities that can make their presence individually felt by other actors, and ANT offers asymmetrical treatment between the technical and the social aspects of technology [10, 11].

---

[1] https://covid19.go.id/id/peta-sebaran.

[2] https://vaksin.kemkes.go.id.

On this study aim to know any actors involved on Covid-19 contact tracing system which are the function, initiative, and support on process of develop the SILACAK system. Analyze the connection between the actors that affect SILACAK system is also the purpose of this work using ANT framework.

2 Method

The case study approach used in to describing collaborative phenomena between stakeholders, the role of organizations and communities in the development of covid-19 Contact Tracing System (SILACAK) in Indonesia [11] was applied because of it allows phenomena to be studied in natural setting to obtain better understanding rather than to find conclusive evidence. The actor-network theory (ANT) was applied as a lens in the analysis of the data. The ANT method can see factors that affect basis of system access [12, 13].

This paper uses concept of translation from Actor Network Theory (ANT) to understand the complex social processes in implementation of health information systems. ANT is role as a way of telling stories about networks and actors - both human and non-human - and the processes by which technology is established. In the context of ANT, actors and networks cannot be independent of each other [14].

The core of ANT analysis is to examine the process of translation where actors align the interests of others with their own. Translation is explained as a four-stage transitional process that consists of problematization, interessement, enrolment and mobilization, through which events are carried out within a network of actors [14, 15].

The first phase is problematization to initiate a problem as well as to propose a solution. The focal-actor renders itself indispensable by defining a process under its control that must occur for all actors to achieve their interests. Interessement is a process where the focal actor stabilizes the identity of other actors and creates links between them [16].

During the second phase of translation, interessement, the focal actor executes these strategies to convince other actors to accept its definition of their interests. Enrolment is the approaches through which the focal actor attempts to define and interconnect different roles that allow other actors to relate within the network. Enrollment also includes the definition of roles of each actor in the newly created actor-network. The last moment of translation is mobilization, when the focal actors ensure that all representatives or spokespersons act according to what have become their aligned interests [11, 16].

3 Results

Figure 1 indicate analysis of SILACAK implementation process in Indonesia with four main periods. The periods describe main steps of SILACAK development addressing issues of contact tracing including increasing of data, users and actors involved.

4 POINT OF TRANSLATION

PERIOD			
NOVEMBER 2020 – FEBRUARY 2021	**MARCH – MAY 2021**	**MAY – JULY 2021**	**AUGUST 2021 – NOW**
• COVID-19 outbreak handling contact tracing in Indonesia has no exist yet before MoH Decree on 2020 for ContactTracing, Development of Contact Tracing Application with DHIS2 was initiated by the Ministry of Health, INFEM, WHO, and BNPB, the problem is the server was down, implementation in 15-16 districts/cities.	• The intervention of the private sector, and so BNPB stop meddling, the strengthening of Testing, Tracing and Isolation (Intervention of PJTLI and tracer Healthcare Center and Army and Police). Start to be implemented in 34 provinces, there is Helpdesk. • SILACAK mobile apps initiation development for android. • Build server for testing and production SILACAK app testing • SILACAK User's Training	• MoH Decree No. 4641/2021 on Strengthening of Testing, Tracing and Isolation. • Second wave of COVID-19 in Indonesia. • DTO taking the role in collaboration with the Coordinating Ministry for Maritime and Investment Affairs, then the role of the Indonesian Army and Police emerged. • Data migration. • Data evaluation. • Daily system maintenance	• NAR-Silacak Integration • SILACAK - Pedulilindungi Integration • Development of SILACAK V 3.0 • Utilization of SILACAK data for Social Restriction assessment.
PROBLEMATISATION	**INTERESSEMENT**	**ENROLMENT**	**MOBILISATION**

Fig. 1. Series of events for the SILACAK implementation in Indonesia

3.1 Moments of Translation

3.1.1 Problematization Moment

This stage is critical in collecting, accessing and using Silacak because decisions regarding system development are informed and guided by authentic and historical information from users. The key in the initial communication has been established. Actors who make up the type of data set and ultimately influence and influence system development and response [16].

The Ministry of Health, in coordination with BNPB, was improving surveillance data reporting and laboratory capacity to better analyze the COVID-19 situation for more prompt response actions and optimal resource mobilization. Strengthen the surveillance system at primary health facilities. One of the points that has played a key role in breaking the COVID-19 chain of transmission is by contact tracing.

This activity requires contact tracers to continuously record and report cases. For this reason, the use of a contact tracking recording and reporting system (Silacak) is important in determining the policies to be made. Due to, server was remaining issues during this step, complaints from the users increased in this step. Fortunately, this issue was addressed in the next step.

3.1.2 Interessement Moment

It is essential In the SILACAK application development there were found some troubles as the unstable server and the unwhole implementation regions. These caused the MoH (through Emerging Infectious Disease unit or INFEM) took a decision by involving the HIS developer (Private Company/sector) in order to strengthen and stabilize SILACAK app, so that can be used optimally by the users. In line with the involvement of private sector, BNPB has stopped being engaged in SILACAK project.

MoH supported not only from Health Information System (HIS), but also obligated to implement and record contact cases found on SILACAK application as written in Minister Decree number 4641 guidance on implementing the Inspection, Tracking, Quarantine and Isolation For Covid-19 Acceleration of Prevention and Control.

The Health Workers, Data Managers [PJTLI], Army and Police were involved to trace the contact cases. Remind that the tracers should mobile easily and visit the contact cases, MoH and developer initiated the development SILACAK Mobile Application, Moreover, this mobile app can be used in offline mode to avoid any internet access issue.

When the system was ready to use, the Emerging Infectious Disease Unit of MoH conducted users training in each district. Actor process was intensively initiated using the system. Users utilized the apps as they got their username. Complaints around servers and apps used were also necessary during this step. The helpdesk team supported the users to learn more about the apps, deliver multiple trainings, as well as supported the users on data entry and developed manual book and video tutorials [18, 19].

3.1.3 Enrolment Moment

This period indicated the strengthening of multisectoral collaboration by involving the ministry of maritime and investment affairs, Indonesian Army and Police. In addition, to address some technical infrastructure issues, data migration, evaluation, daily maintenance and strengthened system to address some issues were conducted during this period.

Not only policy, multi-sectoral collaboration from various stakeholders also was also strengthened in order to increase covid-19 contact tracing in Indonesia. The helpdesk team, on the other hand, supported to solve some technical issues on the apps [20, 21].

3.1.4 Mobilization Moment

Increasing effort of reducing COVID-19 cases, some apps were developed to address certain issues such as NAR for swab and antigen test, peduli lindungi, and ISOMAN for health quarantine. During this period, all these related apps were integrated to SILACAK to easily support COVID-19 case detection and prevention. Facing some troubles.

As collaboration with ministry of maritime, TNI and Polri was strengthened, additional users and tracers from TNI and Polri also significantly increased during this period. However, as tracers found issues regarding the system, they cannot directly contact the helpdesk. They should first contact the PJTLI in the puskesmas level, city level and provincial level to be followed up to the helpdesk. Due to technical issues that supposed to get fast respond, tracers sometimes directly contact the helpdesk [17, 22, 23].

The ANT connection shows on Fig. 2 the types of actors and networks (units) that were present in Silacak at the time of this study. This includes how the actors were connected through various networks in the use of applications. Within networks, the actors carried out activities, were involved in events and employed processes by using Silacak. at one stage or another during the activities, events and processes were negotiated between the human actors, directly and indirectly, consciously or unconsciously. The connection also describes the role of non-human actors to support the whole activities on the technical and non-technical issues.

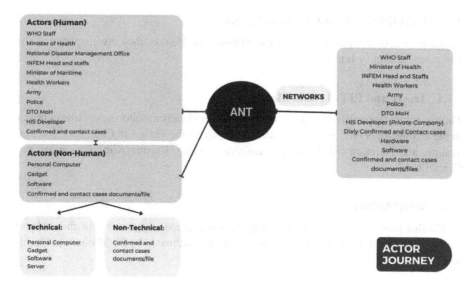

Fig. 2. Actors and Networks of SILACAK

4 Discussion

4.1 Actors

The Ministry of Health consists of the Data and Information Center Department and Emerging Infectious Disease Substance Group (INFEM), Digital Transformation Officer, tracers, PJTLI at province, district/city, healthcare center level. Actors from the SILACAK app as follows:

4.1.1 Emerging Infectious Disease Substance Group (Infem), MoH

Ministry being proactive and able to lead the pandemic at national levels. Despite being heavily criticized for being reluctant by the informed public and academics from inside and outside the country, MoH has been one of the first ministerial level agencies to formally respond to COVID-19 since 4 February 2020. Infem is one of the working units at the MoH that is responsible for the rate of development of emerging infectious diseases in Indonesia, one of which is COVID-19.

4.1.2 Pusdatin (Data and Information Center)

A working unit at the Ministry of Health that acts as a central level health data trustee, has the task of collecting, validating, managing, disseminating and fostering data producers. Ithis case, Pusdatin manages all the healthcare data, including contact tracing data originating from the SILACAK application.

4.1.3 DTO (Digital Transformation Officer)

This one is a new working unit in the Ministry of Health, they are responsible for integrating health systems.

4.1.4 Tracer and PJTLI (Data Manager)

The tracers are responsible to carry out the tracking and daily monitoring of close contacts in the healthcare center, and coordinated in stages by the Person in Charge of Tracing, Testing, and Isolation (PJTLI) at the healthcare center, Regency/City, Provincial and Central levels.

4.1.5 WHO Indonesia

NGOs that provide a lot of funding support and provide suggestions for the use and development of DHIS2 in contact tracing activities coordinated by the Ministry of Health and BNPB.

4.1.6 Private Sector (Castellum Digital Indonesia)

The Private Sector here plays a role as part of the DHIS2-based SILACAK system developer. Where there is a helpdesk and also a system technical team. The helpdesk has an important role in running the troubleshoot from the user's point of view of using the system. Users still find hampers to implement SILACAK, especially for tracer on duty.

The helpdesk divides for each province in Indonesia. Meanwhile, the Technical Team of the Silacak System is tasked with solving technical problems posed by the Helpdesk (sourced from users).

4.1.7 The National Army and Police

The National Army and Police is part of COVID-19 Control Security Task Force, also involved in contact tracing activities. The units involved at the village and sub-district level (Babinsa/Bhabinkamtibmas) which are controlled and coordinated by the healthcare center as a community-based health authority.

The basis for the involvement of them at that time was to meet the adequacy of human resources at the healthcare center and structured in terms of tracking and monitoring close contacts, in the context of accelerating the control of COVID-19.

4.1.8 National Disaster Management Office (BNPB)

Managing an epidemic is not a natural mandate of BNPB. However, given the presidential preference and decision, the Head of BPBP has been tasked as the Chief of the Task Force.

4.2 Networks

4.2.1 Multisectoral (Actors) Collaboration During SILACAK Implementation

The collaboration on multi-sectoral needs on all sector to strengthen coordination and reduce the loss whether cost or human lives. As example, addressing critical global health issues, such as antimicrobial resistance, infectious disease outbreaks, and natural disasters [25].

Investment in collaboration mechanisms enables open and regular communication, and facilitates the mutual understanding, trust, and accountability needed to achieve shared goals. Also important are mechanisms for all stakeholders to provide feedback throughout the process, to inform any adaptations needed. Aligned with a collective logic of inquiry, multisectoral collaboration enabled diverse evidence and ideas to be tested, and encouraged innovation to tackle long standing constraints and achieve greater impact [26].

The Silacak involved multi-sectoral collaboration including Indonesian covid-19 task force, data and information center (Pusdatin), center of infectious and emergency (Infem), world health organization and developer from private sector. WHO initiated to develop Silacak as an integrated tracing system. Encouraged by MoH, a private sector was responsible as a developer of Silacak and coordinated to Pusdatin to provide required server.

The Infem assisted to provide technical and conceptual framework for Silacak system. Infem also encouraged provincial and district office to implement Silacak, while developer trained them on how to operate Silacak, followed by training for tracers and puskesmas.

By July, DTO (Digital transformation office) initiated improvement by involving TNI (National Military of Indonesia) and Polri (National police of Indonesia) to become tracers. For Silacak improvement, coordination is needed between DTO, WHO, infem and private sector.

As the government officially launched the SILACAK as a tracing system, it encouraged all health offices from provincial level, city, district, sub-district, and primary health office (Puskesmas) level to use SILACAK. In the Puskesmas level, tracers were responsible for contact tracing.

They were coming from puskesmas officers, youth group (karang taruna), and TNI. While in the city, district and provincial level, PJTLI were appointed for testing, tracing, and isolation. PJTI also assisted for data entry, ensured data quality and shared the data to tracers for specific case monitoring.

4.2.2 Multiple Apps Integration into SILACAK

The definition of integration as a process of merging small parts or sub-systems into one system that functions as a whole. In the IT industry, integration is 'the end result of a process whose purpose is to connect the different sub-systems into one.

The data, which each of the sub-systems has, becomes part of one bigger system that will share the data easy and fast whenever needed. More specifically, integration is the process of connecting different IT systems, services and/or software so that they can function together [27]. The integration process also can combine into one big or complete system such as SILACAK for contact tracing Covid-19 suspect.

By June to September 2021, the covid-19 in Indonesia reached more than 50.000 confirmed cases in one day. Responding to these issues, SILACAK as a tracing system was strengthened and supported by all parties.

The NAR (New All Record) is an application to record and report Covid-19 confirmed cases including taking and examining specimens, confirmed death, and recovery from COVID-19. It tracks the examination result from 902 laboratories including SWAB PCR test, and antigen test. NAR has been utilized to strengthen migration surveillance of Covid in Indonesia that was fully accessible for all airports, stations, and terminals to ensure health and safe migration for all as well as preventing transmission within the transportation facilities.

Furthermore, SWAB and antigen tests reported through NAR were followed up by ISOMAN apps. As a telemedicine app, people with positive covid received automatic messages and free consultation during their self-quarantine. Prescriptions were provided and patients got medicine for free.

Another app that was also integrated into SILACAK was peduli lindungi. PeduliLindung is an application developed to assist the tracking process to stop the spread of Coronavirus Disease (COVID-19). It relied on community participation to share location data that allowed the government to track contact history. Users also got a notification if they were in a crowd or in a red zone reporting infected people with positive COVID-19 or patients under surveillance.

To increase the close contact tracing rate from 1:0.9 to a minimum of 1:15, TNI, National Military of Indonesia and Polri, National Police of Indonesia also supported the tracing process using integrated systems of NAR, Peduli Lindungi, ISOMAN and Silacak. TNI and Polri responded to the confirmed cases by accessing NAR. They forwarded the list of confirmed cases to TNI and Polri tracer in each sub-districts level. The tracer even supported the data entry into Isoman and Silacak app, ensuring patients to get medicine and to complete their self-quarantine by a negative result of PCR and antigen test.

Collaboration between helpdesk, PJTLI and tracers has supported the learning process where users learn on how IT implementation worked on covid-19 contact tracing, while helpdesk learn on users need. In addition, private sector supported to address any technical issues during system integration between SILACAK, NAR and peduli lindungi.

Not only as data user, Ministry of health has also supported contact tracing process by strengthening policies and daily monitoring conducted by infem. From non-human side, server stability was very important to to ensure sustainability of the system [7, 9, 20]. The four main moments of translation during SILACAK implementation indicated the best practices on how various parties have translated and aligned their interest within the system to achieve goals [17, 24].

As a final statement, Indonesia can learn from countries that have proved successful in controlling pandemics. Taiwan, for instance, has been considered successful in developing effective cooperation between government and business and in communicating transparently to control the pandemic. In collaboration with Taiwan's Centres for Disease Control, two technology companies – HTC and LINE – developed a chatbot that allowed people to report their health status and get advice on the virus. Taiwan's National Health Insurance Administration and National Immigration Agency worked together to identify suspected cases for COVID-19 testing, integrating their databases of citizens' medical and travel history [4].

5 Conclusion

IT use in the health sector has been utilized for certain context including app for covid-19 data based handling management. Indonesia developed apps for contact tracing called SILACAK using DHIS-2 platform. During initial phase, server became issues affecting the system. Fortunately, technical feedback solved the issues and gave better experience on SILACAK. Support from any parties would be required even for any small issues. Coordination between helpdesk is still challenges to ensure accurate information. Various systems have been integrated to strengthen contact tracing process. Fragmentation issues have been addressed within the SILACAK app.

This paper can conclude that inter-connected internal and external socio-technical facets of infrastructure influence the change of HIS. Besides this paper also demonstrates how improvements in one facet will influence other facets of infrastructure, in both negative and positive ways. The application of a different theory, would be of benefit to academics and the healthcare sector of Indonesia in general. There are two primary factors influencing an individual's intention to use this technology: perceived ease of use and perceived usefulness.

6 Limitation Research

There are few limitation on this paper based on the point on this purpose of this work about role of all actors for contact tracing system in Indonesia againts Covid-19 outbreak. This study only described and explained what was happened and who was in charged (actors) for established the contact tracing system and the connection among them, and did not conduct the deep evaluation regarding the impact of each actor. The last limitation was this work focused on described and explained how multi-actors collaboration flattened the covid-19 curve in Indonesia.

7 Recommendation

The researcher could conduct deep evaluation regarding the impact of each actor involved in the process, elaborate more rigorous study method, and migth be elaborated the multi-actor's role deeply.

References

1. Martin, A., Markhvida, M., Hallegatte, S., Walsh, B.: Socio-economic impacts of covid-19 on household consumption and poverty. Econ. Disasters Clim. Change 4(3), 453–479 (2020). https://doi.org/10.1007/s41885-020-00070-3

2. Shadmi, E., Chen, Y., Dourado, I., Faran-Perach, I., Furler, J., Hangoma, P.: Health equity and COVID-19: global perspectives. Int. J. Equity Health **19**, 104 (2020). https://doi.org/10.1186/s12939-020-01218-z

3. Gorbiano, M.I.: BREAKING: Jokowi announces Indonesia's first two confirmed COVID-19 cases. The Jakarta Post (2020)

4. Hsieh, L., Child, J.: What coronavirus success of Taiwan and Iceland has in common. The Conversation **29** (2020)

5. Permatasari, D.: Kebijakan Covid-19 dari PSBB hingga PPKM Empat Level. Kompaspedia (2021)

6. Taufiq, R.I.: Effectiveness of ppkm (enforcement of restrictions on community activities) emergency and levels 1–4 on control of spread covid 19 virus in east java. Percipience J. Soc., Adm., Entrepreneurship J. **1**(1) (2021)

7. Permenkes RI. No HK.01.07/MENKES/4641/2021 tentang Panduan Pelaksanaan Pemeriksaan, Pelacakan, Karantina, dan Isolasi dalam Rangka Percepatan Pencegahan dan Pengendalian Coronavirus Disease 2019 (Covid-19). Jakarta: Menteri Kesehatan Republik Indonesia, No HK.01.07/MENKES/4641/2021 Jakarta: Menteri Kesehatan Republik Indonesia (2021)

8. Syefira, S., Sitompul, T.H., Lian, L., Dewi, E., Meilani, P., Braa, J.: DHIS2 Contact Tracing Application (SILACAK) Tracer Self-Registration System: Pro-active solution using Whatsapp-BOT (AMICA). Dhis2community (2021)

9. Mgudlwa, S., Iyamu, T.: A Framework for accessing patient big data: ANT view of a south African health facility. The Afr. J. Inform. Syst. **13**(2), 65–81 (2021)

10. Manya, A., Braa, J., Sahay, S.: A socio-technical approach to understanding data quality in health information systems: Data quality intervention in Kenya. In: 2015 IST-Africa Conference, IST-Africa (2015). https://doi.org/10.1109/ISTAFRICA.2015.7190582

11. Kimaro, H., Nyella, E.: HIS Standardization in developing countries: use of boundary objects to enable multiple translations. The Afr. J. Inform. Syst. **8**(1), 72 (2015)

12. Myers, M.D.: Qualitative research in information systems. MIS Q. **21**(2), 241 (1997). https://doi.org/10.2307/249422

13. Mörtl, K., Gelo, O.C.G.: Qualitative methods in psychotherapy process research. In: Gelo, O.C.G., Pritz, A., Rieken, B. (eds.) Psychotherapy Research, pp. 381–428. Springer, Vienna (2015). https://doi.org/10.1007/978-3-7091-1382-0_20

14. Teles, A., Joia, L.A.: Assessment of digital inclusion via the actor-network theory: the case of the Brazilian municipality of Piraí. Telematics Inform. **28**(3), 191–203 (2011). https://doi.org/10.1016/j.tele.2010.09.003

15. Callon, M.: Some elements of a sociology of translation: domestication of the scallops and the fishermen of St Brieuc Bay. The Soc. Rev. **32**(1_suppl), 196–233 (2015). https://doi.org/10.1111/j.1467-954X.1984.tb00113.x

16. Heeks, R., Stanforth, C.: Technological change in developing countries: opening the black box of process using actor–network theory. Dev. Stud. Res. **2**(1), 33–50 (2015). https://doi.org/10.1080/21665095.2015.1026610

17. Sitompul, T., Senyoni, W., Braa, J., Yudianto: Convergence of technical and policy processes: a study of indonesia's health information systems. In: IFIP Advances in Information and Communication Technology (2019). https://doi.org/10.1007/978-3-030-18400-1_32

18. Costa, C.C., da Cunha, P.R.: Business model design from an ANT perspective: contributions and insights of an open and living theory. In: Nelson, M.L., Shaw, M.J., Strader, T.J. (eds.) AMCIS 2009. LNBIP, vol. 36, pp. 56–67. Springer, Heidelberg (2009). https://doi.org/10.1007/978-3-642-03132-8_5

19. Sarker, S., Sarker, S., Sidorova, A.: Understanding business process change failure: an actor-network perspective. J. Manag. Inform. Syst. **23**(1), 51–86 (2006). https://doi.org/10.2753/MIS0742-1222230102

20. Bueger, C., Stockbruegger, J.: Actor-network theory. In: McCarthy, D.R. (ed.) Technology and World Politics: An Introduction, pp. 42–59. Routledge (2017). https://doi.org/10.4324/9781317353836-3

21. Latour, B.: Reassembling the social: an introduction to actor-network theory. Oup Oxford, p. 43 (2007)

22. Afarikumah, E.: Deploying actor -network theory to analyse telemedicine implementation in Ghana. Sci. J. Publ. Health 1(2), 77 (2013). https://doi.org/10.11648/j.sjph.20130102.15

23. Arnaboldi, M., Spiller, N.: Actor-network theory and stakeholder collaboration: the case of Cultural Districts. Tourism Manag. 32(3), 641–654 (2011). https://doi.org/10.1016/j.tourman.2010.05.016

24. Braa, J., Sahay, S., Lewis, J., Senyoni, W.: Health information systems in Indonesia: understanding and addressing complexity. In: Choudrie, J., Islam, M.S., Wahid, F., Bass, J.M., Priyatma, J.E. (eds.) ICT4D 2017. IAICT, vol. 504, pp. 59–70. Springer, Cham (2017). https://doi.org/10.1007/978-3-319-59111-7_6

25. Vesterinen, H.M., et al.: Strengthening multi-sectoral collaboration on critical health issues: one health systems mapping and analysis resource toolkit (OH-SMART) for operationalizing one health. PloS one. 14(7), e0219197 (2019)

26. Kuruvilla, S., et al.: Business not as usual: how multisectoral collaboration can promote transformative change for health and sustainable development. Bmj 36, 4 (2018). https://doi.org/10.1136/bmj.k4771

27. Making multiple systems work as one through System Integration [Internet]. [Place Unknow]: Iwconnect; [Updated 2019;Cited 2022 Jun 6] (2019). https://iwconnect.com/making-multiple-systems-work-as-one-through-integr

Government Corruption, ICTs, and the Quest for Inclusion

Education Information System Decentralization: The Introduction of Digital Learner Records in the Gambia

Seedy Ahmed Jallow[✉] and Terje Aksel Sanner

University of Oslo, Oslo, The Gambia
seedy.jallow@edugambia.gm, terjeasa@ifi.uio.no

Abstract. The Gambia EMIS has mainly consisted of a manual, paper based reporting system maintained from the national level. The recent policy changes, which emphasize social inclusion in quality learning, call for an "EMIS shift", which includes the development of a digital national Teacher Register, Learner Records, and the decentralization of key EMIS functions to regions and schools. Empirically, this paper concerns the steps taken towards a decentralized EMIS in the Gambia as we follow the initial implementation of the individual learner admission and registration system in 200 schools. We synthesize previous IS centralization and decentralization literature into an analytical framework, which we apply to make sense of the case findings and provide recommendations for future EMIS decentralization initiatives.

Keywords: Centralization · Decentralization · Social inclusion · Education management

1 Introduction

World development agendas, like the Millenium Development Goals (MDGs) and the Education for All framework (EFA), introduced in 2000 and 1990 respectively, focused on solving global issues of poverty, sanitation, education, health and wellbeing by ensuring access to public services for all. Countries, including developing ones, developed systems to help monitor indicators of access to these services, mainly on a collective level. In 2015, at the end of the MDG period, its final progress report indicated achievements, but also highlighted disparities across age, gender, socio economic and geographic groupings. A key takeaway from the MDG period was the need to tackle the inequalities and uneven progress by targeting interventions and resources in a fair and equitable manner. This set the theme for the ensuing Sustainable Development Goals 2030 Agenda (SDGs).

With the slogan "Leave no one behind" as a core principle, the SDGs promise to reach out to every individual to arrest these inequalities. This creates a phenomena wherein the information needs of countries shifts from the collective to the individual to be able to provide public services in an equitable manner. The Gambia is a developing

Y. Zheng et al. (Eds.): ICT4D 2022, IFIP AICT 657, pp. 159–170, 2022.
https://doi.org/10.1007/978-3-031-19429-0_10

country in sub-Saharan Africa that has aligned its national education policy with SDG4 (SDG for Education) which emphasizes the need to "ensure inclusive and equitable quality education and promote lifelong learning opportunities for all". In particular, SDG Target 4.5 stresses the need to "ensure equal access to all levels of education and vocational training for the vulnerable, including persons with disabilities, indigenous peoples and children in vulnerable situations". The implications are that data needs to be disaggregated by gender, location, wealth quintile and other factors, such as disabilities and income levels (Unicef 2020). Consequently, the national Education Management Information System (EMIS) needs to handle data on individuals disaggregated by a wide range of socio-economic factors (Alvesson and Viñuela 2014) to target individual learners in terms of interventions, track their progress for early warning mechanisms and identifying and capturing the out-of-school learners.

The Gambia's Ministry of Basic and Secondary Education is shifting its EMIS to collect individual level data. This includes a *granularization* of EMIS data and tools, *digitalization* of EMIS process, and *decentralization* of Key EMIS functions to schools. As the increased volume of information processing is enabled by the digitalization of EMIS routines, the ensuring workload could easily overwhelm the system if key EMIS functions aren't decentralized. This paper zooms in on this and discusses four decentralization dimensions to understand the implications of the EMIS shift.

Empirically, this paper concerns the steps taken towards a decentralized EMIS in the Gambia. First, in section two, we review relevant literature on decentralization and centralization of management information systems. Our literature review synthesizes *four* dimensions along which decentralization and centralization needs to be balanced. In Sect. 3, we describe our methods, which is followed by accounts from our empirical case (Sect. 4). In the discussion part of our paper, Sect. 5, we consider how the implementation of an EMIS, aimed at supporting evidence-based decision-making for inclusive and quality education, brings into play different EMIS decentralization dimensions. Finally, we offer some concluding remarks on the implications of the study.

2 IS Centralization and Decentralization

The centralization versus decentralization of information systems is an important but complex debate with a long history and few simple answers (Ein-Dor and Segev 1978; Hugoson 2009; Rockart and Leventer 1976). Most conceptualizations rely on some notion of distance; distance between unit locations; distance between different levels of organizational hierarchy or operations within an organization; the physical or organizational distance between where decisions are made and where they are enacted (King 1984). There is no clear boundary between centralized and decentralized information systems, but rather a core-periphery continuum (Heeks 1999; Rockart and Leventer 1976). The basic questions regarding centralization and decentralization revolve around tailoring organizational arrangements to meet the constraints of organization size, the nature of the IT involved in organizational operations, and the needs of different organizational actors (King 1984).

Chang (2006) defined IS decentralization from the perspective of decision making as "the act or process of assigning the decision-making authority to lower levels of an organizational hierarchy". The lower the average level at which decisions are made, the greater is the decentralization (Chang 2006). King (1984) divides decentralization into three separate areas: physical location, function, and control. Control concerns the locus of decision-making in the organization. Physical location concerns where operations and responsibilities are located in physical space, whereas function refers to the placement of a responsibility within the organizational structure (King 1984).

Dimension of Decentralization of MIS

Norton (1972) argues that the term "centralization" is meaningless with reference to an information system as a whole. Instead, it must be "approached in terms of the specific functions which make up the operations and management of an organization's information system" (Rockart and Leventer 1976). Accordingly, Norton clusters information systems related activities into three categories: Systems Operations, Systems Development, and Systems Management.

Norton (1972) further points out that centralization of system operations include the applications that need information crossing hierarchical boundaries. Against centralization, the complexity of operating systems, high risk of failure, high communication costs, and competition for priority of service in centralized systems are argued (Rockart and Leventer 1976). Norton subdivides systems development into its analysis, design and programming phases. According to Norton, there is "fair consensus" that the analysis phase should be decentralized. For the design and programming phases, with the level of expertise and specialization involved in mind, centralization is peddled (Rockart and Leventer 1976). Concerning system management, there is no clear consensus in literature except for development of standards where the argument is in clear favor of centralization (Rockart and Leventer 1976). Depending on changes in technology, economic situation, available capacity and political interests (King 1984), the different aspects of an MIS can be either centralized or decentralized at a given point in time.

(Ein-Dor and Segev 1978) identified five elements, the position of which should be considered on the centralization-decentralization axis according:

1) Organizational structure: As Pick (2015) argued, the choice of centralization vs decentralization may be influenced by the overall structural design of the organization housing the information technology. In the case of systems development for example, decentralized organizations have been found to have problems of inconsistency in data due to problems of syncing updates and reports.
2) MIS development and implementation: the degree to which MIS plans and projects are formulated and executed centrally.
3) MIS unit: This element has two sub elements; a) the degree to which MIS resources are controlled centrally. This included specialized personnel resources. b) The degree to which the decentralized MIS units are centrally controlled. The MIS units might have discretion with their decision-making or they could be an extension, implementing decisions of the central MIS unit at headquarters.
4) IT resource: The degree to which IT infrastructure and computer equipment is geographically concentrated. In a decentralized system, the bulk of the infrastructure could be located at the headquarters with smaller computers and devices at the lower levels.

5) Data and Data Management in the organization. Redundancy is minimized by use of a centralized database. Decentralized databases could result in lack of data element standardization that is a major problem when it comes to synchronizing, processing and analyzing data.

(Heeks 1999) identified 8 'areas of responsibilities' in dealing with public sector organization information systems. These areas are; information systems planning, organizational structures and staffing, data management, computing and data management architecture, information systems development, information technology acquisition, training, and technical support. He goes on to argue that centralization or decentralization of any of these responsibilities have both merits and challenges. Centralization generally promotes sharing of resources across the organization, avoids duplication and wastage, supports learning and control, and lowers acquisition costs through bulk purchases. However, centralization increases information system dependencies and vulnerabilities and weakens responsiveness as information needs to flow all the way between the central unit and the periphery to inform actio. There is also limited ability to accommodate heterogenous local information system needs.

In contrast, decentralization is praised for its closer distance between the users and the IS developers, easing IS designs around the local users' needs and enabling rapid development cycles. However, decentralization could create a barrier to sharing of data and other resources, including human resources, due to the different information systems that are incompatible. It also limits central planning and control which results in duplication of efforts and data redundancy reducing the efficiency of the information system.

Instead of identifying where each of these areas of responsibility would fall on the centralization-decentralization axis, Heeks recommended a different approach: a core-periphery one. In this, he reconciles the centralization and decentralization approaches into one where both the central and local actors would be involved in all areas of responsibility.

Heeks' in addition to Ein-Dor and Segev's paper, among the papers we reviewed, provided the most practical decomposition of information systems functions and responsibilities that can be mapped to practical issues in the organization. Heeks' paper is further endeared to us by the fact that it's from a similar public sector context. As a result, we synthesize the two papers into a framework that is both practical and focuses on the key components to shed light on the decentralization process from our case.

Our synthesis of the IS centralization-decentralization literature, with an emphasis on the public sector, results in a framework with 4 key dimensions to consider:

1. Organizational structures and staffing, including the structure of the MIS unit
2. Information systems planning, development and implementation
3. Computer architecture, hardware resources (management and acquisition)
4. Data management

3   Methods

The Gambia is a relatively small developing country in a good position to experiment with individual learner records on a national scale. Learnings from The Gambia may inform similar initiatives in other parts of the world. The EMIS decentralization initiative is country driven and as such no buy-in was necessary, open access - no struggles in gaining or maintaining access - to resources, people, documents, offices etc. One of the authors has good access as a member of the national EMIS team and is involved in the design and implementation of the action research project as well.

The purpose of this research is centered around understanding the steps taken by the ministry towards the decentralization of the Gambia EMIS to the school level. We employed a case study methodology within the interpretive research paradigm as we follow the ministry's decentralization process and how it has been interpreted by the various stakeholders along the decentralization chain. The research covers the start of the project in January 2019 to its current state with the two authors very much involved from the beginning. The first author is more hands-on as a member of the local team that conceived the project and also one of the leaders of the implementation team. The second author follows the project from a distance, which allows for a birds eye view on project activity and findings. The authors balance out each other's positional shortcomings granting the research project both analytical rigor and local relevance.

3.1   Case Background

In the Gambia, a political progression towards decentralization is based on the 1997 Constitution, the Local Government Act (2002) and the Local Government Finance and Audit Act (2004). These legislations set out to fundamentally restructure the public sector through extensive fiscal and functional decentralization. Local government areas (2 Municipalities and 5 Councils), structures and officers, were granted authority to provide basic services in education, health, agriculture, road maintenance, sanitation and animal husbandry (Alam 2009). The Education Sector has attempted to decentralize its functions, such as control of schools, through Regional Education Directorates located in each municipality and council. The two municipalities, both in urban areas, were able to open new schools. However, due to lack of expertise and constrained finances, the control of schools was transferred back to the central government shortly thereafter. The councils, mostly in rural areas, found themselves unable to even open new schools. The education sector, like other sectors, still remains under central government control.

The ministry of education in the Gambia has recognized the importance of EMIS to support decentralization and make strides towards the policy goal of inclusive quality education for all. This is why the EMIS is being decentralized to the school level in tandem with a shift from aggregate to individual level data about learners.

In early 2019, the ministry of education in the Gambia invited Health Information Systems Programmes Center from the University of Oslo, Norway (HISP UiO) and and its regional arm, HISP West and Central Africa(HISP-WCA), to a workshop at the MoBSE offices in to discuss the current state of EMIS in Gambia, ongoing EMIS strengthening efforts by the ministry and to identify the implementation scope of the

EMIS-HISP UiO support project. Among the key outcomes of the workshop was an agreement to experiment with eRegisters for students and teachers in schools.

The Ministry of Basic and Secondary Education in the Gambia has customized and implemented the Free and Open Source DHIS2 software application as the new platform for the Education Management Information System (EMIS) in the Gambia. The Health Information Systems Programme (HISP) research group, located at the Department of Informatics, University of Oslo, is coordinating the development of the DHIS2 software and is providing support to implementation teams in various countries. HISP West and Central Africa as a regional organization and a partner of HISP/Department of Informatics, University of Oslo is responsible for coordinating and carrying Information System implementation, assessment, planning, capacity building and research activities in the West and Central Africa region within the HISP network. HISP-WCA trained the core EMIS staff of the ministry on the DHIS2, and supported the ministry during the configuration of the platform for tracking students and teachers to be implemented at the school level.

The education management system has three main levels, the central ministry of education, the regional education directorates, and the schools. There is a fourth level, in between the regional education directorates and the schools, called "Clusters" which are composed of clusters of schools for easier management and supervision, by cluster monitors (school inspectors). The cluster monitors are attached to the regional education directorates as there are no permanent structures that represent the cluster level. Due to resource constraints, only public Lower Basic Schools, Upper Basic School and Senior Secondary Schools are targeted in the initial EMIS decentralization initiative.

3.2 Data Collection and Data Analysis

Data collection started in January 2019 when the planning and development of tools began to around June 2021 when pilot implementation in two regions was concluded. Along the way, a pre-pilot test was held where teachers were trained and then observed while they used the system to register students. During the pilot, head teacher meetings were held to inform about the planned shift and notes were taken of their comments and reactions. Interviews were held with senior officials of the ministry - head of EMIS unit, EMIS advisor to the ministry and a former permanent secretary of the ministry - to identify their motivations and expectations with the EMIS shift. Discussion sessions were also held with regional officers to understand what their needs and concerns are and how this shift could affect their roles.

Document studies were also conducted covering the national education policy and strategic plan, national development plan and local government acts. These documents provided context and some background into the project giving us better understanding of the motivations and vision of the 'EMIS shift'.

We began to make sense of the data early into the data collection process. We applied qualitative data analysis to identify key themes that were coded and grouped. The grouping helped distinguish the main dimensions along which we could analyze the data using the synthesized framework and Heeks core-periphery concept.

4 EMIS Decentralization in the Gambia

Currently, the central EMIS unit is overwhelmed with more schools opening each year and continuously expanding national and international data requirements. The ongoing shift to individual learner data poses significant data processing demands that cannot be handled by the central unit alone. The central EMIS unit would ideally spend its time and resources on making sense of the data and designing programs and interventions to improve the quality of education and mitigate barriers to social inclusion. EMIS decentralization has the potential to strengthen local ownership and enhance the utilization of data for decision-making at regional, cluster and school level.

4.1 Implementation of the "EMIS Shift"

HISP UiO, through its regional arm, HISP-WCA, has supported the central EMIS unit in designing a solution to collect individual level student data at school level. Amongst the key processes in school administration are the admission and registration of children into the school, recording of student attendance, monitoring of performance, tracking of disciplinary records of students etc. The solution designed by the EMIS team incorporated all of the above key processes, but the ensuing pilot only focused on the admission and registration of students, as this is the entry point to student management processes in the schools.

The initial phase involved 200 schools of all primary and secondary education levels in two regions consisting of both urban and rural communities. Findings from the first phase were expected to inform a subsequent national implementation as the two chosen regions contained all the demographics in the country. Each of the 200 schools was supplied with a Chromebook to be used during enrollment of students. Chromebooks were chosen to leverage the offline capabilities of the DHIS2 android tracker app, as many of the schools have very limited access to the internet. This allows the schools to enroll students as they show up and periodically synchronize data with the server when there is internet access.

During the implementation, regional officers were invited to discuss the planning of the teacher training and help in the configuration of the Chromebooks. They supported the central EMIS team on conducting the training and served as regional support staff to schools. A head teacher meeting was organized to present the idea of the shift to individual data. Each head teacher was then tasked to delegate three (3) representatives from the schools, on account of the risks involved in 'putting all our eggs in one basket', to be trained on enrolling students using the chromebooks and synchronizing data. It was also suggested that schools use the trainees to train other teachers in their schools to further mitigate against capacity issues due to teacher transfer, promotion etc. Most of the trainees identified were teachers because they are mostly responsible for the admission and registration of students as many of the schools don't have auxiliary staff to take up these responsibilities.

Through the use of managerial Dashboards on the DHIS2 platforms, both the central ministry and the regional offices now have real time access to enrolment data and analysis based on various demographics of the students. However, there is a plan to conduct an extended training of the regional officers on the use of DHIS2 as a reporting and analysis tool to support their monitoring and oversight functions. The schools can access the dashboards too, either through the web or through the DHIS2 dashboard android app, installed alongside the tracker app in the chromebooks. The schools, however, need internet connectivity to access the DHIS2 Dashboards. Internet connectivity is one of the main constraints facing the implementation.

4.2 Institutional Reception

The initiative, as expected, was well received at the central and regional levels, although the regional officers pleaded for more involvement in shaping the project and for increased capacity building to use and manage the system to meet their information needs.

At the school level, the reaction was mixed. Some schools appreciated the initiative as they saw the need for progress and the role of IT in it. Some envisioned that the solution would help bring about their routine activities in the schools. Others were able to relate to the need for individual data and motivations for the "shift", while others recognized the digital innovations ongoing in other sectors and were glad education was not being left behind. Nevertheless, a few schools were concerned with the implications for their existing data systems: would they need to throw them out in favor of this new initiative? This also resulted in concerns for interoperability between systems at the school level.

However, almost an equal number of school representatives doubted the feasibility of the initiative citing the history of the central units designing seemingly well thought out plans only to fail during implementation. Some bemoaned the unavailability of critical resources in some schools including internet access, electricity and staff. A few made reference to more pressing matters – dilapidated structures, learning materials, teacher motivation, performance issues (~ learning crisis) - that needed more urgent attention. From an operational point of view, concerns were raised regarding the authority of the ministry to collect individual data on learners and the legal grounds for it. A few schools, all private, blatantly refused to participate in the exercises, citing international laws on data privacy, confidentiality and security. Some argued that digital registration of students using the devices are not part of the teachers' Terms of Reference and that they are not qualified to handle the data analysis and reporting needs of the schools. Instead, they suggested qualified personnel to be trained and posted to each school.

Drawing on the synthesized framework, we outline the ongoing EMIS decentralization in the Gambia and the apparent trade-offs between centralization and decentralization. System development includes analysis, design and development of information systems pertaining to the EMIS shift. Due to the level of expertise required and shortage of distributed capacity to develop components of the information system, this component is largely centralized. However, the development process is nonetheless informed by a participatory approach involving a combination of HISP WCA (mentioned in background above) for technical support and training, MoBSE technical and organizational stewardship, and representation of different stakeholders and user groups from the regional, cluster and school levels.

System management includes the administrative aspects of planning, developing, operating and controlling of the system. For the sake of uniformity of reporting, standardization of tools and procurement of electronic equipment, this component is largely centralized. There are specific procurement rules public institutions in the Gambia must follow when purchasing equipment. Decentralization of this process tantamount to unnecessary repetition of the same procurement process that might result in delays and procurement of sub-standard, incompatible or heterogenous equipment that will be hard to maintain.

System operations comprises the infrastructure, including the hardware, operations and human personnel. This component is largely decentralized because of huge processing tasks demanded by the shift in the data system. Computers will be provided at all public schools with the new information system available locally to handle the daily information processing needs. Network infrastructures will be provided to enable the transfer of information between the schools, regional directorates and the central EMIS unit at the ministry of education headquarters. Support staff will also be trained and made available either at the schools or at the regional directorates to support data processing activities and the maintenance of the information system.

5 Analysis

5.1 Framework Analysis

The synthesized framework when applied to our empirical case emphasized four dimensions.

5.1.1 Organizational Structures and Staffing, Including the Structure of the MIS Unit

This dimension concerns how the organization partitions the responsibilities of development efforts and data management along its hierarchy between the central and local staff. In the case we studied, the central ministry trained staff at the school level to handle local data processing needs while handling their routine tasks in school in what Heeks (1999) dubs "hybrid staff". In supporting the school level users on maintenance and making best use of the information systems, regional staffs were identified as focal points for the schools but the central ministry is yet to fully train them on supporting schools and managing the data systems to relieve the stress on the schools of challenges related to remote support and decentralize that responsibility away form the central staff.

5.1.2 Information Systems Planning, Development and Implementation

The IS development dimension concerns the involvement and level of participation of end users and local units in the planning, development and implementation of the information system. It also includes the planning and coordination of training packages and the support rendered to the end users which always follows the development and implementation of any information system. During the planning stages, research work was conducted at the school level studying the data needs and the flow of information. Stakeholders were interviewed, which contributed to the design of the information system. The design and development of the information system was mostly handled centrally. However, a participatory evaluation of the system was carried out in a couple of schools generating invaluable feedback for the developers. The implementation and training was conducted with the full participation of the regional staff with the ongoing support also their responsibility.

5.1.3 Computer Architecture, Hardware Resources (Management and Acquisition)

The computer architecture in practice is a client/server model as is most common in core-periphery approaches (Heeks 1999). The server is hosted on the internet and accessible to the end users via the web or mobile applications. The purchase of hardware is handled centrally as is their replacement but feedback and suggestions from user experiences is invaluable for the central team to fulfill its coordinating and supportive role.

5.1.4 Data Management

Data management dimension consists of defining the division between the central and end users on the creation, alteration, usage and control of data items within the information system. Data management was mostly handled centrally with the more 'generic' data relevant across all the levels and the more 'specific' data most relevant to the schools. The schools, however, are very homogenous across the country with close similarities in terms of structure, operation and information needs. Introducing specific data needs for each would increase the complexity of the system many fold. This makes the study cited above more important as specific data items common to the schools were introduced (many socio-economic indicators of the student) which has more relevance to the school than the central level.

6 Discussion

Centralized management is deeply rooted in the colonial history of the Gambia. Most sectors, including education, practiced centralized management until the local government act (2002) was passed. The implications of decentralization in such "a historically embedded system" (Sahay et al. 2010, p. 31) is highly dependent on the commitment and will of the top authorities, which, in the case of the Gambia, is very strong.

The central EMIS unit has long used the EMIS for generating statistics and reports for central management. The new individual learner information system offers much more than mere generation of statistics. The system is intended to facilitate administrative processes in the school like student admission and registration, assessment, disciplinary records and class allocations/timetabling. In addition, it is a monitoring tool to aid the regional education directorates in their planning and oversight functions over the schools.

With the introduction of ICT in all public schools, it is highly unlikely that a resource-constrained country will afford to place ICT technicians and information processing clerks in all schools, at least not in the short term. The bulk of the data processing responsibilities, including attendance and assessment, will be placed on the teachers who, others might argue, are already overburdened. The fact that data processing is technically not part of their "TOR" makes this issue complicated. The implications of this contradiction could be devastating for the project as a whole as data processing is an integral part of any information system.

7 Conclusion

The four decentralization dimensions, which we identified and developed into a framework and applied analytically in this case study, are all significant in the process of implementing an individual learner information system vis-a-vis an existing aggregate education management information system. Awareness around IS decentralization and its tradeoffs and interdependencies across different dimensions is critical as public sectors in developing economies move towards collecting more and more granular and individualized education data. The determination and will of education sector authorities to decentralize EMIS functions, to ensure progress towards social inclusion and equitable quality learning, are essential to this end, but is not sufficient on its own.

In the education sector, the push for data is informed by aspirations to make learning socially inclusive and equitable. This will need to go hand-in-hand with decentralization of key EMIS functions. Yet, decentralization of data handling tasks needs to be weighed against the availability of qualified staff at the school level. In theory, decentralization means distribution of power. However, it can also simply mean that overburdened teachers get even more data to collect, without time for reflection and self improvement. Here, we have identified and described four key dimensions along which EMIS can be centralized or decentralized along a continuum:organizational structures and staffing, information systems planning, development and implementation, computer architecture and hardware resources, and data management. We believe decentralization along these dimensions need to be weighted carefully to ensure sustainable local empowerment without overburdening of local staff. Furthermore, decentralization needs to involve all organizational levels, including middle management levels, such as education sector regions, so that they can actively support the new decentralized responsibilities of the level below.

References

Alam, M.: Decentralisation in The Gambia. 129 (2009)

Alvesson, H.M., Viñuela, L.: The gambia case study: ministry of basic and secondary education. In: Institutions Taking Root: Building State Capacity in Challenging Contexts, pp. 71–107. The World Bank (2014). https://doi.org/10.1596/978-1-4648-0269-0_ch3

Chang, M.-H.: Decentralization (2006)

Ein-Dor, P., Segev, E.: Centralization, decentralization and management information systems. Inf. Manag. **1**(3), 169–172 (1978). https://doi.org/10.1016/0378-7206(78)90004-6

Heeks, R.: Centralised vs. Decentralised Management of Public Information Systems, vol. 25 (1999)

Hugoson, M.-Å.: Centralized versus decentralized information systems. In: Impagliazzo, J., Järvi, T., Paju, P. (eds.) HiNC 2007. IAICT, vol. 303, pp. 106–115. Springer, Heidelberg (2009). https://doi.org/10.1007/978-3-642-03757-3_11

King, J.L.:. Centralized vs. Decentralized Computing: Organizational Considerations and Managementttptions (Tecnical Report No. 199). University of California, Irvine. https://escholarship.org/content/qt3sf533d6/qt3sf533d6.pdf (1984)

MoBSE: Education Policy 2016–2030 (2016)

Norton, D.P.: Information systems centralization: the issues. Harv. Bus. Rev. (1972)

Pick, R.A.: Shepherd or servant: centralization and decentralization in information technology governance. Int. J. Manag. Inf. Syst. (IJMIS) **19**(2), 61 (2015). https://doi.org/10.19030/ijmis.v19i2.9173

Rockart, J.F., Leventer, J.S.: Centralization vs decentralization of. Information systems: a critical survey of current literature. Sloan WP 845–76, 23(CISR) **25** (1976)

Sahay, S., Sæbø, J.I., Mekonnen, S.M., Gizaw, A.A.: Interplay of institutional logics and implications for deinstitutionalization: case study of HMIS implementation in Tajikistan. Information Technologies **6**(3), 14 (2010)

Unicef:. UNICEF, Oxford Policy Management, Ministry of Education Malaysia—2019—Review of Education Management Information Systems (EMIS) that track individual students. Unicef (2020)

Including the Excluded: Achieving Representation Through Strengthening Health Information Systems in Lao PDR

Elaine Byrne[1]([⊠]) [iD], Jørn A. Braa[1], John Lewis[2], Sam Boupha[2],
and Chansally Phommavong[3]

[1] HISP Centre, University of Oslo, Oslo, Norway
`elaineb@ifi.uio.no`
[2] HISP Vietnam, Ho Chi Minh, Vietnam
`{johnlewis,samboupha}@hispvietnam.org`
[3] Ministry of Health, Ho Chi Minh, Vietnam
`hsipchansaly@etllao.com`

Abstract. Making it possible to identify and include marginalized population groups in routine health information systems is a means of digital inclusion. Our study examined the question of *How can health information systems be designed and implemented to enable the representation of marginalized population groups*? Through a series of iterative quality improvement assessments (2016–2019) of the health information system in Lao PDR a number of substantial changes were made to the routine health information systems. In our analysis we use Zuboff's notion of representation to illustrate how the development and implementation of a digital register in combination with the family information system enables digital representation of marginalized populations and communities. The impact of the changes implemented over the 4 years has addressed many challenges within the health information that enables representation. But we argue that addressing social exclusion requires more than representation.

Keywords: Lao PDR · DHIS2 · Representation · Improvement science · Zuboff

1 Introduction

Exclusion is a complex and multifaceted condition and focuses attention on what Sen calls the'relational roots of deprivation' [1]. The term exclusion is often used to identify various types of social disadvantage in employment, education, housing, health, and social networks: 'generally it describes the state of disadvantage faced by particular groups who are felt to be removed from mainstream society, and who cannot fully participate in normal life' [2, p.17]. Exclusion means many vulnerable people do not have access to health and social services. Health seeking and care-giving practices are generally poor [2]. Knowledge of their rights and entitlements is often limited and that exacerbates their inaccessibility of health services [3]. Often, vulnerable populations do

© IFIP International Federation for Information Processing 2022
Published by Springer Nature Switzerland AG 2022
Y. Zheng et al. (Eds.): ICT4D 2022, IFIP AICT 657, pp. 171–184, 2022.
https://doi.org/10.1007/978-3-031-19429-0_11

not have the necessary documentation to access the services [4]. Additionally, vulnerability is not a state of being, but a continuum - a pathway that can be taken and exited from as the context changes [5, 6].

The rationale underpinning the implementation research presented in this paper is that to address exclusion from health care services there needs to be awareness and visibility of the situation. A Health Information System (HIS) can be used to identify the excluded. With HIS highlighting or making visible those not serviced by the health facilities the HIS can be used for advocating and influencing decisions and policies for the rights of inclusion of vulnerable populations. From this visibility stakeholders and services can then be mobilized to address the situation by acting effectively on the information being produced.

Making it possible to identify and include marginalized population groups are key aspects of the case of developing and assessing the HIS in Lao PDR. This paper explores the process and results of iterative assessment cycles for the quality improvement of Lao PDR HIS. In describing the process and outcomes of the assessments, we highlight key interventions and the approaches adopted by the Lao PDR Ministry of Health (MoH) to improve the HIS. These interventions included the development of digital registers for immunized children and a family folder project aimed at establishing a register of the entire population. In this way this article highlights the process and actions taken that address the question of: *How can HIS be designed and implemented to enable the representation of marginalized population groups?*

2   Exclusion, Representation and HIS

Worldwide, nearly 230 million children under 5 years old do not have a birth certificate [4]. More than 24 million Indonesian children remaining undocumented [7]. As noted above this lack of documentation is linked with reduced access to health, social services, and education [4, 8]. For Lao PDR it is estimated that less than 90% of all children have been vaccinated for any childhood vaccine [9]. Various strategies have been developed to attempt to guide services to address this gap and improve coverage, such as Reaching Every Child (REC). This has led to a number of community based interventions such as door-to-door vaccination, delivering vaccines beyond infancy, focusing on marginalized populations [10]. Often the process of identifying the unreached is labor intensive. For example, in Kenya low performing facilities were mapped using DHIS2 and Quantum Geographical Information System (QGIS) and then a 3-day door-to-door defaulter tracing by community health volunteers was conducted with defaulters being immunized by a nurse [11]. Additionally, identifying the zero dose children can be difficult to calculate if the target population denominators are not accurate. Challenges related to denominator data often relate to disputes over official census data and changes in the geography of administrative and health subdivisions in countries. This can lead to alternative denominator data being used across programs and between levels of the health system [12]. The challenges for estimating denominators are also attributable to catchment area calculations and care-seeking behaviors [13]. Even when there is a reliable catchment area population estimate using the census people often seek care from health facilities outside their district of residence resulting in some districts having coverage of over 100% and others have very low coverage [13] - this is commonly referred to as the 'numerator/denominator mismatch'.

ICTs have also been argued as a useful means to include excluded or marginalized populations. Heeks discusses how the 'bottom billion' of the world's population can be socially, politically, economically and psychologically excluded and that ICTs can assist in decreasing this exclusion [14]. However despite the proliferation of different community based information systems the majority of routine national HIS have data from the health facilities as the lowest level of data collected [15, 16]. Consequently, data is not captured on those not accessing formal health services. Even for HIS that partially include community sourced data the quality and coverage can mean that data is still missing [17] and the marginalized are still not represented in the formal HIS [18]. However, there are a number of examples where information systems have been historically used to address vulnerability, often with NGO's acting as intermediaries [19]. Improved information infrastructure in these marginalised communities, can lead to better health services because of increased transparency and increased opportunity for political and social pressure. Through a parable (Annapurna wanting somebody to dig her garden, but finding it difficult to choose one of three laborers, as each would be chosen if different criteria, such as poverty, unhappiness and illness, was used to inform the making of the decision) Sen explains how decisions made are dependent on the informational base and indicators selected [1, p. 54]. So the process of IS development clearly determines the picture created and views expressed. Equally important to the information that is included is the information that is excluded.

In our analysis we use Zuboff's [20] notion of representation as derived from her two terms automate and informate, which are used to capture the distinction between technology in general and digital technology specifically. While automating refers to computational power, informating refers to the ability of information technology to represent and textualise work being performed. In Zuboff's analysis, all technologies, digital ones included, come with the potential to automate. What makes digital technologies distinct are their additional potential to also informate and that they do not consume their 'input factors' i.e. data and their outputs (information) may be used as input to open-ended purposes still without consuming the 'input factor'. The 'textualisation' or datafication, is then, typically, an (unintended) bi-product of digital technology. With this, Zuboff recognized a potential for empowerment, user participation and processes of learning. Informate creates the potential for additional uses of digital technology supplementing the intended ones that cater for the immediate automation related efficiency concerns of the users.

3   Setting: Lao PDR HIS

Under the framework of the health sector reform, the Lao PDR MoH approved the introduction of DHIS2 – a web-based, open source software for health information system (HIS) in early 2014 replacing the previous Excel based system [see 21 for more detail]. By the end of 2017, the HIS aggregated data from 9 health programmes and all the public health facilities nationally were collected within DHIS2. Lao PDR also gradually developed modules and sub systems in DHIS2 for a number of additional health program specific digital interventions, such as case based tracking of tuberculosis and HIV, and systems supporting the elimination of malaria. Mother and Child Health (MCH) and Immunization (EPI) are two of the priority programmes in the MoH.

Lao PDR had EPI coverages amongst the lowest in the region[1] with EPI data mainly being used for reporting purposes rather than for action or decision making [22]. EPI continued to use their Excel based reporting in parallel to DHIS2 for several years longer than the other programs (until 2018), despite a Ministerial Decree stating that all data should be integrated in DHIS2. An important reason for the parallel reporting was that the DHIS2 and the Excel systems generated different data and indicators. DHIS2 generated lower values for indicators than the values generated by the long standing Excel based systems for EPI which lead to managers and health workers unsure of which data source to use. Having duplicate data collection systems also increased the burden of data collection and reporting at health facilities.

Additional differences were that DHIS2 is designed to provide health facility service coverage data whereas EPI needs population coverage. The EPI programme also required data, such as vaccines stocks and campaign data, that was not included in DHIS2. There were also data quality problems stemming from the numerous data collection tools health workers needed to consult to generate indicators. For example, to track the vaccination for each child both the child's record at their residence and a chain of records needed to be checked requiring considerable back and forth checking in the facility hierarchy. This process of data collection and calculation of indicators compromised data quality.

4   Methodology

The overall design adopted in this project was *Improvement Science*. Improvement science focuses specifically on healthcare improvement with the goal to determine which improvement strategies work whilst simultaneously assuring effective and safe patient care. *Improvement Science* embraces many of the principles of other research designs such as implementation science, knowledge translation, and action research, but it is specifically designed to focus on what works best in complex situations, such as a healthcare setting. The overriding goal of improvement science is to ensure that quality improvement efforts are based on evidence (the theoretical gap mentioned above) as well as best practices [23]. Like implementation science and action research improvement science makes a specific contribution in the research setting itself. However, improvement science places a strong emphasis on the process of change and more involvement and buy-in from stakeholders is expected than in other research approaches. The rationale being that with increased involvement and capacity development results in more sustainable processes and outcomes. There have been a wide array of approaches that relate to improvement science, such as ' translational research targets, evidence-based care, accreditation and external accountability for quality and safety, risk management, error prevention, organizational development, leadership and frontline enhancement, and complex adaptive systems frameworks' [24]. Our approach was based on The Model for Improvement developed by Associates in Process Improvement [25].

---

[1] https://www.gavi.org/programmes-impact/country-hub/west-pacific/lao-pdr.

Over four years, assessments of the routine health information systems resulted in recommended changes. The process of assessments undertaken was iterative - where results of initiated changes based on previous assessments were evaluated and further improvements made. Results from several assessment cycles are presented in this article. Assessments took place with a different focus annually from 2016 to 2019 (see Table 1), but also used a common assessment framework. Each assessment looked at:

- Legal and policy framework: data governance, coordination, legislation and support
- Human Capacity: training, supportive supervision, back up, guidance and aids
- Standardization: metadata standards, SOPs, analytic dashboard, data quality assurance
- Funding: planning, partners/donors harmonization, costing
- Infrastructure: computers, internet, electricity, mobile phones, 3G
- Data use: reports, feedback, review

The main focus of the assessments was on quality improvement where after each assessment the various stakeholders discussed and agreed on a number of actions to address the challenges or bottlenecks identified. The following year the assessment would identify whether the interventions or activities previously identified had addressed the challenges and if further improvements could be made. The process in general was to use the common assessment framework to review the routine reporting as well as having stakeholder's meetings throughout the assessment. For example, having meetings with stakeholders at Ministry of Health, WHO and the EPI program at central level and then also including some provincial, district and facility visits. For example, in 2018. Luang Prabang and Champasak provinces as well as 6 districts and 8 health facilities in these provinces.

Table 1. Specific focus of evaluation 2016–2019

Year	Focus of assessment
2016	Data quality and governance
2017	MCH
2018	EPI and addressing the parallel data collection systems (DHIS2 and Excel)
2019	Reviewing the previous implementation and whether recommended actions had been taken

were visited. In health facilities, and district and province offices the evaluation team studied all aspects of data registration, collection and reporting as well as routines for data validation and data use. Teams generally comprised representatives from the program under review, WHO, World Bank, MoH and University of Oslo (see Table 2 for details for all years).

In the provinces, the assessment started with a larger meeting where objectives and methods were presented and discussed and a similar meeting was conducted after the assessment to present and discuss findings. Generally, people from the provincial health information unit took part in the assessment at district and facility levels. In the districts, managers and staff from all program areas took part in a joint meeting to review all data collection and reporting routines and challenges before going into the details of the particular focus of the evaluation.

In the health facilities all the facility and village register books and reporting tools were reviewed and there was a discussion and demonstrations on how the registers, tools and data are used. Usually there was a large number of registers (see Fig. 1). Observations and discussions took place on how data was validated and compiled from the various log books at field level and facility level and how this was reported and entered into electronic systems.

5 Findings and Interventions

The main challenges identified and the actions taken each year are summarized in Fig. 3. The actions listed were agreed upon with the MoH and concerned partners during the feedback sessions following the evaluations to address the priority issues raised. Often one action taken would necessitate another action or intervention, such as facility data collection in DHIS2 required addressing the connectivity challenges facility staff had. A number of changes made as a result of these evaluations had a major impact in identifying the excluded population groups from health services. These changes involved the development of a digital register and a family folder.

5.1 Digital Register

The Lao PDR MoH has divided villages into three zones where zone 2 and 3 represents areas that are hard to reach and which are a priority for health programs such as the EPI and MCH. A problem identified with DHIS2 was that reliable area or population based coverage indicators data on immunized children or ANC visits could not be calculated. This was because the data reported was based on the health facility where the child was immunized or ANC attended and not the village where the child or woman came from. In this way only service level coverages could be calculated. The provincial hospitals, for example, carry out a significant number of immunizations and many children immunized are from villages in districts outside the provincial capital.

To address this problem there was a move to case based rather than aggregate data reporting so that individual cases could be linked to areas – or more concretely to a village. This necessitated recording the village the individual was from/living in. This would enable then service provision coverages as well as population based/ geographical based coverage for EPI and MCH. The event capture functionality in DHIS2 was used. Event means that there is one data entry for every time the child comes for immunization. Each case could then be registered with date of birth, sex and vaccines given and linked to the village the child lived in rather than where the place where they received the service.

A similar, but somewhat simpler solution was suggested for the MCH ANC program where only the ANC first visit cases, linked to the village, would be included. This would

Table 2. Meetings and visits conducted as part of annual assessments

Year	Meetings	Observational visits
2016	• Annual DHIS2 review meeting with health program managers, stakeholders, development partners and HISP Vietnam team • Millennium Development Goals (MDGs) Lao PDR status dashboard demo and meeting with all the health departments and stakeholders towards publishing health data for public view • Workshop and meetings on data administration, data collection and verification principle with Central and province health staff, DHIS2 core staff, WHO Lao team members, Development Partners and HISP Vietnam	• 6 provinces • 12 districts • 15 health facilities
2017	• Annual DHIS2 review meeting with health program managers, stakeholders, development partners • Meeting with WHO staff, MOH and development partner on Lao PDR status on UHC (Universal Health coverage) and SDGs (Sustainable Development Goals) • Data quality review workshop with central and province level health manager, WHO staff and HISP Vietnam	• 4 provinces • 8 districts • 12 health facilities
2018	• Annual DHIS2 review meeting with health program managers, stakeholders, development partners • Introduction meeting with EPI department on parallel system and advantage of online system • Review meetings of EPI data collection registers and forms with MOH central level staff, WHO Lao team members, EPI managers and GAVI members • Province and district level data quality meeting with Province and district health managers, WHO Lao team members, Central level MoH Staff	• 3 provinces • 6 districts • 8 health facilities
2019	• Data uses and analysis meeting and workshop for central and province level health program managers • Meeting with EPI, GAVI, WHO Lao team members, MOH staff on EPI data collection review and status • Province and district level data quality meeting with Province and district health managers, WHO Lao team members, Central level MoH Staff	• 2 provinces • 9 districts • 10 health facilities

enable the key ANC related indicators to be calculated and, given that each case would be registered electronically, validated.

In order to achieve this shift in data collection, two challenges needed to be addressed:

1. *A current and up to date village list*: the current 9200 villages in Lao PDR that are included in DHIS2, were the official list and used as enumerator areas for the census, but a standardized list was not in place - different users used different names for the same villages and different programs have different lists. Standardizing the village list was needed.

Fig. 1. Collection of active log books and paper tools in one health center

2. *Connectivity issues and unique patient identifiers:* Internet is not available or is unreliable in most of Lao PDR, but internet would be required for case based reporting. Poor internet connectivity could mean that individuals with similar names could be entered without the system being able to detect the conflict, or the same person could be entered multiple times with slightly different spellings of the name. There is no unique person identifier in Lao PDR. This challenge was addressed by developing and implementing an *offline* case based *event* capture app – a data capture app that could push data to DHIS2 when the Internet was available. Off-line data entry meant that the data could be entered on a laptop and then synced when there was a connection. The offline app is programmed to locally generate unique identification (DHIS2 event UID) for each case, so that when user make any changes in offline mode can be synchronized to online DHIS2 instance and vice versa. If data is purely entered in online, health facility user can synchronize their data locally when they have internet connection. SOPs were created in coordination with MOH staff, EPI department and WHO Team members on duration of data synchronization.

The app was developed by the HISP Vietnam team and implemented in all health facilities in 2 provinces in 2018. The offline app includes the entire list of 9200 villages in Lao PDR with coordinates, so cases can be linked to the correct village. When the Internet is available, the online app can be used. Later evaluations showed that this online feature became the most important part of the app. The app was developed for initially for MCH and offered the potential of identifying for example # deliveries and ANC1 visits per facility/zone. The main purpose was to enable entering of data at the level of collection - previously data was entered at district level which required all the paper records, folders and registers to be transported to the district and often there were too many to carry. So data entry changed from district entry to systematic facility level DHIS2 data entry which is then validated at district level (Fig. 2).

The 2018 evaluation explored the use of parallel systems (Excel and DHIS2) in EPI data collection. The reasons for this as noted above were issues with service versus population coverage, and confusion on which system to use as data from the two were

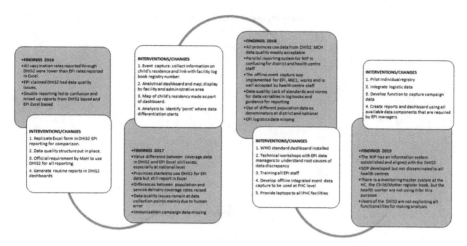

Fig. 2. Timeline of the DHIS2/HIS integrated system in Lao PDR

not the same. During the evaluation it was discovered that in fact data was being exported from DHIS2 to an excel file and that this was being used for the excel calculations, so in fact there was confidence in DHIS2 as a system. By addressing the coverage problem, and ability to work offline, excel was no longer needed nor used as a parallel system.

5.2   Family Folder Project

Another change in the HIS was the use of tracker in DHIS2 to collect family and household data. The family and household data is obtained through an annual paper-based survey conducted by the community health worker for every village. In Lao PDR village boundaries are coterminous with facility catchment boundaries so using the data from the survey facilities generate a household profile for each household in their catchment area. However, in urban areas there are a number of villages that do not match facility level directly and these villages are entered into the system as separate organizational units at district level.

The data from the survey is compared with the census estimates which are calculated for the facilities by the district staff. As illustrated in Fig. 3 most of the households are included in DHIS2.

Additionally, there is a good match with the census estimates and village level survey data in relation to denominators (see Fig. 4). However as can be seen in Fig. 4 there are larger discrepancies in urban areas. This is largely due to the mobility of the urban population, but is also impacted by the migrant workforce.

The challenge of a standardized village list has also been addressed. This list is maintained by the Department of Home Affairs and the MoH is responsible for linking the villages to facilities.

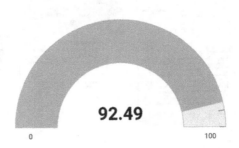

% Members registered vs LSB population
2019 - Lao PDR

92.49

0   100

Fig. 3. Households registered versus census estimates

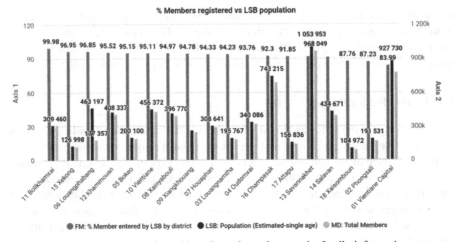

% Members registered vs LSB population

● FM: % Member entered by LSB by district ● LSB: Population (Estimated-single age) ● MD: Total Members

Fig. 4. Comparison of population with registered members on the family information system

6 Discussion

Data about immunized children and pregnant women in each village is now available and these clients are now digitally represented and included in the registers online or offline. But what about the children that have not been immunized? As a director of the GAVI vaccine alliance said when being presented the case based register: "I am not interested in the children in the register", as they have got their vaccines. "I am only interested in those children not in the registers - the zero dose children". 'Zero dose' is defined as children missing one or more doses of vaccination.

Indirectly, by combining the data with the population linked to the villages, the representation of the immunized children could reveal information about those not having been immunized; by combining the number of immunized children with estimated number of children in the villages, areas of low immunization coverage may be identified, and consequently also "zero dose children". The family folder project aiming at digitally representing the entire population is providing a more accurate population number including infants in the villages. As village boundaries are coterminous with catchment areas for facilities all children should then be included in the family survey. Combining the immunization register with the population register will then better enable the identification of the children that not being vaccinated. By combining number of doses given the first month of life with the number of doses being given at the 11th month of life, a drop-out rate of infants missing doses of vaccination, by village, can be calculated, as yet another informating aspect relating to the non-represented. Additionally, with the development of the 'family folder project', all families in all villages and towns in Laos are being registered in a DHIS2 application. The entire population will in this way be digitally represented and enrolled in the census. This development will help develop more accurate population figures for the villages. Linking the family folders to the immunization register will facilitate all newborns being enrolled for immunization and thereby further reducing the zero-dose problem.

However, for digital representation and inclusion for societal transformation to become a reality, there are cultural, social and health service barriers to be overcome. In visiting a health center in rural Laos as part of an evaluation of the information systems, the registers and reports were investigated. The data for ANC clients having had their first visit compared with the estimated number of pregnant women revealed that a significant number of pregnant women had not attended the services. Asking the health workers to what extent they had analyzed the data and notified the low service coverage, and if so, how they had acted upon the data to reach out, identify and enroll the women missing their ANC services. The response was that the women in the areas in question belonged to an ethnic minority group, which had a general low attendance and participation in the health services. Culture, ethnic differences and political issues alongside education and knowledge about health are among the factors creating barriers between marginalized groups and the health services. In this case also, the informating aspects of the representation of those women attending the ANC services, led the attention to those not attending the services. However, contrary to the immunization example, addressing the non-served is not as simple as just identifying them and then providing the services. Needed action would involve overcoming cultural barriers by active health promotion and education among the groups with low participation as well as engaging community leaders and the political levels. The transformative aspects of digital inclusion for social justice are therefore not only about digital representation, but need to be understood through the wider aspects of automating and informating dynamics addressing the societal level.

In relation to addressing the 'zero-dose' by combining the number of immunized children with estimated number of children in the villages, areas of low immunization coverage may be identified, and consequently also "zero dose children". This digital representation was achieved through the combination of automating and informating, which reflected Zuboff's third dilemma of technique, providing new combinations of information and new potentials for use. Providing proactive health services and a receptive population, we have illustrated here that digital representation may lead to the inclusion in terms of provision of health services both for those digitally represented and not represented.

In Zuboff's conceptualizing of informating she highlights three sets of dilemmas: 1) of knowledge stemming from the representation of work performed which risks deskilling workers and meaning being lost or changed; 2) of authority; knowledge affords power and changes in knowledge may change the basis of power; 3) of technique; informating aspects are not fully controllable by management or health services who may initially focus only on those represented, open for unintended consequences of inclusion of those indirectly represented. The transformative aspects of digital inclusion for social justice is therefore not only about digital representation, but needs to be understood through the wider aspects of automating and informating dynamics addressing the societal level. The examples illustrate that digital representation may lead to inclusion of the marginalized at increasing levels of informating and social action; 1) digital representation leads to direct enrollments for health services when included in the immunization or ANC registers, 2) indirect inclusion through informating; data on those digitally represented shed light on those not represented and enable their representation, and 3) informating reveals social in-justice and may lead to collective action at the societal level for inclusion and social justice for the marginalized. Whether the knowledge, power and technique leads to collection action goes beyond digital representation, but without representation it is not possible. In our case, the representation of vaccinated children indirectly helps identify non-vaccinated children, which is further facilitated through the family folder project. Digital representation, in this way, may be seen as digital inclusion of marginalized populations.

The implications for practice are:

- Different denominators are needed for service and population coverage indicators
- Different population denominators can result in different indicators
- Comparisons of data using different denominators enables conversations for better understanding of what the indicators are measuring.
- Confidence in the data is needed for the data to be used.
- Using different sources of data facilitate representation of all families in HIS.

7   Conclusion

The development and implementation of a digital register that could be use offline and online in combination with the family information system has addressed many of the challenges exposed during the annual evaluation of Lao PDR's HIS. Addressing service and population coverage indicators and enabling comparisons of data using census based denominators versus family survey denominator has meant the DHIS2 is now the only system used for EPI and ANC. This saves time for the facility staff but also builds confidence in the HIS. However more broadly it enables representation of all families in DHIS2.

Zuboff's analytical approach may be of equal, if not greater, relevance today as "it may have an even stronger story to tell now than it did when first published" [20,

p. 7] as a result of the expanding scope and reach of digitalization. As illustrated in our examples, digital representation is of direct relevance to marginalized populations and communities, and may be important factors in their societal inclusion and development. The capacity to informate is an open-ended ability for repurposing, aggregation, and further manipulation stemming from the fact that digital representations are not consumed but "renders events, objects, and processes…visible, knowable, and shareable in a new way" [2, p. 9]. However, a two pronged strategy is needed - first is through the creation of awareness and visibility of the situation - representation in the system - and the second through mobilizing the stakeholders and services to address this situation by acting effectively on the information being produced. Overall these strategies can be supported by designing an IS for action - an IS that can be used for advocating and influencing decisions and policies for the rights of inclusion of vulnerable populations.

References

1. Sen, A.: Development as Freedom. Oxford University Press (1999)
2. O'Donnell, P., O'Donovan, D., Elmusharaf, K.: Measuring social exclusion in healthcare settings: a scoping review. Int. J. Equity Health **17**(1), 15 (2018)
3. Scheil-Adlung, X., Kuhl, C.: Social security for all: Addressing inequities in access to health care for vulnerable groups in countries of Europe and Central Asia. In: Social Security Policy Briefings. Social Security Department, International Labour Office Geneva. pp. 47 (2011)
4. United Nations Children's Fund: Every Child's Birth Right: Inequities and Trends in Birth Registration. United Nations Children's Fund (UNICEF), New York (2013)
5. Grabovschi, C., Loignon, C., Fortin, M.: Mapping the concept of vulnerability related to health care disparities: a scoping review. BMC Health Serv. Res. **13**(1), 94 (2013)
6. Beck, E., Madon, S., Sahay, S.: On the margins of the "Information Society": a comparative study of mediation. Inf. Soc. **20**(4), 279–290 (2004)
7. Australia Indonesia Partnership for Justice and Center on Child Protection: Indonesia's missing millions: AIPJ baseline study on legal identity. https://getinthepicture.org/resource/aipj-baseline-study-legal-identity-indonesias-missing-millions (2014). Accessed 12 Apr 2022
8. Setel, P.W., et al.: A scandal of invisibility: making everyone count by counting everyone. Lancet **370**, 1569–1577 (2007)
9. World Health Organization: National Immunization Coverage Scorecards Estimates for 2017. World Health Organization. Available from: https://apps.who.int/iris/bitstream/handle/10665/276969/WHO-IVB-18.12-eng.pdf (2018). Accessed 12 Apr 2022
10. World Health Organization: Reaching every district (RED): a guide to increasing coverage and equity in all communities in the African region. A. World Health Organization. Available from: https://apps.who.int/iris/bitstream/handle/10665/260112/9789290233954-eng.pdf (2017). Accessed 12 Apr 2022
11. Shikuku, D.N., et al.: Door - to - door immunization strategy for improving access and utilization of immunization Services in Hard-to-Reach Areas: a case of Migori County, Kenya. BMC Public Health **19**(1), 1064 (2019)
12. Adane, A., et al.: Routine health management information system data in Ethiopia: consistency, trends, and challenges. Glob. Health Action **14**(1), 1868961 (2021)
13. Maïga, A., et al.: Generating statistics from health facility data: the state of routine health information systems in Eastern and Southern Africa. BMJ Glob Health **4**(5), e001849 (2019)
14. Heeks, R.: ICTs and the World's Bottom Billion in Development Informatics Short Paper. Centre for Development Informatics, IDPM, SED, University of Manchester, UK (2009)

15. Chaulagai, C.N., et al.: Design and implementation of a health management information system in Malawi: issues, innovations and results. Health Policy Plan. **20**(6), 375–384 (2005)
16. Krickeberg, K.: Principles of health information systems in developing countries. Health Inf. Manag. J. **36**(3), 8–20 (2007)
17. Kanjo, C.: Pragmatism or policy: implications on health information systems success. The Electronic Journal Of Information Systems In Developing Countries **48**(1), 1–20 (2011)
18. Byrne, E., Sahay, S.: Participatory design for social development: a South African case study on community-based health information systems. Inf. Technol. Dev. **13**(1), 71–94 (2007)
19. Madon, S.: International NGOs: networking, information flows and learning. J. Strateg. Inf. Syst. **8**, 251–261 (1999)
20. Zuboff, S.: In the age of the smart machine: the future of work and power. Basic Books (1988)
21. Chu, A., Phommavong, C., Lewis, J., Braa, J., Senyoni, W.: Applying ICT to health information systems (HIS) in low resource settings: implementing DHIS2 as an integrated health information platform in Lao PDR. In: Choudrie, M.J., Islam, S., Wahid, F., Bass, J.M., Priyatma, J.E. (eds.) Information and Communication Technologies for Development: 14th IFIP WG 9.4 International Conference on Social Implications of Computers in Developing Countries, ICT4D 2017, Yogyakarta, Indonesia, May 22-24, 2017, Proceedings, pp. 536–547. Springer International Publishing, Cham (2017). https://doi.org/10.1007/978-3-319-59111-7_44
22. World Health Organization Regional Office for the Western Pacific: Overview of Lao Health System Development 2009–2017. Manila, Philippines (2018)
23. Shojania, K.G., Grimshaw, J.M.: Evidence-based quality improvement: the state of the science. Health Aff. **24**(1), 138–150 (2005)
24. Grol, R., Baker, R., Moss, F.: Quality Improvement Research: Understanding the Science of Change in Health Care. BMJ Publishing Group Ltd, pp. 110–111 (2002)
25. Langley, G.L., et al.: The Improvement Guide: A Practical Approach to Enhancing Organizational Performance, 2nd edn. Jossey-Bass Publishers, San Francisco (2009)

Human-Computer Interaction for Ethical Value Exchange and Social Inclusion

Where There is No CISO

Johan Ivar Sæbø[1]([⊠]) [iD], Andre Büttner[1] [iD], Nils Gruschka[1] [iD], Bob Jolliffe[2], and Austin McGee[2]

[1] University of Oslo, Oslo, Norway
{johansa,andrbut,nilsgrus}@ifi.uio.no
[2] HISP Centre, University of Oslo, Oslo, Norway
{bob,austin}@dhis2.org

Abstract. Globally, health information security and associated topics have received considerable attention from both professionals and the academic community. The literature on the threats and mitigations when it comes to developing countries is scarce, and tends to focus on issues such as cryptographic techniques for secure safe data transmission or patients' perceptions of data confidentiality. However, investigation of health information threats in relation to the local context has received less attention. In this paper we reflect on a long-term and global action research project that presents different perspectives on information security. Operating in environments of absent or obsolete relevant jurisdiction, poor institutional capacity for adherence and oversight, and limited awareness of appropriate security and confidentiality issues, we note unique security and confidentiality threats "where there is no CISO". We reflect on mitigations adopted over the years to counter rising threats, and provide recommendations for practice and further research in this regard.

Keywords: Information security · Digital platforms · Data privacy · Data confidentiality

1 Introduction

Information security is usually defined by the so-called CIA triad, i.e. the properties confidentiality, integrity, and availability, or more precisely the safeguarding of these properties. Examples of security-critical situations in the context of health information systems (HIS) are: medical diagnoses shall only be accessible to authorized health personnel and shall be kept confidential otherwise; an electronic medical prescription shall not be changed, i.e. the integrity of the data set must be ensured; in case of an emergency immediate access to medical data (e.g., possible drug allergies) is important, therefore, uninterrupted availability of the health service is required. Violation of the security goals in the aforementioned examples can have different consequences from blackmailing with the threat of publishing medical conditions (or reputation loss due to actual publication) to illness or death due to taking the wrong drug or dose. The reasons for violation of information security are diverse. It can be caused by natural

© IFIP International Federation for Information Processing 2022
Published by Springer Nature Switzerland AG 2022
Y. Zheng et al. (Eds.): ICT4D 2022, IFIP AICT 657, pp. 187–200, 2022.
https://doi.org/10.1007/978-3-031-19429-0_12

disasters, accidental misbehavior, malicious actions or other causes. The goal of information security is the development and implementation of protective measures against these violations. Typical examples are redundancies of services, backup of critical data, control mechanisms to restrict access to data, cryptographic measures like encryption or digital signatures to ensure confidentiality and integrity, and network monitoring to detect and prevent remote attacks.

This paper reports from a large international effort to strengthen national health information systems in developing countries. It centers around the development and implementation of the open source platform DHIS2. Development of DHIS2 is coordinated by the University of Oslo, Norway, and implemented in a range of countries around the world [1]. As a web-based system, DHIS2 is typically set up on local servers in the respective countries, or deployed using commercially available cloud services [2]. As a digital platform in the public sphere, DHIS2 also potentially has a "dark side" [3]. While issues of confidentiality and adverse effects of user data have seen some exploration, for instance related to behaviorall data [4], we in this paper look at aspects of information security as such platforms are developed and implemented globally, also where the context offers challenges considerably different than what has been hitherto examined.

Systems using DHIS2 contain various types of health data, from aggregate statistics to registries containing personal health data. Security issues can thus be broadly categorized in three groups; those relating to the data itself, such as correct handling of confidential data; those relating to hosting the system, including server monitoring and back-up plans; and those related to the software platform and its development, such as community contributions through apps, ensuring secure code, and routines for handling threats. Building on the authors' own involvement for the past two decades, we reflect on the special nature of the project, events and threats experienced, and the measures employed to counter them.

Our title is a nod to David Werner's classic book "Where there is no doctor: A Village Health Care Handbook" [5], which has been a strong influence and motivation for the HISP project in it's aims to strengthen primary health care in communities around the world. It is also an acknowledgment that in many of the settings where we are involved, there is in fact no CISO (Chief Information Security Officer). While we do not aim to provide here a "handbook" for resource-constrained settings, we are intrigued by the apparent lack of focus on contextual health information security issues in the literature.

Our research questions are; What is the nature of information security threats in public health information systems in the Global South, and how can they be mitigated?

2   Methods

This research builds on two main methods. First, we as authors are involved in the HISP project, which coordinates the development of DHIS2 and its implementation in several countries. Working with implementing agencies, typically ministries of health, we have nearly 2 decades of action research from which to reflect on the topic of this study. Second, some of the authors are conducting a comprehensive scoping review of information security and confidentiality issues in health in developing countries. While the scoping review is not completed at the time of writing, it forms the basis for the included review of relevant literature here. We start by describing the process of the review.

2.1 Scoping Review

We have been conducting a scoping review [6] to get an overview of the research that has been done regarding security and privacy of health information systems with particular focus on developing countries. The review was split into four different stages: (1) collecting articles, (2) reviewing titles and abstracts, (3) reviewing full-texts and (4) summary of results.

In the first stage, a search query was defined that was used against relevant databases to collect a list of potential articles. The query was constructed as a combination of various IT-security and privacy terms, different health terms and terms describing the developing context and a list of low- and middle-income countries. The general structure of the query used was as follows: (<security-terms> OR <privacy-terms>) AND <health-terms> AND <developing-countries-terms>. After applying the query to the Web of Science, Scopus, IEEE and ACM digital libraries, putting the results into one list and removing duplicates we had a list of 3486 articles. All titles and abstracts were then read by at least two reviewers each for inclusion or not. When there was a conflict between the decision of the two reviewers, this was solved by a third reviewer. In order to be included, the titles and abstracts should indicate that the article addresses security or privacy in the context of health IT-systems for developing countries. Articles written in a language other than English were excluded. The same applies to articles that were only a summary of conference proceedings or that clearly did not cover all relevant topics. This procedure resulted in a list of 198 included articles for full-text reviewing.

At the time of writing, the full-text review by two reviewers has not been completed. Even though the review is not completed, we lean on the preliminary results as they provide interesting insights into the research trends and can be compared to the reflections coming out of our long-term engagement in the field of health information systems in developing countries.

2.2 Reflections from Action Research

As practitioner-researchers engaged in both developing and maintaining the DHIS2 software, as well as providing direct or indirect support to tens of implementations of it in the health sector in the Global South, we categorise our main research approach as action research [7]. We did not begin by framing a research project with the aim of collecting data on security incidents. In that sense it is a reflection on past activities which were geared primarily towards supporting implementations and providing troubleshooting support as requested. The security related incidents emerged through these activities in a non-systemic way and alongside many other issues. The DHIS2 core team at the time did not maintain any sort of incident register.

For this study, we draw on two perspectives of this action research; first, the larger Health Information Systems Programme (HISP), a project not bound in time or space, but an AR-project with global reach and of a networked nature [8]; second, a range of more specific engagements with formalized structures typically focused on collaboration with ministries of health in the Global South. For the sake of anonymity we do not list countries or partners here. Taken together, our empirical basis spans tens of countries over several continents for 15 years, where we hold and have held various roles. Most important for this study has been that some of the authors have been active in helping countries with all issues related to hosting, held training sessions and workshops related to hosting and information security management, and been the first line of support when countries need assistance with their DHIS2 instances. One of the authors is also engaged with improving security management internally in HISP, working to improve not just the software but the routines and structures appropriate for handling the myriad security issues of a global network.

3   Related Literature

Information security is a broad discipline that covers different levels from software implementation details to organizational and governmental security management. Confidentiality, integrity and availability (CIA) are important properties to protect software systems and in particular its users [9]. The term confidentiality refers to the goal of making data available to authorized parties using cryptography and authentication. Integrity means that it must be ensured that data has not been modified without being noticed. The goal of availability is to make sure that applications and data are accessible and thus to avoid downtime. Similarly, user awareness and acceptance for information security is critical, and capacity building about security risks when using digital systems is important [10]. In particular, health information is very sensitive and requires the highest security standards [11]. A number of regulations have been developed in response to this, such as the EU General Data Protection Regulation (GDPR)[1] or the US Health Insurance Portability and Accountability Act of 1996 (HIPAA)[2] to protect their citizens.

We now turn to findings from the in-process scoping review. A main observation is that there is a large and growing literature related to information security originating in the global south. However, a large part of this deals little with contextual factors and focuses on technical solutions with global applicability. One strand of the literature concerns development of security protocols and cryptography (see for example [12, 13]). Another strand looks at the potential of blockchain technology, which can have a role to play in fragmented health information systems which plague countries both rich and poor (see for example [14, 15]).

Of studies that engage with the development context, many point out that awareness and skills around information security vary greatly, with several pointing out that this is generally lacking. Jack et al. [16] conducted a survey among health care providers in South Africa on information privacy and security, and found that many are ignorant or lack the ability to follow even simple info security procedures. A study from Sri Lanka found that security awareness was actually quite good among health staff, but that their less secure behavior contradicts with their actual concerns [17]. A survey of 15

---

[1] https://eur-lex.europa.eu/eli/reg/2016/679/oj.

[2] https://www.govinfo.gov/app/details/CRPT-104hrpt736/CRPT-104hrpt736.

countries in Africa, Asia, and the Americas on HIV clinics notes that some sites do not backup their data regularly [18]. Gesicho et al. [19] does not cover security explicitly, but finds that, despite increased activity to implement national health data warehouses in developing countries, little attention has been paid in these implementations to ethical issues, including providing data confidentiality and security.

A second strand of studies look at the legal framework, its existence, its relevance, and how it is enforced with various sanctions. Namara et al. [20] find that only a few countries in Africa have developed comprehensive legal frameworks and have meaning-ful enforcement policies. Interestingly, they do point out that privacy values are cultural, and differ significantly across countries. They fail to provide any examples of this how-ever. Being more specific, they mention how lack of oversight leads health staff to ignore regulations by for instance conversing around patients on facebook and whatsapp, and in general store data outside the patients' jurisdictions. Related to the relevance of legal framework, Antonio et al. [21] looks at health information privacy in the Philippines and concludes that technological development has outpaced policy and practice in this regard. In a review of security assessment frameworks such as HIPAA, Gerson and Shava [22] examines the applicability to Namibia's public health sector and calls for security controls to conform with international standards.

One notable topic on which little is written is security incidents, apart from anecdotal reference to data loss and virus more generally. Antonio et al. [21] mentions a few cases from the Philippines where for example videos from students attending operations were publicly circulated. Moreover, some attacks on health records in India were addressed by Misra et al. [12]. There are some studies that contextualize security management. For instance, a delay tolerant architecture, with emphasis on latency, is found to be important in resource-constrained countries [23]. Pankomera and van Greunen [24] does point to some of the challenges in developing countries, such as poor funding and infrastructure, and a shortage of qualified staff. They also point to natural hazards such as floods, fires, tornados, which can be a larger threat to physical security infrastructure than in more resourced environments. A relevant contextual finding is that as health staff in general do not have access to computers, they use memory sticks for their personal files, introducing malware to their office computers [25]. On the impact of development agencies, Hai et al. [26] looked at how the short-term funding of development projects can negatively impact confidentiality and security. When donor-funded special HIV clinics closed down at the end of the project, patients had to shift to general clinics which were seen as not adhering to the same data confidentiality standards, negatively impacting the patients. Khan and Hoque point out that Bangladesh is lacking a centralized method of identification such as the social security number, making it difficult to link data from separate databases. They propose an approach to solve this problem in a secure and privacy preserving manner [27].

4   Empirical Findings

The project from which we report, the Health Information Systems Programme (HISP), has its roots in participatory action research in South Africa in the 90s. It is a global net-work engaged in software development and implementation with stakeholders, typically ministries of health in developing countries, to strengthen HIS. Over the last two decades, the network has grown globally, and the software developed has progressed from an early standalone desktop application to a flexible, web-based HIS platform called DHIS2, now in use in more than 70 countries. Participatory approaches are still applied to both software development and systems implementation [28]. The University of Oslo, Norway, is leading the development, and is also supporting, sometimes extensively, the implementation of DHIS2 in country HIS'. Our case then, is not only of a software developer, but also of a community who are morally, and sometimes also formally, engaged in country HIS implementation activities. This places a special responsibility on the community given that many of the implementing countries have comparatively weak institutions, and poor information security management in the public sector. We now move to some observations from the last decade, coinciding with the move from desktop to online technology, and an increase in scale and scope of the implementation activities.

The shift that happened from around 2011 from the earlier version of DHIS as a desktop system towards a DHIS2 web-based system that ran over the public internet brought with it human resource and physical infrastructure challenges which few countries were well positioned to address. The IT staff in ministries of health and the technical support from regional support entities by and large did not have the linux technical system administration skills nor the organisational structures to effectively manage security. Critically, even today, there are very few country deployment teams who have amongst them a defined security role of any sort. This has led to a reality that most deployments live with a considerable amount of unmanaged risk. A significant one in many deployments is the over-dependence on a single person who has all the knowledge and all the keys to the system. In risk identification exercises carried out in three countries, this emerged as the highest scoring risk in each. Given this, the actual incidents of data loss, exposure or breach have been relatively few. Below is a short summary of typical incidents:

4.1 Some Incidents We Are Aware of

The following is a short list of incidents which are in some way security related which have occurred in the past decade. Note that we (the authors) are not actively maintaining any production DHIS2 system. Some of us are involved in advising, training and occasionally assisting with incident response. We are not at liberty to disclose details which would allow the system to be identified.

4.1.1 Physical Infrastructure Related

In one country the national Health Management Information System (HMIS) was running on a server in a national government data centre. One evening there was a fire caused by an overloaded electrical connection and the server was badly damaged. The disk on which the data was stored was apparently unreadable. In the aftermath of the fire it was discovered that the Ministry of Health had no functioning backup of the data that was less than six months old.

In another country, the Ministry of Health hosted the national system in a purpose built data centre within the Ministry main building. The building had an ongoing problem with rodents and at one stage the rodents penetrated the data centre. Intermittent faults, breakdowns and performance degradation was finally, on physical inspection, traced to rodent damage to the insulation on network cables.

Where systems have been implemented on physical infrastructure, for example in ministry or government data centres, there have also been challenges related to the management and monitoring of the surrounding network environment (for example domain name services) and the reliability of the internet connection. It has been observed in a number of settings that the single internet connection to the service provider is shared by both the servers in the data centre and also all of the office dwellers in what is often a multi-storey, multi-ministry building. With the result that there is massive congestion during working hours effectively rendering the system unusable from the outside.

4.1.2 Cloud Hosted Systems

Whereas it is clear that systems can be fragile when hosted in poorly commissioned or poorly managed physical infrastructure, just moving them to "the cloud" has not been without its own risks. A handful of incidents stand out over the past few years.

In one case an external consultant was providing technical support by managing a national HMIS on a VPS from a commercial cloud infrastructure provider. At the end of his contract, after what seems to have been a misunderstanding over whether the country had brought up to date backups on-shore, the consultant deleted the VPS, resulting in the loss of one year's data.

In another case, a Ministry of Health in a country set up their own account with a cloud VPS provider and secured funding for one year to provision a VPS for running both the national HMIS and an HIV/AIDs patient monitoring system. At the end of the year when the bill became due, it was discovered that no budgetary provision had been made for renewal. The services were cut off and remained inaccessible for approximately 6 weeks while the government department scrambled to find alternative payment sources to cover the bill. (There have been a number of variations on this same scenario over the past few years, where the Ministry of Health have temporarily lost access to their systems and data).

There are other issues which are more particular to the geo-political context of the systems and system owners. Most of the commercial cloud providers operate off a credit card payment system. One of the authors has direct experience of trying and failing to open cloud based accounts from various West African countries and also from India. The transactions were automatically failed without explanation, but presumably linked to the origin IP address. When the same transaction was made through a VPN back through Europe, it succeeded. When the same "trick" was tried by a colleague using a local West African credit card it proved impossible to open an account. The commercial world of private cloud hosting is not a flat world and all credit cards are not created equal.

We have also seen cases where countries have been denied access to commercial cloud services (and SSL/TLS certificates) due to economic sanctions.

An unusual event in 2012 confirmed that the laws of physics and geography can still play a part in the modern age. Following the successful installation of the Kenya system on Linode in 2010, Rwanda also rolled out a national DHIS2 system in 2011, but this time hosted locally within the MOH. One morning a ship trailed anchor through the harbour of Mombasa and snagged the undersea fibre optic cable linking Kenya to the world. The Kenya system was effectively offline for a week. During that same week the connectivity to the Rwanda system was excellent, particularly as the network within the country was generally quieter than normal.

4.1.3 Security Breaches

There have been numerous incidents of data exposure due to misconfiguration of database access control or breach of the server backend through compromised ssh user accounts. We have seen no evidence to date that the data itself was targeted in any of these cases. Of course we cannot conclude this with any certainty, but we haven't seen any obvious subsequent use of the data (e.g. for extortion). We can guess that, particularly given the low resource environment, the commercial value of the data is not sufficiently high to attract more determined attackers with criminal intent to engage in identity theft or ransomware attacks. Though, given the political importance of many of these national systems, the possibility of ransomware attacks is a very real concern. Given that many DHIS2 implementations are in areas experiencing significant internal and external conflict, there is also a real dimension of concern that attackers might seek out personal data for purposes that might threaten their physical rather than financial well-being.

What we have seen in all of the breaches that we know about is that the attackers have seen the machine as a more attractive target than the data, being recruited into bit-coin mining or being taken over to potentially attack other systems. It should be noted that intrusion detection systems of any sort are usually absent, so there is no definitive way to claim that data has not been targeted.

Examples of known deliberate security breaches:

- Successful attacks on the backend using ssh. In one case we know that a superuser account was legitimately created in the afternoon and credentials were shared with the new user over the mobile phone (whatsapp or email). Later that evening there were three successful logins from two different countries (China and France). The account had been setup to allow password authentication. Given that the user was an administrator, effectively full access to the machine had been gained by one or more parties.
- Zero-day vulnerabilities. A critical vulnerability was discovered in March of 2017 in the Apache Struts library that is used within DHIS2. It was a particularly nasty vulnerability that potentially gave an attacker the ability to execute arbitrary commands on the server. The vulnerability was being actively exploited around the world and a number of DHIS2 systems were effected. Although a patch was produced by the DHIS2 core developer team within 24 h, they did not at that time have a formal process for dealing with such events so there was some delay between patching and announcing publicly (during which time there was vigorous internal discussion on what action to take regarding public disclosure). Even after patches were released and announcements made publicly, we were receiving reports for some months afterwards of un-patched systems getting attacked.

Again we don't believe that systems affected by either of the above were deliberately targeted for their data, but cannot prove either way.

Actors who are really interested in the data have not always had to rely upon attacking the system physically or with code. One country has reported that it is a common practice amongst foreign backed NGOs to recruit people from within the public health service (with credentials in the system) in order to access data which they would not otherwise have had access to. Processes around user management, particularly the disabling of user accounts on leaving of the service are usually absent.

5 Discussion

Our point of departure was a review of relevant literature on information security in the health sector in developing contexts. Our study adds to all the strands of the literature identified earlier. In particular, we highlight more detailed accounts of how for instance infrastructural and environmental hazards are significant [24].

5.1 Incidents and Nature of Threats

As discussed above, we are not aware of any significant targeted breaches of production DHIS2 systems or the data they contain. The rapid adoption and high profile of large-scale DHIS2 implementations addressing the COVID-19 pandemic has likely increased the size, value, and visibility of security penetration for systems built upon DHIS2, increasing the likelihood that a serious breach might be perpetrated in the future.

The nature of threats do not seem to spring out of any perceived value of the data itself, though ransom could be an issue as the data is necessary for the functioning of the health services. What has been documented is more about using the servers for other purposes, i.e. the hardware and processing power is more attractive than the data. Access to data is a concern due to the role of foreign organizations, who may be interested in the data for reporting or research purposes, where access can be gained without necessarily having the formalities in place.

This empirical observation (which we cannot readily prove) that attackers seem not to be trying to get at the data is not a reason to be complacent. Even if we theorize that the financial value of the data is low, we also need to take into account that the consequences of abuse of data relating to extremely vulnerable individuals who are somehow marginalised or living on the edge of legality in society can be severe.

5.2 Hosting Issues

When deploying a service, one of the most important questions is: shall the service be hosted locally on our own hardware or shall we rent resources at a cloud provider? Since the introduction of Amazon Web Services in 2006, cloud computing has become the most widespread hosting platform. More and more small, medium and large enterprises are outsourcing their resources to platforms such as Google, Microsoft and of course Amazon, who is still the market leader. Cloud computing promises mainly economic advantages including reduced investment costs, easy self-service setup, and rapid scalability of resources. However, in addition cloud computing has many security benefits, at least when operated professionally. For example, the large cloud providers' data centers have very good redundancies in terms of power supply and Internet connectivity and high standards regarding physical access to the servers. Further, they offer "standard" security measures, like backup, anti-virus scanning, firewalling etc. as easy to use services and usually for an additional fee.

HISP implementers have explored these cloud hosted Virtual private Server (VPS) options since the early days of DHIS2 going "live" on the internet. When the DHIS2 was rolled out nationally in Kenya in 2010 it was hosted on a VPS from a company called Linode. Besides using the large cloud providers, DHIS2 implementers have a long history of working with smaller providers such as Linode, Dediserve and Contabo who all offer various niche advantages. For example Dediserve allowed the setting up of an account without a credit card which had proved to be a major stumbling block for government procurement working with the larger providers. Contabo offers rock bottom prices which have proven extremely popular in Africa.

Another phenomenon that has emerged in recent years is the rise of private companies adding value to the basic cloud VPS and offering DHIS2-as-a-service.

Despite the many touted (and actual) benefits of the new cloud business models, as we saw in the cases above, country systems which have been deployed on commercial cloud environments have faced different types of problems. There is still a risk of data loss without a costed and tested backup plan. Security still needs to be managed, but the types of risk to be managed are different. For example a missing budget item for cloud "rent" can lead to unavailability of the system.

As an illustration of the complexity of factors around this question, one author recalls attending a workshop of WAHO (the West African Health Organisation) on server management in Bobo, Burkina Faso, 2018. Of the ten or so WAHO member states who were represented in the meeting, they were split down the middle on the current state and future plans. One half were hosting systems physically in the country and were without exception looking forward to moving to the cloud. The other half were hosted on the cloud, which they, again without exception, viewed as temporary contingency as they aspired to bring the systems back into the country.

5.3 User Data

The management and protection of users in the system (mostly employee data) has received very little attention, including until quite recently in the software itself. There is a growing awareness of the obligation to protect vulnerable groups in the health sector, like HIV+, sex workers, refugees etc., and in general for patient data. However user data, including telephone numbers, email, internal messages etc. have not been seen as high value data and have sometimes been available indiscriminately to any other user of the system. This should be a cause of considerable concern. In particular aggregate routine reporting systems which contain no individual patient data are generally considered non-sensitive, yet they contain details of often 10s of thousands of health workers. In addition to the potential exposure of the personal information of these users themselves, personal information such as phone number and email could be abused to conduct phishing attacks against system administrators. This could in theory allow unprivileged users to maliciously gain access to credentials providing them access to much more sensitive information and controls within the system. The exposure of user details to other users of the system has been removed from recent versions of the software, but this type of data has not received significant attention as a privacy concern or as a vector for attack on the larger system.

5.4 The Need for Global Awareness

The role of funders of health information system projects has also been given limited attention in relation to security. The core DHIS2 development team works to develop the DHIS2 software platform, supporting increasing numbers of high-profile implementations around the world. The organic growth of DHIS2 software complexity and global adoption yielded a culture lacking in many fundamental security controls within the core development team. This has largely been the result of limited resources, and limited interest from funding organizations in allocating those resources to champion security practices in a context which undervalues them. Largely as a result of muted interest in and awareness of security within the governments and international development organizations implementing and funding DHIS2, the need for strong security practices and policies has not been emphasized within the core team. Additionally, the nature of DHIS2 as an open-source, freely available software platform provided without warranty or guarantee has limited the political and financial pressures which often incentivize commercial enterprise software products to reduce their own legal risk by investing in security practices.

There is a need for leadership within the global health implementation and vendor communities. The identification of security risks and pressure to limit them have to date not been championed by implementing countries or funding organizations. This dearth of conventional incentive should not reduce the moral obligation of community members such as DHIS2 to push for increased security and privacy controls. A small set of high-impact changes have the potential to significantly reduce security risks in production software implementations and increase awareness of those risks amongst implementers and funders.

6   Conclusion

The main conclusion is that, consistent with the literature above, we have found there are a range of organisational factors, infrastructure fragilities and perhaps cultural factors related to risk acceptance which conspire to make it difficult to adequately secure health information systems in many developing countries. We have conjectured that the low financial value of the data might be a factor in explaining why attacks on such systems have not been more widespread.

To add to the difficulty, the DHIS2 software itself has been a complex and difficult system to maintain securely, even by experienced implementers. Great strides have been made in recent years in improving the development process as described above. One positive indication of progress has been the different impact of the Apache Struts vulnerability in 2017, and the more recent and equally critical log4shell[3] vulnerability which was discovered in December 2021. Whereas the former created considerable chaos and a scramble to reach consensus on a response from the core team, by the time of the latter in December 2021 there was a team ready to mitigate and manage communication and a vulnerability management plan to follow.

But the expansion of the global project and subsequent "industrialization" of the software development process has in some ways moved us away from the strong participatory tradition of the early years. One consequence of this has been that developers are perhaps only weakly aware of the security challenges in the field. The security challenges are so enormous and growing, that it is only through a stronger collaborative and informed effort, that the software development process itself can better support the software implementation process. A drive towards increasingly sophisticated digital technology risks leading to a DHIS2 that is increasingly difficult to manage and secure in practice.

As a leader in the public health space, the DHIS2 core development team endeavors to champion security within HISP as well as in the larger community. Within the past year the team has embarked on this journey by creating and implementing thorough software vulnerability management and transparent public disclosure processes, some of the first in the sector. In addition, two experienced information security managers have been recruited to serve in the CISO role within the University of Oslo. This role will have the mandate to promote secure development and implementation practices within the core team and more broadly within the international development and global public health ecosystem.

Having dedicated CISO roles both at the HISP Centre of the University of Oslo, which coordinates the development of DHIS2, and amongst system implementer teams will not necessarily solve these problems, but the hope is that they will reinforce the effort to bring these into view and provide more strategic and systemic responses.

In summary, documentation of the nature and prevalence of security threats against health information systems in developing contexts is under-developed. Security incidents and risks are not well understood, largely due to limited understanding and awareness of security in the organizations and government departments implementing health information systems. The increasing prevalence of individual data in the systems and the high-profile use of them to address, as an example, the global COVID-19 pandemic are likely to increase the risk of malicious security breaches. In addition to malicious action, accidental confidentiality, integrity, and availability degradation continues to be a cause for concern. More study of security risks and mitigations in this context is needed, as is increased awareness and advocacy from stakeholders in the public health space.

References

1. Adu-Gyamfi, E., Nielsen, P., Sæbø, J.: The dynamics of a global health information systems research and implementation project. In: Proceedings of the 17th Scandinavian Conference on Health Informatics, Oslo, Norway, 12–13 November (2019)

---

[3] https://www.fortinet.com/blog/threat-research/critical-apache-log4j-log4shell-vulnerability-what-you-need-to-know.

2. Jolliffe, B., Poppe, O., Adaletey, D., Braa, J.: Models for online computing in developing countries: issues and deliberations. Inf. Technol. Dev. **21**(1), 151–161 (2015). https://doi.org/10.1080/02681102.2014.902354

3. Nicholson, B., Nielsen, P., Saebo, J.: Special issue: digital platforms for development. Inf. Syst. J. **31**(6), 863–868 (2021). https://doi.org/10.1111/isj.12364

4. Zuboff, S.: The Age of Surveillance Capitalism: The Fight for a Human Future at the New Frontier of Power. PublicAffairs, New York (2019)

5. Werner, D., Thuman, C., Maxwell, J.: Where there is no doctor: a village health care handbook. Hesperian Health Guides (2020)

6. Arksey, H., O'Malley, L.: Scoping studies: towards a methodological framework. Int. J. Soc. Res. Methodol. **8**(1), 19–32 (2005). https://doi.org/10.1080/1364557032000119616

7. Baskerville, R.L.: Distinguishing action research from participative case studies. J. Syst. Info. Tech. **1**(1), 24–43 (1997). https://doi.org/10.1108/13287269780000733

8. Braa, J., Monteiro, E., Sahay, S.: Networks of action: sustainable health information systems across developing countries. MIS Quarterly **28**(3), 337 (2004). https://doi.org/10.2307/251 48643

9. Solomon, M.G., Chapple, M.: Information security illuminated. Jones and Bartlett Publishers (2004)

10. Siponen, M.T.: A conceptual foundation for organizational information security awareness. Inf. Manag. Comput. Secur. **8**(1), 31–41 (2000). https://doi.org/10.1108/09685220010371394

11. Hulkower, R., Penn, M., Schmit, C.: Privacy and confidentiality of public health information. In: Magnuson, J.A., Dixon, B.E. (eds.) Public Health Informatics and Information Systems Health Informatics HI, pp. 147–166. Springer, Cham (2020). https://doi.org/10.1007/978-3-030-41215-9_9

12. Misra, M.K., Chaturvedi, A., Tripathi, S.P., Shukla, V.: A unique key sharing protocol among three users using non-commutative group for electronic health record system. J. Discret. Math. Sci. Cryptogr. **22**(8), 1435–1451 (2019). https://doi.org/10.1080/09720529.2019.1692450

13. Kamble, P., Gawade, A.: Digitalization of healthcare with IoT and cryptographic encryption against DOS attacks. In: 2019 International Conference on contemporary Computing and Informatics (IC3I), pp. 69–73 (2019 Dec). https://doi.org/10.1109/IC3I46837.2019.9055531

14. Sari, P.K., Yazid, S.: Design of blockchain-based electronic health records for indonesian context: narrative Review. https://ieeexplore.ieee.org/abstract/document/9255571?casa_t oken=aPIf9bowQucAAAAA:JOJd5MYSIOa6l2Hn3ic_i0HgOevIFgCyvVYyzY6I9G8k1 eKXijDkYBWkCHvoUEgz_qb7WuZ33A. Accessed 17 Jan 2022

15. Osebe, S., et al.: Enabling care continuity using a digital health wallet. In: 2019 IEEE International Conference on Healthcare Informatics (ICHI), pp. 1–7 (Jun 2019). https://doi.org/10.1109/ICHI.2019.8904625

16. Jack, C., Singh, Y., Mars, M.: Pitfalls in computer housekeeping by doctors and nurses in KwaZulu-Natal: no malicious intent. BMC Med. Ethics **14**(Suppl 1), S8 (2013). https://doi.org/10.1186/1472-6939-14-S1-S8

17. Tissera, S.R., Silva, S.N.: Attitude towards health information privacy and electronic health records among urban sri lankan adults. Nursing Informatics **2016**, 1003–1004 (2016). https://doi.org/10.3233/978-1-61499-658-3-1003

18. Forster, M., et al.: Electronic medical record systems, data quality and loss to follow-up: survey of antiretroviral therapy programmes in resource-limited settings. Bull World Health Organ **86**(12), 939–947 (2008). https://doi.org/10.2471/BLT.07.049908

19. Gesicho, M.B., Moon, T.D., Heitman, E., Were, M.C.: Ethical issues in implementing national-level health data warehouses in developing countries. MEDINFO 2017: Precision Healthcare Through Informatics, pp. 718–722 (2017). https://doi.org/10.3233/978-1-61499-830-3-718

20. Namara, M., Wilkinson, D., Lowens, B.M., Knijnenburg, B.P., Orji, R., Sekou, R.L.: Cross-cultural perspectives on eHealth privacy in Africa. In: Proceedings of the Second African Conference for Human Computer Interaction: Thriving Communities, New York, NY, USA, pp. 1–11 (Dec 2018). https://doi.org/10.1145/3283458.3283472

21. Antonio, C.A.T., Patdu, I.D., Marcelo, A.B.: Health information privacy in the philippines: trends and challenges in policy and practice. Acta Med. Philipp. **50**(4) (Dec 2016). https://doi.org/10.47895/amp.v50i4.760

22. Gerson, N., Shava, F.B.: A review of security system assessment tools - ProQuest. https://www.proquest.com/docview/2455896172/fulltextPDF/237C474A4684F42PQ/1. Accessed 17 Jan 2022

23. Zainudin, A., Sudarsono, A., Prakoso, B.M.: An implementation of secure medical data delivery for rural areas through delay tolerant network. In: 2016 International Electronics Symposium (IES), pp. 414–419 (Sep 2016). https://doi.org/10.1109/ELECSYM.2016.7861042

24. Pankomera, R., van Greunen, D.: Mitigating vulnerabilities and threats for patient-centric healthcare systems in low income developing countries. In: 2017 IST-Africa Week Conference (IST-Africa), pp. 1–11 (May 2017). https://doi.org/10.23919/ISTAFRICA.2017.8102384

25. Koivu, A., Mavengere, N., Ruohonen, M.J., Hederman, L., Grimson, J.: Exploring the information and ICT skills of health professionals in low- and middle-income countries. In: Brinda, T., Mavengere, N., Haukijärvi, I., Lewin, C., Passey, D. (eds.) SaITE 2016. IAICT, vol. 493, pp. 152–162. Springer, Cham (2016). https://doi.org/10.1007/978-3-319-54687-2_15

26. Hai, N.K., Lawpoolsri, S., Jittamala, P., Huong, P.T.T., Kaewkungwal, J.: Practices in security and confidentiality of HIV/AIDS patients' information: a national survey among staff at HIV outpatient clinics in Vietnam. PLoS One **12**(11), e0188160 (2017). https://doi.org/10.1371/journal.pone.0188160

27. Khan, S.I., Hoque, A.S.Md.L.: Health data integration with secured record linkage: a practical solution for bangladesh and other developing countries. In: 2017 International Conference on Networking, Systems and Security (NSysS), pp. 156–161 (Jan 2017). https://doi.org/10.1109/NSysS.2017.7885818

28. Roland, L.K., Sanner, T., Sæbø, J.I., Monteiro, E.: P for Platform. Architectures of large-scale participatory design. Scand. J. Inf. Syst. **29**(2), (Dec 2017). [Online]. Available: http://aisel.aisnet.org/sjis/vol29/iss2/1

Digital Entrepreneurship
for Development

Negotiating Inclusion and Digital Entrepreneurship in a Zambian Innovation Hub: A Post-colonial Perspective

Andrea Jiménez[1]([✉]) [iD] and Christopher Foster[2] [iD]

[1] Information School, University of Sheffield, Sheffield, UK
a.jimenez@sheffield.ac.uk
[2] Global Development Institute, University of Manchester, Manchester, UK
christopher.foster-2@manchester.ac.uk

Abstract. The goal of this paper is to look at the inclusion agenda in digital entrepreneurship through a postcolonial lens. While recognising that inclusion has long been embedded in development models relevant to digital entrepreneurship, most literature assumes an economic logic of inclusion, through incorporating people so they can benefit from being a part of a globalised economy. However, this viewpoint ignores the underlying historical, political, economic, and social dimensions that influence how inclusion occurs in digital entrepreneurship. To accomplish this, we draw on postcolonial theory to examine how a Zambian innovation hub negotiates inclusion dynamics between the hegemonic Western narrative as well as local understandings, needs and preferences. We describe the hub's tensions in trying to fit into the global innovation agenda, and how this impacted inclusion within the hub. In doing so, we hope to provide a broader and more critical framework for thinking about inclusion in digital entrepreneurship.

Keywords: Innovation · Inclusion · Post-colonial · Digital entrepreneurship · Global South

1 Introduction

Digital entrepreneurship has become increasingly central to innovation, given the impetus of information and communication technology in an increasingly interconnected world [1–3]. With emerging digital technologies (i.e., big data, blockchain, 3D printing, data analytics) digital innovation provides a rich area for new venture opportunities [3]. It has also transformed the entrepreneurial process into less bounded, less predefined and more diverse phenomena [2]. Digital entrepreneurship is taking place all over the world, promoting and producing digital technologies that feed into the digital economy [3].

In the African context, digital entrepreneurship has become highly visible and often celebrated with the mainstream and business press [4, 5]. The rise of digital entrepreneurship in Africa is aligned with assumptions of the 'flattened world' - that because digital

© IFIP International Federation for Information Processing 2022
Published by Springer Nature Switzerland AG 2022
Y. Zheng et al. (Eds.): ICT4D 2022, IFIP AICT 657, pp. 203–216, 2022.
https://doi.org/10.1007/978-3-031-19429-0_13

entrepreneurship can be done by anyone and anywhere, it creates a level playing field [4].

Within Africa, in line with other regions, the orientation of digital entrepreneurship has increasingly moved beyond firm profit to encompass broader economic and social inclusion agendas [4, 5]. In this context, development discourses emphasise the ideas of innovation and entrepreneurship in meeting development goals [6]. This is particularly evident through the types of funding available for start-up firms in Africa, articulations of entrepreneurs and firm goals, and the emergence of institutions supporting and guiding digital entrepreneurship which push inclusive goals [4]. Digital entrepreneurship and digital technologies are presented as '[…] globally homogeneous, ubiquitous, openly accessible, and inclusive' [5, p.20].

This 'inclusion turn' within digital firms and innovation ecosystems gives to rise to tensions. On one hand, global norms of digital entrepreneurship remain at the centre, grounded within entrepreneurism, innovation and profit (as exemplified by the stories of successful global tech firms). The prevalence of inclusion agendas, on the other hand, suggest orientations and goals in Africa that imply different configurations and worldviews. The growing reference to inclusion within digital entrepreneurship has led to emerging research in the global South that has explored tensions where overlapping economic and inclusion goals exist [7, 8]. Such scholarship provides important insights through unpacking cases of digital entrepreneurship in the global South.

We draw from these views to argue that research needs to think more holistically about the assumptions and tensions linked to the 'inclusion turn' in digital entrepreneurship. To understand and affect genuine inclusion in innovation and entrepreneurship, it is not possible to consider firm-level tensions without linking these into broader patterns of development in the global South. We need to think more critically around the broader structures that underlie the inclusion agenda, moving beyond 'surface level' actions of firms in Africa to consider the way ambitions and goals of individuals and organisations align to norms of digital entrepreneurship. This approach aligns with others recent studies that have begun to investigate the embeddedness of digital entrepreneurship in Africa in broader geopolitical, economic, and historical contexts (e.g. [4, 6, 9]).

Of particular importance in an Africa context, and less understood, is how assumptions around digital entrepreneurship are shaped by, and embedded within long running legacies of global inequalities and dominance that still play a key role in shaping the assumptions and dynamics. As Jack and Avle [10] state, the digital turn represents a continuation of power and privilege structures, mirroring colonial histories and unbalanced representation in decision-making in many ways.

The paper approaches digital entrepreneurship and innovation from a discursive perspective. It looks to move beyond positivist ideas of 'best practice' that 'solve' the tensions between economic growth and inclusion. Rather, closer attention is paid to assumptions embedded within notions of digital entrepreneurship in Africa - how they are invoked across range of innovation actors and what this means for power and agency within North-South relations. Our research question is therefore "How is the process of inclusion influenced by global discourses within organisations supporting digital entrepreneurship and innovation?" Our goal is to provide a broader and more critical frame for thinking of digital entrepreneurship. We aim to recast discussions of 'profit vs inclusion' and 'reality vs practice' into broader discussion of structure and relations. The discussion follows recent IS calls for more intense study new digital work environments, and to better theorise inclusionary and exclusionary practices (e.g. [11]).

We support the theoretical discussion of inclusion through the analysis of one particular type of organisation supporting digital entrepreneurship in the global South: innovation hubs. Technology and innovation hubs are coworking and support spaces for those who are seeking to develop digital innovations such as mobile applications, software development, 3D printing, robotics and more. They also support digital enterprises, including online shopping and more [4]. Innovation hubs provide an insightful example that embody some of the tensions we describe above - they are seen in some contexts as an entrepreneurial space (i.e. as innovation incubators, business accelerators) and in others as a space promoting inclusive transformation and development through entrepreneurship [12]. In this sense, innovation hubs assist us in examining how digital entrepreneurship and the discourse of inclusion in development intersect, how these two aspects interact and complement one another, and any tensions that may arise.

The remainder of the paper is organised as follows. We begin by looking at what inclusion as a discourse involves, and highlight current limitations in how structure and long-standing inequalities within inclusion. We then introduce postcolonial approaches to further strengthen the discursive form of inclusion, recasting innovation as discourses within larger patterns of power and uneven development. This theoretical discussion will be supplemented by an empirical study conducted at a technology and innovation hub in Lusaka, Zambia's capital city. Detailed analysis of this innovation hub has already been discussed elsewhere (see [12–14]). However, in this paper we focus on two specific internal organisational processes of the hub that relate to inclusive/exclusive practices: tensions between global/local dynamics and gender relations.

This analysis sheds light on the challenges that global South organisations supporting digital entrepreneurship face to become inclusive spaces and challenges as they look to help enter Africa into the global entrepreneurship ecosystem. Through our more discursive framework that centres power and uneven relationships, we highlight that tensions around inclusion represent a space by which individuals look to negotiate between powerful global norms and their lives and goals. Studies of inclusion then cannot be seen merely as incorporating people into already existing processes, but need to focus on how actors are challenging the broader structural conditions of power which reproduce uneven relations and reinforce the limitations for inclusion. This is particular brought home in the how organisations supporting digital entrepreneurship and innovation are faced with distinctive challenges where inclusion is something that is desired, yet ultimately limited by the broader contexts of norms, expectations and funding.

2 Inclusion as a Discourse Within Processes of Uneven Development

Inclusion has long been embedded in development processes, including development models relevant to digital entrepreneurship policy and practice. Concepts like inclusive growth [15]; inclusive development [16]; and inclusive innovation [14, 17] provide conceptual approaches to frame how innovation goals and research might align to inclusion and development. Digital entrepreneurship projects have often mirrored such ideas, for example France's Development Agency (AFD) Digital Challenge's which focuses on 'the promotion of entrepreneurial initiatives managed by women and/or men, tackling the challenges of women's inclusion and gender inequalities [...]'[1] has led to the creation of organisations and initiatives suited to promote inclusion in the global South. Inclusion can be orientated around initiatives that include poor people in the development of a 'participatory' innovative agricultural project [18]; to develop grounded innovation platforms (GRIPs) [19], and more.

Inclusion, both social and economic, is embedded in different ways within the broader framework of the Sustainable Development Goals (SDGs). With the goal to 'leave no one behind', inclusion is predominantly focused on the poorest and most marginalised groups being incorporated into the process of socioeconomic development [20]. Such approaches have been critiqued in that in practice, inclusion in the global South is often rendered as economic [21]. Common ideas of economic inclusion and development often aligns with the 'post-Washington consensus' following neoliberal structural adjustment. The assumption here is that inclusion comes through market reform and improved fiscal policy for countries of the global South to reap benefits from being part of a globalised economy. This inclusionary discourse risks new forms of exclusion or/else adverse incorporation for the marginalised [22].

Overall, in these different conceptualisations, inclusion is often seen as a value-neutral process to solve local problems, which 'overlooks the underlying political, economic dimensions of poverty and exclusion, choosing to treat these instead as essentially local problems…devoid of historical materiality… [and] actively script-out larger historical context.' [23, p. 528]. It is crucial to further augment the inclusion literature with a recognition that inclusion often plays a role as a discourse that embeds assumptions and expectations, and a need to highlight historical aspects as important. This implies recognising tensions between the local context, and ideas around culture with Western discourses and narratives, which are dominant in a globalised world [24]. The next section introduces postcolonial theories as an overarching approach from which to think about inclusion critically.

3 Postcolonial Theories

We focus on postcolonial theory as a perspective to examine how the global dimension and hegemonic Western narrative affects processes of inclusion. Postcolonial theories and approaches examine 'a range of social, cultural, political, ethical and philosophical questions that recognize the salience of the colonial experience and its persisting aftermath.' [25, p. 277]. It stems from the premise that certain practices and discourses from colonial times still have legacies and underlying institutions and assumption prevail, dominating our systems today. This school of thinking has been heavily influenced by poststructuralism, through seminal contributions by Edward W Said, Homi K Bhabha and Gayatri C Spivak, among others [26]. In broad terms it suggests that postcolonial states need to break from neocolonial ties to develop independent thinking and practice.

A key contribution of postcolonial's theory is considering the gap between the 'local' and the 'global', by challenging the notions of 'the centre' and 'the margin' as reproduced

---

[1] https://vc4a.com/afd/innovation-for-women-in-africa/ [Accessed 13.04.2022].

in Eurocentric accounts of development [27]. Alternative concepts have been proposed that disrupt such hegemonic narratives that situated certain countries (and types of knowledge) in subordination from others. Concepts like, hybridity [29] are understood as a way to understand knowledge and culture not as universal, but as dynamic, translatable and specific. Within this more plural perspective, one can observe different processes and tactics by which those in colonised positions may adopt the coloniser's cultural and linguistic codes to destabilise power, through actions like translation, mimicry and appropriation.

According to Bhabha [28], for instance, mimicry is a strategy of colonial power and knowledge strategy in which the colonial subject is encouraged to mimic the coloniser by adopting the coloniser's cultural habits, assumptions, institutions, and values. Furthermore, the contribution of postcolonial theory relies on signalling the significance of the global dimension of colonisation, and connecting it to 'the micropolitics of context, subjectivity, and struggle, as well as to the macropolitics of global economic and political systems and processes' [31, p. 501]. Importantly, it examines the global effect of colonisation and sees globalisation as historically informed, with strong roots in colonial relations. As a result, contemporary societies cannot be analysed and understood without acknowledging colonial legacies [30]. This is of particular relevance when looking at digital entrepreneurship in Africa. Authority is given to 'universal' norms of innovation, managerialist and best practises for entrepreneurship. African entrepreneurs are seen as needing to adopt these as a way to support digital entrepreneurship [6].

Postcolonial approach provides with a roadmap for inclusion because it looks at systemic power in a global scale. It seeks to destabilise the Western dominance and hegemonic viewpoint for alternative perspectives. In this sense, it is constantly challenging perceptions that look at the global South in need to mirror global North. Instead, it centres the needs and perspective from postcolonies, their standpoint and their complexity. Importantly, rather than assuming that an inclusive approach will bring positive benefits, it questions what inclusion means, inclusion of what, for who and for what purposes, as well as what happened that caused the exclusion in the first place.

4 Approach

Analysis comes from the case study of a technology and innovation hub in the city of Lusaka, capital of Zambia. This hub was founded in 2011 and throughout the years has been transforming and adapting its organisational structure to adjust to both local conditions as well as external aspects, such as evolving funding and global innovation networks. We describe these changes in relation to different dimensions of inclusion that were experienced by members of the hub. In doing so we are highlighting, in line with postcolonial perspectives, how these different aspects of inclusion are influenced by broader structural inequalities that stem from global South contexts.

Research was undertaken as an interpretivist qualitative case study which followed an ethnographically informed approach by the first author through immersion in the research setting in two different time periods [31, 32]. First in a period of 3 weeks, almost at the beginning of the hub inauguration in 2012, a second time for over a period of three months, 3 years after the launch. Data collection included semi-structured interviews to hub members, hub co-founders, managers and also people outside of the hub that were involved in the Zambian technology ecosystem. Interview questions with hub members followed a flexible structure divided into three main areas: their experiences prior to the hub (what brought them to the hub); the impact of the hub in their lives (careers, personal); and their perception of the hub, the people and the interactions. Some questions for hub co-founders and managers evolved around the strategic challenges faced in structuring the hub, and decision-making. Participant observation was also conducted by visiting the hub on a daily basis and using their workspace, as well as attending the events they organised and events they were invited to. Through participant observation, it was observed that understanding gender dynamics was important. Thus, additional interviews with female participants were focused around gender dynamics and challenges faced at the hub and society at large. Interviews were conducted to understand members' experiences of their work alongside participant observation.

Interviews were supplemented with ethnographic observation of daily practises, events with members, and management meetings, which resulted in the creation of research diaries. Following both visits, a review of online sources to keep up with the hub's activities was conducted. The data was organised and coded in the qualitative data analysis software Nvivo, with a focus on what the respondents perceived to be their experience and their work within the hub. Initially, the data was analysed adopting theoretical lenses based on ideas from innovation, entrepreneurship and gender/intersectionality[2]. Reflection on the categories that emerged from the interviews led to further analysis of the case from a postcolonial perspective, with a specific emphasis on the gender aspects of the case, which was identified as an important element in participant's responses. This stage enabled an iterative process of deepening the analysis and generating additional insights from the data. The names of respondents, as well as the name of the organisation, are kept confidential, and pseudonyms are used instead.

5 Findings

Findings show different tensions between the need to think globally (mainly related to adopting Western strategies of innovation and looking outside for expertise) with an interest in developing local content and strengthen the community. These tensions resulted in different forms of inclusion and exclusion, which will be detailed next.

Inspired by a proliferation of technology and innovation hubs in other parts of Africa, the innovation hub was founded in 2011. The founders were technologists turned entrepreneurs who wanted to provide a space for people interested in innovation to connect and work. Initially it was based next to a Belgian NGO, who offered funding, space, free internet and some computers. And so it often gathered young people, the majority of them with strong interest in technology but insufficient training. Throughout the years the hub has functioned as a coworking space for entrepreneurs and innovators to connect, collaborate and work on their projects to turn them into reality [33]. Hub membership was free and diverse, with

---

[2] Data analysis was initially undertaken as part of the first authors PhD based on these frameworks.

young people interested in learning skills like programming, editing, as well as entrepreneurial skills.

The hub has strongly focused on developing local talent and contributing to the local ecosystem over the years. They set up a team within the hub to teach members programming and coding through workshops. As part of this training led by local experts, members of the hub have developed a number of projects focused on local content, including an app to translate local languages, an app containing the main tenets of the Zambian constitution, an online shopping platform, and more. This shows evidence that from inception there was a strong desire to promote local knowledge and become independent from external sources. The following presents different dimensions that created challenges for inclusion within the hub.

6   Funders vs Local Ambitions

Significant tensions were experienced due to the way that external discourses around entrepreneurship, often shaped by Silicon Valley rhetoric, led to internal changes within the hub. This change had an impact on who was included as a member, as well as how members felt included in the hub (see [14]). For example, the hub relied predominantly in funding from international development organisations, which is a common trend for hubs in Africa [34]. These international organisations had specific expectations for the hub around scaling startups rapidly. This led to tensions between how to fulfil the funders expectations against internal goals related to capacity building and developing local content. In this context, the hub adopted a series of strategies to negotiate the fit between the local agendas and a logic of business and international development.

In some of these strategies, we see a strong need to align with Western model of organisation and development [35]. For example, several hub members referred to the work being done at the hub as a means of assisting Zambia "catching up with the rest of the world" in terms of technology, entrepreneurship and development. Designing/working with technology and development are both considered to be interconnected:

> "and it does give a good name for our country as a whole, and it just helps us compete on a global level so I think that besides making money we push ourselves for our technology and our development." (Charlotte).

In this endeavour, the hub would provide training for those seeking to pioneer in emerging technologies (e.g. robotics, programming), thinking that there would be a future market and investment for these. In some cases this became a reality, but despite many efforts to improve their readiness for new technologies, investment was slow to arrive. As one of the management members explained:

> "So first of all, the most common thing that is always been the, like a problem for ever, is access to capital. And we looked at that in the beginning I never thought it was going to take a while to sort that out." (Timothy)

This situation – between training for the future technology and a general lack of investment –resonates with what others have identified in other African contexts [4–6].

Access to capital is a significant challenge, yet many hubs are following Silicon Valley rhetoric of looking to market pioneering tech to drive investment, only to discover a very different reality [6]. Moreover, even where there has been such investment in Africa, data is showing that these are often obtained by international and white funder-led startups, many of them with less engagement on the ground [36, 37].

Another strategy of the hub was promoting risk-taking and failure as natural parts of entrepreneurship, a very common discourse in the Silicon Valley culture [44]. A member explained that in Zambia, most have been educated to seek safe employment opportunities and not take risks. As explained by one member.

" In [University], if you're in the sciences classes, in exams for example, if you get a question wrong, they deduct marks. If you get it right, you get extra marks, if you don't try, you just get zero. So you're already being told that you'll be penalized for trying if you get it wrong. And by the time you are graduating, you're already feeling like 'mmm, let me take the safe option, because it's guaranteed. If I lose, I just get zero. But I'm not going to take any risks" (Mariani).

To change the idea of risk taking as problematic, they'd invite successful entrepreneurs from other parts of the world to share their stories. In one of these cases, they invited a white South African to speak about her successful business. She discussed her experiences working diligently and being extremely disciplined, as well as how this contributed to her success. During conversations with several hub members after the talk, it was noted that they reflected on how her experience was significantly different from their own, partly due to positionality and context (Research diary).

Such tensions had to be negotiated. In some cases the hub looked adapt their organisation. For example, they diversified some of their events, moving away from entrepreneurship 'capacity building' and knowledge towards more diverse workshops. Such workshops might look to better connect with more relevant entrepreneurship directions for hub members, such as hair treatment and fashion, even though they were a technology and innovation hub. In other cases, however, the tension between what the funders wanted and what the hub thought was relevant resulted in a stronger alignment with the funders' interests.

Following postcolonial thinking, their lack of autonomy also resulted in aspects of translation and mimicry. The discourse began to shift from a strong emphasis on capacity building for aspiring technologists and entrepreneurs to predominantly startup development, which had an impact on the hub's membership demographics [13].

7 Gender Inclusion

One of the aspects where the hub had a strong focus was on gender inclusion. Since its inception, the hub has hosted a female-led organisation that aims to empower and encourage more women to work in technology. This network defined itself as seeking to increase the meaningful participation of women and girls in technology, providing free training in ICT skills, exposure to emerging technologies, mentorship, networking and career progression opportunities. They targeted three different groups: girls in high school, in college and young professionals.

As a result of the trainings and workshops a significant number of women and girls learned digital skills, including coding languages like PHP, website design and robotics. Several of them also developed mobile applications targeting a female audience (e.g. a mobile application for women's rights, a group of women developing gaming applications, etc.). They also made training videos to discuss women's issues and organised workshops before bigger events to target specifically women. Not only did they organise IT related events and work, but through the women's network a number of events were held at the hub that included sectors characterised by more gender-balanced or female dominated, like fashion events and events for natural hair.

Given the broader societal challenges in Zambia, co-founders of the network considered that often women who wanted to learn digital skills did not have the financial resources. To be as inclusive as possible, their organisation applied for grants to provide their services for free. This allowed them to visit a wide range of schools, both in rural and urban areas, where they provided training for younger girls as well as talks to encourage them to study digital related fields. During their visits to rural areas, members of the network became aware of the significant differences between Lusaka and the rest of the country. As described by one of the network's co-founders:

"And then in November we had a chance to go to Soezzi and to Kitwe, and for me I think that was the biggest reality check that I've had recently. [...] I'm more aware of the economic differences and what's actually going on. And even when you look at the statistics, about 40-45% of Zambian women are getting married under the age of 13, it's hard to believe that when you're in Lusaka and you're interacting with people your age who are not yet married or who are getting married by choice. But then when you get outside of Lusaka, is a completely different story." (Mariani).

Interviews with the network co-founders led to interesting insights around gender inclusion. They recognise the gender imbalance around technology and were focused on improving that. They experienced dilemmas around how to achieve this in a way that would be both effective and as inclusive as possible. Their approach considered that training women and girls needed to go alongside working to improve the technology ecosystem. As explained by one of them:

"And if the tech ecosystem is working for guys, then it means that it's going to start working for the girls as well, and start working for everyone." (Mariani)

These distinctions influenced how they perceived the hub as an inclusive or exclusive organisation. According to Jack and Avle [10], how people perceive their own sense of marginality, privilege, and inclusion is critical to how they live out the geopolitics of technology in their daily lives. In this case, those who identified as being raised in the capital spoke about the hub as an inclusive organisation, which welcomed them and allowed them to do their work in equal terms in comparison to male counterparts. However, those who identified as coming from rural areas often described the hub as a predominantly male-centred organisation, where they did not feel always included [14].

The experience of this network demonstrates an attempt from the hub to emphasise on a gender inclusive approach, with many benefits. There was a tension here between wanting to address gender imbalances and support the technology sector in Zambia. This occasionally caused frictions, as some female members felt excluded, while more active members interpreted a lack of attendance as a lack of interest in the work. Some respondents attributed a lower number of female members to individual's responsibility, rather than structural factors. When asked about the lack of female attendance, some of the more active female members responded that girls "are not interested in that sort of thing" (Vicky) and "obviously they didn't see how important it was" (Rouse).

Even though the hub adopted a gender inclusion approach (by providing the space, training and support to the women's network), there were still challenges experienced by some. Here we can also see what Rönnblom [38] describes as the process of inclusion focused on targets, where gender inclusion translates into women becoming objects of inclusion. This is informed in many ways by the way Western discourses around inclusion, which neglects wider structural inequalities, and instead speaks of inclusion as a problem that is mostly in the hands of the individuals. Here we can see what Ahmed [39] describes as a 'happy diversity model' whereby the hub, by hosting the network of women and visibly having more women as members provided a positive image of the organisation, consequently allowing inequalities to be 'concealed and thus reproduced' (p. 72). This process of inclusion did not recognise the complexity of the female members, and thus did not see the differences between them.

From a postcolonial lenses, this raises the issue with the hybridity as a way of obscuring uneven power relations. Findings show that a group of female members experienced a privileged position in comparison to others. This privileged position was not shared by all women, even though the hub adopted an inclusive approach to gender.

8   Discussion

Our analysis of this innovation hub led us to understand that it has been operating within a complex set of relationships, discourses and funding mechanisms that lead to multiple forms of inclusion/exclusion at different levels: within tensions between broader global discourses and funding practices; and within internal gender relations and dynamics. These, we argue, are often shaped by broader aspects of inequality found in society due to various structures of power that continue until today [10].

Inclusion and exclusion processes are heavily influenced by social and historical forces dimensions [40]. Although digital entrepreneurship in Africa is proposed to be beneficial for inclusion, there are many challenges faced. Findings revealed that different aspects affected how inclusive the hub was at different points in time. Following postcolonial thinking, there is a distinction between broader global dimensions, characterised by funders' interests, which influenced how the hub moved to become more for startup development. As mentioned previously, throughout the creation of the hub there has been a tension between a need to think globally and get external sources of funding, and the desire to develop local content, improve people's skills from both rural and urban areas.

We also distinguish broader cultural structures, which influenced inclusion in relation to intersectional dimensions. More specifically, wider gender and class structures in Zambian society, influenced who felt included within the hub. Sometimes these tensions resulted in successful innovations, with the development of successful mobile applications regarding local content, like the local languages app and the Zambian con-stitution app. In other situations, these tensions revealed further practices of exclusion. For example, having to adapt to the expectations of the Western funding organisations.

Overall, the process of inclusion within the hub reflected the broader context and structures of disadvantage in society. For example, the logic of inclusion around gender involved providing a space for women, training and also developing grants with a gender approach. Furthermore, the hub initially adopted an inclusive approach by providing a free space and offering free training to anyone who wanted to attend. With donor funding, it changed its strategy to only consider working with those who create startups and can develop innovations, placing Zambia in the global discourse of innovation. The focus on local content was still relevant, however, it became more of an expert-based, income specific target.

Even though most literature on inclusion within organisations are informed by includ-ing people by adopting managerial strategies and promoting a logic of economic growth, what inclusion means in innovation hubs is influenced by existing power structures that position them as dependent on external funding and support. This then reveals the need to adopt a theoretical framework that deconstructs those wider dimensions affecting the way organisations are framed [27]. In other words, what happens in a hub demon-strates that inclusion should consider structural and historical dimensions that recognise exclusion is not entirely the result of individual action, but of centuries of inequalities becoming institutionalised [29].

In this sense, the innovation hub organisation is part of a global discourse of inno-vation, where members look outside their boundaries to learn, implement ideas and get inspired. Often these are coming from the West because historically, innovation and tech-nology are fields that have been developed in the West mostly, the South being recipients of said dispositives [41].

9   Conclusion

The purpose of this paper was to explore inclusion from a discursive perspective in organisations supporting digital entrepreneurship and innovation in the global South. It follows scholars who challenge the analysis of southern empirical phenomena based on the assumption of transferring ideas and models from the 'developed' countries to Southern ones [4]. Furthermore, it is also based on the assumption that countries in the South are lagging behind but are certainly following the same trajectory of modernisation [42]. These assumptions orientate the various ways in which uneven power relations are impacting forms of inclusion in Southern organisations such as the innovation hub discussed.

Inclusion in organisations is embedded in a wider social, historical and organisational context, resulting in multiple social categories in which individuals are positioned. What form inclusion takes then is not devoid of those wider structures which shape the day to day of an organisation. In this sense, in inclusion sometimes we focus on one spe-cific category, thinking we are moving forward/progressing in making organisations more inclusive. Yet inclusion is a complex process with multiple meanings, that indi-viduals, groups and organisations need to negotiate. Often development organisations have crudely though of inclusion in terms of numbers or specific processes. While this may provide a degree of inclusion, with positive benefits it rarely thinks more broadly about these terrains of inclusion. Structural inclusion is about dealing with the wider dimensions society faces, because they do not stop when you enter the workspace of the organisation [43].

This paper makes two important contributions. It studies the emerging phenomena of digital entrepreneurship and innovation and the growing role of inclusion in these processes. It develops theoretical considerations on inclusion through adopting postcolonial theory, to show the existing challenges around inclusion in digital entrepreneurship and innovation in the global South. In this sense, we argue that if inclusion is detached from a recognition of power and inequality, then it loses its power to be a transformational process and instead becomes a managerial tool [39].

Organisations supporting digital entrepreneurship and innovation are springing up all over the world, with a great number of these just in the African continent, where the discourse is it will help address inclusion challenges. As Friederici et al. [4] state 'As misguided as Silicon Valley comparisons may be, people and enterprises across Africa are forced to engage with them'. We agree with this view, but we further argue that this engagement can help to focus on how much of the challenges digital entrepreneurship faces in Africa are from global forces of inequality, as a result of colonial histories. Such discussions should be at the centre or funding applications, policy recommendations and practice that place emphasis on inclusion agendas.

Rather than assuming digital entrepreneurship in Africa will provide a level-playing field in the global digital entrepreneurship scenario, we could consider how it may continue to amplify existing inequalities and the global North/South divide. Our contribution lies in exploring organisations supporting digital entrepreneurship and innovation and expanding theoretical implications of inclusion in the global South, and showing how inclusion in the global South should consider global dimensions. Inclusion, we argue, is contextual, embedded in context, and related to how people perceive themselves. It is, however, influenced by larger historical and geopolitical dimensions. This implies that we must approach inclusion holistically, viewing it as a discursive practise rather than an outcome of digital entrepreneurship.

References

1. Mutua, W.; Mbwana, A.: Innovative Africa: The New Face of Africa, Essays on the Rise of Africa's Innovation Age (Sambuli, N. (ed.); Afrinnovator) (2012)
2. Nambisan, S.: Digital entrepreneurship: toward a digital technology perspective of entrepreneurship. Entrep. Theor. Pract. **41**(6), 1029–1055 (2017)
3. Shen, K.N., Lindsay, V., Xu, Y.: Digital entrepreneurship. Inf. Syst. J. 28(6), 1125–1128 (2018)
4. Davidson, E., Vaast, E.: Digital entrepreneurship and its sociomaterial enactment. In: Proceedings of the Annual Hawaii International Conference on System Sciences (2010). https://doi.org/10.1109/HICSS.2010.150
5. Friederici, N., Wahome, M., Graham, M.: Digital Entrepreneurship in Africa: How a Continent is Escaping Silicon Valley's Long Shadow. The MIT Press (2020). https://doi.org/10.7551/mitpress/12453.001.0001

6. Ndemo, B., Weiss, T. (eds.): Digital Kenya: An Entrepreneurial Revolution in the Making. Palgrave Macmillan UK, London (2017). https://doi.org/10.1057/978-1-137-57878-5
7. Pollio, A.: Acceleration, development and technocapitalism at the Silicon Cape of Africa. Econ. Soc. **51**(1), 46–70 (2022). https://doi.org/10.1080/03085147.2021.1968675
8. World Bank Enhancing Access to Finance for Technology Entrepreneurs in Southern Africa. Washington, DC (2014).https://openknowledge.worldbank.org/handle/10986/21073
9. Silvia Masiero, M.N., Ravishankar,: Exploring hybridity in digital social entrepreneurship. In: Nielsen, P., Kimaro, H.C. (eds.) ICT4D 2019. IAICT, vol. 551, pp. 295–306. Springer, Cham (2019). https://doi.org/10.1007/978-3-030-18400-1_24
10. Paxling, L.: Exploring technology design among mobile entrepreneurs in Kampala: an open space workshop. Electron. J. Inf. Syst. Dev. Countries. **86**(2), 1–11 (2019)
11. Jack, M., Avle, S.: A feminist geopolitics of technology. Glob. Perspect. **2**(1), 1–18 (2021)
12. Trauth, E., Joshi, K.D., Yarger, L.K.: ISJ Editorial. Inf. Syst. J. **28**(6), 989–994 (2018)
13. Jiménez, A., Zheng, Y.: Tech hubs, innovation and development. Inf. Technol. Dev. **24**(1), 95–118 (2017). https://doi.org/10.1080/02681102.2017.1335282
14. Jiménez, A., Zheng, Y.: Unpacking the multiple spaces of innovation hubs. Inf. Soc. **37**(3), 163–176 (2021). https://doi.org/10.1080/01972243.2021.1897913
15. Jiménez, A.: Inclusive innovation from the lenses of situated agency: insights from innovation hubs in the UK and Zambia. Innov. Dev. **9**(1), 41–64 (2019). https://doi.org/10.1080/215 7930X.2018.1445412
16. George, G., McGahan, A.M., Prabhu, J.: Innovation for inclusive growth: towards a theoretical framework and a research agenda: innovation for inclusive growth. J. Manage. Stud. **49**(4), 661–683 (2012). https://doi.org/10.1111/j.1467-6486.2012.01048.x
17. Gupta, J., Pouw, N.R.M., Ros-Tonen, M.A.F.: Towards an elaborated theory of inclusive development. Eur. J. Dev. Res. **27**(4), 541–559 (2015). https://doi.org/10.1057/ejdr.2015.30
18. Foster, C., Heeks, R.: Conceptualising inclusive innovation: modifying systems of innovation frameworks to understand diffusion of new technology to low-income consumers. Eur. J. Dev. Res. **25**(3), 333–355 (2013)
19. Swaans, K., Boogaard, B., Bendapudi, R., Taye, H., Hendrickx, S., Klerkx, L.: Operationalizing inclusive innovation: lessons from innovation platforms in livestock value chains in India and Mozambique. Innov. Dev. **4**(2), 239–257 (2014)
20. Refsgaard, K., Bryden, J., Kvakkestad, V.: Towards inclusive innovation praxis in forest-based bioenergy. Innov. Dev. **7**(1), 153–173 (2017)
21. Armstrong, D., Armstrong, A.C., Spandagou, I.: Inclusion: by choice or by chance? Int. J. Inclusive Educ. **15**(1), 29–39 (2011). https://doi.org/10.1080/13603116.2010.496192
22. Cookson, T.P.: Working for inclusion? conditional cash transfers, rural women, and the reproduction of inequality. Antipode **48**(5), 1187–1205 (2016)
23. Hickey, S., du Toit, A.: Adverse incorporation, social exclusion, and chronic poverty. In: Shepherd, A., Brunt, J. (eds.) Chronic Poverty, pp. 134–159. Palgrave Macmillan UK, London (2013). https://doi.org/10.1057/9781137316707_7
24. Scheba, A., Scheba, S.: REDD+ as 'inclusive' neoliberal conservation: the case of Lindi. Tanzania. J. Eastern Afr. Stud. **11**(3), 526–548 (2017)
25. Mignolo, W., Walsh, C.: On decoloniality: concepts, analytics. Duke University Press, Praxis (2018)
26. Jack, G., Westwood, R., Srinivas, N., Sardar, Z.: Deepening, broadening and re-asserting a postcolonial interrogative space in organization studies. Organization **18**(3), 275–302 (2011). https://doi.org/10.1177/1350508411398996
27. Bhambra, G.K.: Postcolonial and decolonial dialogues. Postcolonial Stud. **17**(2), 115–121 (2014)

28. C T Mohanty,: "Under western eyes" revisited: feminist solidarity through anticapitalist struggles. Signs: J. Women Culture Soc. **28**(2), 499–535 (2003). https://doi.org/10.1086/342914

29. Bhabha, H.K.: The Location of Culture. Routledge (2012). https://doi.org/10.4324/9780203820551

30. Bhabha, H.K.: Of mimicry and man: the ambivalence of colonial discourse. In: Literary Theory and Criticism. Routledge India (2021).

31. Ponzanesi, S.: Touchstones. In: Paradoxes of Postcolonial Culture: Contemporary Women Writers of the Indian and Afro-Italian Diaspora. State University of New York Press (2004).

32. Quijano, A.: Coloniality and modernity/rationality. Cult. Stud. **21**(2–3), 168–178 (2007). https://doi.org/10.1080/09502380601164353

33. Atkinson, P., Hammersley, M.: Ethnography and participant observation. Handb. Qual. Res. **1**(23), 248–261 (1994)

34. Myers, M.D., Newman, M.: The qualitative interview in IS research: examining the craft. Inf. Organ. **17**(1), 2–26 (2007)

35. Gathege, D., Moraa, H.: Draft Report On Comparative Study On Innovation Hubs Across Africa (Issue May) (2013)

36. Friederici, N.: Innovation hubs in Africa: what do they really do for digital entrepreneurs? In: Taura, N.D., Bolat, E., Madichie, N.O. (eds.) Digital Entrepreneurship in Sub-Saharan Africa. PSEA, pp. 9–28. Springer, Cham (2019). https://doi.org/10.1007/978-3-030-04924-9_2

37. Rafi Khan, F., Westwood, R., Boje, D.M.: "I feel like a foreign agent": NGOs and corporate social responsibility interventions into third world child labor. Hum. Relat. **63**(9), 1417–1438 (2010)

38. Briter Bridges. Africa Investment Report (2021). https://briterbridges.com/reports. Accessed 14 Apr 2022

39. Musse, E.R.: UN-SILICON VALLEY: Lessons on Entrepreneurship, Diversity, and the Movement to Build an Alternative Startup Paradigm. Off Path Ventures LLC (2019).

40. Rönnblom, M.: Bending towards growth: discursive constructions of gender equality in an era of governance and neoliberalism. In: The Discursive Politics of Gender Equality: Stretching, Bending and Policymaking, pp. 105–120. Routledge (2009)

41. Ahmed, S.: On Being Included: Racism and Diversity in Institutional Life. Dure Press (2012)

42. Cornell, S., Hartmann, D.: Ethnicity and Race: Making Identities in a Changing World (2nd editio). Sage Publishing, New York (2007).

43. Jimenez, A.A., Roberts, T.: Decolonising neo-liberal innovation: using the andean philosophy of 'Buen Vivir' to reimagine innovation hubs. In: Nielsen, P., Kimaro, H.C. (eds.) ICT4D 2019. IAICT, vol. 552, pp. 180–191. Springer, Cham (2019). https://doi.org/10.1007/978-3-030-19115-3_15

44. Alcadipani, R., Khan, F.R., Gantman, E., Nkomo, S.: Southern voices in management and organization knowledge. Organization **19**(2), 131–143 (2012)

45. Carrim, N.M.H., Nkomo, S.M.: Wedding intersectionality theory and identity work in organizations: South African Indian women negotiating managerial identity. Gend. Work. Organ. **23**(3), 261–277 (2016)

46. Cook, K.: The psychology of silicon valley: ethical threats and emotional unintelligence in the tech industry. Springer International Publishing, Cham (2020). https://doi.org/10.1007/978-3-030-27364-4

Leveraging Blockchain Technology for the Empowerment of Women Micro-entrepreneurs

Fazeelah Isaacs$^{(\boxtimes)}$ ⓘ, Grant Oosterwyk ⓘ, and Rebecca Njugana ⓘ

University of Cape Town, Cape Town, South Africa
{iscfaz001,njgreb001}@myuct.ac.za, grant.oosterwyk@uct.ac.za

Abstract. Despite the fact that scholars have identified blockchain technology as a powerful tool that can facilitate financial inclusion and empower marginalized people, there is a lack of research regarding its use amongst women, specifically women micro-entrepreneurs. This criticism lends itself to the issue of gender imbalances and inequality in some sections of IT/IS. This study aims to determine the benefits, risks and challenges associated with using blockchain technology for empowering women micro-entrepreneurs. A qualitative research strategy was adopted by using an interview approach, and data collection which focused on the perspectives of professionals employed in the blockchain sector. Using an affordance lens as a guideline, the findings and analysis from the interviews show that blockchain technology both directly and indirectly affords financial inclusion amongst women micro-entrepreneurs in particularly access to financial products and services to promote active participation. We found that many participants motivated that a blockchain solution will not be feasible in the context of a single micro-entrepreneur, but that women should form a network where they will be able to support each other and benefit from economies of scale.

Keywords: Blockchain technology · Women empowerment · Gender inequality · Theory of affordances · Financial inclusion · Micro-entrepreneurs · Development · Digital connection · Challenges · Benefits · Risks · Digital divide

1 Introduction

Women empowerment and gender inequality are key issues which are currently being addressed globally [4]. Women empowerment is the process of improving the assets of women and enhancing their capabilities; allowing them to influence and engage with the institutions which directly and indirectly impact their livelihoods [2]. Empowering women allows them to overcome the barriers they face and increases their socio-economic status within society. Women make up 56% of the worlds unbanked population, which inhibits them from participating within their countries emerging economies [25]. A major challenge women face is financial exclusion and the inability to easily transfer assets, which limits their financial opportunities [7].

© IFIP International Federation for Information Processing 2022
Published by Springer Nature Switzerland AG 2022
Y. Zheng et al. (Eds.): ICT4D 2022, IFIP AICT 657, pp. 217–236, 2022.
https://doi.org/10.1007/978-3-031-19429-0_14

Scholars have identified Information and Communications Technology (ICT) as a powerful tool which facilitates women empowerment in developing countries [9]. Blockchain technology is regarded as a disruptive technology which has the potential to contribute to socio-economic transformation within developing economies [11]. By breaking down socio-economic gender barriers, blockchain technology facilitates the empowerment of women by allowing them to participate in their nations' growing economies [3]. Blockchain has the potential to remove some of the current barriers faced by these disempowered women and can promote financial inclusion through access to financial resources, micro-lending opportunities, trade finance, supply chain finance and investment opportunities, to name a few [3, 12]. Financial inclusion refers to the availability and access to affordable financial services, for those that have not been supported by the formal agents within the traditional financial system [1]. This will enable women micro-entrepreneurs to have more financial opportunities and grow their enterprises.

We conduct an empirical study on how financial inclusion enabled by blockchain technology holds the potential for women empowerment. The study identifies barriers for financial inclusion and suggests blockchain technology-based solutions to overcome these barriers. The use of blockchain technology is still growing within developing countries, it is thus important to recognize its potential for the development of women and allow them to access this technology, to ensure that the digital divide amongst men and women is not accelerated as blockchain adoption becomes more mainstream. This criticism lends itself to the issue of gender imbalances and inequality in some sections of IT/IS which further emphasizes the issue of digital divide [19].

Thus, it is important to determine how the digital divide can be reduced and marginalized women can be included within economies. More studies are needed to critically analyze how women can overcome this digital divide and to actively participate to be part of the decision-making process in the creation of digital tools. This is to ensure that the solutions being designed to combat issues that women face are sustainable and fit women's existing skills, knowledge, and resources. If effective regulations are not put in place, the continued usage of blockchain could accelerate the relative return to sophisticated technology skills that men are more likely to have and further increase the digital divide between men and women [3]. Using an affordance lens as a backdrop to guide how financial inclusion can be realized with the use of blockchain technology and to identify the factors which enable and inhibit this affordance's realization. We consider affordances as a "concept that enabled a middle ground between technological determinism and social constructivism" [14]. To understand how a blockchain technology could empower women, the following research questions were formulated:

Primary Research Question:

RQ: In what ways does blockchain technology afford financial inclusion for women empowerment?

Secondary Research Questions:
SRQ-1: What are the potential benefits and risks of blockchain for women?
SRQ-2: What are the challenges faced when trying to empower women through blockchain technology?

Research Contribution:
This research aims to contribute to the limited body of knowledge and discourse on blockchain technology for the empowerment of women and serve as a foundational understanding for the application of blockchain technology as a sustainable solution for women micro-entrepreneurs. It aims to explore blockchain as a phenomenon beyond its applications in current research.

2 Literature Review

Methods

We performed an in-depth systematic literature review of existing literature to determine the current state of literature regarding the use of blockchain technology to empower women. This was followed by a quality selection assessment and finally, analysis of data in keeping with the hermeneutic cycle [5]. These steps were not performed in a rigorous, sequential fashion; but rather steps were reiterated as determined by the researcher's interpretation and analysis [5]. In the following section, some of the key claims from the synthesis will be explained (Figs. 1 and 2).

2.1 Challenges Faced by Women Micro-entrepreneurs

A major challenge faced by women micro-entrepreneurs is the lack of access to financial products and services [7, 26]. This hinders their ability to grow and invest in their businesses. Considering these challenges, it is important to understand the benefits financial inclusion holds for women. When women have access to adequate and affordable financial products and services, it does not only benefit themselves but their families and communities as well [25, 26].

By leveraging ICT, women can transform their social, political, and economic lives. ICT enables opportunities for growth and development, with the potential to bridge the gaps in socio-economic development [9, 21].

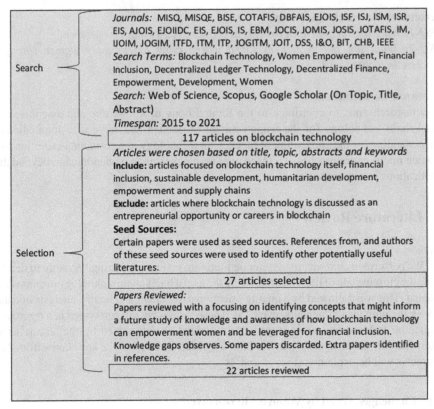

Fig. 1. Search and selection process (after the fashion of [15])

2.2 Blockchain Technology

Blockchain is an emerging technology which continues to attract significant interest from scholars. It is seen as a revolutionary and potentially disruptive technology [13]. Blockchain is a decentralized, digital ledger that facilitates peer-to-peer transactions without the need for third party intervention and enables a range of digital interactions [24, 28]. By eliminating the need for third parties, blockchain technology lowers uncertainty when exchanging value.

2.2.1 Blockchain Technology Risks, Issues and Limitations

Considering that blockchain technology is relatively new; ergo the risks of blockchain have not been extensively tested and it is slightly complex for non-IT specialists to fully understand [26]. This lack of understanding, or rather lack of knowledge on how to use the technology, could be harmful [3]. There are certain challenges which could cause reluctance for the use of blockchain and make it too expensive to deploy. There is no clarity as to whether the costs will be low enough to make it affordable in developing economies and whether there are ways in which these costs can be contained [8]. Affordability of the technology therefore needs to be considered. Blockchain technology also consumes a high amount of energy [11]. There are currently existing attempts to min-imize the energy costs but blockchain will always need servers and computers for the processing of transactions – which means it will always have a high-energy consumption. Most of the blockchain processes need access to the internet [3]. As a result, countries with unreliable internet access and poor energy infrastructure have more limitations for the use of blockchain [18].

Blockchain can aid in overcoming some of the barriers faced in accessing trade and commerce by women. However, it can also further aggravate gender inequality due to the type of skills required for operating the technology [3, 28]. It requires highly specialized skills. Lack of these skills on how to operate blockchain-based applications might create even higher barriers to trade for women [3]. Blockchain technologies potential benefits are recognized amongst scholars; however, it is noted that there is an evident risk due to the lack of regulations and legislation regarding the use of the technology [26]. If not regulated correctly, blockchain could increases the digital divide between men and women, resulting in more gender inequality [3].

2.2.2 Governance

Blockchain successfully removes the need for a third party, as it does not require any authentication or verification [26]. Blockchain technology can be considered "trust less", as there is no need to trust an intermediate organization in performing a transaction [10]. Instead, trust is spread across the peer-to-peer network. However, there is currently an absence of a central authority which authorizes and regulates blockchain. There is also a lack of legislation and no effective regulatory frameworks in place [3, 26]. Blockchain is regulated differently in different parts of the world [3]. Without a globally accepted regulatory framework or legislation, marginalized players in trade, such as women micro-entrepreneurs, could be marginalized even further [3]. An internationally accepted global standard or regulatory framework is required to ensure that this does not happen.

2.3   Blockchain Technology for Empowerment and Development

Research on blockchain is starting to enter the fields of humanitarian action, develop-ment aid, and economic and social development [28]. The technology is currently being used in areas of land titling, financial inclusion, sending remittances, providing identity services, improving the transparency of donations, reducing fraud and corruption, trans-forming governance systems, micro-insurance, micro-loans, cross-border transfers, cash programming, grant management, along with organisational governance [17].

The following table is a collection of projects and companies which are currently using blockchain technology for development (Tables 1 and 2):

Table 1. Use cases of blockchain technology for development

Project/Company name	Use case
Building Blocks – Piloting blockchain with refugee women in Jordan	The UN Women and the World Food Programme have launched Building Blocks for Syrian refugee women who are seeking asylum in Jordan. Building Blocks is a blockchain application which uses a private, permissioned blockchain, to shift from traditional cash transfers. The application enables them to have an online account without the need for any financial intermediaries [3]. Many refugees struggle with access to finance because they do not have documentation to confirm their identity. The application removes this barrier by allowing women to access their accounts via an eye-scan at supermarkets and receive cash [3, 26]
Spenn	Spenn is a start-up which is reviewing ways to make instant financial transfers through SMS. The company aims to create a service that doesn't need an internet-backed smartphone. This allows women who live in villages, far from bank branches to have access to finance and purchasing power by allowing them to transact and apply for loans [3]
EtherLoan and WeiFund	EtherLoan and WeiFund are platforms which enables women entrepreneurs to build up creditworthiness. Monetary transactions are recorded in their individual blockchain-based identity. These platforms can help women in developing countries secure loans without having to go through lengthy bank procedures [3]
Buy from Women – A UN blockchain based initiative	Buy from Women aims to provide female farmers in developing countries with important information on the overall size of their cultivable land, production and weather forecasts, and market prices of their products via SMS. This will enable female farmers to connect to global value chains, thus increasing their market access and ability to negotiate better deals. It could enable them to track the journey their produce undertakes before it reaches the final consumer [3]

(continued)

Table 1. (*continued*)

Project/Company name	Use case
Alice	Alice creates a series of incentives for social organizations to report on their impact reliably and in a transparent way. It incentivizes social organizations to run projects transparently. Donors can track their donations as well as the performance of each project they donated to. The company aims to restore trust in charities and make it easier to identify and help scale projects [10]
BanQu	BanQu was founded in 2015. The company's goal is to solve extreme poverty, by providing the poor with a verifiable identity. They believe it will give the poor greater access to participate in the economy and global supply chains, providing them with greater opportunities, thus improving their livelihoods [10]
Building Blocks – Piloting blockchain with refugee women in Jordan	The UN Women and the World Food Programme have launched Building Blocks for Syrian refugee women who are seeking asylum in Jordan. Building Blocks is a blockchain application which uses a private, permissioned blockchain, to shift from traditional cash transfers. The application enables them to have an online account without the need for any financial intermediaries [3]. Many refugees struggle with access to finance because they do not have documentation to confirm their identity. The application removes this barrier by allowing women to access their accounts via an eye-scan at supermarkets and receive cash [3, 26]

Table 2. Participant demographics and professional experience

Participant code	Gender	Professional position	Professional experience with blockchain
F#01	Female	Freelance blockchain developer	4 years

(*continued*)

Table 2. (*continued*)

Participant code	Gender	Professional position	Professional experience with blockchain
F#02	Female	CCO of blockchain product development company	4 years
F#03	Male	CTO of blockchain based food supply chain	2.5 years
F#04	Male	CEO of AI and blockchain company	7 years
F#05	Female	CEO of blockchain product development company	6 years
F#06	Male	CEO of mobile payment company	2 years
F#07	P1: Male, P2: Female	P1: Blockchain consultant, P2: CEO of micro-finance institutions	P1: Research: 10 years Corporate: 1 year, P2: 0
F#08	Female	COO of blockchain B2B2C marketplace	3 years
F#09	Female	Project manager at blockchain product development company	Research: 1 year Corporate: 3 months
F#10	Male	Identity research engineer	4.5 years

2.4 Blockchain Technology for Financial Inclusion

Financial inclusion is a crucial component of women empowerment. Under the UN's Sustainable Development Goals, increased financial inclusion is a major goal as it increases resilience and captures economic opportunities amongst poorer households and informal economies [20]. Financial inclusion can be viewed as a catalyst to lift women out of poverty by giving them a safe place to save money, build assets, and make their daily lives easier [1]. Financial inclusion is not a means to an end, but it is universally recognized as a critical component to reducing the current high levels of poverty and achieving inclusive and sustainable economic growth.

An inclusive financial system has the possibilities for a greater volume of resources for investment purposes and for the promotion and development of women micro-entrepreneurs [17]. Blockchain technology has the potential to foster greater financial inclusion, encourage economic participation and democratize and decentralize financial services in a new disruptive way.

Blockchain technology can be leveraged to create a more accessible and open financial system. It enables decentralized financial services, which have the potential to broaden financial inclusion, promote permissionless innovation, and create new opportunities for entrepreneurs [6, 23]. It can decrease information asymmetries, increase transparency and reliability in the system. The removal of the need for financial intermediaries significantly reduces costs [16]. Thus, due to these reduced costs, previously excluded participants will now be able to participate.

Blockchain technology can remove the barrier women currently face in the economy, and make foreign trade more inclusive, by including unbanked women in the formal financial system, reducing the credit gap which women micro-entrepreneurs face, enhancing transparency and the decentralized creation of records, and reducing transaction costs and time involved in doing business [3]. There is great potential to increase women's participation within the economy. Blockchain can help women micro-entrepreneurs overcome the costs associated with exporting and importing, and allow these women to interact easily with consumers, other businesses engaged in the supply chain, customs officers, and regulatory bodies [3, 8]. Blockchain technology allows for the automation of credit checks and verification measures throughout the entire supply chain process, which impacts the costs of the financial sector and the shipping industry. These reduced costs encourage women micro-entrepreneurs to participate in their economies [3, 27]. Reduced costs across the supply chain and for financial services allows women micro-entrepreneurs gain competitiveness in foreign markets at higher profitability. This can increase their overall market access within the economy.

3   Research Methodology

The aim of the research was to create new, richer interpretations of how blockchain technology can facilitate women empowerment. The study was guided by an interpretivist, inductive approach, focusing on the narratives and interpretations of participants in order to create these new understandings [22]. This study began by analyzing existing literature on blockchain technology for development and the empowerment of women to identify current use cases of blockchain for empowerment and development. The study did not examine the data collected in terms of theory-derived presumptions; theories have thus been developed based on the themes present within the data after it has been analyzed and interpreted. The study did, however, make use of the theoretical framework of affordances to guide the interpretation of the empirical findings.

Qualitative methods were used to collect data through semi-structured interviews in order to learn and report on participants perceptions and emotions of how blockchain technology can facilitate financial inclusion among women micro-entrepreneurs. Thematic analysis using NVivo software was used to analyse the data. The sample comprised of only blockchain professionals, as opposed to women micro-entrepreneurs. This is because these experts understand blockchain and its potential for empowerment. Blockchain companies are likely to facilitate more empowerment impact as they know the capacity of the technology. The participants selected work on solutions that have potential for women empowerment. There was a preference for female participants to gain first-hand perspectives on women empowerment issues. However, due to the limited number of females in the blockchain industry, it was not possible to only have females in the study. Male participants were included in order to bring a different perspective to the study and avoid any biases.

A total of 12 interviews were conducted, of which only 10 interviews were considered to have valuable data. To comply with the ethical considerations of this study, participants were given a code to ensure that they remained anonymous.

4 Data Analysis, Findings and Discussion

The table below presents the participants demographic characteristics.

All participants have at least one year of experience with blockchain technologies. Many of the participants have high ranking job roles; and were thus able to provide valuable insights due to their levels of experience and a deeper understanding of blockchain technology.

4.1 Empirical Findings

The findings consist of themes which aid in building further context as well as answering the research questions.

4.1.1 Challenges Faced by Women Micro-entrepreneurs

As identified in the initial literature review, women micro- entrepreneurs face many challenges which offset their economic growth. These being: no proof of record. Lack of formal identity, financial exclusion, and limited access to information.

4.1.1.1 No Proof of Record

Currently, many of these women micro-entrepreneurs are not leveraging their existing business data. Without this proof or record, they are unable to prove that they are running sustainable and successful businesses. Thus, they cannot get access to financial services which rely on this proven track record.

4.1.1.2 Lack of Formal Identity

The lack of formal identity was another challenge mentioned in interviews. Participant **F#04** noted that *"[there are] still a lot of women who do not have identity and that's a big challenge, because men don't really struggle with that problem"*. This lack of identity restricts them from registering their businesses, entering into contracts, opening bank accounts and being able to access financial services [3].

4.1.1.3 Financial Exclusion

The lack of banking history, not having access to financial services and lack of funding can be grouped into one larger theme and described as financial exclusion. Financial exclusion was the most common challenge mentioned amongst the participants. Women micro-entrepreneurs have difficulties accessing traditional financial services; *"they have no banking history, and they have no access to financial services"*. (**F#03; F#04; F#05**).

4.1.1.4 Limited Access to Information

Because these women have limited access to information, they are not able to empower themselves with an understanding of how the value chains they are operating within work and do not have the resources to better position themselves for opportunities available, *"woman entrepreneurs don't necessarily have access to or full understanding of the supply chains"*. (**F#04**). This lack of access to information creates information asymmetries within their value chains [3].

4.1.2 Benefits

The potential benefits for women if they were to adopt blockchain technology are that its accessible and has less barriers to entry than traditional systems. Participants noted that blockchain allows women to grow their businesses, it is censorship resistant, reduces costs, increases credibility, promotes financial inclusions, reduces discrimination, and allows women to create a track record of their operations.

4.1.2.1 Reduced Barriers to Entry

Participants noted that one of the main benefits of blockchain is because within the traditional systems there was a *"need to be able to lower barriers to entry"* (**F#08**). Unlike traditional financial services and other traditional products, blockchain allows for fewer barriers to entry as there are not as many requirements to participate. Many participants described blockchain based solutions as *"more accessible"* (**F#01; F#02, F#05, F#08**). And participant **F#10** said that *"the barriers of entry are lower or almost like non-existent in comparison [to traditional systems]"*. It was also noted that you would not need a bank account of credit history.

4.1.2.2 Business Growth and Job Creation

Another benefit identified was the ability for these women to grow their businesses exponentially. Participant **F#01** noted that *"data is very empowering"*. Having access to data allows women to leverage this data to make informed business decisions and ultimately grow their businesses, by gaining competitive advantage, allowing them access to markets, and increasing their market share. As these women's businesses grow; it will lead to job creation. With business growth and increased demand, there will always be a need for more labour as businesses start to expand. As these women's business start to scale up, there will be *"job creation"* (**#F08**).

Blockchain can increase women's access to information, thus improving their bargaining position [3]. The access to information about other contracts will allow these women to better position themselves to *"negotiate with suppliers as they know the contracts other businesses are getting"* (**F#08**). Decreasing information asymmetries and allowing women access to important information will enable women micro-entrepreneurs to be connected to global value chains, thus increasing their market access and knowledge to be able to negotiate better deals [3, 6].

Blockchain technology *"helps [women] have access to markets"* (**F#08**). Because blockchain removes barriers to entry and removes the obstacles of cross border purchases and sales, it holds considerable promise to boost women's participation in international trade [3]. This allows women to access foreign markets. Blockchain also lowers the cost of cross-border payments, which in turn make these markets more accessible to these women [3]. Women can *"use it as a as a method to make international payments as* *a way to store money specifically if [they] don't have access to traditional financial mechanisms"* (**F#05**).

Another way these women can grow their businesses is by increasing their market share.

Participant **F#05** gave an example in the African context. *"Because, if we look at marginalized women in certain sectors, sorry, of certain countries, right. So, you would basically increase the market share of that woman in a country where women are probably not perceived to be valuable in the market space, right? Women don't have equal and fair opportunities to participate in that specific country. Right. So, the moment you put a platform like ours, you put it on the block, and this woman now has access instead of saying for instance, her country has 10 million people, right, of which her market share is so low or so small, that she can't really make a better business in that market.*

Now, the moment she goes on to the block, for instance, and it's spread throughout the whole of Africa. Now, she's got a billion population, the size of a market [share] now is about a billion, you know, on a macro scale, but obviously, you segment the market now, maybe her market is now 100 million, as an example, you know, so which is 10 times more than then her country or entire country.

So, then she can then build her business, she can export products to countries where whatever she produces is actually valued, you know, and it's not because she's a woman, not because she's not a woman. You know, it becomes irrelevant, you know, the agenda. Then becomes irrelevant, because now people are not buying from a person anymore, are they buying from a brand.

You know, they're buying a product, you know, from a brand. So, so I think there's a, there's a whole bunch of value.

So, firstly, increase my market [share]. And then also, obviously, by way of increasing the market [share], I would be scaling my business, right so this is an opportunity for them to scale the business and scale themselves out of just being a micro entrepreneur into really starting to set up a proper business at the end of the day. The advantage that you have with a with engaging or subscribing to or joining some sort of blockchain based solution is the cryptocurrency advantage that comes along with that you say, because the moment you do that, you open yourself to the possibilities of not just receiving Fiat payments and pay payments in fiat currency, but also in cryptocurrency".

4.1.2.3 Cost Reduction

Another significant benefit is the reduction in costs. Traditional services generally have many fees and middleman costs. The removal of the need for financial intermediaries significantly reduces costs [8, 16]. With blockchain *"you don't need to pay ridiculous service fees"*, *"you don't need to pay all those middleman fees"*. (**F#01; F#07**), *"there's fewer intermediaries. Right. And this results in cost savings that are significant that can be passed on to, to the participants, or to the consumers"*. (**F#03**). Due to these reduced costs, previously excluded participants will now be able to participate [6].

Blockchain also *"reduces the costs of operations"* (**F#04**). It can also allow these women to *"save on costs for travel, because [you are able to] buy on [your] phone"*. (**F#08**). These women would generally travel to buy their products.

4.1.2.4 Financial Inclusion

The main benefit identified in the analysis, and the main benefit which this study aimed to uncover, is the financially inclusivity of blockchain. This was the most common theme present amongst participants' responses. Participants noted that blockchain enables access to decentralized loan platforms, alternative credit scoring platforms, grant funding, alternative payment, and transaction mechanisms, and has the potential to unlock traditional financial services through digital identities and documented business records.

Participant **F#04** stated that *"being able to give them access to funding"* is the first step towards financial inclusion as it allows women to invest in their businesses.

Participant **F#03** and **F#06** shared similar sentiments of using digital identities as the first step for financial inclusion.

Participant **F#03** shared *"I think I think whenever I look at financial inclusion in the unbanked space, I think that the ideas around this are like, initially, how can you give somebody a means to transact? Right to transact, in a digital manner. And then beyond that, how they do they give them access to a savings product or to loan and so but like, at the core, they need first level to transact, just send and receive.*

So, with blockchain, because the requirements to participate are not as rigid as traditional finance, you can onboard someone with minimal identification, or with alternative identification, right? The infrastructure at least allows for this. Once they've been given an identity, they can then suddenly, instantly receive send and receive value via digital assets. Right. So, this is like the very first step in the financial inclusion. So, I think the fact that you can create the fact that you can create an identity and use that identity to send and receive and have minimal regulatory hurdles. I think those are the building blocks to accelerate financial inclusion. So, once you have identity, and you can send and receive, I think this is like, you know, like you've already done the heavy lifting in terms of financial inclusion, any other product you add on top of that is a bonus".

Another perspective offered by participant **F#06** was that it *"leaves room for blockchain development, you know, where we will be pushing payments on the block to allow for decentralized finance mechanisms on this on the blockchain, you know, and then from there is, there's a whole bunch of things that that you can do, you know, on the blockchain.*

So firstly, that would be number one, you know, so that everyone in the informal sector, in the SME or micro entrepreneur space can benefit from that.

Because that's the biggest stumbling block. So what I would, what I would do, I would, if I would then like I would push to have my identity digitized, and go to the financial institutions and present this to them as an alternative or if I were the university, I would engage with the financial institutions and open the pathway for informal traders, for SMEs for an identifiable individuals at this stage, to be included through some sort of mechanism of digital identification. So that's, that's One".

Both participant **F#03** and **F#08** emphasized the importance of using business records to enable financial inclusion. *"I think blockchain potentially can help to, to, in* *complementing the digitization of these day-to-day operations of some of these women, which in turn helps to unlock financial services".* (**F#03**).

Participant **F#08** explained how it helps to unlock access to insurance policies. *"Definitely, definitely. Remember blockchain technology how it started from the word go was because there was a financial crisis. That happened because a small group of people have created a system that only they can control and created barriers to entry for many people making financial services to be exclusive to a certain calibre of people. So, the people that discovered or invented blockchain, [identified] a need a system that will be decentralized, meaning that you won't have somebody controlling the entire supply chain or the entire system.*

That's why they have to use it for financial inclusion, because at record keeping you needed to submit it to the banker, you submit to the insurance company". The participant then goes on to discuss a practical example of how this can be done, *"for example, when a company wanted us to talk them [about] hair, we had to have insurance because if you want to have products at 200 stores, that product has to be insured, but it could not because insurance companies said that there's no records here that proves that this hair is what you say it is. They asked how do we ensure this thing just based on your word that you say this is what it is? Then again, it was not insurable.*

Insurance is a part of financial inclusion. For businesses, you need that insurance. But insurance [companies] don't insure anything that is not documented, they won't even show a car that doesn't have papers. Therefore, they won't ensure any asset that doesn't have papers and a proof of where it came from. If it's a laptop, they want a serial number, they want all those kinds of things that actually prove the existence and the creation of the product itself. So that's [how blockchain will] help them with that, [access to insurance].

So, when it comes to that financial inclusion aspect, being able to prove that you are running a sustainable business [is important]".

4.1.2.5 No Discrimination

It was clear amongst participants responses that women face discrimination when applying for loans or credit. Blockchain is able to reduce these levels of discrimination as the technology allows you to only share certain credentials and *"it is kind of like pseudo anonymous to a degree".* (**F#01**); *"if I just have your wallet address, I can't tell if you're a woman or a man. So, I can't actively discriminate against you".* (**F#01; F#02**).

4.1.3   Risks

Three risks of using blockchain were identified amongst participants responses. There was a concern that the lack of regulation could pose a risk to already marginalized people [3]. Participants offered different perspectives within their responses. Some participants stated that *"the nice thing about blockchain is that it allows for self-regulation"* (**F#08**), while others were worried the lack of regulation could pose as a risk, and one participant stated they were unsure of whether it would have any negative effects.

Participant **F#03** and **F#04** felt that the *"lack of regulation can put these women at risk".* Participant **F#03** stated that *"because there is no regulation, it opens things up* *to counterparty risk, which is the risk that you're like, the other person in a transaction won't fulfill the end of the transaction".*

Participant **F#05** stated that they did not know whether this would pose a risk, sharing that they were unsure. *"I'm not sure. Possibly"* (**F#05**), however, they also mentioned that within the blockchain space, people would not accept a solution which actively discriminates against a certain group of people.

The lack of private key management was the most common risk present within the responses. Blockchain does not have any ways to recover your keys; *"if you lose your key. That's it, it's gone".* (**F#01; F#02; F#04; F#06; F#10**). This is not an ideal situation, especially in the case that this would be their entire investment and poses a great risk. For marginalized people who are already struggling with their finances, these women cannot even afford to lose access to their money with no way of recovering it.

Similarly, as with not being able to afford losing your keys, *"these women will not be able to take the hit should the cryptocurrency they are using or inv ested in had to massively drop".* (**F#01; F#04**). Thus, the volatility of cryptocurrencies is another major risk; in the case that women should accept cryptocurrency as a payment method or investment opportunity.

Although there are many benefits associated with the use of blockchain technology, the risks of using blockchain cannot be ignored and need to be explored before considering whether to adopt blockchain.

4.1.4   Challenges

Although blockchain technology has been described as disruptive and revolutionary, it is not a panacea to all these 'women's problems' and is not without its limitations. There are several concerns that are important to consider. This theme addresses the challenges which come with the use of blockchain technology.

4.1.4.1 Lack of Awareness and Understanding

Participants stated that many women micro-entrepreneurs would not even know that blockchain is an option for them. Other participants noted that *"blockchain is a complex technology"* (**F#08**), and many people do not understand it. This would negatively influence the adoption of a blockchain solution, as without awareness and understanding, one would not know how it could benefit you. The lack of understanding should not be overlooked, as it is important to understand how new technologies can be used, to reduce the risk of more harm being done than good [3, 26].

4.1.4.2 High Costs

The operational costs and cost of adopting a blockchain solution can be extremely high. Majority of participants noted that the high costs was the biggest challenge, especially because these women do not have excess finances available. Many participants stated that *"it needs to be more affordable"* (**F#01; F#02; F#09**). Participant **F#07** and **F#08** shared similar sentiments, stating that it will not be a feasible for a single woman micro-entrepreneur to adopt or develop a blockchain solution, as the costs would be far too high. Participant **F#07** stated that *"it can be [too] costly",* while participant **F#08** offered a solution to overcoming this problem.

F#08 *"Firstly, blockchain, it works a lot with macro-economics. So, with micro-economics, if I was a small business by myself, I wanted somebody to build me a blockchain solution for myself, it will be too expensive. So, you have to know that before you build a blockchain [solution], you are building it for a community of more than 1000 business users that are going to use it otherwise cannot be an expensive exercise that will not be able to be sustainable".*

4.1.5 Potential Use Cases for Financial Inclusion

The majority of participants focused on the direct financial aspects. Alternative perspectives included use cases which indirectly focus on financial inclusion, which were using blockchain to digitize business operations, digital identities, create a consistent track record to prove their sustainability and build credibility, proving authenticity and supply chain management.

4.1.5.1 Credit Scoring

Blockchain has the potential to create an effective "credit scoring system" (**F#02, F#03, F#05**). It can track payment histories [3, 17]. Participant **F#02** stated they *"believe credit score systems can be very biased"*, a blockchain enabled solution will provide a transparent way of calculating credit scores.

4.1.5.2 Cryptocurrency

Using cryptocurrency will allow women to participate in foreign trade [3, 16]. Transacting with cryptocurrency gives women access to global markets, because when transacting *"with fiat currency's, women are restricted to their local markets"*. (**F#06**). Using cryptocurrencies also *"removes the need for financial intermediaries, which results in savings which are directly felt by the user"*. (**F#03**).

4.1.5.3 Digital Identity

A blockchain enabled digital identity was a common use case mentioned for financial inclusion. Participant **F#09** offered a perspective which ties into some of the previous themes discussed. *"So digital credentialing, I feel like would be a very good alternative because it allows the person to also to provide information they wish to provide. You could exclude your name which may or may not reveal your gender and also your gender but as all of the rest of the information has been verified and backed, then this will not influence and this your application".*

4.1.5.4 Supply Chain

Using blockchain technology within supply chains was mentioned to indirectly contribute to financial inclusion; as it lowers costs by removing middlemen, having access to information gives women bargaining power, and having a deeper understanding of their supply chains allows them to make informed financial decisions. Blockchain technology allows for the automation of credit checks and verification measures throughout the entire supply chain process, which impacts the costs of the financial sector and the shipping industry. These reduced costs encourage women micro-entrepreneurs to participate in their economies [27]. Reduced costs across the supply chain and for financial services allows women micro-entrepreneurs gain competitiveness in foreign markets at higher profitability.

5 Conclusion

This study was conducted to determine the ways blockchain technology can be leveraged to empower women micro-entrepreneurs through financial inclusion. The study focused on answering the main research question; 'in what ways does blockchain technology facilitate financial inclusion for women empowerment?'.

It is evident that the way blockchain technology can empower women is many-fold. Blockchain is able to assist in overcoming many of the current challenges women micro-entrepreneurs are facing regarding financial inclusion. The findings reveal that blockchain technology both directly and indirectly affords financial inclusion amongst these women. The proposed model below summarises the key findings using an affordance lens.

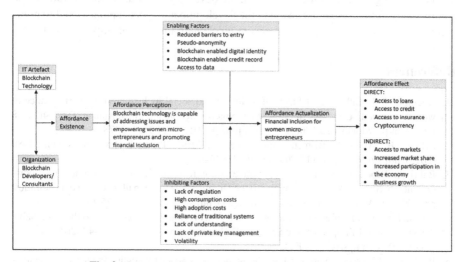

Fig. 2. Summary of the key findings using an affordance lens

The use of blockchain technology allows women micro-entrepreneurs to grow their business and affords them the opportunity to access both local and foreign markets, increase their market share and increase their participation within the economy. As their business grows, their revenues will increase, and they will be able to scale their businesses. Being financially included does not only mean having access to financial products and services, but rather being able to financially participate as well. It is, however, important to note that a blockchain solution will not be feasible in the context of a single micro-entrepreneur, and that these women should rather form a network where they will be able to support each other and benefit from economies of scale.

5.1 Limitations

There were certain factors which limited this study, the first one being the limited research on blockchain technology for women empowerment. In certain instances, the paper relied on blog posts to explore how blockchain is currently being used to empower women. However, the researchers ensured that these were from reputable websites and that the author of the blog had knowledge and experience with blockchain technology. Secondly, the most evident limitation was that this study does not have the perspectives of women micro-entrepreneurs. It was, however, decided that the study would have more grounding coming from the organizational context and by analysing the perspectives of blockchain experts who understand the technologies potential.

5.2 Future Research

Considering that this study did not include the perspectives of women micro-entrepreneurs; future research can be conducted which analyses factors which influence adoption amongst these women and aid in the development of an adoption framework. Alternatively, future research can aid in the development of a conceptual model to guide organizations on how to apply strategies in blockchain for women empowerment.

References

1. Ademola, S.S.: Influence of financial inclusion and social inclusion on the performance of women - owned businesses in lagos state, Nigeria. Scholedge Int. J. Manag. Dev., 4(3), 18 (2017). https://doi.org/10.19085/journal.sijmd040301, ISSN 2394–3378
2. Adjei, S.B.: Assessing women empowerment in Africa. Psychol. Dev. Soc. 27(1), 58–80 (2015). https://doi.org/10.1177/0971333614564740
3. Bahri, A.: Blockchaining international trade: a way forward for women's economic empowerment? In: Smeets, M. (ed.) Adapting to the Digital Trade Era: Challenges and opportunities, pp. 300–319. World Trade Organization (2021). https://doi.org/10.30875/137d7993-en
4. Bayeh, E.: The role of empowering women and achieving gender equality to the sustainable development of Ethiopia. Pacific Sci. Rev. B Humanit. Soci. Sci. 2(1), 37–42 (2016). https://doi.org/10.1016/j.psrb.2016.09.013
5. Boell, S.K., Cecez-Kecmanovic, D.: A hermeneutic approach for conducting literature reviews and literature searches. Commun. Assoc. Inf. Syst. 34(12), 257–286 (2014). https://doi.org/10.17705/1cais.03412
6. Chen, Y., Bellavitis, C.: Blockchain disruption and decentralized finance: the rise of decentralized business models. J. Bus. Ventur. Insights 13, 1–8 (2020). https://doi.org/10.1016/j.jbvi.2019.e00151
7. Chinomona, E., Maziriri, E.: Women in action: challenges facing women entrepreneurs in the gauteng province of South Africa. Int. Bus. Econ. Res. J. (IBER), 14(6), 835 (2015). https://doi.org/10.19030/iber.v14i6.9487
8. Chod, J., Trichakis, N., Tsoukalas, G., Aspegren, H., Weber, M.: On the financing benefits of supply chain transparency and blockchain adoption. Manage. Sci. 66(10), 4378–4396 (2019). https://doi.org/10.1287/mnsc.2019.3434
9. Crittenden, V., Crittenden, W., Ajjan, H.: Empowering women micro-entrepreneurs in emerging economies: the role of information communications technology. J. Bus. Res. 98, 191–203 (2019). https://doi.org/10.1016/j.jbusres.2019.01.045

10. Cunha, I.N.S.: Beyond the hype: embracing blockchain for social change. An analysis of how blockchain is fostering social innovation [Unpublished master's thesis]. Copenhagen Business School (2019)
11. da Cunha, P., Soja, P., Themistocleous, M.: Blockchain for development: preliminary insights from a literature review. Aisel.aisnet.org (2020). https://aisel.aisnet.org/amcis2020/adv_info_systems_research/adv_info_systems_research/10/
12. El Kasri, G.: Why blockchain technology is empowering women. Policy Center 25 April 2019. https://www.policycenter.ma/opinion/why-blockchain-technology-empowering-women#.YLZYFqgzYdV
13. Frizzo-Barker, J., Chow-White, P., Adams, P., Mentanko, J., Ha, D., Green, S.: Blockchain as a disruptive technology for business: a systematic review. Int. J. Inf. Manage. **51**, 102029 (2020). https://doi.org/10.1016/j.ijinfomgt.2019.10.014
14. Fromm, J., Mirbabaie, M., Stieglitz, S.: A systematic review of empirical affordance studies: recommendations for affordance research in information systems. Research-in-Progress Papers. 42 (2020). https://aisel.aisnet.org/ecis2020_rip/42
15. Günther, W.A., Rezazade Mehrizi, M.H., Huysman, M., Feldberg, F.: Debating big data: a literature review on realizing value from big data. J. Strat. Inf. Syst. **26**(3), 191–209 (2017). https://doi.org/10.1016/j.jsis.2017.07.003
16. Larios-Hernández, G.: Blockchain entrepreneurship opportunity in the practices of the unbanked. Bus. Horiz. **60**(6), 865–874 (2017). https://doi.org/10.1016/j.bushor.2017.07.012
17. Mavilia, R., Pisani, R.: Blockchain and catching-up in developing countries: the case of financial inclusion in Africa. Afr. J. Sci. Technol. Innov. Dev. **12**(2), 151–163 (2020). https://doi.org/10.1080/20421338.2019.1624009
18. Norta, A., Leiding, B., Lane, A.: Lowering financial inclusion barriers with a blockchain-based capital transfer system. In: IEEE INFOCOM 2019 - IEEE Conference on Computer Communications Workshops (INFOCOM WKSHPS), pp. 319–324 (2019). https://doi.org/10.1109/infcomw.2019.8845177
19. Ostern, N.: Toward a joint theory on social identity and individual differences of gender and it: the case of women in blockchain (Paper presentation). In: Twenty-Eighth European Conference on Information Systems (ECIS2020), A Virtual AIS Conference 6 June 2020
20. Patwardhan, A.: Financial inclusion in the digital age. Handb. Blockchain Digital Finan. Inclusion **1**, 57–89 (2018). https://doi.org/10.1016/B978-0-12-810441-5.00004-X
21. Sanap, M.: Role of information and communication technology in the women empowerment. Chronicle Neville Wadia Inst. Manage. Stud.Res. **4**(1), 300–306 (2015)
22. Saunders, M., Lewis, P., Thornhill, A.: Research Methods for Business Students (8th ed.). Pearson Education (2019)
23. Skogvang, E.M.: Blockchain: uniting aid and trade? a case study of the UN women blockchain project to empower women and girls in humanitarian settings [Unpublished master's thesis]. University of Oslo (2018)
24. Tang, C.: Innovative technology and operations for alleviating poverty through women's economic empowerment. SSRN Electron. J. (2020). https://doi.org/10.2139/ssrn.3748862
25. Thompson, J.: Tech can reach the world's unbanked women – but only if they tell us how it should work. World Economic Forum, 22 January 2021. https://www.weforum.org/agenda/2021/01/women-banking-digital-divide/#:~:text=Lack%20of%20formal%20ID%20is%20one%20common%20barrier%20to%20accessing%20financial%20services.&text=Understanding%20the%20needs%20of%20end,to%20banking%20or%20insurance%20products
26. Thylin, T., Duarte, M.: Leveraging blockchain technology in humanitarian settings – opportunities and risks for women and girls. Gend. Dev. **27**(2), 317–336 (2019). https://doi.org/10.1080/13552074.2019.1627778

27. Yang, Y., Chen, X., Gu, J., Fujita, H.: Alleviating financing constraints of SMEs through supply chain. Sustainability **11**(3), 673 (2019). https://doi.org/10.3390/su11030673
28. Zwitter, A., Boisse-Despiaux, M.: Blockchain for humanitarian action and development aid. J. Int. Humanitarian Action **3**(1), 1–7 (2018). https://doi.org/10.1186/s41018-018-0044-5

Digital Resilience in Adversity

Digitalisation of Indigenous Finance Institutions in Sub-Saharan Africa: A Critical Discourse Analysis

Rebecca Njuguna$^{(\boxtimes)}$ (ID), Pitso Tsibolane (ID), and Ulrike Rivett (ID)

University of Cape Town, Cape Town, South Africa
njgreb001@myuct.ac.za, {pitso.tsibolane,ulrike.rivett}@uct.ac.za

Abstract. This paper conducted a Critical Discourse Analysis (CDA) on top IS publication outlets in Sub-Saharan Africa. The aim was to identify and critically evaluate taken-for-granted assumptions contributing to the marginalisation of indigenous finance institutions (IFIs). The scarcity of literature suggested absence of a discourse on IFIs in the ICT4D domain. Consequently, no substantive deductions were made on violations of validity claims. Habermasian CDA was nonetheless applied to the selected literature to highlight issues relating to comprehensibility, truth, sincerity and legitimacy. Majority of the literature extended the narrative of IFIs as part of the transient informal economy that is expected to dissipate as viral digital technologies such as mobile money aid the mainstream financial system to achieve total financial inclusion. Alternative perspectives were missing from this body of literature. Appropriate definitions, diverse research questions and methodologies are required to better understand IFIs, their history, contemporary practices and role in sustainable development.

Keywords: Indigenous finance institutions · Informal finance · Digitilisation · Digital technologies

1 Introduction

Digitalisation "refers to the structuring of many and diverse domains of social life around digital communication and media infrastructures" [1, p. 5]. The concern of this paper is to explore how indigenous finance institutions (IFIs) are interacting with, influencing, and being influenced by digital technologies. The term 'indigenous' is elusive to define. From an African perspective, indigenous knowledge is regarded as that which is embedded in African philosophy and practices that have existed for centuries [2]. To define indigenous finance institutions, a brief review of the informal sector is necessary. The informal sector has been the subject of debates, particularly among economists and policymakers. Even the definition of what the informal sector is, is not conclusive [3]. Broadly, the informal sector is a 'grey market economy' that is not governed by the formal and legal frameworks outlined for businesses in a certain jurisdiction [4].

© IFIP International Federation for Information Processing 2022
Published by Springer Nature Switzerland AG 2022
Y. Zheng et al. (Eds.): ICT4D 2022, IFIP AICT 657, pp. 239–251, 2022.
https://doi.org/10.1007/978-3-031-19429-0_15

From a macroeconomic viewpoint, governments have related to the informal sector in either of two ways [5]. The first is by embracing and supporting it. The second is attempting to bring it under their regulatory purview to enforce various standards such as labour and tax laws. The rationale for businesses in the informal economy is to avoid high operational costs that come with formalisation, and this allows them to provide affordable products and services to large sections of the population [4]. While unregulated by formal legal frameworks, the informal sector has its own internal system created and enforced by various stakeholders within the ecosystem. The entire phenomenon can, in one way, be considered a response to the brutal and bureaucratic formal system that constrains personal initiative particularly among groups with limited socio-economic capital. The informal sector thus creates a "shadow" economy that offers a path out of poverty. In the place of written laws and contracts, the informal economy is governed by mutual cooperation, collaboration and reciprocity.

The informal sector is vast, but this article is only concerned with one aspect of it: informal finance institutions. Origins of informal finance institutions such as rotating savings and credit associations (ROSCAs) and accumulating savings and credit associations (ASCAs) have been traced to urban immigrant groups needing a source of capital to build new livelihoods in new environments [4, 6]. In pre-monetized societies in Africa, similar practices existed prior to European contact with the continent [2]. There were activities coalesced around families, communities, or kingdoms whose objective was communal welfare. This is consistent with one of the most prominent African philosophies, Ubuntu, which posits that a person is a person through other people, thus placing the community's interests above the individual.

Modern day community-based finance institutions that still espouse Ubuntu philosophy can be found across Africa [2]. Chama, Chilemba in East Africa, Esusu, Susu, Tontines, Djanggi in West and Central Africa, stokvels, Chilimba in Southern Africa. Although in literature these institutions are typically referred to as informal finance institutions, it is owing to their links to pre-colonial practices that the term 'indigenous finance institutions' is preferred in this article. By so doing, the virtues of indigenous socio-economic practice such as mutual co-operation and communal welfare are given higher credence than the notoriety and lack of governance that the term 'informal' invokes [3].

2   Contextualising Indigenous Finance Institutions

Indigenous finance institutions (IFIs) are significant contributors to household income and employment in developing countries [3]. Specifically, IFIs provide bootstrap financing for small businesses as well as other needs among financially marginalised communities in the global South [2]. Unlike mainstream bank financing, the IFI channels have lower repayment cost and do not have strict requirements such as collateral as prerequisites. This source of capital is crucial particularly to start-ups before they develop the track record that can qualify them for credit with banks.

Despite its centrality in the lives of the financially excluded, the IFI sector has historically been viewed as "temporal", "fringe" or a "waiting room" in the transition process from traditional, rural to the formal, urban economy [3]. This persistent informalization of IFIs has delegitimized their existence, which served to worsen their exclusion in the global financial discourse. In this paper, we view the IFI sector as existing of its own accord, not solely because of marginalisation and exclusion [2, 7]. IFIs have been largely associated with rural, urban poor, low literacy, low-income populations [8]. These groups also tend to be underserved by the mainstream financial system and thus forced to depend on alternative means of accessing capital and other financial services. Although these groups depend more on IFIs, proliferation of IFIs among urban, educated and banked groups suggests that access to the mainstream financial system does not obliterate the role of IFIs.

Although financial inclusion in the mainstream financial system has increased steadily in Sub-Saharan Africa, the widespread use of IFIs has remained. In West African countries such as Ghana and Nigeria, usage ranges between 50–95% of the adult population [9]. In South Africa, access to mainstream financial services is above 70%, which is one of the highest in Africa [10, 11]. Nonetheless, 11.5 million people, which is more than half of the adult population, use IFIs regularly [12]. While the number of those with access to banks is large, only about 33% use them for savings and 12% for borrowing [10]. These are among the services IFIs offer with more flexibility and lower costs than banks. This shows, at least in the case of South Africa, that mere access to the mainstream system does not eliminate people's use of IFIs.

Whether viewed as transition states or lasting institutions, the current role of IFIs in socio-economic development is self-evident. Additionally, the fact that they have survived attempts to formalise and 'civilise' them for decades speaks to the resilience of communal practices and institutions. Resilience in IS discourse has been approached from several perspectives. Heeks and Ospina [13, p. 75] define resilience as "the ability of a system to withstand, recover from, and adapt to short-term shocks and longer-term change." One way of assessing resilience is by looking at before, during and after a disturbance to a system has occurred [14]. Although the technological revolution has affected IFIs, the largest shock they have faced and prevailed against so far is colonialism. Colonialism significantly disrupted livelihoods and socio-economic structures in Sub-Saharan Africa. Thus, it is possible to look at IFIs before, during and after colonialism to get insights about the resilience of these indigenous information systems.

The second approach of assessing resilience is using three attributes: robustness, self-organisation and learning [13]. Robustness is a measure of how well a system can maintain its characteristics and performance in spite of external shocks and disturbances. The current principles, activities, and practices of IFIs are very similar to pre-colonial practices which included among other things regular meetings and contributions in one form or another for the mutual benefit of all members. Self-organisation measures how well a system can recover by rearranging its functions and processes to adapt to external disturbances. IFIs shifted from non-monetary to monetary contributions when the traditional African ways of subsistence were disrupted, and most people transitioned to the cash economy [6]. Learning refers to the system's ability to generate feedback and use it to build new skills, attitudes, and competencies necessary for experimentation and innovation. Ongoing appropriation and domestication of ICTs in IFIs [12, 15] is evidence of a system that is capable of engaging with external knowledge and incorporating it where it is found to improve the system.

By the metrics of resilience outlined by Heeks and Ospina [13] and Atinaf, Molla and Anteneh [14], IFIs are resilient indigenous financial systems. This should interest the ICT4D community to understand IFIs and their relationships with ICTs and development goals better. This is particularly important because of the fundamental differences between the philosophies underpinning IFIs and digital technologies. IFIs are rooted in African philosophy, that puts *we* (the community) ahead of *I* (the individual) [16]. Digital technologies are underpinned by Western philosophies centred on the individual. Although IFIs are appropriating some digital technologies, there is a fundamental misalignment. This misalignment is worth investigation so that IFIs can be offered ICT solutions aligned with the African way of *knowing* [16, 17], to support them to play their role in socio-economic development.

ICT4D practitioners have been called upon to engage deeper with various stakeholders, including community organisations playing a role in poverty and inequality eradication among other development goals [3]. In 2019, the Electronic Journal of Information Systems in Developing Countries (EJISDC) ran a special issue on "IT for the informal sector in developing countries". This issue appealed to the IS community to provide nuanced IT solutions that can support the informal sector "beyond the conventional straight-jacketed technology, economic, and policy solutions for the informal sector" [5, p. 1]. Bhattacharya [3] further proposed that ICT has much to offer the informal sector when it is not used solely as a tool to formalise the sector. The rallying call in the special issue and the propositions made therein back this article's interest to examine the discourse around ICT tools designed for and used by IFIs.

The next section discusses critical discourse analysis as the approach that was chosen for this review and the rationale for the choice.

3   Critical Discourse Analysis (CDA) Review Methodology

Critical discourse analysis (CDA) is one of the methods of conducting systematic literature review. Specifically, it is a critical review method applied when the objective is to examine and challenge ideological assumptions existing in literature [18]. By analysing a discourse, CDA brings out ideological hegemonies that may have been reproduced in literature in a domain. The two most common perspectives in CDA are Foucaldian and Habermasian CDA. While both seek to identify and challenge ideological hegemony with emancipatory ends, they approach it from different perspectives. Foucaldian CDA examines a communicative utterance, the context, and power structures between actors. Further, it examines historical discourse and how it influences current norms and practices. Habermasian CDA on the other hand analyses communicative utterances between actors in a communicative process. This scope limit assumes an ideal speech situation, a transcendental condition where all actors participate in the communication process freely, with no coercion from hegemonic powers.

However, it is acknowledged that the ideal speech situation is rarely achieved due to power imbalances [18]. Thus, communicative utterances are assessed to identify how actors have deviated from the ideal speech situation. This deviation could be a result of conscious or unconscious hegemonic participation. Conscious hegemonic participation is intentional manipulation of communication while unconscious participation constitutes adopting and advancing dominating ideologies in a taken-for-granted manner. Habermasian CDA is concerned with the latter. Habermasian CDA was selected to assess the IFI digitalisation discourse. Applying Foucaldian CDA and assessing conscious hegemonic participation involves direct criticism of individual and institutional actors advancing hegemonic participation. The discourse assessed in this review comprises of publications. It is not part of the objective of this review to assess the authors and affiliated institutions. Rather, the interest is to analyse the discourse itself to identify the various perspectives and assess any unconscious deviations from the ideal speech situation.

Unconscious hegemonic participation is identified by assessing the discourse against four validity claims: comprehensibility, truthfulness, legitimacy, and sincerity [19]. To be comprehensible, utterances should be linguistically simple, free of technical jargon that makes it difficult to understand. Truthfulness refers to the content of an utterance, where arguments should be factual and complete. Legitimate discourse is inclusive of all perspectives. Sincerity is the disparity between the speaker's utterance and what they intend to communicate.

CDA is value laden. Thus, it is not entirely free of the researchers' bias, beliefs and assumptions [18]. To support the researchers' interpretation and judgement of the discourse assessed, empirical evidence is required [18, 19]. This prevents researchers from making conclusions that are not a truthful representation of the analysed text. Wall et al. [18] outline four principles of conducting Habermasian CDA on publication discourse. First is to assume that the publication process aspires towards the ideal speech situation by being open to debate and allowing researchers to present alternative, even unpopular ideas without fear of any negative consequences. The second is to assume that hegemonic participation existing in a domain is unconscious. Hence, focus and criticism is directed towards concepts and not the authors and their institutions. Thirdly, researchers should test each text against the four validity claims but draw conclusions based on the body of literature assessed and not a single publication. Lastly, the review can be conducted on a sub-discipline or across several disciplines depending on the nature of the topic at hand.

The body of literature selected for this review comes from five publication outlets: the Information Technologies & International Development Journal (ITID), Electronic Journal of Information Systems in Developing Countries (EJISDC), African Journal of Information Systems (AJIS), Information Technology for Development (ITD), and IFIP Working Group 9.4 (IFIP). Bai [20] identifies ITID, EJISDC and ITD as the top 3 ICT4D journals globally. AJIS was selected for it's speficic focus on IS research from within the African continent. IFIP WG 9.4 was selected alongside the journals for being one of the longest running top conferences globally, and is specifically dedicated to research on social implications of ICTs for development. Wall et al. [18] recommend top journals for critical reviews as they have a wider audience and are more cited, hence have more ideological influence on the community. The four journals and one conference selected are among the top reputable publication outlets for IS researchers in developing countries, particularly those researching ICT4D. They are therefore a good sample of advances in ICT4D, the dominant ideologies around digitalisation and innovation in developing countries.

Before embarking on a critical review, a likelihood that some ideological hegemony exists ought to have been first identified. "A simple review of a representative sample of the literature based on a specific and simple set of criteria may be sufficient to demonstrate the need for a full-scale critical review" [18, p. 11]. The authors' first conducted a literature review as part of a proposed co-design study to develop an ICT solution for IFIs. It was then that it became apparent that digitalisation of IFIs was scarcely discussed in literature. The literature was extended to the broader informal sector to understand how it is being supported by ICTs. That further supported the intuition that the informal sector is under researched in general, and ICT practitioners' attention has been called towards the sub-domain [3]–[5]. The EJISDC special issue in early 2019 emphasised the need for more empirical research in the informal sector. This forms the backdrop against which this review will be attempting to establish a discourse in the sub-domain by assessing articles for the period 2019, 2020 and 2021.

The next section presents the analysis and findings based on the four validity claims. The coding schema developed by Wall et al. [18] for conducting CDA was followed for this analysis. It includes guidelines such as which speech elements to analyse for each validity claim as well as the section of publication these elements are likely to be found.

4 Empirical Analysis and Findings

After the 5 publication outlets were identified, the authors searched each of them manually, browsing each issue from 2019 to 2021 and identified topics related to the informal sector or informal finance. This yielded only six papers after full paper screening. Due to this low number, the authors searched Scopus for additional papers using the key words 'informal financ*' 'digitisation' and 'digitalisation'. This yielded an additional six papers. All the papers analysed are presented in Table 1. The six papers from the supplementary search on Scopus are marked with an *.

Table 1. A summary of the papers analysed

Authors	Publication	Country/context	Paradigm	Methods
[21]	ITD	Ghana	Positivist	Quantitative
[22]	ITD	Zambia	Positivist	Quantitative
[23]	EJISDC	Zambia	Interpretivist	Qualitative
[24]	EJISDC	Sub-saharan Africa		Qualitative
[25]	ITD	Nigeria		Quantitative
[26]	ITD	44 African countries		Quantitative
[27] *	Journal of Enterprising Communities: People and Places in the Global Economy	42 African countries	Positivist	Quantitative

(*continued*)

Table 1. (*continued*)

Authors	Publication	Country/context	Paradigm	Methods
[16] *	1st Virtual Conference on Implications of Information and Digital Technologies for Development		Critical	Qualitative
[28] *	Telecommunications Policy	Burkina Faso	Positivist	Quantitative
[29] *	1st Virtual Conference on Implications of Information and Digital Technologies for Development	Malawi		Qualitative
[12] *	International Development Informatics Association Conference	South Africa	Interpretivist	Qualitative
[30] *	International Conference on Information Resources Management	South Africa	Interpretivist	Qualitative

For the analysis, the screening was done manually and NVivo 12 was thereafter utilised for coding and analysis. Table 2 presents some of the assumptions extracted in papers, which form the basis of identifying a discourse in the literature analysed.

The main deduction that was made from the search and analysis was that there is no discourse on IFIs in Sub-Saharan Africa within the ICT4D domain. This conclusion was arrived at based on the lack of literature on the subject from the top publication outlets. The extended search on SCOPUS did not yield much either. While the papers found provide knowledge on some studies and perspectives on the informal sector, they are insufficient as a corpus for discourse analysis. This lack of discourse can be viewed as a form of unconscious hegemonic participation where a research sub-domain has been neglected by researchers without conscious intention on their part. Based on this deduction, no conclusions were drawn on violations of validity claims. Instead, CDA was used to map out issues related to each validity claim, from which implications and recommendations for future research were later derived.

The comprehensibility claim is concerned with the ease of understanding terms. Although the informal sector concept was fairly clear, informal finance was not clearly defined. In one instance IFIs such as rotating savings and credit associations and self-help groups (SHGs) were classified under microfinance institutions and in another, the same were classified together with practices such as hiding cash at home, using predatory loan sharks, using bus drivers as remittance channels, and keeping livestock. Thus, the concept of informal finance, the variety of practices and institutions within it is unclear. Truthfulness is concerned with factual accuracy in a discourse. The fact that very few studies engaged with IFIs empirically challenges some of the assumptions extended in conceptual papers. For instance, while some conceptual articles on financial inclusion reported that the use of informal finance is declining, the studies that were dedicated to

Table 2. Examples of assumptions extracted from the analysis

Validity Claim	Underlying assumption	Testing Criteria	Findings
Comprehensibility	Informal finance reflects a lack of formal financial services and regulations	Definition of informal finance institutions	Only 3 studies described informal finance institutions according to their practices as opposed to being the opposite of formal, regulated financial institutions
Truth	Financial inclusion studies capture IFI perspectives	Empirical situation	Only two out of 12 studies engaged directly with IFIs to capture first-hand perspectives
Sincerity	Informal finance will disappear as more people move to the formal financial system	Connotations	Informal finance was not discussed much and when it was, it was only a few remarks in passing
Legitimacy	Informal finance is mostly used by the poor and unbanked	Lack of diverse perspectives	Poor, poverty, unbanked, rural, excluded appeared frequently
	Methods		There were no design or evaluation studies
	Focus on registered microfinance and SMEs		All except two empirical studies engaged with registered microfinance and small enterprises
	Mobile money as the ultimate financial inclusion innovation		Mobile money had the highest occurrences across the studies

IFIs and surveyed IFI users reported a different picture, both in qualitative findings and national statistics. The confusion between the diffusion of mainstream financial services coupled with innovations such as mobile money, and the decline of informal finance usage reflects some unconscious deception on the assumed future of informal finance.

The sincerity claim looks at connotative language that might result in confusion. Only 3 articles had sections expounding on informal finance and their various forms. While there was a recurring acknowledgement of the role informal finance has been playing especially among the unbanked, it was mostly followed by an elaborate discussion on mobile money as a panacea for the financially marginalised. 'Mobile' was by far the most frequently used word in the publications (1021 instances). On the other hand, 'informal', which comprised also of non-finance mentions of the informal sector had 348 mentions and 'rotating' which captured rotating savings and credit associations (ROSCAs) had only 19 mentions. In one instance, when highlighting the gap in financial inclusion, ROSCAs and ASCAs were classified as informal services that the marginalised resort to. In the same article in another section highlighting the impact of mobile money, ROSCAs and ASCAs were classified as formal savings channels that have benefited from mobile money alongside banks. The authors don't take this as intentional distortion of the place of IFIs but a result of the lack of clarity pointed out under the comprehensibility claim.

The legitimacy claim concerns the inclusion of different perspectives. First, most studies in their background and literature review sections acknowledged the informal sector, and the existence of both registered (and regulated) and unregistered (and unregulated) institutions. However, when sampling, majority went for the registered institutions, be it SMEs or microfinance institutions (MFIs). One of the assumptions advanced was that informal finance is mostly for the poor, rural and unbanked. Among the keywords in this domain, 'poor', 'poverty', 'rural' appeared frequently. Only two studies presented profiles of educated, urban and tech savvy IFI users. Thirdly, participation in informal finance was also predominantly presented as a survivalist endeavour for the unbanked. The alternative perspective of IFI users which was only represented by two studies suggests there are social-cultural reasons why people choose to use IFIs despite having steady income and access to mainstream financial services. Informal finance tended to be reduced to remittances, with multiple instances referring to insecure ways of sending and receiving money, and cash storage in lockboxes. There was a lack of other perspectives on IFIs such as easy sources of low-cost credit for personal and business needs, social capital and insurance mechanism [8]. Lastly, innovation in informal finance was predominantly discussed in relation to mobile money as the solution. Apart from discussions of how IFI users are appropriating and domesticating popular ICTs such as mobile devices and social media, the entire body of literature analysed lacked any mention of niche innovation for or within IFIs by the ICT4D community.

5   Implications and Recommendations for Future Research

Overall, the literature analysed reflects a nascent debate in ICT4D on indigenous finance, its role in socio-economic development and its future. The difficulty to define the informal sector applies to the IFIs too. The paucity of literature dedicated to innovations in IFIs may be because of the dominant view of their transitory nature. If one regards the informal sector, IFIs included, as survivalist transitory states that will eventually dissolve naturally as people transition to the formal system, then it might not be worth investing in ICT solutions for. There are exceptions to this dominant view, such as the conceptual discussion by van Stam [16] and empirical studies by Biyela, Tsibolane and Van Belle [12], Menze and Tsibolane [30] and Kariuki and Ofusori [15].

Comprehensibility can be enhanced by having more studies in the vein of Aliber [7], Ojera, [2] and van Stam [16], dedicated to in-depth exposition of IFIs, their history, contemporary practices and the role of ICTs in supporting them to promote socio-economic development. IFIs and other informal sector institutions are usually described on the basis of what they are not, such as not regulated, nor registered [7, 31]. As a starting point, appropriate definitions and descriptions can be debated and agreed upon. Truth and sincerity can be addressed by openly acknowledging that deeper perspectives of IFIs exist and encouraging more research to understand them. Terms such as 'unregulated' in defining IFIs only consider the legal frameworks that apply to mainstream financial systems, while disregarding that IFIs have their own form of governance that has sustained their existence for centuries.

Legitimacy can be enhanced by IT/IS researcher's broadening the scope of empirical investigations. The informal sector is seen as generally meeting a demand for products and services that the formal economy is unable to meet. From this viewpoint, the existence of IFIs signals financial intermediation needs among populations that are underserved by the mainstream financial system. However, there is evidence of IFI use cutting across demographics [8, 12], and in Sub-Saharan Africa, such practices preceded the establishment of the mainstream financial services on the continent [2, 7]. Different questions therefore need to be asked such as why people choose to use IFIs even when banked, what the role of IFIs is in sustainable development and how ICTs can support that. While there is no shortage of innovation around mobile money, mobile banking and other financial technologies aligned with the mainstream financial system, the lack of innovation for IFIs reflects the view of indigenous finance systems as subaltern. Other areas of the informal sector such as street trading have received diverse attention, including design science research to understand their unique challenges and build responsive ICT solutions [32]. Such methodological variety can also be applied in researching IFIs which would be in line with da Silva's [33, p. 693] call for "...new studies to develop more native and indigenous theories of ICT4D". Lastly, a lot of ICT4D literature is underpinned by assumptions of individual agency and empowerment [34]. IFIs are established and run based on collective empowerment. Studies that explore this notion of communal or collective capabilities would enhance our understanding of ICT adoption and use in contexts where groups can have more empowerment and emancipatory impact than the individual.

6 Conclusion and Limitations

The IT/IS space is a fast-paced environment. Thus, three years since the EJISDC special issue called for innovation in the informal sector was deemed a sufficient timeline to examine what steps the ICT4D community has taken in response to the call. Among the top publication outlets selected, the findings indicate a scarcity of both conceptual and empirical studies regarding IFIs. Focusing on the five publication outlets that were deemed among the top voices of IS in Sub-Saharan Africa limited finding more literature that may have been published in other venues. Future research can expand the number of outlets to capture more perspectives.

CDA is rooted in the critical paradigm which calls for self-reflexivity as part of the research process [19]. Methods used, analysis and interpretation in interpretive and critical research is usually limited by the researcher's experiences and worldview [35]. In this case, the authors are interested in the preservation of indigenous knowledge systems, of which IFIs are a part, and how ICTs can support these alternative ways of knowing that may not be compatible with mainstream ideologies and artefacts. Therefore, the interpretations and conclusions arrived at from this review can be challenged from other viewpoints. Opening a debate is one of the goals of critical research, to spur discussions that would result in a deeper understanding of the phenomenon.

Appendix

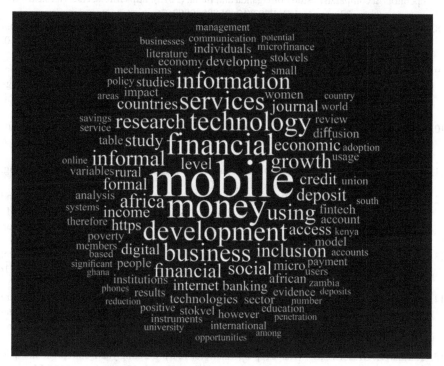

Fig. 1. Word frequency from the 12 papers analysed

References

1. Brennen, J.S., Kreiss, D.: "Digitalization." Int. Encycl. Commun. Theory Philos. pp. 1–11. (2016). https://doi.org/10.4324/9780203736319-36
2. Ojera, P.: Indigenous financial management practices in Africa: A guide for educators and practitioners. Adv. Ser. Manag. **20**, 71–96 (2018). https://doi.org/10.1108/S1877-636120180 000020005
3. Bhattacharya, R.: ICT solutions for the informal sector in developing economies: What can one expect? Electron. J. Inf. Syst. Dev. Ctries. **85**(3), 1–7 (2019). https://doi.org/10.1002/isd2. 12075

4. Rangaswamy, N.: A note on informal economy and ICT. Electron. J. Inf. Syst. Dev. Ctries. **85**(3), 1–5 (2019). https://doi.org/10.1002/isd2.12083

5. Seetharaman, P., Cunha, M.A., Effah, J.: IT for the informal sector in developing countries: A broader perspective. Electron. J. Inf. Syst. Dev. Ctries. **85**(3), 1–5 (2019). https://doi.org/10.1002/isd2.12093

6. Verhoef, G.: Informal Financial Service Institutions for Survival: African women and stokvels in urban South Africa, 1930–1998. Enterp. Soc. **2**(2), 259–296 (2001). https://doi.org/10.1093/es/2.2.259

7. Aliber, M.: The importance of informal finance in promoting decent work among informal operators: a comparative study of Uganda and India. (2015). https://ilo.userservices.exlibrisgroup.com/view/delivery/41ILO_INST/1242589840002676

8. Mduduzi, B., Khumalo, N.: The role of stokvels in South Africa: a case of economic transformation of a municipality. Probl. Perspect. Manag. **17**(4), 26–37 (2019). https://doi.org/10.21511/ppm.17(4).2019.03

9. Kounou, G., Akpona, C., Ahouantchede, H., Gohoue, R., Belqasmi, F., Glitho, R.: A social network-based architecture for on-line RoSCAs in the developing world. In: 2013 Proceedings of 4th Annual Symposium on Computing. Dev. ACM DEV, pp. 10–11. (2013). https://doi.org/10.1145/2537052.2537070

10. Louis, L., Chartier, F.: Financial Inclusion in South Africa: an integrated framework for financial inclusion of vulnerable communities in south africa's regulatory system reform. J. Comp. Urban Law Policy **1**(1), 13 (2017)

11. The Banking Association South Africa, "Financial Inclusion," (2021). https://www.banking.org.za/financial-inclusion/. Accessed 03 Jan 2022

12. Biyela, N., Tsibolane, P., Van Belle, J.-P.: Domestication of ICTs in Community Savings and Credit Associations (Stokvels) in the Western Cape, South Africa. In: Krauss, K., Turpin, M., Naude, F. (eds.) IDIA 2018. CCIS, vol. 933, pp. 35–47. Springer, Cham (2019). https://doi.org/10.1007/978-3-030-11235-6_3

13. Heeks, R., Ospina, A.V.: Conceptualising the link between information systems and resilience: a developing country field study. Inf. Syst. J. **29**(1), 70–96 (2019). https://doi.org/10.1111/isj.12177

14. Atinaf, M., Molla, A., Anteneh, S.: Towards a resilient information system for agriculture extension information service : an exploratory study. In: 2021 Proceedings. of 1st Virtual Conference on Implications of Information and Digittal Technologies for Development, pp. 696–708. (2021)

15. Kariuki, P., Ofusori, L.O.: WhatsApp-operated stokvels promoting youth entrepreneurship in Durban, South Africa: experiences of young entrepreneurs. In: Proceeding of ACM International Conference on Ser., vol. Part F1280, pp. 253–259. (2017) https://doi.org/10.1145/3047273.3047397

16. van Stam, G.: Appropriation, coloniality, and digital technologies. In: Proceedings of the 1st Virtual Conference on Implications of Information and Digital Technologies for Development, pp. 709–721 (2021)

17. Pérez-García, L.: The ICT4D-Buen Vivir Paradox: using digital tools to defend indigenous cultures, In: 2021 Proceedings of the 1st Virtual Conference on Implications of Information and Digital Technologies for Development, pp. 722–733 (2021)

18. Wall, J.D., Stahl, B.C., Salam, A.F.: Critical discourse analysis as a review methodology: An empirical example. Commun. Assoc. Inf. Syst. **37**, 257–285 (2015). https://doi.org/10.17705/1cais.03711

19. Cukier, W., Ngwenyama, O., Bauer, R., Middleton, C.: A critical analysis of media discourse on information technology: preliminary results of a proposed method for critical discourse analysis. Inf. Syst. J. **19**(2), 175–196 (2009). https://doi.org/10.1111/j.1365-2575.2008.00296.x

20. Bai, Y.: Has the global south become a playground for western scholars in information and communication technologies for development? Evidence from a three-journal analysis. Scientometrics **116**(3), 2139–2153 (2018). https://doi.org/10.1007/s11192-018-2839-y

21. Coffie, C.P.K., Hongjiang, Z., Mensah, I.A., Kiconco, R., Simon, A.E.O.: Determinants of FinTech payment services diffusion by SMEs in sub-Saharan Africa: evidence from Ghana. Inf. Technol. Dev. **27**(3), 539–560 (2021). https://doi.org/10.1080/02681102.2020.1840324

22. Tang, Y.K., Konde, V.: Differences in ICT use by entrepreneurial micro-firms: evidence from Zambia. Inf. Technol. Dev. **26**(2), 268–291 (2020). https://doi.org/10.1080/02681102.2019.1684871

23. Wakunuma, K., Siwale, J., Beck, R.: Computing for social good: supporting microfinance institutions in Zambia. Electron. J. Inf. Syst. Dev. Ctries. **85**(3), 1–16 (2019). https://doi.org/10.1002/isd2.12090

24. Nan, W., Zhu, X., Lynne Markus, M.: What we know and don't know about the socioeconomic impacts of mobile money in Sub-Saharan Africa: a systematic literature review. Electron. J. Inf. Syst. Dev. Ctries. **87**(2), 1–22 (2021). https://doi.org/10.1002/isd2.12155

25. Owoseni, A., Twinomurinzi, H.: Evaluating mobile app usage by service sector micro and small enterprises in Nigeria: an abductive approach. Inf. Technol. Dev. **26**(4), 762–772 (2020). https://doi.org/10.1080/02681102.2020.1727825

26. Chatterjee, A.: Financial inclusion, information and communication technology diffusion, and economic growth: a panel data analysis. Inf. Technol. Dev. **26**(3), 607–635 (2020). https://doi.org/10.1080/02681102.2020.1734770

27. Kelikume, I.: Digital financial inclusion, informal economy and poverty reduction in Africa. J. Enterprising Communities **15**(4), 626–640 (2021). https://doi.org/10.1108/JEC-06-2020-0124

28. Ky, S.S., Rugemintwari, C., Sauviat, A.: Friends or Foes? Mobile money interaction with formal and informal finance. Telecommun. Policy **45**(1), 102057 (2021). https://doi.org/10.1016/j.telpol.2020.102057

29. Malanga, D.F., Banda, M.: ICT Use and livelihoods of women microenterprises. In: 2021 Proceedings of 1st Virtual Conference on Implication of Information and Digital Technologies for Development, pp. 877–889 (2021)

30. Menze, A., Tsibolane, P.: Online Stokvels : the use of social media by the marginalized. In: International Conference on Information Resources Management (CONF-IRM), p. 26 (2019)

31. Galdino, K.M., Kiggundu, M.N., Jones, C.D., Ro, S.: The informal economy in pan-Africa: review of the literature, themes, questions, and directions for management research1. Africa J. Manag. **4**(3), 225–258 (2018). https://doi.org/10.1080/23322373.2018.1517542

32. Rumanyika, J., Apiola, M., Mramba, N.R., Oyelere, S.S., Tedre, M.: Mobile technology for street trading in Tanzania: a design science research approach for determining user requirements. Electron. J. Inf. Syst. Dev. Ctries. **87**(5), 1–21 (2021). https://doi.org/10.1002/isd2.12176

33. da Silva, A.P.: Sharing wisdoms from the east: developing a native theory of Ict4d using grounded theory methodology (Gtm) – experience from timor-leste. In: 2021 Proceedings of the 1st Virtual Conference on Implications of Information and Digital Technologies for Development, no. 1, pp. 685–695

34. Lorini, M.R., Chigona, W.: ICTs for inclusive communities : a critical discourse analysis introduction , aim and significance research problem and context. In: 2014 Proceedings of the 8th International Development Informatics Association Conference, no. 2014, pp. 78–94

35. Wall, J.D., Stahl, B.C., Salam, A.F.: Critical discourse analysis as a review methodology: an empirical example. Commun. Assoc. Inf. Syst. **37**, 257–285 (2015). https://doi.org/10.17705/1cais.03711

Reimagining Socio-technical ICT4D Interventions: Nexus Between Context, Resilience, and Sustainability

Muluneh Atinaf[✉] [iD]

IT-Doctoral Program, Addis Ababa University, Addis Ababa, Ethiopia
muluneh.atinaf@uog.edu.et, mulunehatinaf@yahoo.com

Abstract. Information technology for development (ICT4D) is embedded in complex socio-technical contexts. This presents challenges to resilient and sustainable of the ICT4D interventions. The problems is partly rooted in the lack of fully understanding context of the local development practices and transform it to resilient and sustainable interventions and in the gap to understand the relationships between context, resilience, and sustainability. The purpose of this research is to address how context, resilience, and sustainability relate to each other. The research draws empirically from the literature to develop propositions to show how the concepts relate and from review of the extant literature and qualitative data collected from a local agriculture extension information service to support the claims. The results contribute to theory by conceptualizing the links between context, resilience, and sustainability and inform practice through the recommendations made on how resilient and sustainable socio-technical information systems interventions be approached.

Keywords: Context · Resilience and sustainability · The socio-technical context of ICT4D interventions · Resilient and sustainable ICT4D interventions · Socio-technical ICT4D

1 Introduction

Context, resilience, and sustainability are becoming the core pillars of mainstream information systems (IS) and ICT4D research and practice. Yet, the relationship between these triple concepts is not explored sufficiently. Thus the purpose of this research is to explore how the triple concepts of context, resilience, and sustainability relate each other in the context of ICT4D interventions. The research adopts the definition of ICT4D [45, 46] as the attempt to use information and communication technology (ICT) tools to undertake their actions and exploit opportunities for societies; the concept of "development" to refer the "long-term societal transformation" which recognizes the historical and spatial diversity of countries [38] expressed in terms of technological infrastructure and institutional arrangements [47]. The importance of ICT4D in enabling the multifaceted, dynamic, and contentious socio-technical processes of societies is a well-recognized fact

© IFIP International Federation for Information Processing 2022
Published by Springer Nature Switzerland AG 2022
Y. Zheng et al. (Eds.): ICT4D 2022, IFIP AICT 657, pp. 252–269, 2022.
https://doi.org/10.1007/978-3-031-19429-0_16

[38] though the social and technical factors continue to be critical for its success [1]. For instance, the frequent technological change, the complex social dynamics, and development processes are presenting challenges to ICT4D interventions and research [38]. The socio-technical approach has been applied to grasp the factors in complex socio-technical systems as a means to analyze the problems and the solutions [2] as socio-technical systems. However, many ICT4D initiatives are criticized for the techno-centric focus over the social-centric aspect of the intervention [11] assuming that providing access to technology creates the required capability [11] which resulted in a socio-techno divide [9]. This is against the widely accepted conceptualization of socio-technical systems which perceives socio-technical systems as involving human and technology components and the interactions between the two [3]. Recent work has produced useful knowledge on the triple concepts of context [4, 5], resilience [6–8], and sustainability [9] of ICT4D interventions but the relationship between the concepts and attempt to build on the existing socio-technical knowledge is rare. ICT4D research can benefit from consideration of prior cumulative socio-technical knowledge to contribute to ICT4D and mainstream IS research [53]. Moreover, resilience and sustainability should unlock the potential of the socio-technical to take advantage of both the digital and the social components.

Context, resilience, and sustainability are attracting ICT4D scholars and the concepts are becoming core conceptual and practical research agendas in major IS and ICT4D conference proceedings and journals. However, the concepts are treated in isolation limiting our understanding of the links existing between the triple concepts. Context refers to "the processes and conditions, other than the constituent causal sociomaterial interactions (or intra-actions) of IS phenomena, that affect their formation and are affected by them [36, p. 13]. Context-based research in the ICT4D domain rarely goes beyond understanding and describing the lived experiences of stakeholders to incorporate the local development practices and the existing information systems artifacts [13]. Resilience on the other hand refers to the ability of a system to perform its objectives in the face of challenges through different mechanisms to continue to thrive [15]. One can understand from these definitions that resilience is related to maintaining the functions and operations of a system during stress either through unlocking potential from the technology or human potential. Sustainability refers to enduring those interventions, specifically the ICT4D interventions in the development arena and keeping target users to continue using the interventions [10] effectively so that users can attain their desired goals through the systems they apply [18]. The concept of sustainability adds the notion of development to the above explanation. Those to whom the intervention is for would not continue using it unless it adds value to their livelihoods in any way. Context, resilience, and sustainability are related to the three foundational premises of ICT4D research and practice, i.e., context, technology, and socio-economic development [36]. Therefore, ICT4D research and practice needs to address these concepts together. This has importance in achieving sustainable ICT4D interventions that are transformed from and considered local development contexts having the properties of resilience during times of external stress.

Context matters to any information systems interventions [4, 5] regardless of the methodological challenge associated with it in IS research in general and ICT4D in particular [4, 5]. The impact of ignoring context when the interventions are for enabling development is serious. For instance, many ICT4D interventions in African countries fail because the interventions are a-contextual which lack adequate reflections of the cultures and values of local realities [56]. Hence, disregarding context in ICT4D research and practice leads to failures of the interventions [57] which again limit understanding of how contexts in ICT4D should be theorized [14]. The consequence of risks that may arise is not predictable during this time of socio-technical dynamism. The problem is serious in an interconnected environment such as in the agriculture extension information service system considered in this research context. Ethiopia, where the context of this research is conducted is being challenged by external shocks presenting pressure to the resilience of the agriculture extension information service system in different locations. The agriculture extension information service has to deal with multiple and overlapping shocks and treats such as the recurrent climate change, the COVID 19 pandemic, pests and diseases, local conflicts including the current civil war, economic slowdowns and the role that the agricultural sector is expected to play. These have impacts on the local agricultural development practices and on the economy at large. Putting resilient ICT4D interventions in place to communities where there are differences in accessing technology, digital literacy, and cognitive issues to apply the information content received is another issues be dealt with cautiously. Provision of technical telecom infrastructure, for instance, to a socio-technical problem without providing the required capability to the diversity of stakeholders cannot be a resilient intervention [16]. However, those systems are expected to be sustainable assisting users to achieve their development goals. The general sustainability literature looks at sustainability from the perspective of efficient use of resources, i.e., from the economic, institutional, social, and environmental dimensions through innovative use and reuse of the resources [9, 33]. ICT-enabled development interventions pose an enduring question as to how these initiatives can become sustainable at the community, regional, country, or global levels.

This research follows a multi-method and multi-theoretical approach to conducting ICT4D research as suggested by [32] for applications involving such interconnected issues of context, resilience, and sustainability. Therefore, a socio-technical analysis of the local agriculture extension information service system will enhance and further our understanding about the relationships between the triple concepts of context, resilience, and sustainability of ICT4D interventions. Hence, research on ICT4D needs to be reimagined back to the socio-technical foundations and move from descriptions of silo conceptual explorations to linking up the concepts with a purpose of holistic knowledge creation. This research will address the following research question: how do context, resilience, and sustainability relate to one another.

The rest of the paper is structured as follows. The next section discusses the literature to assess and develop the conceptualizations of context, resilience, and sustainability. This is followed by a discussion on the research methodology applied to address the research question in this study. Then the paper presents preliminary results followed by discussion of the results. Finally, the research is presents the conclusion and next steps to be done during the next iteration the research.

2 Review of the Literature

ICT4D research targeting development goals in specific settings should not be studied in isolation but together with a deep investigation of the historical processes of development and governance that have evolved in that context [44]. This approach offers advantage to emphasize and ask the question of how, under what circumstances, and for whom do ICTs, embedded in social practices and processes lead to development? [38] This is a critical question for ICT4D research because the interventions are meant for those who need them which in turn help to abstract it to the local context. Such closer abstraction to those who need it or to the context reveals local truths [52] and the impact of information technology in this interconnected world often depends on context [5]. Zheng et al. [38] explicitly acknowledged context and the socio-technical nature of development processes in ICT4D interventions. Such agreements by the scholarly and practitioner community on foundational ICT4D questions should be furthered to the trending ones too. Hence, we have to also ask how resilient and sustainable the ICT4D interventions are given the contexts within which the interventions are planned for implementation. The understanding we had so far about the issue of context reveals that ICTs do not provide linear solutions and there is no one-size-fits-all kind of solution [44] to all settings rather attention needs to be given to the complex socio-technical contexts of the interventions [12]. ICT is considered as part of the context and as an ensemble artifact encompassing the conditions and processes in the environment of an observed phenomenon [48]. This emphasizes ICT4D interventions need to have a holistic view and conceptualized as embedded in a system, a network, a project, or social structure [38]. This positions ICT4D research extending contextual research from organizational perspectives in which the systems are implemented and used in domains of inquiry such as communities, countries, or global institutions [36] to resilient systems concepts.

Protection of information systems has been an issue of decision-makers to safeguard the organizations information systems from risks [7] than resilience. However, recently emerging risks become borderless and unpredictable limiting the capabilities of traditional or a priori risk mitigating plans implying the need for other assumptions than following classical risk and security management [7]. Though resilience is getting greater attention both in the ICT4D and ISs research, there is no common agreement on what resilience means for development projects [10]. Resilience has been approached from the technical, the social, and the socio-technical perspectives by different authors and disciplines. There are initial works which tried to treat context and resilience together via some mechanisms in a way to inform the technical aspect of resilience so it can be materialized into digital interventions for its effective use [6]. Effective use can be understood through [18]: (i) understanding how a network of affordances supports the achievement of organizational goals, (ii) understanding how the affordances are actualized, and (iii) using inductive theorizing to elaborate these principles in a given context. Effective use of socio-technical information systems to be deployed in resource-constrained environments need more than what is suggested by Burton-Jones and Volkoff such as understanding the context and how the interventions could be made resilient. However, most sustainability studies ended up with understanding sustainability factors than looking at such links. For example, Baduza and Khene [10] see the sustainability of projects from three important factors: technological, social, and financial sustainability. A wider perspective of sustainability is given by Liu [17] who categorized the factors of sustainability into financial/economic, cultural/social, technological, political/institutional, and environmental sustainability. Each of these explanations deals with the social and technical components of sustainability. If we look at each of the technological, social, and financial sustainability they tell us about the continuity of technology use, continuity of social practices, or continuity of financial sources or funding which of course have importance to sustaining the intervention. However, what should be done for instance on ICT as an enabler of all or some of these sustainability elements is not clear.

2.1 Information Systems as Context-Specific and Socio-technical Systems

The practices of stakeholders in agriculture are expected to operate within a network of interdependencies that apply ICTs in a bottom-up and top-down logic to incorporate indigenous knowledge into their farming practices or nurture value-chain integration [54]. According to Karanasios and Slavova [54] the nature of ICT4D initiatives in agriculture are step-wise processes to be attained gradually. Similarly contextualized knowledge needs to be founded on the existing socio-technical one and built over a longer-term gradually. In reality, many ICT4D interventions experience failures resulting in design-reality gaps because the interventions are still a-contextual [55]. Hence, one of the key steps toward successful ICT4D interventions is a deep understanding of the contexts [19] such as the information requirements, access to technology, digital literacy levels of stakeholders, institutional and social structures, the processes of information generation, and dissemination, the values and objectives of the stakeholders in the local agricultural development practices, and the staffing and skills of employees [12]. This further support the argument that explains all research models and theories are restricted within their contextual applicability where the impact of the outcome depends on the context [5]. A gap in fully understanding context challenges the transformation of user needs into desired solutions [10]. Traditional software development approaches such as systems analysis and design cannot be easily adapted to suit contexts implying the need for contextual development methodologies to meet the needs of communities and stakeholders [10].

The socio-technical dimension involves people, task/process, structure, technology, and data [2]. The people dimension refers to human subjects characterized by certain behavior, skills, and values; task/process describes any form of action having certain goals and deliverables; structures describe the hierarchical relationships in individual projects, social groups, or entire organizations; technology refers to the application of knowledge through machines, digital methods, and processes such as development tools or technical platforms; data refer to the values and observations that are recorded, processed, and analyzed using information systems [2]. Avgerou [36] suggested the need for addressing two decisions to contextualize within a specific setting: the first is the choice of conditions and processes in the environment of a focal phenomenon to be investigated. The second is the choice of domains to be researched as issues in the environment. According to Avgerou [36], the choice of domains refers to the domain of application of the information system which would be implemented either to empower the stakeholders with information and information processing or change the behavior of their actions such as the impact of their actions on the environment, the way they use a certain infrastructure, utility, and natural resources. Therefore, information systems as enablers of some behavior or actions that people want to take to achieve their goals or objectives need to considerate of the above socio-technical aspects.

2.2   Context, Resilience, and Sustainability as Socio-technical Phenomenon

Most ICT4D literature focuses on technocratic projects implemented by government agencies, NGOs, or international donors [38] for a mare description and understanding of the interventions [14, 50]. This makes ICT4D interventions in Africa, where most of those interventions are situated, a-contextual contradict the local development realities, cultures, and values [55] resulting in failures [56]. Thus, context is determinant to the sustainability of ICT4D interventions. The nature of ICT4D being embedded in a system, a network, a project or a social structure [38] implies its operation within a socio-technical context. In other words, ICT4D interventions are expected to function as systems involving stakeholders, their networks, and the social and institutional structures within a certain context. However, the notion of context in ICT4D is being challenged due to the components it involves and the interactions between the components that require our understanding of context [38]. Context varies from setting to setting though there could be common elements such as technology, usage, and users [49]. Culture, socio-political and geopolitical space, novel ICT communities, ICT characteristics, and novel ICT users are also relevant contexts in ICT4D research [49]. Therefore, context is a key socio-technical phenomenon in the study of ICT4D interventions. Similarly sustaining the interventions, sustainability in other words, is considered as a socio-technical [20] phenomenon.

Resilience is approached from different perspectives. Some literature treated it from the technical point of view [8] and others tried to look at resilience from the social dimensions only [7]. From the social dimension, resilience is an emergent property enabling the organization's capacity to continue its functions in the face of external stressors through mindfulness, agility, elastic infrastructure, and recoverability [7]. But resilience combines technical design features [8] too along with organizational features. There is limited literature that covered both the technical and social together or from the socio-technical perspective. Such literature emphasized the importance of putting resilient development within the communities and the technical systems they applied [6]. This approach is in line with the argument by Baduza and Khene [10] who narrated that resilience for development projects represents the materialization of local learning and community ownership focusing on human capability development than on technological development only. Hence, resilience is a socio-technical phenomenon involving the two components where both the technical infrastructure and the social structures need to be maintained in the face of external shocks. Therefore, placing resilience in the context of ICT4D research can be rooted in the study of ICT4D interventions in the context of development practices and stakeholders to enable sustainable societal changes. It is this socio-technical nature of resilience that is attracting scholars' attention [7] in addition to its potential to enable sustainable development. Therefore, new strategies are needed for organizations and communities to sustain their services, associated technology assets, people, and facilities [7].

Sustainability of ICT4D projects has been a core argument and most of the findings on sustainability are related to factors for sustainability [10]. Such knowledge is important because ICT4D research is applied within specific contexts where the applications require a nuanced understanding of the socio-technical processes [38] and factors to make them sustainable. Socio-technical changes may take place in a certain context where individuals are not only recipients of development benefits but also agents of change [38] implying the social, technical, and interaction between the two is key to a socio-technical phenomenon. Therefore, the technical component in the socio-technical ICT4D is important to enable the interaction and ICT can play an instrumental role in facilitating social interaction [51]. The interaction between the social and the technical offers the advantage of enabling engagement and ownership as the social is the primary owner of their development practice. An important point related to the whole concept of ICT4D interventions is suggested by Zheng et al. [38] who stressed researchers and practitioners in the ICT4D domain should critically reflect on their implicit assumptions about development and technology, consider where the research or practice is situated in the broader picture of social transformation, and what may be missing in their implicit theory of change (societal transformation) of ICT4D as the phenomenon is a contentious socio-technical process. In other words this refers to context, sustainable development, and ICT as sociotechnical phenomenon. Avgerou [36] described this in the ICT4D context as the phenomena in ICT4D are constituted by a dynamic human and technology entanglement (intra-actions) where neither the technical nor the social have an independent, self-contained existence but they are epistemologically inseparable, i.e., impossible to understand by studying them as independent entities. Development in this regard should embrace multiplicity, heterogeneity, and openness as a concept and as a socio-technical process [38].

3   Research Methodology

The purpose of this research is to explore the relationships between the triple concepts of context, resilience and sustainability in ICT4D interventions. To meet its objectives, the research is conducted in two phases. The first phase is devoted to explore the conceptualizations of context, resilience, and sustainability and draw propositions that show the links existing between the triple concepts. Hence, this phase explores the meaning of the concepts along with the relationships existing between them as a socio-technical phenomenon. The extant literature is used as a source of data in this phase. The second phase provides empirical evidence for the propositions given in the first phase above. The purpose of this step is to show support of the propositions about the relationships between context, resilience, and sustainability using evidence from empirical data. The case study method is adopted for this round of the research. A case study has the advantage of deeply understanding the real-life experience of different stakeholders and their context of action [57]. Empirical data were collected from a multi-stakeholder and multi-context agriculture extension information service system in Ethiopia.

3.1 Research Context and Data Collection

As discussed above, the research draws from two types of data for the two phases of the research. The research applies data collected from the extant literature and empirical data collected from stakeholders in the agriculture extension information service system. For the first phase, articles from mainstream information systems and ICT4D specialist journals and conference repositories were accessed. The materials were retrieved from the following journal databases and conference proceedings: Information Technology for Development, Information Technologies & International Development, Electronic Journal of Information Systems in Developing Countries, the proceedings of the series of conferences on ICT in developing countries organized by the IFIP WG9.4, and the AIS eLibrary. Cross-references and keyword search strategies have been used to retrieve relevant literature. Content evaluation of the sources accessed is done by the author. As the research is interested in the relationships between the triple concepts, research articles that cover one of the concepts and connects to one or more of the concepts is considered for further analysis. In addition to this, which of the socio-technical components (the social, the technical, or the interaction between the two) does the research gave focus is also considered for analysis. According to this criteria, a research article that focuses on context but doesn't mention the socio-technical nature of context and didn't connect it to either resilience or/and sustainability is not a target for review. This phase produces the propositions to show the links between context, resilience, and sustainability.

A case study method is adopted as an approach for the second phase of the research. Case study offers an advantage to focus on the lived life experiences of stakeholders [29, 30]. This is useful to analyze the contexts in the research setting as deeply as possible. Specifically, it is important in environments where users' context of action is critically important [31] inquiry in the research. The agriculture extension information service is one of the socio-technical kinds involving networked stakeholders interacting to support stakeholders' daily agriculture extension development practices. The agriculture extension information service in the country is characterized by multifaceted socio-technical contexts involving multiple stakeholders with different characteristics. The stakeholders can be individuals, collectives, or institutional support systems involved in the public agriculture extension service. A holistic understanding of the triple concepts of context, resilience, and sustainability is not easy through a single research approach. For this reason as well as to harness the issues holistically, the research has adopted a multi-method approach [32].

Data has been collected from stakeholders following snowballing technique and data were analyzed following qualitative data analysis techniques. A total of 37 subjects were involved as subjects for data collection. Data were collected in two rounds and in different years. The first round of data collection and the research context was done during Feb, 2017; it is included in [12]. The second round of data collection was done between Dec 2020 and Aug 2021. The second round of data collection was made to substantiate the first round by adding data from the supply side of ICT4D interventions, i.e., information systems developer. This phase involves a total of eight subjects who are expert information systems developers and managers in agriculture extension information systems development and management from four organizations. The subjects were selected purposefully as they are the ones who have been involved and are with the highest experience in rolling out information systems to be applied in the agriculture extension information services. Analysis of this second round data is in progress and the primary purpose of this paper is to establish the links between the triple concepts and communicate that to the wider ICT4D research and practice community. Part of the data along with the context of the agriculture extension information service is presented in prior published manuscript, hence can be found in [12].

4 Findings

The first round of the research is completed at this stage and the research's report on these preliminary results is presented below. In this round, the research has tried to look at existing work in terms of the focus and approaches being followed by the author to explore the context, resilience, and sustainability of ICT4D interventions. A total of 58 papers were assessed based on the criteria set but only few were qualified for further analysis. The literature analysis is done in terms of the socio-technical components (the social, the technical, the interaction between the social and technical) the work has covered and how it relates to the other concepts. This is supported with the arguments drawn from the literature to show the links between context, resilience, and sustainability. It is a well-accepted understanding that most of the ICT4D literature focuses on context as the work of Davison and Martinsons [5] boldly noted "context is king". However, most of the research done treated context independently from the concepts of resilience and sustainability research. Table 1 below presents the results from the categorization of the literature reviewed according to the methodology discussed above. The categorization is made according to the focus of the research work selected, i.e., technical, social, or socio-technical, and the specific dimension the work have focused on.

The literature surveyed on context, resilience, and sustainability is presented in a table of matrix according to the components of the socio-technical dimensions, the dimensions seen, and the triple concepts of context, resilience, and sustainability. According to the data, there is significant work related to contexts in the ICT4D literature done to explore the lived experiences of stakeholders' local development practices. However, the number of works that tried to link context to resilience or sustainability is limited. The limited number of work under context in Table 1 above doesn't mean there is little work done on context rather very few of them connect context to resilience and sustainability. There is a voluminous literature on context but it focuses on describing the phenomenon than incorporating it to the designs of information systems needed [37] or transforming it into digital solutions without connecting it either to one of or both of the other concepts. On the other hand, good size of work explores the concepts of resilience and sustainability together.

Different issues have been raised under the technical, social, and interactions of the social and technical components. Research done on technical and social components of the socio-technical phenomenon discusses the concepts explicitly. However, research papers that discuss the interactions between the social and technical components do not explicitly mention it. Concepts raised under the technical component include the purely technical aspects that tried to conceptualize resilient information systems [8, 24], the intensions of stakeholders to use the ICT4D interventions [9], scalability of the

Table 1. The focus of prior research on context, resilience, and sustainability

The focus of the Socio-technical Dimension	Dimensions seen	Context	Resilience	Sustainability
The Technical	Technical		[8, 24]	
	Scalability		[10, 35]	[10, 35]
	Digital resiliency		[35]	[35]
	Information systems architecture		[40]	
	Infrastructure		[41]	
	Model		[43]	
The Social	Social (organizational/institutional)		[7, 33]	[33]
	Economic/financial		[10, 33, 35]	[10, 33, 35]
	Ecology/ecosystem		[25, 33]	[33, 35]
	Social-ecological		[26]	
	The intention of stakeholders to use ICT	[9]	[9]	
The Social and the Technical	Emergency management		[34]	
	IT use		[42]	
	Human-computer interaction (HCI)		[6, 20, 39]	

information systems [10, 35], digital resilience [35], information systems architecture [40], resilient infrastructure [41], and building a resilient model [43]. The concepts raised under the social dimension include the social (organizational/institutional) in general, the financial/economic aspects [10, 33, 35], ecology/ecosystem [25, 33, 35], and social-ecological [26]. The works that indicated the interactions between the social and the technical components raise issues of emergency management [34], IT use [42], and human-computer interaction [39]. Others have covered issues that involve both the social and technical components. For instance, [10] and [35] have raised the importance of financial or economic resources for scaling ICT4D projects. These are the preliminary results to show how context, resilience, and sustainability relate each other and how the concepts are treated in the literature. Further research is required to support the propositions given in the model based on empirical data that reflect the socio-technical nature of the three concepts.

4.1 The Link Between Context, Resilience, and Sustainability in ICT4D Interventions

As it is presented in Table 1 above, there are few sources that linked context to resilience. The size of the papers is reduced due to the criteria being used to consider the papers for further analysis. That is, only research work that deals with either to two or three of the triple concepts is considered. Had it considered work that has dealt with only one of the concepts, the size would have been huge. Context is about the phenomenon taking place in the research setting, and exploration of such phenomenon is not a new one. One of the reasons for this could be because resilience is an emerging research domain in the both the mainstream and ICT4D. Hence, prior research gave focus to sustainability than to resilience of the interventions where resilience is a trending research in ICT4D. Such understanding is reflected in Marais [9]. The other potential reason could be existing information systems were not considered as part of studying context rather understood as constraints [13]. Information systems development as a means of intervention in any context is known to be both situated and socio-technical [21] where the situated action perspective implies the form and nature of IS development activities are interrelated with, and inseparable from its contextual setting [22]. Therefore, the existing artifacts applied by the stakeholders operating within a contextual boundary [13] are part of the socio-technical context surrounding the research setting [5]. However, existing ICT4D interventions are often treated as black boxes serving as resources or constraints on development giving much focus primarily to the new intervention for development [13]. This contradicts the prevailing knowledge that states newer designs of IS can be shaped from the experiences and learning of the material constraints [13]. Therefore, the inclusion of existing information systems artifacts in the study will offer an opportunity to understand the details of the sophisticated socio-technical ICT4D phenomena. Existing information systems discussed above can be analyzed in a way to understand the gaps in implementing the socio-technical requirements [12]. The literature offers independent assessments on design and reality gaps though it doesn't try to explicitly connect it to either resilience or sustainability. The design reality gap analysis framework offers the dimensions of analysis: objectives and values, processes, technology, information, management systems and structure, investment resources, staffing and skills, milieu (OPTIMISM) [23]. Given the above rich analysis dimensions, the OPTIMISM framework is appropriate to understand the context in terms of the gaps and the fit between the current information systems and the socio-technical requirements [12].

In the literature, resilience is approached from different domains such as from a technical dimension [8, 24], a social (organizational/institutional, individual, collectives) dimension [7] ecological perspective [25], and social-ecological perspectives [26]. This research adopts the perspective of the perspective proposed by the wider ICT4D research but with a view from the socio-technical foundations. Thus, the socio-technical issue is what defines both contexts of local development practices and resilience. Context emerging from the social dimension influences the technical resilience and context in the technical context guides the technical resilience for a sustainable intervention. This needs to prioritize the development of new knowledge paying attention to the socio-technical elements than focusing solely on the social or technical aspects [27]. As ICTs are primarily enablers of human development, such development strategies should be discussed where self-reliant relationships are built via networks from the bottom-up spanning local, regional, and national levels [9]. Therefore, it is when the interventions are resilient and when resilience is mapped from the socio-technical contexts of the stakeholders and local development practices that sustainability of the ICT4D interventions be ensured. Hence, ICT4D interventions can be sustainable when they are resilient both from the social and technical dimensions. However, it should be noted that sustainability is one of the many factors for successful ICT4D interventions [9]. Recent research on resilience has produced attributes and markers that characterize and define information systems resilience from the technical perspective [8]. Heeks and Ospina [8] have tried to attach their framework meant for analyzing the technical resilience of information systems to a social component just listing the markers. That is a good start to consider the social component but it only lists some features as markers for the attributes of resilience. It would have been very informative to research and practice as well as change both practices if it is presented in a way how those markers can be transformed into technical resilient information systems. According to Heeks and Ospina [8], the information systems resilience attributes are grouped into foundational and enabling attributes. Foundational attributes include robustness, self-organization, and learning whereas the enabling attributes include redundancy, rapidity, scale, diversity and flexibility, and equality each of them having resilient attribute markers.

Given the above discussion, it is important to look at the details of the proposed model for sustainable ICT4D interventions depicted in Fig. 1 below. The literature shows the existing relationship between the concepts of context, resilience, and sustainability. To summarize it once again, the arrow from context to resilience shows that resilience is informed by the context of the local development practices and the stakeholders. Context is socio-technical as it is discussed above. Therefore, the resilience of the technology is reflected from the socio-technical context in that it should be either to maintain the social resilience or support it through a resilient technical system. The technical context and the interaction between the social and the technical inform resilience in a way that both resilient solutions should consider the social and technical contexts of the local development practices and the stakeholders. Hence, resilience is also socio-technical which refers either to maintaining the continuity of organizations and their services to operate smoothly in the face of external stressors or the technical systems to resist and continue functioning during external stressors. This is a dyadic relationship between context and resilience, hence the double arrow between them. In turn, sustainability is informed by the combined socio-technical context and resilience. However, as ICT is one of the components to be considered in ICT4D research the properties of sustainability in this research case the ones to motivate users continued use of the artifact should be embedded in it.

Based on the literature review made and the discussions that follow the research proposes the following diagram presents the link between the concepts.

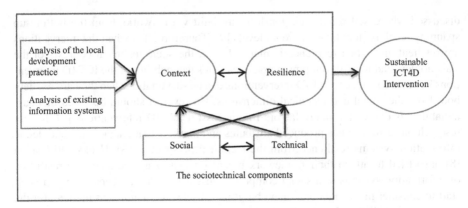

Fig. 1. Relationship between context, resilience, and sustainable digital solution

5 Discussions

In the literature, there is no clarity on the dimensions that constitute resilience and the factors that have importance for sustainability. The different concepts raised under resilience imply the lack of agreement between scholars on the dimensions of resilience. This is mainly due to the emergence of resilience as a new pillar of ICT4D research and the continued development of the technology. Most of the literature in the ICT4D domain focuses on technical resilience. Work that focuses on the technical dimensions of resilience has been published recently by Heeks and ospina [8]. Though there are sources that focus on the social component of resilience there is also inclination to treat resilience and sustainability as one and the same. This is in line with the findings of [58] who reported that most of the ICT4D literature is approaching resilience and digital resilience synonymously emphasizing the technical component only. The dimensions of the technical resilience suggested by [8] are useful attributes but the framework needs further evaluation for the purpose of whether the it is complete as a generic tool to be applied in any context and whether each of its attributes are in line with the purpose and definition of resilience.

The reviews made show that only a few of the papers discussed two or more concepts together. This is evident between the concepts of resilience and sustainability or the concepts of context and resilience. However, those papers which raised resilience and sustainability do not discuss the links between the concepts but most of them viewed the concepts either as related concepts or as a necessary condition for the other. For instance, [10, 35] discussed the importance of economic/financial availability to sustainability and resilience of projects but didn't discuss how the two relate and the relational factors between them. One may also ask a reasonable question about the links between context and sustainability. There is a lot of work on context both in the mainstream and ICT4D outlets. However, most of it focuses on description of the context [14] than transforming it into sustainable interventions.

Unlike the link between context and resilience, some ICT4D literature claims resilience and sustainability have relationships and differences as well. For instance, Zhang and Lin [28] reported that sustainability and resilience are related where the two can learn from each other; however, they also differ in that resilience measures regeneration of resources and sustainability focuses on supplying the resources. Regeneration of resources is the continued existence of the services or resources via different forms, media, or mechanisms to the stakeholders whereas supplying the resources makes available or existence of the resource with no interruptions. Therefore, if one of the properties of resilience is regenerating the resources then that act will lead to the sustainability of the ICT4D intervention. This is one implication of how resilience and sustainability reinforce and influence each other as well. Even in most cases, what is being discussed as sustainability is the sustainability of ICT itself, i.e., continuity of ICT use which cannot be a new concept or construct if we have context, resilience, and sustainability altogether.

Moreover, there are also shared attributes between resilience and sustainability from the technical perspective, for instance scale/scalability. The work of Baduza and Khene [10] tried to look at the resilience and sustainability of ICT4D along with the need for scalability. However, the link between the two and the importance of context either to resilience or sustainability or to both of them is not given. Resilience is dynamic and the capacity for adaptation to adversity is distributed across systems where individual resilience depends on the resilience of other systems [16]. This makes resilience similar to the concept of sustainability [10] through the intentions of stakeholders to use the intervention [9]. But this would be possible only when the stakeholders' resilience intents (the social) are mapped into the intervention solution. As discussed above there is a match in some of the dimensions of context, resilience, and sustainability. Though this can be taken as what makes the concepts similar it doesn't mean that they are one and same to be treated together. Rather more research is needed to clarify how the concepts differ or relate each other. ICT4D intervention can benefit from embracing the three foundations of ICT4D research, i.e., context, technology, and socio-economic development.

Context of the ICT4D interventions can be explored from the local development practices and the stakeholder's which takes the existing IS into account. Moreover, the technical component of resilience can support sustainability of the local contextual development practices. The link between context and resilience shows two points: first, the link from context to resilience shows that context informs the development of resilient information systems, and second, resilience on the other hand ensures the continuity of the functioning of the context that is the social component. It is therefore within the interventions that one can embed the sustainability action behaviors as sustainability doesn't have material existence. Some unique attributes to be drawn from the socio-technical analysis of the contexts of the local development practices and the stakeholders and resilience analysis of the information system will add to this. For example, technical resilience cannot be a solution for a community that is challenged with digital divides, connectivity issues, access to digital content, and gaps in applying the content received into its context. Therefore, looking at the triple concepts together will offer a holistic view of the ICT4D intervention than conducting isolated research on each of the concepts can contribute. The proposed model can be further evaluated with empirical data to test the propositions given in the model. Further research is needed to test the propositions using empirical data that reflect the socio-technical nature of context, resilience, and sustainability.

6 Conclusion

Context, resilience, and sustainability are becoming the pillars of ICT4D research and practice. Hence, the research concludes ICT4D research and practice needs to be reimagined in accordance with the three core issues discussed and the foundational socio-technical components. These core concepts are attracting attention both in mainstream information systems and ICT4D research domains. Approaching the triple concepts in a holistic way has an advantage to understand the required interventions in a holistic way and to reinforce the concepts in the interventions. Hence, context, resilience, and sustainability in ICT4D research should be approached together than in isolation. For instance, technical resilience cannot be treated without considering the context in an environment where there are issues of literacy, access or digital divide, connectivity, etc. Therefore, while considering the triple concepts of context, resilience, and sustainability in an ICT4D intervention the concepts should be explored within the foundations of the socio-technical framework. One reason for this is because; ICT4D interventions are shaped by the social, the technical, and the interactions between the social and technical components. The other is such an approach offers a systemic level of understanding encompassing the socio-technical (social and technical/artifact) components. The concepts are interrelated and one influences the other in the process of putting a sustainable ICT4D intervention in place. The second round of the research and the findings and the discussion that follows will improve and complete this research. This research in progress work contributes to both theory and practice. For theory, it contributes by developing a sustainability model showing the conceptual links between context, resilience, and sustainability of ICT4D interventions. The research contributes to practice through the outputs which provide insights to practitioners to understand the socio-technical contexts of the community's local development practices and the socio-technical nature of resilient ICT4D interventions leading to sustainability.

References

1. Luna-Reyes, L., Zhang, J., Gil-Garcı́a, J., Cresswell, A.: Information systems development as emergent socio-technical change: a practice approach. Eur. J. Inf. Syst. **14**, 93–105 (2005)https://doi.org/10.1057/palgrave.ejis.3000524
2. Bostrom, R.P., Heinen, J.S.: MIS problems and failures: a socio-technical perspective, part II: the application of socio-technical theory. MIS Q. **1**, 11–28 (1977)
3. Baskerville, R., Baiyere, A., Gregor, S., Hevner, A., Rossi, M.: Design science research contributions: Finding a balance between artifact and theory. J. Assoc. Inf. Syst. **19**(5), 358–376 (2018). https://doi.org/10.17705/1jais.00495
4. Avgerou, C.: Contextual explanation: Alternative approaches and persistent challenges. MIS Q. **43**(3), 977–1006 (2019). https://doi.org/10.25300/MISQ/2019/13990
5. Davison, R., Martinsons, M.: Context is king! considering particularism in research design and reporting. J. Inf. Technol. **31**(3), 241–249 (2016). https://doi.org/10.1057/jit.2015.19
6. Atinaf, M., Molla, A., Anteneh, S.: Towards a resilient information system for agriculture extension information service: an exploratory study. In: Proceedings of the 1st IFIP 9.4 Virtual Conference on Implications of Information Technology and Digital Technologies for Development (2021) https://doi.org/10.48550/arXiv.2108.09748

7. Abramowicz, W. (ed.): BIS 2013. LNBIP, vol. 160. Springer, Heidelberg (2013). https://doi.org/10.1007/978-3-642-41687-3

8. Heeks, R., Ospina, A.V.: Conceptualising the link between information systems and resilience: a developing country field study. Inf. Syst. J. **29**(1), 70–96 (2018). https://doi.org/10.1111/isj.12177

9. Marais, M.A.: ICT4D and sustainability. Int. Encycl. Digit. Commun. Soc. 1–9 (2015)

10. Baduza, G., Khene, C.: A holistic view of ICTD and up-scaling of community development projects.In: Proceedings of the 12th annual pre-ICIS SIG GlobalDev Workshop. Munich, Germany, December 15 (2019)

11. Chigona, W., Pollock, M., Roode, J.D.: South Africa's socio-techno divide: a critical discourse analysis of government speeches. S. Afr. Comput. J. **44**, 3–20 (2009)

12. Atinaf, M., Molla, A., Karanasios, S., Anteneh, S.: Digitalizing agriculture extension service in Ethiopia: a design-reality gap Analysis. In: Twenty-Third Pacific Asia Conference on Information Systems, Dubai, UAE (2020)

13. Chae, B., Poole, M.: The surface of emergence in systems development: agency, institutions, and large-scale information systems. Eur. J. Inf. Syst. **14**, 19–36 (2005)

14. Sein, M.K., Thapa, D., Hatakka, M., Sæbø, Ø.: A holistic perspective on the theoretical foundations for ICT4D research. Inf. Technol. Dev. **25**(1), 7–25 (2019). https://doi.org/10.1080/02681102.2018.1503589

15. Barasa, E., Mbau, R., Gilson, L.: What Is resilience and how can it be nurtured? A systematic review of empirical literature on organizational resilience. Int. J. Health Policy Manag. **7**(6), 491–503 (2018)

16. Masten, A.: Ordinary Magic: Resilience in Development. Guilford publications, New York (2015)

17. Liu, C.: Sustainability of rural informatization programs in developing countries: a case study of China's Sichuan province. Telecommun. Policy. **40**(7), 714–724 (2016). https://doi.org/10.1016/j.telpol.2015.08.007

18. Burton-Jones, A., Volkoff, O.: How can we develop contextualized theories of effective use? A demonstration in the context of community-care electronic health records. Inf. Syst. Res. **28**(3), 1–22 (2017). https://doi.org/10.1287/isre.2017.0702

19. Borzaga, C.: Bodini, R,: What to make of social innovation? Towards a framework for policy development. Soc. Policy Soc. **13**(3), 411–421 (2014). https://doi.org/10.1017/S14747464 14000116

20. Weber, M., Hacker, J., vom Brocke, J.: Resilience in information systems research – A literature review from a socio-technical and temporal perspective. In: 2021 Proceedings of ICIS (2021)

21. McLeod, L., Doolin, B.: Information systems development as situated socio-technical change: a process approach. Eur. J. Inf. Syst. **21**, 176–191 (2012)

22. Gasson, S.: A social action model of situated information systems design. Data Base Adv. Inf. Syst. **30**(2), 82–97 (1999). https://doi.org/10.1145/383371.383377

23. Bass, J.M., Heeks, R.: Changing computing curricula in African universities: evaluating progress and challenges via design-reality gap analysis. Electron. J. Inf. Syst. Developing Countries **48**(1), 1–39 (2011). https://doi.org/10.1002/j.1681-4835.2011.tb00341.x

24. Wang, J.W., Gao, F., Ip, W.H.: Measurement of resilience and its application to enterprise information systems. Enterp. Inf. Syst. **4**(2), 215–223 (2010). https://doi.org/10.1080/175175 71003754561

25. Holling, C.S.: Resilience and stability of ecological systems. Annu. Rev. Ecol. Syst. **4**(1), 1–23 (1973). https://doi.org/10.1146/annurev.es.04.110173.000245

26. Walker, B., Holling, C.S., Carpenter, S., Kinzig, A.: Resilience, adaptability and transformability in social-ecological systems. Ecol. Soc. **9**(2) (2004)

27. Sarker, S., Chatterjiee, S., Xiao, X., Elbanna, A.: The sociotechnical axis of cohesion for the IS discipline: Its historical legacy and its continued relevance. MIS Q. **43**(3), 695–719 (2019). https://doi.org/10.25300/MISQ/2019/13747

28. Zhang, W.J., Lin, Y.: On the principle of design of resilient systems – application to enterprise information systems. Enterp. Inf. Syst. **4**(2), 99–110 (2010). https://doi.org/10.1080/175175 71003763380

29. Yin, R.K.: Case Study Research: Design and Methods Applied Social Research Methods. Sage, London and Singapore (2009)

30. Eisenhardt, K.M., Graebner, M.E.: Theory building from cases: opportunities and challenges. Acad. Manag. J. **50**(1), 25–32 (2007). https://doi.org/10.5465/amj.2007.24160888

31. Benbasat, I., Goldstein, D., Mead, M.: The case research strategy in studies of information systems. MIS Q. **11**(3), 369–386 (1987)

32. Masiero, S.: Should we still be doing ICT4D research? Electron. J. Inf. Syst. Developing Countries. (2022). https://doi.org/10.1002/isd2.12215

33. Schoormann, T., Kutzner, K.: Towards understanding social sustainability: an information systems research-perspective. In: Forty-First International Conference on Information Systems (2020)

34. Sakurai, M., Kokuryo, J.: Design of resilient information system for disaster response. In: Thirty Fifth International Conference on Information Systems. (2014)

35. Tim, Y., Cui, L., Sheng, Z.: Digital resilience: how rural communities leapfrogged into sustainable development. Inf. Syst. J. **31**(2), 1–23 (2020)

36. Avgerou, C.: Theoretical Framing of ICT4D Research. In: Choudrie, J., Islam, M.S., Wahid, F., Bass, J.M., Priyatma, J.E. (eds.) ICT4D 2017. IAICT, vol. 504, pp. 10–23. Springer, Cham (2017). https://doi.org/10.1007/978-3-319-59111-7_2

37. Heiden, P., Beverungen, D.: A renaissance of context in design science research. In: Proceedings of the 55th Hawaii International Conference on Systems Sciences, pp. 5758–5767 (2022)

38. Zheng, Y., Hatakka, M., Sahay, S., Andersson, A.: Conceptualizing development in information and communication technology for development (ICT4D). Information Technology for Development. 1–14 (2018). https://doi.org/10.1080/02681102.2017.1396020

39. van Biljon, J.: Knowledge mobilization of human-computer interaction for development research: core issues and domain questions. Inf. Technol. Dev. **26**(3), 551–576 (2020). https://doi.org/10.1080/02681102.2020.1767022

40. Zhang, W., Lin, Y.: On the principle of design of resilient systems – application to enterprise information systems. Enterprise Information Systems. **4**(2), 99–110 (2010). https://doi.org/10.1080/17517571003763380

41. Scholl, H., Patin B.: Resilient information infrastructures: mobilizing adaptive capacities under extreme events. In: Proceedings of the Eighteenth Americas Conference on Information Systems (2012)

42. Nemeth, C.Nunnally, M., O'Connor, M., Cook, R.: Creating resilient IT: how the sign-out sheet shows clinicians make healthcare work. In: Proceedings of AMIA 2006 Symposium, pp. 584–588 (2006)

43. van der Aalst, W., Hinz, O., Weinhardt, C.: Resilient digital twins: organizations need to prepare for the unexpected. Bus. Inf. Syst. Eng. **63**(6), 615–619 (2021)

44. Madon, S., Sharanappa, S.: Social IT outsourcing and development: Theorising the linkage. Inf. Syst. J. **23**(5), 381–399 (2009). https://doi.org/10.1111/isj.12013

45. Avgerou, C.: Information systems in developing countries: a critical research review. J. Inf. Technol. **23**(3), 133–146 (2008)

46. Walsham, G.: ICT4D research: reflections on history and future agenda. Inf. Technol. Dev. **23**(1), 18–41 (2017). https://doi.org/10.1080/02681102.2016.1246406

47. Yang, G.: The co-evolution of the internet and civil society in China. Asian Surv. **43**(3), 405–422 (2003). https://doi.org/10.1525/as.2003.43.3.405
48. Orlikowski, W., Iacono, S.C.: Research commentary: desperately seeking the "IT" in IT research – a call to theorizing the IT artifact. Inf. Syst. Res. **12**(2), 121–134 (2001)
49. Andoh-Baidoo, F.: Context-specific theorizing in ICT4D research. Information Technology for Development. **23**(2), 195–211 (2017). https://doi.org/10.1080/02681102.2017.1356036
50. Sein, M.K., Thapa, D., Hatakka, M., Sæbø, Ø.: What theories do we need to know to conduct ICT4D research? In: Proceedings of SIG GlobDev Ninth Annual Workshop. Dublin, Ireland, December 11 (2016)
51. Davison, R.M., Díaz Andrade, A.: Promoting indigenous theory. Inf. Syst. J. **28**(5), 1–6 (2018). https://doi.org/10.1111/isj.12203
52. Sarker, S.: Building on Davison and Martinsons' concerns: a call for balance between contextual specificity and generality in IS research. J. Inf. Technol. **31**(3), 250–253 (2016)
53. Sahay, S., Sein, M.K., Urquhart, C.: Flipping the context: ICT4D, the next grand challenge for IS research and practice. J. Assoc. Inf. Syst. **18**(12), 837–847 (2017)
54. Karanasios, S., Slavova, M.: How do development actors do "ICT for development"? A strategy-as-practice perspective on emerging practices in Ghanaian agriculture. Inf. Syst. J. **29**(4), 888–913 (2019). https://doi.org/10.1111/isj.12214
55. Krauss, K.: Demonstrating critically reflexive ICT4D projects conducted in rural South Africa. Information Technology for Development. (2021). https://doi.org/10.1080/02681102.2021.1928588
56. Heeks, R.: Information systems and developing countries: failure, success, and local improvisations. Inf. Soc. **18**(2), 101–112 (2002). https://doi.org/10.1080/01972240290075039
57. Yin, R.K.: Case Study Research Design and Methods Applied. Social Research Methods Series 5. Sage Publications, Thousand Oaks (2003)
58. Boh, W., et al.: Digital resilience during covid: fleeting or enduring. In: 2021 Proceedings of ICIS (2021)

The Use of a User-Centric Smart Mobile Application Prototype for Supporting Safety and Security in a City: A Design Science Method

Maxine Mathijssen and Maureen Tanner[✉] [iD]

University of Cape Town, Cape Town, South Africa
MTHMAX005@myuct.ac.za, mc.tanner@uct.ac.za

Abstract. Cities are the drivers of innovation, growth, and change, and are rapidly expanding, especially in Africa. Cape Town is one of those cities, with high urbanization rates and persisting crime levels. There is a need to design 'smart' ways of growth which includes facilitating a safe and secure city for citizens. This study focuses on smart city initiatives in Cape Town, placing citizens at the center of the development process. Crowdsourcing techniques are utilized to develop a smart mobile application prototype that focuses on enhancing community engagement, resilience and increased perceived feelings of safety and security for citizens. The study uses a Design Science Research method with Cape Town citizens as the main stakeholders, to propose an artifact based on their wishes and needs with regards to safety and security in the city.

Keywords: Smart city · Cape Town · Mobile application · Safety and security · Community

1 Introduction

Cities have always been the drivers of innovation, growth, and change [1]. Urban populations are rapidly increasing, and interestingly, 95% of urban expansion are expected to take place in developing countries on the Asian and African continents [2]. As urbanization rates in these countries are high, there is a growing demand to relieve pressure off urban areas, facilitate economic growth and improve safety and security for citizens [3]. Smart city technologies are a potential solution to urbanization-related issues and are furthermore argued to attract new business and city investments, create job opportunities, and improve productivity [4]. Smart cities are usually argued to deploy Internet of Things (IoT) and Information and Communication Technologies (ICT) to connect information, people, and city elements for the benefit of creating a better manageable, sustainable, and livable city, while maintaining a competitive edge [1]. To facilitate this, a smart city is dependent on its citizens and participatory governance and should take a user-centered approach as it is focused on enhancing livability [5].

Although investigated quite extensively across Western and Asian contexts [6], smart city concepts have remained relatively unexplored within developing countries on the

© IFIP International Federation for Information Processing 2022
Published by Springer Nature Switzerland AG 2022
Y. Zheng et al. (Eds.): ICT4D 2022, IFIP AICT 657, pp. 270–294, 2022.
https://doi.org/10.1007/978-3-031-19429-0_17

African continent, despite African cities' attempts to pursue smart city agendas (see [7]). As there is no one-size-fits-all model, smart city implementations across Western or Asian countries cannot simply be duplicated to apply to African cities.

Developing countries are characterized by rapid urbanization, social and economic inequality and high urban crime rates [7, 8]. Research has shown that when pursuing smart city developments, developing nations have not focused enough on delivering a 'smart and safe' city that fights crime and ensures public safety for its citizens [8–11]. An inclusive and safe city should be a prime focus when addressing smart city strategic developments, especially in developing countries [8]. In the longer run, a safe and secure city environment is critical for a smart city that wants to be sustainable and attract foreign business and investments [12].

Therefore, this study adopts community-based, crowd-sourcing approach to technology design, that is focused on increasing perceived safety and security of citizens in developing cities. The focus is on developing countries that are characterized by high urbanization rates, high urban crime rates and fear of crime. One such smart technology is the use of mobile applications for the benefit of smart urban development. Literature has increasingly covered the role of mobile services in harnessing safety and security of citizens in the urban context (see [13, 14]. Studies show that people are willing to download safety apps that include live tracking capabilities [15], reliability and transparency in terms of where data is stored, and functionalities that allow users to send emergency signals to loved ones [16] to enhance perceived feelings of personal safety [17]. Furthermore, personal safety apps are argued to be usable to the community because they are local and belong to the citizens as the end users [16].

In developing smart technologies, citizen involvement is unmissable, as establishing trust amongst citizens is a key factor to ensure the success and longevity of the ecosystem [8]. This research aims to design a proof-of-concept smart mobile application that focuses on increasing feelings of safety and security of citizens in the urban, smart city context. This smart mobile application falls within the realm of a smart city application. The implementation of smart city application is characterized by requirements related to communication, information sharing and real-time information [25]. The proposed smart mobile application will abide by these three characteristics. The research takes Cape Town as its case study, which is South Africa's third largest city with approximately 3.7 million residents and argued to be the crime capital of South Africa, while furthermore ranking as one of the world's highest in terms of homicide rates [8, 18]. Western Cape crime rates are the highest and fastest growing in the country, making crime prevention and control a concern and high priority for city management [12] to which this research aims to contribute.

To strive towards a city that is perceived safer by citizens, this research offers an alternative perspective that takes on a user-driven approach for developing a smart mobile application prototype with the aim of increasing perceived feelings of safety and security. This approach is taken on using a Design Science Research (DSR) methodology, which is realized through creating an artifact with the goal of solving practical problems, which here relate to disproportionally high crime rate and increased perceived feelings of a lack of safety and security among citizens.

The following research question is introduced: How can a 'smart' community-based crime-focused mobile application influence feelings of safety and security for Cape Town citizens?

The study aims to contribute to research and practice by applying results from the case to cities on the continent with similar urban characteristics and developmental traits to expand knowledge on smart city developments across the African continent. In doing so, this research takes on a user-centric approach aiming at addressing, understanding, and detailing the needs and wishes of citizens with regards to fear of crime and feelings of safety and security in the context of a smart city.

As mobile phone penetration is high across the continent and access to Internet is rapidly expanding, a mobile prototype ought to contribute to research and practice by introducing a smart application that is accessible to its users. As the mobile prototype proposed in this research aims to use crowdsourcing and is dependent on user input as well as existing crime-related city data, the prototype provides a technology intended to facilitate greater community engagement and feelings of safety.

2   Literature Review

2.1   Smart Cities

The United Nation Population Fund states that since 2008, more than half of the world's population lives in cities and this percentage is expected to rise to 70% by 2050 [19]. Growing cities bring challenges that local authorities need to respond to. Such challenges are concerned with public safety and security, quality of living, public transportation and infrastructure, employment and economy and environmental performance [20]. As a result, questions arise with regards to how a city could be "smart" and designed in such a way that the implementation of technologies can facilitate public safety and security for citizens thereby positively impacting the overall quality of living [21].

It is commonly argued that a smart city is an urban area that deploys IoT and ICT for the benefit of creating a better manageable, sustainable, and livable city, while maintaining a competitive edge [1, 22]. Smart cities commonly focus on a variety of dimensions, such as safety, economy, people, governance, mobility, environment and living, and comprises of people, businesses, organizations, and processes to achieve the desired goals for the city [23]. The end goal of a smart city is to increase quality of living for citizens and deliver benefits for governments on a national and provincial level, as well as for local city-level municipalities [6]. The use of smart mobile devices such as smartphones and wearables, is rapidly increasing and form a huge potential for future smart cities designed at meeting citizens' demands [24], which is the focus of this study.

Previous studies have explored the wide variety of smart city applications, which include smart energy, smart public services, smart water and waste management, smart mobility, and smart security, amongst others [25]. Smart city applications are necessary for communication and sharing of real-time information that facilitate the implementation and growth of the smart city [25]. This study focuses on one area of smart city applications, which is that of smart security.

2.2 The City of Cape Town and the Smart City

Cape Town is the second largest city in South Africa with approximately 3,4 million inhabitants and an important center for trade, especially with respect to tourism and the mobile IT sector [8]. In 2002, the City of Cape Town launched their "Smart City Strategy", as part of the wider City Development Strategy (CDS) for Cape Town. The focus of the strategy included leadership, policy and regulation, e-government, IT enabled development and IT enabled governance [2]. A decade later, the Integrated Development Plan was launched, serving as a five-year strategic framework that guides decision making within the municipality [2]. The plan was built around five 'pillars' which include the opportunity city, the safe city, the caring city, the inclusivity city and the well-run city [2]. The city has recently improved internet speed and overall access, introduced the use of digital platforms for access to digital public services, and opened data sources for utilization by businesses [2]. However, it is the 'safe city' pillar that this study aims to explore further. There is a need to develop smart city objectives in Cape Town involving the city's population in project planning and implementation. This research aims to further built on existing literature and applications for enhanced inclusivity and contributing to technological advancements that are community-based and use crowd-sourcing solutions in the context of a smart city.

2.3 Safety and Security in Cape Town

Public safety and security are highly intertwined with crime rates, in such that they are compromised when city crime rates are high, and cities are not actively putting in measures to combat crime [26]. Especially in developing countries, where resources for combating crime are generally less widely available than in developed countries, deterring crime and realizing a safe and secure city is one of the main objectives for a smart and safe city [27].

In South Africa, crime cases are a national health priority as the country reports a six times higher homicide rate than the global average [18]. Recent official statistics show that Western Cape crime rates are the worst in the country and in many categories identified by South African Police Services (SAPS) [28].

Considering the above-mentioned points, there is a need for urban integration that is inclusive and focuses smart developments around addressing safety and security related issues at the level of citizen's wishes and needs, which will aid cities to function better through distributed problem-solving decisions [25, 29]. The safe city must be considered vital for enhancing effective city management, handling crime, and facilitating a healthy living environment for citizens [30]. Various research has explored interventions in developing countries that seek to support safety by improving old systems using smart technologies (e.g., [31, 32]). However, it is important to gauge how citizens perceive urban security to promote smart city management. This not only prevents or responds to safety concerns, but also ensure a that the city is an attractive place to reside in [30]. Smart safe applications in urban spaces are crucial and help improve urban governance and planning as well as provide a better living environment for citizens [30].

2.4 Personal Safety and Fear of Crime

Most studies acknowledge the relationship between personal safety and crime, both of which have significant theoretical and empirical commonalities [33]. Like crime committed against an individual, personal safety is said to be jeopardized when intentional harm is being done to an individual or their property [34]. Said, then, is that the perception of personal safety is threatened by a fear of crime [35]. Some research identifies that fear of crime occurs when people can imagine themselves falling victim to crime, partly because of hearsay from people they know [36]. In addition, fear of crime is fed through physical environmental factor such as poor lighting, hiding places for criminals, poor state of buildings, and a high frequency of abandoned streets within areas, as well as social factors such as the lack of police control, surveillance cameras and people in the street/area [37].

Previous research shows that providing crime related information to citizens and involving them in effective policing is assumed to be socially beneficial and leads to better public service transparency [13, 38]. Although a 'safe city' constitutes one of the five pillars for city development in Cape Town according to the IDP [2], it is commonly argued that citizen involvement by authorities for the benefit of safer cities has been lacking [38]. As a result, this research aims to involve end-users in the development of a mobile application prototype that attempts to increase community involvement and empowerment, as well as increased feelings of safety and security, partly because of reduced fear of crime and victimization.

2.5 Citizen Involvement and User-Centered Design

Smart cities are first and foremost associated with the implementation of a set of technologies for the benefit of a livable city [39]. However, various research has argued that smart city applications often put too much focus on just the technologies, and less on citizens and engagement with society [22], while communities and individuals should be considered as key stakeholders in the smart planning process [22]. The danger of failing to consider citizens and societal engagement in these applications could result in wasting expenditures that were initially budgeted to facilitate the implementations [22]. In addition, the leverage of smart technologies is often provided by corporate giants, regularly leading to monopolization of the smart city because of a shift in power dynamics from the city to corporate companies [22]. Consequently, smart cities could lose their creative edge [1]. For this reason, a design science research method is explored in this research, where end-users are placed at the center of the development process and new knowledge is created from the lived experiences, wishes, and needs from end-users.

3 Methodology

3.1 Research Strategy

A qualitative research method was chosen for this research to assist in the elicitation of the requirements for the application. This was relevant as this study is aimed at understanding the "lived experiences" and perceptions of people to gain a deeper understanding of the problem at hand and gaining insights from its meaning [40]. These insights then form the basis of constructing the prototype, for which creativity and co-creation are the most important values.

3.2 Design Science Research Methodology Framework

This study uses the DSR methodology. DSR is defined as "the scientific study and creation of artifacts as they are developed and used by people with the goal of solving practical problems of general interest" [40]. The artifact that is developed during the study is a mobile application prototype. In answering the research questions using a DSR method, the research draws on the methodological framework from [40]. The different stages of the design science method framework are addressed in the next subsections.

3.2.1 Activity 1 - Explicate Problem

To define the requirements for building the mobile application prototype, the problems must be defined precisely [40]. To achieve this, interviews with respondents were held in line with DSR, with the purpose of identifying lived experiences of the participants in relation to their current safety and security-related challenges. To achieve the above, a total of 12 semi-structured interviews were conducted. More details about the interviews, how they were conducted and how their results were analyzed are described in the data collection section.

3.2.2 Activity 2 - Define Requirements

Where the previous activity elicited the problem, this stage evaluated the application requirements as proposed by the stakeholders and assessed their completeness and feasibility for implementation [40].

3.2.3 Activity 3 - Design and Development of Artifact

The third activity is Design and Develop Artifact with the aim of fulfilling the requirements as proposed in the previous stage. This activity was concerned with "creat[ing] an artifact that addresses the explicated problem and fulfils the defined requirements" [40] (p.117). The input used in this stage consisted of the insights gathered from the participants and knowledge from literature. This phase comprised of three sub-activities. In the first sub-activity, a brainstorm session was conducted, leading to the design of sketches for the user interface. The second sub-activity included a more elaborate design of the mobile application prototype. Use case diagrams and user stories were used to visualize the skeleton of the prototype with its main functionalities and actors. Lastly, in the third and final sub-activity, the prototype was designed using the software Sketch which was used to demonstrate the artifact, and to obtain user feedback in the evaluate artifact phase.

3.2.4 Activity 4 - Demonstrate Artifact

The aim of this phase was to demonstrate the mobile application prototype that had been designed in the previous phases [40]. In this phase, descriptive insights were gathered from participants, by asking them to engage with the prototype through user stories describing real-life scenarios. Each user story contained one or more acceptance criteria, which were in line with the application. The user stories defined how the application was expected to behave and how these behaviors should be satisfied.

3.2.5 Activity 5 - Evaluate Artifact

This activity determined how well the artifact solved the explicated problem and how well it satisfied the requirements set out in the second stage. In this phase, participants were interviewed and asked for their feedback after which alterations were made to the artifact accordingly. Four users from the initial pool of participants were asked to participate in the second round of interviews in which they were given access to the prototype and asked to carry out a set of tasks (activity 4). Semi-structured interviews were then conducted, guided by the Technology Acceptance Model for evaluation.

The research used Davis' TAM as a model as theoretical underpinning for gathering and analyzing user feedback on the mobile prototype during the evaluation phase [41]. TAM is one of the most widely used models for user acceptance and use of technology in the Information Systems field [42].

The model assumes that users come to accept a technology when there is a high level of Perceived Usefulness (PU) and Perceived Ease of Use (PEU) of the technology [42]. This study assumes that PEU is achieved when the user of the application believes that using the smart city mobile application prototype would be free of effort. PU refers to the user believing that the smart city mobile application prototype would enhance their feelings of safety and security in the city. PU and PEU are the most important factors in determining an individual's attitude towards the system and whether they will use it [43].

Participants were asked to perform a set of tasks, in line with the system's main functionalities. These tasks are identified as the external variables for evaluating the technology's acceptance by the interviewees. The following external variables were chosen:

- Task 1: Create a new account and log in
- Task 2: Start a safe route
- Task 3: File an incident report
- Task 4: Become member of a community
- Task 5: Add a safety resource to your folder
- Task 6: Send out an emergency signal

Incorporating the task assessments into the technology acceptance model for evaluation, the research proposes an applied TAM (see Fig. 1). The following section addresses how this model was used for artifact evaluation.

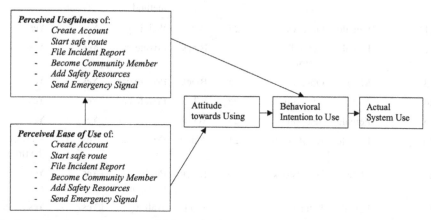

Fig. 1. Technology acceptance model for evaluating smart mobile application prototype - adapted from [41]

3.3 Sampling Strategy and Size

The overarching sampling method used in this research is that of nonprobability purposive sampling. The strategy chosen is purposive in nature, because it does not involve random selection of participants and the study aims to include participants from the different strata identified. Within the purposive sampling method, the study specifically utilized nonproportional quota sampling. In quota sampling, the population, in this case Cape Town's population, is divided into strata which are relevant to the study's topic of interest. The strata chosen for the quota sampling in this study include gender and location. These strata are considered most important for evaluation based on previous literature on crime, safety and security in the context of Cape Town as a smart city (see [45]). Literature suggests women are less likely to defend themselves against perpetrators and further experience higher fear of crime than their male counterparts [49], hence why gender is chosen as a stratum. To determine the difference in perceptions of safety across the city and success of the application, location is chosen as the second stratum for sampling.

The total number of respondents during the first round of interviews is N = 12. The sample overview can be found in Table 1.

Table 1. Sample overview interviews round 1

Respondent No	Gender	Living location	Age	Race	Home-work travel method	Accessto Phone	Accessto internet
R1	Female	Observatory	27	White	Walking	Yes	Yes
R2	Female	Centralbusiness District	28	Black	Private car	Yes	Yes
R3	Male	Observatory	25	Black	Private car	Yes	Yes
R4	Male	Sea point	25	White	Private car	Yes	Yes
R5	Female	Sea point	25	White	Private car	Yes	Yes
R6	Female	Kenilworth	21	Asian	Private car	Yes	Most of the time
R7	Male	Woodstock	29	Black	Public transport	Yes	Yes
R8	Female	Salt river	24	White	Walking	Yes	Yes
R9	Female	Observatory	24	White	Public transport	Yes	Yes
R10	Female	Rondebosch	26	Black	Public transport	Yes	Yes
R11	Male	Green point	28	Black	Public transport	Yes	Yes
R12	Male	Salt river	30	Black	Walking	Yes	Most of the time

The total number of respondents during the second round of interviews is N = 4 (see Table 2). After that, data saturation was reached. Respondents kept their case number from the first round of interviews.

Table 2. Sample overview interviews round 2

Respondent No	Gender	Living location	Age	Race	Home-work travel method	Accessto Phone	Accessto internet
R4	Male	Sea point	25	White	Private car	Yes	Yes
R6	Female	Kenilworth	21	Asian	Private car	Yes	Most of the time
R8	Female	Salt river	24	White	Walking	Yes	Yes
R11	Male	Green point	28	Black	Public transport	Yes	Yes

3.4 Data Collection Method

Interviews were chosen as the preferred data collection method as they allow for high engagement with respondents and facilitate greater creativity which are important objectives for development of the prototype. Rounds of interviews were performed twice, during the first stage and fifth stage of the design period, in the explicating problem and artifact evaluation stage, respectively. Interviews were conducted via WhatsApp because of the Covid-19 restrictions active at the time of data collection. All interviews were recorded. Additionally, field notes were taken by the researcher during the interviews.

3.4.1 Interviews Round 1

As the research follows the DSR method, the main purpose of the interviews was to go into depth on the lived experiences of users and consequently get an understanding of the problem. In the first part, respondents were asked general questions addressing demographic characteristics, namely age, gender, race, housing status, place of residence, job status and employment location, work-home travel method, income, access to mobile device and access to the Internet. Thereafter, the research focused on gathering individuals' perception of crime threat, perceived safety in the neighborhood, trust in local crime prevention authorities, and degree of neighborhood integration. Participants are encouraged to openly share their experiences with regards to feelings of safety and security in the city and their neighborhood.

In the second part of the interview, participants were informed about the proposed design of a mobile application prototype and its function as a smart city application that is focused on enhancing feelings of safety and security of Cape Town citizens. The notion of a smart city was explained in the interview. Participants were asked to share their wishes and needs when it comes to enhancing feelings of safety and security through mobile application prototype features and requirements. Particularly, the participants are asked to translate their experiences with regards to safety and security threats as identified earlier in the interview and fit them within a set of requirements to enhance their feelings of safety and security.

Lastly, participants are asked how they foresee the success of a prototype with the purpose of enhancing citizens' feelings of safety and security, which potential drawbacks could be identified.

3.4.2 Interviews Round 2

Following the DSR method, a second round of interviews was performed during evaluation stage. The purpose of the second round of interviews was to gather feedback from participants on the developed prototype and to what degree it conformed to the participants' expectations with regards to feeling safe and secure in their neighborhoods in Cape Town as set out in the initial round of interviews. The in-depth interviews provided rich insights in the perceived usefulness and ease of use of the artifact. Furthermore, because of the structure and determined content of the interview protocol, saturation of knowledge could be reached after these interviews.

The mobile application prototype was made available on Sketch cloud. The participants interviewed for the in-depth evaluation were sent an open link to the prototype. The prototype was made available to interviewees just before the start of the interview. Participants were asked to open the link on their mobile device to have the best mobile application prototype experience, while keeping the interview call on loudspeaker.

During the first part of the interview, participants were given the opportunity to explore the different screens to get an impression of the general look and feel of the prototype as well as the available screens and menu options. Participants were asked to provide comments on their first impression. During the second part of the interview, participants were requested to perform a set of six tasks derived from the main use cases. The protocol for the task assessment and evaluation follows the Technology Acceptance Model, where users were asked to assess intention to use and ease of use for each of the tasks. The six tasks were the same for each of the participants to facilitate comparison and implement any feedback accordingly. In addition to commenting on the perceived usefulness of the different system functions, participants were further asked to specifically assess the perceived usefulness of the system functions in terms of its effect on enhancing feelings of safety and security.

3.5 Data Analysis

All interviews were transcribed. The approach chosen for qualitative data analysis is that of thematic analysis (44). Specifically, this research engaged in inductive thematic analysis. As the design science research method aims to generate new knowledge, insights, and explanations from the perspectives of users central to the problem, inductive thematic analysis was performed to refrain from fitting the data in a pre-existing frame, but rather linking the themes to the data themselves.

NVivo was used to analyze the qualitative data gathered in the interviews. Coding of the interviews was performed in two phases. The first phase included the coding of the first half of the interview, going into challenges with regards of feeling safe and security in the neighborhood and the city. This part is called "Perceptions of safety" and a total of 16 nodes were used to code this section. Nodes were subdivided into the following themes: challenges influencing safety and security, attitudes towards safety, neighborhood development, and external factors impacting safety.

The second phase included the coding of the second part of the interview, going into wishes and needs with regards to enhancing safety and security in the neighborhood and the city in the context of the mobile application prototype development. This part is called "Wishes and needs" and total of 14 nodes were used to code this section. Nodes were subdivided into the following themes: Application requirements, attitudes towards using the app, challenges for using the app, and factors impacting use and success of the app.

The second round of interviews, in which four participants were interviewed to obtain feedback on the developed mobile application prototype as a result from the requirements deriving from the first round of interviews, have been coded into a code book called "Application Evaluation". A total of 10 nodes is used to code this section.

4 Findings

4.1 Explicate Problem – Challenges with Regards to Feelings of Safety and Security

This section discusses the results from the first part of the interviews. The participants' challenges are discussed with regards to their feelings of safety and security in the neighborhood.

4.1.1 Fear of Night-Time

The first challenge experienced by interviewees that negatively impact feelings of safety and security for participants relates to the daytime versus night-time divide. All people interviewed identify that they feel less safe or completely unsafe at night in their neighborhood. The reasons for the feelings of unsafety at night-time range from a lack of visibility in their surroundings, streets becoming quieter and a feeling of vulnerability: *"Times I feel unsafe would definitely be when it gets darker, at nighttime, because the roads generally become more quite in Sea Point, so I feel more vulnerable, less safe"* [R5].

4.1.2 Mode of Transportation Restrictions

Respondents mention mode of transportation as a factor impacting their feelings of safety in their neighborhood, leading to a decrease in feeling safe and secure. The respondents with access to a car stress that driving a private car gives them a safe or safer feeling because it is a personal space that is not likely to be compromised. Taxi services such as Uber are perceived somewhat safe by those respondents that use this mode of transportation. However, in a few cases, these private taxi services are also considered unsafe: *"I'm okay with using an Uber but there are sometimes some issues with Ubers attacking females or kidnapping people or stuff like that. So, I'd rather just use my own car most of the time"* [R2]. Some respondents also stated they feel uncomfortable whilst using public transport as it limits the possibility of being in one's own space. Word-of-mouth pertaining to the risks associated with public transport also limit their feelings of safety and security. Lastly, walking decreases respondents' feeling of safety, especially while carrying valuables: *"I would walk and I would see weird people following me and I would literally have anxiety attack due to that, because I would never feel safe knowing that there is somebody potentially following me and if there is nobody in the street and then also it does really affect me"* [R9].

4.1.3 Feeling Unsafe Around Strangers

The third challenge relates to feelings of unsafety around strangers: "So at night when I see maybe a group of men, usually, I feel less safe. And then safer if I see couples, or groups of all kinds of different people who don't look poor, then I feel safer, I guess, to be honest". Respondents mention that they feel safe(r) when there are more people around (e.g., in shopping centers, the promenade, and beaches). Touching upon feelings of unsafety, respondent R2 mentions that the presence of beggars gives her an increased feeling of unsafety: "There is a lot of them around in the area, especially by our apartment block there is a lot of people always begging and stuff. You never know their real intentions. Because some of them might want to steal but some of them might really actually be begging for food innocently".

4.1.4 Street Architecture and Infrastructure

The fourth challenge relates to the design of the streets and overall infrastructure. For instance, open and visible spaces, proper streetlights, greenery, the presence of bars and restaurants, and cleanliness of the area contribute to increased feelings of safety and security: *"If you look at Camps Bay there is a lot of visibility, it's a big suburb, there is greater infrastructure there and the lights and patrols are higher"* (R7). The inability to look far ahead also diminishes participants' feelings of safety: *"I feel like in Observatory, there is a main road and there are a lot of street corners and as soon as I'm approaching a corner I'm always stressing out, because there is a lot of stories where people are hiding in these small streets and waiting for victims and attack them as soon as they cross the corner" [R3].*

4.1.5 Lack of Police Support and Follow-up

The fifth challenge identified by interviewees refers to the lack of police involvement and follow up when incidents are reported: *"when we had the break in, we literally investigated on our own and we found out who did it through the body corporate, the building managers, and we found pictures of the person who did it. We literally told the police that we have pictures, but they didn't do anything with the case and didn't get back to us like they said they would"* [R2].

4.2 Define Requirements

This section addresses the application requirements as proposed by the interviewees, with each requirement discussed in a different sub section linking back to the challenges with regards to feelings of safety and security for participants in the study.

4.2.1 Emergency Panic Button

All participants mentioned the need for an emergency button. How this functionality should function was dependent on the respondent. Overall, most respondents conclude that the emergency panic button should be easily accessible and easy to navigate, as the respondents mention such a functionality would be ideal to use in case of emergency: *"I think that I would probably at the top of my head want something like a panic button, something that I can react to really quickly in instances where I am being attacked, or somebody is trying to attack me, or somebody is trying to rape me"* [R2]. With regards to the easy navigation of such a functionality, because of time constraints in a situation of emergency, two participants came up with the idea of a "hot key" or "assistive touch" which sits on the screen when it is locked: *"I guess basically having an always on function to the app where it's kind of sitting on your screen whether or not the phone is locked or unlocked so you can press it in a panic situation"* [R3]. Another participant proposes a code word functionality that listens only to the person owning the device: *"So you for example choose your own code word and no one else also knows it. And then whenever you use that, or you have to say it twice so something like that, it activates"* [R8].

Among participants, there was no consensus on who should be buzzed once the emergency button has been activated. The range of options includes family members or friends, neighborhood watch, private security companies, and local police officers. For most of the participants, the signal should preferably go out to the security (community) team nearest to the destination of where the emergency has been reported, so a fast response is guaranteed: *"Depending on which area you're on, it sends a signal to community safety or police that are in that area, I think that would be the most valuable feature that the app would have"* (R3). The mobile app emergency button could be linked to physical emergency buttons installed in homes, so it is accessible through the mobile device anywhere and at any moment. Such a functionality relates back to the challenge of time of day, and specifically, a fear of night-time, fear of strangers, challenges relating to certain modes of transportation, and feeling unsafe in certain streets and areas: *"If you don't feel safe at a particular occasion, you click help and then it alerts a security team that patrols in the area to come to your location to escort you to wherever your destination that you would like to reach. So, I think that's one of the important things"* [R10].

4.2.2   Crime Heat Map

The second requirement for the app was that of a crime heat map which enables citizens to log incidents and suggests neighborhood to be avoided and accessed based on previously logged information: *"I think it would be really helpful, a crime heat map, because some instances you want to go somewhere but you are not necessarily sure what the crime rate is like there because you've never been there before. So, I think it would be really helpful and it wouldn't really scare me"* [R2]. Some participants suggested that the logged incidents be filed in a database which would be used to make long term algorithms available for safe route planning for citizens, as well as being able to (re)allocate law enforcement resources to those areas identified as crime hotspots to tackle and diffuse criminal activity.

Flowing from the idea of a crime heat map was the suggestion for a safe route planning system. Some participants indicated that planning a route in the app could be relevant to avoid certain areas that are associated with high crime and incidents. Participants would be able to enter their destination point and be directed towards their destination in the safest manner, building on logged incidents from the crime heat map.

Such a safe route planning system, building on the crime heat map, could primarily tackle the time of day and mode of transportation challenge faced by participants: *"Like maybe trends can be developed from that, so let's say all incidents are happening between 10 at night and 2 am, then you're kind of like it's just not a good idea to walk at night whether you're in a group or alone"* [R5]. A crime heat map could also recommend where to drive and park a car safely: *"I think for a long-term thing it's definitely positive for them to track down if there has been car break in"* [R1].

4.2.3 Community Chat Room

A third requirement suggested by participants related to a community chat room, to enable the user to speak to people in the neighborhood or obtain updates: *"People can post updates (...) or if I see something sketchy and I'm just going to ask on the app like "did anyone else see this? I would just like to clarify that wasn't anything serious"* [R6]. The community chatroom functionality was dependent on the involvement of the community to raise awareness in the community and facilitate the community buy-in for use of the app: *"I think the community would need to be involved in that they need to obviously have a forum to speak about these things that are happening, share information on who's been mugged and what's been happening. Maybe like an active forum and people just sharing their experiences of what they've gone through. And not just sharing, but also just information that helps the community in a way"* [R11]. Whether users are afraid of movement at night, walking alone, accessing certain streets or parks, or being confronted with strangers, the application's community chatroom would function as an awareness platform to promote vigilance in the neighborhood and look out for other members of the community.

4.2.4 Safety Resources

A fourth application requirement touched upon the availability of safety resources. Participants mentioned local police office numbers, rape response numbers, and other emergency contact numbers such as ambulance and police: *"It's also a typical South African problem of not knowing how to contact ambulances or police or stuff like that in times of emergency. Cause the number that we all use which is 10111 which would take you to the police dispatch is now used for something else, and it's quite confusing. So, to be in a setting where the app would be linked to a, not a distribution center, but for a lack of better term, to a room or outpost that would then deal with your query would be a lot better"* [R3]. The fifth suggestion for an application requirement was that of a live police map: *"also obviously knowing where the security guards are positioned on the map will also make me safer because then I know if I'm using that street like there is a security guard so then I would feel a bit safer"* [R1]. Participants suggested that knowing where police are stationed or where police cars are driving, would allow participants to remain in the vicinity of police which increases their feelings of safety and security. The suggestion of safety resources within the application tackles the challenge of a lack of police involvement and follow-up.

4.3   Design and Development of Artifact

Based on the previous section which defined the requirements for the application, the sketches and first build of the prototype were designed. To give a representation of the functions, a use case diagram was developed which was accompanied by user stories. The user stories helped articulate how the user would interact with the artifact. These were also used during the evaluation phase when the participant was asked to complete as set of tasks with the mobile application prototype and share their opinions regarding perceived usefulness and ease of use of the system in accordance with the Technology Acceptance Model (TAM).

The use cases based on participant input for the design of the application was visualized in an initial set of sketches (see example in Fig. 2). Details about the use cases and user stories are shown in Table 3. The sketches were designed into the prototype using Sketch software. After completion of the initial prototype (see example in Fig. 3), the files were pushed to Sketch Cloud to make it accessible to participants.

Fig. 2. Example of sketches   **Fig. 3.** Example of screens

4.4   Demonstrate Artifact

The user stories that guided the demonstration of the artifact can be found in Table 3. Each user story had a range of acceptance criteria, examples of which are also included in Table 3. Each user story is mapped to the corresponding use case.

Table 3. Use cases, user stories and example acceptance criteria

Use case	User story	Example acceptance criteria
Login	I would like to sign into my account so that I can access my personal app	Given that I am a returning user, when I open the app, I expect to be able to log in with my email and password credentials, so that I can access my personal app
Reset password	I would like to reset my password so that I can log in to my account even if I forgot my password	Given that I am a returning user, when I try to log in but cannot remember my password, I expect to reset my password, so that I can log in
Create account	I would like to create a new account so that I can use the app when I am a new user	Given that I am a new user, when I am a new user, I expect to have a clearly visible "sign up" button at the bottom of the screen so that I can create a new account
Create account	I would like to see the progress of my sign up so that I am not discouraged to use the app	Given that I am a new user, when I sign up, I expect to see a progress bar
Searchincident reports	I would like to see previous incidents on a map so that I can explore the safety in different neighborhoods	Given that I am a user, when I go on the Safe Map, I expect to see pins indicating a previously reported incident
Fileincident report	I would like to file my own incident report so that I can report a crime and help other neighborhood members stay vigilant	Given that I am a user, when I am on the Safe Map, I expect to be able to click a button to file an incident
Start safe route	I would like to start a route planner so that I can navigate from point A to point B in the safest way possible according to my personal values	Given that I am a user, when I am on the Safe Map, I expect to start a Safe Route by clicking a Safe Route button that is clearly visible
Viewsafety resources	I would like to have easily accessible safety resources so that I can call them if I need assistance	Given that I am a user, when I am on the Safety Resources map, I expect to add a safety resource to my personal safety resources folder

(continued)

Table 3. (*continued*)

Use case	User story	Example acceptance criteria
Access/View communities	I would like to become a member of a community so that I can see community-logged incidents and view and chat with other members of my community	Given that I am a user, when I navigate to "communities" in the main menu, I expect to see my personal communities or add a new one
Viewsafety category weights	I would like to have an overview of my settings so that I can edit and set personal account details	Given that I am a user, when I go to settings, I expect to see an overview of settings options in a listing view
Send emergency signal	I would like to have an S.O.S. button in the map section which I can click to send an emergency signal	When I click on the S.O.S. red button, I expect to get a push notification with the choice of sending the emergency signal or cancelling the action
Respondto emergency request	I would like to be able to respond to an emergency request to help a co-community member	When I am a member of a community, I would like to get a pop up when a user within my community sends an emergency signal and have the option to respond or decline it

4.5 Evaluate Artifact

To evaluate the artifact, participants were asked to provide feedback about the artifact in accordance with the Technology Acceptance Model. According to this model, users are asked to assess perceived ease of use (PEU) and perceived usefulness (PU) for each of the system variables. This is accomplished through guiding the participants through a set of tasks in line with the use cases and user stories. An overview of the user feedback in line PEU and PU can be found in Table 4. The prototype was enhanced in line with the participants' recommendations.

288 M. Mathijssen and M. Tanner

Table 4. Application feedback according to Technology Acceptance Model

System variables	Perceived ease of use	Perceived usefulness
Accounts	-Increase font size of sign-up button	
Category weights	-Change naming convention on slide bar ends	-Remove crime category weights from view -Add more subcategories to movement weights -Add a user explanation as an introduction
Safe routes and crime map	-Amend the menu wording -Change the color of the pins to red	
Incident reports	-Change the color of the pins to red -Add a filter for finding recent reports	-Add the option to upload picture in incident report -Add follow up button options after submitted report -Add a date filter to minimize exposure to previous crime reports
Communities	-Add filter for finding recent reports	-Add "report user" option -Add scan profile functionality for new profiles
Safety resources		-Add "tips and tricks" section for feeling safer -Start personal chat with community user
Emergency buttons		-Offline emergency signal option

5 Discussion

The design science research method used in this study aimed to address the explicated problem of participants experiencing challenges with regards to feeling safe and secure in the city. The study found that the most important requirement for the application as voiced by participants is the presence of an emergency button that can be quickly and easily accessed. This finding is supported by literature, as various studies touch upon the use of mobile services in harnessing safety and the importance of a silent signal to be send out to police, which is one of the most echoed wishes [45]. This study provided more insights into this by revealing that ideally, the panic button should be accessible when the phone is locked which can be accomplished when the prototype is built into a working mobile application.

In terms of the destination of the signal, literature suggests the signal to be sent to community members or family and friends [46]. This research carefully evaluated the destination of the GPS emergency signal based on user interviews, and proposed something similar, where community members take on a central role as the first point of contact for emergencies in the community-based application. Interviewees stress the importance of having the community engaged in the mobile application prototype, because the success of the mobile applicated is dependent on community buy-in. This finding finds support in other studies, such as the study by [14] which observes that communities actively use online platforms to share information with co-members with a similar interest, with crime being one of those popular conversational topics.

Additionally, the study found that for the application to be successful, an important requirement is the implementation of a crime heat map from which users can view previously logged incident reports on a live map and start a safe route based on their personal wishes and needs. The study recommends a logging incident system as another unmissable feature. The incident reports are mapped for use of the safe route functionality, and additionally available in the crime heat map and communities' maps. This is in line with literature which suggests that keeping citizens informed about crime incidents will provide them with knowledge to be more careful navigating through their neighborhoods [14].

As shown in Table 5, the prototype offers a combination of capabilities that are unique compared to the current availability of personal safety apps in South Africa, while keeping user friendly and easy to use according to participants. Looking at Table 5, this prototype offers functionalities that are rarely seen in other applications, including the possibility to add personal resources, plan a safe route based on previously filed crime reports, and the focus on community involvement and crowdsourcing. The latter is considered an important requirement by the participants in this study for the application to be successful. The possibility to engage with community members, share knowledge and call out community members during emergency is what separates this application from others in the field.

It is important to reflect on how the proposed mobile application prototype can lead to greater community resilience within a smart city. The study found that participants feel most resilient and confident about co-members of the community assisting in the case of an emergency as opposed to the police or friends, because there is a lack of trust in the police and friends, or family contacts could likely not be in the neighborhood. Provided there is a large community buy-in, the app would be used by many people and in effect, the likelihood of an active community member being in close vicinity of where an emergency signal is being sent is also high. The research further found that participants believe community engagement and social cohesion within the neighborhood have a positive effect on feelings of safety in the neighborhood because it shows a member can rely on the neighborhood and to help you when in need. This further helps build community resilience. The community chat room is necessary here to play a central role in facilitating communication and awareness between community members.

Previous research has shown that crowdsourcing, where information gathering through the internet is done by individuals, is often very successful because technologies that are based on crowdsourcing show to have an overwhelming participatory crowd

Table 5. Application prototype functionalities compared to existing personal safety apps in South Africa

Feature/Use Case	Research App	Namola	MySAPS	Life360	BullHorns	Safe Community App	MySOS	bSafe
Log in/sign up	✓	✓	✓	✓	✓	✓	✓	
Log incident	✓		✓		✓	✓		
Safe route	✓							
Personal safety Resources	✓		✓					
Community room	✓					✓		
Emergency signal	✓	✓		✓	✓	✓	✓	✓
Private armed response	✓	✓			✓	✓	✓	
Response from community members	✓					✓		
Response from trusted friends/family	✓	✓		✓	✓	✓	✓	✓
Live GPS tracking and sharing	✓	✓		✓		✓	✓	✓
Ambulance services		✓						
Live streaming of incident								✓

[14, 47, 48]. Studies in Latin America and Brazil have shown that mobile applications using crowdsourcing related to crime prove successful in reducing the number of crimes in those areas [47]. The applications addressed here use a similar functionality where incidents are alerted to co-community members in the near vicinity [47]. This study's proposed mobile application prototype makes use of the same crowd-sourcing methods for collecting crime-based data. Community members in the research have addressed their confidence in a large community buy in which could lead to the use of the mobile application prototype having a snowball effect for participation, for the purpose of feeling more safe and secure in the neighborhood with the help of the community, and therefore the study concludes that the smart mobile application will have a positive effect on community engagement.

6 Conclusion

This study provided insights into the design of a smart mobile application that can help citizens manage their fear of crime and improve their personal safety. Previous research has shown that issues relating to safety, security and fear of crime negatively impact urban life for citizens, and several studies suggest that improving the social engagement within communities might alleviate such issues [13, 45]. To strive towards a city that is perceived safer by citizens, this research offered an alternative perspective that takes on a user-driven approach for developing a smart mobile application prototype according to the Design Science Research method with the aim of increasing feelings of safety and security. The study taps into Cape Town's high mobile phone penetration rate and existing local government's initiatives for building on smart pillars by proposing a mobile application prototype for citizen use. In doing this, the study places participants, who are in turn Cape Town citizens, at the front of the analysis and development process.

This study addressed the following research question: "How can a 'smart' community-based crime-focused mobile application prototype influence feelings of safety and security for Cape Town citizens?" Addressing the research question involves several aspects. Citizens must actively be involved in addressing smart-community solutions for the benefit of increasing the quality of life for citizens, which is one of the main objectives of the smart city [1, 22]. This research accomplished this, giving citizens a central role in the problem description, requirement analysis and evaluation of the mobile app.

For the application to be successful, there is a need for community buy-in on a large scale, as the application is only argued to work when there is a large group of users to rely on for building a crime database and helping community members when in need. The application should be easily accessible, both in terms of quick access to the emergency signal as well as accessibility in terms of pricing, data, and connectivity, so it can be used by members from all types of communities in the City of Cape Town. However, most importantly, this research found that facilitating more safety and security for Cape Town citizens through the mobile application prototype is a first step in aiding citizens in being more informed on the levels of crime in the neighborhood and share thoughts with different members related to safety. This is an essential step to building community resilience.

The research identified a few research limitations. Firstly, due to time and resource constraints, the study only included neighborhoods from the inner parts of Cape Town in its case study for research and analysis and excluded the wider areas of Cape Town which include the Klipfontein District, Helderberg, Northern Suburbs and the South Peninsula. Additionally, the study could have benefitted from a larger pool of interviewees if resources and time would have allowed it. Lastly, a limitation of the study can be identified relating to data connectivity and accessibility. Although mobile phone penetration is high across the continent and access to Internet is rapidly expanding, citizens are currently dealing with limited access to data because of the high costs as well as connectivity issues, especially in the outskirts of the city. This reduces the availability of the application to all citizens in the city and has a negative effect on large-scale community buy-in, one of the requirements of success for the application.

Emerging from the first limitation addressed in the previous subsection, future research could conduct large-scale interviews with citizens from all suburbs and neighborhoods in Cape Town, to get an understanding of their wishes and needs. In addition, future research on the topic could focus on performing interviews with all smart city stakeholders including local government and municipalities, to get an understanding of the smart city plans with regards to a safe and secure city. Results of these interviews should focus on alignment between citizen wishes and needs and municipal and local government plans to identify the gap between stakeholder interests. This will drive a mutual beneficial smart and safe city that is built on urban technologies and human experience. Future research should furthermore focus on linking logged incidents to law enforcement crime databases to analyze large scale crime data and tackle crime issues more efficiently going forward.

References

1. Albino, V., Berardi, U., Dangelico, R.: Smart cities: definitions, dimensions, performance, and initiatives. J. Urban Technol. **22**(1), 3–21 (2015)
2. City of Cape Town. Five-Year Integrated Development Plan 2012–2017. *2015/2016 Review and Amendments* (2016)
3. Letaifa, S.B.: How to strategize smart cities: revealing the SMART model. J. Bus. Res. **68**(7), 1414–1419 (2015)
4. Galdon-Clavell, G.: (Not so) smart cities?: the drivers, impact and risks of surveillance-enabled smart environments. Sci. Public Policy **40**(6), 717–723 (2013)
5. Oliveira, Á., Campolargo, M.: From smart cities to human smart cities. In: 2015 48th Hawaii International Conference on System Sciences, pp. 2336–2344. IEEE (2015)
6. Deloitte. Africa is ready to leapfrog the competition through Smart Cities Technology. Johannesburg (2014)
7. Backhouse, J.: Smart city agendas of African cities. In: Proceedings of 1st African Conference on Information Systems and Technology (ACIST), Accra (pp. 7–8) (2015)
8. Ni Loideain, N.: Cape Town as a smart and safe city: implications for governance and data privacy. J. Int. Data Priv. Law, (41) (2017, forthcoming)
9. Lemanski, C.: A new apartheid? The spatial implications of fear of crime in Cape Town South Africa. Environ. Urbanization **16**(2), 101–112 (2004)
10. Bornheim, M., Fletcher, M.: Public safety digital transformation: the internet of things (IoT) and emergency services. In: 2020 Predations Document IoT and Emergency Services 3 European Emergency Number Association (2020)
11. Lacinák, M., Ristvej, J.: Smart city, safety and security. Procedia Eng. **192**, 522–527 (2017)
12. Isafiade, O.E.: Ubiquitous intelligence for smart cities: a public safety approach (2017)
13. Kadar, C., Te, Y.F., Rosés Brüngger, R., Pletikosa Cvijikj, I.: Digital neighborhood watch: to share or not to share? In: Proceedings of the 2016 CHI Conference Extended Abstracts on Human Factors in Computing Systems, pp. 2148–2155 (2016)
14. Ariffin, I., Solemon, B., Bakar, W.M.L.W.A.: An evaluative study on mobile crowdsourcing applications for crime watch. In: Proceedings of the 6th International Conference on Information Technology and Multimedia, pp. 335–340. IEEE (2014)
15. McCarthy, O.T., Caulfield, B., O'Mahony, M.: How transport users perceive personal safety apps. Transport. Res. F: Traffic Psychol. Behav. **43**, 166–182 (2016)
16. McGrath, S.: Mobile apps can enhance personal safety efforts. Student Aff. Today **19**(1), 6 (2016)

17. Maxwell, L., Sanders, A., Skues, J., Wise, L.: A content analysis of personal safety apps: are they keeping us safe or making us more vulnerable? Violence Against Women **26**(2), 233–248 (2020)
18. Jabar, A., Bjorkman, S., Matzopoulos, R.: Modified delphi study to determine optimal data elements for inclusion in a pilot violence and injury observatory in Cape Town, South Africa. Afr. J. Emerg. Med. **9**(1), 30–35 (2019)
19. UNFPA United Nations Population Fund (2020). https://www.unfpa.org/
20. Giffinger, R., Fertner, C., Kramar, H., Meijers, E.: City-ranking of European medium-sized cities. Cent. Reg. Sci. Vienna UT **9**, 1–12 (2007)
21. Choi, J., Hwang, M., Kim, G., Seong, J., Ahn, J.: Supporting the measurement of the United Nations' sustainable development goal 11 through the use of national urban information systems and open geospatial technologies: a case study of south Korea. Open Geospatial Data, Softw. Stan. **1**(1), 1–9 (2016). https://doi.org/10.1186/s40965-016-0005-0
22. Kloppers, J.: Citizen engagement in Cape Town's transition towards a smart city. In: 2016 IST-Africa Week Conference, pp. 1–13. IEEE (2016)
23. Nam, T., Pardo, T. A.: Conceptualizing smart city with dimensions of technology, people, and institutions. In: Proceedings of the 12th Annual International Digital Government Research Conference: Digital Government Innovation in Challenging Times, pp. 282–291 (2011)
24. Walid, A., Kobbane, A., Ben-Othman, J., El Koutbi, M.: Toward eco-friendly smart mobile devices for smart cities. IEEE Commun. Mag. **55**(5), 56–61 (2017)
25. Novotný, R., Kuchta, R., Kadlec, J.: Smart city concept, applications and services. J. Telecommun. Syst. Manage. **3**(2), 1–5 (2014)
26. Brodie, N.: Understanding crime statistics in South Africa - what you need to know (2015). http://www.unfpa.org/swop
27. Baud, I.S.A., Scott, D., Pfeffer, K., Sydenstricker-Neto, J., Denis, E.: Digital and spatial knowledge management in urban governance: emerging issues in India, Brazil, South Africa, and Peru. Habitat Int. **44**, 501–509 (2014)
28. SAPS South Africa SAPS Crime Statistics (2020). https://www.saps.gov.sa/
29. Turok, I.: Persistent polarisation post-apartheid? Progress towards urban integration in Cape Town. Urban Stud. **38**(13), 2349–2377 (2001)
30. Laufs, J., Borrion, H., Bradford, B.: Security and the smart city: a systematic review. Sustain. Cities Soc. **55**, 102023 (2020)
31. Ahir, S., Kapadia, S., Chauhan, J., Sanghavi, N.: The personal stun-a smart device for women's safety. In: 2018 International Conference on Smart City and Emerging Technology (ICSCET), pp. 1–3. IEEE (2018)
32. Moreira, B., Cacho, N., Lopes, F., Cavalcante, E.: Towards civic engagement in smart public security. In: 2017 International Smart Cities Conference (ISC2), pp. 1–6. IEEE (2017)
33. Austin, D.M., Furr, L.A.: The effects of neighborhood conditions on perceptions of safety. J. Crim. Just. **30**(5), 417–427 (2002)
34. Waters, J., Neale, R.H., Mears, K.: Perceptions of personal safety in relation to the physical environment of university campuses. In: CIB Joint Symposium on Advancing Facilities Management and Construction through Innovation, pp. 230–242) (2005)
35. Bilsky, W., Pfeiffer, C., Wetzels, P. Feelings of personal safety, fear of crime and violence and the experience of victimization amongst elderly people: research instrument and survey design. Fear Crime Crim. Victimization, 245–267 (1993)
36. Gray, E., Jackson, J., Farrall, S.: Feelings and functions in the fear of crime: applying a new approach to victimisation insecurity. Br. J. Criminol. **51**(1), 75–94 (2011)
37. Ceccato, V., Nalla, M.K.: Crime and fear in public places: towards safe, inclusive and sustainable cities, p. 486. Taylor & Francis (2020).
38. Wallace, A.: Mapping city crime and the new aesthetic of danger. J. Vis. Cult. **8**(1), 5–24 (2009)

39. Wortmann F, Flüchter K.: Internet of Things Technology and Value Added. Springer Fachmedien Wiesbaden. Online (2015) ISSN, 57, 221.
40. Johannesson, P., Perjons, E.: An Introduction to Design Science. Springer, Cham (2014). https://doi.org/10.1007/978-3-030-78132-3
41. Davis, F.D.: Perceived usefulness, perceived ease of use, and user acceptance of information technology. MIS Q. **13**, 319–340 (1989)
42. Cheung, R., Vogel, D.: Predicting user acceptance of collaborative technologies: an extension of the technology acceptance model for e-learning. Comput. Educ. **63**, 160–175 (2013)
43. Iriberri, A., Leroy, G., Garrett, N.: Reporting on-campus crime online: user intention to use. In: Proceedings of the 39th Annual Hawaii International Conference on System Sciences (HICSS 2006), vol. 4, pp. 82a–82a. IEEE (2006)
44. Braun, V., Clarke, V.: Using thematic analysis in psychology. Qual. Res. Psychol. **3**(2), 77–101 (2006)
45. Blom, J., Viswanathan, D., Spasojevic, M., Go, J., Acharya, K., Ahonius, R.: Fear and the city: role of mobile services in harnessing safety and security in urban use contexts. In: Proceedings of the SIGCHI Conference on Human Factors in Computing Systems, pp. 1841–1850 (2010)
46. Yu, A., Bamis, A., Lymberopoulos, D., Teixeira, T., Savvides, A.: Personalized awareness and safety with mobile phones as sources and sinks. UrbanSense **08**, 26 (2008)
47. Mancini, F., et al.: New technology and the prevention of violence and conflict. Int. Peace Inst. UNDP, USAID (2013) (2013)
48. Domdouzis, K., Akhgar, B., Andrews, S., Gibson, H., Hirsch, L.: A social media and crowd-sourcing data mining system for crime prevention during and post-crisis situations. J. Syst. Inf. Technol. **18**(4), 364–382 (2016)
49. Hollander, J.A.: Vulnerability and dangerousness: the construction of gender through conversation about violence. Gend. Soc. **15**(1), 83–109 (2001)

Building Digital Resilience to Combat Pandemics: Comparison of South Korea, Sri Lanka and Rwanda

Pamod M. Amarakoon[1]([⊠]) [iD], Jørn A. Braa[1] [iD], Kyung Ryul Park[2] [iD],
Sundeep Sahay[1] [iD], and Andrew Muhire[3] [iD]

[1] HISP Centre, University of Oslo, Oslo, Norway
{pamodma,jbraa,sundeeps}@ifi.uio.no
[2] Korea Advanced Institute of Science and Technology, Daejeon, South Korea
park.kr@kaist.ac.kr
[3] Ministry of Health, Kigali, Rwanda

Abstract. Use of digital technologies for management of COVID-19 pandemic was widely observed across the globe. However, building resilient digital systems to better manage the pandemic based on country contexts was a challenge. The objective of this study is to identify socio-technical determinants of building resilient digital technologies based on a comparative study or three countries. Case study method was utilized with qualitative data collection methods to identify thematic areas for comparison. The study revealed that resilient digital pandemic responses will rely on a plurality of technologies, and on agility, flexibility and capacity in producing these solutions.

Keywords: Sri Lanka · South Korea · Rwanda · Resilience · COVID-19 · Pandemic

1 Introduction

Resilience in health IT has been defined as "institutions' and health actors' capacities to prepare for, recover from and absorb shocks, while maintaining core functions and serving the ongoing and acute care needs of their communities" (Haldane et al. 2021). The resilience of health systems in low- and middle-income countries (LMICs) has become an increasingly important research topic since the 2014 Ebola Virus Disease (EVD) outbreaks in West Africa (Haldane et al. 2017) and is now magnified with the current COVID-19 pandemic.

A basic vulnerability-resilience duality characterizes the process of creating and deploying resilience, comprising aspects of both a 'bounce back' to re-establish stability and a 'bounce forward' to adapt to changing situations. This duality is exemplified in the Paris Climate Agreement, where the term "climate-resilient development" refers to both mitigation of climate change hazards and adaptation by "fully realizing technology development and transfer to improve climate change resilience and reduce greenhouse

Y. Zheng et al. (Eds.): ICT4D 2022, IFIP AICT 657, pp. 295–309, 2022.
https://doi.org/10.1007/978-3-031-19429-0_18

gas emissions" (The Paris Agreement I UNFCCC 2015). The COVID-19 epidemic, which is still sweeping the globe and disproportionately affecting communities, has comparable issues in terms of resilience, in that it necessitates quick action to mitigate the vulnerabilities produced by this shock. This goes hand in hand with the need to provide creative and agile solutions to respond to the changing environment.

In response to the COVID-19 pandemic, a 2020 WHO policy brief highlighted the need for effective 'information systems and flows' and strong epidemiological surveillance as key resilience-building strategies (Thomas et al. 2020). The pandemic has been characterized by high levels of uncertainty with rapid changes in policies and urgent demand for data and digital technology responses. In early 2020, Sri Lanka developed an effective digital platform for responding to the emerging pandemic using the open source DHIS2 platform (*District Health Information Software 2*, n.d.). The system provided an effective and agile response, with the ability to support case surveillance and contact tracing, and integrating disparate information systems to ensure critical lab test results could be used in the COVID-19 response (Kobayashi et al. 2021). Using the same DHIS2 platform and having developed strong capacity in its application, Rwanda quickly adopted the Sri Lanka COVID-19 apps, which were distributed in the global DHIS2 network, and managed to establish a resilient digital pandemic response. In this paper we present and discuss the successful digital responses using the open-source platform approach by these two LMICs, and compare them with the case of South Korea, which was also able to provide a resilient digital pandemic response through a plethora of different solutions fostered through a private-public partnership and better economic strength to power digital innovation. In the discussion, the three cases will be used to identify key determinants for digital resilience and to indicate the advantages of South-South-North network and platform approaches in building digital resilience, in particular in the global south. We hypothesize that in order to achieve an efficient digital response in times of a pandemic agility and plurality of digital solutions are required in contexts of LMIC or developed countries. In addition, such efficient responses may be backed by low-cost, opensource solutions in a LMIC setting with community driven implementations while high-tech technology with better resources can be used in the context of developed countries. The paper primarily focus around testing the above hypothesis and to understanding the socio-technical determinants of building resilient digital technologies to better manage the pandemics.

2 Review of Literature

2.1 Resilience

Resilience is a term that has been studied across numerous fields such as ecology, sociology, engineering, public health, psychology, etc. The phrase 'resilience' comes from the Latin root "resilire", which refers to the ability to 'bounce back' from adversity as well as 'bounce forward' to altered systems that can cope with changing circumstances (Longstaff et al. 2013). The term "resilience" was used in ecology to characterize complex natural systems that can absorb perturbations and yet maintain equilibrium, as well as the speed at which equilibrium is reestablished (Rose 2017).

Folke et al. (2010) propose a 'resilience thinking' process framework for complex social–ecological systems (SES) that integrates resilience, adaptation, and transformability. The ability of the SES to evolve and adapt while staying within crucial thresholds is referred to as resilience. The capacity to alter reactions to changing environmental factors and internal processes is referred to as adaptability. Finally, transformability refers to the ability to cross boundaries and embark on new development paths. Change at lesser scales allows for greater resilience at significantly larger scales, while crises provide windows of opportunity for uniqueness and invention.

Since the 2014 Ebola outbreaks in West Africa, discussions on resilience have dominated health systems research, and the current COVID-19 pandemic has amplified this trend (Haldane et al. 2017). As essential resilience-building initiatives, a WHO strategy brief from 2020 emphasized the importance of efficient "information systems and flows" as well as strong epidemiological surveillance (Thomas et al. 2020). The Lancet defines resilient health systems as having the ability to plan for and respond to crises, sustain normal fundamental operations when a crisis occurs, and reconfigure itself based on lessons learned (Kruk et al. 2015).

As an 'active process inside a dynamic health system that is continually navigating problems by getting better', resilience is an emergent property of Complex Adaptive Systems (CAS), requiring adaptation, learning, and transformation (Barasa et al. 2017). Blanchet et al. (2017) describe resilience as a health system's ability to absorb, adapt, and transform when subjected to stress while maintaining control over its structure and functions, based on ecology and complexity research.

Many scholars define resilience in terms of traits or properties such as robustness, redundancy, resourcefulness, and speed (Bruneau et al. 2003). An attribute-focused approach, it is said, is too broad, undermining the concept's analytical precision, and labeling anything as "resilience" is redundant. Adaptive capacity, as proposed by Klein et al. (2003), is an umbrella concept for resilience that includes difficulties outlined by Bruneau et al (2003). Decreased vulnerability, flexibility, adaptability, agility, and self-organization were all mentioned (Erol et al. 2010; Heeks and Ospina 2019). However, the process of establishment of resilience of digital systems from a socio-technical perspective is still an under-researched area specially in the domain of the health sector. We try to focus on exploring this dimension with three case studies from the Global North and South.

3   Methods

For this article, we used a case study methodology since it allowed us to delve at the context and dynamics of the phenomena – agile development of resilient digital technologies in a pandemic situation – in three different countries. According to Darke et al. (1998), such an approach is advantageous in emerging and less researched research areas, such as the phenomena studied in this paper. According to Yin's (2014) definition of a case study, our method was an empirical investigation of a current occurrence in a real-life setting.

To test the hypothesis we needed to select countries representing LMIC and developed settings. South Korea, Sri Lanka and Rwanda were selected based on convenience and access to conduct qualitative research during times of a pandemic by the authors. The authors in general have had long-term academic and information system engagements in the 3 countries involved with the case studies. Two of the authors were actively engaged with the implementation process of the COVID-19 related digital health response in Sri Lanka and Rwanda. According to Yin, the data collection methods in this case were diverse, covering socio-technical methodologies. Some of the authors had personal anecdotes with system development efforts, which they shared in the form of narratives. Memos were also compiled from observations made during stakeholder meetings throughout the implementation of the digital solutions. Interviews were conducted with key stakeholders at national and district level engaged with the implementations. Secondary data sources included publications released by public health organizations, materials presented at stakeholder meetings, and notes taken during informal discussions with stakeholders. The data collection methods devised in the three countries are summarized in the Table 1 below.

Table 1. Data collection methods used in the 3 settings

South Korea	Sri Lanka	Rwanda
Interviews • Government Officer, Ministry of Science and ICT • Administrator, National Information Society Agency • ICT Developer • Public Health expert in academia	Interviews • National level health and ICT sector administrators • National level system implementers • District level health administrators • District level system implementers • Field level system users	Interviews • Key implementers and administrators at national, district levels and at Rwanda Biomedical Centre • System end users at vaccination centres and clinics, immigration at airport
Document Analysis • Government policy reports • Press release • Government's website • KCDC's statistics	Meeting Notes • Notes from high level policy and system design meetings	Meeting Notes • From high-level meetings with national task force and health administrators • System design meetings
	Observations • Stakeholder engagement at planning meetings • End user training programs • System use at field level	Observations • Stakeholder meetings related to policy and system design • Training programs • End user engagement at field level
	Document Analysis • Government policy documents • Government website with official statistics	Document and data analysis • Following the daily updates of cases and vaccination

Throughout the data analysis process, we were continually communicating our experiences and perspectives on the information we had acquired. The case story was then jointly developed, and thematic analysis techniques were employed to identify patterns appearing in the presentation of this study, as indicated by Braun et al. (2014).

4 Case Studies

We present the three cases and thereafter we compare and discuss their implications.

4.1 South Korea

4.1.1 Background

South Korea's pandemic strategy, particularly during the early stages, has been lauded by international organizations and the media (World Health Organization 2020). The first patient confirmed as a case of COVID-19 was announced on January 20, 2020. Korea was successfully able to control and mitigate the spread of the epidemic without the need for a lockdown or restrictions on movement (Lee et al. 2020). The case of Korea case provides several important policy implications and empirical evidences on effective data governance and digital resilience. First of all, the government responded to the COVID-19 pandemic in an agile and collaborative manner (Moon 2020). During its response, various digital technologies were applied (Government of the Republic of Korea 2020). Conducting an interpretive case study of Korea, Park et al. (2021) identify key features of digital resilience including agility, plurality - enabled by active roles of diverse stakeholders including citizens, research communities, and private sector.

4.1.2 Massive Applications of Digital Technologies

The utilization of various digital innovations including information systems, mobile applications and medical devices was crucial in testing, tracing, and treatment. This study particularly focuses on the use of ICTs in sharing information and improving government's response as well as in treatment of COVID-19. First, in order to enhance government to government (G2G) and government to citizen (G2C) communications, Ministry of Land and Transportation (MOLIT) developed the Smart Management System (SMS) in collaboration with the Korea Disease Control and Prevention Agency (KDCA) and the Ministry of Science & ICT (MSIT) (– (Ministry of Science & ICT - Republic of Korea - Republic of Korea 2020). Since February 2020, sending emergency alerts and messages via mobile phone text messages has been a promising communication tool to rapidly disseminate information and promote preventive behavior among the public during the pandemic outbreak in South Korea. The SMS collects big data, such as mobile phone location, hot spot usage, CCTV recordings, and credit card usage within 10 min (Ministry of Health & Welfare: News & Welfare Services 2020). Second, artificial Intelligence played an important role in supporting the diagnosis and treatment. AI based medical imaging including x-ray and CT scan analysis devices were developed to detect major lung abnormalities, and assist doctors in making quick diagnosis during the pandemic (Ministry of Science & ICT - Republic of Korea 2020).

4.1.3 Agility

Learning from the MERS outbreak, the government had significantly ramped up its testing capacity drawing upon all available resources and supported by advanced ICTs to geo-locate positive cases (Moon 2020; Park et al. 2020). The government enacted a policy on emergency use authorization which enabled the use of pre-approved diagnostic kits in conditions of emergency. The agility was built by the use of multiple apps for different purposes, each built through multiple actors and partnerships. Different forms of learnings contributed to providing the basis for agility in both target and object system responses, which were socio-technical in nature (Amarakoon et al. 2020).

Regarding the institutional change in governance, it is also notable that each local government established a Local Disaster and Safety Management Headquarters to secure the capacity of healthcare services and beds (Ministry of Foreign Affairs- Republic of Korea 2020). The government established drive-thru and walk-thru screening stations by late February which shortened testing time and scaled testing capacity nationally, without putting health workers at risk (Lee and Lee 2020; Ministry of Health & Welfare 2020; Moon 2020). Tests lasted 10 min on average, per person, whereas previous tests and registration lasted 30 min (Ministry of Health and Welfare 2020). Korea was capable of conducting over 23,000 diagnostic tests free of charge per day.

4.1.4 Citizens' Participation

Although using ICTs for sharing information is not new in the crisis, citizen generated applications of the Korea case is quite unique. A couple of notable geographic information system (GIS)-based applications and websites developed by citizens aimed to support people access and share information on COVID-19 and masks. Among them, 'Corona Map' attracted many users as supplementary sources for information. After the first outbreak in Korea in 2020, the KDCA published the trajectory history of patients on its website. After 10 days of the first case, a college student developed 'Corona Map', a web-based map services that visualizes COVID-19 patients' travel history. The service hit 2.4 million views on its first day and attracted a large number of users. Later, he information on the map was also found on the website provided by KDCA. In addition, the developer and other civil society leaders were invited to engage with shaping process of government policy. In order to tackle concerns over privacy and human rights, the government worked together with civil society and tried to set up policy balancing public health needs and human right issues. Although the service gradually lost its attention, it served as one of the agile information providing channels during the pandemic. Understanding citizens' participation and how this transforms knowledge, and social norms is crucial for analyzing the effective response to the pandemic. Citizen participation can provide alternative way of information sharing and suggest implications for the data governance policy in public health crisis.

4.1.5 Public-Private Partnerships (PPP)

PPP were effectively leveraged to support different interventions in an agile manner. A key intervention was the Epidemic Investigation Support System (EISS), which enabled information sharing between government authorities and private sector including credit card companies and mobile network operators. Park et al. (Park et al. 2020) state that about 2,000 daily cases were tracked by mobile tracking applications, which reduced the time of epidemiological investigation to 10 min, using information based on latitude and longitude, as well as of visit duration (Park et al. 2020; You 2020). In addition, the government collaborated with private sector in the making of COVID-19 treatments and vaccines. In order to widely implement the diagnostic method, the KDCA collaborated with the biotech industry. Ministry of Food and Drug Safety (MFDS) approved the fast review for six diagnostic companies including Seegene, Kogene Biotech, SolGent, SD Biosensor, Bioseum and Biocore) and granted emergency use authorization for COVID-19 detection kits (MFDS 2020). Later, the number of exports of these test kit as well as export destinations including Vietnam, the US, Italy, and Spain increased rapidly. The total value of the Korean-developed test kits exported has grown to exceed 250 million USD as of January 2022 (Statista 2022).

In April 2021, the KDCA announced the launch of COOV (Corona Overcome), an electronic vaccination certificate for COVID-19 vaccines. With the PPP between KDCA and Blockchain Labs Inc. a decentralized identifier (DID), a blockchain-based identification technology was applied to prevent forgery and falsification of the COVID-19 electronic vaccination certificate and to confirm its authenticity (COOV 2021)[1]. Citizens were able to reserve vaccinations through social media such as Naver and Kakao applications as well. Another key aspect of the context relevant for the COVID-19 response was the government's investment in research and development in science, technology and innovation (Park 2022). The government, collaborating with private sectors, was able to effectively respond to the pandemic by investing in technology and facilitating diverse stakeholders' engagement.

4.2 Sri Lanka

4.2.1 Background

The COVID-19 pandemic that emerged in China in December 2019 rapidly spread across several countries in the Southeast Asia in first two months of the year 2020. Sri Lanka, being a country that heavily depends on tourism was at risk of COVID-19 in early 2020 due high number of incoming tourists especially from China. Controlling the COVID-19 required rapid detection and action by multiple stakeholders led by the health sector. The country lacked a digital information system for such surveillance activities which was typically present in most of the developed countries. Establishing such a system in the light of a pandemic in the context of a low and middle-income country was challenging. However, the Ministry of Health together with the multisector stakeholders were able to establish a digital surveillance system for COVID-19 in a short span of time backed by open-source solutions, existing country capacity and governance mechanisms.

4.2.2 Agility in Design and Implementation

In January 2020 the Ministry of Health had a crucial meeting to decide on the technical aspects of designing a digital surveillance system. It was identified that the development

---

[1] COOV System, Apr. 2022, [online] Available: https://en.coov.kr.

of the system had to be rapid and subjected to frequent changes following the implementation due to poor understanding of the requirements of a pandemic surveillance system at that time. The existing capacity of the country as well as training requirements were also considered. Having analyzed these requirements the ministry decided to use the free and open source health management information platform DHIS2 to design the backbone of the surveillance system. The country already had capacity and experience in using this platform for aggregate and case-based data collection in multiple use cases in the domain of health. In addition, medical officers of health informatics were the key human resources backing the implementation of this platform at national and district level. The first module of the platform was aimed at fulfilling requirements at ports of entry to track tourists for COVID-19 once they arrive in the country. This module was designed and implemented by end of January 2020, one day before the country reported its first COVID-19 confirmed case. The core team driving the design and implementation consisted of HISP Sri Lanka, the local node of the global HISP (Health Information Systems Program) network driving the implementation of DHIS2, health informaticians from the Ministry of health as well as the ICT agency of Sri Lanka. The team was quickly able to customize the DHIS2 platform for the changing epidemiological requirements of the country. Within a period of three months, the team was able to incorporate data modules into the system to cover the requirements around quarantine, case registration and tracking, contact tracing, community surveillance, laboratory data collection and ICU bed monitoring. In the meantime, when inbuilt features of DHIS2 was not sufficient to serve the requirements, the national core team worked with the ICT agency to organize a hackathon to find volunteer developers to design web apps that ran on top of the DHIS2 platform. Contact mapping visualization, ICU bed monitoring and contact tracing using mobile tower location are examples of the applications developed from the hackathon. The drive for customization and implementation continued in the third quarter of 2020 even though the disease burden was much less. The continuing efforts helped the country to develop a steady response to strengthen laboratory monitoring and integration of community testing platforms in the second wave of COVID-19 in fourth quarter of 2020. The team was able to integrate a laboratory information system to the central DHIS2 platform for COVID-19 to establish an integrated ecosystem of COVID-19 digital systems. The platform expanded further in 2021 with the addition of the immunization module with preregistration of the entire adult population of Sri Lanka (close to 19 million). The module, which was rapidly developed, was ready to be used on the first day the COVID vaccination campaign was launched in Sri Lanka. The vaccination module was expanded further in mid-2021 with the inclusion of a component to produce cryptographically verifiable digital vaccination certificates. The team with the support of ICT Agency, implemented the global digital public goods platform, DIVOC, for generating certificates and integrated it with the vaccination module of the DHIS2. The integrated solution provided a robust digital system to capture and visualization COVID vaccination information to track the rapid vaccination program as well to produce digital vaccination certificates for citizens for travel purposes.

4.2.3 Local Capacity and Multisector Engagement

The COVID-19 surveillance system was an advanced implementation of DHIS2 which had customised DHIS2 components, custom-made web applications as well as integrations with government-owned systems and third-party solutions making it a robust information ecosystem with multisector collaboration. The salient features which enabled this ecosystem was the agile and dedicated collaboration between the ministry of health, the government stakeholders, private sector as well as international networks backed by the governance and leadership of the COVID-19 steering committee headed by the president. The long-term capacity building in health informatics by the country was a key driver in designing and implementing the system within the resources of the ministry. The major impact brought about by the system was the availability of up-to-date dashboards customized to the role of the user, which provided decision-makers the information to take proper actions.

The solution developed in Sri Lanka was not nurtured solely with in-country resources. There was constant communication with the open source DHIS2 community and the experts at the University of Oslo, Norway that facilitated rapid development and implementation. The experience in Sri Lanka and the metadata that was developed was shared with the DHIS2 community and the University of Oslo which was further developed and released as a generic metadata package. This package has facilitated more than 50 countries in adopting DHIS2-based solutions for COVID-19 surveillance. The feedback received from the DHIS2 community further contributed to enhancing the products that were developed in Sri Lanka such as the contact tracing web application.

Information Systems implementations in Sri Lanka were traditionally involved with extensive training programs that were conducted at the district level. However, COVID-19 related restrictions brought about major challenges in conducting physical training programs. The country quickly adopted video conferencing platforms coupled with simple user guides and instant messaging support groups as solutions for facilitating training and the provision of support. Quite surprisingly, the health care workers rapidly responded to the change brought about by new technologies and adopted the platform.

ICT infrastructure that was required for data collection at different levels of institutes including hospitals, laboratories, community centers, quarantine centers as well as ports of entry was a constant challenge for scaling up the implementation. In addition, the constant requirement for integration with the existing and emerging information systems was a challenge that the core team successfully managed. Prioritization of requirements and managing the existing administrative and hierarchical establishments has been one of the toughest challenges in implementation.

4.3 Rwanda

4.3.1 Adapting Global Solutions to Local Context

Sharing solutions and experience from the Sri Lanka case through the DHIS2 global network, Rwanda also embarked on a process to develop a digital health response to COVID-19 using the DHIS2 platform. From March 2020, the Rwanda DHIS2 team implemented a case surveillance and contact tracing system, using software developed through the Sri Lanka initiative and enhanced through global collaboration, and included in the new WHO digital health packages (Poppe et al. 2021). These open-source packages consist of health program specific standardized metadata sets that can be downloaded and installed in DHIS2. The Rwandan Ministry of Health reported that they saved considerable time by downloading the WHO metadata and then adding additional data variables they already used in their paper based reporting, and which were not part of the standard package:

"We saved time by not having to argue too much with multiple stakeholders on what data to include or not, since the standards were recommended by WHO and it was easy to include additional needed data variables."

Rwanda Ministry of Health (MoH) Team Member

The lab system work-process, from taking the sample, transporting to the lab, and the dissemination of results, however, turned out to be the biggest bottleneck. Turnaround times of up to one week made real time surveillance impossible. The MoH team then embarked on a full revamp of the lab system at the Rwanda Biomedical Centre, reducing and optimizing the work-processes, deploying Android tablet computers for end users, installing workstations in the labs, and establishing a public portal for booking a COVID-19 test, online payment, and checking of results. The entire system was based on the Open Source DHIS2 platform.

When vaccination became possible in March 2021, the MoH team started to develop a vaccination support module in the DHIS2 linked to the lab module with the same unique identifier. There were initially several competing systems suggested by development partners and one of these was first selected as the COVID-19 vaccination system. With developers based in the US and with little local knowledge, this "development from a distance" approach, however, failed to respond to the needs of the MoH and the evolving requirements of the COVID-19 vaccination campaign, such as the need for QR coded certificates and interoperability with the lab system. Given this development and the positive results from the implementation of the DHIS2 lab system, the MoH selected the DHIS2 platform for COVID-19 vaccination support and later decided that all Covid related systems should be based on the DHIS2 platform. The need for local ownership, control and experience of the technology were seen as key reasons leading to this decision.

4.3.2 Expansion of Solutions

An entire ecosystem of COVID related apps, modules and services has now been developed and are currently in operation for such tasks as: tracking of cross-border trucks and drivers, QR coded certificates, self-registration for travelers to Rwanda for their health declaration, uploading of documents, payment for rapid test at arrival, and for SMS text messaging of results. The vaccination campaign targeted the adult population of approximately 7.5 million people and had reached 7 million doses by mid-November, 2021. Several vaccines were used, including: Pfizer, Moderna, Johnson & Johnson, and Sputnik, with the majority requiring two doses.

During one week in November, 1 million doses were given, providing pressure on server and team, as the approach of using real-time online registration of vaccination, meant that if the server was down, users had to change their work process and keep notes on paper, which is complicated because each dose is to be linked to a unique identifier. Response time was critical, and the global DHIS2 open-source network was engaged in supporting the Rwanda team in addressing server bottlenecks, such as to terminate processes lasting more than one minute, and removing the autocomplete function on search fields which can create high server loads.

The Rwanda DHIS2 team has provided an effective and agile information and digital response to the pandemic and thereby contributed greatly to the resilience of the Rwanda health system and society during the COVID-19 pandemic (see rbc.gov.rw for daily updated data on cases and vaccination). The open-source capacity and quality of the DHIS2 platform have been a prerequisite for building capacity in developing and mastering systems in the Rwanda team as well as for establishing a reciprocal collaborative global network for sharing digital solutions, best practices, support and learning. The platform aspects of the DHIS2 have also been important in building a plurality of apps needed for responding to the pandemic on top of the DHIS2 and interacting through the open API.

5 Discussion

The case studies reveal that the selected countries used slightly different methods in deploying digital technologies based on availability of resources and country strategies. The success of digital tools in controlling the pandemic in the 3 settings have been documented in several publications. Rwanda's success during the pandemic, especially in COVID-19 vaccination has been highlighted as a lesson for the entire Africa and use of digital tools has been attributed as a key determinant of the success (*Vaccinating Africa: What Governments Can Learn From Rwanda's Effective Rollout | Institute for Global Change*, n.d.). Sri Lanka's COVID-19 control and vaccination has been highlighted as extremely efficient in the South Asian region and this was driven by several digital tools acting in synergy (*WHO Dialogues: Sri Lanka Shares Digital Innovations Made during Pandemic - Sri Lanka | ReliefWeb*, n.d.). World bank spotlights effective use of digital tools in Korea as an example other countries can learn from (*Learning from Korea's Digital Response to COVID-19: Details on Public Health Measures through Open Data and the Contact Tracing System (English) | World Bank Group*, n.d.).

The case studies from the 3 countries depicts that an efficient digital response at a pandemic situation requires plurality of factors whether it be a LMIC like Sri Lanka or Rwanda, or a developed country like South Korea. The analysis of the case studies enabled us to identify 3 broader themes based on which we could prove the hypothesis and identify the enabling factors for digital resilience. We discuss the case studies along the following perspectives; agility, flexible use of digital technologies and networks; and optimum use of local capacity.

5.1 Agility of Response

COVID-19 surfaced in the world in a completely unexpected manner in the late 2019. Countries had to prepare for the adversities imposed by the pandemic, the livelihood and the economy of the people. In the preparation for the pandemic information plays a pivotal role and the countries had to decide on best use of information in an agile manner amidst the uncertainties caused by the pandemic. The case study from Korea depicts how the country built upon the experiences and preparations from the MERS epidemic and deployed its resources in ramping up testing, developing and deploying multiple apps by the government as well as partnerships with the private sector stakeholders. This highlights the agility of response in the early phase of pandemic which could be attributed to the application of learnings from the previous pandemics and adoption and implementation of the policies in a high resource, developed country context.

However, the case studies from Sri Lanka and Rwanda reveal that these countries did not have prior preparation, governance or policies to deploy digital technologies to monitor and manage the limited resources in times of a pandemic. However, while it is generally expected that such countries in the Global South with low resources and poor governance would collapse in the context of a pandemic, we observe the agility in decision-making, governance of information management as well as engagement with the stakeholders observed in the early phase of the pandemic. Sri Lanka set up a steering committee to engage with different ministries and the private sector to deploy the available resources to design a variety of apps on an open source platform and deployed across the countries. Rwanda materialized on learnings from deployments in other countries such as Sri Lanka and adopting the solutions which better suited the country context within short span of time. The swift response observed in these two case studies highlights how countries with limited resources could build resilient informatics solutions to manage the pandemic to a satisfactory level as well as contribute these learnings to sustain routine information systems.

5.2   Flexible Use of Digital Technologies and Networking

South Korea spearheaded development of digital technologies to manage COVID 19 related information based on state of the art technologies adhering to robust privacy standards. These enabled the country to design and implement the systems in the early pandemic which was also supported by extensive public private partnerships and citizen driven approaches. However, this is contrasting with the LMIC context of Sri Lanka and Rwanda which did not possess the technologies or the resources to build solutions that can be designed from the scratch. Instead, they built on their own solution on the widely established open-source platform DHIS2 which was robust and flexible enough to cater the changing requirements around COVID-19. The platform supported customization using the front-end tools and development of web applications and integrations to serve additional requirements. The knowledge sharing and integral connectivity of these countries with the global open-source community made it possible to leverage lack of in country expertise by connecting with a pool of experts from around the globe. Thus, use of flexible open source digital platforms and networking with the global communities supported these countries to rapidly develop and implement digital solutions for COVID-19 at the same pace of that of developed countries such as South Korea.

The COVID-19 DHIS2 contact tracing tool of Sri Lanka, which is utilized by numerous countries, is a prime example of a product of hackathon, which is a classic example of agile software development process (Alkema et al. 2017). Kruk et al. (2015) define health system resilience as the ability to both effectively respond to crises and retain fundamental functioning when a crisis occurs, based on lessons learned from Ebola. When the pandemic struck, we faced similar issues in stabilizing and maintaining normal systems ('bouncing back'), as well as developing new digital capabilities to respond to the pandemic ('bouncing forward'). While South Korea displayed its bouncing back and bouncing forward characteristics of use of digital technologies from the lessons learned from previous MERS epidemic, the use of technologies in Sri Lanka and Rwanda reveals how they used frugal digital technologies to efficiently manage the pandemic while they also helped continue the routine information systems at level of pre-pandemic status.

5.3 Optimum Use of Local Capacity

Folke et al. (2010) define resilience as a capability that evolves through time as a result of establishing readiness, using it, and evolving it to produce transformability potential. Resilience and adaptability, which they consider to be part of resilience, as well as transformability, reflect many sorts of capacities that emerge over time, frequently in response to external events such as the COVID-19 pandemic.

The case studies from both Global North and South reveals that the optimum use of local capacity was a key determinant of successful implementation of digital technologies for COVID-19. South Korea utilized its existing knowledge and resources in technology for development of the digital solutions. In addition, the citizens and the academia were actively involved in designing as well as contributing in testing and deployment of the solutions. The government was keen to provide sufficient resources for the private sector to develop technologies and conduct research. Research and development was a key focus on the governments' involvement in providing support for digital interventions for COVID-19.

In the context of Sri Lanka, its leveraged on long-term capacity building in health informatics in the government sector for leading the development of solutions with the contribution of other stakeholders in the government as well as the private sector. The health informatics is produced from the long-term capacity building efforts were also the key resources driving the implementation is at the district level. In the case of Rwanda, the local HISP team which was instrumental in implementing digital solutions in the health sector led to the interventions which was closely connected to the global open-source community. Therefore, the LMICs mostly utilized their human resources and long-term capacity building in open-source solutions and support networks in achieving resilience in building and implementing digital solutions.

6 Conclusion

The three cases show that resilient digital pandemic responses will rely on a plurality of solutions, and on agility, flexibility and capacity in producing these solutions. While South Korea was able to provide an effective digital pandemic response by mobilizing its industrial, technological and economic base through a public-private partnership, Rwanda and Sri Lanka were able to provide a similarly resilient digital pandemic response through an open-source platform approach combined with in-country capacity and global networking to enable a plurality of apps and solutions.

References

Alkema, J.P., Phillip Levitt, S., Chen, J.Y.J.: Agile and hackathons: A case study of emergent practices at the FNB codefest. In: ACM International Conference Proceeding Series, Part F1308, pp. 1–10 (2017). https://doi.org/10.1145/3129416.3129430

Amarakoon, P., Braa, J., Sahay, S., Siribaddana, P., Hewapathirana, R.: building agility in health information systems to respond to the COVID-19 pandemic: the Sri Lankan experience. In: Bandi, R.K., Ranjini, C.R., Klein, S., Madon, S., Monteiro, E. (eds.) IFIPJWC 2020. IAICT, vol. 601, pp. 222–236. Springer, Cham (2020). https://doi.org/10.1007/978-3-030-64697-4_17

Barasa, E.W., Cloete, K., Gilson, L.: From bouncing back, to nurturing emergence: Reframing the concept of resilience in health systems strengthening. Health Policy Plann. 32(suppl_3), iii91–iii94 (2017). https://doi.org/10.1093/heapol/czx118

Blanchet, K., Nam, S.L., Ramalingam, B., Pozo-Martin, F.: Governance and capacity to manage resilience of health systems: towards a new conceptual framework. Int. J. Health Policy Manag. 6(8), 431–435 (2017). https://doi.org/10.15171/ijhpm.2017.36

Braun, V., Clarke, V.: What can "thematic analysis" offer health and wellbeing researchers? Int. J. Qualit. Stud. Health Well-being 9 (2014). https://doi.org/10.3402/qhw.v9.26152

Bruneau, M., et al.: A framework to quantitatively assess and enhance the seismic resilience of communities. Earthq. Spectra 19(4), 733–752 (2003). https://doi.org/10.1193/1.1623497

Darke, P., Shanks, G., Broadbent, M.: Successfully completing case study research: combining rigour, relevance and pragmatism. Inf. Syst. J. 8(4), 273–289 (1998). https://doi.org/10.1046/j.1365-2575.1998.00040.x

District Health Information System 2 (n.d.). https://www.dhis2.org/. Accessed 8 Dec 2015

Erol, O., Henry, D., Sauser, B., Mansouri, M.: Perspectives on measuring enterprise resilience. In: 2010 IEEE International Systems Conference Proceedings, SysCon 2010, pp. 587–592 (2010). https://doi.org/10.1109/SYSTEMS.2010.5482333

Folke, C., Carpenter, S.R., Walker, B., Scheffer, M., Chapin, T., Rockström, J.: Resilience thinking: integrating resilience, adaptability and transformability. Ecol. Soc. 5(4) (2010)

Government of the Republic of Korea Flattening the curve on COVID-19: How Korea responded to a pandemic using ICT. The Government of the Republic of Korea (2020)

Haldane, V., et al.: Health systems resilience in managing the COVID-19 pandemic: lessons from 28 countries. Nat. Med. 27(6), 964–980 (2021). https://doi.org/10.1038/s41591-021-01381-y

Haldane, V., Ong, S.E., Chuah, F.L.H., Legido-Quigley, H.: Health systems resilience: meaningful construct or catchphrase? Lancet 389(10078), 1513 (2017a). https://doi.org/10.1016/S0140-6736(17)30946-7

Heeks, R., Ospina, A.V.: Conceptualising the link between information systems and resilience: a developing country field study. Inf. Syst. J. 29(1), 70–96 (2019). https://doi.org/10.1111/isj.12177

Klein, R.J.T., Nicholls, R.J., Thomalla, F.: Resilience to natural hazards: how useful is this concept? Environ. Hazards 5(1), 35–45 (2003). https://doi.org/10.1016/j.hazards.2004.02.001

Kruk, M.E., Myers, M., Varpilah, S.T., Dahn, B.T.: What is a resilient health system? Lessons from Ebola. Lancet 385(9980), 1910–1912 (2015). https://doi.org/10.1016/S0140-6736(15)60755-3

Lee, D., Heo, K., Seo, Y.: COVID-19 in South Korea: Lessons for developing countries. World Dev. 135, 105057 (2020). https://doi.org/10.1016/j.worlddev.2020.105057

Lee, S.M., Lee, D.H.: "Untact": a new customer service strategy in the digital age. Serv. Bus. 14(1), 1–22 (2020). https://doi.org/10.1007/s11628-019-00408-2

Learning from Korea's Digital Response to COVID-19: Details on Public Health Measures through Open Data and the Contact Tracing System (English) | World Bank Group (n.d.). https://olc.worldbank.org/content/learning-korea%E2%80%99s-digital-response-covid-19-details-public-health-measures-through-open-data. Accessed 10 Apr 2022

Longstaff, P.H., Koslowski, T.G., Geoghegan, W.H.: Translating resilience: a framework to enhance communication and implementation. In: 5th International Symposium on Resilience Engineering (2013)

Ministry of Food and Drug Safety- Republic of Korea: Press Release: "Corona diagnostic test kit for post COVID-19" 20 May 2020 (2020)

Ministry of Foreign Affairs- Republic of Korea: Korea's Response to COVID-19 and Future Direction View|Key Strategies (2020). http://www.mofa.go.kr/eng/brd/m_22591/view.do?seq=11&srchFr=&srchTo=&srchWord=&srchTp=&multi_itm_seq=0&itm_seq_1=0&itm_seq_2=0&company_cd=&company_nm=&page=1&titleNm=

Ministry of Health & Welfare: News & Welfare Services: Press Release-COVID-19 Response Meeting Presided Over by the Prime Minister (2020). https://www.mohw.go.kr/eng/nw/nw0101vw.jsp?PAR_MENU_ID=1007&MENU_ID=100701&page=1&CONT_SEQ=352978

Ministry of Science & ICT - Republic of Korea: How We Fought COVID-19: Perspective from Science & ICT (2020)

Moon, M.J.: Fighting <scp>COVID</scp> -19 with agility, transparency, and participation: wicked policy problems and new governance challenges. Public Adm. Rev. **80**(4), 651–656 (2020). https://doi.org/10.1111/puar.13214

Park, K.R., Sahay, S., Braa, J., Amarakoon, P.: Digital resilience for what? Case study of South Korea. arXiv preprint arXiv:2108.09950 (2021)

Park, K.R.: Science, technology, and innovation in sustainable development cooperation: theories and practices in South Korea. In: International Development Cooperation of Japan and South Korea, pp. 179–208. Palgrave Macmillan, Singapore (2022)

Park, Y.J., et al.: Development and utilization of a rapid and accurate ephttps://doi.org/10.24171/j.phrp.2020.11.3.06idemic investigation support system for covid-19. Osong Public Health Res. Perspect. **11**(3), 118–127 (2020).

Poppe, O, Sæbø, J.I., Braa, J.: WHO digital health packages for disseminating data standards and data use practices. Int. J. Med. Inform. **149**, 104422 (2021). https://doi.org/10.1016/j.ijmedinf.2021.104422

Rose, A.: Defining resilience across disciplines. In: Rose, A. (ed.) Defining and Measuring Economic Resilience from a Societal, Environmental and Security Perspective. IDRM, pp. 19–27. Springer, Singapore (2017). https://doi.org/10.1007/978-981-10-1533-5_3

Statista: Export value of coronavirus (COVID-19) test kits from South Korea as of December 2021, by country of destination (2022). https://www.statista.com/statistics/1112556/south-korea-covid19-test-kits-export-value-by-country/. Accessed 30 Mar 2022

The Paris Agreement | UNFCCC (2015). https://unfccc.int/process-and-meetings/the-paris-agreement/the-paris-agreement

Thomas, S., Sagan, A., Larkin, J., Cylus, J., Figueras, J., Karanikolos, M.: Strengthening health systems resilience: Key concepts and strategies (2020)

Vaccinating Africa: What Governments Can Learn From Rwanda's Effective Rollout | Institute for Global Change (n.d.). https://institute.global/advisory/vaccinating-africa-what-governments-can-learn-rwandas-effective-rollout. Accessed 10 Apr 2022

World Health Organization: Sharing COVID-19 experiences: The Republic of Korea response (2020)

WHO Dialogues: Sri Lanka shares digital innovations made during pandemic - Sri Lanka | ReliefWeb (n.d.). https://reliefweb.int/report/sri-lanka/who-dialogues-sri-lanka-shares-digital-innovations-made-during-pandemic. Accessed 10 Apr 2022

Yin, R.K.: Case study research : design and methods (2014). https://books.google.lk/books/about/Case_Study_Research.html?id=Cdk5DQAAQBAJ&redir_esc=y

You, J.: Lessons from South Korea's Covid-19 policy response. Am. Rev. Public Adm. **50**(6–7), 801–808 (2020). https://doi.org/10.1177/0275074020943708

Digital and Language Inequalities in Disseminating COVID-19-Related Health Campaigns in Uganda: The Effects of Confinement and Social Distancing Strategies

Milburga Atcero[1]([⊠]) [iD] and Maureen Ayikoru[2] [iD]

[1] Department of Leisure and Hospitality Management, Makerere University Business School, Kampala, Uganda
matcero@mubs.ac.ug
[2] Department of Strategy, International Business and Entrepreneurship, School of Business and Management, Royal Holloway, University of London, London, UK
Maureen.ayikoru@rhul.ac.uk

Abstract. This article unveils existing gaps in the use of digital technologies and local languages in the context of official COVID-19 pandemic communication strategies in Uganda. It entails an analysis of a purposively drawn sample of official COVID-19 communication from the Ministry of Health through its website, notably in English and translations into few native Ugandan languages, to argue for the need for a more diverse and inclusive language strategy in pandemic containment and prevention communication strategy. Interviews were also held with a convenient sample of Ugandans from diverse ethnolinguistic and socio-demographic backgrounds to explore the way in which social distancing, a dominant strategy used in COVID-19 infection prevention control was understood by sections of the population and factors influencing their understanding, acceptance or rejection of this strategy. Discursive thematic analysis was employed to examine the ways in which important public health information and strategies aimed at controlling the spread of COVID-19 are communicated to the culturally and linguistically diverse Ugandan population. The study critically analyses the implications of the cultural interpretations and multiple meanings of strategies such as social distancing and the use of sanitizers amongst a linguistically and socio-economically diverse population. The study argues that local languages, including specialist languages such as braille and sign language play a pivotal role in spreading information and raising awareness about the current global pandemic. It highlights the need to create an inclusive, responsible and ethical mass media and internet communication and content in local Ugandan languages in addition to English which is the official language.

Keywords: Coronavirus · Local languages · Braille and sign languages · Responsible and ethical communication · ICT inequalities · Vulnerable communities

© IFIP International Federation for Information Processing 2022
Published by Springer Nature Switzerland AG 2022
Y. Zheng et al. (Eds.): ICT4D 2022, IFIP AICT 657, pp. 310–331, 2022.
https://doi.org/10.1007/978-3-031-19429-0_19

1 Introduction

The COVID-19 is the infectious disease caused by the most recently discovered coronavirus. According to the World Health Organization (WHO) (2020), this new virus and its pathological characteristics were unknown before the outbreak began in Wuhan, China, in December 2019. COVID-19 pandemic has affected all countries in the world, with severe impacts on society, particularly vulnerable communities and overwhelmed healthcare systems. The pandemic has caused widespread social and economic disruption and dramatic re-shaping of the world. Recent studies have shown that in the absence of reliable vaccines, acute shortage of essential supplies, including personal protective equipment, diagnostics, and medical products, social distancing, hand washing, mask-wearing, and disinfecting are the only feasible approaches to fight against this pandemic in order to reduce viral transmission (Huremović 2019).

Globally, there have been combined efforts to fight the COVID-19 pandemic through preventive measures such as country border closures, national lockdowns, and schools' closures among other examples. In Uganda, similar measures have been implemented, including placing infected individuals in isolation or those potentially exposed but asymptotic (e.g. returnees and travelers from other countries) in quarantine, closure of the international airport, non-food shops, places of worship, workplaces, schools, cancellations of mass gatherings, lobbying for donations and increased awareness campaigns through special COVID-19 messages, advertisements (hereafter, adverts) and songs (ibid). However, each of those measures comes with complex legal, ethical, logistical, linguistic and cultural challenges, but also mental health challenges associated with isolation and uncertainty (ibid). For instance, in Uganda, where over 70% of the population is informally employed (Uganda Bureau of Statistics, UBOS, 2014), there has been a negative collective reaction to some of the COVID-19 guidelines by the informal traders in downtown Kampala whose livelihoods depend on daily transactions with their customers. The situation is exacerbated in the informal settlements or slums, which are defined as "contiguous settlement(s) where the inhabitants are characterized as having inadequate housing and basic services, [settlements which are] often not recognized and addressed by public authorities as an integral part of the city" (UN Habitat, 2003, p. 10). In slum areas of Kampala, strategies such as social distancing, one of the non-pharmaceutical measures of combating the spread of COVID19 is simply impossible to operationalize due to overcrowding which is an inherent characteristic of such settlements (Richmond et al. 2018).

The extant literature underscores the significance of communication and the need for best practice in emerging infectious diseases that represent risks and crisis to public health (e.g. Covello 2003; Reynolds and Seeger 2005; Holmes et al. 2009). Various best-practice models have developed as a result of the previous pandemics such as the anthrax, sudden acute respiratory syndrome (SARS) and the Avian flu among others, for example Covello's (2003) seven-point checklist of best practices that should be included in any public health risk and crisis communication plan or the well-known crisis and emergency risk communication (CERC) model proposed by Reynolds and Seeger (2005).

However, one of the emerging complications of the COVID-19 pandemic is that linguistically and culturally diverse peoples have inadequate information about how to keep themselves and their communities safe and secure or indeed the seriousness of the pandemic (WHO 2021). Following the WHO global response plans for COVID-19, it identified risk communication and community engagement as a priority. Consequently, all those with responsibility to the public are requested to communicate effectively with communities, counter misinformation, and make sure people can hold them accountable. According to Uganda's constitution of 1995, there are 65 known indigenous languages in Uganda with varying numbers of native speakers. In order to promote knowledge to operationalize epidemic mitigation mechanisms, as evidenced in the current fight against COVID-19, it is imperative to develop an effective COVID-19 communication strategy that covers most if not all indigenous Ugandan languages. The UBOS (2016) indicates that Uganda's population is made up of different ethnic groups with varying unique customs and norms which play a major role in shaping behaviour and ways of life of the people in the country. Besides, several externally displaced persons (refugees) have settled in Uganda, in addition to those who have come to live in the country voluntarily due to business, charity or religious and other non-conflict related reasons. These foreign residents also speak diverse languages from their countries of origin, notably from Rwanda, Sudan, Congo DRC, Somalia, Burundi, South Africa, Malawi, Zambia, Kenya, Tanzania, Cameroon, Ethiopia, Eritrea, Tunisia, Morocco, Lebanon, India, China, Turkey and Europe, to mention but a few examples. Our analysis of the mass media campaigns and advertising, the guidelines, the Radio and Television Talk shows about COVID-19 pandemic show that majority of the local and foreign languages, as well as braille and sign languages are silent (in other words less used).

An ethnolinguistic map of Uganda

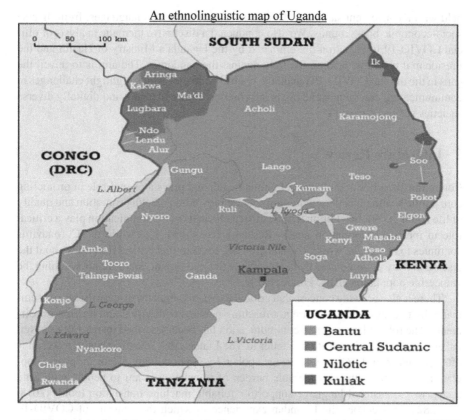

The magnitude of the language challenge is undisputable. According to the WHO (2020), the COVID-19 pandemic continues to evolve rapidly and this heightens the need for accurate, trusted information adapted to changing scenarios. This is even more important in the context of the lessons learnt in Liberia and Sierra Leone, during the 2014 Ebola outbreak, during which more women died partly because they had less access to accurate information about the virus in their own languages.

Languages aside, research has shown that in some countries, the digital platforms (DP) have contributed tremendously in keeping citizens informed (Jiang and Ryan 2020).The DPs have enabled public participation and/or offered open data and digital applications to enable public participation. In Uganda, if someone wants to obtain updated information about COVID-19 crisis, the Ministry of Health (MoH) Website stores such information on its website and social media (twitter and Facebook) pages but this is generally in English language. Little effort has been put in place to translate the COVID-19 campaign documents into the different local languages or the non-Ugandan languages. Every public entity ranging from telecommunication companies, hospitals, banks, markets, local government offices, public places, transport services, post offices, academic institutions etc., have adverts mainly in English or in Luganda yet it is a known fact that Uganda as a country has more than 60 languages (The Constitution of Uganda 1995 amended in 2005).We explore these anecdotes in public understanding, construction and (mis)interpretation of COVID-19 official messages through interviews held with a convenient sample of Ugandans speaking various languages, from diverse socio-economic backgrounds. We also conducted a discursive thematic analysis of official COVID-19 information disseminated by the Uganda's Ministry of Health and the Presidential taskforce leading the fight against the pandemic. The aim is to unveil the gaps in the official COVID-19 pandemic control strategies which highlight challenges in communicating emergency and crisis information in linguistically and digitally diverse societies such as Uganda's.

2 Literature Review

Communication lies at the 'heart of public health and plays a pivotal role in promoting core public health objectives including disease prevention, health promotion and quality of life (Badr 2009). In addition to this, trusted channels of communication play a critical role in meeting information needs. Research has shown that while the Coronavirus continues to ravage the world, there is growing concern that critical messages about the disease that are disseminated by health authorities and broadcasters are not reaching the vulnerable population (BBC Future, n.d.).

There is also growing concern that critical messages about the disease that are disseminated by telecom companies are not reaching persons with visual and hearing impairments. The role of languages in communication has been described insightfully by Neil Pakenham-Walsh, who wrote in a letter to The Lancet, that scientific health research is often presented in English, a language spoken by approaximely 5% of the world population and where "the considerable burden of translation is left to people with little access to professional language support or reliable machine translation tools" (2018, p. e1282). This echoes the Ugandan experience in which the majority of COVID-19 guidelines published in English, represent a potential disadvantage to speakers of other languages spoken in a country that is linguistically diverse. Similar observations were made by Salman Waqar, an academic GP registrar at the University of Oxford and the general secretary of the British Islamic Medical Association, who averred in 2020, that much of the initial public health guidance around Covid-19 has been in dominant languages, potentially bypassing those less able to understand such language particularly at grassroots (BBC Future, n.d.). However, as recommended by the OECD, in the short term, public communication and transparency are needed to reinforce compliance with emergency measures and fight disinformation. In addition, inclusive participation is fundamental to the creation of a sustainable, socially cohesive society (OECD 2012).

Therefore, in such pandemics, communication is a critical component of helping individuals prepare for, respond to, and recover from emergencies. Effective communication can help to prevent crisis from developing (WHO 2020). By definition, communication is about "building relationships with others, listening and understanding them, and conveying thoughts and messages clearly and congruently; expressing things coherently and simply, in ways that others can understand, and showing genuine knowledge, interest and concern; bringing these aspects together to make change happen" (Government Information and Communication Service website 2018).The crisis and emergency risk communication (CERC) field is defined by the Centers for Disease Control and Prevention (CDC) as, "an effort by experts to provide information to allow an individual, stakeholder, or an entire community to make the best possible decisions about their well-being within nearly impossible time constraints and help people ultimately to accept the imperfect nature of choices during the crisis" (CDC 2002, p. 6).

In order to create public awareness about the pandemic, African governments are using mass media, notably radio and television, as well as ICT, particularly social media and mobile telephone platforms (Mobile phone data and COVID-19). This approach is broadly consistent with the emerging scholarly research on the role of social media in global crisis communication in which five main potential roles of social media have been synthesized from the extant literature (Eriksson 2018). Specifically, Eriksson found that 'effective crisis communication is associated with using social media's potential to create dialogue and to choose the right message, source and timing; performing pre-crisis work and developing an understanding of social media logic; using social media monitoring; and continuing to prioritize traditional media in crisis situations [as well as simply] using social media in its own right during crises' (2018, p. 540).

In Uganda, with 42 million people (UBOS 2020) in lockdown and mostly confined in their homes, ICTs are becoming a necessity, as they represent one of the main ways to communicate and access information and services, but also one of the only remaining vectors for social interactions during the national lockdowns and periods of compulsory confinement (ibid). The present article maintains that in the current COVID-19 crisis, much as ICTs are helping to reach wider audiences globally, Uganda, like other Sub-Saharan African countries, still faces several challenges which directly or indirectly affect communication about COVID-19 pandemic. For instance, the 2019 communication sector report by the Uganda Communications Commission (UCC) shows that the country's internet penetration stands at 37.9% with over 23 million internet users, who mostly use mobile phones. According to the same report, mobile internet subscription stood at between 14.3 to 15.2 million persons out of the 42 million Ugandans. At the same time, about 1.1 million to 1.4 million Ugandans have actively subscribed to pay-TV services. This clearly shows the digital gap as of 2020, given that a large proportion of the population (estimated at 62–96%) does not have access to the internet or pay-TV.

As mentioned earlier, some of the most vulnerable people such as the majority living in rural communities, people living with disability, those who are elderly, homeless, or recent immigrants/refugees, are the most difficult to reach if ICTS serve as the main instrument of communication (Lee et al. 2008). This implies there is an ethical responsibility to ensure social media platforms such as WhatsApp, Twitter and Facebook among others are augmented with equivalent options, or the most vulnerable will face further inequalities in communication of COVID-19 information and hence miss out on essential, life-saving messages from the Ministry of Health, an information void that could be filled with mis or disinformation (e.g. Vijaykumar et al. 2021). Equally, the few local languages in use and sign languages seem to promote knowledge to operationalise pandemic mitigation mechanisms.

As evidenced in the current fight against COVID-19, arguably, languages have become an asset in dealing with pandemics, peace and security issues within the region. A recent research finding in the area of challenges of translating and disseminating HIV/AIDS messages in a multilingual and multicultural nation: the case of Uganda indicates that among these challenges is the question of translating HIV/AIDS materials in the absence of a standardized terminology and disseminating them in multilingual and multicultural communities. Recent surveys have also shown that Refugee communities still lack the basics in the fight against the spread of the Coronavirus, especially the information component (see World Vision 2020). In the same vein, according to Ugandan newspaper, the Daily Monitor (April 2020), with limited access to radio, television, newspapers, the internet and the impediment of language barrier, sharing vital information in the refugee settlements remains a big challenge. Therefore, a regular communication with the public and at-risk populations is one of the most important steps to help prevent infections, save lives and minimize adverse outcomes (World Vision Uganda, UNICEF 2020). Information must be provided in multiple formats and local languages to address the barriers which older people often face, related to literacy, language and disability. In such cases, the use of door to door awareness drives across all the villages in the settlements, using mobile public address systems and megaphones is indispensable (ibid). Since COVID-19 has been declared a global health emergency, trusted, clear and effective communication and engagement approaches are critical to ensure that fear, panic and rumors do not undermine response efforts and lead to COVID-19 spreading to the vulnerable communities.

Research has advised that Communication lies at the "heart of public health" and plays a pivotal role in promoting core public health objectives including disease prevention, health promotion and quality of life (see Covello 2003; Holmes et al. 2009). Undeniably speaking, Uganda's MOH and national COVID-19 taskforce would do well to employ a multi-faceted approach to its public health communication as a measure to improving communication for vulnerable communities in Uganda through their different indigenous languages used on mass media, flyers, brochures the internet.

By and large, language is the primary issue in times of crisis, Betsch (2020) argues that in the current absence of medical treatment and vaccination, the unfolding COVID-19 pandemic can only be brought under control by massive and rapid behaviour change. In this regard, what is more important than being able to communicate with its multilingual and multicultural citizens in their language in order to inform them about: what Coronavirus is, where it comes from, how it spreads, who is most at risk, what it's signs and symptoms are and what is the difference between coronavirus and common flu. (https://communityengagementhub.org/what-we-do/novel-coronavirus/) Furthermore, what could be more crucial than giving the local communities instructions to follow, reassuring and reminding them that all together we will overcome the pandemic (ibid). How crucial is it to include the marginalized and vulnerable people in the know of COVID -19 (ibid) How then can the citizens be informed about the pandemic and above all about the preventive measures (covid-19-response-bulletin-ethiopia-3) if majority do not get the correct scientific information about the pandemic due to limitations in language and technological mediums used to convey such messages? Framed in this way, it is reasonable to argue that local languages, incontestably promote comprehension, and increase appreciation of the prevailing environment around a given community (2004 Tony Reed report). The argument here is that local languages are a tool for socialization that helps to shape people's understanding of their environment, identifies and the role they play within it. In the light of the latter, COVID-19 pandemic becomes more than a health issue. The pandemic in Uganda will not be just a crisis of public health or the economy. It risks becoming a language and digital emergency that threatens the access of, the understanding and interpretation of information about COVID-19 across all the 135 districts of Uganda.As documented by the IHR (2005), Uganda needs to recognize risk communication as a critical pillar for developing national core capacity during emerging infectious diseases and other IHR (2005) related events.

3 Methodology

3.1 Participants and Data Sources

Data for this study were collected using secondary analysis of a purposively drawn sample of official COVID-19 communication from the Ministry of Health, Office of the Prime Minister and the Presidential Address as well as directives to the country. In addition, data was also gathered and reviewed from print media, websites, and social media in Uganda to understand the type of information that is circulating, and the possible impact this may have on the knowledge, attitudes, beliefs, and cultural practices, particularly those likely to be from rural or vulnerable communities.

The focus on official communication was justified on the basis that they were delivered to Ugandans using one or more of the mass media and social media platforms such as the national and pay-TV channels, Ugandan daily newspapers (print media), Ministry websites and twitter among others as described in the previous two sections. The purpose of the secondary analysis is to highlight the gaps in such official communication which is released in English with limited translations into the various languages spoken in Uganda and to show the implications in terms of inclusiveness in a country with diverse linguistic and digital characteristics.

Telephone interviews were also conducted with a total of 50 Ugandans from various socio-economic backgrounds, who speak diverse local [and specialist] languages constituted the Sampling Frame. The aim of the interviews was to understand how participants make sense out of social distancing, which is one of the main public health strategies employed to minimise the spread of COVID-19 in Uganda. We focused on social distancing because it is one of the most difficult strategies to employ in a communitarian society where the cultural norms cherish social cohesion with people living together, and in some cases reinforced by socio-economic challenges arising from poverty as seen in informal settlements (slums) in urban areas.

3.2 Procedures

Participants were asked four open-ended questions about the languages they spoke, their knowledge of English, the meaning of 'social distancing' and what, if any cultural or other lens they use to make sense of 'social distancing' as seen here below in Table 1.

The interviews were not designed for an objective assessment or evaluation of participants experiences in as much as aiming to elicit their distinctive individual understanding and sense making of social distancing, the most common social COVID-19 containment strategy (cf. Holmes et al. 2009). As mentioned above, the linguistic diversity in Uganda meant non-pharmaceutical measures used in containing the pandemic in its early days

Table 1. Interview questions

---

a. What is your primary language of communication?
b. Do you speak English?
c. What three things come to mind when you hear the word 'social distancing'?
d. Are these views on social distancing based on your customs/culture, everyday experiences in life or anything else?

---

were not always easily understandable and in some cases agreeable to sections of the population, including those likely to be vulnerable. The interviews were therefore conducted with the aim of understanding how participants made sense of social distancing, which was one of the main public health strategies employed to minimise the spread of COVID-19 in Uganda and across the world. The interviews which were conducted by the first author lasted between 15–30 min, they were not audio-recorded, to save phone battery in a context of unpredictable availability of electricity and also to protect the Author from contracting covid-19. Instead, the interviewer manually recorded each response in notebooks, which were eventually typed and analysed thematically. In other words, the interviewer used non-verbatim transcription because this helped to ensure that the transcriptionist could transcribe and translate for readability rather than keep taking a verbatim approach. The interview data and official communication (secondary) data were subjected to thematic analysis, a common method used in qualitative analysis (see Braun and Clarke; Bryman and Bell 2011). The approach used in this study followed closely from Braun and Clarke (2006, p. 79) who describe thematic analysis as a 'method for identifying, analysing and reporting patterns or themes within data and for minimally organising and describing data in rich detail'. Themes were identified due to their prevalence within the data, as well as their potential in explaining contextual issues relevant to social distancing and the role of language in communicating COVID-19 control messages to diverse populations in Uganda. The study findings are summarised in Table 2 below.

4 Results and Discussions

4.1 Introduction

The results section includes presentation of examples of official COVID-19 communication from the Ministry of Health summarised in Fig. 1, in Sect. 4.2. It also presents a summary of key findings from interviews with convenient sample of Ugandans from diverse language and socio-demographic backgrounds in Sect. 4.3. Four main themes are covered within Sect. 4.3 as a basis to demonstrate the language and cultural gaps in official COVID-19 communication in Uganda. The first theme addresses the influences of socio-cultural factors in mediating public understanding of key strategies such as social distancing; the second theme focuses on socio-cultural and contextual factors, followed by the role of professional interlocutors in facilitating understanding for special groups such as people with disabilities and refugees and last theme highlights the role of social and political factors in influencing public understanding of official COVID-19 containment strategies such as social distancing as typified by the excerpts and descriptions presented in Table 2 below.

Table 2. Illustrative example linking data to thematic categories and explanations [empirical data in the first column is where respondent views or quotations can be found, this is orgnised to show how data and themes are linked so we did not use separate quotations beyond the deteailes covered here in Table 2

Empirical data	Description	Thematic categories
Social distancing, well, ○ People living in the village say these are habits of town (urban) people; ○ They don't trust reasons for social distancing because they have never had experience of such a thing. ○ Usually during funerals or functions, they come together (not stay away from each other). The above 3 issues are as a result of culture and certain mindset and experience that has been there for a long time ○ For instance, Mr. A said people are saying that they drink *nguli* (locally distilled alcohol) and they eat bitter indigenous	Social distancing is understood through socio-cultural lens that defines ways of living in a community in rural urban settings and ways of treating ailments using traditional herbal medicine which seems to be valued and (in)appropriately considered a competing alternative to modern medicine in the treatment of COVID-19. The magnitude of the COVID-19 which has brought about the need for social distancing among other strategies are weighed through a mindset that requires 'proof' of how dangerous it is as 'no one has experienced it or died	socio-cultural influences on public understanding of social distancing in Uganda

(*continued*)

Table 2. (*continued*)

green vegetables such as *ijiribi, kulubu, kiliwere* [and] *palabi* which can fight the so-called COVID-19, o That they used to use *pati izaaki* (tree roots), pounded and mixed with [wood fuel] ashes to heal someone with a headache (which is one of the symptoms of COVID-19), so they can use such local methods and herbs to treat COVID-19 o That they can take herbs such as liquid squeezed out of eucalyptus leaves to heal a positive covid-19 case (Mr.A, 45-55-year old, male native speaker of *Lugbarati*, one of the 8 area languages spoken in North-western Uganda, western Congo DRC and parts of South Sudan, he has basic understanding of English and works as driver of a top local politician. He spoke to people in his local social network and his village in Arua district about social distancing, he reflects their views in this varied perspective)	from it'	
What does social distance mean? • People don't care much about it because they have no experience of death arising from COVID-19 • People say this is *wolokoso* (meaning gossip) • That social distancing are habits of the urban people These meanings are based on established mind set. (Mr B, 55-65-year-old male from South-Eastern Uganda living in Kampala and a native speaker of *Lusoga*, one of the 8 area languages and a fluent speaker of English), preferred to obtain his elderly (above 75-year-old) mother's views on social distancing. He had gone to the village for the burial of his niece and relatives were rushing to shake his hands and to hug him. But when he kept his distance [due to ongoing requirements for social distancing] it annoyed all of them, who told him off for being antisocial. This might explain these views from his mother)	Social distancing is understood through socio-cultural and contextual distinctions employed in judging behaviour based on rural vs urban living, where the rural communities seem to observe social norms around communal living, established over time, whilst urban living is associated flouting these norms. Social distancing is reduced to a mere 'gossip', not something to be taken seriously as there is no 'proof' of its existence or effects on the referent community	Socio-cultural and contextual influences on public understanding of social distancing in Uganda
What three things come to mind for a person who is either hard of hearing or completely deaf when they are told or read about social distancing? ◊ When it is signed [use of sign language], they understand what it means and they also observe it. This is for the deaf but with no signs, they don't understand [what is meant by social distancing] ◊ For the blind, deafblind and those with severe disability who need one to one [support], they have challenges with social distancing because they have to move in close contact with each other [dependence on others]. These views are not based on culture but an understanding of the special needs of the people with these specific disabilities (loss of hearing). (Dr. P, 45—55 years old holds a PhD in special needs education, and she speaks *Luganda, Lunyankore* and *Luo*, three main area languages spoken in central,	Social distancing is understood through the avenue of those with responsibilities for teaching or looking after people with disabilities, whose knowledge of the special needs and special languages help to explain it and to provide instructions. Their role as special language speakers or guides helps to ensure both understanding and observation of the guidelines	The role of professional interlocutors in facilitating public understanding of social distancing for people with disability

Table 2. *(continued)*

southern and northern Uganda. Like Ms G; her views on social distancing are based on her experiences with a few of her students with wide range of disabilities, including hearing, sight and a combination)		
What does social distancing mean to them? ⇒ They say it is one way of pulling them away (especially the men) from their communal and social way of drinking *malua* or *lacwi* (local millet-based alcoholic beverage normally consumed communally by men, using bamboo straws) from the same pot or from sharing a drink from the calabash (gourds) ⇒ The Boda-boda (local motorcycle taxi operators) say it is a political warfare meant to stop those boda-boda who support opponents of the ruling government. They argue that when an NRM candidate is canvassing support for their own candidate, boda-bodas are not suppressed but when the opposition canvasses support for their members and boda-bodas support them, Police suppresses the boda-bodas. ⇒ Social distance amounts to practicing anti-social behaviour yet in the villages they are used to staying together (social cohesion) Ms C says that the above meanings depict the value attached to communal way of socializing in the TESO culture. The issue of bad attitude and propaganda are also playing a role. As mentioned by Mr. D yesterday, Ms C said the TESO are also saying government is deceiving about COVID-19 given the experience of people who were in quarantine for Nothing. That They Were Being Given Medication They Didn't Know Very Well, That They Were Not Sick, In Conclusion That These Were Tricks to Keep People Away So That Votes Can Be Stolen. (this information has gone viral) (Ms C, 35-45 years old, native speaker of Ateso, one of the 8 area languages in Uganda, and fluent in English sharing her experiences of speaking about social distancing with people from her home region in Eastern Uganda)	Social distancing is understood and interpreted through shared social and cultural norms which are well-established amongst the referent community. Social distancing is associated with breaking these norms through acting in ways considered to be 'anti-social'. Another layer of interpretation is the contextual political environment in which there is mistrust of politicians' motives for implementing social distancing	Socio-cultural and political influences on public understanding of social distancing in Uganda
What does social distancing mean to them? ♦ They ask for an explanation to know why they should [keep] social distance ♦ They ask to know what *Tonsemberera* means (it is a Ministry of Health COVID-19 advert on social distancing in Luganda, the most dominant Ugandan language) ♦ They ask if "it [*Tonsemberera*] is your football club" or what you mean [when you use the term]? ♦ They ask if "is it a football club or "People Power" [the latter being the slogan of a popular Ugandan opposition politician's new political movement]?" ♦ Even yesterday, they still asked if it was a football club? NB: Mr. D claimed he laboured to explain that social distancing or *Tonsemberera* means "'don't touch	Social distancing is interpreted through social and contextual experiences such as the growing distrust of politicians' motives in implementing it, as presidential and parliamentary elections are due to be held in January 2021. The need for 'proof' is used as a proxy to indicate the falsity of claims about COVID-19 as no one has seen it or those on quarantine were isolated for 'nothing'. Social distancing is reduced to a mere game, or a new 'football club' or 'politics' but not something to be taken seriously	Socio-cultural and political influences on public understanding of social distancing in Uganda

(continued)

Table 2. (*continued*)

people', 'don't come near people'", surprisingly in conversations with ordinary people who speak Luganda, the language from which the uncommon word derives. Mr D conjectures that these meanings are based on mindset and propaganda [read misinformation] from those who were quarantined when they had no covid-19, for instance:
 	
   ♦ that some people think that because the president wants to keep them in the lockdown in order to get votes, he keeps telling them to social distance
   ♦ that no one has so far died of COVID-19 from their community [seeing is believing]
   ♦ that people who were in quarantine told some of their relatives and friends that they were kept in there for nothing, that they were being given medication they didn't know very well, that they were not sick
   ♦ that these were tricks to keep people away so that votes can be stolen.
   ♦ they think it is a game
 	
(Mr D., a 25-35-year-old male, informally employed, native speaker of Luganda, with basic fluency in English. Mr D's views were based on his experiences of speaking with people in his social network and within his neighbourhood in the out skirts of Kampala)		

The meaning of social distancing for Sudanese refugees:
 	
   ➢ Awareness was created so this helped the refugees to understand Social distancing.
   ➢ For examples when a person coughs near other people, they quickly keep a distance.
   ➢ Posters were used to simplify the social distancing campaigns [in a visual way]
   ➢ Translations helped.
 	
NGO's [working with refugees recruited] about 4 people [who spoke *Barr, Juba Arabic* and *Kakwa*] to translate [official COVID-19] guidelines from English into the above 3 languages and later these languages were used for sensitizing the refugees.
 	
(Ms V, 35-45-year old Ugandan female, graduate logistics officer working with NGOs near refugee settlements, native speaker of Lugbarati, fluent in English. Ms V's experiences of what social distancing means to Sudanese refugees in North-Western Uganda are based on vicarious observations and conversations with staff of NGOs who work with the refugees)
	Social distancing is understood through the role of those with responsibilities for the refugees, who realise the need for official guidelines to be translated in languages spoken by the referent community. Their role in recruiting native speakers to translate official guidelines used in raising awareness among refugees from South Sudan is taken as a proxy in helping them make sense out of social distancing	The role of professional interlocutors in facilitating public understanding of social distancing for externally displaced people

Source: summarised by the authors, based on insights from Ayikoru & Park (2019)

4.2 Discursive Thematic Analysis of Official Communication on COVID-19 in Uganda

From the analysis of COVID-19 campaign messages on MOH webpage and Twitter page and the print media, it can be argued that Ugandans received most of the online messages in English. The message ranged from "social distancing-avoid close contact with people who are visibly sick with a cold or flu-like symptoms (fever, cough, sneeze)", "wash your hands often with soap and running water for at least 20 s. If soap and water are not available, use an alcohol-based hand sanitizer", "don't touch the soft parts of the face", "The entire population will put on fabric masks", "wear a medical or face masks if you are sick or someone around you is sick" as seen in the extracts in Fig. 1 below.

It can be inferred that the public communications about COVID-19 pandemic including use of social media, the press (newspapers, posters) and media (television stations) and other informational materials have been majorly provided in English. This is a major concern when Ugandans are so diverse from a linguistic and a cultural perspective (Ethnologue 2020). It is only fair that the Ministry of Health and the Ugandan government translate all public communications and information about the coronavirus into multiple languages that represent the people and communities currently living in Uganda. It can therefore be argued that it is crucial for the indigenous communities of Uganda to receive clear information about the virus and control measures and this is Ugandan government's responsibility.

Therefore, taking into account the millions of people who speak multitudes of local languages within Uganda, the COVID-19 risk is compounded by the lack of health materials in a language they understand. In the same vein, people in the grassroots level, the visually impaired, the vulnerable and marginalized are not well informed about the dangers of the pandemic either due to challenges of not having a radio or a TV set or even due to technical difficulties families encounter as they try to listen to these devices. The argument here is that it isn't just enough to say "wash your hands" if this pandemic is to be combatted and wiped out successfully. The current guidelines seemingly favour a limited number of people who understand the English language and the few area (local) languages into which translations have been made, and yet the guidelines were meant to be used by all health care providers in Uganda, including those working in the public and private sectors, the grassroots local community health workers as well as the Elderly and people living with disabilities. In order to ensure that the country responds adequately and mitigates the impact of the COVID-19 pandemic the country needs to adopt an inclusive approach and translate COVID-19 guidelines in th known 65 local languages including sign and braille languages and languages spoken by the immigrants and refugees (the ethnologue 2020).The argument here is that lack of a language policy impedes communication. If Ugandan policy makers had put in place a language policy that considers all the existing languages in Uganda, this would have contributed to producing resources on COVID-19 in the numerous languages and closing the existing enormous information gap.

Furthermore, Local languages would have helped in developing guidelines and Standard Operating Procedures (SOPs) on mass media and social media for vulnerable communities during the pandemic, they could have helped to engage with communities and to produce information for local, national and regional needs hence saving lives of millions of people that are at stake. The eminent challenge is that SOPs are mostly produced in English language which is accessible by 23% of Ugandans who are ICT literate. Despite the fact that UNICEF developed resources to present facts, guidelines for prevention of COVID-19 and translated into 30 different languages including eight spoken by refugees, a big chunk of the population is still left out.

But the main argument here is that the COVID -19 pandemic has shown that languages are essential, more so to the vulnerable people, those with special needs because the languages help to communicate preventive measures that should be adhered to during the coronavirus disease pandemic. In addition, making the dissemination of COVID-19 pandemic information disability inclusive including the use of sign language interpreters is unquestionable (WHO guidelines on Disability considerations during the COVID-19 outbreak). The use of correct language for the visually impaired and engaging the local communities in the discourse about COVID-19 operations is crucial.The predominant languages used on mass media (television, radios, mobile phones, social media) or in the print press, posters or even on digital space, are English and the Area languages (Constitution of Uganda 1995 amended 2005) namely: Ateso, Jhopadhola, LebAcoli, LebLango, Luganda, Lugbarati, Lumasaba, Lusoga, Runyankore-Rukiga and Runyoro-Rutoro). Besides that, for people with disabilities for instance, the Television readers are too fast but also the visually impaired cannot see the advertising and campaigns or comedies/drama about COVID-19 crisis (the information broadcast on the National and private TV stations by the Ministry of Health cannot be seen by the visually impaired neither can they be heard by those hard of hearing). Besides this, official presidential addresses to the nation or Ministerial briefings to the media often happen in English without any translation. The deaf blind cannot listen and visualize adverts about COVID-19. The rural population where literacy levels are quite low do not easily understand adverts in English or in the few Area languages in use by the press and the media. Even at community levels, the different dialects and cultures worsen the situation because SOPs can be interpreted differently.

In addition, words such as "confinement and social distancing" or quarantine can be interpreted differently in different dialects and different cultures. More so the isolated underprivileged communities such as the elderly, the people with disability, refugees, impoverished households in rural and urban settings do not have the access to devices such as TVs, smart phones or radios, even if some of these might seem to be reasonably priced and viable technologies for spreading life-saving information about the pandemic. It is therefore a deplorable condition of social impact or relationship between the communities and the mobile technology.

4.3   The Influences of Socio-cultural, Contextual, Political and Professional Factors in Mediating Public Understanding of Social Distancing in Uganda

Like most health sectors on the global scene and within Sub Saharan Africa, Uganda's health system was ill-prepared for COVID-19 pandemic, partly due to limited resources and weaknesses in the core competencies of the International Health Regulations (IHR) namely the ability to detect, prevent and respond to public health threats. The COVID-19 outbreak unveiled multiple challenges and weaknesses within Uganda's health sector, among them language and cultural barriers and ICT gaps. This is even more poignant in contexts where public understanding of the pandemic is suffused with misinformation, doubt or mistrust in the authoritative or official information (cf. WHO 2020; Nguyen and Catalan 2020). For example, there is an emerging sense that the shared belief amongst majority of the population in Uganda about COVID-19 is that it is a faked crisis, or worse still, a pandemic for the Western World or for the urban population and therefore they tend to underestimate the significance of health promoting behaviour such as social distancing, frequent handwashing, mask wearing, staying home, ranking them lower than other pressing needs for food for example. Some misinterpret the emphasis on the need to use alcohol based sanitisers to mean it is a matter of drinking locally brewed alcohol and in there lies the 'cure' for COVID-19. As a result, the initial efforts of MoH to respond to concerns of the urban and the rural population were overwhelmed by resentment and distrust. Most especially the vulnerable people who have been living by hand to mouth trade, the communities living in slum areas, those living near the border points thus contributing to increased rapid spread of transmission among population living along the Border points and the cargo lorry drivers and in communities at present.

The initial response to the COVID-19 pandemic was characterized by high levels of public denial, misconceptions, misinformation (risk-communication/infodemic-management) and resistance at the community level, especially by the informal sector comprising of market vendors, hawkers, motorcycle riders (popularly known as boda-bodas), large scale and small-scale traders. The majority of households under this category were, and are still unable to survive without some form of daily trade given that they hardly have disposable income. In such contexts, going outside ones home in search for work, water, or food, is a necessity, but one which clearly increases the risk of spreading the coronavirus due to running counter to preventive and containent measures from public health officials.

From Community perspective, many community members attributed their initial disbelief of COVID-19 to a social belief that it was a simple flu that could be cured by drinking local alcoholic beverage called Uganda waragi or by using a cocktail drink made of garlic, lemon, orange, ginger and traditional herbs. Consequently, many micro, small and medium-sized enterprises (MSMEs) have continued their activities in defiance of official guidance (Seitz 2020). The clinical presentation of the disease, which had symptoms similar to common flu or influenza could not worry majority of the population for whom lack of food and other basic necessities of life were an urgent need compared to a virus they perceived to be less dangerous. Additionally, several conspiracy theories were circulating and suggested that COVID-19 was a politically framed disease or money-making scheme by the local and international elite, aimed at duping or controlling the already suffering population.

Besides the MoH recently launched a campaign on COVID-19, called "Tonsember-era" in Luganda, one of the dominant Ugandan languages, which means "don't come near me or give me space" which runs on state media, including television and radio. Political leaders have also recorded messages in local languages to sensitize communities. Local leaders also broadcast COVID-19 information to their neighborhoods, sometimes with loudhailers. The argument here is that the languages in use are not representative of languages spoken in Uganda yet there is need to develop inclusive response to reduce the spreading of COVID-19 (OECD report), let alone the misinformation and misinterpretation about the pandemic which apparently is rampant in Uganda (UNICEF 2020). Above all, it becomes crucial to engage with communities and larger population in the response to COVID-19.

According to COVID-19 Partners Platform Pillar 2, it is critical to communicate to the public what is known about COVID-19, what is unknown, what is being done, and actions to be taken on a regular basis. Preparedness and response activities should be conducted in a participatory, community-based way that are informed and continually optimized according to community feedback to detect and respond to concerns, rumours and misinformation (UNICEF 2020). Debatably, COVID -19 pandemic has shown that languages are essential. For instance, in order to mitigate the crisis, designing online and print copies of adapted communication campaigns that focus on symptoms identification and preventive measures while remaining particularly mindful of local languages, braille and sign language culture and customs have become unquestionably crucial given that it is important to understand the needs of specific groups who might experience barriers to accessing lifesaving information in appropriate multiple and accessible formats such as Braille and large print for people who are visually-impaired (ibid).

According to UNICEF guidance on COVID-19 Response, information should be provided orally (e.g. through loudspeakers in the community). Easy-to-read version or plain text accompanied by pictures/ diagrams, which are more accessible for people who have intellectual disabilities and also benefit many other children, including those with low literacy or who use different languages. Written formats or video with text captioning and/or sign language, for people with hearing impairment. Accessible web content for people using assistive technologies such as screen reader. The key to improving accessibility is to provide all information in multiple formats- written, oral and pictorial, to reach people with diverse communication needs and preferences.

4.4 Discussions

Information and communication have long been shown to play a crucial role in disease prevention, promotion of health and wellbeing, raising public awareness in crisis situations and more recently, in the fight against the ongoing COVID-19 pandemic (e.g., Covello 2003; Erikson 2018; Holmes et al. 2009; Jiang and Ryan 2020). To gain insight into this from a Ugandam context, this article discusses the implication of language in use for communicating on mass media, the printed press and social media during COVID-19 crisis and its unprecedented impact on confinement and social distancing strategies. It is argued that the Covid-19 pandemic has changed expectations of the population through an overwhelming access to information that became widely available through official government messages on prevention and control, disseminated through mass and social media, to encourage behaviour change to reduce the risk of spreading the infection. Notable also, is the plethora of information or rather what the WHO (n.d.) describes as an 'infodemic', by which is meant the overabundance of information during disease outbreaks, including those that are false or misleading, emerging from diverse sources, both digital and physical, with the capacity to undermine public health messages aimed at combating the outbreaks. However, it has been shown that the official government messaging about the coronavirus, while well-intentioned, tended to favour mostly the segment of Ugandan population that has access to digital technologies and those that understand the English language as well as few of the area languages into which official public health messages on the pandemic had been translated. This inadvertently excluded a large majority of particularly vulnerable communities in Uganda who are not equipped to use digital technologies let alone the ethnolinguistic diversity highlighted previously. This is contrary to the emerging literature that emphasizes the role of inclusive language in making essential health information accessible (e.g. Royston et al. 2020; Pakenham-Walsh 2018). The public health crisis resulting from the coronavirus pandemic has been exacerbated by the effects of misinformation (Mian and Khan 2020), with anecdotal evidence from the interviews summarised in Table 2 above suggesting how efforts to control the pandemic maybe undermined through poor and sometimes culturally mediated misunderstandings or misinterpretation.

In Uganda, the installation of broadband in villages has dramatically improved thanks to the expansion of mobile phone ownership, the use of village phones and the setting up of wireless broadband networks. However, this does not mean widespread access to and usage of such technologies across the population (e.g., UCC Report, 2019). Specifically, some endemic challenges such as low bandwith, the high cost of broadband and differing levels of digital literacy all indicate that availability of such infrastructure does not necessarily equate to better connectivity or access, particularly in rural areas (ibid). In addition to this, the proportion of the population that has access to the internet is limited, to less than 40% (UCC 2019), in spite of the fact that ICTs are crucial to development. In the minds of most citizens, the broadband policy seems not to carry much importance; it does not have a direct link to their most basic concerns, which, for the poorest, boils down to essential necessities (food, water, shelter and medicines) (UN- Uganda 2020). Yet broadband affects other areas which are critical for development. Since the majority of Uganda's citizens are not engaged in the discourse about ICTs, a significant section of the population is left out of broadband policy development. The challenge here among other factors is that all these innovations are mostly presented in English and the grass-roots men and women are mainly ICT illiterate. In order to engage a larger section of the vulnerable population in broadband policy development, there is need for information repackaging from source language text to target language text in order to benefit the different clientele. This is likely to facilitate a clearer understanding of the challenges of using ICTs in rural areas, moreso during such times as the ongoing COVID-19 pandemic. Besides, the overreliance on digital technologies which are not available to majority of the population limits the capacity of such technologies in delivering information at scale that would have been desirable during public health emergencies. The effects of such disparities on dissemination of essential public health messages during a global health crisis will need to be considered in order to respond better in future pandemics.

5 Conclusion and Recommendations

This article sought to unveil existing gaps in the use of digital technologies and local languages in the context of official COVID-19 pandemic communication strategies in Uganda. It emerged clearly, that official communications from the Ministry of Health, which seeks to convey scientific and life-saving information to Ugandans is undermined by overreliance on the English language, with minimum efforts made at translating to other native Ugandan and specialist languages. It also found that public understanding of key strategies such as social distancing are strongly mediated by a range of factors, including social, cultural, contextual, political and professional, with varying implica-tions for how serious or otherwise the strategies are viewed. An important outcome of such gaps in the choice of language used in dissemination of COVID-19 messages is that misinformation sets in from poorly explained or translated scientific messages, which undermine efforts made to combat the pandemic. It seems reasonable to suggest that all stakeholders fighting the coronavirus pandemic collaborate and promote scientific evidence and unity over misinformation and conjecture (Calisher et al. 2020), to ensure protection of those that might otherwise be mislead or who might reject life-saving health messages about prevention and control of infections through engaging in non-santioned behaviours (e.g. rejecting face masks wearing or social distancing or succumbing to improper use of alcohol instead of prescribed usage of hand sanitisers).

Ensuring that the public has access to the right information about COVID-19 is not only of critical importance to decision makers and the national taskforce formed to fight the pandemic, but it can be considered a human right that should be observed especially during such a global health crisis (Royston et al. 2020; Pakenham-Walsh 2018). The main emphasis here is that a well-informed population is better able to protect itself from pandemics and any other emergencies, and that the role of diverse and inclusive languages is therefore paramount in ensuring access to and effective response to the messages being communicated by those in positions of authority. For instance, most elderly and disabled persons who are more likely to be on the margins of society (e.g. UN-Uganda 2020) have limited access to television sets, radio, social media and telephone messages, implying that they rely mainly on second-hand information which may or may not be accurate translation of official public health messages. Televised programmes that feature experts discussing Covid-19 should have sign language interpreters and transcriptions to enable persons with visual and hearing impairments to benefit from the expert knowledge. Debatably, accessing information through such media has become a luxury for many vulnerable families in Uganda.

Despite the fact that mobile technologies have enabled the closing of the gap of continued access to healthcare services during the COVID-19 pandemic in Uganda, there are still notable challenges including language used for communicating on the media (e.g. the use of Twitter by the Ministry of Health and encouraging the public to check updates through this social media platform or the Ministry's website, all of which are inevitably published in the English language). Risk communication and health promotion strategies form an integral part of any public health response to a global pandemic of the current magnitude. They provide life-saving information to people in affected communities for proactive actions to protect themselves. COVID-19 pandemic clearly shows that health promotion and risk communication strategies in indigenous languages can be useful in publicizing key messages, engaging communities, and managing rumors, misinformation/misinterpretation so that people can take informed decisions to mitigate the threats to public health. Going forward, it is important to incorporate linguistically and culturally appropriate health promotion and risk communication strategies in Uganda's preparedness and response efforts during pandemics of the current nature. This, along with well-known CERC models will provide the basis for an effective communication to the public during such public health emergencies, with better outcomes for the majority.

Future research will need to consider how an integrated approach that seeks to leverage advances in digital technologies at grass-roots, community levels, combined with usage of inclusive and diverse languages can be prioritized in managing public health crises. It will also be helpful to understand how conceptualising access to essential health information as a human right can be translated into language and wider developmental policies in countries with diverse ethnolinguistic populations. Undertaking such research before any future emergencies will assure better preparedness and potentially effectiveness of risk communication. Such future research is likely to benefit from an interdisciplinary framework that examines the complexities embedded in language, culture, socio-political contexts and digital technologies, with the potential to yield much more insight for better disaster and emergency preparedness and policy-making.

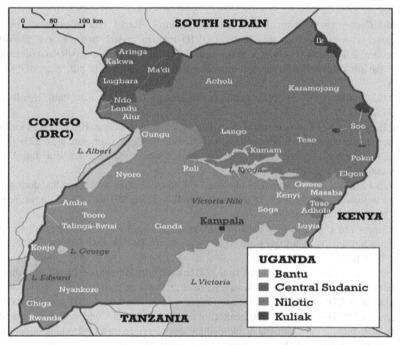

Fig. 1. Selected samples of official Covid-19 communication from Uganda's Ministry of Health

References

Badr, E.: Public health communication: some lessons for effectiveness. Sudanese J. Public Health **4**(3), 313 (2009)

BBC Future: Coronavirus: Why some racial groups are more vulnerable (n.d). https://www.bbc.com/future/article/20200420-coronavirus-why-some-racial-groups-are-more-vulnerable

Calisher, C., et al.: Statement in support of the scientists, public health professionals, and medical professionals of China combatting COVID-19. Lancet **395**(10226), e42–e43 (2020)

Communication in the time of covid-19 some reflections on ethics. https://www.scu.edu/ethicsspotlight/covid-19/communication-in-the-time-of-covid-19-some-reflections-on-ethics/?

Community Engagement. https://communityengagementhub.org/what-we-do/novel-coronavirus/

Coronavirus disease (COVID-19) advice for the public. https://www.who.int/emergencies/diseases/novelcoronavirus-2019/advice-for-public

Betsch, C.: How behavioural science data helps mitigate the covid-19 crisis (2020)

Covello, V.: Best practices in public health risk and crisis communication. J. Health Commun. **8**, 5–8 (2003)

Eriksson, M.: Lessons for crisis communication on social media: a systematic review of what research tells the practice. Int. J. Strateg. Commun. **12**(5), 526–551 (2018). https://doi.org/10.1080/1553118X.2018.1510405

European Centre for Disease Prevention and Control. Guidance on community engagement for public health events caused by communicable disease threats in the EU/EEA. Stockholm: ECDC (2020)

European Centre for Disease Prevention and Control. Rapid risk assessment: outbreak of novel coronavirus disease 2019 (COVID-19): increased transmission globally – fth update. 2020. https://www.ecdc.europa.eu/sites/default/les/documents/RRA-outbreak-novelcoronavirus-disease-2019-increasetransmission-globally-COVID-19.pdf. Accessed 06 Apr 2020

Glik, D.C.: Risk communication for public health emergencies. Ann. Rev. Publ. Health **28**(1), 33–54 (2007)

Griffin, E.: A First Look at Communication Theory, 6th edn. McGraw-Hill (2006). Health and science controversies: fresh perspectives from Covid-19. Media Commun. **8**(2), 323–328

Health Crisis Communication and Post-Ebola Virus Disease Containment Era. Int. J. Crisis Commun. **4**(1), 31 (2020)

Holmes, B.J., Henrich, N., Hancock, S., Lestou, V.: Communicating with the public during health crises: experts' experiences and opinions. J. Risk Res. **12**(6), 793–807 (2009). https://doi.org/10.1080/13669870802648486

How refugees are coping with Covid-19 lockdown, 27 April 2020. https://www.monitor.co.ug/News/National/How-refugees-are-coping-with-Covid-19-lockdown/688334-5535628-2esry5z/index.html

Huremović, D.: Social distancing, quarantine, and isolation. In: Huremović, D. (ed.) Psychiatry of Pandemics, pp. 85–94. Springer, Cham (2019). https://doi.org/10.1007/978-3-030-15346-5_8

Imperial College COVID-19 Response Team. Impact of non-pharmaceutical interventions (NPIs) to reduce COVID19 mortality and healthcare demand. Imperial College, London, 16 March 2020. 2020. https://www.imperial.ac.uk/media/imperialcollege/medicine/sph/ide/gidafellowships/Imperial-College-COVID19-NPI-modelling-16-03-2020.pdf

Infodemic Management-Infodemiology. https://www.who.int/teams/risk-communication/infodemicmanagement

Lunn, P., et al.: Using behavioural science to help fight the coronavirus. ESRI Working Paper No. 656, March 2020. http://aei.pitt.edu/102644/ (2020)

Jiang, N., Ryan J.: How does digital technology help in the fight against COVID-19? (2020). https://blogs.worldbank.org/developmenttalk/how-does-digital-technology-help-fight-against-covid-19

Mian, A., Khan, S.: Coronavirus: the spread of misinformation. BMC Med. **18**, 89 (2020). https://doi.org/10.1186/s12916-020-01556-3

National Guidelines for Management of Covid-19. https://www.health.go.ug/covid/document/nationalguidelines-for-management-of-covid-19/

Nguyen, A., Catalan, D.: Digital mis/disinformation and public engagement with (2020)

OECD: Transparency, communication and trust: the role of public communication in responding to the wave of disinformation about the new coronavirus. OECD, Paris (2020). https://www.oecd.org/coronavirus/en/#policy-responses

OECD: COVID-19 Policy Brief on Well-being and Inclusiveness (2020). http://www.oecd.org/coronavirus/en/

OECD, Perspectives on Global Development 2012: Social Cohesion in a Shifting World (2011)

Public Health England. Guidance on social distancing for everyone in the UK, 20 March 2020. PHE, London (2020). https://www.gov.uk/government/publications/covid-19-guidance-on-socialdistancing-and-for-vulnerable-people/guidance-on-social-distancing-for-everyone-in-the-uk-andprotecting-older-people-and-vulnerable-adults

Pakenham-Walsh, N.: Improving the availability of health research in languages other than English. Lancet Glob. Health **6**(12) (2018). https://doi.org/10.1016/S2214-109X(18)30384-X

Reynolds, B., Seeger, M.: Crisis and emergency risk communication as an integrative model. J. Health Commun. **10**, 43–55 (2005)

Richmond, A., Myers, I., Namuli, H.: Urban informality and vulnerability: a case study in Kampala, Uganda. Urban Sci. **2**, 22 (2018). https://doi.org/10.3390/urbansci2010022

Royston, G., Pakenham-Walsh, N., Zielinski, C.: Universal access to essential health information: accelerating progress towards universal health coverage and other SDG health targets. BMJ Glob. Health **2020**(5), e002475 (2020). https://doi.org/10.1136/bmjgh-2020-002475

Uganda: Calls for Disability-friendly Lockdown Measures. https://globalaccessibilitynews.com/2020/04/09/uganda-calls-for-disability-friendly-lockdownmeasures/

UN-Uganda: Leaving No One Behind: From the COVID-19 Response to Recovery and Resilience-Building. An Inter-agency Report on the Analyses of the Socioeconomic Impact of COVID-19 in Uganda. Prepared by the UN-Uganda, June 2020. Kampala (2020)

UNICEF guidance on COVID-19 Response: Considerations for Children and Adults with Disabilities UNICEF informational videos. https://www.unicef.org/disabilities/index_90418.html; page 83 of UNICEF Guidance For practical tips on how activities can be modified for children with disabilities, p. 82. http://training.unicef.org/disability/emergencies/downloads/UNICEF_General_Guidance_English.pdf; and CBM Humanitarian Hands-on-Tool at https://hhot.cbm.org/en/card/communication

UNICEF Uganda: Frontline line fight against COVID-19 (2020). https://www.unicef.org/uganda/stories/front-line-fight-against-covid-19-uganda

Vijaykumar, S., et al.: How shades of truth and age affect responses to COVID-19 (mis)information: randomized survey experiment among WhatsApp users in UK and Brazil. Humanit. Soc. Sci. Commun. **8**, 88 (2021). https://doi.org/10.1057/s41599-021-00752-7

WHO outbreak communication guidelines. World Health Organization, Geneva (2005). WHO/CDS/2005.28.   http://apps.who.int/iris/bitstream/10665/69369/1/WHO_CDS_2005_28_eng.pdf?ua=1&ua=1

WHO outbreak communication planning guide, 2008 edn. World Health Organization, Geneva (2008). http://apps.who.int/iris/bitstream/10665/44014/1/9789241597449_eng.pdf?ua=1&ua=1

WHO: Disability considerations during the COVID-19 outbreak. World Health Organization (WHO). Coronavirus disease (COVID-19) (2020). https://www.who.int/emergencies/diseases/novel-coronavirus-2019

WHO: Infodemic (n.d.). https://www.who.int/health-topics/infodemic#tab=tab_1

Exploring Notions of Resilience and Adaptability in the Context of Piloting a Mobile App for Risk Awareness During Covid-19

Arlene Bailey[1]([✉]), Larissa Pschetz[2], Marisa Wilson[2], Michaela Hubmann[3], Jonathan Rankin[2], Yhanore Johnson-Coke[1], Jessica Enright[4], Sara Jakubiak[4], Luke Buchanan[5], Sandra Latibeaudiere[1], Evan Morgan[2], Michael Heneghan[2], and Parris Lyew-Ayee[5]

[1] University of the West Indies, Kingston, Jamaica
{arlene.bailey,sandra.latibeaudiere}@uwimona.edu.jm
[2] University of Edinburgh, Edinburgh, UK
{L.Pschetz,Marisa.Wilson,Jonathan.Rankin,E.Morgan}@ed.ac.uk
[3] University of Manchester, Manchester, UK
michaela.hubmann@manchester.ac.uk
[4] University of Glasgow, Glasgow, UK
jessica.enright@glasgow.ac.uk
[5] Mona GeoInformatics Institute, Kingston, Jamaica
{lbuchanan,admin}@monainformatixltd.com

Abstract. This paper explores notions of resilience and adaptability in the context of the design, development and pilot of a mobile phone application, COVID-Aware, for enhancing risk awareness during the COVID-19 pandemic. Through an interdisciplinary team approach, we explore the utilization of an information and communications technology platform in supporting resilience and wellbeing at the individual and collective levels among community members. The study integrated data models, that were developed in Jamaica to predict the risk of COVID-19, with existing epidemiological models developed for COVID-19 in different parts of the world. Participants' perspectives on adapting to the use of the app on their mobile devices assisted with exploring ways to share visualisations of this data, and their views of adaptations to health protocols provided feedback for participatory development of the app. The use of the mobile application to support risk awareness, assessment and potential choices, and implications for resilience are discussed.

Keywords: ICTs · Mobile app · COVID-19 · Risk · Data modelling · Community · Health · Adaptation · Resilience

1 Introduction

This study investigates the potential for information and communication technologies to support information sharing to facilitate risk awareness and mitigation of the impact of

© IFIP International Federation for Information Processing 2022
Published by Springer Nature Switzerland AG 2022
Y. Zheng et al. (Eds.): ICT4D 2022, IFIP AICT 657, pp. 332–344, 2022.
https://doi.org/10.1007/978-3-031-19429-0_20

COVID-19. There have been a number of initiatives globally to develop technological applications to mitigate the spread and impact of COVID-19. Mobile applications have focused on aspects such as contact tracing, digital proximity, travel and border processing, health and safety protocols, vaccination status, and symptom checking. Applications have also been developed to support the transition to virtual modes or enhance activities such as online learning, telemedicine activities, and delivery services. While some technologies developed for the COVID-19 context had a positive impact, others have not been widely adopted and some have generated discussions regarding efficacy and ethical issues of privacy and consent (Alanzi 2021; Dearden and Klein 2021; Luciano 2020). In addition, considerations related to information technology for development implementations should include reflections on aspects of sustainability, resilience and scalability (Baduza and Khene 2019). These discussions are important as well in the context of rapid responses to crisis situations such as the pandemic. Furthermore, the direct translation of such technologies into different contexts can be problematic and potentially exacerbate vulnerabilities and inequalities (Qureshi 2021). This paper explores social and cultural aspects involved in the adoption of risk-mitigating technologies through the development of a pilot application and its assessment by a sample of respondents who participated in the pilot. The app depicts the potential spread of COVID-19 in a community based on the level of observation of health and safety measures such as social distancing.

In the context of the pandemic and related impacts, the importance of resilience-building has been highlighted (Zinser and Thinyane 2021). With calls for additional research, Heeks and Ospina (2019) explore the existing and potential contributions of ICT4D research to community resilience and e-resilience, highlighting the synergies and role of ICTs in supporting resilience in communities. The research project explores the development of crisis-response technologies that may enhance individual and community resilience, particularly taking into account local practices, social constructs and values. Resilience looks at ways of managing during the pandemic, with the supporting resources and information to inform decisions around the implications for lives and livelihoods, and the societal perspectives on this balance. The role of infomediaries and information sources becomes increasingly critical in supporting resilience (Zinser and Thinyane 2021).

This interdisciplinary project, which comprised team members from the fields of anthropology, computer science, design informatics, development studies, geography, ICTs for development, and social work, included the development of three distinct activities: one focused on the development of predictive data models, one concentrated on the design and development of an application, and a final one dedicated to qualitative analysis and testing.

A qualitative assessment of people's perceptions of current practices to mitigate the spread of COVID-19 in Jamaica, supported the exploration of ways to integrate data models that have been developed by Mona GeoInformatics Institute (MGI) to predict risk of COVID-19 spread in different areas in Jamaica (models that took the make-up of different communities into account) with existing epidemiological models developed for COVID-19 in different parts of the world, looking at ways to interpret this data and facilitate visualization in the most informative way possible. We developed a mobile phone application to share this information, and have piloted this application with participants from different communities.

As discussed below, while technological solutions can have an impact on mitigating the spread of the COVID-19, as with other technologies that aim to support social change (Pschetz et al. 2020), they also need to take into account the needs and challenges of the contexts they are implemented in (Tolani et al. 2020). The pilot of this application was conducted when Jamaica was at the early stages of COVID-19 spread, where dedicated technological solutions could potentially assist in mitigating the number of people affected by the virus. Such solutions, however, can face many challenges, ranging from varying levels of Internet access and data literacy. If carried out without due consideration of constraints, technological solutions may also exacerbate inequalities between characteristics such as demographic groups and geographic locations.

Through social analysis and practical technical experimentations that combine data modelling and prototype testing, we have investigated the potential of a digital tool to mitigate the spread of COVID-19.

The paper proceeds as follows: in the next section we explore related literature. The methodology is then discussed, followed by a presentation of findings, discussion and conclusion.

2 Related Literature

The significant changes and disruptions that have arisen from the pandemic have resulted in the continued need for ongoing development of mechanisms to support and enhance resilience at the individual, community and societal levels. UNDP Jamaica (2021) has highlighted the importance of risk assessments in informing plans for growth and recovery to support increased resilience. Sakurai and Chughtai (2020) note that resilience entails working towards supporting the entire community or ecosystem, and understanding the diverse contexts, including under-resourced situations. It is further noted that resilience involves being able to handle the effects of disruptions while maintaining the ability to continue core practices and work towards planned goals.

Marais and Vannini (2021) emphasize the role of participatory approaches which consider the local context, socio-cultural perspectives and values. A key to resilience and sustainability also reflects co-design and the dynamics related to the role of the researchers. The importance of efforts to build risk awareness levels during the pandemic has been highlighted, which was seen as a key input in prevention and mitigation strategies (Chatterjee et al. 2020). Applications related to sharing information on risk modelling were being developed and tested (Chande et al. 2020), and ways of visualizing risks in accessible forms were being considered (Padillaa et al. 2021). Representations and interpretations of the visualizations, as well as the level of interactivity and types of device on which the information would be shared, were considered key (Goldberg et al. 2021). Additionally, data, information and knowledge visualizations have an important role in facilitating knowledge transfer, supported by design considerations for ICTs to support communication (van Biljon and Osei-Bryson 2020). Some applications have looked at supporting the health sector with information sharing on current policies and protocols (Helou et al. 2022). Goldberg et al. (2021) further noted the potential impact of the use of health apps to mitigate risks, and the need for further research and development of risk assessment apps in diverse contexts, noting for example issues of technology access and user demographics.

A number of apps have been and continue to be developed to try to support a range of activities in mitigating the spread of COVID-19 (WSIS 2020). The urgent situation also resulted in the need for rapid analyses of the interventions which can facilitate further development of initiatives (Rowe et al. 2020). There have been continued calls for the use of ICTs and expertise in epidemiology to support the management of crises and build resilience (Madon 2005; Sakurai and Chughtai 2020). The use of apps to support the building of resilience during the pandemic has also been explored (Golden et al. 2021; Nicolaidou et al. 2021).

Prosser et al. (2020) highlight the role of choice in decisions to observe COVID control and prevention guidelines such as wearing a mask, physical distancing, quarantine and isolation measures. They note that these choices have implications for individual and collective action, and the guidelines that are issued in relation to mitigation practices as COVID-19 measures are eased or further restricted. The role of individual and collective action continues to form part of the discussion on choices to be made for the economy and society in the short and long terms. Manyika (2020) reflects on the historical impact of choices made by societies, the shifting of responsibilities between institutions and individuals and the need for greater collective action and socially inclusive choices. There has been interest in the ways in which options and risks are assessed, and choices are made at the individual and collective levels during this pandemic.

James et al. (2021) noted that in a survey of taxi operators in Jamaica during the pandemic, risk perceptions varied based on the types and number of information sources, including the use of ICTs and social media. U-Report Jamaica, a UNICEF-supported youth platform and messaging tool, carried out a survey about people's perception of COVID-19 in Jamaica with 1,062 respondents, most between 20–30 years old. When asked about which issues they were most unsure or knew the least about COVID-19, most responded "risks and complications" (22%) followed by "recognising symptoms" (17%), "preventing covid-19" (11%) and "what to do if I have symptoms" (11%). About a third of the youth respondents indicated that they did not feel they were at risk. The survey reinforced the relevance of supporting risk awareness.

3 Research Methods

Based on an initial assessment of the context, needs and available resources to work towards mitigation of the impact of COVID-19, through interactions with stakeholders, and a review of current developments, a number of ideas were considered by the research team (see Pschetz et al. 2022). The review entailed identifying existing known or reported initiatives, discussions with stakeholders involved in planned national or community initiatives, and the experiences of team members. Given the considerations related to the potential impact of the use of ICTs to support COVID-19 mitigation, the concept of providing information on the risk of spreading COVID-19 was selected. By combining a data model constructed by Mona GeoInformatics Institute, who were members of the research team, with models derived from the spread of COVID-19 elsewhere, the application would predict the risk of the spread of COVID-19 in different communities based on different potential situations. Individuals could then use the model to access advice that is specific to them and understand how their actions have an impact on their communities. Community leaders could also find opportunities to use the app as a tool and discussion point to visualize and illustrate potential risks.

To streamline the implementation of the defined concept, the team focused on three areas: 1) contextual analysis, 2) development of predictive data models, and 3) design and development of the application interface, as explained below. The research approach reflected considerations in design science for development (Osei-Bryson and Bailey 2019; Pal 2017).

3.1 Contextual Analysis

With awareness of both the benefits and complexities of participatory design approaches in engaging and empowering users (Pschetz et al. 2020; Thinyane et al. 2020), and cognizant of the role of researchers and all participants in the research process (Jimenez et al. 2022), the team explored the best approaches to facilitate interaction virtually with community members and representatives during the design phase due to COVID-19 guidelines. Working with communities, we defined a series of everyday scenarios that may impact social distancing or involve increased social interaction, ultimately increasing the risk of spread of COVID-19. These scenarios aimed to give a more naturalistic basis to define the number of people, proximity, and potential contact points between individuals, which would then be used to create parameters for designing the application. We defined fifteen scenarios that could take place under mild or medium lockdown restrictions, which were: shopping at an outdoor food market, queuing to withdraw money from a bank machine, attending church services, going to a traditional or faith-based healer, going to a community gathering, paying taxes at a tax office, using public transportation, visiting a barber shop or hairdressing activities, caring for the elderly, persons with disabilities and/or children in rural and urban areas, attending dance hall sessions, participating in group sporting activities, attending funerals, going to public wi-fi hotspots to access school material or other data, and joining lines to collect benefits through the Government's COVID-19 grant assistance programme. We further delineated parameters for people to tailor each of these scenarios. For example, shopping at an outdoor food market could be refined by defining the average number of people present at a given time of day, the average time people spent there, how likely they were to observe social distancing advice, etc.

In addition, we conducted a literature review of ethnographic studies related to cultural and gendered understandings of illness and the body, Jamaican folk medicine, and the anthropology of the state. Frames of analyses from this literature review were set against media analysis of newspapers and responses to the COVID-19 pandemic in Jamaica. This background qualitative information shaped the development of risk scenarios for the application, and helped us to formulate questions for feedback interviews.

3.2 Development of Predictive Models

The data infrastructure that supported the application resulted from the combination of four different sources:

a) *Determinations of population vulnerability:* based on existing predictive models of risk developed by the MGI. These models took into account the composition of communities in Jamaica through data on population density, age, and occurrence of health issues, such as diabetes and hypertension, to identify groups most at risk;

b) *Infection data,* including the probability of transmission through different levels of contact and the rates of progression through disease states. At the time, the probability of transmission was estimated based on data from China (Verity et al. 2020), and other transitions that had been estimated from world data[1], and Scotland data (Banks et al., 2020). This allowed us to give the probability of transmission, given contact between an infectious individual and a susceptible individual, and to specify the probability of movement from a disease state at a single time step (notionally, one time step is a day), where these probabilities varied by age group. We used a compartmental model, a common approach in basic epidemiological modelling in which there are various disease-state compartments that individuals move between with specified rates. In our compartmental mode, there were seven states: Susceptible, Exposed, Asymptomatic, Infected, Hospitalised, Recovered, and Dead, as inspired by (Carcione et al., 2020), and similar to the model used by Banks et al. (2020). Susceptible people are uninfected and can catch the disease. Exposed people have caught the disease but are not yet infectious. Asymptomatic and Infected people are able to infect others, and can either progress to a more serious state of illness, i.e. Hospitalised or Dead, or can recover.

c) *Simulation configuration,* which was derived experimentally, based on network-based epidemiological models for COVID-19, according to which the spread of infection doubled over approximately two days. The simulation was run for each combination of app inputs provided; this was saved on datasets as cookies on users' mobile phones.

d) *Input from users:* "community" chosen from a list of communities, "behaviour" chosen from a list of behaviours, e.g. food shopping, which were drawn from a series of scenarios as defined above, "num_visits": which included "behavior_name": list of possible values of number of visits per week, and "num_people".

3.3 COVID-Aware Interface and Visualisation

The mobile phone interface aimed to use the data above to communicate varying levels of risks of spreading/contracting the virus in different communities according to the predefined scenarios. It was designed to be interactive, allowing people to change the parameters of the epidemiological models (input from users above) and visualize how these changes can affect transmission rates. It was expected to be used by anyone, while considering the central role of community leaders who could provide support and advice.

---

[1] https://www.worldometers.info/coronavirus/coronavirus-incubation-period/.

This way, the visualisation and parameter inputs would need to be clear and accessible. The application also assumed that phones accessing the application would be connected to the Internet but that this connection could be slow.

Aspects of digital adaptation were seen in relation to the design of the app, and adjustments that needed to be made during the design phase to accommodate data processing times, minimizing the number of datasets and streamlining the scenarios for visualizations.

Our first step to reduce the number of generated datasets was to generalise the sizes of different communities to small (up to 1,000 residents), medium (from 1,000 to 4,000 residents) and large (over 4000). In this way, when people selected their communities after opening the application, they would be informed about which population size the model was based upon, e.g. "You have selected Community A with a population of 3,878. The model will use the medium sized population dataset." The system would then take into account the age structure of each community to modify the number of predicted hospitalisations and deaths.

The second step was to reduce the number of scenarios that could be selected in the application. The need to minimise the number of datasets led us to look for ways to cover most scenarios through parameters that could be combined to define a situation as close as possible to real-life. The scenarios were then simplified to accommodate three main input options: food shopping, small gatherings (up to 15 people) and large gatherings (up to 100 people). Within each of these options, people would set how many times each week they thought others would do these activities, and, for each activity, how many people they thought would come within six metric feet of each other. With the restriction to three general scenarios we were able to produce all data for the application to be tested by four communities (generating 2,788 datasets in total, 697 for each community).

Figure 1 depicts screenshots of the COVID-Aware application.

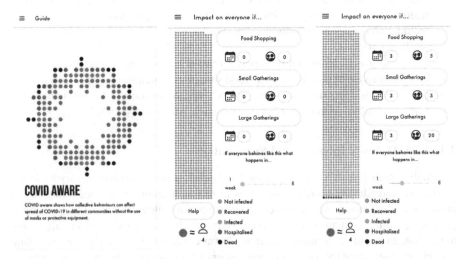

Fig. 1. Screenshots of COVID-aware mobile application

Wakunuma et al. (2020) highlight the socio-ethical implications in relation to the use of technologies for health initiatives, including during the pandemic. In the design and implementation phases of the study, there were a number of ethical considerations. These included the utilization and storage of the data models and qualitative interviews, and the process of interacting with participants given the health and safety protocols and physical distancing measures. The implications of the design of the interface and messages to be conveyed were also considered, as well as the interview questions, particularly during this time of the pandemic. The interviews were conducted by phone, with initial connections made via phone or WhatsApp. Phone/data credit was provided to participants to assist with accessing the Internet for use of the app. Conducted by phone, interviews explored participants' interpretation of the application and their impressions of the design and functionality, likelihood of sharing app or information with their communities and networks, as well as also social and cultural factors influencing COVID-related behaviours and understandings of risk, such as sources of information, choice options, support networks, household structure, levels of risk perception, preventive practices, and levels of trust. Characteristics of participants are outlined in Table 1 below.

Table 1. Characteristics of COVID-aware pilot participants

Number of participants	28 (4 communities; 7 persons each)
Gender	Female: 16 Male: 12
Age groups	19–29: 6 30–39: 6 40–49: 7 50–59: 6 60–69: 3

Interviews were recorded, then transcribed from the recordings, and the research team analysed the transcripts through content analysis exploring reflections on the app's design, content and participants' perspectives of the overall potential of the COVID-Aware app for risk assessment and mitigation towards wellbeing during the pandemic. For this paper, notions of resilience and adaptation reflected in the project were assessed.

4   Findings

In this section we highlight some of the participants' perspectives in relation to the app, the perception of risks during the time of the pandemic, and connect these to the notions of resilience and adaptability.

Reflecting on the information shared in the app, and their existing and new knowledge, participants shared their experiences with adapting to the evolving health and safety protocols, containment measures and restrictions:

"Yes, it's very difficult.... [it] is going to take a heck of a time to adapt that social distance". (Participant R2)

"It is very difficult for you consistently not to embrace, not to shake your hand because most of the time, you who is disciplined. You have to keep putting out your hand, pulling your hand and giving them the elbow or whatsoever. Most of the time you see a friend or what, you put your hand out, you stretch your hand out. We grow up that way". (Participant S1).

In some cases, adaptations included adjusting to the move to virtual social interactions. These were also discussed in relation to the research process, which included virtual interactions, and the existing protocols and recommendations, such as gathering limits, depicted in the app.

"Automatically the human beings [are] social creatures, and because of norms and cultures it's hard to resist....It won't be so easy to stop [gathering] and even the virtual sense of reality now, virtual existence of things now. In reality, some persons don't feel that." (Participant W2).

Participants shared perspectives on the potential of the app to support education and knowledge sharing towards increasing risk awareness. This would have implications for building resilience and adapting as the context and available information evolved.

"App useful in educating people what socialising could do in terms of transmissions in community, Good for visualising spread of COVID". (Participant A1).

A participant further shared that given the current context, the app could provide useful support:

"I'm saying in my situation; it will be good for us (the app)" (Participant D1).

The need for mobility to facilitate necessary activities was highlighted in terms of navigating the adaptations needed. ICTs were seen as a possible means to support carrying out these activities.

"I would say why? - Let me use myself in that question. I would actually go to the supermarket, supermarket canteens, the cashiers, other employees, other buyers, other customers and all of that so you might -- We have to eat, we have to get something, we have to have food in the house. We have to have - in the sense of we cannot always stay in. Yes, some persons have to also work". (Participant C1).

Some of the respondents noted their thoughts on the ongoing risk, and assessment of the risk. The adaptability of the app to reflect scenarios or the selection of scenarios for inclusion was a consideration in the design and participant assessment of the app. One respondent indicated.

"Some people still don't maintain the distance. None of them don't maintain the distance. I don't think the distance has anything to do with it. If you are at a distance, if you have to catch it, you will catch it the same way. If you wear the

mask and you still have to catch it, you will catch it the same way. It's just a risk we've got to take." (Participant W1).

Having explored the app, participants indicated some areas where they thought the risk awareness assessment would be useful. This would reflect ideas related to adaptability and building resilience in mitigating the effects of the pandemic.

"Because I don't want to go close to anyone that have the virus and I don't know, because the virus doesn't show on everyone so you don't catch the virus so you have to keep your social distance." (Participant T1)

"Why choose to go to a large gathering? They [are] basically social events, so a lot of them [are] funerals and sometimes they have parties. The restriction is being lifted now, so persons are feeling now more free, so they want to go out and try to feel some sense of normalcy" (Participant R2).

"You're saying what you'd want to see-- It would have been nice to have a symptom link or symptom page, so you go on and it says if you have these symptoms, you contact your local authorities" (Participant C2).

In response to questions related to perceptions of the app, participants shared views of the existing features and the implications for awareness of risks and responses to the risks. The participants' responses reflected continued adaptations to the COVID-19 context, and ways in which the information shared via the mobile app could contribute to enhancing resilience during the pandemic.

"App useful to learn how one could be infected/infect others when attending gatherings. [My friends] they really think it is a good thing because at least they can use something for a measure of it. Use something as a measurement. Now, what if we are all there? It make them even be more aware. Even my friends when I spoke to about it and they said it's automatic." (Participant T1).

"The app now is useful because every time you think about you remember you're supposed to wear a mask, keep social distance or something like that". (Participant A2).

"It's a good app and I would say it will help me so I could know that "All right then, if there is 50 persons." If I come on 50 persons on a daily basis within six feet, I can get affected with the virus and it maybe takes-- Well as far as what the app is showing me, it's a possibility where you may not live because you have shows that you have deaths, you have recoveries, you have hospitalized. I would say you got-- It will give me and my family a chance to know what can take place or what do take place or what can happen". (Participant I1).

"In the case of-- For instance, COVID-19 itself, again, when I use the app, I think it can help others to really understand the importance of following the guidelines of social distancing and wearing a mask and so forth because for instance, if you are not following the guidelines, you are going to ruin a lot of people exposing yourself to other persons who might be infected with the disease". (Participant C2).

"App very interesting, and it's informative. I'm glad I really- because I knew COVID-19 was a very deadly virus but I didn't stop to think about how it could spread and how fast in a period of time. The app was very, very informative and it is an eye-opener". (Participant S2).

5 Discussion and Conclusion

This paper explores aspects involved in the adoption of risk-mitigating technologies through the development of a mobile application, COVID-Aware, to support information sharing and visualization of health and safety protocols, and the implications for individuals and communities based on the decisions made during the pandemic. Participants' perspectives on adapting to the use of the app on their mobile devices assisted with exploring ways to share visualisations of this data, and their overall views of adaptations to the health protocols provided feedback for participatory development of the app. Ethical considerations during the research included the work with the data for the app, the approaches to interpretation, presentation and visualization of the data, and the field work conducted virtually with participants using mobile platforms. Throughout the study, concepts of technology adaptations and resilience (both digital and human), and the connections between them in relation to the development of the COVID-Aware mobile app were explored. At a time where there is continued focus on individual and collective responsibilities for managing the pandemic and balancing lives and livelihoods, with some persons expressing the need for additional guidance on safety measures to be adopted in a given context, approaches to visualizing and sharing information can be helpful in mitigating risks. The data modelling and visualization within a community context is also useful for research and practice.

Reflections on the process of design, development and participatory assessment of the COVID-Aware app also illustrate some of the "bounce forward" resilience pre-conditions discussed by Russpatrick et al. (2021). The existence of locally developed data models based on community information facilitated the development of the predictive models combined with the epidemiological models for other countries. It is recognized that the ability to respond to the shocks requiring rapid adaptation and innovation also facilitates learning and resilience for future crises or pandemics (Russpatrick et al. 2021).

The continued calls for increasing the messaging and communication around risks, particularly given the length of the pandemic, highlights the considerations around effective use of technologies to support risk awareness as we work towards increased resilience. The resilience of the technology and the users is also a key factor in exploring means of depicting the risks which may provide useful perspectives in the context of the debates on balancing lives and livelihoods within the recommended health protocols.

As indicated by Sakurai and Chughtai (2020, p. 591) "Digital technology should be used in a productive and ethical way to develop long-term resilience in society". This COVID-Aware app, through a multidisciplinary team approach, sought to utilize technology to facilitate risk awareness and measures to mitigate the spread of COVID-19, thereby increasing individual and collective resilience in a development context.

Acknowledgements. This study was funded by the Scottish Funding Council – Global Challenges Research Fund (SFC-GCRF) COVID-19 Urgency Research Fund. We thank the SFC-GCRF for the support for the study, and all collaborators, participants and reviewers for the valuable insights shared and contribution to the research process.

References

Alanzi, T.: A review of mobile applications available in the app and google play stores used during the COVID-19 outbreak. J. Multidiscip. Healthc. **14**, 45 (2021)

Baduza, G., Khene, C.: A holistic view of ICTD and up-scaling of community development projects. In: Proceedings of the 12th Annual Pre-ICIS AIS SIG GlobDev Workshop, Munich, Germany, 15 December 2019 (2019)

Banks, C.J., et al.: Disentangling the roles of human mobility and deprivation on the transmission dynamics of COVID-19 using a spatially explicit simulation model. medRxiv (2020)

Chande, A., Lee, S., Harris, M., et al.: Real-time, interactive website for US-county-level COVID-19 event risk assessment. Nat. Hum. Behav. **4**, 1313–1319 (2020)

Chatterjee, R., Bajwa, S., Dwivedi, D., Kanji, R., Ahammed, M., Shaw, R.: COVID-19 risk assessment tool: dual application of risk communication and risk governance. Progr. Disast. Sci. **7**, 100109 (2020)

Dearden, A., Kleine, D.: Interdisciplinarity, self-governance and dialogue: the participatory process underpinning the minimum ethical standards for ICTD/ICT4D research. Inf. Technol. Dev. **27**(2), 361–380 (2021)

Goldberg, E.M., Bingaman, C.S., Perera, S., Ranney, M.L.: MyCOVIDRisk app: development and utilisation of a COVID-19 risk assessment and mitigation application. BMJ Innov. **7**(2) (2021)

Golden, E.A., et al.: A resilience-building app to support the mental health of health care workers in the COVID-19 era: design process, distribution, and evaluation. JMIR Formative Research **5**(5), e26590 (2021)

Heeks, R., Ospina, A.V.: Conceptualising the link between information systems and resilience: a developing country field study. Inf. Syst. J. **29**(1), 70–96 (2019)

Helou and Waltmans–den Breejen, C. M., Severin, J. A., Hulscher, M. E. J. L., & Verbon, A. , 2022.Helou, R.I., Waltmans–den Breejen, C.M., Severin, J.A., Hulscher, M.E. J.L., Verbon, A.: Use of a smartphone app to inform healthcare workers of hospital policy during a pandemic such as COVID-19: a mixed methods observational study. PloS One **17**(1), e0262105 (2022)

James, K., Thompson, C., Chin-Bailey, C., Davis, K.D., Nevins, D.H., Walters, D.: COVID-19 related risk perception among taxi operators in Kingston and St. Andrew, Jamaica. J. Transp. Health **22**, 101229 (2021)

Jimenez, A., Abbott, P., Dasuki, S.: In-betweenness in ICT4D research: critically examining the role of the researcher. Eur. J. Inf. Syst. **31**(1), 25–39 (2022)

Luciano, F.: Mind the app—considerations on the ethical risks of COVID-19 apps. Philos. Technol. **33**(2), 167–172 (2020)

Madon, S.: Governance lessons from the experience of telecentres in Kerala. Eur. J. Inf. Syst. **14**(4), 401–416 (2005)

Manyika, J.: In "how will the world be different after COVID-19?" finance & development, June 2020 – Policies, Politics and Pandemics. International Monetary Fund (2020). https://www. imf.org/external/pubs/ft/fandd/2020/06/pdf/fd0620.pdf

Marais, M.A., Vannini, S.: Network weaving to foster resilience and sustainability in ICT4D. In: Proceedings of the 1st Virtual Conference on Implications of Information and Digital Technologies for Development, pp. 43–56 (2021)

Nicolaidou, I., Aristeidis, L., Christodoulou, C., Lambrinos, L.: Co-creating a gamified app for enhancing students' emotional resilience in times of crisis (COVID-19). In: 15th annual International Technology, Education and Development Conference, 8–9 March 2021 (2021)

Osei-Bryson, K.M., Bailey, A.: Contextual reflections on innovations in an interconnected world: theoretical lenses and practical considerations in ICT4D–Part 2. Inf. Technol. Dev. **25**(1), 1–6 (2019)

Pal, J.: CHI4Good or Good4CHI. In: Proceedings of the 2017 CHI Conference Extended Abstracts on Human Factors in Computing Systems, pp. 709–721. ACM (2017)

Pschetz, L., Bailey, A., Rankin, J., Enright, J., Wilson, M.: situating the Covid aware app: challenges of designing with predictive models. In: Morton, S. (ed.) Designing Interventions to Address Complex Societal Issues. Routledge (2022)

Pschetz, L., et al.: Designing distributed ledger technologies for social change: the case of Cari-Crop. In: Proceedings of the 2020 CHI Conference on Human Factors in Computing Systems (2020)

Prosser, A.M., Judge, M., Bolderdijk, J.W., Blackwood, L., Kurz, T.: 'Distancers' and 'non-distancers'? The potential social psychological impact of moralizing COVID-19 mitigating practices on sustained behaviour change. Br. J. Soc. Psychol. **59**(3), 653–662 (2020)

Qureshi, S.: Pandemics within the pandemic: confronting socio-economic inequities in a datafied world. Inf. Technol. Dev. **27**(2), 151–170 (2021)

Rowe, F., Ngwenyama, O., Richet, J.L.: Contact-tracing apps and alienation in the age of COVID-19. Eur. J. Inf. Syst. 1–18 (2020)

Russpatrick, S., Sæbø, J., Monteiro, E., Nicholson, B., Sanner, T.: Digital resilience to Covid-19: a model for national digital health systems to bounce forward from the shock of a global pandemic. In: Proceedings of the 1st Virtual Conference on Implications of Information and Digital Technologies for Development, pp. 67–80 (2021)

Sahay, S.: Are we building a better world with ICTs? Empirically examining this question in the domain of public health in India. Inf. Technol. Dev. **22**(1), 168–176 (2016)

Sakurai, M., Chughtai, H.: Resilience against crises: COVID-19 and lessons from natural disasters. Eur. J. Inf. Syst. **29**(5), 585–594 (2020)

Thinyane, M., Bhat, K., Goldkind, L., Cannanure, V.K.: The messy complexities of democratic engagement and empowerment in participatory design–an illustrative case with a community-based organisation. CoDesign Int. J. CoCreat. Design Arts **16**(1), 29–44 (2020)

Tolani, A., Owoseni, A., Twinomurinzi, H.: Designing for context versus the lock-in effect of 'free' global digital platforms: a case of SMEs from Nigeria. In: Hofmann, S., Müller, O., Rossi, M. (eds.) DESRIST 2020. LNCS, vol. 12388, pp. 321–332. Springer, Cham (2020). https://doi.org/10.1007/978-3-030-64823-7_29

UNDP Jamaica: Year in Review 2021 – UNDP Multi Country Office in Jamaica (2021). https://www.jm.undp.org/content/jamaica/en/home/blog/2021/2021_s-top-4-lessons-in-growth---resilience--lessons-from-our-pe.html

van Biljon, J., Osei-Bryson, K.M.: The communicative power of knowledge visualizations in mobilizing information and communication technology research. Inf. Technol. Dev. **26**(4), 637–652 (2020)

Verity, R., et al.: Estimates of the severity of coronavirus disease 2019: a model-based analysis. Lancet. Infect. Dis **20**(6), 669–677 (2020)

Wakunuma, K., Jiya, T., Aliyu, S.: Socio-ethical implications of using AI in accelerating SDG3 in Least Developed Countries. J. Responsible Technol. **4**, 100006 (2020)

WSIS: The Coronavirus (COVID-19) Response – ICT Case Repository, WSIS Stocktaking, World Summit on the Information Society (2020). https://www.itu.int/net4/wsis/stocktaking/Content/doc/surveys/15863048637525604/WS_COVID-19Response-ICTCaseRepository-MidtermReport.pdf

Zinser, S., Thinyane, H.: Organizational resilience between competing networks of infomediaries: a case study in civil society resilience in Hong Kong. In: Proceedings of the 1st Virtual Conference on Implications of Information and Digital Technologies for Development, pp. 6–18 (2021)

Artificial Intelligence, Inequalities, and Human Rights

Artificial Intelligence for Quality Education: Successes and Challenges for AI in Meeting SDG4

Tumaini Mwendile Kabudi(✉) ⓘD

University of Agder, Kristiansand, Norway
`tumaini.kabudi@uia.no`

Abstract. The application of artificial intelligence (AI) in education has brought significant transformations to traditional models of education. Despite its potential to provide quality education, AI applications in education raise significant concerns. The goal of this paper is to understand how to increase AI implementation in education by identifying practical benefits and challenges that must be addressed if AI is to be harnessed to achieve Sustainability Development Goal 4. Twenty-two interviews were conducted with AI experts. Several rounds of analysis of the interviews revealed five main themes: 1) the role of the teacher in AI in education (AIEd); 2) the inclusion of students with intellectual disabilities; 3) racial and data bias in AIEd; 4) design issues of AI-enabled learning systems; 5) and commercialization of AI-enabled learning systems. The findings of this study contribute to the ongoing research on AI in education and help build a better understanding of AI's role in achieving SDGs.

Keywords: Artificial intelligence · AIEd · Sustainability development · SDGs · SDG4 · Education

1 Introduction

The recent wave of technological innovation is based on artificial intelligence (AI). AI is considered to be a system that uses machine learning, data mining, computer vision, language recognition and natural language generation to collect data and to predict, recommend or decide the best line of action [1]. More recently, the United Nations acknowledged that this pervasive emerging technology can rapidly accelerate progress in pursuing its global agenda of sustainable development [2]. UN's global agenda goals regarding sustainable development, known as Sustainable Development Goals (SDGs), cover a range of social, economic and environmental matters. Given the role of education as an enabler of economic development, one of the SDGs deals specifically with education, namely SDG4, that is, "Ensure inclusive and equitable quality education and promote lifelong learning opportunities for all" [2, 3]. AI is already changing the education sector. Students now have the capability to find information at their fingertips through educational software and reactive products such as Leapfrog, Amazon's Siri

Y. Zheng et al. (Eds.): ICT4D 2022, IFIP AICT 657, pp. 347–362, 2022.
https://doi.org/10.1007/978-3-031-19429-0_21

and Google's Alexis [4, 5]. AI offers unprecedented opportunities to humanity and thus solves educational challenges, such as expanding the availability of education, making learning more interactive and personalising learning [6]. AI applications are increasing in the field of education, from laboratory setups to contemporary and complex learning systems. A great example of such systems is AI-enabled adaptive learning systems (AI-ALS) and Intelligent Tutoring Systems (ITS), which promote adaptive learning. The application of AI in education (AIEd) has increased due to its promising potential to provide personalised and adaptive learning, provide instant and correct feedback, facilitate meaningful interactions and improve students' engagement. Moreover, AI has the potential to have a major effect on administrative tasks, data mining and data analytics due to its powerful processing capabilities. AI is also used in learning assessments, such as grading essays [7]. AI offers other great opportunities, such as the integration of serious games into ITS and intelligent agents in the form of chatbots. Thus, AI has been transforming the ways of teaching and learning in education and has contributed to maintaining high-quality teaching during global crises, such as the pandemic [8].

The potential and importance of such systems is well established; however, AI-enabled learning interventions and applications, especially AI-ALS, remain largely at the experimental stage [9, 10]. A recent literature review noted a critical gap between what AI-ALS could be and can do and what the current systems do in terms of how they are implemented in real educational environments [11]. There is a severe discrepancy, which has been consistently noted between the potentials of AI-ALS and their actual implementation in real teaching and learning settings [12–14]. The increased need for AI-ALS to be further utilised and adopted more quickly in education demands more empirical research on the implementation and evaluation of these systems. Moreover, AI has yet to be adopted in most of the poorest regions of the world. AI can provide financial and intellectual superiority to some countries, while other countries will be left behind [4]. Thus, the provision of more inclusive access to education to all students using AI in less affluent countries is a persistent challenge, as AI is still an unknown concept in such a context [15]. Moreover, research reports such as UNESCO (2021) have connected AI and SDG4, but little research has been done on the evidence-based implications of AI in schools and universities. With AI evolving rapidly in the education field, issues such as the integration of AI-ALS systems within real education contexts need to be addressed. Hence, more research is needed to understand how to increase the implementation and adoption of AI in education (AIEd).

Thus, this article identifies the existing practical benefits of AI in education and the challenges that need to be addressed in harnessing AI to achieve this SDG. Therefore, the motivation for this research is to investigate the following research question:

RQ: *How can researchers, developers and designers successfully integrate and implement AI technologies in education to accomplish SDGs in quality education?*

To address our RQ, in-depth interviews with AIEd technological experts who are knowledgeable about the design and development of AI-ALS. The findings of the study contribute to the ongoing research on AI and show how IS research can lead the way in harnessing AI to achieve SDG4. Moreover, it contributes to ongoing research on the digitalisation of education and shows how IS research can lead the way in designing the learning systems of the future. Better education, especially in a developing context, would lead to significant benefits for such societies and positively affect other SDGs, such as SDG5, SDG10, SDG9 and SDG16. Henceforth, this article will help the AI in Education (AIEd) community build a better understanding of AI and SDGs. In the following sections, the theoretical background is provided. The author provides a literature review of the opportunities and challenges of AI in education. Then, the author describes the research design of the study in detail. The data collection and analysis steps are described and elaborated upon in detail. Finally, the findings are inductively derived and discussed in the context of what happens in practice and in the existing literature. This paper then concludes with the implications of the study and recommendations for future research.

2 State of the Art: Vis-à-vis Opportunities and Challenges of AI in Education

Artificial intelligence (AI) has advanced and has been widely adopted in various fields, including education. With AI technology thriving in recent years, its applications in the form of AI-ALS have increased [16, 17]. AI-ALS are generally digital learning tools enabled by AI that "adapts, as well as possible, to the learner, so that the learning process is optimized, and/or the student performance improve" [18]. AI-enabled adaptive learning systems (AI-ALS) are platforms that adapt to the learning strategies of students, changing and modifying the order and the difficulty level of learning tasks based on the abilities of students [17, 19]. These systems support adaptive learning (i.e., personalisation of learning for students in a learning system) in a way that allows the system to deal with individual differences in aptitude [16]. Most recent AI-ALS include Smart Sparrow, Knewton, Fishtree, INSPIREus, ProSys, QuizBot, OPERA, LearnSmart, Connect ™, ACTIVEMATH and Student Diagnosis, Assistance, Evaluation System based on Artificial Intelligence (StuDiAsE) [11]. AI-ALS was developed to help address most challenges that occur in technology-enhanced learning environments. These include resource limitations, difficulty in students attaining and mastering their learning skills, variety in learning abilities of students and diverse student backgrounds [11, 20]. AI-ALS motivates students to embark on their own learning journeys through automated feedback cycles in these systems. The ability of AI-ALS to enable the personalised learning of students sparks in them interest in the field of education and thus increases students' enthusiasm [16]. This is mainly due to the promising potential of the systems, such as providing customised learning to students (adaptive learning), offering fast feedback and dynamic assessments and facilitating meaningful group collaboration and engagement in learning settings [21]. In addition to AI-ALS, other AIEd technologies include ITS, expert systems and chatbots [22].

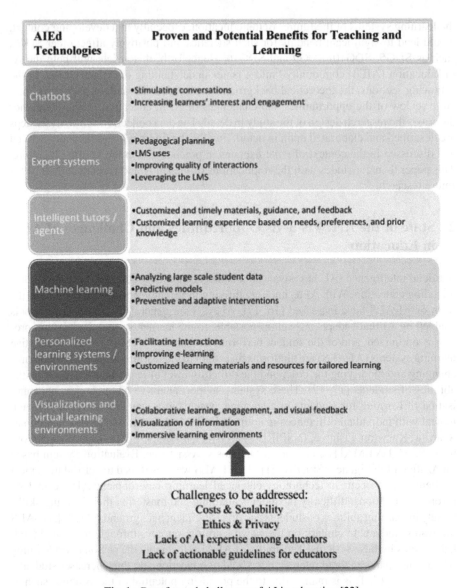

Fig. 1. Benefits and challenges of AI in education [22]

Such advances in contemporary educational technologies and digital education have sparked increased interest in enhancing teaching and learning [23, 24]. Figure 1 illustrates the potential or proven benefits of AI in education. AI-ALS and other AIEd technologies facilitate learner engagement, varied interactions with learners, and improvement of learning outcomes, in addition to helping lecturers and administrators identify gifted and at-risk students, monitor learning progress and provide feedback [22]. AI offers other great opportunities to meet SDGs for quality education globally. For example, issues such as teacher modelling and multimodal interaction, emphatic systems and the use of educational robots offer unprecedented opportunities for research into issues such as diversity, inclusive education, equitable quality education and ethical concerns [25]. Moreover, AI in education contributes to addressing long-term educational targets (i.e., as part of SDG4). These include attaining and learning 2st Century skills; universal access to global classrooms; lifelong and life-wide learning; interaction data to support learning; and mentors for every student [26].

Although AI holds great promise for providing quality education for all, its application in education comes with challenges. [2, 3] have pointed out several challenges and risks of implementing AI in education that can thus affect SDG4's realisation. These challenges include ensuring the equity and inclusion of AI in education. The least developed nations, as it stands, risk suffering other technological, social and economic disadvantages due to AI [3]. In addition, developing quality and inclusive data systems is another concern. Other concerns in implementing AIEd include ethics and transparency in the collection and use of learners' data; preparing teachers for AIEd while preparing AI to understand education; and developing a comprehensive public policy on AIEd for sustainable development. AI has raised significant worries and ethical concerns, such as replacement of teachers, job loss and algorithmic bias [27]. Furthermore, AI has the potential to aggravate inequality and further entrench the control and supremacy of big tech companies [28]. Access to affordable electricity, internet and smart devices, which are prerequisites for AIEd, are not equally distributed in developing contexts and may instead present new forms of inequalities. There has been little demonstrable positive impact of AI on education in terms of enhancing equity and quality [29]. In addition, although the provision of quality education is at its core, the role of digital infrastructure and technology in the realisation of SDG 4 is not addressed commendably in the SDG4 targets. Therefore, the impact of AI on students, teachers and society in general has yet to be determined [2]. Issues such as the effectiveness of AIEd interventions, the choice of pedagogies used in these interventions, gender-equitable and AI for gender equality and data ethics have yet to be addressed. Thus, this research aims to address the above-mentioned gaps by identifying the practical benefits and challenges that must be addressed to increase AIEd implementation.

3 Research Design and Methodology

I followed Yin's [30] argument that qualitative research methods address "how" questions. Therefore, the research design for this study is based on a qualitative research methodology. Grounded theory was used to guide the study, as it served to explain in conceptual terms what actually occurs in practice. The theory also helped in interpreting the collected data and extracting the literature during the study [31]. The author conducted an empirical examination of the DPs using expert interviews and content analysis. AI technology experts involved in the design, development and extensive research on AI in education were interviewed. Content analysis was used to code phrases, sentences and paragraphs. The results obtained were used to discuss the benefits of implementing AI in education and the challenges that need to be addressed. In the following sections, the data collection techniques and analysis are described and discussed.

3.1 Data Collection via Expert Interviews

Throughout a 3-month period, a series of semi-structured interviews with experts were conducted. This method was used to explore and understand the perspectives of AI technology subjects involved in developing, designing and implementing AI-ALS. Moreover, this method was considered suitable because the author could collect in-depth information from several experts across the world during the pandemic. The experts were selected using the snowball sampling technique based on their publications and work. This technique was quite practical, since it allowed us to collect data during a pandemic. Relying on a literature search and Google Scholar profiles, the author identified 143 experts who had published research on AI-ALS and appeared to be active in the AIEd community. They were randomly selected using a convenience sampling technique. The experts were then contacted via email. Data were collected until theoretical saturation was achieved on various aspects of participant experiences and perspectives regarding the development, design and implementation of AI-ALS—the focus of this study. The demographic profiles of the experts are presented in Table 1. The interviews were conducted face-to-face using a video conferencing tool. All interviews were anonymous and confidential. The expert interviews lasted between 45 min and 1 h. The questions in our interviews were used to help answer the main research question. The semi-structured interview questions focused on the implementation status of AI-ALS, its major benefits and the perceived challenges in its implementation. The interviewer asked probing questions for further elaboration based on the information provided by our experts. The interviews were conducted in English, although some of the interviewees and the interviewer's first language was not English. Thus, some of the nuances of the language may have been lost during the transcription of the interviews.

Table 1. Profile of the respondents

#	Organisation	Expert category	Role	Country
1	University	Researcher, Designer, Developer	Academic	Australia
2	University	Designer, Developer	PhD Student	Switzerland
3	Consulting Company	Researcher	Project Manager	France
4	Research Lab	Researcher	Academic	Tunisia
5	University	Researcher	Academic	Switzerland
6	Industry	Designer, Developer	Software Engineer	UK
7	University	Researcher	Academic	Germany
8	Research Centre	Researcher	Co-Director	UK
9	University	Researcher	Academic	USA
10	University	Designer, Developer	PhD Student	USA

(*continued*)

Table 1. (*continued*)

#	Organisation	Expert category	Role	Country
11	Research Lab	Developer, Researcher	Head of Research Lab	Russia
12	University	Researcher	Academic	China
13	University	Researcher	Academic	UK
14	University	Designer, Developer	Academic	USA
15	University	Researcher	Academic	Brazil
16	University	Designer, Developer	Academic	Singapore
17	Research Lab	Designer, Developer	Academic	Morocco
18	University	Developer, Researcher	PhD Student	South Korea
19	University	Researcher	Academic	Ukraine
20	Research Centre	Researcher	PhD Student	USA
21	Research Lab	Researcher	Academic	UK
22	Research Centre	Researcher	Academic	USA

The semi-structured interviews were conducted from July to November of 2021. These interviews took place mainly at the most convenient time for the interview subjects. The interviews were conducted face-to-face using a videoconferencing tool. The interviews were transcribed verbatim, focusing mainly on spoken words. The text transcripts were stored on a secure file served and identifying labels were removed from the file names.

3.2 Data Analysis

After the interviews were conducted, they were transcribed. The interviews were recorded, both in video and audio formats, and represented in total approximately 22 h of conversation. This was a large amount of qualitative data, and each recording took 6–8 h of transcription work. The author independently transcribed the English-language transcriptions using qualitative data analysis software (NVivo). The transcriptions were then reviewed and inspected for accuracy and corrected if needed. The coding and evaluation of the expert interviews were then conducted through qualitative thematic analysis. This method is the most comprehensive and precise approach to analysing data collected qualitatively [32]. An open coding process, according to [33], that generates first order codes/themes was used. An initial list of generated codes was first developed based on the identified sentences and paragraphs. Pattern coding was employed for the categorisation of the coded data. Pattern coding was used to move from an unrelated list of codes to central themes that could be explored. This was done through a process of constant comparison between the initial codes, where common patterns were detected and thus organised into first-order themes. In any IS research, it is important to build on the obtained prescriptive knowledge to provide solid grounding [34, 35]. Through an iterative approach of developing, revising, comparing and recategorizing codes, five major themes and their multiple sub-themes emerged.

4 Discussion of Findings

This section presents the findings of the data collection. The findings reported in this paper are based on the analysed data collected from 22 interviewees. Of the 22 experts who were interviewed, 6 were female and 16 were male. The majority came from the USA (5), followed by the UK (4) and Switzerland (2). Moreover, the majority of these experts came from universities and research groups (Fig. 2).

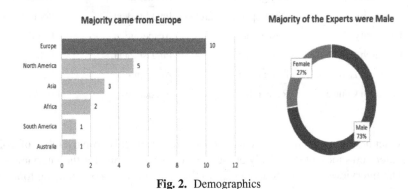

Fig. 2. Demographics

Five major themes emerged after the analysis. The themes were based on experts' perspectives on the implementation status of AI-ALS, significant practical benefits of AI-ALS and the challenges perceived during the implementation of AI-ALS. The themes included 1) the role of teachers, 2) racial and data bias, 3) inclusion of students with intellectual disabilities, 4) commercialisation of AI-ALS, and 5) cultural design issues. Each of these themes is further detailed in the remainder of this section.

4.1 The Role of the Teacher in AIEd

The value and role of the teacher in AIEd was a prominent theme discussed by the experts in this study. The majority explained that the intention of building AI-ALS was not to replace teachers in educational settings. The following are excerpts of experts' statements on the value of the teacher:

> "There are some people in AI and education who kind of see themselves as replacing teachers, which I think is nonsense. Even if it sorts of worked, it would be nonsense, you know, because actually, education is preeminently a social interaction between teachers and learners in in a social context". (Expert 12)

> "And I just think that's important to reinforce is there's nothing in learning analytics as a paradigm that seeks to replace a teacher". (Expert 21)

"One of the things that I strongly believe is that we're not trying to develop a system that replaces teacher. It would be something teachers use to help them and that would be with the teachers being present a lot of the time as well. So it's not like how our students have had to suffer during COVID restrictions, where they've just been stuck in front of a screen on their own... (so) we didn't envisage a system that will replace a teacher...". (Expert 13)

"I don't know about your country or other countries, but there are still teachers here who feel they are being replaced and they don't like it at all. With the ones who build it, we never thought of replacing teachers. I mean, teachers have an incredible and difficult job to do, and I've never thought of replacing them". (Expert 20)

"...If we're going to talk about any kind of artificial intelligence that exists within the field... it should be artificial intelligence that is applied to that specific problem.... (And thus) of how do we use artificial intelligence not to replace teachers, but to assist teachers in doing their job better". (Expert 20)

Hence, teachers play an important role in AIEd. Some teachers understand the benefits of using AI in their classrooms. Expert 13 gave good examples of teachers' positive perspectives on AI-ALS. She stated: *"As the positives for the teachers were that they thought it would actually free them up to do other things. They thought it would be, you know, when you're trying to share your time between lots of different students, you could maybe take your eye off the ball with ones that were doing well and spend more time with those that were struggling. And the fact that they will be developing their own versions, as the idea is to give them a platform that they could then tailor themselves"*. Expert 20 also highlighted how teachers enjoyed uploading their own content on these systems, specifically the ASSISTMENTS system. ASSISTMENTS has been successfully and widely adopted in the USA because *"it gave teachers templates for creating new content that teachers can use to make their own problems... that their students can work on, and that they can share with other teachers. They don't have to do the rigorous skill mapping or the misconception mapping because that takes a load of time and teachers don't have time to do that"*. Thus, these advantages, in addition to providing teachers with information about their students using learning analytics, encourages them to use AI-ALS. This helps harness AI to achieve SDG4.

Nevertheless, teachers also displayed negative attitudes towards AI. The overwhelming negative attitudes of teachers towards AI-ALS were defined by the heavy workload related to designing each course or discipline with a modular approach, and thus populate the different aspects of the platform (Experts 2, 11 and 13). Most teachers tended to be busy and had specific plans and thus felt that AI could be disruptive (Expert 10). Teachers also felt that they needed to have some sort of incentive to do such work (Expert 1) or have technical support to help develop their content in these systems (Experts 1 and 5). Moreover, teachers felt that the systems enabled by AI were too advanced, complicated or hard to understand. Unlike learning management systems such as Canvas, AI-ALS resemble a "black box" that was inflexible for teachers to use (Expert 9). Teachers not being technologically and pedagogically skilled to use AI-ALS discouraged them from embedding such systems in their classrooms (Experts 2, 14 and 21). Thus, it was challenging to find lecturers who were willing to use AI-ALS in their curricula.

4.2 Racial and Data Bias in AIEd

Other significant themes that emerged in this study were data bias and racial and inequality issues. Several researchers, such as [36] and [37] have explicitly identified case issues related to data, racial and other ethical concerns in AIEd. Expert 20 provided reasons for the existence of such racial and data bias: *"I'm sure that you know a common critique of the field is that it's predominantly white and male, and a lot of the algorithms that we produce are really good at predicting people who are white and male but tend to struggle in a lot of different areas"*. Moreover, due to racism and inequality existing in most countries, there has been unequal access to quality education. Expert 14 highlighted this: *"Because of the racial split in the United States, it's the poor and the urban, the people whose parents had to go out and work... parents who had a frontline job or we're in the service sector...that didn't get any support to study and work online...Is the same in the United States as anywhere else, you know, poor people...urban people get an inferior education. In the United States, especially because of COVID, the country is starting to admit that's a huge racial bias and huge lack of resources for students of color"*. Gupta et al. (2020) indicated that access to affordable broadband internet and smart devices, which are prerequisites for digital education, are not equally distributed and thus may introduce new forms of inequalities. Therefore, racial bias and inequality affect SDG targets related to providing free, affordable and quality education to all women and men (Targets 4.1 and 4.3). Other barriers that affect AI implementation in terms of meeting SDG4 were incorrect use of data and issues relating to modelling false negatives and false positives (Experts 12 and 21). Expert 12 elaborates on this: *"Let's take the example of looking for evidence that a student is not doing too well and need extra help. They look over past data about students and they try to find patterns in the data which say these students look like they need help. So, they compare the new student against data for those previous. Now that can kind of go wrong because you can get false positives and false negatives; you can end up offering a student who's doing perfectly well extra help which he or she doesn't need. That's not too dangerous, but it's a waste of resource"*. Thus, the wrong application of AI models and racial and data bias are crucial issues to be addressed.

4.3 Supporting Students with Intellectual Disabilities and Autism

One of the other interesting insights identified in this study was the application of AI in assisting students with autism and intellectual disabilities. Much research has been conducted that reveals the positive outcomes of using AI in the field of intellectual disabilities (Kazimzade, Patzer, & Pinkwart, 2019). Expert 13, for instance, conducted research to determine whether adopting technology in AI-ALS can help people who have cognitive challenges with school-based learning. Expert 6 also employed AI-ALS in two vocational schools for students who needed special educational assistance. Inclusive education is a target promoted in SDG4, with the explicit objective of ensuring equal access to all levels of education for persons with disabilities (Target 4.5). Thus, AI demonstrated effectiveness in meeting SDG4. However, several barriers were identified in using AI to assist such students. One major barrier was capturing students' data issues. Expert 13 gave the following example: *"There was one (student) that I was working with who wouldn't look at the camera, so we couldn't pick up lots of things. She sat sideways the whole time"*. Expert 6 identified this as well: *"Students with special education needs might not want to sit behind a computer patiently for a very long period of time; they might find it boring"*. Such cases impede the collection of student data, which could build a better future for AI-ALS systems. Other barriers highlighted were time and money issues. Again, Expert 6 elaborated on this: *"There is a lot of popular tools that teachers might already have in a special educational needs environment. They might not be translatable very easily to this (AI-ALS) system (in terms of content etc.), which might cause the adoption to be very expensive and time taken so it's all of that"*. Such barriers impede the role of AI in implementing SDG4.

4.4 Culturally Sensitive Design Issues of AI-ALS

Culturally sensitive design issues have also been identified as another theme. Mohammed and Watson [25] has explicitly identified and examined issues related to challenges faced when AIEd technologies aim to incorporate culturally sensitive design features. Contemporary learning systems, such as AI-ALS, are sometimes not adopted simply because of cultural design aspects. For instance, there are cases of contemporary learning systems that were built for one ethnicity being used for another. A good example of this was given by Expert 12: *"Let's say university has got a lot of Chinese students but the (learning system) model was built on European students. Now it could be that a Chinese student who maintains you know much calm face no matter what, is not helped. Because the model has been built on European students. So, I mean, we've gone offside bit sideways slightly, that is an educational consequence of building models you know"*. Thus, a lack of insufficient data for other ethnic groups impedes ensuring the provision of quality education for all (SDG4, Targets 4.1 and 4.3). Another example of cultural design mistakes was highlighted by Expert 5, in which they conduct projects for German companies that produce and develop systems in China: *"Their way about thinking and training is of course a German way of thinking about teaching and learning. So, what they do is they translate everything to Chinese and deploy it there. And (then they) are surprised that it doesn't work because apparently the culture refrain for a Chinese person. We know from interface design that Asian cultures have a different preference for interfaces. It's much more blinking and shining...So you need to translate that also to learning systems, right...And out of the blue you end up with what we would call cultural design of such systems"*.

4.5 Commercialisation of AI-ALS

There have been efforts to adopt AL-ALS widely and to commercialise it, which were initially developed in research. Expert 1 gave an example of Pearson acquiring the Smart Sparrow system. This system was initially developed by the University of New South Wales by the Adaptive eLearning Research Group at the School of Computer Science and Engineering. Expert 13 also discussed the commercialisation of AI-ALS: *"It was interesting...actually one of the aims of EU funding is try get you to the stage where companies are just ready to bite your hand off and take this product for commercial development. And we did have lots and lots of contacts, so when we had the final review meeting, the people who were responsible for commercialisation of it gave lots of companies...".* The commercial development of AI-ALS has assisted in the wide adoption of these novel learning systems and can thus help achieve SDG4 by ensuring equal access to quality education (Target 4.3).

However, despite the significant efforts, there are still issues that challenge the ability of AI to meet SDG4. One identified issue is the fact that some AI-ALS have become proprietary systems and thus no longer affordable and free. Expert 1 expressed his disappointment in detail: *"And I believe...a major reason why these systems are not widely adopted. First, because they are expensive because they are proprietary, so they are closed systems and people want things that are more open, that they can develop something, that they can reuse, you know, and export. And that's a major problem, because if I look back and I see the work that was involved and then I cannot really take advantage of it, it it's really disappointing"*. Expert 13 also noted that she did not see anything being done by companies responsible for the commercial development of AI systems after their review meeting during the EU funding process.

5 Implications and Recommendations

A nation's development is generally determined by the quality of education its society provides. This is substantiated by the United Nations' decision to formulate SDGs, including SDG4, which focuses on education [38]. To achieve SDG4, three key areas need to be addressed: education facilities and learning environments that are safe and equipped with advanced technology, support for students to obtain regular access to education (financial and otherwise) and an adequate supply of qualified and motivated teachers [39]. At present, AI is becoming increasingly important and integral to supporting global sustainability trends and quality education. Researchers and innovators using AI-ALS are advancing education and assisting in achieving SDG4. [2–4, 40] and [15] show the importance of AI in SDG4. We extend these findings by conducting a qualitative case study on the role of AI and identifying benefits and challenges for AIEd implementation. This study contributes to ongoing research on how AI can provide quality education for all. The study also contributes to the literature by identifying challenges impeding AIEd implementation, such as algorithmic bias and poor representativeness. The study provides important insights for practitioners and educators who are interested in using AI to achieve SDG4. In this section, the implications of the study and recommendations for future research are discussed.

One of the practical implications of this study involves the role of AI and teachers in education. More research should be done to reinforce the role of AI in assisting teachers, not replacing them. Several studies, such as [41, 42] and [43], have discussed this issue. Moreover, there should be more research on the benefits of AIEd implementation. These benefits include helping reduce the teachers' workload, communicating with students, helping students, and improving the effectiveness of systems in tutoring students (Experts 10 and 21). Another recommendation is to train teachers on how to use AI-ALS so that they can improve their teaching and productivity (Expert 5). Teachers should be encouraged to learn new digital skills to use AI in a pedagogical manner, while AI-ALS developers should also learn how teachers work to create sustainable solutions in real educational settings [3]. Further research on the pedagogical aspects of AI-ALS should also be conducted. Expert 18 stated that the above is possible through more collaboration (interdisciplinary work) between educational (pedagogy) and technical experts. Thus, the call for invitations for AI experts and educational researchers to fully collaborate in the technological innovation process will further advance AIEd [22].

Moreover, developers and researchers in AIEd should have a contextual understanding of the learning systems enabled by AI. It is noteworthy to consider and understand education in its social context. Education is preeminently a social interaction between teachers and learners in social contexts (Expert 21). The main objects of any educational setting are human learners and teachers. Thus, there needs to be more attempts to develop systems that take account of all the main players in a complex educational ecosystem [44]. In terms of data and racial bias, it is preferable to develop algorithms based on groups of people rather than on an individual level. According to expert 20, it is more effective to find meaningful statistical differences at the group level and personalise around that information than to personalise down to the individual level. Programming for four or five different groups is much easier and also makes it easier to evaluate outcomes. AI-ALS designers and developers will be better equipped to produce positive education outcomes if they are more willing to think about the different kinds of people their systems serve [45, 46]. In addition, algorithms should be tested to determine how they affect specific groups of people (such as those defined by race and gender) before deployment [47]. Furthermore, members of communities affected by algorithms should be involved throughout the development process and the use of algorithms in education [36, 48].

Finally, the other barrier identified in this study that needs to be addressed is time, financial and other resource constraints, such as poor internet connectivity. Developing and designing AI-ALS involves a lot of investment in terms of time, finances and even human resources (Experts 21, 1, 19 and 2). Moreover, limited time can lead to developers acting negatively, as they "kind of cut corners and so don't necessarily reach the full potential of AI-ALS" development projects (Expert 10). In addition, AI-ALS rely on good internet; hence, poor internet connectivity can limit the implementation of AIEd. Therefore, it is recommended that administrative and financial support should be provided to support AIEd implementation. In the USA, for instance, during the pandemic, there was a major effort to ensure students have the resources to study online. Some students in resource-constrained environments were handed with computers and internet installed in their homes (Expert 14). The State Department also provided teachers with money to purchase online learning systems that helped teach their students during the pandemic. Moreover, the use of existing resources, such as iPhones, for facial tracking data collection will help alleviate cost and integration barriers (Expert 6). Moreover, collaboration among different research groups and institutions can render the issue of a lack of administrative and financial support (Experts 4, 19 and 18). The above-mentioned recommendations are only a few examples of how AI could help make education more inclusive and accessible.

This study has several limitations due to its nature. The sample population chosen might hinder the transferability and generalizability of the study, given that the author worked with a small sample, who were primarily from developed countries. Thus, given the small sample size of the study, further research should focus on incorporating more perspectives from other experts in the AIEd community. Moreover, further research should include more perspectives from experts in developing countries.

References

1. Nguyen, G., et al.: Machine learning and deep learning frameworks and libraries for large-scale data mining: a survey. Artif. Intell. Rev. **52**(1), 77–124 (2019). https://doi.org/10.1007/s10462-018-09679-z
2. UNESCO: AI and education guidance for policymakers (2021)
3. Pedro, F., Subosa, M., Rivas, A., Valverde, P.: Artificial intelligence in education: challenges and opportunities for sustainable development. Work. Pap. Educ. Policy **7**, 46 (2019)
4. Goralski, M.A., Tan, T.K.: Artificial intelligence and sustainable development. Int. J. Manag. Educ. **18**(1), 100330 (2020)
5. Winkler, R., Soellner, M.: Unleashing the potential of chatbots in education: a state-of-the-art analysis. Acad. Manag. Proc. **2018**(1), 15903 (2018)
6. Makala, B.B., Schmitt, M., Caballero, A.: How artificial intelligence can help advance post-secondary learning in emerging markets (2021)
7. Tyson, M.M., Sauers, N.J.: School leaders' adoption and implementation of artificial intelligence. J. Educ. Adm. **59**(3), 271–285 (2021)
8. Pappas, I.O., Giannakos, M.N.: Rethinking learning design in IT education during a pandemic. Front. Educ. **6**, April 2021
9. Verdú, E., et al.: Intelligent tutoring interface for technology enhanced learning in a course of computer network design. In: Proceedings - Frontiers in Education Conference, FIE, vol. 2015, February 2015
10. Baker, R.S.: Stupid tutoring systems, intelligent humans. Int. J. Artif. Intell. Educ. **26**(2), 600–614 (2016). https://doi.org/10.1007/s40593-016-0105-0
11. Kabudi, T., Pappas, I., Olsen, D.H.: AI-enabled adaptive learning systems: a systematic mapping of the literature. Comput. Educ. Artif. Intell. **2**, 100017 (2021)
12. Somyürek, S.: The new trends in adaptive educational hypermedia systems. Int. Rev. Res. Open Distance Learn. **16**(1), 221–241 (2015)
13. Cavanagh, T., Chen, B., Lahcen, R.A.M., Paradiso, J.: Constructing a design framework and pedagogical approach for adaptive learning in higher education: a practitioner's perspective. Int. Rev. Res. Open Distrib. Learn. **21**(1), 172–196 (2020)
14. Imhof, C., Bergamin, P., McGarrity, S.: Implementation of Adaptive Learning Systems: Current State and Potential, pp. 93–115. Springer, Cham (2020)
15. Vincent-Lancrin, S., van der Vlies, R.: Trustworthy artificial intelligence in education: pitfalls and pathways. OECD Education Working Paper No. 218 (2020)
16. Park, H., College, G.G., Robertson, C.: The impact of active learning with adaptive learning systems in general education information technology courses. In: SAIS 2018 Proceedings (2018)
17. Nguyen, A., Gardner, L., Sheridan, D.: Data analytics in higher education: an integrated view. J. Inf. Syst. Educ. **31**(1), 61–71 (2020)
18. van der Vorst, T., Jelicic, N.: Artificial Intelligence in Education: Can AI Bring the Full Potential of Personalized Learning to Education? International Telecommunications Society (ITS), Calgary (2019)

19. Xie, H., Chu, H.C., Hwang, G.J., Wang, C.C.: Trends and development in technology-enhanced adaptive/personalized learning: a systematic review of journal publications from 2007 to 2017. Comput. Educ. **140**, 103599 (2019)
20. Wambsganss, T., Rietsche, R.: Towards designing an adaptive argumentation learning tool. In: 40th International Conference on Information Systems, ICIS 2019 (2019)
21. Addanki, K., Holdsworth, J., Hardy, D., Myers, T.: Academagogy for enhancing adult online learner engagement in higher education. In: Proceedings of the 2020 AIS SIGED International Conference on Information Systems Education and Research (2020)
22. Zhang, K., Aslan, A.B.: AI technologies for education: recent research & future directions. Comput. Educ. Artif. Intell. **2**, 100025 (2021)
23. Loebbecke, C., Picot, A.: Reflections on societal and business model transformation arising from digitization and big data analytics: a research agenda. J. Strateg. Inf. Syst. **24**(3), 149–157 (2015)
24. Hopkins, N., Tate, M., Sylvester, A., Johnstone, D.: Motivations for 21st century school children to bring their own device to school. Inf. Syst. Front. **19**(5), 1191–1203 (2016). https://doi.org/10.1007/s10796-016-9644-z
25. Mohammed, P.S., 'Nell' Watson, E.: Towards inclusive education in the age of artificial intelligence: perspectives, challenges, and opportunities. In: Knox, J., Wang, Y., Gallagher, M. (eds.) Artificial Intelligence and Inclusive Education. PRRE, pp. 17–37. Springer, Singapore (2019). https://doi.org/10.1007/978-981-13-8161-4_2
26. Woolf, B.P., Lane, H.C., Chaudhri, V.K., Kolodner, J.L.: AI grand challenges for education. AI Mag. **34**(4), 66–84 (2013)
27. Ryan, M., Antoniou, J., Brooks, L., Jiya, T., MacNish, K., Stahl, B.: Technofixing the future: ethical side effects of using AI and big data to meet the SDGs. In: Proceedings - 2019 IEEE SmartWorld, Ubiquitous Intelligence and Computing, Advanced and Trusted Computing, Scalable Computing and Communications, Internet of People and Smart City Innovation, SmartWorld/UIC/ATC/SCALCOM/IOP/SCI 2019, pp. 335–341 (2019)
28. Smith, M.L., Neupane, S.: Artificial intelligence and human development toward a research agenda. In: IDRC, p. 63 (2018)
29. Lim, C.P., Kumar Bhowmik, M.: Digital learning for developing Asia countries: achieving equity, quality, and efficiency in education (2018)
30. Yin, R.R.K.: Case Study Research: Design and Methods, 4th edn. Sage, Thousand Oaks (2009)
31. Fernández, W., Lehmann, H.: Achieving rigour and relevance in information systems studies: using grounded theory to investigate organizational cases. Grounded Theory Rev. **5**(1), 79–107 (2005)
32. Creswell, J.W., Creswell, J.D.: Research Design: Qualitative, Quantitative, and Mixed Methods Approaches. Sage, Thousand Oaks (2017)
33. Saldaña, J.: The Coding Manual for Qualitative Researchers. Sage, Thousand Oaks (2009)
34. Braun, R., Benedict, M., Wendler, H., Esswein, W.: Proposal for requirements driven design science research. In: Donnellan, B., Helfert, M., Kenneally, J., VanderMeer, D., Rothenberger, M., Winter, R. (eds.) DESRIST 2015. LNCS, vol. 9073, pp. 135–151. Springer, Cham (2015). https://doi.org/10.1007/978-3-319-18714-3_9
35. Feine, J., Morana, S., Maedche, A.: Leveraging machine-executable descriptive knowledge in design science research – the case of designing socially-adaptive chatbots. In: Tulu, B., Djamasbi, S., Leroy, G. (eds.) DESRIST 2019. LNCS, vol. 11491, pp. 76–91. Springer, Cham (2019). https://doi.org/10.1007/978-3-030-19504-5_6
36. Baker, R.S., Hawn, A.: Algorithmic bias in education. Int. J. Artif. Intell. Educ. 1–41, November 2021
37. Williamson, B., Eynon, R.: Historical threads, missing links, and future directions in AI in education. Learn. Media Technol. **45**(3), 223–235 (2020)

38. Meroyi, S.I.: Operationalising sustainable development goal (SDG) 4 in Nigeria: artificial intelligence and employability of graduates. Sapientia Found. J. Educ. **2**(2), 146–152 (2020)
39. Tatto, M.T.: Comparative research on teachers and teacher education: global perspectives to inform UNESCO's SDG 4 agenda. Oxford Rev. Educ. **47**(1), 25–44 (2021)
40. Kazimzade, G., Patzer, Y., Pinkwart, N.: Artificial intelligence in education meets inclusive educational technology—the technical state-of-the-art and possible directions. In: Knox, J., Wang, Y., Gallagher, M. (eds.) Artificial Intelligence and Inclusive Education. PRRE, pp. 61–73. Springer, Singapore (2019). https://doi.org/10.1007/978-981-13-8161-4_4
41. Guilherme, A.: AI and education: the importance of teacher and student relations. AI Soc. **34**(1), 47–54 (2017)
42. Holstein, K., McLaren, B.M., Aleven, V.: Co-designing a real-time classroom orchestration tool to support teacher – AI complementarity. J. Learn. Anal. **6**(2), 27–52 (2019)
43. Felix, C.V.: The role of the teacher and AI in education. In: International Perspectives on the Role of Technology in Humanizing Higher Education, pp. 33–48. Emerald Publishing Limited (2020)
44. du Boulay, B.: Jim Greer's and Mary Mark's reviews of evaluation methods for adaptive systems: a brief comment about new goals. Int. J. Artif. Intell. Educ. **31**(3), 622–635 (2020). https://doi.org/10.1007/s40593-020-00198-z
45. Bellamy, R.K.E., et al.: AI fairness 360: an extensible toolkit for detecting and mitigating algorithmic bias. IBM J. Res. Dev. **63**(4–5) (2019)
46. Sahlgren, O.: The politics and reciprocal (re)configuration of accountability and fairness in data-driven education. Learn. Media Technol. (2021)
47. Sun, W., Nasraoui, O., Shafto, P.: Evolution and impact of bias in human and machine learning algorithm interaction. PLoS One **15**(8), e0235502 (2020)
48. Kuhlman, C., Jackson, L., Chunara, R.: No computation without representation: avoiding data and algorithm biases through diversity. arXiv preprint. arXiv:2002.11836 (2020)

Machine Learning in Sub-Saharan Africa: A Critical Review of Selected Research Publications, 2010–2021

Judy van Biljon[✉]

University of South Africa, Pretoria, South Africa
vbiljja@unisa.ac.za

Abstract. Machine learning, a field of artificial intelligence application, will profoundly impact countries in sub-Saharan Africa (SSA) in the next few decades. The extent of the impact will depend largely on the countries' readiness. Roadmaps and research agendas towards implementing machine learning for development (ML4D) exist, but little is known about the state of ML4D research in sub-Saharan Africa. Guided by an existing ML4D roadmap, we conducted a critical literature review on selected research publications papers published from 2010 to 2021 with the aim of describing the status of SSA ML publications and informing future research. This should be of interest to researchers and funding organizations investigating the potential impact of ML4D projects in the SSA region.

Keywords: ML4D · AI4D · Machine learning · Development · Artificial intelligence

1 Introduction

The relationship between information and communication technologies (ICTs) and international development is dynamic and constantly evolving (Heeks 2020a). The geopolitical discourses on technology adoption have evolved from techno-centric approaches aimed at replacing human capacity, to more holistic design perspectives aimed at augmenting human capacity and enabling meaningful human practices in which technology plays a part. Digitalisation has paved the way for datafication, the masses of digital traces left by people and technologies in online spaces and the proliferation of advanced tools for the integration, analysis, and visualization of data patterns for purposes of decision making and commercialization (Flyverbom et al. 2019). Nonetheless, society still needs to come to terms with artificial intelligence (AI) applications where those applications are used to augment and, increasingly replace human decision making in data intensive, socially sensitive decision processes like loan-approvals, hiring and granting parole to people (Mehrabi et al. 2021). This is especially challenging for sub-Saharan African (SSA) countries, some of which are still coming to terms with issues surrounding the first three industrial revolutions, e.g. problems relating to universal access to electricity, mechanization of production, and industry automation (Butcher et al. 2021).

© IFIP International Federation for Information Processing 2022
Published by Springer Nature Switzerland AG 2022
Y. Zheng et al. (Eds.): ICT4D 2022, IFIP AICT 657, pp. 363–376, 2022.
https://doi.org/10.1007/978-3-031-19429-0_22

Against the background of SSA countries having severe challenges in preparing for the optimal and sustainable use of AI, it is imperative to align the efforts of the different stakeholders by having a shared conceptualisation of what is feasible and what is advisable. The focus of this paper is on Machine learning (ML), a subset of AI that refers to the ability of computers to process information relating to a specific task and use the results to adjust their behaviour to maximise their chances of achieving their goals without being explicitly programmed to do so (Mann and Hubert 2020). There are clear benefits to algorithmic decision-making. Machines can take into account orders of magnitude more factors than humans can and machines do not become tired or bored (Mehrabi et al. 2021). However, like humans, algorithms are vulnerable to biases (Ferrer et al. 2021). This can lead to digital discrimination, which means users are treated unfairly, unethically or just differently based on their personal data that is automatically processed by an algorithm (Criado and Such 2019).

Africa has been a playground for Western researchers (Bai 2018). While their involvement has produced significant positive outcomes in terms of research impact (van Biljon and Renaud 2019) it is important to guard against Africa becoming a dumping ground for perceived challenges, imposed problems and barriers which limit the use of AI in the attainment of sustainable development objectives. In trying to make sense of the AI value proposition and the consequences of adoption, researchers can become polarized along disciplinary lines. Researchers in the physical sciences may focus on AI-related solutions and progress which creates a positive AI narrative, while researchers in the humanities focus on the biases and discrimination which create a negative AI narrative. As noted, finding solutions to bias and discrimination in AI requires robust cross-disciplinary collaboration (Ferrer et al. 2021). Therefore, the different stakeholders need to interact to ensure a contextually sensitive, holistic approach; if there is no shared awareness and interdisciplinary knowledge exchange is not managed, then it can lead to siloed thinking, ill-advised actions and policies.

The advancements of AI are set to continue and impact all countries, regardless of their geography, actual or perceived readiness to benefit from the use of AI and other emerging (Butcher et al. 2021). ML applications have proven valuable in addressing some problems associated with less developed contexts and there is the undeniably potential to extend human capabilities. However, to harness the benefits of technology and to blunt its worst disruptions, developing countries will need to take rapid action to ensure they can compete in the economy of the future, specifically by investing in health and education as the building blocks of human capital (World Bank Report 2019). Accordingly, the potential of ML technology when investigating SSA problems merits attention but there are numerous challenges to consider (Mann and Hubert 2020). Besides the problems with data availability, computing capacity and relevant skills (Weber and Toyama 2010), there is the risk of introducing bias, in the data and/or the algorithm. To manage the complexities of adopting ML4D solutions research it is necessary to formulate theorizations that can guide the consideration of goals, prerequisites, stakeholders etc. To address this problem, research agendas (Butcher et al. 2021; Smith and Neupane 2018) and a ML4D roadmap (De-Arteaga et al. 2018) have been developed to guide the adoption of AI technologies. Given the dynamic, ever-evolving nature of ICT4D a critical overview of SSA literature published on ML4D could be useful to improve our understanding of what has been published and to inform future research in the domain. The rest of the paper is organised as follows: Sect. 2 will provide an overview of the relevant literature, Sect. 3 will present the research design, results and findings with the conclusion being discussed in Sect. 4.

2 Overview of Related Literature

2.1 ICTs and International Development

Information and communication technology for development (ICT4D) refers to the academic field concerned with the use of ICTs for international development with the focus on the so-called developing countries and particular emphasis on the less materially advantaged members of those societies (Walsham 2017). Sein et al. (2019) argue that three concepts, namely ICT, D and the catchall term '4' or 'for' lie at the root of the definition of the interdisciplinary ICT4D field. Related to each concept is a specific group of theories, the first group focuses on Development theories i.e., What is development (D)? The second group focuses on theories conceptualizing ICT, i.e., What is ICT in the context of development? The third and final group of theories focus on transformative processes linking ICT to D i.e., How does ICT make D happen?

An in-depth discussion of these groups of theories and the three ICT4D components are beyond the scope of this paper where the focus is on the ML research that has been conducted in the ICT4D domain. Digital information and communication technologies (ICTs) impact international development on the micro and the macro levels. At the macro level, many studies have employed quantitative data analyses to investigate the impact of digital information and communication technologies (ICTs) on international development. For example, Bankole and Mimbi (2017) used previous research in the domain to propose a research direction for macro/micro level impact of ICT on national development on the African continent while Gwagwa et al. (2020) considered policy responses to AI. At the micro (individual) level, impact can be viewed through one or more of the following lenses: (1) economic development as accumulation of financial capital, (2) livelihood development as accumulation of livelihood assets; including not just money but also health, skills, information, etc., and (3) capabilities development as greater freedom on what to be and to do (Heeks 2014). From the livelihoods and the capability view of the micro level, the core development concept of context comes into play. Sein et al. (2019) argue that any holistic understanding of the use of ICT for development needs to include a contextual understanding of the theoretical premise of ICT, development and the transformative process by which ICT may lead to development. Taking a cultural view of context, Davison and Martinsons (2016) argue that in an increasingly globalised world, the context of locally distinctive values and behaviours will become more important.

As noted, the relationship between ICTs and development is constantly evolving (Heeks 2020a). Considering poverty alleviation as the main driver in ICT4D 1.0 marginalized the poor in developing countries allowing a supply-driven focus characterising users largely as passive consumers; ICT4D 2.0 focuses on centralizing them thereby creating a demand-driven focus which characterized them as active producers and innovators (Heeks 2020b). Now ICT4D 3.0, also described as *digital-for-development,* is emerging as a new paradigm between digital technologies and international development. Several factors support the 'digital-for-development' drive. The shift in focus, from the proliferation of communication and information to the extraction of knowledge from the resulting data (Mann and Hubert 2020). The interest in and the availability of open-source data (Kitchin 2014), the advent of deep learning, and the proliferation of machine learning tools (Kumar and Sharma 2021). These developments created the expectation that AI as a tool could be used to solve many of the developing world's problems like the unrealistic expectations once associated with ICT4D.

Considering the issues and contentions in responsible business and digital transformation, Flyverbom et al. (2019) consider the most common ethical issues at the upstream level to be the violation and intrusion of privacy, the consent of the data provider, and the transparency with which big data companies collect the information. Clearly, those issues could apply to developing contexts too. Given the potential risk of bias in the datasets selected and in the algorithms applied (Ferrer et al. 2021), we are at risk of perpetuating historical and contemporary socioeconomic disparities if the research problem, design and interpretation of the findings are not contextually sensitive. The next section will briefly review AI, ML and International Development.

2.2   Artificial Intelligence, Machine Learning and International Development

Weber and Toyama (2010), when considering on-the-ground projects in development, highlight the following challenges to using artificial intelligence techniques to impact a poor community (a) finding large-scale data in an appropriate format, (b) the low cost of labour and (c) the fact that a lack of intelligence is often not the bottleneck. Mann and Hilbert (2020) identified the tension between global efficiency and local needs as one of the issues at the crossroads of AI/ML and development. For example, automating labour conflicts with local need for jobs. Resolving, or at least, balancing these tensions is pivotal in the quest to harness the potential of AI/ML techniques and practices for designing at the margins. For example, the ability to perform automatic pattern recognition may prove useful when experts are either costly or unavailable in a specific country or region (Weber and Toyama 2010). While acknowledging the real challenges mentioned regarding AI4D (with ML4D as sub-field) we argue that there is value in researching the use of AI for development by researchers in developing contexts. Resource-constrained contexts have implications for socio-economic development efforts in the sense that resources are scarce and should not be wasted in pursuit of non-practicable and unsustainable solutions.

To guide future investments in capacity building for responsible AI development and deployment, (Butcher et al. 2021) investigated the AI landscape in SSA, specifically what capacity already exists and what measures stakeholders in the region are taking to ensure that they are AI-ready. They identified the stakeholder groups as Centres of Higher Education and Training, Members of the AI Community and Government and made recommendations on AI-related Academic Activities, Research and Development, Policy Environment, Challenges and Capacity Building Needs and Diversity in AI-related Activities. Researchers applying AI in Developing Contexts have to consider context-specific challenges in terms of data, usability and resources (Weber and Toyama 2010). Furthermore, Smith and Neupane (2018) suggest that the digital and analogue foundations required for an ethical and equitable application of the technology in many countries in the Global South are largely absent while salient power asymmetries remain. The constraints and challenges mentioned may lead us to question the feasibility of applying AI in Developing Contexts. On the other hand, the proliferation of software tools allows even naive users to develop ML-based models for their respective problem domains (Kumar and Sharma 2021). Therefore, the more useful question to engage on is: What research has been done on the topic of applying ML to Developing Countries, specifically SSA?

Accordingly, De-Arteaga et al. (2018) proposed the following key properties for ML allocations in the developing world (ML4D).

- Applications and data are geographically constrained to developing countries.
- Problems concern a critical development area for the region of interest.
- Substantially uses ML as an integral element
- Problems being addressed or contextual elements necessitate solutions that differ from existing or plausible solutions in developed regions, and the proposed solution effectively addresses these differences.

The ML4D research roadmap proposed by De-Arteaga et al. (2018) as depicted in Fig. 1, suggests three technical stages where ML4D can play an essential role and meaningfully contribute to global development, namely to (1) improve data reliability, (2) provide direct solutions and deployed systems, and (3) to inform policy and decision makers. Each of the three stages is then linked to novel ML methods to be applied in the ML4D context.

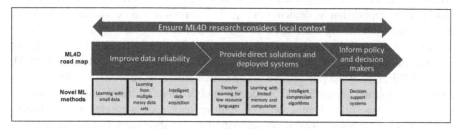

Fig. 1. ML4D Roadmap (De-Arteaga et al. 2018)

This roadmap was used as a point of departure in analyzing the findings of the literature review as described in Sect. 3.3. The next section will discuss the research design.

3 Research Design

The research design involved a critical review (as a type of systematic literature review) on ML4D in SSA based on a selected set of papers from 2010 to 2021. The aim of systematic literature reviews is to go beyond aggregating existing evidence toward constructing lessons from the accumulated literature (Kitchenham et al. 2009) and support the analysis of the literature in a research domain. Grant and Booth (2009) proposed a topology of literature reviews whereby, the most basic type of review (literature review) is useful for building on previous work, avoiding duplication and identifying gaps in the literature. Chatterjee and Davison (2021:228) argue that the gap-spotting approach is built on a fallacious argument since it assumes the fact that a research study has not been done, implies that there is value (a contribution) in doing it. Therefore, we opted for the critical review which has the descriptive purpose of a literature review but goes beyond that, i.e. it aims to demonstrate that the literature has been researched extensively and reviewed critically to include a degree of analysis and conceptual innovation which typically results in a hypothesis or model (Grant and Booth 2009; Bandara et al. 2015). Bramer et al. (2018) propose a systematic search strategy to develop literature searches starting with clear and focused questions. Considering the purpose mentioned, this research question is formulated as: What research has been done on the topic of applying ML to Sub-Saharan Africa? The review procedure is explained in Sect. 3.1 and the results in Sect. 3.2 and Sect. 3.3 respectively. Ethical clearance for this study was obtained from the College Research and Ethics Committee of the University of South Africa.

3.1 Literature Analysis

The literature review was carried out to construct a corpus of papers representative of ML4D research conducted in SSA for the period 2010 to 2021. Grant and Booth (2009) characterize the review types in terms of the purpose of the search, appraisal, synthesis and analysis but do not prescribe the relevant procedures. Therefore, we followed the PRISMA (Page et al. 2017) guidelines to be transparent in the reporting of the methods and facilitate replication as depicted in Fig. 2. The review was conducted in the week of 6 August 2021, using the search string: "Machine Learning" AND ("Developing Countries" OR "Developing World") for the period 2010 to 2021. Due to the wide and interdisciplinary scope of interest in ML, we included the following databases ACM, Inspec, IEEE, DBLP, Scopus and WoS. The search criteria were set to include only conference and journal papers and 1706 records (publications) were identified as meeting said criteria. These titles were screened to remove items such as patents, magazine articles, abstracts from books, workshops and bulletins published in conference proceedings because the scope and format of these items were not comparable to the conference and journal publications. Removing these 555 items, 1151 records remained for retrieval. Considering these 1151 records, the location where the research was done was captured using the title, abstract or the full paper if necessary. For 337 publications the region was not specified and for 717 publications the research was from other parts of the world (not conducted in SSA). Having removed those, 98 publications remained for analysis on ML research done in SSA. Considering the 98 records of studies conducted in SSA, 4 were inaccessible so the final corpus consisted of 93 papers.

Bandara et al. (2015) suggest the inductive approach for coding when the themes to be reported on are purely derived from the literature analysis and the deductive approach when the themes to be reported on are predetermined to some extent by using coding schemes or theorizations like theoretical lenses, models, frameworks or alignment with

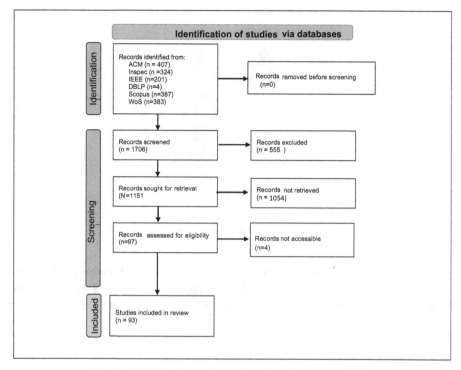

Fig. 2. PRISMA Flow diagram based on Page et al. (2017)

specific research questions. Bramer et al. (2018) concurs on the usefulness of prede-termined themes and suggests finding articles appropriate for guiding the research and analysis strategy. The most appropriate paper in this regard was the ML4D roadmap (De-Arteaga et al. 2018) as depicted in Fig. 1 and hence those themes were applied in guiding the analysis (see Sect. 3.3).

3.2 Publication's Overview

The 93 publications were first analysed to provide an overview in terms of the distribution across years, domains, and countries. Figure 3 depicts the number of publications per country. It can be observed that most studies were done in South Africa (16). Kenya (14) has the same number as the group of cross-border studies (not indicated on the map), followed by Nigeria (12) and Ethiopia (10). This is followed by Ghana (4), Mozambique, Senegal and Tanzania each three with a number of countries contributing two or less studies. It is unknown how many publications appear in other languages but having the English language as an inclusion criterion is possibly a limitation in providing a holistic view of SSA research publications.

Figure 4 depicts the papers per year, showing significant growth in the number of papers since 2010, especially since 2017. Note that the year 2021 was captured only until 6 August 2021, so the number of publications in 2021 is likely to exceed all previous years. A simplistic extrapolation would put the final number for 2021 at 19. The

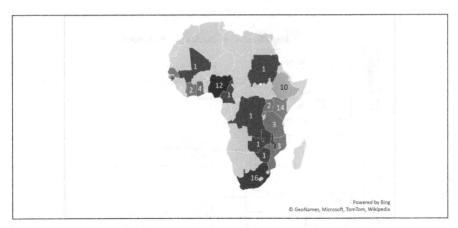

Fig. 3. Number of publications per-country

publications selected consist of 58 conference publications and 35 journal publications. This resonates with the fact that the field is dynamic, and researchers might need the quicker turnaround times associated with publishing in conference proceedings.

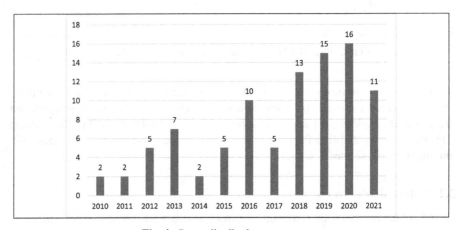

Fig. 4. Paper distribution across years

The distribution of the publications across domains is presented in Fig. 5. The highest concentration of publications was found in Manufacturing (28%) which includes Engineering and several publications where ML techniques were used to optimise systems. This is followed by Health (21%) and the Environment (12%) of the publications with the rest all below 10%. The relatively few papers on Education is noteworthy, considering that Health and Education were highlighted as priority fields in the World Bank report on the changing nature of work (World Bank Report 2019). The challenges with data availability and quality received from the Education systems as well as the political and cultural challenges with the classification of students according to their performance

(Archer and Prinsloo 2020) would be some of the factors limiting research in the Education domain. Research on the social aspects would fall into the *Other* category. The papers in that category includes the use of ML techniques to address social challenges like illuminating the working of an informal industry on one of the poorest countries (Björkegren 2020). The paper on narratives and counternarratives on data sharing in Africa (Abebe et al. 2021) engages with issues arising from power imbalances and identify recurring barriers to data sharing as well as inequities in the distribution of data sharing benefits.

Based on a literature survey (Mehrabi et al. 2021) propose a taxonomy on bias and fairness in Machine Learning which includes 23 types of bias and six types of discrimination. Their paper provides evidence of a dynamic body of research into the social impacts of ML, but apart from a few examples like the paper by Abebe et al. (2021) the latter is not evident from the ML4D SSA literature surveyed in this study. This could be indicative of the complexities involved in classifying interdisciplinary research into distinct categories. However, more research is needed to investigate whether the research on ethical and responsible AI is being published in electronic databases not included in this study or whether this points to an actual gap in the ML4D literature. Assuming that research is published elsewhere this still raises questions about the apparent lack of interdisciplinary research on the ML4D topic.

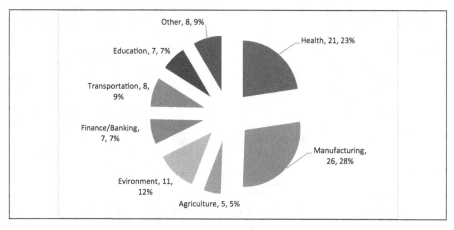

Fig. 5. Research domains

3.3 ML4D Roadmap

Another approach is to consider the elements of the ML4D roadmap De-Arteaga et al. (2018) as a point of departure in making sense of the results of the critical review. Notably, the roadmap was suggested for ML4D and not for ML4D research, so it is necessary to consider how, if at all, those elements can inform research. Therefore each of the constructs depicted in Fig. 1 (De-Arteaga et al. 2018) are now considered in terms of their relevance for ML4D research.

Considering the *ML4D road map* and *novel ML Methods* components in Fig. 1, these constructs could be useful in informing research goals. Therefore, these were used as initial codes in analysing the data with Atlas.ti version 9. For example, the publications related to the code, *limited memory or computational capacity* as depicted in Fig. 6. There is evidence of publications related to each of these initial codes as depicted in Fig. 7 (the number in brackets indicates the number of sub-categories), additional categories such as *data accessibility* also emerged from the data. Besides confirming the relevance of the suggested categories, the importance of data-related issues when considering ML4D in the SSA context became evident. The data issues, as depicted in Fig. 8 include but are not limited to, data availability, absent data source, unbalanced data, collection challenges, quality issues and accessibility issues. Based on the number of data-related issues the construct *data availability* should be added since that cannot be assumed in SSA. Furthermore, it is a prerequisite for *data reliability* and the rest of the constructs mentioned in Fig. 1.

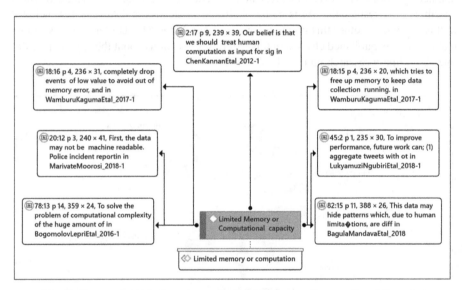

Fig. 6. Papers related to the category limited Memory or Computational Capacity

3.4 Summary

The insights based on the roadmap presented in Fig. 1 and the findings from the literature review are presented in Fig. 9. As with all research in developing countries, the context is imperative (Davison and Martinsons 2016) and this is also evident in the theoretical lenses applied by Sein et al. (2019). Therefore, the context element is presented not as a single construct but rather a pervasive, overarching and encompassing phenomenon. Concerning *Research Goals, Data Availability* has been added to the goals of *Data Reliability* and *Solutions and deployed Systems*. The papers relating to Education were

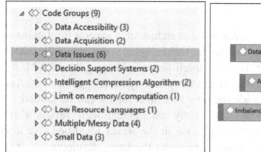

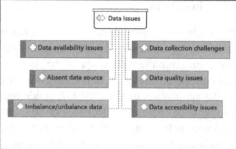

Fig. 7. Goals as code groups   **Fig. 8.** Data issue categories

focused on predicting academic performance (Mgala and Mbogho 2015) and a diversity of other projects e.g. a cloud-based infrastructure for digital content delivery (Mlitwa and Simbarashe 2019) not specifically on improving ML skills. However, Butcher et al. (2021) highlighted the importance of skills development in the Sub-Saharan regions and therefore *Skills Development* has been added to Fig. 9. *Decision Support* is a fundamental goal of ML research and has been retained. *Policy* encompasses all the ethical policies and requirements to mitigate bias and discrimination in the data capturing and the ML procedures applied. The *Methodological Considerations* retained the ML methods from Fig. 1 with the addition of Ethical considerations and Other to provide for new methods being added. Not to imply that the set of goals proposed are immutable, but methods are more reliant on technology and hence more susceptible to change.

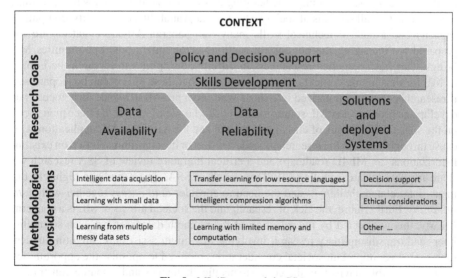

Fig. 9. ML4D research in SSA

3.5 Limitations

The study has a number of limitations. Keyword searches have several limitations in particular where keywords are related to specific technologies (Levy and Ellis 2006). However, given the wide scope of the Artificial Intelligence field using the term ML4D was considered necessary in focusing our efforts. Despite a rigorous approach enforced by the application of the PRISMA guideline, any literature survey can be faulted for having made contestable decisions (both intentionally and unintentionally) about which works to include and which elements to emphasise in the works identified. We also acknowledge the ambiguity and limitations surrounding the term 'development' (Sen 2001; Toyama 2010) but limit the discussion to aligning our perspective with the holistic perspective provided by Sein et al. (2019). For the purpose of this paper, we consider human development as going beyond socio-economic development toward increased freedom of choice (Sen 2001). ML is merely a tool whereof the application is determined by the researchers, consequently their theoretical lenses and goals determine what ML methods are relevant. Likewise, De-Arteaga et al. (2018) used specific lenses and granularities in suggesting the methodological considerations in their roadmap thereby making it difficult to evaluate and extend that. Adding a taxonomy of ML methods was considered but linking a taxonomy of methods to a context may be limiting. How to represent the relevant methods as part of informing future ML4D research could be considered towards future refinements of ML4D research roadmaps.

4 Conclusion

Artificial intelligence, with machine learning as sub-field is like a tidal wave spreading out and affecting all sections of society. Due to data availability, data quality, computing capacity and a lack of technical skills many Sub-Saharan African countries are ill-prepared for managing the possible disruptions or optimizing the opportunities ML brings. This has compelled researchers in different disciplines to research the impact of ML for developing contexts. Our contention is that these efforts can be jeopardised if researchers become polarized into those who seem pro-ML4D since their focus is to develop and promote new ML solutions and those who seem anti-ML4D since their focus on the societal challenges of classifying people and the harm that ML applications can cause through biases in the research procedures, data or the algorithms. Based on existing theorizations (an ML4D roadmap) and a critical literature review of SSA research we share insights towards guiding ML4D research in SSA. These findings highlight the many data-related challenges and the need to consider *data access* together with *data reliability*. Furthermore, the lack of research into the societal affects of ML is a concern. Clearly, this is affected by the selection of the research databases but even so multi-, inter- and transdisciplinary research involving ML might assist in highlighting under-represented yet important societal considerations required to optimise the opportunities while responsibly navigating the context-specific challenges and resource constraints. As noted a contextual understanding of what is feasible and desirable in the SSA context is essential as resources are scarce and should not be wasted in pursuit of impracticable and unsustainable projects.

Acknowledgement. This paper is based on the research supported by the South African Research Chairs Initiative of the Department of Science and Technology and National Research Foundation of South Africa (Grant No. 98564).

References

Abebe, R., et al.: Narratives and counternarratives on data sharing in Africa. In: Proceedings of the 2021 ACM Conference on Fairness, Accountability, and Transparency, pp. 329–341 (2021). https://doi.org/10.1145/3442188.3445897

Archer, E., Prinsloo, P.: Speaking the unspoken in learning analytics: troubling the defaults. Assess. Eval. High. Educ. **45**(6), 888–900 (2020). https://doi.org/10.1080/02602938.2019.1694863

Bai, Y.: Has the Global South become a playground for Western scholars in information and communication technologies for development? Evidence from a Three-Journal Analysis. Scientometrics **116**(3), 2139–2153 (2018)

Bandara, W., Furtmueller, E., Gorbacheva, E., Miskon, S., Beekhuyzen, J.: Achieving rigor in literature reviews: insights from qualitative data analysis and tool-support. Commun. Assoc. Inf. Syst. **37**, 154–204 (2015). https://doi.org/10.17705/1cais.03708

Bankole, F., Mimbi, L.: ICT infrastructure and it's impact on national development: a research direction for Africa. Afr. J. Inf. Syst. **9**(2), 1 (2017)

Björkegren, D.: Measuring informal work with digital traces: mobile payphone operators in Rwanda. PervasiveHealth Pervasive Comput. Technol. Healthc. (2020). https://doi.org/10.1145/3392561.3397576

Bramer, W.M., de Jonge, G.B., Rethlefsen, M.L., Mast, F., Kleijnen, J.: A systematic approach to searching: an efficient and complete method to develop literature searches. J. Med. Libr. Assoc. **106**(4), 531–541 (2018). https://doi.org/10.5195/jmla.2018.283

Butcher, N., Wilson-strydom, M., Baijnath, M.: Artificial intelligence capacity in Sub-Saharan Africa. Compendium report (2021)

Chatterjee, S., Davison, R.M.: The need for compelling problematisation in research: the prevalence of the gap-spotting approach and its limitations. Inf. Syst. J. **31**(2), 227–230 (2021). https://doi.org/10.1111/isj.12316

Criado, N., Such, J.: Digital discrimination. Digit. Discrim. (2019). https://doi.org/10.1093/oso/9780198838494.003.0004

Davison, R.M., Martinsons, M.G.: Context is King! J. Inf. Technol. **31**(3), 241–249 (2016)

De-Arteaga, M., Herlands, W., Neill, D.B., Dubrawski, A.: Machine learning for the developing world. ACM Trans. Manag. Inf. Syst. **9**(2) (2018). https://doi.org/10.1145/3210548

Gwagwa, A., Kraemer-Mbula, E., Rizk, N., Rutenberg, I., De Beer, J.: Artificial Intelligence (AI) deployments in Africa: benefits, challenges and policy dimensions. Afr. J. Inf. Commun. **26**, 1–28 (2020)

Ferrer, X., Nuenen, T.V., Such, J.M., Cote, M., Criado, N.: Bias and discrimination in AI: a cross-disciplinary perspective. IEEE Technol. Soc. Mag. **40**(2), 72–80 (2021). https://doi.org/10.1109/MTS.2021.3056293

Flyverbom, M., Deibert, R., Matten, D.: The governance of digital technology, big data, and the internet: new roles and responsibilities for business. Bus. Soc. **58**(1), 3–19 (2019). https://doi.org/10.1177/0007650317727540

Grant, M.J., Booth, A.: A typology of reviews: an analysis of 14 review types and associated methodologies. Health Info. Libr. J. **26**(2), 91–108 (2009). https://doi.org/10.1111/j.1471-1842.2009.00848.x

Heeks, R.: ICTs and poverty eradication: comparing economic, livelihoods and capabilities models. In: IDPM Development Informatics Working Paper no. 58, University of Manchester, UK (2014)

Heeks, R.: ICT4D 3.0? Part 1—The components of an emerging "digital-for-development" paradigm. Electron. J. Inf. Syst. Dev. Ctries. **86**(3), 1–15 (2020a). https://doi.org/10.1002/isd2.12124

Heeks, R.: ICT4D 3.0? Part 2—The patterns of an emerging "digital-for-development" paradigm. Electron. J. Inf. Syst. Dev. Ctries. **86**(3), 1–13 (2020b). https://doi.org/10.1002/isd2.12123

Kitchenham, B., Brereton, O.P., Budgen, D., Turner, M., Bailey, J., Linkman, S.: Systematic literature reviews in software engineering - a systematic literature review. Inf. Softw. Technol. **51**(1), 7–15 (2009). https://doi.org/10.1016/j.infsof.2008.09.009

Kitchin, R.: The Data Revolution: Big Data, Open Data, Data Infrastructures and Their Consequences. Sage, Thousand Oaks (2014)

Kumar, P., Sharma, M.: Data, machine learning, and human domain experts: none is better than their collaboration. Int. J. Hum. Comput. Interact. **38**(14), 1307–1320 (2021). https://doi.org/10.1080/10447318.2021.2002040

Levy, Y., Ellis, T.J.: A systems approach to conduct an effective literature review in support of Information Systems research. Inf. Sci. J. **9**, 1–32 (2006)

Mann, S., Hubert, M.: AI4D: artificial intelligence for development. Int. J. Commun. **14**, 4385–4405 (2020)

Mehrabi, N., Morstatter, F., Saxena, N., Lerman, K., Galstyan, A.: A survey on bias and fairness in machine learning. ACM Comput. Surv. (CSUR) **54**(6) (2021). https://doi.org/10.1145/3457607

Mgala, M., Mbogho, A.: Data-driven intervention-level prediction modeling for academic performance. In: ACM International Conference Proceeding Series, vol. 15 (2015). https://doi.org/10.1145/2737856.2738012

Mlitwa, N.B.W., Simbarashe, M.: A cloud-based architecture for a regional trans university learning management system collaboration on digital content delivery across Southern Africa. In: EDULEARN 2019 Proceedings, 1 July 2019, pp. 7819–7827 (2019). https://doi.org/10.21125/edulearn.2019.1903

Page, M., et al.: The PRISMA 2020 statement: an updated guideline for reporting systematic reviews. BMJ Br. Med. J. **372**(n71) (2017). http://www.prisma-statement.org/PRISMAStatement/FlowDiagram

Sein, M.K., Thapa, D., Hatakka, M., Sæbø, Ø.: A holistic perspective on the theoretical foundations for ICT4D research. Inf. Technol. Dev. **25**(1), 7–25 (2019). https://doi.org/10.1080/02681102.2018.1503589

Sen, A.: Development as freedom. Oxford Paperbacks (2001)

Smith, M.L., Neupane, S.: Artificial intelligence and human development toward a research agenda. International Development Research Centre (IDRC/CRDI) (2018). https://idl-bnc-idrc.dspacedirect.org/handle/10625/56949

Toyama, K.: Human-computer interaction and global development. Found. Trends Hum. Comput. Interact. **4**(1), 1–79 (2010). https://doi.org/10.1561/1100000021

van Biljon, J., Renaud, K.: Human-Computer Interaction for Development (HCI4D): the Southern African landscape. In: Nielsen, P., Kimaro, H.C. (eds.) ICT4D 2019. IAICT, vol. 552, pp. 253–266. Springer, Cham (2019). https://doi.org/10.1007/978-3-030-19115-3_21

Walsham, G.: ICT4D research: reflections on history and future agenda. Inf. Technol. Dev. **23**(1), 18–41 (2017)

Weber, J.S., Toyama, K.: Remembering the past for meaningful AI-D. In: AAAI Spring Symposium - Technical Report, SS-10-01, pp. 97–102, September 2010

World Bank Report: The changing nature of work. World Developemnt Report (2019). http://documents.worldbank.org/curated/en/816281518818814423/2019-WDR-Report.pdf

Datafication, Dehumanisation and Participatory Development

Tony Roberts[1(✉)] and Yingqin Zheng[2]

[1] Institute of Development Studies, Sussex, UK
t.roberts@ids.ac.uk
[2] Royal Holloway University of London, Egham, UK
yingqin.zheng@rhul.ac.uk

Abstract. This paper asks whether datafication practices are dehumanising international development and if a human-centred and participatory datafication is possible. The paper uses Habermas' theory of the different 'knowledge interests' that constitute different forms of social action. Three kinds of datafication projects are explored: humanitarian AI, digital-ID and community mapping. The authors argue that data-science and participatory practices are forms of social action that are shaped by different knowledge-interests. It is argued that the technical knowledge interests shaping datafication projects conflict with high-level policy commitments to participatory development. Ethical Principles of AI are assessed as a route to more human-centred practices of datafication for development. The authors argue that avoiding tokenistic forms of participation will require the incorporation of practical and emancipatory knowledge interests and the use of new monitoring and evaluation tools to trace the achieved levels of participation of different actors at each stage of the project cycle.

Keywords: Datafication · Participation · Dehumanisation · Human-centred · Artificial intelligence · Critical theory

1 Introduction

Datafication is transforming the landscape of international development. Datafication of development refers to the increased use of digital data in development knowledge production and decision-making processes [1]. The algorithmic processing of big data using artificial intelligence is impacting multiple areas of development practice [2]. Development agencies have been under significant pressure from funders to demonstrate innovation in the datafication of development [3, 4]. Humanitarian agencies have been under similar pressure to innovate using data from satellite imaging, remote sensing, biometric identification, social media, and other data sources to inform operational decision-making [5, 6]. The pressure to make digital data central to decision-making is reflected in a range of high-level policy commitments including the Digital Development

Principle[1] to *"be data driven"*. As a result, development agencies are active in supporting states in the datafication of areas including identification (digital-ID), border control, social protection, online government services, and predictive analytics [7, 8]. These data-centred innovations have delivered significant efficiencies and development benefits as well as introducing new risks and challenges. This paper is focused on whether this turn to data-centred development necessarily comes at the expense of existing commitments to human-centred development, and assesses the potential for synergy between the two approaches using participatory practices.

Prior to digitalisation, a citizen might seek development assistance via a face-to-face meeting with a government officer, an agricultural extension worker, or a community meeting. Participatory development aims to enhance the agency of marginalised people to take part in development decision-making that affects their lives through human-centred processes of dialogue and critical reflection [9, 10]. Some datafication processes explicitly aim to 'disintermediate' development processes by removing human intermediaries and the need for face-to-face human dialogue and interaction [11]. We argue that such processes can dehumanise the development process, making it more data-centred than human-centred and less participatory [6, 8]. We examine evidence that such processes of datafication disproportionately increase the agency and power of external actors and private corporations with the unintended consequence of widening inequality, reproducing unequal power relationships, and leaving behind the most marginalized [7, 12–15].

Information systems development has predominantly been considered as the application of the scientific method to increase efficiency and efficacy [16]. Walsham [17] was influential in popularising the use of interpretive theory as a lens to understand information and communication technology for development. There has been less use of critical theory to analyse digital development (see however [18–20]. This paper contributes to the later scholarship by combining Habermas' [21] critical theory from the Frankfurt School with critical participatory praxis from the global South.

Section 2 outlines Habermas' critical theory of knowledge interests and social action to argue that data science is shaped by the desire to predict and control. Section 3 reviews the impact of datafication in international development and the claim that it leads to dehumanization, exclusions, and widening power inequalities. Section 4 reviews the emergence of proposed new ethical principles for AI in international development and assesses them against critical theories of participatory development. Section 5 assesses whether participatory datafication is possible and whether new ethical principles can produce a more human-centred datafication in international development. Section 6 concludes that if marginalised people are to play a decision-making role in development projects affecting their lives then more practical and emancipatory knowledge interests are required alongside new practical tools to guide participation planning and evaluation in datafication projects.

---

[1] The Digital Development Principles were developed by funders, multi-laterals and international development agencies to guide the use of digital technologies in development. https://digitalpr inciples.org/.

2 A Habermasian Perspective on Data-Centred Development

This section introduces Habermas' critical theory of social action and his typology of knowledge interests as a theoretical foundation to examine the datafication of international development.

2.1 The Critical Theory of Habermas

A fundamental issue in digital development is which interests are prioritised and who benefits. This paper explores which interests are prioritised in data-centred approaches to international development. We draw on Habermas' critical theory of social action to illuminate these issues.

Habermas argues that the social action of humans is always constituted by what he called knowledge interests. In his book Knowledge and Human Interests, Habermas [21] (1972) claims that there are three kinds of fundamental human interests that determine three paradigms of knowledge production: *technical, practical and emancipatory*, as illustrated in Table 1. According to this perspective, the human desire to explain, control and predict constitutes the 'technical' knowledge interest that is characteristic of positivist empirical-analytical processes in the natural sciences. The human desire to understand meaning and to communicate constitutes the 'practical' knowledge interest that is characteristic of the interpretivist hermeneutical processes in the humanities. And for Habermas, the human desire to be free from domination constitutes the third category of 'emancipatory' knowledge interests that are characteristic of the critical social sciences. While these are ideal types that are not mutually exclusive, the categories are analytically useful.

Lyytinen and Klein [16] in their analysis of Habermas' critical theory show how the technical knowledge interest serves 'purposive-rational' social action based on empirical science that follows technical rules to maximise efficiency and achieve specific goals. In comparison, practical knowledge interest serves communicative social action to achieve mutual understanding, with an emphasis on common understanding of norms, meaning, values and maintaining social relationships. Achieving agreement through communicative action entails discursive processes that enable the assessment of the truth of statements, sincerity of speech and validity of claims. Emancipatory knowledge interests by comparison use social dialogue to critique the abuse of power; produce knowledge about the causes of social injustice, and guide social action to overcome it. Lyytinen and Klein [16] see the third category as uniting the other two knowledge interests with enquiries that use critical reflection to critique power inequality in order to inform social action to improve equity. Although analytically distinctive, in practice one approach often draws upon methods from the other: for example when critical-emancipatory approaches use discursive communicative action to investigate the validity of knowledge claims and truth statements.

2.2 Epistemological Underpinnings of Datafication in Development

Applying Habermas' critical theory, we can examine which knowledge interests and social actions are served in the processes of datafication and AI application, and what are the implications for international development.

Table 1. Aspects of knowledge interests. Source: [16]

Knowledge Interest	Social Action	Mediating Elements	Sciences	Purpose	Process
technical	purposive-rational	work systems	empirical-analytic	explanation, prediction, control	scientific method, verification
practical	commun-icative action	cultural institutions, natural language	historical-hermeneutic Geisten-wissen-schaften	understanding of meaning, expansion of inter-subjectivity	ideographic method, dialogue rules of hermeneutics
emancipatory	discursive action	power unwarranted constraints	critical sciences, psycho-analysis, philosophy	emancipation, rational consensus, Mundgkeit	reflective method criticism of assumptions

One of the attractions of data-driven development is the impression of scientific neutrality and precision provided by computing data with algorithms to produce what appear to be 'objective' truths. Epistemologically, data-centric development is often premised on big data as the source of knowledge for decision-making in development [4, 22–24]. Flyverbom et al. [25, p. 39] point out that big data "creates a different ground for the evaluation of 'truth'" in international development, by making knowledge claims on the basis of the large quantity of data, especially when they are real-time data. This also gives rise to the tendency of focusing on correlation rather than causation, which is increasingly used for decision-making.

This approach was evidenced when Hernandez and Roberts [8] reviewed 49 projects using predictive analytics in humanitarian work. Predictive analytics uses a form of artificial intelligence called machine learning to operate on big data sets using statistical modelling to make predictions about the probability of future events (ibid). It is used to support decision-making in humanitarian responses to drought and mass population displacements, to inform the allocation of staff and the management of supply chains. Predictive analytics is also used to inform social protection entitlements, employment decisions, policing and criminal justice, and governance decision-making [26–29]. Apart from humanitarian agencies the next most common actor in humanitarian predictive analysis projects was private corporations including Microsoft, Google and the global association of mobile phone companies GSMA [8]. Some concerns have been raised about the increasing role of private corporations in datafication for development and the accompanying shift in power away from disadvantaged people [7]. Privacy International [30] raised serious concerns about the World Food Programme sharing its humanitarian data with private sector data partner Palantir and court cases are pending regarding the role of Facebook data in the Rohinga genocide [31].

It is clear that a rule-bound technical rationality is employed in data-centred development that seeks to optimise efficiency, control and predictability in ways that echo Habermas' first category. The efficient calculation and allocation of human and material resources are no doubt important aspects of international development. While datafication and AI may serve instrumental and strategic purposes in international development, e.g. increasing managerial efficiency and fulfilling strategic objectives of power holders, it is important to recognise that the knowledge created through datafication and machine learning does not necessarily corresponding to any 'objective truth'. The assumption that big data is better than localised, situated, and contextualised 'thick data' is highly problematic. First of all, the term 'raw data' is an oxymoron as data is always already 'cooked' [32, 33]. As Manovich [34, p. 224] puts it, "Data does not just exist – it has to be generated". Data is generated by selectively subtracting from reality, a reductive process resulting in binary ones and zeros. In the sociology of knowledge, it has long been recognised that scientific facts are products of a series of human choices in categorisation, labelling, and measurement, produced in contested processes [35]. As a result, data is always partial, biased, and political. Similarly, machine learning is not neutral, it inherits the ontology, bias, and politics already baked into the data sets on which it relies.

Furthermore, through the extraction and decontextualisation of big data, data-centred development inevitably marginalises *practical knowledge* grounded in the shared understanding of local norms and social relations which have been proven to be imperative in the sustainability and inclusiveness of development projects. This practical knowledge and the human ability to interpret it contextually, is subtracted when big data is collected and fed into machine learning processes. Furthermore, datafication and algorithms that are effectively black-boxed are not transparent or accountable to human questioning; this inevitably diminishes emancipatory knowledge interests' ability to challenge any unwarranted abuse of power. The opacity and the lack of accountability of datafication and algorithmic processes substantially undermines the agency of local participants to: verify the knowledge claims put forward by datafication decision making; examine the underlying power relations; or participate in the knowledge creation and decision-making process; principles which are essential to human-centred development. While machine learning has an emphasis on automated pattern recognition, participatory methods involve disadvantaged people in dialogue designed to uncover the distinct root causes of their disadvantage and overcome it together.

The data-driven development approach is a significant departure from the ideals of participatory human-centred development in which marginalised people are the source of knowledge, and in which participatory dialogic processes are the means and ends of development. The requirement for computational power and data analytics skill means that the process of development knowledge production is not carried out locally by marginalised and disadvantaged people themselves and as a result they can be left without agency and none the wiser. In other words, development decision-making processes are often dehumanised and physically removed from the relevant human contexts, prioritising automated algorithmic analysis of big data over in-depth deliberative, contextualised and participation-based knowledge production [36]. It should be noted that this shift of knowledge paradigm in international development is also likely to lead to the replacement of local expertise, and intermediary issue experts, shifting power relations in the field of international development [7, 25]. As we discuss later the reduced participation of local people and intermediaries in digitalisation processes in often accompanied by the increased participation of external private companies who partner in the extraction of data and its processing.

For this reason, the idea that development should *"be data-driven"* as stated in the Digital Development Principals needs to be problematised, both because data may be gender or racially biased and because marginalised people have the right to voice their opinion and be at the centre of any decision-making about their lives [9, 37]. Although the Digital Development Principals also say *"design with users"*, we argue that it is not only 'users' who have the right to participation, and that the right to participation extends beyond the design stage of development projects.

In the next section, we will review the shift from people-centred to data-centred development, and look at specific examples of datafication and their implications for development.

3   The Impact of Datafication on International Development

Datafication has occurred in multiple sectors of international development. Examples include the digitalisation of microfinance [38], digital governance [39], digital identity [40] and digital social protection 41]. Increasingly, access to healthcare, employment, criminal justice, and decisions about resource deployment are made on the basis of automated analysis of big data sets using artificial intelligence [8, 36].

In the rest of the section we examine the impact of datafication on international development.

3.1   Dehumanisation of Development Process

Datafication often delivers valued benefits of cost reduction, efficiencies that improve speed of service delivery, convenience to citizens and reduction in corruption. However, datafication also brings the risk that local contextual knowledge and expertise is disintermediated. Sharma and Joshi [42] argue that digital development processes tend to design out local knowledge of development settings provided by those with lived experience and the ability to make a situated assessment of development processes.

When human-centred development processes are replaced by data-centred processes the effect is dehumanising. Dialogue and human interaction are replaced by computer-mediated machine calculation. Instead of convening a village meeting or conducting worshops, extracted data can be used to generate algorithmic decision-making. Funders are incentivising development agencies to experiment with satellite data, remote sensing, social media data and artificial intelligence. Although it is often argued rhetorically that the two methods should be complementary, in practice the funding disproportionately incentivises datafication rather than participation. Research from the United Nations has noted that datafication projects are tending to replace, rather than complement, analogue access. As pointed out in a UN special report on extreme poverty and human rights, "[t]he digital welfare state sometimes gives beneficiaries the option to go digital or continue using more traditional techniques. But in reality, policies such as 'digital by default' or 'digital by choice' are usually transformed into 'digital only' in practice" [43, p. 13].

The research in 49 predictive analytics projects by humanitarian agencies [8] examined how historic data of previous humanitarian emergencies is being combined with data from sources including mobile phone records, social media, satellite images, and meteorological data to create the large datasets needed to predict refugee movement, food security, and inform aid deployment. The researchers noted the risks associated with reliance on repurposed datasets containing omissions and biases that lead to algorithms reproducing past errors, prejudices and inequalities (ibid).

McQuillan [44] argues that machine learning is a particular form of knowledge production native to big data. He acknowledges that the technology itself is not inherently good or bad, nor is it inevitable that its use will cause harm. However, he argues that the affordances of machine learning, the ability to recognise patterns in historic data with predictive power, abstracts from human social and political contexts in ways that *"invisibly distorts the distribution of benefits and harm"*. The opacity of machine learning decision-making can cause or obscure harm. The basis on which predictions are made are unknown, as are the gender, race or class biases hidden in the data. This method of opaque knowledge production obstructs people's rights to transparency, participation, and accountability. McQuillan warns that the use of machine learning risks adopting a drone-like perspective on society; a perspective that combines a top-down view of society leading to harmful interventions of dubious legality.

It is thus a serious concern that reliance on big data and automated decision-making has the effect of de-centring the human agency of affected populations and of experienced frontline practitioners and replacing it with the mechanical logic of algorithms. The humanitarian principle to *"keep people at the centre of everything we do"* [6] is at risk by the encroachment of artificial intelligence at the behest of funders and powerful commercial interests. It is therefore imperative to keep humans in the loop to ensure development agencies remain accountable to the populations they exist to serve (ibid).

3.2 The Exclusion of the Vulnerable

Datafication has become an important means of managing population identification systems (Digital-ID). Digital-ID systems are increasingly used a gateway to control social protection systems worldwide, including (un)conditional cash transfers [41, 43]. Access to digital welfare payments is often used to motivate for the creation of identification registries by humanitarian agencies and states. Digital-ID systems increasingly use biometric identification such as fingerprints, iris-scanning or facial recognition [45, 46].

Entitlement to welfare entitlements for refugees, pensioners or mothers is increasingly algorithmically determined and cash is often transferred directly to people's mobile phones, or electronic debit cards. This datafication of affected populations makes them machine readable and machine processable – a significant efficiency gain for humanitarian or state agencies but also another form of dehumanisation compared to the person-centred processes that are replaced. The move to digitalisation of identification is often achieved in partnership with private corporations, raising issues of data ownership, privacy and protection [7, 41]. Global financial corporations and the world's largest data aggregators are partnering with humanitarian organisations in humanitarian datafication projects including Mastercard[2], Goldman Sachs[3] and Experian[4].

The Aadhaar digital-ID system in India is the world's largest digital-ID system. It is the model for many other national identification systems and the subject of a great deal of research including dedicated special journal issues [47]. Digitalised biometric data is recorded about each citizen enabling them to access multiple entitlements and services (Gov of India, n.d.). The Aadhaar ID has become a requirement to access a wide range of welfare services and social protection entitlements and has delivered valuable benefits of convenience and service access to many millions of citizens. However, research shows that the most marginalised citizens are excluded by the systems and as a result suffer deprivations. When visiting ration shops citizens must authenticate biometrically but the system regularly fails as a result of connectivity issues or because of worn fingerprints. Chaudhuri [48] documents how shop owners manipulate the Aadhaar system to make it work, revealing a paradox of (dis)intermediation; although the system is designed to obviate the need for human mediation the systems regularly do not function without the creative improvisation of intermediaries who break the rules and modify the system to secure the intended development outcome. Ironically, Chaudhuri finds that a process of datafication created to design out human errors and corruption only works in practice when humans design out the technology errors to ensure disadvantaged citizens have access to rations (ibid).

3.3 Shifting Power Relations in Development

Datafication is also shifting power and agency away from traditional actors in ways that increase the power and agency of technology corporations [7]. This happens as a result of private-public partnerships that are employed to digitalise government functions and development agency operations. The increased use of commercially owned big data and proprietary algorithms has the effect of making citizens increasingly visible to corporate and government actors resulting in a shift of power to those who hold the most data (ibid.).

In their analysis of datafication Heeks and Shakhar [15] use a data justice lens to assess who benefits from a range of community data mapping initiatives in Kenya, Indonesia, and India. Their analysis found that target communities experienced real incremental benefits, but that external actors and wealthier communities gained the most. Data about the most marginalised communities was not captured at all and the most significant social justice issues were made invisible by the datafication process with the effect that overall, there was an increase in relative inequality. Heeks and Shakhar used an information value chain framework that traces the steps by which data is captured and

---

[2] Mastercard Transforming Humanitarian Response https://www.mastercard.us/en-us/business/governments/find-solutions/humanitarian-aid.html.

[3] IrisGuard funded by Goldman Sachs https://www.irisguard.com/who-we-are/about-us/.

[4] Experian partners with Humanitarian Open StreetMap https://www.experianplc.com/media/4224/experian-sb-report-2021.pdf.

transformed into developmental results. Among their conclusions is the finding that *"In general, then, these pro-equity data initiatives were somewhat 'extractive' in utilising a few community residents as data sources but largely excluding them from all other information value chain processes"* (ibid).

Commercial datasets and proprietary algorithms have been criticised for being black-boxed technologies [49] not open to public scrutiny, and therefore raising issues of transparency and accountability for development processes. Marginalised communities cannot participate meaningfully in development initiatives that affect their lives if the data and decision-making processes that shape them are opaque or regarded as proprietary trade secrets. Studies have shown that big data reflects historical patterns of prejudice and disadvantage along intersecting lines of gender, race and class leading to the finding that use of artificial intelligence often reflects, reproduces, and amplifies historical patterns of (dis)advantage [12, 14, 50]. Where datasets and/or algorithms are not open to public scrutiny there is no transparency, no accountability mechanism, and no route to redress [12, 50, 51]. As a result, human rights groups have actively campaigned against the deployment of facial recognition, predictive policing and smart city technologies that rely on these technologies [52, 53]. Some development agencies including Oxfam UK imposed moratoria and some cities have banned the technologies [54].

In short, datafication delivers clear benefits including efficiency, convenience and expanded service access. Nevertheless, the centralisation of technical knowledge and the domination of techno-rationality take place at the expense of practical knowledge, resulting in the dehumanisation of development processes; and actively suppress emancipatory knowledge interests, as exemplified in the exclusion and exploitation of the most vulnerable groups in society, instrumentalised through the extraction of data by corporate and government agencies.

4   Return to Human-Centred Development

To address these issues, i.e. to re-enact practical and emancipatory knowledge interests in datafication and AI in development, a participatory approach is imperative.

4.1 Beyond Ethical AI

In respons to criticism of bias and lack of accountability in datafication there has been a proliferation of initiatives to develop ethical frameworks to secure the continued use of artificial intelligence in international development. The Montreal Declaration on Responsible AI[5], OECD Principles on Artificial Intelligence[6] and the UNESCO Recommendation on AI[7] are examples of the many recent initiatives in this space. Floridi and Cowls [55] have conducted meta-analysis to distil the growing number of ethical principles into a 'Unified Framework of AI Principles in Society'. The Montreal Declaration on Responsible AI refers frequently to the importance of participation in AI processes. The

---

[5] The Montreal Declaration on Responsible AI.

[6] OECD Principles on Artificial Intelligence.

[7] The UNESCO Recommendation on AI.

OECD Principles do not mention participation but they do refer to human-centred values, although there is little detail about how human-centred AI might be realised in practice. Floridi and Cowls [55] note with concern that the various principles that they studied were either global in scope or address western liberal democracies and that perspectives from Africa and Asia are generally unrepresented or under-represented in the current principles.

As Birhane [56] argues in her paper on algorithmic justice, studies addressing the harm caused by artificial intelligence, predominantly (1) revolve around technical solutions and (2) do not sufficiently centre impacted communities. Birhane argues that it is necessary for practitioners to decentre technical solutions such as fixing the data or algorithms. She proposes a fundamental epistemological shift—from rational to relational approaches—and calls for an approach to ethics that goes above and beyond technical solutions. Her proposal envisages that a more human-centred approach is required with relational processes, involving dialogue and critical reflection with affected populations, as opposed to technical "solutions". Similarly, McQuillan [44] proposes a shift away from opaque and dehumanised machine calculation towards a human-centred process of critical reflection and social dialogue in the form of people's councils for ethical machine learning.

On this basis, in the rest of the section, we will argue for the imperative to return to human-centred participatory development with the aim of overcoming the dehumanising effects of data-centric approaches. We start with a critical review of participatory development and discuss how to move beyond tokenistic practices of participation.

4.2 Participatory Development

Participatory approaches to development emerged from a variety of sources in the 1970s onwards [57, 58]. Scholars from the global South including Freire [58], Fals-Borda [59], and Sen [37] argued for a human-centred model of participatory development that enhanced the agency and control of previously marginalised and disadvantaged people. Swantz [60] and Chambers [61] were among those who popularised these participatory models of development which revolve around group dialogic processes. Participatory approaches aim to engage people with lived experience of poverty and injustice in reflection about their experience of injustice, its root causes, and collective action to overcome it. Participatory practices of development aimed to increase the decision-making role that disadvantaged people play in defining the development initiatives designed to improve their lives. When Amartya Sen embraced participatory development, he stated [37, p. 281] that central to his approach to development was *"the idea of the public as an active participant in change, rather than as a passive and docile recipient of instructions or of dispensed assistance"*. This participatory approach to development is consciously human-centred, arguing that the people most directly affected by social deprivations and disadvantage should play a central role in determining how disadvantage and injustice is mitigated and overcome [37, 58, 59, 61, 62].

In addition to this normative and rights-based case for human-centred development there is also an instrumental argument that participation simply produces better development outcomes [63]. This more pragmatic case for people-centred development argues that this is for two reasons, (a) people with the most lived-experience of a development challenge are well-placed to inform the design of solutions, and (b) active community engagement in early stages of the project cycles can be effective in securing uptake and dissemination [64]. From a gender perspective, scholars have evidenced that women's participation in digital development programmes expands their applicability and development impact [65, 66]. In their study of 121 rural water projects, Ishamn, Naravan, and Pritchett [67] found strong evidence that increasing the representation of intended beneficiaries directly improved project outcomes.

From the 1980s onwards, the dominant development paradigm began embracing and incorporating aspects of this heterodox participatory approach within mainstream approaches to development [68]. Article 2 of the United Nations [69] Right to Development states that

> *"the human person is the central subject of development and should be the active participant and beneficiary of the right to development"* and that interventions should enable *"their active, free and meaningful participation in development and in the fair distribution of the benefits resulting therefrom"*.

By 2015 states and international development agencies unanimously committed themselves to the Sustainable Development Goals (SDGs) including target 16.7: to *"ensure responsive, inclusive, participatory and representative decision-making at all levels"* [70].

The consensus that more inclusive processes produce improved development outputs is reflected in the inclusion of "design with the user" as one of the Digital Development Principles endorsed by funders and international development organisations[8]. It is important however, that participatory development is not confused with 'inclusion'. Participation goes significantly beyond counting the number of people a particular demographic group that are represented in a process. From the outset participation is centrally concerned with the degree of agency and control that participants have in decision-making processes at all stages of the project cycle. The participatory development literature eschews tokenistic participatory process where marginalised people are simply sources of data extraction in the design stage or during the data collection phase but are excluded from other key stages such as project conception, implementation, or evaluation.

From the outset Arnstein [57] argued that in practice it was important to distinguish between 'levels' of participation, ranging from shallow and tokenistic forms of inclusion graduating in normative value up to genuine partnerships in which participants had meaningful decision-making control over development projects that affect their lives. Based on Arnstein's work, many versions of 'ladders of participation' were developed to reflect different operational contexts (Fig. 1.)

Cornwall and Jewkes [71] argued that what distinguishes valuable participation is the extent to which decision-making power is shifted from external experts to local participants. After the turn of the millennium, scholars conducted a sustained critique of the 'tyranny' of shallow and tokenistic forms of participation in which participants had little meaningful influence over project conception, implementation or evaluation [10, 72]. Hickey and Mohan [62] were among those who argued that in order to move from

---

[8] https://digitalprinciples.org/endorse/endorsers/.

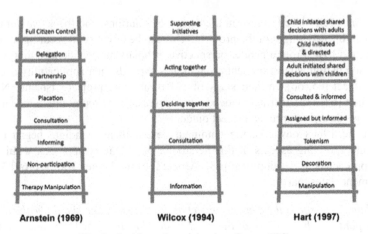

Fig. 1. Ladders of participation. Source [76].

tyrannical to transformative forms of participation it is necessary to increase the agency and decision-making power of marginalised actors themselves in the design, planning and evaluation of development projects.

Although participatory development theory is well established, and a global consensus on its merits is reflected in its explicit inclusion in global development goals, funding and practice have always lagged significantly behind theory. It is much harder to achieve equitable participation than it is to sign up to it in principle. These criticisms apply as much to digital development projects as in other areas. For example, in their evaluation of four digital mapping projects, Heeks and Shakhar [15] concluded that despite their achievements, the projects were largely extractive with community members entirely excluded from most stages of the project cycle.

Recognising the value of participation and human-centred development, some of the recent initiatives to re-orient datafication for development initiatives explicitly include increasing participation among their principles. The UNESCO Recommendations on Ethical AI speak most directly to the importance of participation in international development stating that *"Participation of different stakeholders throughout the AI system life cycle is necessary for inclusive approaches to AI governance, enabling the benefits to be shared by all, and to contribute to sustainable development"*. Although *"designing with the user"* is a component of the previously mentioned Principles for Digital Development, what is distinctive about the UNESCO Recommendation is the insistence on participation not only in the design stage but in all stages of the AI system life cycle. The UNESCO Recommendation is also distinctive in noting the importance of considering which stakeholders should be participants in AI decision-making, stating that *"stakeholders include, but are not limited to, governments ... human rights institutions and equality bodies, anti-discrimination monitoring bodies, and groups for youth and children"*.

Participation scholars have argued that it is important to evaluate participation along three dimensions: (i) who gets to participate [9, 73]; (ii) at which stages in the development process [74, 75]; and (iii) with what level of control over the process [10, 57].

Despite agreement in theory, systematic evaluation of along these three dimensions are rare in the research literature. To address this gap, Roberts [76] developed the participation cube to help practioners visualise, calibrate, and structure a three-dimensional analysis of (a) who gets to participate, (b) at which stages of a project, and (c) with what level of control. Figure 2 illustrates 'participation tracing': a practice of tracing the level of participation achieved by different project participants at key stages in the project life-cycle [77].

The vertical axis is calibrated in levels of control achieved over the decision-making process, following Arnstein's 'ladder of participation'. The horizontal axis reflects the different stages in the project cycle. Then a unique trace is made to reflect the participation of each different project actor in each project stage. Figure 2 reflects a retrospective analysis made of participation levels in a specific project in Zambia [77], however the number of stages, the names of participation levels, and participant actors need to be re-calibrated for each new project to reflect that particular context. This kind of participation tracing can be used as either a planning, monitoring or evaluation tool, to assess the levels of participation of different actors and inform the modification and improvement of project processes. To support the move from principles to measurable practices of participatory digital development more research is necessary to develop tools and methods of participatory planning, monitoring and evaluation.

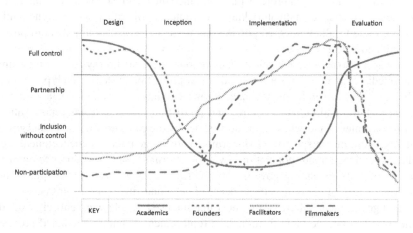

Fig. 2. Participation tracing. Source [77].

5 Discussion

This paper began by framing the discussion of datafication in the context of Habermas' theory of social action and knowledge interests. The evidence shows that data-science and participatory practices are distinct forms of social action that are shaped by different knowledge interests. The shift in priorities of funders, governments and international development towards the datafication of development has involved introducing new actors and new interests. This has had the unintended consequence of dehumanising the datafication of development in three areas: the use of predictive analytics in humanitarian settings, digital-ID programmes, and community mapping projects.

In the case of humanitarian predictive analytics the knowledge interests of control, prediction, and explanation are clear. What Habermas calls our technical knowledge interest for explanation, control, and prediction is understandable in the face of a disaster, as is the desire to use remote sensing and statistical analysis to provide situational analysis in settings where putting 'boots on the ground' may be dangerous or impossible. However, this form of knowledge production appeals to a particular mindset in and outside of emergency settings. Predictive analytics are also being applied by humanitarian agencies in human resource management, water purification, and supply chain logistics. None of the 49 examples of predictive analytics studied involved the participation of affected populations in decision-making roles across different stages of the project cycle. These datafication processes contributed to dehumanisation of humanitarian commitments to human-centred development. One of the key recommendations [8, p. 30] was that *"an opportunity exists at this early stage to actively engage affected populations in the design, implementation and evaluation of humanitarian predictive analytics... The contextual knowledge of affected populations and the experience of humanitarian practitioners [can be] combined with the technical expertise of data scientists to improve both the power relationships and predictive efficacy of future innovations in predictive analytics"*. Datafication projects that combined the technical knowledge interests of data-science with the emanicipatory knowledge interests of critical social sciences might provide a route to allow affected populations to be active decision-makers in projects designed to affect their lives.

The paper also reviewed datafication of national identification systems, which aim to disintermediate government services and social protection systems. Such programmes can be viewed as driven by the technical knowledge interest to extract data, rationalise decision-making, and enhance control and prediction. Many citizens report valuable gains in convenience and access, and nation states secure gains in efficiencies and governmentality. From the perspective of Habermas' knowledge interests, the technical logics produce knowledge about populations by applying rule-based procedures to empirical data, successfully extending government control over operations and outputs. These disintermediation gains come at the expense of dehumanising relationships between citizens and government. Many of the most marginalised people were entirely excluded by the use of biometric identification. The replacement of human mediated processes of governance with automated algorithmic processes had the unintended consequence of removing rights and entitlements. The black-boxed nature of the AI process and the use of external private corporations and proprietary technologies reduced human mediation and removed accountability and means of redress. These logics are not inevitable, a national identification system could be informed by practical knowledge interests: a public dialogue could run in parallel to the technical build that enables citizens to communicate their concerns and priorities to government in ways that practically inform functionality and system modifications.

Exclusion and extraction were also themes in the third set of digitalisation projects - four digital mapping projects [15]. As in the digital identification examples, data about the most marginalised people was not captured and their realities were not represented in the datafication programmes. Heeks and Shakhar [15] characterised the datafication process as excluding the most deprived individuals and ignoring the most challenging injustices. In both the digital-ID projects and the digital mapping projects, the most marginalised social groups, who are the indented focus of international development, are de-centred and excluded by the digitalisation projects. In the digital mapping example the greatest benefits accrued to external agencies and already relatively advantaged actors, resulting in an overall increase in relative inequalities. These findings resonate with findings from other sectors of digital development [13, 39].

These criticisms of datafication have been accepted by a wide range of actors in digital development and as a result new ethical principles have been produced to reorientate and guide practice. These principles are often explicit in seeking to increase participation and produce a more human-centred AI. Increasing participation holds the potential for disadvantaged people to play decision-making roles at the centre of datafication projects. However, we know from non-digital development that achieving this will not be straightforward [57, 72] if we are to go beyond tokenistic levels of participation. It is in ensuring that excluded voices are heard, understood, and are influential that Habermas' practical and emancipatory knowledge interests have a role to play. Practical knowledge interests constitute social action concerned with understanding and communication. To the extent that datafication projects genuinely incorporate and understand the voices, contextual knowledge, and expressed needs of disadvantaged people, they can be said to reflect practical knowledge interests and communicative social action in the Habermasian sense.

Emancipatory knowledge interests require not only understanding the communicated experience of disadvantaged people, they also requires enabling disadvantaged people themselves to identify the causes of the disadvantage that they experience, as well as their active engagement in social action to remove them. Overcoming injustice and securing freedom from unwarranted domination is the human drive that Habermas argues constitutes emancipatory knowledge interests. This form of social action cannot be characterised by extraction or by exclusion, nor can it be characterised by increased levels of inequality or disadvantage. In such projects participation is not judged by whether more disadvantaged people took part but by whether participants engaged in discussion and reflection about their experience of disadvantage and its causes, and in social action to overcome it.

The various sets of new ethical principles for AI are welcome recognition of some of the negative consequences of datafication. Increasing participation and more human centred AI processes are key to countering the dehumanisation of development but it is easier agree principles that to change practices. There have been claims that the proliferation of principles are in part motivated by corporate ethics washing and a desire to avoid regulation [78, 79]. We will soon be able to assess the extent to which principles translate into participatory practices. Experience from non-digital development suggests participatory practice varies in the degree to which disadvantaged people gain decision-making across the different stages of the development cycle.

6   Conclusion

The paper has argued that datafication can dehumanise development. We have shown the relevance of Habermas' concepts of knowledge interests and participatory development to understanding how datafication can dehumanize development and whether more participatory and human-centred datafication projects are possible. A review of datafication projects in three sectors acknowledged that datafication projects have delivered valuable benefits of efficiency, expanded access, and convenience. The authors have argued that datafication has introduced new actors, technologies and knowledge interests that have resulted in extractive processes, exclusion of the most disadvantaged, and disintermediation of human processes that dehumanise development. In the cases reviewed, digitalisation projects had unintended consequences, including a reduction in the human right to participation and accountability and a relative increase in inequality.

The paper argues that the epistemic underpinnings of data science (technical knowledge interests) conflict with the practical-communicative and critical-emancipatory underpinnings of participatory development, but it does not argue that they cannot be reconciled. The new Ethical AI Principles now being agreed for future digitalisation projects provide a potential route to assess whether a synergy of different approaches to datafication is possible that results in more participatory AI and human-centred datafication. The authors argue that translating principles into practices that avoid tokenstic forms of participation will require the incorporation of practical and emancipatory knowledge interests and the development and use of new planning and evaluation tools to trace the achieved levels of participation of different actors at each stage of the project life cycle. People with a lived experience of poverty and injustice have the right to be included in the design, implementation, and evaluation of any development projects intended to benefit them. Not in tokenistic ways but as authors, architects, and arbiters of their own development.

References

1. Heeks, R.: Information and Communications Technology for Development. Routeledge, London (2018)
2. Feeny, T., Elson, O.: Artificial Intelligence in International Development, Results for Development (2019). https://static1.squarespace.com/static/5b156e3bf2e6b10bb0788609/t/5e1f0a37e723f0468c1a77c8/1579092542334/AI+and+international+Development_FNL.pdf
3. World Bank: World Development Report 2016: Digital Dividends. The World Bank, Washington (2016). https://elibrary.worldbank.org/doi/abs/10.1596/978-1-4648-0671-1
4. USAID: Digital Download 2018, Center for Digital Development. United States Agency for International Development, Washington (2018)
5. OCHA: Data Responsibility Guidelines: Working Draft. The Centre for Humanitarian Data: OCHA, The Hague (2019)
6. Roberts, T., Faith, B.: Digital aid: understanding the digital challenges facing humanitarian assistance. Institute of Development Studies, Brighton (2021). https://opendocs.ids.ac.uk/opendocs/handle/20.500.12413/16484
7. Taylor, L., Broeders, D.: In the name of development: power, profit and datafication in the global south. Geoforum **64**, 229–237 (2015)

8. Hernandez, K., Roberts, T.: Predictive analytics in humanitarian action: a preliminary mapping and analysis. Emerging issues, knowledge for development report 33. Institute of Development Studies, Brighton (2020). https://opendocs.ids.ac.uk/opendocs/handle/20.500.12413/15455

9. Chambers, R.: Whose Reality Counts? Putting the Last First. Practical Action Publishing, Rugby (1997)

10. Cornwall, P.: The Participation Reader. Zed Books, London (2011)

11. Foster, C., Graham, M., Mwolo Waema, T.: Making sense of digital disintermediation and development: the case of the mombassa tea auction. In: Graham, M. (ed.) Digital Economies at Global Margins. MIT Press, Cambridge (2019)

12. Eubanks, V.: Automating Inequality: How High-Tech Tools Profile, Police, and Punish the Poor. St. Martin's Press, New York (2017)

13. Hernandez, K., Roberts, T.: Leaving no one behind in a digital world: an extended literature review. Institute of Development Studies (2018)

14. Benjamin, R.: Race After Technology: Abolitionist Tools for the New Jim Code. Polity, Medford (2019)

15. Heeks, R., Shekhar, S.: Datafication, development and marginalised urban communities: an applied data justice framework. Inf. Commun. Soc. **22**(7), 992–1011 (2019)

16. Lyytinen, K.J., Klein, H.K.: The critical theory of Jurgen Habermas as a basis for a theory of information systems. In: Mumford, E., Hirschheim, R., Fitzgerald, G., et al. (eds.) Research Methods in Information Systems, pp. 207–225. North-Holland, Amsterdam (1985)

17. Walsham, G.: Interpreting Information Systems in Organisations. Wiley, London (1993)

18. Zheng, Y., Stahl, B.: Technology, capabilities and critical perspectives: what can critical theory contribute to Sen's capability approach? Ethics Inf. Technol. **13**(2), 69–80 (2011)

19. Lin, C.I., Myers, M.D.: Extending ICT4D studies: the value of critical research. MIS Q. **39**(3), 697–712 (2015)

20. Poveda, S., Roberts, T.: Critical agency and development: applying Freire and Sen to ICT4D in Zambia and Brazil. Inf. Technol. Dev. **24**(1), 119–137 (2018). https://doi.org/10.1080/02681102.2017.1328656

21. Habermas, J.: Knowledge and Human Interests. Heinemann, London (1972)

22. IDRC: Artificial intelligence and human development : toward a research agenda. Canadian International Development Research Centre, Ottowa (2018)

23. IDRC: Data for Development: the road ahead. Canadian International Development Research Centre, Ottowa (2019). https://idatosabiertos.org/wp-content/uploads/2020/10/D4D_report-dig-1.pdf

24. Mann, S., Hilbert, M.: Int. J. Commun. **14**, 4385–4405 (2020)

25. Flyverbom, M., Madsen, A.K., Rasche, A.: Big data as governmentality in international development: digital traces, algorithms, and altered visibilities. Inf. Soc. Routledge **33**(1), 35–42 (2017)

26. Angwin, J., Larson, J., Mattu, S.: Machine bias: there's software used across the country to predict future criminals. And it's biased against blacks (2016). ProPublica, text/html, 23 May 2016. https://www.propublica.org/article/machine-bias-risk-assessments-in-criminalsentencing

27. Brayne, S., Rosenblat, A., Boyd, D.: Predictive policing (2015). datacivilrights.org. http://www.datacivilrights.org/pubs/2015-1027/Predictive_Policing.pdf

28. Fitterer, J., Nelson, T.A., Nathoo, F.: Predictive crime mapping. Police Pract. Res. **16**(2), 121–135 (2015)

29. Stroud, M.: The minority report: Chicago's new police computer predicts crimes, but is it racist? (2014). The Verge, 19 February 2014. http://www.theverge.com/2014/2/19/5419854/theminority-report-this-computer-predicts-crime-but-is-it-racist

30. Privacy International: Palantir and the UN's World Food Programme, London Privacy International (2019). https://privacyinternational.org/news-analysis/3405/palantir-and-uns-world-food-programme-are-partnering-reported-45-million
31. Milmo, D.: Rohingya sue Facebook for £150bn over Myanmar genocide (2021). https://www.theguardian.com/technology/2021/dec/06/rohingya-sue-facebook-myanmar-genocide-us-uk-legal-action-social-media-violence
32. Bowker, G.: Memory Practices in the Sciences. MIT Press, Cambridge (2005)
33. Gitelman, L. (ed.): "Raw Data" Is an Oxymoron. MIT Press, Cambridge (2013)
34. Manovich, L.: Trending: the promises and the challenges of big social data. In: Gold, M.K. (ed.) Debates in the Digital Humanities. University of Minnesota Press (2012)
35. Latour, B., Woolgar, S.: Laboratory Life: The Construction of Scientific Facts. Princeton University Press, Princeton (1986)
36. Pawleke, A., Cañares, M., Hernandez, K., Prieto Martin, P.: Data for development: what's next? Concepts, trends and recommendations for German Development Cooperation. Deutsche Gesellschaft für Internationale Zusammenarbeit (GIZ) (2017). https://opendocs.ids.ac.uk/opendocs/handle/20.500.12413/14154
37. Sen, A.: Development as Freedom. Oxford University Press, Oxford (1999)
38. Siwale, J., Godfroid, C.: Digitising microfinance: on the route to losing the traditional 'human face' of microfinance institutions. Oxf. Dev. Stud. (2021). https://doi.org/10.1080/13600818.2021.1998409
39. Roberts, T., Hernandez, K., Faith, B., Prieto Martín, P.: Key issues in digitalisation and governance. SDC Governance Network, Swiss Development Cooperation, Bern (2022)
40. Masiero, S., Arvidsson, V.: Degenerative outcomes of digital identity platforms for development. Inf. Syst. J. **31**(6), 903–928 (2021)
41. Faith, B., Roberts, T.: Risks and benefits of digital social protection. BASIC Research Working Paper 3. Institute of Development Studies, Brighton (2022). https://doi.org/10.19088/BASIC.2022.003
42. Sharma, P., Joshi, A.: Challenges of using big data for humanitarian relief: lessons from the literature. J. Humanit. Logist. Supply Chain Manag. **10**(4), 423–446 (2019)
43. OHCHR: Report of the special rapporteur on extreme poverty and human rights. No. Seventy-Fourth Session: Item 72(b) of the Provisional Agenda (2019). https://www.ohchr.org/EN/NewsEvents/Pages/DisplayNews.aspx?NewsID=25156. Accessed 27 Nov 2020
44. McQuillan, D.: People's councils for ethical machine learning. Soc. Media Soc. **4**(2), 1–10 (2018)
45. World Bank: Principles on identification for sustainable development: toward the digital age. The World Bank, Washington (2017). http://documents1.worldbank.org/curated/en/213581486378184357/pdf/Principles-onidentification-for-sustainable-development-toward-the-digital-age.pdf
46. Amnesty International: Amnesty International Submission to the Office of the United Nations High Commissioner for Human Rights on the Impact of Digital Technologies on Social Protection and Human Rights (2019). https://www.ohchr.org/Documents/Issues/Poverty/DigitalTechnology/AmnestyInternational.pdf
47. Rao, U., Nair, V.: Aadhaar: governing with biometrics. South Asia: J. South Asian Stud. **42**(3), 469–481 (2019). https://doi.org/10.1080/00856401.2019.1595343
48. Chaudhuri, B.: Paradoxes of Intermediation in aadhaar: human making of a digital infrastructure. South Asia J. South Asian Stud. **42**(3), 572–587 (2019). https://doi.org/10.1080/00856401.2019.1598671
49. Pasquale, F.: The Black Box Society: The Secret Algorithms that Control Society. Harvard University Press, London (2015)
50. Noble, S.: Algorithms of Oppression: How Search Engines Reinforce Racism. New York University Press, New York (2018)

51. O'Neil, C.: Weapons of Math Destruction: How Big Data Increases Inequality and Threatens Democracy. Penguin Books, London (2017)
52. Liberty Human Rights: Predictive policing. Liberty Human Rights (2020). https://www.lib ertyhumanrights.org.uk/fundamental/predictive-policing/
53. Privacy International: IBM (not) ending facial recognition - our quick thoughts. Privacy International (2020). http://privacyinternational.org/news-analysis/3898/ibm-not-endingfac ial-recognition-our-quick-thoughts
54. Lee, D.: San Francisco is first US city to ban facial recognition (2019). BBC News, 14 May 2019. https://www.bbc.com/news/technology-48276660
55. Floridi and Cowls: Unified Framework of AI Principles in Society, HDSR 1.1, MIT Press (2019). https://hdsr.mitpress.mit.edu/pub/l0jsh9d1/release/8
56. Birhane, A.: Algorithmic injustice: a relational ethics approach. Patterns **2**(2) (2021). https://www.sciencedirect.com/science/article/pii/S2666389921000155
57. Arnstein, S.: A ladder of citizen participation. J. Am. Inst. Am. Plann. Assoc. **35**(4), 216–224 (1969)
58. Freire, P.: Pedagogy of the Oppressed. Continuum, New York (1970)
59. Fals-Borda, O.: Investigating reality in order to transform it: the Colombian experience. Dialect. Anthropol. Amsterdam **4**(1), 33–35 (1979)
60. Swantz, M.: Research as education for development, a Tanzanian case. In: Hall, B. (ed.) Creating Knowledge: A Monopoly? Participatory Research in Development. SPRIA, New Delhi (1982)
61. Chambers, R.: Rural Development. Longman, Essex (1983)
62. Hickey, S., Mohan, G.: Participation: From Tyranny to Transformation. Zed Books, London (2004)
63. Mansuri, G., Rao, V.: Does participation improve development outcomes? (2012). https://doi.org/10.1596/9780821382561_CH05
64. World Bank: The World Bank Participation Sourcebook. The World Bank, Washington (1996). https://elibrary.worldbank.org/doi/abs/10.1596/0-8213-3558-8
65. Faith, B., Roberts, T., Berdou, E.: Towards a more gender-inclusive open source community. Digital Impact Alliance, Washington (2018). https://dial.global/wp-content/uploads/2018/11/GenderOSS_v10_PDF.pdf
66. Barker, L., Mancha, C., Ashcraf, C.: What is the impact of gender diversity on technology business performance? National Centre for Women and Information Technology (2014)
67. Ishamn, J., Naravan, D., Pritchett, L.: Does participation improve performance?: Establishing causality with subjective data. World Bank Econ. Rev. **9**(2), 175–200 (1995)
68. Wald, N.: Anarchist participatory development: a possible new framework? Dev. Change **46**(4), 618–643 (2014). https://onlinelibrary.wiley.com/doi/abs/10.1111/dech.12136
69. OHCHR: Declaration on the Right to Development, New York, United Nations (1986). https://www.ohchr.org/en/instruments-mechanisms/instruments/declaration-right-development
70. UNSDSN: Indicators and Monitoring Framework for the Sustainable Development Goals. Geneva, United Nations Sustainable Development Solutions Network (2015). https://indica tors.report/targets/16-7/
71. Cornwall, A., Jewkes, R.: What is participatory research? Soc. Sci. Med. **41**(12), 1667–1676 (1995)
72. Cooke, B., Kothari, U. (eds.): Participation: The New Tyranny. Zed Books, London (2001)
73. Holland and Blackburn: Whose Voice? Participatory Research and Policy Change. Intermediate Technology Publications, London (1998)
74. Pain, R., Francis, P.: Reflections on participatory research. Area **35**(1), 46–54 (2003)
75. Kindon, S., Pain, R., Kesby, M.: Participatory Action Research Approaches and Methods. Routledge, Abingdon (2007)

76. Roberts, T.: Digital affordances in participatory research methods. In: Burns, D., Howard, J., Ospina, S. (eds.) The SAGE Handbook of Participatory Research and Inquiry. SAGE, London (2021)
77. Roberts, T., Howard, J.: The participation cube: retrospective analysis of projects in Zambia and Uganda. In: Conference Paper, Development Studies Association Conference, May 2022 (2022)
78. Wagner, B.: Ethics as an escape from regulation. From "ethics-washing" to ethics-shopping?, pp. 84–88. Amsterdam University Press (2018). https://doi.org/10.25969/mediarep/13281
79. Bietti, E.: From ethics washing to ethics bashing: a view on tech ethics from within moral philosophy. In: Proceedings of ACM FAT* Conference (FAT* 2020), New York, NY, USA, 10 p. ACM (2019). https://doi.org/10.1145/3351095.3372860

Towards a Balanced Natural Language Processing: A Systematic Literature Review for the Contact Centre
Balancing the AI Triple Challenge of *Opportunity*, *Ethics*, and *Opportunity Cost*!

Lungile Binza[✉] and Adheesh Budree[✉]

Department of Information Systems, University of Cape Town, Cape Town, South Africa
bnzlun003@myuct.ac.za, adheesh.budree@uct.ac.za

Abstract. Artificial Intelligence (AI), which is the design, development, and utilisation of iterative and complex algorithmic systems that complete tasks which normally required human intelligence, is rapidly gaining momentum throughout the world. Through Machine Learning these AI systems automatically learn and adapt themselves so that they can offer an even more accurate outcome than humans and this offers many exciting benefits to most businesses and economies. But their introduction has raised ethical questions after some unethical conduct on their part like racism, biasness against women, unemployment (through intelligent automation), and inequality. After these incidents of unethical behaviour by some AI technologies around the globe most public, private, and even non-profit organisations embarked on initiatives to address the unethical conduct of AI systems. They produced a range of ethical AI frameworks, guidelines, and principles, but a properly balanced AI, where *opportunity*, *ethics*, and *opportunity costs* intersect, is still to be achieved or realised. Most AI Practitioners are pressured by their shareholders to prioritise commercial interests over ethical considerations.

The findings from this Systematic Literature Review study, which used meta-analyses for qualitative synthesis, demonstrate that a **Balanced** Natural Language Processing (**NLP**) is possible.

Keywords: Artificial Intelligence · Machine Learning · Balanced AI · Natural Language Processing · Ethical AI · Systematic literature review

1 Introduction

Artificial Intelligence (AI) is the study of the design, development, application, and operationalisation of complex algorithmic systems that train themselves to think and act as intelligently as human beings (Schrader and Ghosh 2018). Powered by Machine Learning (ML) algorithms, where they adaptively interpret and continuously self-learn through analyzing new large datasets (Walsh et al. 2019; Floridi and Cowls 2019; Bankins 2021; Giermindl et al. 2021), these "intelligent virtual agents" recognize and respond

© IFIP International Federation for Information Processing 2022
Published by Springer Nature Switzerland AG 2022
Y. Zheng et al. (Eds.): ICT4D 2022, IFIP AICT 657, pp. 397–420, 2022.
https://doi.org/10.1007/978-3-031-19429-0_24

to specific environments (Acemoglu and Restrepo 2019; Teng 2020) that would have otherwise required human-level intelligence and intervention (Biller-Andorno et al. 2020; Naude and Dimitri 2020). These environments, which require pattern identification in data and the generation of predictions to assist in decision making processes (Nadimpalli 2017; Biller-Andorno et al. 2020; Krijger 2021), include *Knowledge Reasoning'*, *'Machine Learning (ML)'*, *'Robotics'*, *'Computer Vision'*, *'Visual Perception'*, *'Speech Recognition'*, *'Voice Biometrics'*, and *'Natural Language Processing (NLP)'* (Coombs et al. 2020).

NLP as an "interdisciplinary field of AI where the machine can be used to understand and manipulate natural language text or speech" (Bender and Friedman 2018; Li et al. 2021) includes *text generation, speech recognition, question answering, speech to text*, and *text to speech*. In this research study, the term AI would refer mainly to NLP, since the focus is on a Banking Contact Centre suite of AI technologies.

The AI industry forecasts some huge economic promise, potential, and benefits (Brynjolfsson and McAfee 2012), it's resulting in things getting 'easier, cheaper, and abundant' (Naude and Dimitri 2020). AI has the potential to increase human wellbeing, boost most sectors of the economies, improve various societies, and general good quality customer service (Arambula and Bur 2020; James and Whelan 2022). As Dolganova (2021) points out AI increases "customer loyalty, trust, and could boost sales by up 30% per annum".

But, with all these undoubted economic and commercial success stories, AI has the transformative social and cultural influence in society (Mika et al. 2019). AI has also demonstrated a pattern of entrenching social divides and amplifying or worsening social inequality, particularly among historically marginalized groups (Hagerty and Rubinov 2019).

Some few examples that demonstrate AI unethical behaviour in the United States are:

(a). "a job recruiting tools being biased against women" (Hagerty and Rubinov 2019);

(b). "Latin and African American borrowers faced with discriminatory credit algorithms" (Hagerty and Rubinov 2019);

(c). "bias regarding race, gender, and/or sexual orientation in sentiment analysis systems, and natural language processing technologies" (Hagerty and Rubinov 2019); and

(d). "an AI legal system that discriminated against African American and Hispanic men when making decisions about granting parole which has since become infamous" (Taddeo and Floridi 2018).

(e). "the US recidivism prediction algorithm that allegedly mislabelled African American defendants as "high-risk" at nearly twice the rate as it mislabelled white defendants" (Angwin et al. 2016) from Krijger 2021).

(f). "hiring algorithms that, based on analysing previous hiring decisions, penalized applicants from women's colleges for technology related positions" (Dastin 2018).

(g). "a healthcare entry selection program that exhibited racial bias against African American patients" (Obermeyer et al. 2019)

(h). "Google uses AI to identify photos, people, and objects in GOOGLE's Photos Services and always it will not be able to produce the correct results. Also, if any camera misses mark on racial sensitivity then the predicted criminals will be always the black people" (Alotaibi 2018).

All of these incidents and instances led to governments, academics, civil society or non-profit organisations, research institutes, and even the private sector to embark on initiatives to ensure ethical AI behaviour. Ethical AI which broadly refers to "the fair and just development, use, and management of AI technologies" (Bankins 2021) was initiated. Since AI Systems are more socio-technical in nature, considering ethical implications on their design, development, deployment, and operation became of critical importance for the society. Non-governmental organisations like **AI4Good** led to the development of the **AI4People** ethical AI Framework by Floridi et al. in 2018 (Kindylidi and Cabral 2021); initiatives by European Commission's High-Level Expert Group on Artificial Intelligence (AI-HLEG) led to the publishing of Ethics Guidelines for **Trustworthy AI or Sustainable AI** (Kindylidi and Cabral 2021); The Japanese Society for Artificial Intelligence (JSAI) identified the ethical principles to be followed by developers of artificial intelligence systems (Dolganova 2021); The Atomium – European Institute for Science, Media and Democracy white paper on AI ethics outlines five principles of AI ethics (Dolganova 2021); **Responsible AI** which is "concerned with the design, implementation, and use of ethical, transparent, and accountable AI technology in order to reduce biases, promote fairness, equality, and to help facilitate interpretability and explainability of outcomes" (Trocin et al. 2021) was also born.

These initiatives were not only in the non-profit, governmental, or research institutes based only but the private sector also came on board:

(a) IBM launched an "Everyday Ethics for Artificial Intelligence: A practical guide for designers and developers" (Ashby 2020);
(b) Microsoft leadership uses the "six principles mainly derived from the AI4People framework to guide its use of their AIs" (Bankins 2021); and
(c) Google as also formulated "seven principles of artificial intelligence that the company is following in creating and using AI technologies" (Dolganova 2021).

Most AI Practitioners are pressured to prioritise commercial interests over public or ethical consideration (Mittelstadt 2020). This raises a question of whether a **Balanced AI**, where business benefits or commercial viability of AI (*opportunity*); *ethics* in AI design and development, and AI utilisation or operation (*opportunity cost*) are all balanced? So the research question and problem is on whether an ethically designed, developed, implemented, and utilised NLP for Contact Centres in South Africa continue having positive effects on business performance? This question though cannot be fully answered in this SLR publication as the case study is still to be undertaken, but the conceptual framework(s) gained from this exercise will be used as a guide to conduct the case research. The primary goal for this SLR publication was to conduct thematic analysis for academic literature to achieve a *Balanced NLP*.

2 Methodology

A systematic literature review (SLR) (Paré et al. 2015) was conducted to identify relevant research papers with meta-analyses for qualitative synthesis. It followed 8 stages namely: conceptualization and protocol identification, searching the literature, screening the articles, selecting the relevant articles, performing some thematic analysis, presenting the results, developing the framework, and then concluding. These stages are illustrated in Fig. 1 below:

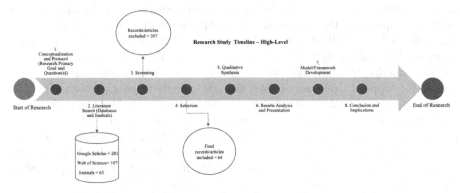

Fig. 1. Systematic literature review and meta-analyses research flow

The literature search, screening, and selection was conducted in 5 steps as shown in Table 1 below. These are sources searched, search keywords, search strategy, inclusion criteria, and exclusion criteria.

(i) Sources Searched
Two main databases, Web of Science and Google Scholar, were used as the main sources for the literature search. Also about 6 mainly IS journal websites were also used. These are Journal for Management Information Systems (JMIS); European Journal of Information Systems (EJIS); MIS Quarterly; Information Systems Journal (ISJ); Journal of Strategic Information Systems (JSIS); and Journal of Information Technology (JIT).

(ii) Search Keywords
The keywords "AI Implementation"; "AI Adoption", "Ethical AI Implementation", "NLP", and "Ethical NLP" were used to conduct the literature search from the above databases and journal websites. A total of over 350 articles were found.

(iii) Search Strategy
All the websites of the 2 identified Databases and Journals were interrogated. Using the combination of the above keywords, the search strategy was for articles from the last 3 years: January 2018 to December 2021. Interestingly, there were about three relevant articles from *MIS Quarterly*, the *International Journal of Information Management*, and *Critical Social Policy* that were already accepted for publishing in 2022 and those 3 papers were also included.

Table 1. Steps for searching and selecting the articles

Step	Step description	Detailed step description	No of articles
#1	Sources searched	**Databases**: (i). Web of Science, and (ii). Google Scholar **Journals**: (a). Journal for Management Information Systems (JMIS); (b). European Journal of Information Systems (EJIS); ©. MIS Quarterly; (d). Information Systems Journal (ISJ); (e). Journal of Strategic Information Systems (JSIS); and (f). Journal of Information Technology (JIT)	Journals n = 63; Databases n = 308
#2	Search terms	The Keywords used during the process were: "AI Implementation"; "AI Adoption", "Ethical AI Implementation", "NLP", and "Ethical NLP"	Journals n = 63; Databases n = 308
#3	Search strategy	Went to all the websites of the 2 identified Databases and Journals. Searched for articles in the last 3 years (2018 to 2021)	Journals n = 20; Databases n = 44
#4	Inclusion criteria	All publications between Jan 2018 and Dec 2021 with ethical AI principles and guidelines	Journals n = 20; Databases n = 44
#5	Exclusion criteria	Articles older than 2018 and those that were not entirely relevant to the ethical AI cause	Journals n = 43; Databases n = 264

(iv) Inclusion Criteria

With the search strategy discussed in (iii) above, the results were ±64 relevant articles selected. From those articles, Google Scholar contributed about 45 articles, which accounts for about 70% of all the included publications, and Web of Science about 19, which accounts for 30% of the articles.

The 2021 calendar year seemed to be the most prominent with over 33% of all ethical AI related articles being published that year. 2020 publications follow with 22% slightly ahead of 2019 articles at 22% were tied second at around 22% each, as shown in Table 2 below.

From the journal, the Association for Computational Linguistics and European Journal of Information Systems had the biggest number of articles with 4 each, as shown in Table 3 below. The Institute for Electronic and Electrical Engineers (IEEE), and Minds and Machines came second tied at 3 articles each. The was a very long tail of 1 publication each from various academic institutions, research institutes, MIS Quarterly, and other journals like Journal of Strategic Information Systems.

(v) Exclusion Criteria

All publications before January 2018 were excluded and also those that were not entirely relevant to the debate of ethical AI. This resulted in around 307 articles being excluded from the SLR. The field of ethical implementation and utilisation of AI tends to be highly

Table 2. Year of article publications included in the SLR

Year	Count	Percentage (%)
2018	11	17%
2019	14	22%
2020	14	22%
2021	22	34%
2022	3	5%
Total	**64**	**100%**

Table 3. Some selected journal publications included in the SLR > 1 article

Publication	Count	H-Index
Association for Computational Linguistics	4	71
AI & SOCIETY	2	
European Journal of Information Systems	4	108
Global AI Ethics	1	
Oxford	2	
Journal of Information Technology	2	79
Minds and Machines	3	39
International Journal of Information Management	2	114

dynamic and Ethical AI is a phenomenon that has recently been thrust into the spotlight, hence the decision to restrict the literature search to the last 3 years.

3 Analysis of Literature Identified

All the literature that has been reviewed came from the 64 relevant articles that have been included in the study using the combination of the keywords "*AI Implementation/Adoption*"; "*Ethical AI Implementation/Adoption*", "*NLP*", and "*Ethical NLP*". These are the articles published in the last 3 years, from 2018, that deal with AI ethical related issues.

Floridi and Cowls (2019) posit that the ethical debate around AI is almost as old as the 1950s and 1960s. However, it is only in recent years that impressive advances in the capabilities and applications of AI systems have brought the opportunities and risks of AI for society into sharper focus (Yang et al. 2018). Just to recap, Table 4 below shows some definitions of artificial intelligence from various authors and researchers:

Table 4. Artificial Intelligence (AI) definitions

No	AI definition	Author	Publisher & (Year)
1	AI are individualized applications being developed by businesses and used by consumers to power human decision-making processes, reduce the time needed to complete everyday tasks, and automatically inform us of events and incidents in the social and political world around us	Schrader and Ghosh	IEEE (2018)
2	AI is a growing resource of interactive, autonomous, and often self-learning agency that can deal with tasks that would otherwise require human intelligence and intervention to be performed successfully	Floridi and Cowls	Harvard (2019)
3	AI is increasing capability of machines to perform tasks, which have been conducted traditionally by people	Mika et al.	VTT Technical Research Centre of Finland (2019)
4	The theory and development of computer systems able to perform tasks normally requiring human intelligence, is widely heralded as an ongoing "revolution" transforming science and society altogether	Jobin et al.	Health Ethics & Policy Lab (2019)
5	AI encompasses various interrelated technologies often underpinned by machine learning algorithms, whereby AI achieves set objectives via supervised (with human guidance) or unsupervised (machine autonomous) learning through analyzing large datasets	Walsh et al.	Ethics and Information Technology (2019)
6	AI refers to 'machines that act intelligently when a machine can make the right decision in uncertain circumstances	Naude and Dimitri	AI & Society (2020)

(*continued*)

Table 4. (*continued*)

No	AI definition	Author	Publisher & (Year)
7	AI has the ability to decide what task to execute under diverse circumstances and sometimes beyond human capabilities and understanding and doesn't use fixed algorithm to perform a tasks	Teng	*AIBotics* (2020)

3.1 Ethical Issues AI

Alotaibi (2018) list 9 leading ethical issues related with artificial intelligence: *Unemployment*; *Inequality*; *Humanity*; *Artificial Stupidity*; *Racist Robots*; *Security*; *Evil Genies*; *Singularity*; *Robot Rights*. These are exactly the same ethical issues that had been raised by Julia Bossmann at the World Economic Forum (WEF) in 2016 which demonstrated that there's some unanimity when it comes to ethical AI issues.

Table 5. Leading ethical issues

Ethical issue	Brief description
Unemployment	Is this the end of jobs? What happens after the end of jobs?
Inequality	How do we ensure the income from AI machines is equitable shared?
Humanity	Can the machines influence our behaviours, interaction or relationship building with others?
Artificial stupidity	How do we prevent mistakes, especially in healthcare industry where it could have catastrophic consequences in human life?
Racist robots	How do we eliminate AI bias and injustice?
Security	Cybersecurity is even more important now, how do we keep AI safe from adversaries?
Evil genies	What if AI itself turns against humanity? How do we protect against unintended consequences?
Singularity	Humans controls dangerous animals because of ingenuity and intelligence. Can they do the same for complex and intelligent systems like AI?
Robot rights	Is there a humane way to treat AI systems? How do we know they require some 'human' rights?

Source: adapted from Bossmann (2016); andAlotaibi (2018)

On unemployment, the rise of Intelligence Automation (IA) – intelligent automation of knowledge and service work (Coombs et al. 2020) – could lead to job substitution especially for office work and clerical tasks, sales and commerce, transport and logistics;

manufacturing industry, construction, some aspects of financial services, and some types of services like translation, and tax consultancy (Degryse 2016). IA differs from previous forms of automation because of machine learning where AI machines can learn, adapt and improve over time, based on new available data (Coombs et al. 2020; Coombs 2020), which could lead *job polarization.* Job Polarization is a phenomenon where "advance technology seems to be displacing workers away from middle-skill/middle-pay jobs down to low-skill/low-wage jobs, where these workers further depress low-skill wages, or for a lucky few who are retrained, up to high-skill jobs where the workers enjoy higher productivity and higher wages" (Dau-Schmidt 2017).

3.2 Global AI Ethical Initiatives

Table 5 above on leading AI ethical issues and the unethical AI behaviours listed in the introduction page have led to the global initiatives to combat unethical AI design, development, implementation, and utilisation, especially in the global north. Ethical AI broadly refers to "the fair and just development, use, and management of AI technologies" (Bankins 2021, 5). Nakata et al. (2021) list some major global initiatives led by governments, national and international organisations, research institutes, civil society (non-profit), and private sector pertaining to AI principles for ethics since 2016 (Jobin et al. 2019). Some selected of those initiatives are listed below:

(i)   5 principles on *"Ethically Aligned Design"* from IEEE in 2017;
(ii)   6 principles on *"Future Computed"* by Microsoft in 2018;
(iii)   9 principles on *"Statement on AI, Robotics, and 'Autonomous' Systems"* by European Group on Ethics in Science and New Technologies in 2018;
(iv)   5 principles on "AI in the UK: ready, willing, and able" by the Select UK Committee on AI in 2018;
(v)   5 principles on *"Everyday Ethics for Planning"* by IBM in 2018;
(vi)   7 principles on *"Sony Group AI Ethics Guidelines"* by Sony in 2018;
(vii) 5 principles on *"An Ethical Framework for a Good AI Society"* by AI4People in 2018
(viii) 7 principles on *"Principles of Human-Centric AI Society"* by the Japan's Cabinet Office in 2019; and
(ix)   4 principles on *"Ethics Guidelines for Trustworthy AI"* by the EU's High-Level Expert Group on Artificial Intelligence on AI (AI-HLEG) in 2019.

Source: adapted from Nakata et al. (2021)

These initiatives and the subsequent principles and guidelines have led to the emergence of terms like AI4Good and AI4People Framework (Floridi et al. 2018; Cowls et al. 2021), Trustworthy AI (Mökander and Floridi 2021; Cowls et al. 2021), Responsible AI (Kindylidi and Cabral 2021), and Emotional AI, (McStay 2019). Some of these will be discussed in detail below:

3.2.1 Responsible AI

Responsible AI is concerned with the design, development, implementation, and utilisation of ethical, transparent, and accountable AI technology in order to reduce biases, promote fairness, equality, and to help facilitate interpretability and explainability of outcomes (Trocin et al. 2021). It is a fairly new phenomena that investigates the ethics of AI to understand the moral responsibility of these technologies (Kindylidi and Cabral 2021).

3.2.2 Trustworthy AI

Ethics Guidelines on Artificial Intelligence ('the Guidelines') were released by the European Commission's High-Level Expert Group on Artificial Intelligence on AI (AI-HLEG) for Trustworthy AI. Developing trustworthy AI by ensuring that systems are lawful, ethical and robust (European Commission 2019).

In general, these frameworks consist of several key themes, exemplified by the HLEG Guidelines for trustworthy AI that lay out seven key requirements: (European Commission 2019; Cowls et al. 2021; Krijger 2021):

(i) **Human Agency and Oversight**, "AI systems should allow humans to make informed decisions and be subject to proper oversight." (European Commission 2019; Cowls et al. 2021; Krijger 2021);

(ii) **Technical Robustness and Safety**, "AI systems need to be resilient, secure, safe, accurate, reliable, and reproducible." (European Commission 2019; Cowls et al. 2021; Krijger 2021);

(iii) **Privacy and Data Governance**, "Adequate data governance mechanisms that fully respect privacy must be ensured." (European Commission 2019; Cowls et al. 2021; Krijger 2021);

(iv) **Transparency**, "The data, system and AI business models should be transparent and explainable to stakeholders." (European Commission 2019; Cowls et al. 2021; Krijger 2021);

(v) **Diversity, Non-discrimination and Fairness**, "Unfair bias must be avoided to mitigate the marginalisation of vulnerable groups and the exacerbation of discrimination." (European Commission 2019; Cowls et al. 2021; Krijger 2021);

(vi) **Societal and Environmental well-being**, "AI systems should be sustainable and benefit all human beings, including future generations." (European Commission 2019; Cowls et al. 2021; Krijger 2021);

(vii) **Accountability** "Responsibility and accountability for AI systems and their outcomes should be ensured." (European Commission 2019; Cowls et al. 2021; Krijger 2021).

3.2.3 Research Institutes on Ethical AI

Below are just some selected research institutes that also developed some ethical AI principles.

(a) The **Capgemini Research Institute** also designed their six core principles and characteristics of ethical (Dolganova 2021): (a). "ethical actions from design to application" (Capgemini Research Institute 2019); (b). "transparency" (Capgemini Research Institute 2019); (c). "explainability of the functioning of AI" (Capgemini Research Institute 2019); (d). "the interpretability of the results" (Capgemini Research Institute 2019); (e). "fairness, lack of bias" (Capgemini Research Institute 2019); (f). "the ability to audit" (Capgemini Research Institute 2019).

(b) The **European Institute for Science, Media and Democracy** published a white paper outlining five principles of AI ethics (Floridi et al. 2020; Dolganova 2021): (a). Promoting human well-being (Floridi et al. 2020); (b). Harmlessness ("confidentiality, security, and 'attention to opportunities'") (Floridi et al. 2020); (c). Autonomy ("the right of people to make their own decisions") (Floridi et al. 2020); (d). Fairness ("respect for the interests of all parties that can be influenced by the actions of the system with AI, the absence of discrimination, the possibility of eliminating errors") (Floridi et al. 2020); (e). Explainability ("transparency of the logic of artificial intelligence, accountability") (Floridi et al. 2020).

Other fields, especially in Health Care, have developed their Frameworks for ethical AI considerations like in Pathology: Transparency, Accountability, and Governance (Chauhan and Gullapalliyz 2021) are of critical importance in an AI System and in Otolaryngology: Consent and Patient Privacy, Beneficence, Non-Maleficence, and Justice (Arambula and Bur 2020) are the principles adopted.

3.2.4 Private Sector Ethical AI Initiatives

The private sector, especially the Tech Companies, also developed some practical standards and guidelines in designing and developing AI within their companies:

(a) IBM's "Everyday Ethics for Artificial Intelligence: A practical guide for designers and developers" (IBM 2018; Ashby 2020) were published in 2018 and are in full operation: (i). Purpose expressed as unambiguously prioritized goals (IBM 2018); (ii). Truth about the past and present (IBM 2018); (iii). Variety of possible actions (IBM 2018); (iv). Predictability of the future effects of actions (IBM 2018); (v). Intelligence to choose the best actions (IBM 2018); (vi). Influence on the system being regulated (IBM 2018); (vii). Ethics expressed as unambiguously prioritized rules (IBM 2018); (viii). Integrity of all subsystems (IBM 2018); (ix). Transparency of ethical behaviour (IBM 2018).

(b) Microsoft also developed and published five principles that their leadership uses in order to guide their use of AI (Bankins 2021). These are mainly linked to the AI4People framework (Bankins and Formosa 2021; Bankins 2021) and are: (i). **fairness** ("aligned to the justice norm") (Microsoft n.d.); (ii). **reliability and safety** ("aligned to the beneficence norm") (Microsoft n.d.); (iii). **privacy and security** ("aligned to the non-maleficence norm") (Microsoft n.d.); (iv). **inclusiveness** ("aligned to the justice norm") (Microsoft n.d.); and (v). **transparency and accountability** ("aligned to the explicability norm") (Microsoft n.d.).

(c) Google as also developed and published *seven* principles that they use to design, develop, and utilise these AI type technologies (Dolganova 2021): (i). "AI should be socially useful" (Pichai 2018); (ii). "it is necessary to strive to avoid unfair influence on people" (Pichai 2018); (iii). "application of best security practices" (Pichai 2018); (iv). "responsibility for the actions of AI in front of people" (Pichai 2018); (v). "ensuring guarantees of confidentiality, proper transparency and control over the use of data" (Pichai 2018); (vi). "maintaining standards of excellence" (Pichai 2018); (vii). "limiting the use of potentially harmful and offensive software products" (Pichai 2018).

3.3 AI4People Framework

The AI4Good initiative led to the development AI4People Unified Framework of Principles for AI in Society (Floridi et al. 2018, 2020; Floridi and Cowls 2019). This framework seem to encapsulate all the earlier ethical AI principles and consolidated them into 5 unified ethical AI principles: (a). **Beneficence**: "Promoting Well-Being, Preserving Dignity, and Sustaining the Planet" (Floridi et al. 2018, 2020; Floridi and Cowls 2019; Beil et al. 2019); (b). **Non-maleficence** "Privacy, Security and 'Capability Caution'" (Floridi et al. 2018, 2020; Floridi and Cowls 2019; Beil et al. 2019); (c). **Justice**: "Promoting Prosperity and Preserving Solidarity" (Floridi et al. 2018, 2020; Floridi and Cowls 2019; Beil et al. 2019); (d). **Explicability**: "Enabling the Other Principles Through Intelligibility and Accountability" (Floridi et al. 2018, 2020; Floridi and Cowls 2019; Beil et al. 2019); (e). **Autonomy:** "The Power to Decide (to Decide)" (Floridi et al. 2018, 2020; Floridi and Cowls 2019; Beil et al. 2019).

3.4 AI Ethical Design

The robustness of the design and the agility of the architecture of Trustworthy AI is extremely important and must be built into the system from the beginning (Mökander and Floridi 2021). That could also lead to a process of continuous improvement of the re-design process. The IEEE has setup 4 Ethically Aligned Design (EAD) standards to address the ethical concerns of AI (Alotaibi 2018): (a). "Model Process for Addressing Ethical Concerns during System Design" (Alotaibi 2018); (b). "Transparency of Autonomous Systems" (Alotaibi 2018); (c). "Data Privacy Process" (Alotaibi 2018); and (d). "Algorithmic Bias Considerations" (Alotaibi 2018).

Also, the Japanese Society for Artificial Intelligence (JSAI) articulated some ethical principles to be followed by designers and developers of the AI systems (Dolganova 2021): These include.

(a) respect for human rights and respect for cultural diversity (JSAI 2017);
(b) compliance with laws and regulations, as well as not harming others (JSAI 2017);
(c) respect for privacy (JSAI 2017);
(d) justice (JSAI 2017);
(e) security (JSAI 2017);
(f) good faith (JSAI 2017);
(g) accountability and social responsibility (JSAI 2017);
(h) self-development and promotion of understanding of AI by society (JSAI 2017).

Leidner and Plachouras (2017) had originally proposed 6 ethical by design principles: (i). "proactive and not reactive"; (ii). "ethical set as a default setting"; (iii). "ethics
embedded into the process"; (iv). "end to end ethics"; (v). "visibility and transparency";
and (vi). "respect for user values". These were further reiterated by Chauhan and Gullapalliyz (2021) in their *Inclusive AI Design and No Bias* design principles. Schrader
and Ghosh (2018) also proposed an ethical AI development Framework which includes
the following five components: (a). "Identify ethical issues of AI"; (b). "Improve human
awareness of AI"; (c). "Engage in dialogical collaboration with AI"; (d). "Ensure the
accountability of AI"; (e). "Maintain the integrity of AI".

3.5 NLP Business Benefits

In most businesses their primary goal or objective when implementing an AI technology
or AI innovation is to enable product and service innovation, enhance the customer experience, improve customer service, increase efficiency and productivity, and also Improve
decision making (Amazon 2020). In some other cases, like financial services industry,
risk assessment and fraud detection and prevention are another priority (Nadimpalli
2017). Because the focus area in this AI study is the NLP, which is mainly utilised in
the services sector, the AI business benefits of interest would be revenue generation and
cost optimisation, customer service, efficiency improvements and high productivity, and
competitiveness.

3.5.1 Revenue Generation and Cost Optimisation

Revenue and sales forecasts with the deployment of the NLP solution are astronomically.
For instance, the NLP can process a thousand times more the queries and transactions that
would have otherwise been done by over 100 people (Nadimpalli 2017). That coupled
with some cost savings and optimisation use cases like "a Bank that saved over $9 million
to customers after implementing an AI tool to scan small business transactions for fake
invoices" (Quest et al. 2018). The scaling of these AI technologies is also simple but the
benefits are so huge. Through AI implementation in the Anti-Money-Laundering space
in banking, the incidents of suspicious activity increased to more than 20 times, but the
resolution is also quicker (Quest et al. 2018).

3.5.2 Customer Experience

The deployment of the AI in customer services environment has significantly enhanced
customer experience (Dolganova 2021) and this became a huge competitive advantage.
The introduction of the NLP in the financial services improved the Customer Satisfaction
Index (CSI) score, improved the Complaints to Compliments ratio, and the Net Promoter
Score (NPS) (Quest et al. 2018). With the forecast that over 80% of consumers are likely
to buy a brand that offers personalised service, the need for AI to enhance customer
experience is even bigger (Arambula and Bur 2020; Amazon 2020).

3.5.3 Efficiency Improvements and Enhance Productivity

The implementation of AI in various areas improves accuracy and efficiencies like in the contact centres the NLP empowered customers through self-service, shortens the Average Handle Time (AHT), especially on query resolution, significantly improves contact quality since upfront authentication enabled, and reduces customer effort (Leins et al. 2020). In the health care sector, AI improves efficiency and accuracy through image analysis, robot-assisted surgery, and drug discovery by augmented the ability to provide quality health care (Hague 2017). These AI models do not only predict the image analysis outcomes, but also identify the specific areas on an image for examination and showing the level of confidence in the prediction (Hague 2017).

3.5.4 Competitive Advantage or Strategic Competition

NLP is a strategic competition tool as it allows you to gain new customers, but also significantly enhance service offering the existing customers, which is a huge competitive advantage (Arambula and Bur 2020).

4 Analysis, Synthesis, and Interpretation

After all the ethical AI initiatives undertaken, Jobin et al. (2019) contended that there are around 84 ethical AI guidelines and around 11 principles: transparency; justice and fairness; non-maleficence; responsibility; privacy; beneficence; freedom and autonomy; trust; dignity; sustainability; and solidarity. But Floridi et al. (2020) team, which were part of the AI4Good initiative, agreed that there's some evidence of convergence of the 11 principles into around 5 principles which are part of the AI4People Ethical AI principles: transparency; justice and fairness; non-maleficence; responsibility; and privacy.

Of the 84 AI guidelines, 43, which makes just over 50%, is shared between 5 countries who are more economically developed: USA, UK, Germany, France, and Finland (Jobin et al. 2019). The rest of the guidelines is shared between EU, EC, Australia, Canada, and EU institutions.

4.1 The AI Triple Challenge

The triple AI challenge is trying to ensure that the AI is designed, developed, and operated in such a way that the business *opportunity*, the *ethical* considerations of the AI, and the *opportunity cost* are all balanced (Floridi et al. 2018). If these three components or themes, as we call them in this thematic analysis study, are fully considered then a Balanced AI (NLP) will be born. The *ethics* - avoidance of overuse or wilful misuse of the AI - and the business benefits - *opportunity* from the NLP (AI) innovation - emanating from the adoption of the AI have been discussed above, but the opportunity cost (underuse) hasn't been fully explored. The primary objective is to avoid the misuse and the underuse of the NLP (AI) technologies (Floridi et al. 2018).

The opportunity cost of the AI is the underuse of the AI technology (Floridi et al. 2018). This is the potential benefit that can be forgone or missed out because of an option that was not chosen in AI. Since it's unseen it is easy to overlook and opportunity cost.

Within AI, the broader risk is that it may be underused out of fear of overuse or misuse, hence the need to balance these in the Balanced NLP (AI) (Floridi et al. 2018).

4.1.1 Opportunity Theme

For the Balanced NLP (AI) to be realized, the NLP must satisfy all the necessary business case metrics, especially on return on investment. Within the NLP realm, Customer Experience, Revenue Generation & Cost Optimization, Competitiveness, and Efficiency Improvements & High Productivity are the best business metrics to satisfy (Table 6).

Table 6. Summary of the SLR outcome of the opportunity theme

Theme	Principle	Guidelines	Authors
Opportunity	Customer experience	• Improved customer satisfaction index; • Good customer service	Dolganova (2021); Quest et al. (2018)
	Revenue generation & cost optimization	• Sales revenues up; • Costs optimised	Quest et al. (2018)
	Competitiveness	• Gain new customers; • Retain existing customers	Arambula and Bur (2020)
	Efficiency improvements & high productivity	• Average handle time on queries improved • Empowered customers through self-service • Good contact quality	Hague (2017); Leins et al. (2020)

4.1.2 Ethics Theme

The outcome of the SLR ethics theme of the AI triple challenge is summarised in Table 7 below. Beneficence & Dignity; Justice & Fairness; Accountability & Responsibility; Human Agency & Oversight; Non-Maleficence, Governance, Privacy, and Security; and Transparency, Autonomy, & Freedom are the ethical principles that are consolidated into.

Beneficence and Dignity

For the AI to achieve the Balanced AI status in the global south it must benefit everyone. In South Africa in particular there's a crisis of *inequality*, *unemployment*, and *poverty* and any AI to be trusted it must create jobs and no job substitution or staff reduction. Job creation and augmentation must be at the centre instead of staff reduction or job polarization. The AI shouldn't further exacerbate the inequality problem instead everyone must benefit equally: company, employees, and customers. Basically, the AI must

Table 7. Summary of the SLR outcome of the ethics theme

Theme	Principles	Guidelines	Authors
Ethics	Beneficence & dignity	Promoting well-being, preserving dignity, and sustaining the planet	Floridi et al. (2018); Beil et al. (2019); Floridi and Cowls (2019); Jobin et al. (2019) European Commission (2019); Arambula and Bur (2020) Floridi et al. (2020)
	Justice & fairness	• Unfair bias must be avoided to mitigate the marginalisation of vulnerable groups and the exacerbation of discrimination • Respect for the interests of all parties that can be influenced by the actions of the system with AI, the absence of discrimination, the possibility of eliminating errors	Floridi et al. (2018); Pichai (2018); Beil et al. (2019); Floridi and Cowls (2019); Jobin et al. (2019); Capgemini Research Institute (2019); European Commission (2019); Arambula and Bur (2020); Floridi et al. (2020); Bankins (2021); Dolganova (2021); Krijger (2021); Microsoft n.d.
	Human agency & oversight	• Promoting human well-being • AI systems should allow humans to make informed decisions and be subject to proper oversight	Jobin et al. (2019) European Commission (2019); Floridi et al. (2020); Cowls et al. (2021); Krijger (2021)
	Non-maleficence, governance, privacy, and security	• No misuse or overuse of the AI systems • AI systems need to be resilient, secure, safe, accurate, reliable, and reproducible • Confidentiality, security, and 'attention to opportunities' Adequate data governance mechanisms that fully respect privacy must be ensured	Floridi et al. (2018); Jobin et al. (2019); Pichai (2018); European Commission (2019); Beil et al. (2019); Arambula and Bur (2020); Floridi et al. (2020); Bankins (2021); Cowls et al. (2021); Dolganova (2021); Krijger (2021); Microsoft n.d.

(continued)

Table 7. (*continued*)

Theme	Principles	Guidelines	Authors
	Transparency, autonomy, & freedom	• The data, system and AI business models should be transparent and explainable to stakeholders • Explainability of the functioning of AI • The right of people to make their own decisions • The power to decide	IBM (2018); Pichai (2018); Floridi et al. (2018); Schrader and Ghosh (2018); Jobin et al. (2019); European Commission (2019); Capgemini Research Institute (2019); Beil et al. (2019); Floridi and Cowls (2019); Arambula and Bur (2020); Floridi et al. (2020); Bankins (2021); Krijger (2021); Chauhan and Gullapalliyz (2021); Microsoft n.d.

be seen to addressing some of the socio-economic issues, which are really endemic in this society.

Justice and Fairness

The AI must also be seen to be helping out in ensuring fairness in society. The global south comes from some painful past of colonisation and exploitation and the AI must contribute in correcting some of those injustices. Racism was rife and AI shouldn't be seen to be furthering some racist behaviours. The languages, dialects, and accents vary from region to region and AI must adept to these through machine learning. There should be no biasness and proper pronunciation of African names would to an AI that could be trusted.

Non-maleficence, Governance, Privacy, and Security

Most countries in the global south are underdeveloped because of lack of service delivery and corruption by elected officials. In order for the Balanced AI to be trustworthy, it must be seen to be exposing these corrupt practices and not to be misused by the corrupt elite. It must comply with the laws like POPIA in South Africa and should stand in solidarity with the marginalised.

4.1.3 Opportunity Cost Theme

From the reviewed literature, the principles that could be grouped under the opportunity cost theme are *Transparency* and *Explainability*, as well as *Accountability* and *Responsibility*. The transparency principle is as an opportunity cost as is the ethics and makes a second appearance. For the balanced NLP (AI) to be a reality, these AI systems should be have people to explain their inner workings (features and functionality) so that they are not underused or underutilized (Table 8).

Table 8. Summary of the SLR outcome of the opportunity cost theme

Theme	Principles	Guidelines	Authors
Opportunity cost	Transparency & explainability	• The data, system and AI business models should be transparent and explainable to stakeholders • Explainability of the functioning of AI	IBM (2018); Pichai (2018); Floridi et al. (2018); Schrader and Ghosh (2018); Jobin et al. (2019); European Commission (2019); Capgemini Research Institute (2019); Beil et al. (2019); Floridi and Cowls (2019); Arambula and Bur. (2020); Floridi et al. (2020); Bankins (2021); Krijger (2021); Chauhan and Gullapalliyz (2021); Microsoft n.d.
	Accountability & responsibility	Responsibility and accountability for AI systems and their outcomes should be ensured	Schrader and Ghosh (2018); Beil et al. (2019); Chauhan and Gullapalliyz (2021); Dolganova (2021); European Commission (2019); Cowls et al. (2021); Krijger (2021)

4.2 Ethical AI Design

Based from the data of the SLR the ethical AI design principles can be consolidated into of *Data Privacy and Security, No Algorithmic Bias, Integrity of Subsystems,* and *Interpretability and Robustness of the AI,* as shown in Table 9 below. All other ethical design considerations can be accommodated with these principles. Therefore, for a Balanced AI to be achieved, these ethical AI design principles must be adhered to.

Table 9. Summary of the SLR outcome of the ethical AI design

Theme	Principles	Guidelines	Authors
Ethical AI design	Data privacy and security	• Security for personal data and access control while working with AI	IEEE (2009); Alotaibi (2018);
	No algorithmic bias	• Inclusive AI Design and no Bias	IEEE (2009); Shahriari and Shahriari (2017); Chauhan and Gullapalliyz (2021)
	Integrity of subsystems	• Visibility and transparency: design process published for public scrutiny and criticism	Leidner and Plachouras (2017); IBM (2018); Schrader and Ghosh (2018);
	Interpretability and robustness of the AI	• Build interpretability and robustness into AI systems from the start • Ethics embedded in the process end to end (E2E)	IEEE (2009); Shahriari and Shahriari (2017); Leidner and Plachouras (2017); Mökander and Floridi (2021);

4.3 Balance NLP Conceptual Framework

Based on the above Ethical AI Challenge themes identified and the ethical AI design principles, Fig. 1 below represents the recommended conceptual framework for the Balanced NLP from this SLR.

The ethical AI design is fundamental in ensuring the future ethical behaviour of the Balanced AI. The integrity of the data and it's privacy is critical since AI depends on the availability of data to continue learning and adapting. Those will lead to robust algorithms that won't end up performing unethical conduct. So the design is the input and the start of this conceptual framework.

The opportunity, ethics, and the opportunity are the outcomes of the model. From an *ethics* perspective, the Balanced AI Balanced AI recommends 5 ethical AI principles instead of the 11 ethical AI principles as suggested by Jobin et al. (2019) and the 5 solid principles suggested by Floridi et al. (2018, 2020), which is not really far from the Floridi et al. (2018, 2020) teams: (i) Beneficence & Dignity; (ii). Justice & Fairness; (iii). Human Agency & Oversight; (iv). Non-Maleficence, Governance, Privacy, and Security; and (v). Transparency, Autonomy, & Freedom. As discussed in their guidelines above, if these ethical principles are adhered to, the Balanced AI would be achieved.

From an *opportunity cost* perspective, there's two main principle to consider that should be the outcome of the Balanced AI: (i). *Transparency* and *Explainability*, and (ii). *Accountability* and *Responsibility*. For fear of underutilising the AI System, the ability to explain and understand all the features and functionality of the system is fundamental, hence transparency and explainability.

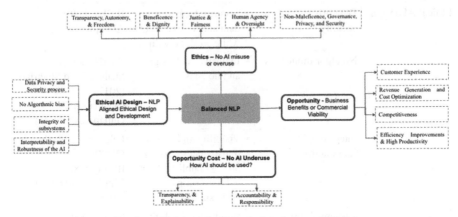

Fig. 2. Conceptual framework for a balanced NLP

The Opportunity theme or business benefits, the Balanced NLP, should be able to meet the return on investment (ROI) targets of Customer Experience, Revenue Generation & Cost Optimization, Competitiveness, and Efficiency Improvements & High Productivity. There are various metrics to test and validate these as part of the operational environment and they would need to be regularly re-visited to check the continued sustainability on the Balanced AI investment.

5   Recommendation

The above conceptual framework in Fig. 2 will be used as a guide for the case research study where the influence of ethical AI will be tested against the business models of the Contact Centre. The approach of the proposed case research study will be inductively conducted with qualitative data collection technique and thematic data analysis to test for the conceptual framework's validity.

5.1   Balanced NLP

For the Balanced NLP to be achieved, the intersection of ethics, opportunity, and opportunity cost should be proven, as seen in Fig. 3 below:

(i) Ethics - Opportunity
From this SLR, the link or intersection between the opportunity and ethics themes is critically important for the Balanced NLP to be achieved. This couldn't be clearly demonstrated in this review as the case research isn't finalised yet, but it will need to be fully explored and explained.

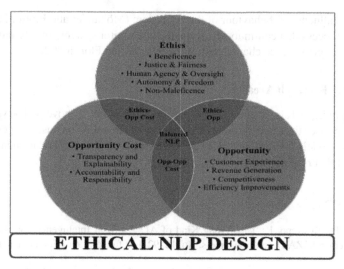

Fig. 3. Balanced NLP - intersection of ethics, opportunity, and opportunity cost

(ii) Ethics - Opportunity Cost

The link between ethics and opportunity cost themes has been demonstrated in this SLR where ethics and opportunity cost principles converge. The *Transparency* and *Explainability* principles, and *Accountability* and *Responsibility* principles are seen as part of the opportunity cost theme, but most authors classify them as ethics principles. In the final research case study, not much emphasis will be put to this intersection.

(iii) Opportunity - Opportunity Cost

From this SLR, the link or intersection between the opportunity and opportunity cost themes is also of critically importance for the Balanced NLP to be achieved. This couldn't be clearly demonstrated in this review as the case research isn't finalised yet, but it will need to be fully explored and explained.

(iv) Balanced NLP

The opportunity theme plays a central role in achieving this Balanced NLP. Its relationship with both the ethics and opportunity cost theme will determine whether a Balanced NLP - where ethics, opportunity, and opportunity cost intersect - is possible. This will be fully explored and explained in the case research study.

6   Concluding Remarks

The ethical AI design process is as important as any of the above themes in ensuring a Balanced NLP outcome. The ethical AI design is encompassing and is overarching for all the 3 other themes as its application is important in guaranteeing the ethicalness of the AI.

Finally, to constantly check if the NLP continues to meet the required standards of Balanced AI, the ethics-based auditing process would be recommended. This a governance mechanism that is used by businesses that design and deploy AI systems so as to control the influence or behaviour of the AI system (Mökander and Floridi 2021). This is an audit process that continuously evaluate and monitor system outputs and report on the system's performance characteristics (Mökander and Floridi 2021).

6.1 Future Research Areas

As already indicated above, the conceptual framework in Fig. 2 above will be validated in the research case study to determine the influence of ethical AI on business performance or business models in the Contact Centre. Other areas of study will be influenced by the outcome of that research case.

References

Acemoglu, D., Restrepo, P.: The Wrong Kind of AI? Artificial Intelligence and the Future of Labor Demand, IZA Discussion Papers, No. 12292, Institute of Labor Economics (IZA), Bonn (2019)

Alotaibi, S.S.: Ethical issues and related considerations involved with artificial intelligence and autonomous systems. Int. J. Adv. Comput. Sci. Appl. 9(4), 35–40 (2018)

Amazon: How Amazon Is Using AI To Better Understand Customer Search Queries (2020). https://analyticsindiamag.com/how-amazon-is-using-ai-to-better-understand-customer-search-queries/. Accessed 15 Jan 2022

Leidner, J.L., Plachouras, V.: Ethical by design: ethics best practices for natural language processing. In: Proceedings of the First Workshop on Ethics in Natural Language Processing, pp. 30–40, Association for Computational Linguistics (2017)

Microsoft: Responsible AI (n.d.). https://www.microsoft.com/en-us/ai/responsible-ai

Nakata, T., et al.: Initiatives for AI ethics: formulation of Fujitsu Group AI commitment. Find. Assoc. Comput. Linguist.: ACL-IJCNLP 56, 3895–3901 (2021)

Angwin, J., Larson, J., Mattu, S., Kirchner, L.: How we analyzed the compas recidivism algorithm. https://www.propublica.org/article/how-we-analyzed-the-compas-recidivism-algorithm. Accessed 22 Sept 2021 (2016)

Arambula, A.M., Bur, A.M.: Ethical considerations in the advent of artificial intelligence in otolaryngology. Head Neck Surg. 162(1), 38–39 (2020)

Ashby, M.: Ethical regulators and super-ethical systems. Systems 8, 53 (2020). https://doi.org/10.3390/systems8040053

Bankins, S.: The ethical use of artificial intelligence in human resource management: a decision-making framework. Ethics Inf. Technol. 23(4), 841–854 (2021). https://doi.org/10.1007/s10676-021-09619-6

Beil, M., Proft, I., van Heerden, D., Sviri, S., van Heerden, P.V.: Ethical considerations about artificial intelligence for prognostication in intensive care. Intensive Care Med. Exp. 7(1), 1–13 (2019). https://doi.org/10.1186/s40635-019-0286-6

Bender, E.M., Friedman, B.: Data statements for natural language processing: toward mitigating system bias and enabling better science. Trans. Assoc. Comput. Linguist. 6, 587–604 (2018)

Biller-Andorno, N., et al.: AI support for ethical decision-making around resuscitation: proceed with care. J. Med. Ethics 48, 175–183 (2020). https://doi.org/10.1101/2020.08.17.20171769

Bossmann, J.: Top 9 ethical issues in artificial intelligence (2016). https://www.weforum.org/agenda/2016/10/top-10-ethical-issues-in-artificial-intelligence/. Accessed 10 Jan 2022

Brynjolfsson, E., McAfee, A.: Race Against The Machine: How The Digital Revolution Is Accelerating Innovation, Driving Productivity, and Irreversibly Transforming Employment and The Economy. MIT Sloan School of Management (2012)

Capgemini Research Institute: why addressing ethical questions in AI will benefit organizations (2019). https://www.capgemini.com/wp-content/uploads/2019/08/AI-in-Ethics_Web.pdf. Accessed 11 Jan 2022

Chauhan, C., Gullapalliyz, R.R.: Ethics of AI in pathology current paradigms and emerging issues. Am. J. Pathol. **191**(10), 1673–1683 (2021)

CNBC: Jack Ma's Artificial Intelligence and Automation Warning [Video] (2017). https://youtu.be/cgAPG3Lh3gQ?t=70/. Accessed 14 Jan 2022

Naudé, W., Dimitri, N.: The race for an artificial general intelligence: implications for public policy. AI Soc. **35**(2), 367–379 (2019). https://doi.org/10.1007/s00146-019-00887-x

Coombs, C., Hislop, D., Taneva, S.K., Barnard, S.: The strategic impacts of intelligent automation for knowledge and service work: an interdisciplinary review. J. Strateg. Inf. Syst. **29**, 101600 (2020)

McStay, A.: Emotional AI and EdTech: serving the public good? Learn. Media Technol. **45**(3), 270–283 (2019). https://doi.org/10.1080/17439884.2020.1686016

Coombs, C.: Will COVID-19 be the tipping point for the Intelligent Automation of work? A review of the debate and implications for research. International Journal of Information Management. Reader in Information Systems, School of Business and Economics, Loughborough University, LE11 3TU, United Kingdom (2020)

Mökander, J., Floridi, L.: Ethics-based auditing to develop trustworthy AI. Mind. Mach. **31**(2), 323–327 (2021). https://doi.org/10.1007/s11023-021-09557-8

Cowls, J., Taddeo, M., Tsamados, A., Floridi, L.: Achieving a 'Good AI Society': comparing the aims and progress of the EU and the US. SSRN Electron. J. **27**, 1–25 (2021). https://doi.org/10.2139/ssrn.3851523

Quest, L., Charrie, A., Roy, S.: The risks and benefits of using AI to detect crime. Risk J. Harv. Bus. Publ. **8**, 2–5 (2018)

Taddeo, M., Floridi, L.: How AI can be a force for good: an ethical framework will help to harness the potential of AI while keeping humans in control. ResearchGate **361**(6404), 751–752 (2018)

Dastin, J.: Amazon scraps secret AI recruiting tool that showed bias against women. Reuters. https://www.reuters.com/article/us-amazon-com-jobs-automation-insight-idUSKCN1MK08 G. Accessed 18 Sept 2021 (2018)

Krijger, J.: Enter the metrics: critical theory and organizational operationalization of AI ethics. AI Soc. 1–11 (2021). https://doi.org/10.1007/s00146-021-01256-3

Dau-Schmidt, K.G.: The Impact of Emerging Information Technologies on the Employment Relationship: New Gigs for Labor and Employment Law. Articles by Maurer Faculty. 2657 (2017)

Degryse, C.: Digitilisation of the economy and its impact on labor markets - European Trade Union Institute - Working Paper (2016)

Schrader, D.E., Ghosh, D.: Proactively protecting against the singularity: ethical decision making in AI. IEEE Comput. Reliab. Soc. **16**, 56–63 (2018)

Dolganova, O.I.: Improving customer experience with artificial intelligence by adhering to ethical principles. Bus. Inform. **15**(2), 34–46 (2021). https://doi.org/10.17323/2587-814X.2021.2.34.46

European Commission: Ethics guidelines for trustworthy AI [Text] (8 April 2019). https://ec.europa.eu/digital-single-market/en/news/ethics-guidelines-trustworthy-ai

Mika, N., Nadezhda, G., Jaana, L., Raija, K.: Ethical AI for the governance of the society: challenges and opportunities (2019). VTT Technical Research Centre of Finland Ltd., Visiokatu 4, Tampere

Floridi, L., et al.: AI4People—an ethical framework for a good AI society: opportunities, risks, principles, and recommendations. Mind. Mach. **28**, 689–707 (2018)

Floridi, L., Cowls, J.A.: Unified framework of five principles for AI in society. Harvard Data Sci. Rev. (1.1) (2019). https://doi.org/10.1162/99608f92.8cd550d1

Pichai, S.: AI at Google: our principles. Google (2018). https://blog.google/topics/ai/ai-princi ples/. Accessed 05 Jan 2022

Floridi, L., et al.: AI 4People's ethical framework for a good AI society: Opportunities, risks, principles, and recommendations (2020). https://www.eismd.eu/wp-content/uploads/2019/03/AI4 People%E2%80%99s-Ethical-Framework-for-a-Good-AI-Society.pdf. Accessed 10 Jan 2022

Statistics South Africa: Quarterly Employment Statistics. Statistical Release - P0277, December, 2019 (2019)

Giermindl, L.M., Strich, F., Christ, O., Leicht-Deobald, U., Redzepi, A.: The dark sides of people analytics: reviewing the perils for organisations and employees. Eur. J. Inf. Syst. **31**, 410–435 (2021)

Trocin, C., Mikalef, P., Papamitsiou, Z., Conboy, K.: Responsible AI for digital health: a synthesis and a research agenda. Inf. Syst. Front. (2021). https://doi.org/10.1007/s10796-021-10146-4

Kindylidi, I., Cabral, T.S.: Sustainability of AI: the case of provision of information to consumers. Sustainability **13**, 12064 (2021). https://doi.org/10.3390/su132112064

Leins, K., Lau, J.H., Baldwin, T.: Give me convenience and give her death: who should decide what uses of NLP are appropriate, and on what basis?. In: Proceedings of the 58th Annual Meeting of the Association for Computational Linguistics, pp. 2908–2913, July 5–10, Association for Computational Linguistics (2020)

Hagerty, A., Rubinov, I.: Global AI ethics: a review of the social impacts and ethical implications of artificial intelligence. Global AI Ethics (2019)

Hague, D.C.: Benefits, Pitfalls, and Potential Bias in Health Care AI (2017)

IBM Developer Staff: AI Fairness 360 (2018). https://developer.ibm.com/technologies/artificial-intelligence/projects/ai-fairness-360/. Accessed 08 Jan 2022

Li, Y., Thomas, T., Liu, D.: From semantics to pragmatics: where IS can lead in Natural Language Processing (NLP) research. Eur. J. Inf. Syst. **30**(5), 569–590 (2021)

Nadimpalli, M.: Artificial intelligence risks and benefits. Int. J. Innov. Res. Sci. Eng. Technol. **6**(6), 4 (2017)

Shahriari, K., Shahriari, M.: IEEE standard review—ethically aligned design: a vision for prioritizing human wellbeing with artificial intelligence and autonomous systems. In: Humanitarian Technology Conference (IHTC), IEEE Canada International, pp. 197–201. IEEE (2017)

Obermeyer, Z., Powers, B., Vogeli, C., Mullainathan, S.: Dissecting racial bias in an algorithm used to manage the health of populations. Sci. **366**(6464), 447–453 (2019)

IEEE: Ethically aligned design: a vision for prioritizing human wellbeing with artificial intelligence and autonomous systems. IEEE (2009)

James, A., Whelan, A.: 'Ethical' artificial Intelligence in the welfare state: discourse and discrepancy in Australian social services. Crit. Soc. Policy **42**(1), 22–42 (2022). https://doi.org/10.1177/0261018320985463

Jobin, A., Ienca, M., Vayena, E.: The global landscape of AI ethics guidelines. Nat. Mach. Intell. **1**(9), 389–399 (2019)

Walsh, T., et al.: The Effective and ethical development of Artificial Intelligence, p. 250. ACOLA (2019). https://acola.org/wp-content/uploads/2019/07/hs4_artificial-intelligence-report.pdf

Teng, C.H.: How to approach ethical AI implementation? A practical guide to implementing ethical Artificial Intelligence (AI), AIBotics (2020)

Paré, G., Trudel, M.C., Jaana, M., Kitsiou, S.: Synthesizing information systems knowledge: a typology of literature reviews. Inf. Manag. **52**(2), 183–199 (2015)

Mittelstadt, B.: Principles alone cannot guarantee ethical AI (2020)

Yang, G.Z., et al.: The grand challenges of science robotics. Sci. Robot. **3**(14), eaar7650 (2018). https://doi.org/10.1126/scirobotics.aar7650

JSAI: The Japanese Society for Artificial Intelligence Ethical Guidelines (2017). http://ai-elsi.org/wp-content/uploads/2017/05/JSAI-Ethical-Guidelines-1.pdf. Accessed 14 Jan 2022

Pushing Boundaries - New and Innovative Philosophical, Theoretical and Methodological Approaches to Researching ICT4D

Understanding Evolution and Progress Towards Academic Maturity - A Review of Ten Years of ICT4D Research

Cecilia Strand[1](✉) and Mathias Hatakka[2]

[1] Uppsala University, Uppsala, Sweden
Cecilia.strand@im.uu.se
[2] Örebro University, Örebro, Sweden
mathias.hatakka@oru.se

Abstract. ICT4D researchers have since the inception of the field engaged in analyzing its emerging contours, as well as continuously pursued critical self-examination to support academic growth. This paper aims to contribute to a better understanding of the outcome of the efforts of pushing a relatively young field forward, by analyzing the field's level of academic maturity. Through a literature review of ten years of ICT4D research (2011–2020), which include all papers published in ITD, ITID and EJISDC as well as all ICT4D papers published in the Senior Scholars' Basket of 8 Journals, the study observes that ICT4D research fulfills several criteria associated with academic maturity. Furthermore, the results indicates that the most cited ICT4D research output is actively contributing to disciplines outside the reference disciplines of IS and development studies, suggesting that ICT4D research has established itself beyond the reference disciplines. The later constitutes a key milestone in disciplinary development.

Keywords: ICT4D · Disciplinary growth · Academic maturity · Literature review

1 Introduction

The use of information and communication technology for development (ICT4D) has a history dating back to the late 80s [1, 2]. The role of ICTs in development, and understanding of ICTs potential contribution to development, has both expanded and shifted over time [1, 3]. Although the general trend has been expansion; the field has also been questioned at its core, that is, whether ICT4D was one of many fads in development practices and research [4]. Early challenges was a direct result of numerous reports of failed ICT4D projects in developing contexts [5, 6]. By the early 2000s the existential debates appear to have settled, and since then the ICT4D field appears to have reconciled with its dual nature as a 'pracademic' endeavor, that is spanning the "somewhat ethereal world of academia as scholars and the pragmatic world of practice" [7], resulting in an orientation towards understanding how, rather than if, ICTs can support development [8–11].

© IFIP International Federation for Information Processing 2022
Published by Springer Nature Switzerland AG 2022
Y. Zheng et al. (Eds.): ICT4D 2022, IFIP AICT 657, pp. 423–439, 2022.
https://doi.org/10.1007/978-3-031-19429-0_25

Gomez [12] argued in 2013 that the "magnitude of the growth in the field of ICTD is unquestionable" (p. 2), and justifies the position by the number of new ICT4D journals and the hundreds of conferences that have taken place in the first decade of the millennium. Notions of growth and evolution is supported in one of the larger systematics reviews of the field, which sets out to understand the content characteristics of the ICTD field in the first decade of the millennium using a multi- variable research design [12]. Gomez's identifies multiple upward trends such as research output levels, contribution to design, policy or theory including formulation, testing and validation of theory.

Several studies have sought to contribute to a better understanding of the field's evolution over time, including critical self- examination concerning the field's research gaps [2, 13, 14]. Areas of neglect include, but is not limited to; lack of theoretical foundation and theoretical maturity [12]; paradigmatic assumption and influences [15], as well as engagement with critical theory including post-colonial theory [16–19]; failure to engage with ICTs impact on gender equality [20]; lack of explicit engagement and failure to unpack "development" as well as outline ICTs role in relation to development goals [21, 22]. Schelenz and Pawelec [23] offers a comprehensive summary of critiques regarding ICT4D research output and contribution to practice, and tries to support ICT4D academics to confront and overcome areas of critique, as well as remind the community of its history as a discipline with an ambition to support practice. To sum up, the community of ICT4D researchers have since the inception of the field, engaged in analysis of not only the field's emerging contours, in terms of thematic, geographical, methodological orientation, but also continuously pursued critical self-examination to support further growth. In line with this tradition, this paper aims to contribute to a better understanding of the outcome of these efforts of pushing the field forward, but does so from a slightly different vantage point than previous work. This paper hope to contribute to a better understanding of evolution over time by engaging in an analysis of the field's level academic maturity.

Serenko and Bontis [24] argues that academic maturity rests on the fulfillment of a number of criteria, such as having an established set of journals, regular academic meetings, distinct subject matter, major scholars, growing body of knowledge, recognized learned societies or special interest groups, well-developed networking channels, a place in the academic teaching curriculum, and recognition of scholarly output, as well as an impact on other disciplines. Wade et al. [25] highlight the importance of making a substantial contribution theoretically and methodlogically to other fields to achieve the status of being a reference discipline. A reference discipline is thus a well-established and recognized academic domain that supports other disciplines' intellectual endeavors [26]. Wade et al. [25] argued that the IS field, at the time had only left "a modest imprint", it cannot be regarded as reference discipline. Although the listed criteria makes no reference to the importance of academic environments to support high quality and impactful research, there is reason to believe that critical mass both in terms of intellectual capacity and other resources, are important factors. Especially in fields with strong international competition, it has been noted that concentration of resources including intellectual capability, is an important factor in achieving internationally recognized research [27]. Furthermore, the existence of critical mass and formalized research groups, appear to be conducive to the quality of individual researchers' output [28], and international visibility, which can be seen as a proxy for research quality [29]. We also interpret it as a sign of institutional recognition of the discipline.

To better understand the ICT4D field's evolution and level of maturity, this paper explores factors associated with academic maturity. Through a review of the past ten years of ICT4D research output, this paper analyzes:

- The existence of major scholars, where major is understood as number of publications and citations.
- The existence of academic ICT4D hubs, i.e., congregation of academic production to specific spaces.
- The existence of key works, understood as frequently cited works.
- The degree of impact on disciplines outside the two reference disciplines IS and development studies, i.e., to what degree is ICT4D research being recognized by other academic disciplines.

2 Method

For the review of the literature we followed the guidelines of journal selection by Webster and Watson [30]. Similar to Gomez [12] we selected the three top ranked peer-reviewed journals from our field of study, ICT4D. Gomez [12] also included two additional ICT4D focused journals, as well as two ICT4D conferences. In this study we supplemented the top ranking ICT4D journals with the top journals in one of our reference fields, IS. The top three ICT4D journals was selected based on Heeks ranking [31][1] and the top IS journals selected are the Senior Scholars' Basket of 8 Journals (SSB8J) [32]. The literature review thus comprised of 11 journals in total. For the three ICT4D journals EJISDC, ITD and ITID all papers between 2011–2020 (except for editorials and book reviews) were included. For articles from the SSB8J a slightly more purposeful sample stagey was applied, which entailed identifying and including only the articles which had a clear focus on ICT4D. The sample processes included a search using the keywords: 'ICT4D', 'ICTD', 'Developing countries' and 'Developing country'. In a second step all abstracts were read to determine if the paper had an ICT4D focus or if ICT4D was cursorily mentioned. We acknowledge that ICT4D is an interdisciplinary field, and scholars publish in a vast number of different outlets, including other IS journals not included in this study. There are for example several regionally oriented ICT4D journals focusing on Africa and Asia that are not included. Similiar to Gomez [12], we choose to exclude region- specific journals. With the aforementioned limitations, we may have missed some highly cited ICT4D papers, which can have had an impact on the results. We recommend that development studies journals, as well as high-ranking conferences, should be included in future studies. A total of 862 papers were included in this study. See Table 1 for selected journals and number of papers.

With almost half of the articles (47%) EJISDC dominate the material in terms of number of published ICT4D papers 2011–2020. Only 6.5% were published in the SSB8J. After identification all papers were coded on:

---

[1] Note that Information Technologies & International Development Journal are currently not publishing any papers. Last issue was in 2020.

Table 1. Selected journal and number of papers

Journal	Number of papers	Average no. of citations
EJISDC	406	17,16
ITD	267	30,41
ITID	133	29,91
ISJ	19	
JIT	13	
JAIS	8	
MISQ	6	
EJIS	4	
JSIS	3	
ISR	2	
JMIS	1	
SSB8J combined	56	54,88

– Journal name, year published, volume and issue.
– Title of the paper.
– Authors (both main and co-authors).
– Author university. (If author was affiliated with multiple universities, only the first listed university was noted).
– The country of the authors' university affiliation.
– Number of citations for each paper.

Google Scholar was used to determine the number of citations as it provides the most comprehensive citation data [33]. The number of citations was collected during one week in September 2020. Since recently published papers have had a shorter time to accumulate citations, we acknowledge that the mapping is skewed in favor of older papers. The entire statistical analysis was done in excel using Pivot tables, and we only use descriptive statistic in the paper.

To explore the field's impact on other disciplines, we mapped citation patterns for the ten most cited papers. A citation identifies the "researchers whose concepts, theories, methods, equipment, and so on, inspired or were used by the author" [34]. Furthermore, a citation of a particular text, reflects the merits of it, that is, its quality, significance, and/or impact [34]. The study approached citations in similar fashion to Wade et al. [25], who explains the rationale behind citation analysis as "[c]itations represent a means by which knowledge is transferred among scholars both within a field and between fields. Citations are the foundational building blocks upon which scientific traditions are formed and advanced" (p. 249).) Given the study's sample size of 862 articles, where each item has accumulated numerous citations, in combination with the study's resources limitations; the citation analysis only included the top ten most cited articles. This purposeful sampling technique, was motivated by the top ten constituting the field's most substantial output. Scientometrics considers a set of the most influential articles as a valid sample-procedure [35]. For each of the top ten cited articles, the citations we assessed and coded as either: a) ICT4D, b) IS, c) Development, or d) Other, i.e., outside the two reference disciplines, such as business administration, political science or pedagogy etc. During the analysis we reviewed each source that we were not immediately able to place within a specific field. The review entailed examining the journal's aims and scope statement, followed by an examination of the papers the journal typically published. Sources in languages other than English, Germen, French, Spanish and Portuguese, were excluded due the authors' language limitations to assess the source's disciplinary home. Further-more, to limit the risk for interpretational error in the coding, all items were coded by both authors.

3 Findings

Several studies have ambitiously analyzed the ICT4D field's growth since the start of the millennium, and concluding it to be a diverse, multi-disciplinary and multi-stakeholder academic field [2, 19, 23]. This study sought to contribute to the understanding of the ICT4D field's evolution, using a different lens than most previous studies.

3.1 Existence of Major Scholars

The existence of major scholars is one criteria to measure disciplinary maturity. Table 2 shows the authors that has published the most papers as main author between 2011–2020. Although one author stands out, Gomez, it is difficult to argue that there is a group of leading scholars. Rather there is a spread of authors publishing in the field (there are 1606 different authors that are either main or co-author of the papers included in the study). With the study including all papers for ten years, one could arge that most of leading authors publishes relatively little. The productivity measure would, of course, change had we included more journals and conferences such as IFIP WG 9.4, ICTD and SIG GlobDev.

The results could also indicate a diverse community where many contribute. Only Agder University and University of Cape Town appear twice in the list for the 14 most published researchers. The results indicate that the field is still a rather male- dominated domain with only three of the 14 most published authors being female.

Looking at the SSB8J specifically (see Table 3) we see that 16 authors have published 2 or more papers from 2011 to 2020. Comparing total number of publications with publications in SSB8J we see that some authors, such as Venkatesh, Sykes and Myers only publish in SSB8J whereas e.g., Gomez only publish in the ICT4D specific journals. We also see that some of the most published overall, such as Heeks and Thapa, publish in both the SSB8J and the ICT4D specific journals.

Table 4 shows the most cited authors (as both main and co-authors) and average number of citations per paper. Not surprisingly, considering he is the most productive in terms of number of publications, Gomez has the greatest number of citations with 529. On second place it is a "tie" between Venkatesh and Sykes. For all their papers they are main author (Venkatesh) and co-author (Sykes) which explains their identical numbers.

Table 2. Most published authors (as main author)

Main author	No. of papers	University	Gender
Gomez, Ricardo	10	University of Washington	Male
Thapa, Devinder	7	Agder University	Male
Heeks, Richard	7	University of Manchester	Male
Samoilenko, Sergey	6	Virginia Union University	Male
Bello-Bravo, Julia	6	Michigan State University	Female
Venkatesh, Viswanath	5	University of Arkansas	Male
Etoundi, Roger Atsa	5	University of Yaoundé	Male
Winley, Graham Kenneth	4	Assumption University	Male
Mariscal, Judith	4	Centro de Investigación y Docencia Económicas	Female
Mooketsi, Bojelo E	4	University of Cape Town	Female
Sein, Maung K	4	Agder University	Male
Bankole, Felix O	4	University of Cape Town	Male
Duffett, Rodney	4	Cape Peninsula University of Technology	Male
Effah, John	4	University of Ghana Business School	Male
18 authors with 3 publications			

Interesting though, while they only have 5 published papers, they have almost as many total numbers of citations as Gomez. As mentioned all of Gomez papers are published in the three dedicated ICT4D journals, whereas Venkatesh and Sykes papers are published in the SSB8J (3 in MISQ, 1 in ISJ and 1 in ISR). Papers publishing in the SSB8J have a higher average number of citations (see Table 1). Similar to most published authors, most of the most cited authors are male (17 of 20).

When combining data for lead and co-authorship, number of total citations, as well as average number of citations per paper (Table 4); it become even more difficult to argue a group of leading scholars. Is an individual a leading scholar based on the number of papers published? Or the total number of citations accumulated? The ICT4D field has a group of six scholars that have accumulated 400 or more citations, but with a range of 5–16 papers contributing to the overall score.

3.2 The Existence of ICT4D Hubs

With established research groups likely to be a conducive environmental factor to research output and quality, as well as a sign of institutional recognition of the discipline; the study sought to explore the existence of research hubs. Table 5 shows the 21 most published universities. There appear to be two main hubs, that in terms of number of peer reviewed articles, are more productive than other environments. These academic environments are University of Cape Town and University of Oslo.

Table 3. Most published authors in SSB8J (as main- or co-author)

Author	No. of papers
Venkatesh, Viswanath	5
Sykes, Tracy Ann	5
Heeks, Richard	3
Rai, Arun	3
Karanasios, Stan	3
Soekijad, Maura	2
Sandeep, M. S	2
Myers, Michael D	2
Cui, Lili	2
Slavova, Mira	2
Cui, Miao	2
Thapa, Devinder	2
Ferguson, Julie	2
Pan, Shan L	2
Ravishankar, M. N	2
Avgerou, Chrisanthi	2

3.3 ICT4D Key Work

A key feature of a mature research discipline is the existence of key works, defined here as frequently cited works. The ICT4D field appear to have a set of key works that are widely cited and most likely to impact the conversations within ICT4D community. Not surprisingly, most (17) of the papers in the list are from 2011–2015. The most cited paper is however from 2017 and published in ITD. No particular academic environment dominate, which could be interpreted as a there are several institutions that provide the right conditions for impactful work to be produced (Table 6).

3.4 Impact Outside the Reference Disciplines of IS and Development Studies

Does ICT4D research draw primarily intra-disciplinary citations from the fields of IS and development, or other disciplines? Wade et al. [25] describe a 80/20 rule in his study of twelve years of published IS management research, where around 80% of citations are intra-disciplinary citations, and the rest come from other fields.

The citation analysis (see Table 7) of the ten most influential articles indicate that ICT4D key works often, but not always surpass the 80/20 rule. The analysis indicates that several of the most cited articles have been successful in reaching an audience outside the two reference disciplines of IS and development studies. A closer look does however indicate that it is primarily research that focus on trade, business- intelligence

Table 4. Most cited authors (as main- and co-author)

Author	No. of citations	No. of papers (main- and co-author)	Avg. citations	Gender
Gomez, Ricardo	529	16	33,06	Male
Venkatesh, Viswanath	518	5	103,60	Male
Sykes, Tracy Ann	518	5	103,60	Female
Heeks, Richard	488	13	37,54	Male
Brown, Irwin	442	9	49,11	Male
Thapa, Devinder	417	11	37,91	Male
Sæbo, Øystein	331	8	41,38	Male
Bankole, Felix O	317	4	79,25	Male
Pather, Shaun	302	6	50,33	Male
Sein, Maung K	295	7	42,14	Male
Walsham, Geoff	290	3	96,67	Male
Graham, Mark	284	5	56,80	Male
Smith, Matthew L	276	3	92,00	Male
Blumenstock, Joshua E	265	2	132,50	Male
Wyche, Susan	241	3	80,33	Female
Zainudeen, Ayesha	240	3	80,00	Female
Carmody, Padraig	232	2	116,00	Male
Venkatraman, Srinivasan	219	1	219,00	Male
Chib, Arul	218	7	31,14	Male
Furuholt, Bjørn	211	3	70,33	Male

and administration, that have been particularly successful in drawing citations outside the two reference disciplines.

4 Discussion and Conclusion

This study sought to contribute to the growing body of research on the ICT4D field's evolution. We belive this study complements some of the previous work most notably, Gomez [12] and Walsham [2], as well as Andersson and Hatakka [36]. We used a slightly different lens than most previous studies that primarily engaged with analyzing the field's key foci, methodological and theoretical approaches, as well as geographical orientation and implication for policy. Academic maturity can be measures based on a number of criteria such as an established set of journals and conferences, major scholars, a growing body of knowledge, well-developed networking channels, a place in the academic teaching curriculum, recognition of scholarly output [24], as well as an impact on other disciplines [25]. In this paper we explored some of the criteria for academic maturity.

Table 5. Affiliation for main authors

University	No. of published papers	Country
University of Cape Town	35	South Africa
University of Oslo	31	Norway
University of Washington	19	United States
University of South Africa	17	South Africa
Cape Peninsula University of Technology	16	South Africa
University of Manchester	14	United Kingdom
University of Agder	13	Norway
University of London	12	United Kingdom
London School of Economics & Political Science	10	United Kingdom
University of Yaoundé	10	Cameroon
Örebro University	9	Sweden
Assumption University	8	Thailand
Michigan State University	8	United States
University of the West Indies	8	Jamaica
Nanyang Technological University	8	Singapore
University of Fort Hare	8	South Africa
University of Ghana Business School	8	Ghana
University of Pretoria	7	South Africa
University of Oxford	7	United Kingdom
Rhodes University	7	South Africa
University of the Western Cape	7	South Africa

The existence of major scholars - the study shows that the field has several established scholars that both have a relatively high production of papers and citations. We can also see that ICT4D research are welcome, and published, in the top IS journals. Hence, there are indications that the field has leading scholars, but the findings are inconclusive, with the configuration of a leading group is difficult to ascertain.

The existence of ICT4D hubs – Our study also reveals that there are number of universities with a high production of ICT4D research. As mentioned, the existence of critical mass and formalized research groups, appear to be conducive to the quality of individual researchers' output [28]. Albeit there exist research environments who are numerically productive, i.e., are responsible for a relatively high number of papers; these research environments were not responsible for any of the top ten most cited work, University of Cape Town, has one paper on the top twenty list. Looking at the list of most published universities it is also apparent there are 4 countries that produces most ICT4D research, South Africa, UK, Norway and the USA.

Table 6. 20 Most cited papers

Journal	Year	Title	Author	Citations	Affiliation of authors
ITD	2017	ICT4D research: reflections on history and future agenda	Walsham, G	264	University of Cambridge
ISJ	2014	Understanding e-Government portal use in rural India: role of demographic and personality characteristics	Venkatesh, V., Sykes, T. A., & Venkatraman, S	219	University of Arkansas, Coastal Carolina University
ISJ	2011	A preliminary study of ecommerce adoption in developing countries	Datta, P	209	Kent State University
MISQ	2015	Bridging the Service Divide Through Digitally Enabled Service Innovations: Evidence from Indian Healthcare Service Providers	Srivastava, S. C., & Shainesh, G	198	HEC, Paris, Indian institute of management, Bangalore
ITD	2015	An Empirical Study of Factors Affecting E-Commerce Adoption among Small- and Medium-Sized Enterprises in a Developing Country: Evidence from Malaysia	Ahmad, S. Z., Abu Bakar, A. R., Faziharudean, T. M., & Mohamad Zaki, K. A	197	Abu Dhabi University, Prince Sultan University, University of Malaya,
ITID	2011	Mobile Phones and Expanding Human Capabilities	Smith, M. L., Spence, R., & Rashid, A. T	191	International Development Research Centre – Ottawa, Economic and Social Development Affilates – Toronto

(continued)

Table 6. (*continued*)

Journal	Year	Title	Author	Citations	Affiliation of authors
EJISDC	2012	ICT Evaluation: Are We Asking the Right Questions?	Gomez, R., & Pather, S	177	University of Washington, Cape Peninsula University of Technology
ITD	2016	Why Don't Farmers Use Cell Phones to Access Market Prices? Technology Affordances and Barriers to Market Information Services Adoption in Rural Kenya	Wyche, S., & Steinfield, C	177	Michigan State University
EJIS	2012	The impact of IT-business strategic alignment on firm performance in a developing country setting: exploring moderating roles of environmental uncertainty and strategic orientation	Yayla, A. A., & Hu, Q	175	Binghamton University, Iowa state university
ITID	2013	Considering Failure: Eight Years of ITID Research	Dodson, L. L., Sterling, S. R., & Bennett, J. K	170*	University of Colorado
ITD	2013	Telecommunications development and economic growth in Africa	Chavula, H. K	167	Economic Commission for Africa
ISR	2013	Digital Divide Initiative Success in Developing Countries: A Longitudinal Field Study in a Village in India	Venkatesh, V., & Sykes, T. A	166	University of Arkansas

(*continued*)

Table 6. (*continued*)

Journal	Year	Title	Author	Citations	Affiliation of authors
EJISDC	2011	Mobile Banking Adoption in Nigeria	Bankole, F. O., Bankole, O. O., & Brown, I	161	University of Cape Town
JMIS	2013	Information Technology and Productivity in Developed and Developing Countries	Dedrick, J., Kraemer, K. L., & Shih, E	161	Syracuse University, University of California, Sungkyunkwan University
ITD	2012	Youth, mobility and mobile phones in Africa: findings from a three-country study	Porter, G., Hampshire, K., Abane, A., Munthali, A., Robson, E., Mashiri, M., & Tanle, A	156	Durham University, University of Cape Coast, University of Malawi,
ITD	2017	Increasing collaboration and participation in smart city governance: a cross-case analysis of smart city initiatives	Viale Pereira, G., Cunha, M. A., Lampoltshammer, T. J., Parycek, P., & Testa, M. G	150	Danube University, Krems Pontifical Catholic University of Rio Grande do Sul
ITD	2012	Inferring patterns of internal migration from mobile phone call records: evidence from Rwanda	Blumenstock, J. E	146	University of California
ITID	2011	Social Influence in Mobile Phone Adoption: Evidence from the Bottom of the Pyramid in Emerging Asia	De Silva, H., Ratnadiwakara, D., & Zainudeen, A	144	LIRNEasia, Louisiana State University

(*continued*)

Table 6. (*continued*)

Journal	Year	Title	Author	Citations	Affiliation of authors
EJISDC	2011	The Developmental Contribution From Mobile Phones Across the Agricultural Value Chain in Rural Africa	Furuholt, B., & Matotay, E	133	University of Agder, Mzumbe University
ITID	2013	Emergent Practices Around CGNet Swara: A Voice Forum for Citizen Journalism in Rural India	Mudliar, P., Donner, J., & Thies, W	132*	University of Texas, Microsoft Research India

*Google scholars do not separate the citations from the journal ITID and the conference proceedings the paper was first published in.

Key works – in our study we also list the top 20 cited papers from 2011–2020. Of the top 20 cited papers there are only two authors that appear more than once -Venkatesh and Sykes (as main- and co-authors of the same papers) - with two papers on the list. When looking at where the papers are published, while the SSB8J papers only represent 6.5% of the papers in our dataset, six of the 20 most cited papers are from SSB8J, including 3 of the top five cited papers.

Impact outside of the reference disciplines - The study's citations analysis indicate that ICT4D research is being recognized beyond its reference disciplines. Some sub-areas are clearly contributing to and influencing other academic disciplines. Following the 80/20 rule [25] we see that eight of the top ten cited papers have more than 20% of the citations outside of the reference fields of ICT4D. For one paper [37], as much as 45,7% of the citations are outside of ICT4D or its reference fields. While, the citation-patterns can be interpreted as a sign of recognition from other disciplines, further bibliometric studies are required to establish to what degree ICT4D research recirprocates and itself embraces pluralism and transdisciplinarity beyond its refence disciplines. Future work should thus explore to what degree the ICT4D field, is defined by an intellectual ideal of a never-ending cycle of wide engagement with other fields, and learning from other disciplines to ensure both continuous relevance of output and rigour [38].

Other criteria for a mature field, not explicitly studied in this paper, would also indicate that the ICT4D field has come a long way since the early 2000s. ICT4D has its own specialized journals (e.g., ITD and EJISDC) and its own regular academic meetings through a set of international conferences and workshops, e.g., IFIP WG 9.4 began already in 1989, followed by ICTD (2006) and SIG GlobDev (2008). ICT4D research status is further verified by e.g., special issues in the SSB8J. For example, at the time of this paper, there is a special issue in MISQ about "Digital Technologies and Social Justice" [39] and in ISJ about "Information Systems and Sustainable Development" [40].

Table 7. Citation analysis of the ten most cited papers

Journal	Title	ICT4D	IS	Development	Other
ITD	ICT4D research: reflections on history and future agenda	47,8%	28,4%	11,7%	12,1%
ISJ	Understanding e-Government portal use in rural India: role of demographic and personality characteristics	28,8%	43,4%	0,5%	27,4%
ISJ	A preliminary study of ecommerce adoption in developing countries	29,7%	44,0%	0,5%	25,8%
MISQ	Bridging the Service Divide Through Digitally Enabled Service Innovations: Evidence from Indian Healthcare Service Providers	17,7%	47,5%	4,5%	30,3%
ITD	An Empirical Study of Factors Affecting E-Commerce Adoption among Small- and Medium-Sized Enterprises in a Developing Country: Evidence from Malaysia	32,0%	18,3%	4,0%	45,7%
ITID	Mobile Phones and Expanding Human Capabilities	31,5%	25,0%	9,0%	34,5%
EJISDC	ICT Evaluation: Are We Asking the Right Questions?	41,2%	31,1%	4,5%	23,2%
ITD	Why Don't Farmers Use Cell Phones to Access Market Prices? Technology Affordances and Barriers to Market Information Services Adoption in Rural Kenya	35,6%	18,6%	8,5%	37,3%
EJIS	The impact of IT-business strategic alignment on firm performance in a developing country setting: exploring moderating roles of environmental uncertainty and strategic orientation	20,6%	42,3%	0%	37,1%
ITID	Considering Failure: Eight Years of ITID Research	46,5%	31,7%	8,8%	13,0%

Finally, ICT4D is an independently taught subject and part of the academic teaching curriculum across the world. ICT4D specific curriculums have been developed [41] and is being taught at universities across the world [42–44].

Mindful of that assessing academic maturity is not a black and white matter, but entirely dependent on how it is measured and when, this study makes no claim to conclusively determine the ICT4D field level of maturity. Nevertheless and despite that several criteria appear to be only partially fulfilled, the community of researchers should take great pride in the field's evolution, and where our research is read and appreciated by audiences beyond the reference disciplines of IS and development studies.

Acknowledgements. The authors wish to acknowledge Sirajul Islam, Associate professor at Örebro University, Sweden for his valuable assistance during a first round of coding.

References

1. Heeks, R.: Do information and communication technologies (ICTs) contribute to development? J. Int. Dev. **22**(5), 625–640 (2010)
2. Walsham, G.: ICT4D research: reflections on history and future agenda. Inf. Technol. Dev. **23**(1), 18–41 (2017)
3. Heeks, R.: ICT4D 2.0: the next phase of applying ICT for international development. Computer **41**(6), 26–33 (2008)
4. Wade, R.H.: Bridging the digital divide: new route to development or new form of dependency? Glob. Gov. **8**, 443–466 (2002)
5. Avgerou, C., Walsham, G.: Information Technology in Context: Studies From the Perspective of Developing Countries. University of North London voices in development management, vol. 303. Aldershot, Ashgate (2000)
6. Heeks, R.: Information systems and developing countries: failure, success, and local improvisations. Inf. Soc. **18**(2), 101–112 (2002)
7. Walker, D.: Being a pracademic–combining reflective practice with scholarship. In: Keynote Address AIPM Conference (2010)
8. De', R., Ratan, A.L.: Whose gain is it anyway? Structurational perspectives on deploying ICTs for development in India's microfinance sector. Inf. Technol. Dev. **15**(4), 259–282 (2009)
9. Sein, M.K., Harindranth, G.: Conceptualizing the ICT artifact: toward understanding the role of ICT in national development. Inf. Soc. **20**(1), 15–24 (2004)
10. Walsham, G., Robey, D., Sahay, S.: Foreword: special issue on information systems in developing countries. MIS Q. **31**(2), 317–327 (2007)
11. Harindranth, G., Sein, M.K.: Revisiting the role of ICT in development. In: 9th International Conference on Social Implications of Computers in Developing Countries, São Paulo, Brazil (2007)
12. Gomez, R.: The changing field of ICTD: growth and maturation of the field, 2000–2010. Electron. J. Inf. Syst. Dev. Ctries. **58**(1), 1–21 (2013)
13. Dey, B., Ali, F.: A critical review of the ICT for development research. In: Dey, B., Sorour, K., Filieri, R. (eds.) ICTs in Developing Countries, pp. 3–23. Palgrave Macmillan UK, London (2016). https://doi.org/10.1057/9781137469502_1
14. Krauss, K., Turpin, M.: The emancipation of the researcher as part of information and communication technology for development work in deep rural South Africa. Electron. J. Inf. Syst. Dev. Ctries. **59**(1), 1–21 (2013)
15. Gomez, R., Day, S.A.: Research questions, paradigms and methods in ICT for development: content analysis of selected ICTD literature, 2000–2010. In: Proceedings of IFIP WG 9.4: Social Implications of Computers in Developing Countries (2013)
16. Pal, A., De, R.: For Better or for Worse? A Framework for Critical Analysis of ICT4D for Women. arXiv preprint arXiv:2108.09947 (2021)
17. De, R., et al.: ICT4D research: a call for a strong critical approach. Inf. Technol. Dev. **24**(1), 63–94 (2018)
18. Lin, C.I., Kuo, F.-Y., Myers, M.D.: Extending ICT4D studies. MIS Q. **39**(3), 697–712 (2015)

19. Walsham, G., Sahay, S.: Research on information systems in developing countries: current landscape and future prospects. Inf. Technol. Dev. **12**(1), 7–24 (2006)
20. Gillard, H., et al.: "Missing women": gender, ICTs, and the shaping of the global economy. Inf. Technol. Dev. **14**(4), 262–279 (2008)
21. Sein, M.K., et al.: A holistic perspective on the theoretical foundations for ICT4D research. Inf. Technol. Dev. **25**(1), 7–25 (2019)
22. Zheng, Y., et al.: Conceptualizing development in information and communication technology for development (ICT4D). Inf. Technol. Dev. **24**(1), 1–14 (2018)
23. Schelenz, L., Pawelec, M.: Information and communication technologies for development (ICT4D) critique. Inf. Technol. Dev. **28**, 1–24 (2021)
24. Serenko, A., Bontis, N.: The intellectual core and impact of the knowledge management academic discipline. J. Knowl. Manag. **17**, 137–155 (2013)
25. Wade, M., Biehl, M., Kim, H.: Information systems is not a reference discipline (and what we can do about it). J. Assoc. Inf. Syst. **7**(1), 14 (2006)
26. Nambisan, S.: Information systems as a reference discipline for new product development. MIS Q. **27**, 1–18 (2003)
27. Johnston, R.: Effects of resource concentration on research performance. High. Educ. **28**(1), 25–37 (1994)
28. Vabø, A., et al.: The establishment of formal research groups in higher education institutions. Nordic J. Stud. Educ. Policy **2016**(2–3), 33896 (2016)
29. Horta, H., Lacy, T.A.: How does size matter for science? Exploring the effects of research unit size on academics' scientific productivity and information exchange behaviors. Sci. Public Policy **38**(6), 449–460 (2011)
30. Webster, J., Watson, R.T.: Analyzing the past to prepare for the future: writing a literature review. MIS Q. **26**, xiii–xxiii (2002)
31. Heeks, R.: An ICT4D journal ranking table. Inf. Technol. Int. Dev. **6**(4), 71–75 (2010)
32. AIS: Senior Scholars' Basket of Journals (2011). https://aisnet.org/page/SeniorScholarBasket
33. Harzing, A.-W.K., Van der Wal, R.: Google scholar as a new source for citation analysis. Ethics Sci. Environ. Polit. **8**(1), 61–73 (2008)
34. Nicolaisen, J.: Citation analysis. Ann. Rev. Inf. Sci. Technol. **41**(1), 609–641 (2007)
35. Larsen, T.J., Levine, L.: Citation patterns in MIS: an analysis of exemplar articles. In: León, G., Bernardos, A.M., Casar, J.R., Kautz, K., De Gross, J.I. (eds.) TDIT 2008. ITIFIP, vol. 287, pp. 23–38. Springer, Boston, MA (2008). https://doi.org/10.1007/978-0-387-87503-3_2
36. Andersson, A., Hatakka, M.: What are we doing? - Theories Used in ICT4D research. In: 12th International Conference on Social Implications of Computers in Developing Countries, Ocho Rios, Jamaica (2013)
37. Ahmad, S.Z., et al.: An empirical study of factors affecting e-commerce adoption among small-and medium- sized enterprises in a developing country: evidence from Malaysia. Inf. Technol. Dev. **21**(4), 555–572 (2015)
38. Kroeze, J.H., van Zyl, I.: Transdisciplinarity in information systems: extended reflections (2014). https://uir.unisa.ac.za/handle/10500/14627
39. Aanestad, M., et al.: Call for Papers MISQ Special issue on Digital Technologies and Social Justice (2021)
40. Tan, B., Nielsen, P.: Information Systems Journal: Special Issue Call for Papers - Information Systems and Sustainable Development (2021)
41. Heeks, R.: ICT4D Course Curriculum and Teaching Materials (2017)
42. Al-Ahmad, W.: The importance of introducing a course on information and communication technologies for development into the information technology curriculum. Int. J. Educ. Dev. ICT **6**(1), 66–75 (2010)

43. Colle, D.: Building ICT4D capacity in and by African universities. Int. J. Educ. Dev. ICT **1**(1), 101–107 (2005)
44. Pade-Khene, C.: Curriculum development of an ICT4D module in the South African context. Issues Inf. Sci. Inf. Technol. **12**, 111–140 (2015)

What is 'Smart' About Smart Village? Emerging Discourses and Future Research Directions

Pragyan Thapa[1]([✉]) [iD] and Devinder Thapa[1,2] [iD]

[1] University of Agder, Kristiansand, Norway
{pragyan.thapa,devinder.thapa}@uia.no
[2] University of South-Eastern Norway, Hønefoss, Norway

Abstract. This paper takes stock of how 'smart' is conceptualized in smart cities literature and how the concept is getting re-appropriated in different smart village initiatives across Europe and the Global South. Emerging discourses on smart village espouse the concept of 'smart' to strategically leverage ICTs to bring inclusive and sustainable rural development, however these visions are ambiguous about the nature of ICT artifacts and its interactions with rural community and people's goals and abilities and how they can shape actions and outcomes of sustainable development. Finally, future research directions for ICT4D researchers are proposed to address the current shortcomings and to expand the knowledge and practice of smart village interventions.

Keywords: Smart village · Smart cities · Smart · Sustainable rural development · ICT4D intervention

1 Introduction

There has been an emergence of 'smart village' interventions for strategic use of ICTs for rural development across Europe [1] and in many parts of the Global South [2, 3]. Many of these interventions come as a response to appropriate and expand the concept of smart cities in a rural context with the aim to facilitate the achievement of sustainable rural development. Authors also highlight smart village as a nascent but potential research area to address the shortcomings of extant smart cities literature [4]. They argue that since smart village has a small scale and limited focus on specific village level communities than large scale smart cities, it potentially offers better and manageable empirical focus on local contextualization of problems and ICT based interventions, benefiting both researchers and practitioners.

Interest in ICTs and rural development isn't a recent trend. Historically, rural studies authors as well as ICT4D authors have explored the potential roles of information technology for rural development [5–8]. For instance, what roles telecommunication and publicly accessible IT infrastructures like telecentres play to diversify the local rural economy and facilitate social change. Therefore, the novelty of smart village must be weighed in a historical context of previous and existing rural ICT interventions.

© IFIP International Federation for Information Processing 2022
Published by Springer Nature Switzerland AG 2022
Y. Zheng et al. (Eds.): ICT4D 2022, IFIP AICT 657, pp. 440–454, 2022.
https://doi.org/10.1007/978-3-031-19429-0_26

However, the discourses on smart village are concurrently emerging in public sector agendas, civil society initiatives, academic literature, and corporate efforts. This paper argues that it is important to identify how these multiple interpretations of smart village overlap and differ, and how this so-called new approach addresses rural issues, the idea of 'development' and the nature of information technology. Given that 'smart' has become a buzzword, uncritically importing the smart agenda from the smart cities approach and applying it to a novel area comes with its own set of drawbacks [9]. Therefore, this paper aims to critically explore how the idea of smart gets re-appropriated in rural context and how this context contributes in re-defining the discourses around smart itself.

This paper is conceptual in nature and bases its evidence on a selective review of existing smart cities and smart village literature, as well as smart village policy documents, project reports, and project websites. Taking an ICT4D (Information and Communication Technology for Development) perspective, it critically questions how the concept of 'smart' is shaped in the smart village discourse. An ICT4D perspective allows us to conceptualize smart village as a socio-technical phenomenon and to discuss not only its technological side but also the social processes and developmental implications [10, 11]. This complements the growing consensus in the related domain of smart cities research that emphasizes a holistic view that crosscuts dimensions of technology, society, economy, and environment [12]. On one hand, this perspective equips us to unpack the underlying assumptions about technological artifact(s) and their interactions with organizational structures, processes, and human agency [13–15]. On the other hand, it enriches our understanding of an ICT4D phenomenon by looking at the role of the context in which it is embedded and by focusing on the phenomenon's role in bringing transformational change at societal level [16].

The paper is organized in the following way. First, it synthesizes how the conceptualization of 'smart' has evolved within the smart cities literature. Second, it highlights selected smart village interventions and smart based rural development literature to make sense of emerging conceptualization of smart in the smart village discourse. Finally, it proposes relevant future research directions to contribute to the practice and research of smart village.

2   Evolution of 'Smart' in Smart Cities

A commonly agreed upon definition of smart cities is hard to find. Numerous survey articles have come up with plethora of definitions. Ismagilova et al. [17] in their literature review note that smart cities are conceptualized with a major focus on technology integrated with related themes of citizens, interaction, sustainability, and quality of life. Another review article [12] found that a techno-centric view of smart cities is promoted through the grey literature published by North American business companies, while a holistic view of smart cities in terms of human, social, economic, environmental and technological dimensions, is generated in peer-reviewed articles published by European universities.

In a now influential paper, Hollands [18] claimed that smart cities initiatives were driven by techno-deterministic values and pro-business and entrepreneurial ethos of high tech corporate companies and municipal governments. He calls for a more progressive conceptualization of smart cities that put people and human capital first and doesn't blindly put its trust solely on technology to drive change. More recent work has followed his call and shifted towards conceptualizing smart cities by integrating the view of sustainability [19–21] and inclusiveness [22–24].

Drawing on these conceptual debates, it can be argued that visions of 'smart' cross-cuts four broad conceptualizations: (1) smart as technological (2) smart as entrepreneurial (3) smart as sustainable (4) smart as inclusive (Table 1).

Table 1. Multiple conceptualizations of 'smart' in the smart cities discourse

Concepts of 'smart' in smart cities	Technological system	Social system	Area of interest
Smart as technological	High focus (supply driven)	Low focus	Supply side needs to build smart systems
Smart as entrepreneurial	Low focus	High focus	Entrepreneurial development, collaborative business networking
Smart as sustainable	Low focus	High focus	Social and environmental values generated in addition to economic values
Smart as inclusive	High focus (demand driven)	High focus	Citizen participation, inclusion of marginalized groups in design, deployment, and evaluation of projects and planning

2.1 Smart as Technological

The dominant imagination of 'smart' in the smart cities discourse connects the concept primarily to the role of ICT infrastructures [25]. This vision of smart largely comes from researchers working in the domains of computer science and engineering, as well as corporate companies that develop, produce, and help municipal governments implement smart technologies and datafication processes like Internet of Things (IoT), cloud computing and Big Data [12, 17]. For instance, a highly cited paper by Zanella et al. [26] on IoT sees the realization of smart city concept through exploitation of advanced technologies for management and optimization of public services and for increasing the transparency and evidence based strategizing of cities.

Angelidou [27] notes that such visions promote a smart city product economy where ICT infrastructures are pushed in a market of smart city products and solutions to pull the demand of cities seeking to address urban problems. For Zanella et al. [26], deployment of IoT system is at the core of smart city initiatives and critical factors for successful deployment are twofold: the technological complexities of integrating and standardizing heterogenous systems to support a dynamic urban IoT system, and a sustainable market mechanism that allows steady investment and commercial demand of smart technological systems. Therefore, 'smart as technological' discourse is of top-down nature with development and marketing of technological systems taking primary attention whereas citizen centric and demand side social processes getting overlooked [18, 24].

2.2 Smart as Entrepreneurial

Entrepreneurial spirit is a recurrent idea in smart cities initiatives that is also closely interlinked with technocentric vision of smart cities [18]. Designated smart cities aim at stimulating economic growth and job opportunities by providing seedbed conditions not only for local enterprises and entrepreneurs to grow but also for attracting foreign investors and expanding non-local markets [28]. Collaboration and innovation are two interconnected themes when discussing about the entrepreneurial spirit of smart cities. Barcelona, one of the pioneer smart cities, puts digital innovation at the fore of its Barcelona Digital City Plan [29]. It claims to support entrepreneurs and businesses by providing them with collaborative networking opportunities through digital hubs and incubators, as well as funding opportunities for innovations with social impacts. Similarly, business and management scholars have investigated the smart city phenomenon as an opportunity to explore the role of smart cities in fostering entrepreneurship [30] and to develop framework for collaborative entrepreneurial ecosystems [31].

Authors note that entrepreneurialism and techno-centrism are dual agendas of a corporate model of smart city promoted by city governments and corporate tech suppliers [9, 24]. Much like the technological conceptualization of smart cities, the entrepreneurial view favours a supply-driven focus and a dominant market logic to boost local economy. Though the entrepreneurial discourse might seem to make up for the shortcomings of the technology discourse by putting attention back to social systems and processes of collaboration and networks, we need to understand that underlying these social systems are strong neo-liberal pursuits of profitmaking and economic growth rather than democratic and pro-public values [32].

2.3 Smart as Sustainable

Recent scholarship has tried to question the holistic and ecological dimensions of smart cities, thereby trying to move away from market-driven urban growth to people-centred and urban ecology-centred concerns. They ask how is the smart city agenda improving the citizen's quality of life and making urban systems sustainable for the future [19]? The integrated concept of 'smart sustainable city' is one such example. Höjer and Wangel [20] define smart sustainable city as "a city that meets the needs of its present inhabitants without compromising the ability for other people or future generations to meet their needs, and thus, does not exceed local or planetary environmental limitations, and where this is supported by ICT" (p. 347). This reorientation also emerges from critical studies that find problems with non-ideological, pragmatic, and commonsensical views [33] when imagining smart as "technological" and/or "entrepreneurial". Authors emphasize the political and non-neutral impacts of neo-liberal corporate management of cities and the dangers of overlooking varying levels of contextual factors across regions when drawing up a one-size-fits-all framework of smart city.

Limited but growing literature on smart cities and sustainable development suggests that sustainability discourse within smart cities should espouse models, frameworks, and indicators that explore and measure better sustainability targets and assessments of impacts, and not just economic indicators and models of growth [19, 21, 34].

2.4 Smart as Inclusive

Closely related to the sustainable development agenda is the growing scholarship that puts social justice and citizen centric agendas at the forefront of smart cities research. They are interested in asking questions like how smart cities will benefit marginal communities? [22], how initiatives may increase urban inequality? [23] and how to improve the role of marginalized groups in conceiving, designing, implementing and evaluating smart cities projects? [35]. Here marginalized groups are any heterogenous groups of people like migrant workers, slum dwellers, ageing population, and people with disabilities.

Building their argument from a European context, Engelbert et al. [36] caution that 'inclusiveness' may be prevalent in the smart city rhetoric, but the underlying logics benefit technologists and experts, de-socialize urban problems through business frames and hold an unproblematic view of participation that in return leads to exclusion of citizen participation and perspectives. It is pertinent to understand that normatively, inclusiveness discourse demands integration of bottom-up approaches to ensure citizens not only the right to use the technology as users but also the right to shape the city with technological solutions for sustainable development as co-designers [24], thus taking account of both technological and social system. Therefore, it can be argued that 'smart as inclusive' discourse puts high focus on technological systems, but this focus is normatively different from the high technological focus in 'smart as technological' discourse. While 'smart as technological' discourse imagines businesses and experts driving and designing technological systems without any input from citizens, 'smart as inclusive' imagines technological systems to emerge from democratic dialogues and deliberations between citizens and technology producers.

In sum, the concept of 'smart' has dynamically evolved in smart cities literature. From the knowledge generated in the last decade itself we can trace the shifting conceptualization of smart cities: from techno-centric values to holistic values of sustainable and inclusive urban development. However, it is challenging to critically assess the discourses around smart village, since the knowledge around the concept is still emerging and not clearly understood. The next section highlights this emerging field of research and practice.

3 Emerging Discourses of 'Smart' in Smart Village

Smart cities literature highlights municipal government and corporate sector as the two main dominant drivers of the smart city initiatives [25, 33], while civil society and academia have recently become important drivers with the need to integrate sustainability and inclusiveness in the conceptualization of smart cities [24]. For critically assessing how 'smart' is operationalized in smart village, this paper therefore sought to present how these different drivers like governments, civil society, private sector, and academic literature were contributing to the ongoing discourses.

This paper takes a strategy to generate a variety of narratives from policy documents, program and project reports, and academic articles to assess their views on technology, people, processes, and rural development. This resulted in identification of five major smart village interventions at a global level. These include two policy guided public sector interventions, two civil society led interventions, and one corporate sector supported intervention. In addition to these practice-based discourse, the paper also briefly presents theoretical discourse of the concept of smart village in the extant academic literature.

3.1 Public Sector

European Union (EU) is one of the few governing bodies that has taken up 'smart village' as a wide scale policy intervention. It defines smart villages as "communities in rural areas that use innovative solutions to improve their resilience, building on local strengths and opportunities" [37]. EU imagines ICTs to play an important but not a defining role in creating innovative solutions. Similarly, it considers smart village as a non-radical strategy that builds upon existing interventions, strategic governance mechanisms and a flexible funding modality that welcomes private and public partnerships. Multiple smart village projects are running in many EU member countries [1]. For instance, innovation in service delivery through community centres and business hubs and mobile clinics, social innovation for rural development through rural hackathon events, crowdsourcing, and co-working space. Some smart village projects are also offering flexible workspace for professionals to telework from villages and make use of local resources. In all this, the overarching purpose is to reconfigure local resources and knowledge primarily with social entrepreneurship and ICTs.

Similarly, International Telecommunication Union (ITU), a United Nations specialized agency for ICTs, and the government of Niger have piloted a multi-million dollars smart village project in some villages in Niger with a long-term aim to expand the project to cover all the villages of the country. The project draws upon Niger 2.0, a national level policy to achieve sustainable development goals (SDGs) by exploiting the opportunities of digital economy [38]. As such, digital technologies play a prominent role in ITU and Niger's definition of smart village. They define smart village as "a community in rural areas that leverages digital connectivity, solutions and resources for its own development and transformation towards the SDGs" [2]. They claim smart village to be a radical departure from previous top-down approaches, focusing on networked and integrated governance, and multi-stakeholder alliances that work to achieve holistic goals, while sharing and reusing resources. The project is also very explicit about ICT driven sustainable development by adopting the nine guiding principles of digital development [39]. These principles advocate user-centric, scalable, and sustainable design, data privacy, local contextualization, data driven decision-making and open standards.

While EU's smart village policy ranges across rural areas of Europe and covers variety of projects in member countries, ITU and Niger's smart village strategy is a developing country specific project that if successful will be spread across Africa and Global South. They both differ in several other ways too. EU's policy intervention is incremental in the sense that it wants its already existing rural development policies to work as building blocks for their smart village actions. In other words, smart village projects do not begin from scratch and work at new set of problems, but they bring about innovative "ways" and "means" to support ongoing processes of rural development programs [40]. Thus, role of digital technologies is secondary, as in deriving from rural development policies, and more broadly defined as "not a pre-condition to become smart village" and "means to innovative solutions and not solutions" [37]. As such, EU's imagination of smart is closer to 'smart as entrepreneurial' iteration where technological system's interaction with social systems is reduced to a tool view [13], while the focus is more on social interactions and processes to improve market and entrepreneurial mechanisms for villages.

On the other hand, ITU and Niger's version of smart village is radical in its ambition and clear on the imperative role of ICTs in achieving sustainable development. As mentioned earlier, smart village is deemed as a complete restructuring of Niger's governance structure to bring a "whole-of-government-approach" that reforms the old governance structure of fragmented policy interventions to move away from narrowly defined goals that lead to duplication of programs and funding [2]. Unlike EU, smart village interventions don't derive from existing policy governance structure, but these interventions aim at reengineering a new "whole-of-government" policy structure with implications to political will and leadership. Furthermore, if EU's intervention can be argued to be innovation-based, ITU and Niger's intervention is more problem-based as it is driven by the "ends" of achieving sustainable development goals [40]. 'Smart as sustainable' and 'smart as inclusive' agendas through combination of ICTs and structural change to meet SDGs drive the vision of smart in ITU and Niger's smart village.

3.2 Civil Society

Numerous smart village projects are spearheaded through civil society initiatives. Among these, two initiatives will be highlighted here. First is the Smart Village Initiatives, funded by Cambridge Malaysian Education and Development Trust and Templeton World Charity Foundation. Second is the Smart Village IEEE, funded by the Institute of Electrical and Electronics Engineers (IEEE).

Both initiatives share similarities in their focus for improving access to off-grid, sustainable energy services to rural communities of Global South and actualizing overall developmental benefits from energy access. They claim sustainable energy access to be a prerequisite to connectivity possibilities offered by ICTs. They also share notable differences. Smart Village Initiatives has so far mainly occupied itself with developing a smart village framework to understand needs and problems of communities through interactions with multiple stakeholders in different developing regions in the form of workshops and capacity building events [3]. The smart village framework advocates certain policy recommendations for governments and donors to create supportive conditions for sustainable technological solutions with access to finance, gender inclusion, capacity building and integrated collaboration as main policy imperatives.

Meanwhile, since 2010 Smart Village IEEE supports and collaborates with community level entrepreneurs and activists. IEEE equips them with technologies to generate sustainable energy, for instance solar panels, chargers, and batteries [41]. IEEE follows an entrepreneurship model of sustainability whereby it looks at enhancing market mechanisms to create user demand for energy. For that it conducts activities and trainings for local entrepreneurs so they can create innovative local services that make diverse use of clean energy, thus increasing its demand and ensuring financial stability to maintain and upgrade off-grid energy services [42].

The imagination of smart as sustainable, inclusive, and entrepreneurial is evident in the two civil society-led smart village initiatives. Even though they don't explicitly discuss about digital technologies, they see technology through a holistic approach as they are simply not looking at villages adopting sustainable energy services but how communities take ownership of these energy services, how they activate their agency to create new services from energy access and how their action benefits the community at large.

3.3 Private Sector

It was highlighted earlier that private and corporate sector have had prominent stake in promoting and defining the smart city agenda. But in the case of smart village, corporate sector's presence is still very negligible. Nokia, a multinational telecommunications company, is one rare example. The company has embraced smart village, albeit in the capacity of corporate social responsibility. Its smart village project in India, named Smartpur, claims, "The Smartpur model has been theorized in a way that redefines the existing ideas of smart villages, by not only deploying digital infrastructures but also integrating the use of the infrastructure into their daily lives thereby promoting socio-economic growth" [43]. The project is still in early phase and spans across seven Indian states and ten districts.

The central idea of Smartpur is to build a village ecosystem connecting a hub village to nodal villages [44]. A hub village is where primary services are provided by rural entrepreneurs and nodal villages are where these services will be redistributed through local rural entrepreneurs of these nodal villages. Smartpur's entrepreneurship model is like Smart Village IEEE's model with the underlying assumption that local entrepreneurs will help create locally appropriate services and help sustain services, while donors will facilitate conditions for entrepreneurial growth. As such, Smartpur too strongly links entrepreneurship and sustainable development in its conception of 'smart'. Nevertheless, it should be pointed out, Smartpur's position in broader Indian policy domains remains unclear. Given its status as a corporate social responsibility initiative, it would be just wishful thinking to expect Smartpur to engage in dialogues to reform or inform policy actors.

3.4 Academia

Only limited academic deliberation about smart village has taken place so far. Exceptions include two edited volumes [45, 46] that have tried to discuss the area at length. Within and outside these volumes, we find variety of academic lens exploring the smart village phenomenon. Some investigate the more computational side of smart technologies in rural contexts. Like studies on precision farming or smart farming with focus on using IoT and Big Data to improve agricultural production and management [47]. Then there are scholars who argue to broaden the scope of smart technologies to nonagricultural domains like healthcare, transportation, and waste management [48]. Meanwhile researchers from rural planning and development, and geography lead the academic discussion on smart village [4, 45] investigating its implications for sustainable development. IS and ICT4D have much to offer in the theoretical and empirical development of smart village but so far IS and ICT4D researchers have given little explicit attention to the phenomenon. This is same for smart cities as well. In their survey of smart cities research in the IS domain, Ismagilova et al. [17] note smart cities research is still at a nascent stage in IS. For instance, they found 43 IS journals publishing articles on smart cities but more than half of the journals had published not more than one article, while the remaining had published not more than three articles (Table 2).

Table 2. Emerging discourses of 'smart' in smart village across multiple levels

Sector	Example(s)	Smart as	Area of interest
Public	*European Union's Smart Village* *ITU and Niger's Smart Village*	'entrepreneurial' 'sustainable' and 'inclusive'	Rural entrepreneurship, innovative services, collaborative partnerships, Digital development for sustainable development, integrated and networked governance
Civil society	*IEEE Smart Village* *Smart Village Initiative*	'entrepreneurial', 'sustainable' and 'inclusive'	Accessing sustainable and affordable energy and generating socio-economic returns from energy access
Private	*Nokia's Smartpur*	'entrepreneurial' and 'sustainable'	Rural entrepreneurship based and digital technology-based innovation of rural services
Academia	*Visvizi et al. [46] and Patnaik et al. [45]*	'technological', 'entrepreneurial', 'sustainable' and 'inclusive'	IoT based smart systems in agriculture, rural entrepreneurship, links with sustainable rural development

4   Implications and Future Research Directions

Visions of smart village across sectors share some commonalities, but also significant differences. Sustainability and inclusiveness remain two intersecting agendas. Similarly, role of ICTs, in general, is to facilitate broader sustainable development of villages and rural areas. But the link between ICTs, sustainable development, and villages remains unclear and contested. Moreover, relevant differences exist between smart village initiatives in terms of the strategic role of ICTs. As mentioned earlier, most smart village policies and projects view technologies as "tools" or "means to an end" while setting greater interest on social processes like building entrepreneurial capacity. They narrow smart village projects as opportunities to digitalize processes and project activities within existing governance structure. Therefore, de-centering digital technologies, in other words nominalizing their role.

To understand why digital technologies are de-centered in rural development thinking, we need to take a turn towards rural development scholars' view of technology driven development in general. Contemporary rural development thinking is highly critical of the modernist model of rural development. In the modernist view, rural development was equated to industrializing agriculture [49]. Farmers were expected to intensify their agricultural production through highly specialized seeds, chemical fertilizers, and irrigation facilities. Technological determinism afflicted the planning strategies as hopes for rural prosperity were hooked on genetically modified agricultural inputs and big irrigation projects that didn't pan out to bring expected economic benefits but worsened the environmental impact of technology driven development projects [50].

The new rural development paradigm seeks to depart from the monopoly of agriculture, individual entrepreneurial capacity, and economies of scale. The shift is towards rural livelihood strategies that combine farm activities with non-farm activities, focus on collective actions that emerge from networking and partnership and widen the economies of scope [51]. In sum, the new rural development rectifies techno-determinism inherent in the modernist view, but it does so through social determinism. Technology in rural development gets refashioned into a monolithic, homogenous black box [52]. In other words, technology is relegated as a backdrop in much of the rural development literature.

But when we reduce technologies to neutral artifacts or relegate them as nominal entity of interest, we overlook the political nature of technologies [53], as in who designs technologies and what values and purpose shape them. Also, considering technologies as opportunities to automate, doesn't fully explore the opportunities to redesign processes and strategies [54]. It is thus important to understand the dynamic relationships between technologies and multiple actors, and how they shape and not determine each other. This socio-technical approach sits in the middle, neither techno-determinist nor socio-determinist, and is suitable to explore the phenomenon of smart village, where the meeting point is the notion of using ICTs for sustainable development of rural communities and villages. Future smart village research has opportunities to explore issues that highlight how multiple stakeholders interact with ICT interventions and how do these interactions enhance or can be enhanced to achieve sustainable rural development goals.

This is where the fields of information systems (IS) and particularly ICT4D has relative potential to contribute to the theoretical development of the concept of 'smart village' as a phenomenon mutually shaped by technological artifacts and social processes and having developmental implications. We do not claim that an ICT4D approach is the only and the right way to make theoretical contributions on smart village. We acknowledge the prevalence of socio-determinist (studies that only theorize social processes and development implications of interventions) trends and techno-determinist (studies that are only interested in theorizing the design and adoption of ICT artefacts) trends within ICT4D research itself [10, 11]. However, we argue that an ICT4D framework offers smart village researchers a socio-technical-developmental orientation and direction. Smart village scholars can draw from a rich body ICT4D literature that is focused exists at the intersection of rural development and ICTs. Secondly, the theoretical implications that emerge from such smart village research can be fed back for further development and refinement of the holistic ICT4D framework. Therefore, investigating the socio-technical phenomenon of smart village not only uses an ICT4D framework but also contributes to the theoretical development of an ICT4D approach that take account of all three elements of ICTs, social processes, and developmental outcomes.

This article proposes three future research directions for ICT4D researchers and smart village researchers to broaden scientific knowledge and practice of smart village.

4.1 Theorizing Smart Village as a Rural ICT4D Phenomenon

For long, ICT4D researchers have been interested in generating knowledge about rural and community driven ICT interventions. Investigating smart village interventions presents two opportunities for ICT4D researchers in this area. Firstly, relevant literature on rural ICT4D interventions, for example research on telecentres and digital transformation of rural businesses, has significantly theorized lessons from past failures of rural ICT4D projects. This knowledge can be used to critically appraise the promise and 'newness' of existing smart village interventions and redress the past flaws in future smart village interventions. Secondly, as smart village espouses values of inclusive and sustainable development, ICT4D researchers can theoretically contribute new knowledge about the interrelationship of ICTs and sustainable rural development.

As suggested earlier, ICT4D researchers need to bridge the divide between techno-deterministic visions of 'smart' and the underlying social constructivism of many rural and ICT4D empirical scholarship that fails to engage with the material agency of IT artifacts. Therefore, future theoretical contribution on smart village needs to better illustrate how materiality of IT artifacts, goals and abilities of rural people and community, and contextual conversion factors shape but do not determine future actions, practices, and outcomes of sustainable development.

4.2 Conducting Interdisciplinary and Modest Scale Field-Based Studies

Kitchin [33] argues to move the academic debate around smart cities beyond analysis of government and corporate documents, and to undertake fieldwork in cities and interview stakeholders to reveal underlying power dynamics, multi-level effects, costs, and benefits of initiatives. Similarly, he also urges more cross disciplinary collaborations between social science researchers and technical researchers to produce critical scholarship within technology driven initiatives.

These points are relevant to research in smart village as well. It is time for knowledge around smart village to come from empirical and field-based evidence and not from anecdotal and synoptic evidence reported in grey literature published by governments, donors, and NGOs. Likewise, many authors have been arguing on behalf of more modest and small size smart initiatives than large scale technological solutions [24]. Smart village with its focus on specific rural and marginalized community has scope for researchers to conduct such delimited and manageable empirical study that will also benefit from rich local contextualization [4].

4.3 Adopting Action Research (AR) Methodology for Constructive Knowledge

Studies on rural ICT4D interventions, but ICT4D interventions in general, take an interpretive stance to better understand and evaluate already established projects despite several recent calls to diversify the discipline with more action and intervention driven methods [11, 55]. Based on his survey of ICT4D researchers, Harris [56] claims that though ICT4D researchers express their desire to communicate and share their research with policymakers, practitioners, and the general public, very rarely ICT4D researchers get involved in engaged scholarship for collaborative action planning and problem solving. This finding contradicts with the most commonly understood knowledge within ICT4D that it is imperative to collaborate and partner with local stakeholders for the success and sustainability of ICT4D interventions [57].

Therefore, adopting an action research (AR) approach in studying and developing smart village, future studies should address the gap within ICT4D research on collaborative partnerships between researchers and local practitioners to build ICT4D interventions. For instance, within an AR framework researchers and practitioners can engage in dialogic communication where researchers bring in their theoretical understanding of smart village based on academic literature whereas local practitioners bring in their understanding of local contexts, knowledge, and lived experiences to define problems and design actions for change [58–60]. AR potentially enables researchers to generate and make relevant the scientific knowledge about how to support local communities to strategically leverage ICTs for sustainable development goals.

5 Conclusion

In this paper, we discussed how the framing of 'smart' in the smart cities literature has evolved from a techno-deterministic view (smart as *technological*) to that of a holistic view that takes into consideration the goals of social justice and sustainable development of urban settings. As we turned to the discussion of smart village, we found out that the emerging discourses tied the concept of 'smart' to *sustainable* and *inclusive*. However, adopting an information systems perspective to assume smart village as an ICT4D phenomenon, it was revealed smart village initiatives avoid techno-deterministic visions by putting more emphasis on social processes. They nonetheless overlook the ways technological system interact with social system and how they are co-shaping each other. Therefore, this paper urges future smart village researchers to take a holistic theoretical lens to conceptualize smart village as a rural ICT4D phenomenon, while engaging in more collaborative, field based empirical studies with local practitioners that are not only limited to understanding the problems of smart village but are interested in generating constructive and problem-solving actions.

References

1. European Network for Rural Development: Thematic Groups on Smart Villages: Collection of projects, p. 37 (2018)
2. International Telecommunication Union: Building Smart Villages: A Blueprint. International Telecommunication Union (2020)
3. Holmes, J.: The Smart Villages Initiatives: Findings 2014–2017 (2017)
4. Visvizi, A., Lytras, M.D.: It's not a fad: smart cities and smart villages research in European and global contexts. Multidisciplinary Digital Publishing Institute (2018)
5. Grimes, S.: Exploiting information and communication technologies for rural development. J. Rural. Stud. **8**(3), 269–278 (1992)
6. Grimes, S.: Rural areas in the information society: diminishing distance or increasing learning capacity? J. Rural. Stud. **16**(1), 13–21 (2000)
7. Roman, R.: Diffusion of innovations as a theoretical framework for telecenters. Inf. Technol. Int. Dev. **1**(2), 53–66 (2003)
8. Bailur, S.: Using stakeholder theory to analyze telecenter projects. Inf. Technol. Int. Dev. **3**(3), 61–80 (2006)
9. Grossi, G., Pianezzi, D.: Smart cities: utopia or neoliberal ideology? Cities **69**, 79–85 (2017)
10. Avgerou, C.: Theoretical framing of ICT4D research. In: Choudrie, J., Islam, M.S., Wahid, F., Bass, J.M., Priyatma, J.E. (eds.) ICT4D 2017. IAICT, vol. 504, pp. 10–23. Springer, Cham (2017). https://doi.org/10.1007/978-3-319-59111-7_2
11. Sein, M.K., et al.: A holistic perspective on the theoretical foundations for ICT4D research. Inf. Technol. Dev. **25**(1), 7–25 (2019)
12. Mora, L., Bolici, R., Deakin, M.: The first two decades of smart-city research: a bibliometric analysis. J. Urban Technol. **24**(1), 3–27 (2017)
13. Orlikowski, W.J., Iacono, C.S.: Research commentary: desperately seeking the "IT" in IT research - a call to theorizing the IT artifact. Inf. Syst. Res. **12**(2), 121–134 (2001)
14. Lee, A.S.: Thinking about social theory and philosophy for information systems. Soc. Theory Philos. Inf. Syst. **1**, 26 (2004)
15. Avison, D., Elliot, S.: Scoping the discipline of information systems. Information systems: the state of the field, pp. 3–18 (2006)
16. Avgerou, C.: Discourses on ICT and development. Inf. Technol. Int. Dev. **6**(3), 1–18 (2010)
17. Ismagilova, E., et al.: Smart cities: advances in research—an information systems perspective. Int. J. Inf. Manag. **47**, 88–100 (2019)
18. Hollands, R.G.: Will the real smart city please stand up? City **12**(3), 303–320 (2008)
19. Bibri, S.E., Krogstie, J.: Smart sustainable cities of the future: an extensive interdisciplinary literature review. Sustain. Cities Soc. **31**, 183–212 (2017)
20. Höjer, M., Wangel, J.: Smart sustainable cities: definition and challenges. In: Hilty, L.M., Aebischer, B. (eds.) ICT Innovations for Sustainability. AISC, vol. 310, pp. 333–349. Springer, Cham (2015). https://doi.org/10.1007/978-3-319-09228-7_20
21. Ahvenniemi, H., et al.: What are the differences between sustainable and smart cities? Cities **60**, 234–245 (2017)
22. Lee, J.Y., Woods, O., Kong, L.: Towards more inclusive smart cities: reconciling the divergent realities of data and discourse at the margins. Geogr. Compass **14**(9), e12504 (2020)
23. Shelton, T., Zook, M., Wiig, A.: The 'actually existing smart city.' Camb. J. Reg. Econ. Soc. **8**(1), 13–25 (2015)
24. Hollands, R.G.: Critical interventions into the corporate smart city. Camb. J. Reg. Econ. Soc. **8**(1), 61–77 (2015)
25. Caragliu, A., Del Bo, C., Nijkamp, P.: Smart cities in Europe. J. Urban Technol. **18**(2), 65–82 (2011)

26. Zanella, A., et al.: Internet of Things for smart cities. IEEE Internet Things J. **1**(1), 22–32 (2014)
27. Angelidou, M.: Smart cities: a conjuncture of four forces. Cities **47**, 95–106 (2015)
28. Alawadhi, S., et al.: Building understanding of smart city initiatives. In: Scholl, H.J., Janssen, M., Wimmer, M.A., Moe, C.E., Flak, L.S. (eds.) EGOV 2012. LNCS, vol. 7443, pp. 40–53. Springer, Heidelberg (2012). https://doi.org/10.1007/978-3-642-33489-4_4
29. de Barcelona, A.: Barcelona Digital City: Putting technology at the service of people. Barcelona Digital City Plan (2015–2019). Ajuntament de Barcelona, Barcelona (2019)
30. Barba-Sánchez, V., Arias-Antúnez, E., Orozco-Barbosa, L.: Smart cities as a source for entrepreneurial opportunities: evidence for Spain. Technol. Forecast. Soc. Chang. **148**, 119713 (2019)
31. Appio, F.P., Lima, M., Paroutis, S.: Understanding smart cities: innovation ecosystems, technological advancements, and societal challenges. Technol. Forecast. Soc. Chang. **142**, 1–14 (2019)
32. Morozov, E., Bria, F.: Rethinking the smart city. Democratizing Urban Technology, vol. 2. Rosa Luxemburg Foundation, New York (2018)
33. Kitchin, R.: Making sense of smart cities: addressing present shortcomings. Camb. J. Reg. Econ. Soc. **8**(1), 131–136 (2015)
34. Trindade, E.P., et al.: Sustainable development of smart cities: a systematic review of the literature. J. Open Innov.: Technol. Market Complex. **3**(3), 11 (2017)
35. Boni, A., et al.: Initiatives towards a participatory smart city. The role of digital grassroots innovations. J. Glob. Ethics **15**(2), 168–182 (2019)
36. Engelbert, J., van Zoonen, L., Hirzalla, F.: Excluding citizens from the European smart city: the discourse practices of pursuing and granting smartness. Technol. Forecast. Soc. Chang. **142**, 347–353 (2019)
37. Smart Villages Pilot Project, Briefing Note, p. 2 (2019)
38. World Bank, Niger: Smart Village for rural growth and digital inclusion (2018)
39. Principles for Digital Development. Principles n/d [10 October 2021]. https://digitalprinciples.org/principles/
40. Peppard, J., Ward, J., Daniel, E.: Managing the realization of business benefits from IT investments. MIS Q. Exec. **6**(1), 1–11 (2007)
41. Mackenzie, D.: IEEE smart village: sustainable development is a global mission. IEEE Syst. Man Cybern. Mag. **5**(3), 39–41 (2019)
42. Anderson, A., et al.: Empowering smart communities: electrification, education, and sustainable entrepreneurship in IEEE smart village initiatives. IEEE Electr. Mag. **5**(2), 6–16 (2017)
43. Nokia: Nokia Annual CSR Report: Indian Market 2019–2020 (2021)
44. Digital Empowerment Foundation. Smartpur: A digital ecosystem (2021). https://smartpur.in/
45. Patnaik, S., Sen, S., Mahmoud, M.S. (eds.): Smart Village Technology. MOST, vol. 17. Springer, Cham (2020). https://doi.org/10.1007/978-3-030-37794-6
46. Visvizi, A., Lytras, M.D., Mudri, G.: Smart Villages in the EU and Beyond. Emerald Publishing Limited, Bingley (2019)
47. Wolfert, S., et al.: Big data in smart farming – a review. Agric. Syst. **153**, 69–80 (2017)
48. Cowie, P., Townsend, L., Salemink, K.: Smart rural futures: will rural areas be left behind in the 4th industrial revolution? J. Rural Stud. **79**, 169–176 (2020)
49. Ellis, F., Biggs, S.: Evolving themes in rural development 1950s–2000s. Dev. Policy Rev. **19**(4), 437–448 (2001)
50. Todaro, M.P.S., Stephen, C.: Economic Development, 11th edn. Pearson, New York (2012)
51. Van der Ploeg, J.D., et al.: Rural development: from practices and policies towards theory. Sociol. Rural. **40**(4), 391–408 (2000)

52. Sein, M.K., Harindranath, G.: Conceptualizing the ICT artifact: toward understanding the role of ICT in national development. Inf. Soc. **20**(1), 15–24 (2004)

53. Winner, L.: Do artifacts have politics? Daedalus **109**, 121–136 (1980)

54. Hammer, M.: Reengineering work: don't automate, obliterate. Harv. Bus. Rev. **68**(4), 104–112 (1990)

55. Heeks, R., Ospina, A.V., Wall, P.J.: Combining pragmatism and critical realism in ICT4D research: an e-Resilience case example. In: Nielsen, P., Kimaro, H.C. (eds.) ICT4D 2019. IAICT, vol. 552, pp. 14–25. Springer, Cham (2019). https://doi.org/10.1007/978-3-030-191 15-3_2

56. Harris, R.W.: How ICT4D research fails the poor. Inf. Technol. Dev. **22**(1), 177–192 (2016)

57. Kleine, D., Unwin, T.: Technological revolution, evolution and new dependencies: what's new about ICT4D? Third World Q. **30**(5), 1045–1067 (2009)

58. Nielsen, P.A.: IS action research and its criteria. Information Systems Action Research, pp. 355–375. Springer (2007). https://doi.org/10.1007/978-0-387-36060-7_15

59. Baskerville, R.L.: Investigating information systems with action research. Commun. Assoc. Inf. Syst. **2**(1), 19 (1999)

60. Mathiassen, L., Chiasson, M., Germonprez, M.: Style composition in action research publication. MIS Q. **36**, 347–363 (2012)

Digital Public Goods for Development: A Conspectus and Research Agenda

Brian Nicholson[1] , Petter Nielsen[2](✉) , Johan Ivar Sæbø[2] ,
and Ana Paula Tavares[3]

[1] Alliance Manchester Business School, University of Manchester, Manchester, UK
brian.nicholson@manchester.ac.uk
[2] HISP-Centre and Department of Informatics, University of Oslo, Oslo, Norway
{pnielsen,johansa}@ifi.uio.no
[3] e-Lab: Research Laboratory on E-Government and E-Business, Getulio Vargas Foundation, Rio de Janeiro, Brazil

Abstract. Digital public goods (DPGs) for development is a relatively new discourse in the field of information technology for development (ICT4D). DPGs are currently portrayed by international organisations and donors as key enablers towards the accomplishment of the Sustainable Development Goals (SDGs). However, there is a paucity of research that establishes the link between the DPGs and the SDG and examines the contribution of DPGs to development. This paper introduces the DPG discourse and relevant theoretical concepts. We then present a case illustration of the UN-centred discourse on DPGs, showing a technology orientation in the goals and mission statements. Drawing on research on DHIS2, commonly used in the discourse as a prominent example of DPGs, we develop a research agenda related to the methods, theory and philosophy we find appropriate for advancing our understanding of DPGs, the link between DPGs and the SDGs and for development in general.

Keywords: Digital public goods · Sustainable development goals · DPG · Research agenda

1 Introduction

The purpose of this paper is to contribute to a relatively new global discourse based on digital public goods (DPGs) as central to ICT for socio-economic development. DPGs are defined as digital technologies and content that "are freely and openly available, with minimal restrictions on how they can be distributed, adapted, and reused" [1: p. 17]. Examples of DPGs can be found across multiple sectors in low and middle-income countries (LMICs), including the electronic medical record OpenMRS[1] the foundational

---

[1] https://openmrs.org/.

© IFIP International Federation for Information Processing 2022
Published by Springer Nature Switzerland AG 2022
Y. Zheng et al. (Eds.): ICT4D 2022, IFIP AICT 657, pp. 455–470, 2022.
https://doi.org/10.1007/978-3-031-19429-0_27

identity system MOSIP[2], and the health information system DHIS2[3]. More examples can be found at Digital Square[4] and the Digital Public Goods Alliance[5].

More specifically, this paper is motivated by the portrayal of DPGs by international organisations and donors as key enablers towards accomplishing the Sustainable Development Goals (SDG), both directly as contributors to solving concrete challenges, and indirectly as serving as digital building blocks to foster further innovation[6]. It is well recognized that the well-being of citizens relies on the provision of public goods by national governments [2]. The extension of public goods to increase the provision of DPGs secured by international cooperation is also posited by some as contributing to the SDGs [3]. SDGs are a collection of 17 global goals designed to be a "blueprint to achieve a better and more sustainable future for all", which succeeded the Millennium Development Goals. The SDGs were set in 2015 by the United Nations General Assembly and intended to be achieved by the year 2030.

This focus on DPGs in relation to development has already influenced funding opportunities and endorsements via curated lists of DPG principles, and reference implementations that highlight selected DPGs made available for countries and agencies involved in ICT4D (for example [4]). However, we posit that in this nascent stage there is limited empirical data and theoretical knowledge to support the relationship between DPGs and SDGs and how these technologies may facilitate or inhibit development outcomes [3, 5, 6]. There are many examples in the field of ICT4D of technological determinism as a feature of failure such as in the case of the One Laptop per Child (see for example [7]). Indeed, technology and society are intertwined [8], and it becomes paramount for researchers to understand the social, political, institutional and cultural contexts, which shape DPGs and their relations to development [9]. We are thus concerned here with directing a critical focus on DPGs and related initiatives.

Concurrently, initial research on the new discourse of DPGs for development has pointed out numerous challenges and tensions. For example, [3] emphasised the impact of globalisation, which entails growing interconnectedness that increases the number of critical challenges affecting mostly those living in the poorest nations. Indeed, the power asymmetries between groups of people (e.g., gender, geography, resources distribution), along with policy-practice gaps, namely, knowledge, governance, procurement, participation, capacity, and financial gaps - prevent the normative ideal of DPGs to be achieved. Additionally, Nicholson et al. [10] pinpoint the scaling challenges of DPGs through a case analysis identifying paradoxes of DPGs: using sophisticated tools for relatively simple analysis; prioritising voices that tend to be unheard; and building software simultaneously relevant for global and local contexts. Those paradoxes reveal the competing effects with the macro and micro and the impact of collective action and governance to promote DPGs effectively. In the context of these debates, this paper aims to contribute to advance our understanding of DPGs and the SDGs. We do so by developing a research agenda and by focussing on the following research question:

---

[2] https://www.mosip.io/.

[3] http://dhis2.org.

[4] https://digitalsquare.org/.

[5] https://digitalpublicgoods.net/.

[6] See https://digitalpublicgoods.net/.

How can DPGs contribute to sustainable development and what are the underlying challenges and opportunities to achieve the SDGs?

The authors of this paper are actively engaged in action research into DPGs in relation to the Health Information Systems Programme (HISP) on the District Health Information System (DHIS2) at the University of Oslo[7]. Our theoretical position is broadly aligned with the social constructionist perspective and that implies viewing human activity in organisations as being context-bound. Thus, there is an emphasis in the work of our group on consideration of the local, emergent and contingent and on understanding how attitudes are shaped by particular historical, political and/or cultural circumstances [12]. Our theoretical position opposes the technological determinist view and we posit that we best understand DPGs as an ideal, a socio-technical accomplishment that is ongoing rather than as embedded into a repository of static and transferrable technological artefacts.

The paper is organised as follows: First, we review prior literature in public goods and DPGs and outline some concepts related to technological determinism. There follows a case illustration of an international organisation that is promoting DPGs - the Digital Public Goods Alliance and our analysis of it. Finally, the paper develops a research agenda to help establish the relationship between DPGs and SDGs.

2   Literature Review and Conceptual Framing

The following section outlines public goods, DPGs and the central tenets of technological determinism.

2.1   Public Goods

The body of research on public goods is extensive, relating back to the ground-breaking work of Samuelson [13] and more recently Nobel laureate Elinor Ostrom on the governance of commons and the fundamental principles of non-rivalry and non-exclusion [14, 15]. One individual's consumption of public goods does not influence what is available for others and exclusion from consumption is impossible or prohibitively expensive. A well-cited example of a public good is a lighthouse, where one navigator's use of the light does not reduce availability to other navigators, nor can one effectively charge for use, as exclusion is impossible.

While having individual and societal benefits, a challenge is how to produce adequate levels of public goods in the absence of market mechanisms. In her research, Ostrom showed that under certain conditions individuals can overcome the lack of a functioning market or regulations, to obtain benefits in a sustainable way through collective action. Achieving this on the large scale needed for *global* public goods, available and relevant across groups of people, geographies, and generations [2], adds another level of complexity in terms of design and governance.

Public Goods are goods that members of a group benefit from regardless of whether they contribute towards creating and sustaining them. Public Goods, such as education

---

[7] See for example [11] or http://dhis2.org.

and healthcare, are acknowledged to promote social change through inclusion and a shared sense of citizenship [16]. A challenge with these goods is that their provision may be unreliable due to inadequate incentives to supply them, and the need for government interventions or collective actions. Furthermore, there may be variations due to the nature of services provided which could be public, private or hybrid yielding complexity to the conceptualization [3].

Prior research has demonstrated that public goods provision has a role in the progression towards the SDGs including overcoming poverty, improving health, education, security and protecting the natural environment [17].

2.2 Digital Public Goods

DPGs, like other public goods, are goods that anyone can benefit from, regardless of whether they contribute towards creating or sustaining them. They are in the form of software, data sets, AI models, or content that are generally free and contribute to sustainable national and international digital development. As such, the digital world today offers a large number of public goods globally, thus becoming digital global public goods (DGPGs). Despite the costless nature of accessing DPGs, they are only available to users that have Internet access generating a digital divide between who have and who do not have access to digital infrastructure.

Evidence suggests that digital technologies share characteristics with public goods, however the "digital" has a particular dynamic different from that of the non-digital, for example a lighthouse. Bonina et al. [18] define digital innovation platforms as facilitating the production of content, products or services developed by one or more parties, and serving as the foundation upon which other external actors can effectively build further derivative and complementary innovations. Thus, by following this logic open digital platforms (e.g., open-source software, open data and artificial intelligence models) are considered DPGs by enabling non-rivalrous and non-excludable access. These traits, however, are not the default and not necessarily permanent fixtures as with other types of public goods but because of an ongoing design effort.

For some stakeholders, extending the concept of public good to DPGs is seen as fundamental to attaining the SDGs. For example, the 2021 Sustainable Development Goals Report shows the potential of DPGs related to information access[8]. Another example is in SDG3 (Good Health and Well-Being) where the lack of data is a key obstacle to assessing the impact of Covid-19. DPGs are claimed to address this by promoting a collaborative form of social value creation by distributing system development costs and supporting agility and rapid propagation of innovations by being freely available for all to modify, deploy, and promoting interoperability and other practices including open data [19].

Thus, it is crucial for both the research and practice of ICT4D to understand the nature of DGPs for development. Conceptually understanding the nature of DPGs will potentially contribute to ICT4D discourses, particularly on how the potential of digital technologies can be better materialized for development. There is an emerging, nascent literature in this domain of DPG for development summarised in Table 1 above.

---

[8] https://unstats.un.org/sdgs/report/2021/.

Table 1. Summary of DPGs studies in the ICT4D literature

Authors	Study method	Main findings
Sahay, S (2018) [3]	Case study in the public health sector in India	A core policy issue is ensuring collective action at the global level to facilitate the production of, and access to, goods, and yield significant external benefits, across multiple nations. Two key characteristics have been identified to successful Global Public Goods: (i) design based on principles of platforms and, (ii) a governance strategy that enables platform principles in design and practice. Also, there are six policy-practice gaps that have been identified to move closer to the normative ideal of a GPG, addressed with context-specific strategies
Nicholson, B., Nielsen, P., Sæbø, J., and Sahay, S. (2019) [34]	Case study of digital platform installed in over 80 countries globally, primarily used in the health sector (DHIS2)	Four tensions have been identified in global public goods based on the case of digital platforms for innovation: (i) between serving those that can pay for functionality and those that cannot, (ii) between DHIS2 as a generic software and an appliance, (iii) between supporting the platform core and supporting innovation in the fringes; (iv) between global and local accountability. The theory of contradictions helps illustrate some of the tensions, confronting simplistic and linear views that implementing GPG health management platforms will translate unproblematically to efficiency gains. Cultivating a GPG mindset in the users as well as platform owners is necessary which may imply a cultural change

(*continued*)

Table 1. (*continued*)

Authors	Study method	Main findings
Sæbø, J. I., Nicholson, B., Nielsen, P., and Sahay, S. (2021) [10]	Case study of digital platform installed in over 80 countries globally, primarily used in the health sector (DHIS2)	The potential for translating and contextualizing digital platforms for the purpose of socio-economic development remains understudied. The theory of paradoxes help to capture the dynamics of the Digital Global Public Goods (DGPG) phenomenon as they evolve over time and space to understand their scaling challenge in health. The study identified 3 main paradoxes: (i) using sophisticated tools for relatively simple analysis; (ii) prioritising voices that tend to be unheard; and (iii) building software simultaneously relevant for global and local contexts. Those paradoxes reveal the competing effects with the macro and micro and the impact of collective action and governance to promote DGPGs effectively

2.3 Technological Determinism

The relationship between technology and society can be understood from a technological determinism perspective where technological change determines social changes in an established way [20–22]. Technological determinism has been considered a controversial theory [23] stating: "... the development of technology proceeds in an autonomous manner, determined by an internal logic independent of social influence" [23: p. 15495].

Over the years, technological development and innovation have become an important motor of social, economic or political change [24]. Conversely, evidence suggests that technology is a major cause but not the sole determinant of social change [23]. Scholars rather argue that technological design is the outcome of negotiations between several social groups and between the social and the technical, rather than the product of an internal, technical logic [25]. Despite the criticism, Winner [26] emphasised the relevance of technology's social effect, arguing that determinism should not be rejected as "technology does constrain human activities" [27: p. 77].

Technology determinism can take the form of "an idea, theory or a way of explaining technology development in history or the present, but it can also take the form of actual material structures that—implicitly or explicitly—permeate and influence society" [28].

It is therefore a result of what is societally desirable and what is technically possible. Thus, while DPGs can be an essential enabler for accomplishing the SDGs, we still need to understand their properties, how they relate to other technologies and how they influence and are influenced by the social setting in which they are implemented and used.

3   Case Illustration: The Emerging UN-Centred Discourse on DPGs

We illustrate why a research agenda on DPGs for development is needed by looking at recent developments led by various international collaborations and spearheaded by the United Nations system. Below we track the emergence of a discourse among international agencies that hold significant power of funding and legitimacy in the ICT4D field.

In 2014 the Digital Impact Alliance (DIAL) was formed, culminating more than a decade of work by international development organisations on how to include digital tools in their programming for improved outcomes. DIAL is a community of development agencies, both from the UN system and philanthropist organisations such as the Bill and Melinda Gates Foundation, country development agencies such as SIDA from Sweden and USAID, and various NGOs and companies. A flagship project is the Principles for Digital Development, widely endorsed globally. One of the tenets of these principles is "invest in software as a public good".

In 2018, the UN Secretary-General convened a high-level panel on digital cooperation, which released its report the year after. It noted that DGPs are important for the innovation of inclusive digital products and services, but that there is no 'go-to' place for such DPGs. A clear recommendation was the establishment of "a broad, multistakeholder alliance, involving the UN, [to] create a platform for sharing DGPs, engaging talent and pooling data sets, in a manner that respects privacy, in areas related to attaining the SDG" [29: p. 4]. Here DPGs were defined as digital technologies and content that are "freely and openly available, with minimal restrictions on how they can be distributed, adapted and reused" [29: p. 11]. As a strategic response to this call, the Digital Public Goods Alliance (the Alliance) was formed.

The Alliance is a "multi-stakeholder initiative with a mission to accelerate the attainment of the SDGs in LMIC by facilitating the discovery, development, use of, and investment in digital public goods" (https://digitalpublicgoods.net, accessed 16.01.2022). Its board includes UNICEF and UNDP, the development agencies of Germany and Norway, and the Government of Sierra Leone. The Alliance has taken the lead in the focus on DPGs over the last few years, as it has developed a standard for DPGs, as well as maintaining a registry of certified DPGs that meet this standard. While the definition of DPGs according to the Alliance has naturally evolved since the early phases, the current one states that they are "… open source software, open data, open AI models, open standards and open content that adhere to privacy and other applicable laws and best practises, do no harm, and help attain the Sustainable Development Goals" [30]. This definition is broad in terms of what manifestation of the digital it includes, but introduces an explicit link to the SDGs, as well as carrying other normative values. The registry the Alliance maintains of DPGs is making it easier for interested parties to discover them, the "to-go" place as the high-level panel on digital cooperation envisioned. For inclusion in this registry, there is a formal application process using the DPG standard, which follows the definition mentioned above.

A few points are noteworthy here. The first is the requirement of documentation of relevance to SDGs. Another is linked to licences, where the Alliance does accept stricter licences when it comes to prohibiting commercial reuse while at the same time encouraging licences allowing for commercial reuse. Lastly, a few well-intentioned aspects are related to data privacy, security, adherence to applicable laws, and last but not least that the projects "have taken steps to ensure the project anticipates, prevents, and does no harm by design"[9].

DIAL also maintains a list of relevant digital tools. This list explicitly links which SDGs they address, but is not exclusively for DPGs. Some digital tools that are well known in the ICT4D sphere appear in both lists. For instance, the health-related DHIS2 platform is listed in both, as a certified DPG and as relevant for SDG 3 (health and well-being), 4 (quality education), and 17 (partnerships for the goals). Together these lists potentially carry a lot of weight, on the one side linking digital technologies to SDGs, and on the other side functioning as a gatekeeper for what the Alliance considers as "good" technologies.

The DPG standard and curated list are two of the tools the Alliance applies to reach their goals of improving the discoverability, uptake, and sustainability of DPGs in LMICs. In addition, the Alliance takes a proactive role in advancing high impact DPGs by providing funding resources to strengthen DPG ecosystems. A stated aim is to work with governments in LMICS and regional hubs to change the power balance around technology solutions and DPGs are seen as an unprecedented opportunity to achieve this [30].

The Alliance, despite the first impression of being technology-focused, also calls for local ownership and local capacity to fully leverage digital technologies' innovative potential. This point is echoed by the Lancet and Financial Times Commission on governing health futures 2030: Growing up in a digital world, which argues that DPGs, due to their defining characteristics and associated values of sharing and openness, can play a strong role in enabling domestic ownership and control of digital public infrastructure cultivation [31].

Some challenges with DPGs are recognized by the Alliance. For instance, while digital technologies hold the potential to support development, they may likewise exacerbate inequalities. Further, the Alliance emphasises that the success of DGPs is not only related to its software features but also requires transformations of other systems, structures and practises in the context in which it is implemented.

The rhetoric of DPGs is rapidly permeating other relevant agencies. Digital Square, a 'marketplace' for health technology solutions, is funded by a similar set of investors; UNICEF and WHO, national development agencies such as GIZ of Germany, USAID and PEPFAR from USA, and the Swiss Agency for Development and Cooperation, as well as other NGOs like Bill and Melinda Gates Foundation and Rockefeller Foundation. They earlier worked with so-called global goods, defined as "digital health tools that are adaptable to different countries and contexts"[10], but now increasingly link to and

---

[9] https://digitalpublicgoods.net/standard/, accessed 14.01.2022.

[10] https://digitalsquare.org/digital-health-global-goods, accessed 14.01.2022.

refer to DPGs throughout their websites. Indeed, their current material seems confused, caught in the middle of updating their global goods references to DPGs, signalling a shift towards a public goods perspective.

The last organisation we briefly introduce here, though not the only one adopting a DPG rhetoric, is Co-develop, springing out of a convening by the Rockefeller Foundation, the Alliance, and the Norwegian Ministry of Foreign Affairs[11]. They aim to be a resource mobilisation platform with a focus on Digital Public Infrastructure (DPI), which can be supplied by either proprietary technology or DPGs. It is still in the establishment phase and their material may not be representative of the final destination. While being more agnostic as to what business model is behind the technology, a linear causality from digital technologies to SDGs is implied through quotes on their banners and a 5-step DPI development model.

4 Analysis

The rise of the discourse among the actors described above will inevitably have an influence on the broad field of ICT4D. As funding, legitimacy, and attention are steered towards DPGs, developers of technology, practitioners and implementers alike will be likely to adapt. Many of the same organisations are behind several of the collaborations mentioned above and thus it is not surprising that similar material and rhetoric appear across the related websites. However, we also note that these organisations combined make up a significant power constellation in the field of ICT4D and our short case illustration brings attention to some of the potential pitfalls and current shortcomings of this discourse. Three main points are particularly relevant:

First, DPGs are still poorly understood, as evidenced by the definitions used. Drifting away from the more classical definitions of public goods and global public goods, the SDGs are included, as are other normative values like "do no harm". This is not necessarily a bad thing as trading some definitional clarity for normative prescription may be very much in the interest of the organisations mentioned. However, we note a lack of clarity and in particular a lack of understanding of the *digital* aspects of DPGs.

Our contention is that exploring the potential of DPGs to support achieving the SDGs is a worthy goal, however, the design and use of digital technologies are different from other technologies (goods). The basis of DPGs are digital technologies [32] that are reprogrammable and thus multi-purpose, and their architecture is flexible, modular and layered. Digital technologies promote open innovation [33] based on assembling and re-assembling digital components of various kinds over time, allowing for an agile, cyclic and infinite process of design to meet diverging and emerging needs. While sharing many traits with digital technologies, DPGs are also uniquely different, which warrants studying them specifically and critically. For example, DPGs must be usable across multiple contexts and relevant both on a global scale (across different sites and generations) and locally (flexible enough to fulfil local and idiosyncratic needs) to be inclusive [34].

A second point to induce from the case is a tendency towards technological determinism and this takes several forms. The agenda of the DPG Alliance is based on DPGs

---

[11] https://www.codevelop.fund/aboutfaq, accessed 14.01.2022.

supporting the achievement of the SDGs. However, this relationship and the mechanisms to release the potential of DPGs for the SDGs remain unexplored. While certain 'qualities' of different DPGs can be assessed before it is eventually approved and included in the registry, the effect and value of a DPGs towards the achievement of SDGs can only be realised when it is put into use and used over time. The DPGs will not be implemented in a vacuum, but in a context where use is influenced by existing practises, institutions, other technologies and politics. Whether the DPG will 'do harm' or not is not an attribute of the technology alone, but a consequence of how it is implemented and used and may change over time. While the Alliance promotes successful examples (for example DHIS2), there is limited theoretical knowledge about how to design, scale, govern, and use DPGs in practice and how to reduce and not magnify inequalities. Thus, the broad goal of "accessibility for all" to digital tools [30] risks a similar outcome to previous initiatives that were criticised for technological determinism and ultimately failed. The Alliance do acknowledge the need for capacity building, fostering ecosystems of businesses and academia etc., for sustainability. Overall, the discourse is unbalanced; focusing predominantly on the promises of technology while not engaging with the socio-political aspects of making it work, of unintended consequences, and of local appropriation.

Our third point concerns the link between DPGs and the SDGs that relates to the consumption side of the goods, which tends to be implicit, as discussed above. The link between the organisations engaging in the discourse and the production of the technology is at the same time more explicit. Digital Square is set to be a marketplace where technology developers, funders, and implementing agencies can find each other. DPGs are by definition the result of market failures (as are any public goods), and establishing mechanisms to supply them and scale them over time is crucial. The involved organisations are well placed to be the future "international public sector" that provides DPGs.

While DPGs may accelerate the move towards a more inclusive future for all, they can also reinforce and magnify existing inequalities. The growing gender gap in Internet use is one example in this respect (see for example UN 2020). These design and use traits indicate how DPGs are unique and their design requires particular approaches, financing mechanisms and governance structures. There is currently a paucity of knowledge about how to scale, govern, and implement DGPGs successfully to reduce and not magnify inequalities. Thus, the link between the DPGs and the accomplishment of the SDGs is by large missing in this discourse.

5   Towards a Research Agenda for Digital Public Goods

In this section, we outline a research agenda on DPGs, we emphasise consideration of the global, local, emergent and contingent related to DPGs and their link to the SDGs. We posit and reaffirm our position that DPGs should be understood as an ideal, a sociotechnical accomplishment that is ongoing rather than as embedded into a repository of static and portable technological artefact. We hope that this agenda can support the ICT4D community in developing a stronger empirical basis on DPGs, a better conceptual understanding of DPGs and a clearer link between DPGs and the SDGs.

The substantial work on digital transformation in information systems research has facilitated insight into the characteristics of the 'digital' dimension of a DPG mentioned above that extends the relatively static public goods examples of a lighthouse, traffic lights, flood defences etc. Open digital platforms are considered DPGs because they enable non-rivalrous and non-excludable access. At the same time, the flexibility enabled by the digital characteristic means that a DPG status could be more fluctuating and temporary compared with other categories of public goods (e.g. flood defences). To illustrate, an example we encountered involved a software application previously distributed freely in line with DPG principles of non-rivalry, non-excludability. However, a decision was made by the organisation management to monetise the application and access to download it was changed in the space of just a few days via a paywall. Thus, reaching the status of DPG is a result of design and a continuing accomplishment. DPGs can be seen as a particular type of digital technology, and with particular traits and challenges, for example, the supply-side challenges related to funding and sustaining them. This has not been addressed in the digital transformation literature and remains a gap in our knowledge.

In the following sections, we develop key themes that form a proposed research agenda on DPGs. For each theme, we propose a central research question. We are actively engaged in action research into DPGs in relation to the Health Information Systems Programme (HISP) on the District Health Information System (DHIS2) at the University of Oslo. DHIS2 is commonly used as an archetypical example of DPGs, and we will thus draw on our insights to support the research agenda.

5.1 Global Versus Local Relevance

In a previous publication in the IFIP 9.4 W.G. proceedings [34] we used a paradoxes lens to explore tensions of DPGs. A key facet of this analysis related to DHIS2 was that the 'global' i.e. a generic public good fulfilling the greatest number of possible implementations over time is in tension with the 'local' i.e. fulfilling the current needs of local ministries of health at the 'fringes', without overwhelming amounts of functionality that is not required and at the same time enabling innovation from the same 'fringes'. We argued that instead of focusing on DPGs, the focus should be on Digital Global Public Goods (DGPG) relevant locally and on a global scale. The power of international organisations and donors in shaping the core application was revealed as a major force in defining the roadmap and functionality of the DHIS2 implementations. A knowledge gap remains in the role and realisation of subsidiarity (making decisions on the lowest possible level, see e.g. [2]) in DGPGs when by definition applying capitalist free market mechanisms on the supply side is not the solution. Potentially, much can be learned from the extensive previous work on public goods that has discussed collective action when managing natural resources. How this translates to digital technologies and how to conceptualise and practically realise the relevance of the DPGs locally and globally remains unknown.

RQ: How to develop and sustain the relevance of DPGs related to subsidiarity and collective action, and their relationship?

5.2   Local Capacities and Capacity Building

DPGs have much in common with digital technologies in general when it comes to reach and scale and the marginal cost of reproduction. Digital technologies are different from physical as well as other informational goods in that they are malleable and flexible and may come as half-finished products requiring substantial efforts and thus capacity to set parameters, customise and integrate with other components to make them relevant locally. This is also not a one-time effort but requires continuous updates to accommodate new versions and new functionality as well as maintaining the integration with other systems. It is crucial to understand what capacities in terms of human expertise are needed to implement, scale and maintain DPGs locally over time. This capacity will also depend on the particular DPGs and the local design infrastructure they offer including boundary resources. The capacity requirements for physical infrastructure such as hosting, networks and end-user equipment is another element.

> *RQ: What are the needs for capacity to support DPGs locally and how to build and retain them in LMIC settings?*

5.3   The Economy of DPGs

Public goods are a result of market failures, i.e. market mechanisms will not support their production. DPGs are also a result of market failures but by design. DGPs such as DHIS2 are funded by donors including aid agencies, global development funds, NGOs and philanthropists. A question is whether this is an efficient and sustainable model over time. For example, there is a risk that donors may change their priorities and end their funding. This eventuality could lead to the demise of the DPG, or change its public good status by introducing a fee-based business model. Other relevant aspects of the economy of DPGs relate to scaling, the cost of free-riders and the value of generativity when the DPG is triggering local innovations (such as locally developed apps distributed on an app store) that are brought back into the DPG and shared among all its users. There is thus a two-way relationship between the DPGs and sustainable development. On the one hand, DGPs can contribute to the SDGs by, for example, enabling government agencies to serve their citizens better in terms of improved health and education services. On the other hand, sustainable development involves expanding, preserving, and maintaining digital public goods.

> *RQ: What is the particular economy of DPGs and how to achieve sustainable donor-based funding arrangements?*

5.4   DPGs and Scaling

In a recent article [10], we analysed the challenges of scaling DPGs using the case of DHIS2. A conclusion of the paper was that public sector DPG implementations in LMICs require alternative conceptualizations to that of commercial digital platforms in the global North. This is because of differences in incentives, institutional context and resource constraints [35, 36]. Gaps remain in our knowledge of scaling and DPGs, the ecosystem supporting DPGs across various settings is highly complex and hetero-geneous. Building on the insights of Jacobides et al. [37] from the commercial domain would enable in-depth analysis of the symbiosis and challenges presented by the various supporting actors and networks in a DGPG.

RQ. How may DGPGs effectively scale?

5.5 Understanding and Responding to Digital Global Public 'BADs'

The costs or 'public bads' associated with DPGs are largely neglected by the organisa-tions descried in the case illustration. We posit that interventions intended to generate DPGs can, and often do, generate 'bads' that are also non-excludable and non-rivalrous and therefore can adversely impact a significant number of people. These 'bads' are evi-dent in Zuboff's [38] criticisms of the major digital platforms relating to surveillance, privacy, and security and Masiero's [39] exclusion of vulnerable groups in Aadhaar, inter-net crime, fraud, web viruses, denial of service attacks, hate speech etc. The authors' prior analysis of DHIS2 also identified a 'bad' conceptualised as "Global vs. Local Account-ability" [34]. A recurrent theme in country implementations of DHIS2 is to collect data on various user groups, such as key populations and certain diseases (for example sex workers and HIV), or for any social program use which in some jurisdictions is illegal to collect. There have been instances where data is collected on religion and caste, and such data has the potential to be misused in the wrong hands. One starting point may be to link DGP 'bads' to governance procedures from the commercial platform literature (see e.g. [40]) but as previously stated, this must take into account the developing country resource-constrained contexts.

RQ: How can public bads be identified, conceptualised and controlled in a DPG?

While our theoretical knowledge about DPGs is scant, the catalogue of DPGs clas-sified by the Alliance are already playing an important role in public health in LMICs, including DHIS2, OpenMRS, MOSIP and DIVOC. Countries have already begun to implement these DGPGs, but scaling them up nationally and globally still hinges on unexplored territories of standardisation, interoperability frameworks, sharing models, infrastructure for adaptation, capacity building and international digital cooperation.

There is a substantial body of already existing knowledge related to the design and use of DHIS2 concerning non-rivalrous processes of sharing, information exchange, global collaboration and interaction and spillover effects between organisations, coun-tries and continents. However, this knowledge and related implications for policy and practice primarily relates to DHIS2, health information systems in LMICs and is dis-seminated primarily within the global health domain. At the same time, there is limited empirical research on other DPGs. Thus, to build a stronger theoretical foundation for understanding DPGs, we also call for empirical research on a range of DPGs beyond the public health domain in LMICs, both on how DPGs are funded and developed and how they are implemented and used and their link with the SDGs.

A central element of the DPG discourse is openness represented by open-source software, open data, open standards etc. The existing literature on *open development* in

ICT4D research addresses the potential and the challenges of openness related to socio-economic development (see for example [41]). A central theme in the open development literature is the actual value of openness for development and critical discussions of the real positive and negative impact of open technologies. The research agenda we suggest in this paper relates to openness, but each theme also goes beyond and argues that it is not enough for DPGs to be open to make an impact. We thus question the merits of openness and identify five core areas where more research is needed to understand DPGs as a particular type of digital technology and with certain traits of openness. Our hope is that the research agenda presented here with themes and related research questions can inspire and act as a platform for further research to advance our understanding of DPGs.

References

1. UN: Report of the Secretary-General: Roadmap for Digital Cooperation (June 2020). https://www.un.org/en/content/digital-cooperation-roadmap/assets/pdf/Roadmap_for_Digital_Cooperation_EN.pdf. Accessed 14 Jan 2022
2. Kaul, I., Grunberg, I., Stern, M.: Global public goods. In: Kaul, I., Grunberg, I., Stern, M. (eds.) Global Public Goods: International Cooperation in the 21st Century, pp. 450–498. Oxford University Press, Oxford (1999)
3. Sahay, S.: Free and open source software as global public goods?: What are the distortions and how do we address them? Electron. J. Inf. Syst. Dev. Ctries. **85**, 4 (2019)
4. Serat, V.G.: UNICEF boosts digital public goods - time to boost our team! 25 February 2021. https://www.unicef.org/innovation/stories/unicef-boosts-digital-public-goods-boost-our-team. Accessed 14 Jan 2022
5. Birdsall, N., Diofasi, A.: Global Public Goods for Development: How Much and What for. Center for Global Development, Washington DC (2015)
6. Walsham, G.: ICT4D research: reflections on history and future agenda. Inf. Technol. Dev. **23**(1), 18–41 (2017)
7. Robertson, A.: OLPC'S $100 Laptop Was Going to Change the World - Then it All Went Wrong. The Verge (2018). https://www.theverge.com/2018/4/16/17233946/olpcs-100-laptop-education-where-is-it-now. Accessed 16 Jan 2021
8. Poveda, S., Roberts, T.: Critical agency and development: applying Freire and Sen to ICT4D in Zambia and Brazil. Inf. Technol. Dev. **24**(1), 119–137 (2018)
9. Heeks, R.: ICT4D 3.0? Part 1 - The components of an emerging "digital-for-development" paradigm. Electron. J. Inf. Syst. Dev. Ctries. **86**(3), e12124 (2019)
10. Nicholson, B., Nielsen, P., Sæbø, J., Sahay, S.: Towards a Conceptual Understanding of Digital Global Public Goods Platforms for Development, forthcoming in the Information Society (2022)
11. Adu-Gyamfi, E., Nielsen, P., Sæbø, J.I.: The Dynamics of a Global Health Information Systems Research and Implementation Project. In: Scandinavian Conference on Health Informatics. Linköping University Electronic Press, Oslo (2019)
12. Jimenez, A., Roberts, T.: Decolonising neo-liberal innovation: using the Andean philosophy of 'Buen Vivir' to reimagine innovation hubs. In: International Conference on Social Implications of Computers in Developing Countries, IAICT, vol. 552, pp. 180–191. Springer, Cham (2019). https://doi.org/10.1007/978-3-030-19115-3_15
13. Samuelson, P.A.: The pure theory of public expenditure. Rev. Econ. Stat. **36**(4), 387–389 (1954)
14. Ostrom, E.: Governing the Commons: The Evolution of Institutions for Collective Action. Cambridge University Press, UK (1990)

15. Ostrom, V., Ostrom, E.: Public goods and public choices. In: Savas, E.S. (ed.) Alternatives for delivering public services: toward improved performance. Westview Press, Boulder (1977)
16. Ferdman, A.: Why the intrinsic value of public goods matters. Crit. Rev. Int. Soc. Pol. Phil. **21**(5), 661–676 (2018)
17. Rubens, A., Yiu, L., Bardy, R., Saner, R.: Public Goods Sustainable Development and the Contribution of Business. Cambridge Scholars Publishing (2021)
18. Bonina, C., Koskinen, K., Eaton, B., Gawer, A.: Digital platforms for development: foundations and research agenda. Inf. Syst. J. **31**, 869–902 (2021)
19. O'Neil, K., Rasul, N.: Co-Develop: Digital Public Infrastructure for an Equitable Recovery (2021). https://www.rockefellerfoundation.org/wp-content/uploads/2021/08/Co-Develop-Digital-Public-Infrastructure-for-an-Equitable-Recovery-Full-Report.pdf. Accessed 14 Jan 2022
20. Staudenmaier, J.M.: Technology's Storytellers: Reweaving the Human Fabric. MIT Press, Cambridge (1985)
21. Misa, T.J.: How machines make history and how historians (and others) help them to do so. Sci. Technol. Hum. Values **13**, 308–331 (1988)
22. Bimber, B.: Three faces of technological determinism. In: Smith, M.R., Marx, L. (eds.) Does Technology Drie History? The Dilemma of Technological Determinism. MIT Press, Cambridge (1994)
23. Kline, R.R.: Technological determinism. In: Smelser, N.J., Baltes, B. (eds.) International Encyclopedia of the Social and Behavioral Sciences, pp. 15495–15498 (2001)
24. Macmillan, P.: Global Politics. Palgrave Macmillan, UK (2015)
25. Pinch, T.J., Bijker, W.E.: The social construction of facts and artefacts: or how the sociology of science and the sociology of technology might benefit each other. Soc. Stud. Sci. **14**, 399–441 (1984)
26. Winner, L.: Technology as Forms of Life. Readings in the Philosophy of Technology. David M. Kaplan, pp. 103–113. Rowman & Littlefield, Oxford (2004)
27. Winner, L.: Autonomous Technology: Technics-Out-of-Control as a Theme in Political Thought. MIT Press, Cambridge (1977)
28. Hallström, J.: Embodying the past, designing the future: technological determinism reconsidered in technology education. Int. J. Technol. Des. Educ. **32**(1), 1–15 (2020). https://doi.org/10.1007/s10798-020-09600-2
29. UN: Report of the UN Secretary-General's High-level Panel on Digital Cooperation: The age of digital interdependence (2019). https://www.un.org/en/pdfs/DigitalCooperation-report-for%20web.pdf. Accessed 16 Jan 2022
30. Nordhaug, L.M., Harris, L.: 5 Year Strategy (2021–2026). Digital Public Goods Alliance (2021)
31. Kickbusch, I., et al.: The lancet and financial times commission on governing health futures 2030. Lancet Comm. **398**(10312), 1727–1776 (2021)
32. Yoo, Y., Henfridsson, O., Lyytinen, K.: Research commentary: the new organizing logic of digital innovation: an agenda for information systems research. Inf. Syst. Res. **21**(4), 724–735 (2010)
33. Chesbrough, H.W.: Open Innovation: The New Imperative for Creating and Profiting from Technology. Harvard Business Press, USA (2006)
34. Nicholson, B., Nielsen, P., Saebo, J., Sahay, S.: Exploring tensions of global public good platforms for development: the case of DHIS2. In: Nielsen, P., Kimaro, H.C. (eds.) ICT4D 2019. IAICT, vol. 551, pp. 207–217. Springer, Cham (2019). https://doi.org/10.1007/978-3-030-18400-1_17
35. Bonina, C., Koskinen, K., Eaton, B., Gawer, A.: Digital platforms for development: foundations and research agenda. Inf. Syst. J. **31**(6), 869–902 (2021)

36. Nielsen, P.: Digital innovation: a research agenda for information systems research in developing countries. In: Choudrie, J., Islam, M.S., Wahid, F., Bass, J.M., Priyatma, J.E. (eds.) ICT4D 2017. IAICT, vol. 504, pp. 269–279. Springer, Cham (2017). https://doi.org/10.1007/978-3-319-59111-7_23

37. Jacobides, M.G., Cennamo, C., Gawer, A.: Towards a theory of ecosystems. Strateg. Manag. J. **39**(8), 2255–2276 (2018)

38. Zuboff, S.: The Age of Surveillance Capitalism: The Fight for a Human Future at the New Frontier of Power. Public Affairs, New York (2018)

39. Masiero, S., Arvidsson, V.: Degenerative outcomes of digital identity platforms for development. Inf. Syst. J. **31**(6), 903–928 (2021)

40. Gawer, A., Cusumano, M.A.: Industry platforms and ecosystem innovation. J. Prod. Innov. Manag. **31**(3), 417–433 (2014)

41. Smith, M.L., Elder, L., Emond, H.: Open Development: a new theory for ICT4D. Inf. Technol. Int. Dev. **7**(1), iii–ix (2011)

Investigating Mid-level IT Affordances as Drivers for Societal Change: Addressing the Education Data Challenge in The Gambia

Bjørnar Valbø$^{(\boxtimes)}$ (iD) and Terje Aksel Sanner (iD)

University of Oslo, Oslo, Norway
{bjornarv,terjeasa}@ifi.uio.no

Abstract. Affordance perspectives have gained traction among information systems (IS) scholars and have seen recent adoption in ICT4D research. Although scholars recognize the need to differentiate between mere technology use and higher-level organizational and societal IT affordances, no clear terminology for the representation of affordance granularity exists. This paper introduces "mid-level IT affordances", which, we argue, emerge from technology use and serve as prerequisites for the actualization of higher-level affordances. To illustrate, we draw on a case study of education management information systems in The Gambia. International development agendas encourage public sector actors to produce increasingly granular data. Yet, the capacity to utilize the data is not strengthened correspondingly. This introduces a disconnect between policy and practice, whereby investments in technology use affordances fail to translate into IT affordances for monitoring progress towards complex policy goals. A mid-level IT affordance perspective allows for the identification and potential mitigation of such gaps.

Keywords: Mid-level IT affordances · Education management · SDGs

1 Introduction

A theoretical challenge identified by information systems (IS) scholars pertains to the level of granularity of affordances. DeSanctis and Poole [1] introduce the term "repeating decomposition problem", pointing at the fact that "there are features within features (e.g., options within software options) and contingencies within contingencies (e.g., tasks within tasks)" and raise the question, "how far must the analysis go to bring consistent, meaningful results?" (p. 124). To date, there is no clear consensus on how best to conceptualize the aggregation of affordances from "simple" (e.g., tagging [2]; inputting data [3]; searching [4]) to more complex composite affordances at the organizational and societal level (e.g., clinical decision-making [3]; developing concepts [4]; organizational memory affordance [5]; Enhancing Knowledgeability and Autonomy [6]). Accounting for the intricate relationship between technology use and its implications for social

Y. Zheng et al. (Eds.): ICT4D 2022, IFIP AICT 657, pp. 471–489, 2022.
https://doi.org/10.1007/978-3-031-19429-0_28

development is at the heart of the ICT4D research agenda. Further development of an affordance perspective is promising in this regard.

Technology is not a panacea for development [7, p. 12]. Yet, the development landscape is fraught with ICT interventions to improve the lives of the world's poor (e.g., [8]). Faik et al. [6] point out that there is limited attention to "how [societal consequences] emerge from the development, deployment, or use of IT" (p. 1361). To this end, the authors attempt to develop an analysis that ties IT use affordances directly to societal changes. Inspired by this recent work, we argue that the recognition of "mid-level IT affordances" allows us to trace and account for the action possibilities that emerge from basic technology use (lower-level affordances). In turn, we argue, "mid-level IT affordances" are constitutive of higher-level affordances that are associated with social development, such as improved health and wellbeing of populations or equitable access to quality education.

This study reports from the Gambian education sector, where the Ministry of Basic and Secondary Education (MoBSE) has engaged in an "Education Management Information Systems shift", a stepwise digitization initiative, that entails the transition from reliance on surveys and aggregate statistics to individual learner records. Until recently, the EMIS was an aggregated and paper-based data system, managed at the national level and characterized by fragmented data [9, p. 129]. The existing information system could not explain why learning outcomes in the country remained low while the proportion of qualified teachers increased. More recently, it could not respond to information needs regarding the effect of school closures during the Covid-19 pandemic, nor guide interventions to alleviate the situation for out of school learners.

MoBSE, like many other ministries of education, were unable to produce data to monitor progress towards some of the key Sustainable Development Goals (SDGs), which aim to "ensure inclusive and equitable quality education and promote lifelong learning opportunities for all" [10]. This includes ensuring "equal access to all levels of education and vocational training for the vulnerable, including persons with disabilities, indigenous peoples and children in vulnerable situations". Consequently, "data needs to be disaggregated by gender, location, wealth quintile and other factors" [11, p. 9]. This necessitates processing of individual learner data. MoBSE experienced a policy-practice gap, whereby national and international policies called for increasingly granular data, while the education system's capacity to record, interpret and utilize the data for local action remained scarce.

This paper draws on and extends an affordance perspective [12], to explore the action possibilities the "EMIS Shift" affords education management in The Gambia. Our main contribution is the introduction of "mid-level IT affordances" to IT affordance research. An affordance perspective allows us to study action possibilities associated with IT adoption, implementation and use at an organizational "mid-level" (e.g., [13–17]). In ICT4D research, affordance perspectives are hitherto underutilized, although there are recent promising examples (e.g., [18–20]). A widely adopted definition of affordances in IS research, is that an affordances is "the potential for behaviors associated with achieving an immediate concrete outcome and arising from the relation between an artifact and a goal-oriented actor or actors" [16, p. 69, 17, p. 823].

In this paper, we map the interdependence between "simple", or lower-level, technology feature use affordances (e.g., inputting data) to mid-level affordances (i.e., organizational IT capabilities) such as *decentralizing data access*. Finally, we relate these mid-level affordances to higher-level affordances, which afford the education sector in The Gambia the ability to *monitor progress* towards the SDGs and national policy goals (i.e., societal changes [6]). The structure of the paper is as follows. In the next section, we provide an overview of relevant IT affordance literature. Next, we present our method. In Sect. 4 we present our empirical case and discuss the case findings before we in Sect. 5 consider how the Gambian EMIS case underscores the importance of understanding the composite, interdependent, and delicate nature of IT affordance realization in public sector organizations in the Global South.

2 IT Affordances at Different Levels of Granularity

Gibson [21, 22] first introduced the concept of affordances to the field of evolutionary psychology while arguing that animals do not perceive the objects' physical properties, but rather what objects can provide: "The *affordances* of the environment are what it *offers* the animal, what it *provides* or *furnishes*, either for good or ill" [22, p. 127]. A shelter affords sheltering to animals, and a knife affords cutting to people. Since different actors have different capabilities, affordances are not the same for all actors. For instance, stairs afford climbing to most people, but not to infants or people with certain disabilities. While affordances can be easy to perceive and actualize for "simple" objects (e.g., a knife), the application of AT to the IS field has proven difficult. In an organizational context, a complex information system affords a plethora of different action possibilities to an array of different actors.

Markus and Silver [23] warn that repeating decomposition of IT feature usage might pose analytical challenges and suggest to "hypothesize that the system as a whole, rather than one or more component parts, provides an affordance" (p. 628). Nonetheless, a complex information system in an organization setting affords a number of desirable action possibilities that somehow needs to be perceived and realized by organizational actors. Gutek et al. [24] notes that most computer systems are really "sets of loosely bundled capabilities and can be implemented in many different ways" (p. 234, as cited in DeSanctis & Poole [1, p. 126]). Leidner et al. [14] urge researchers to look beyond mere technology use, while Volkoff and Strong [25] highlight that researchers should study affordances at an appropriate level of granularity. To date, there is no clear guidance on how to identify and label such different granularity levels of IT affordances. This is needed, we hold, to study the relationship between changing IT use affordances and societal development and to generate a coherent body of knowledge.

2.1 Towards an Ensemble View of IT Affordances

The decomposability of affordances has given rise to several theoretical constructs in IS research. Strong et al. [16] illustrate affordances' interdependency through the *affordance dependency diagram*. Similarly, Burton-Jones and Volkoff's [3] *affordance network* explains how affordances are interrelated. Both these concepts allude to how the actualization of an affordance can lead to the emergence of another affordance. Thapa and Sein [19] extend this line of reasoning and introduce the *trajectory of affordances*, that is, the trajectory along which affordances travel, "specifying the process and conditions through which affordances are perceived leading to actualisation of affordances" (p. 811). They also argue that affordances form *ensembles*. Interestingly, these notions all resemble ideas introduced by Gaver [26] more than two decades earlier: "Complex actions can be understood in terms of groups of affordances that are *sequential in time* [emphasis added] or *nested in space* [emphasis added]" (p. 79).

As an illustration of sequential affordances, Gaver [26] explains how a door handle affords turning *after* the grasping affordance (i.e., grasping the door handle) has been actualized. He distinguishes sequential affordance (in time) from nested affordances (in space), as he explains how the *door opening* affordance consists of the affordances *pulling the door handle* and *pulling the door*. Drawing on Gaver, Bernardi [27] refers to nested affordances as *composite affordances* and provides an example of how the *building a support network* affordance is a composite of the *self-presentation* and *narration* affordances. We have visualized Gaver's ideas in Fig. 1, and in Fig. 2 we have replaced Gaver's affordances with generic terms. This simple framework served as a starting point for our study of affordances in the Gambian EMIS Shift implementation.

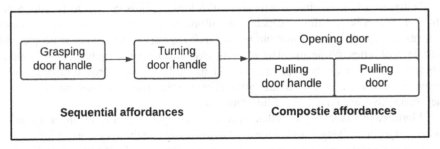

Fig. 1. Conceptual framework derived from Gaver [26], using Gaver's affordances

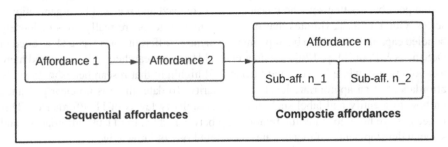

Fig. 2. Conceptual framework derived from Gaver [26], using generic terms

2.2 Gaps

Although IS scholars have shown that there is interdependency between affordances and that the IT affordances of most interest reside on a higher level of abstraction, there is a gap in the literature on how to identify and characterize these affordances. Extant literature mentions lower and higher level (e.g., [3]), first- and second-order [14], and individual- and organizational-level [16] affordances. In this paper we introduce "mid-level IT affordances" to signify affordances that emerge as a consequence of technology use and are constitutive to the higher-level affordances.

In the following methods section, we describe the case context, and in the subsequent section we argue how IS scholars may investigate affordance interdependencies, by recognizing their *composite* and *sequential* nature, across three different levels of granularity (low, mid, and high).

3 Method

3.1 Case Background

This study reports from an ongoing research endeavor in The Gambia, coordinated by the Health Information Systems Programme (HISP) center at the University of Oslo. The Gambia, like many other ministries of health in low- and middle-income countries, has been using the open-source District Health Information Software 2 (DHIS2[1]) as a nation-wide health management information system (HMIS) since 2010 [28] and is now expanding the usage of DHIS2 into the educational domain, implementing it as their national education management information system (EMIS). To meet the demand of individual data reporting, put forth by the SDG4 and national goals of improved learning outcomes across social stratifications, the need for an information system which could disaggregate data to individual level was identified. The positive experience from the health domain and the establishment of relevant in-country technical capacity resulted in the selection of DHIS2 as a backbone for the nationwide EMIS implementation. Despite its historical association with the public health sector, DHIS2 offers a set of generic data models and customizable modules that are deliberately domain agnostic. The on-going appropriation of DHIS2 to the education sector is driven by countries that already have developed a strong national capacity to utilize DHIS2 for health and wish to capitalize on this also in education.

As part of the digitalization initiative MoBSE has implemented DHIS2 as the backbone of its national EMIS. DHIS2 is a modular and complex digital platform system, consisting of a software core onto which new contents, applications or services can be developed. The development and implementation of such compliments are facilitated by DHIS2's software development kits, design systems, documentation and open application programming interfaces (APIs). To utilize the flexibility of DHIS2, MoBSE in The Gambia needs to obtain local capacity to configure and customize existing DHIS2 modules and develop and maintain complimentary applications when necessary.

3.2 Data Collection and Analysis

Through field trips, interviews, and recurrent biweekly online meetings with representatives from MoBSE, the authors have continuously engaged with the Gambian implementation of DHIS2-EMIS over a period of 16 months. We reviewed relevant official

---

[1] https://dhis2.org/.

Table 1. Data sources

Data source	Type
Education Sector Strategic Plan 2016-2030 [9]	Official Gambian government publication
The shift from aggregate to individual-level data system in the case of The Gambia EMIS (Internal project document)	PhD Proposal to the University of Oslo by a MoBSE employee
Meeting the global learning crisis with data: a research agenda on digital platforms for education management [29]	Research opinion article (manuscript in preparation)
Information system centralization and decentralization: The introduction of digital learner records in The Gambia [30]	Conference article (manuscript in preparation)

17 Bi-weekly EMIS status and update meeting
Participants:
• The EMIS project manager (HISP center)
• 3 scientific staff (HISP center, including second author)
• 1 PhD Research fellow (first author)
• Representatives from national EMIS implementations
    o The Gambia (2)
    o Uganda (4)
    o Mozambique (1)
    o Sri Lanka (1)
    o Togo (2)
	Recurrent meeting with local stakeholders for EMIS implementations in The Gambia, Uganda, Mozambique, Sri Lanka, and Togo

20 Bi-weekly EMIS project coordination meeting
Participants:
• The EMIS project management team
    o The EMIS project manager
    o 1 Professor
    o 1 Associate professor (second author)
    o 1 Senior engineer
• 1 PhD Research fellow (first author)
	Recurrent meeting for HISP's EMIS project management team at the HISP center (UiO)

18 Bi-weekly research meeting.
Participants:
• 3 scientific employees at the HISP center
    o 1 Professor
    o 2 Associate professors (including second author)
• 3 PhD research fellows
    o 1 MoBSE employee currently doing a PhD at UiO studying the Gambian *EMIS shift* towards individual data collection and reporting.
    o 1 HISP Uganda employee involved in the expansion of DHIS2 from the health sector to the education sector. Doing a PhD studying disaggregation of decision-making in the Ugandan education sector.
    o 1 PhD research fellow at the HISP center, studying the implementation of DHIS2-EMIS in The Gambia and Uganda (first author).
	Recurrent meeting among PhD research fellows studying EMIS implementations in The Gambia and Uganda

6 interviews of employees at different levels of the educational system in The Gambia. The average interview duration was approximately 30 minutes.	Semi-structured interviews. Snowballing used to identify interviewees.

documents to further contextualize the case study. Table 1 gives an overview of the data sources. We identified a set of affordances related to the ongoing DHIS2-EMIS implementation and organized these into themes, with the help of the conceptual framework we derived from Gaver's [26] work (Fig. 2). This allowed us to engage with the clustered and sequential nature of the identified affordances and explore the interdependencies between lower- and higher-level affordances. Our analyses revealed the need for a terminology that can describe affordances that are neither basic lower-level affordances nor very abstract higher-level affordances. Hence, we introduce the notion of "mid-level affordances" to bridge this gap.

4 Case Description

4.1 Configuring DHIS2 for Education Management

DHIS2 is an open-source management information software platform, used by 73 ministries of health [31] and six ministries of education [32]. DHIS2 development is coordinated by the HISP center at the University of Oslo. HISP is a research and implementation network, with 15 recognized HISP groups around the world and numerous other contributors. Recently, DHIS2 has been adopted in several new domains, such as agriculture, road safety, logistics management, and education management [33]. For more than a decade, The Gambia has been using DHIS2 as an HMIS. The Ministry of Basic and Secondary Education (MoBSE) have since 2019 adopted DHIS2 as a backbone for its EMIS. DHIS2 can be used for both individual records keeping and aggregate data collection and analysis. MoBSE wishes to leverage DHIS2 to meet EMIS requirements put forth by the SDG4 and national goals of improved learning outcomes across social stratifications.

DHIS2 is a rather complex piece of software, with a platform architecture. This grants local design flexibility, for those who have the necessary capacity to configure DHIS2's "bundled applications" or develop platform extensions themselves. A freshly installed instance of DHIS2 requires configuration in terms of setting up organizational hierarchies and creating data elements and indicators which data collectors will report against and analysts will monitor. By taking advantage of DHIS2's software development kits, APIs, design tools and documentation it is possible to create software extensions or applications that can be loosely integrated with the platform core. These apps can also be uploaded to the DHIS2 App Hub, which makes them available for other user organizations to download and install on their DHIS2 instances.

Since DHIS2 is open source, the entire source code can be modified by anyone with the right skill sets. However, as the DHIS2 core is maintained and governed by HISP at the University of Oslo (HISP UiO), actors with core software requirements engage with the HISP UiO development team to have their requirements recognized in the DHIS2 roadmap. Through two decades of north-south-south university collaborations, a large network of experts has emerged to cater for public sector DHIS2 implementation needs. Implementations are often organized as participatory co-creation projects involving HISP UiO, a local regional or national HISP group and a ministerial department as partners. In addition to knowledge sharing through projects, there are formalized training structures referred to as DHIS2 Academies as well as a vibrant online community of practice, where local problem owners can find advice and support from experienced members of the community.

4.2 Gambian DHIS2-EMIS Configurations

Data Visibility at All Levels. DHIS2 affords education sector administrators the possibility of creating custom analytics dashboards and analysis tools using for example pivot tables, graphs, or maps. Nine members of the MoBSE national level team received training from HISP West and Central Africa (HISP WCA) on how to configure relevant thematic dashboards and analysis tools. The national team can now design their own thematic dashboards and share these with users at sub-levels. Ideally, given sufficient organizational capacity, each organizational level could be trained to develop custom dashboards for the level below themselves in the hierarchy. Hence, the national level would make dashboards for the regions and the regional offices would make dashboards for schools in their regions. Furthermore, each level can make their own dashboards or adjust the dashboards received from a higher level to account for local priorities and circumstances. Given sufficient training in software configuration and data analysis, each school can visualize its own data and inspect relevant indicators for their own planning and management (e.g., teacher and student attendance, dropout, and completion rates by relevant group disaggregations, etc.). Similarly, cluster monitors – school inspectors responsible for following up a cluster of schools within a region – have access to a different dashboard and analysis setup and can inspect school performance and reporting rates. At national level, MoBSE has access to all data in the system and has yet another dashboard and data visualization setup to be able to monitor broad trends and evaluate national education sector programs. Figure 3 provides an example of a DHIS2-EMIS dashboard.

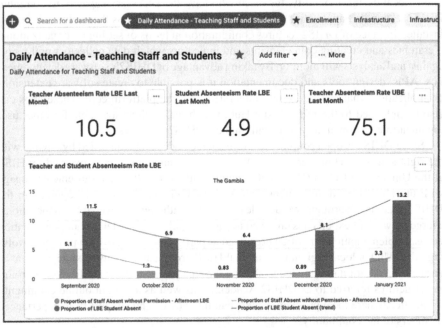

Fig. 3. DHIS2-EMIS dashboard showing daily attendance trend in lower basic education (LBE) units in The Gambia. Demo data may not correlate with actual figures.

Data Disaggregation. MoBSE in The Gambia decided to redesign its EMIS, which was essentially based on Microsoft Excel, Access databases and paper-based data collection tools, in order to cater for the novel socio-economic disaggregation requirements of education data. Internally, this process has been called the "EMIS shift", as it entails a shift from handling purely aggregated data (statistics) to also maintaining individual learner records.

MoBSE perceived the possibility of using DHIS2's Tracker module - a generic module for capturing data over time about any type of tracked entity - to capture and store educational data on individuals. The Tracker module is used in public health implementations of DHIS2 to store medical information on patients from their recurring visits to a clinic or to record data about trajectories of blood samples or health commodities. The module supports storing (constant) information about the tracked entity as well as data that varies over time. Thus, MoBSE decided to use the Tracker module to collect and store socio-economic data, attendance history, and continuous assessment data about learners.

Exploiting the design flexibility of DHIS2, MoBSE, in collaboration with HISP WCA, configured individual learner modules to be able to follow-up individual students. The modules were designed through participatory methods where HISP WCA first engaged in capacity building workshops in order to inform MoBSE about the different design possibilities. In the configured modules, MoBSE captures the learners' socio-economic data, attendance history, continuous assessment, and disciplinary record. During 2020, MoBSE implemented individual learner admission and registration by employing a combination of DHIS2, mobile data traffic, and Chromebooks in 200 schools. The technical resources from the initial phase were further leveraged to collect and register students throughout public schools in the entire country. Beyond individual record keeping, the individual data can be anonymized and aggregated to provide useful information for secondary administrative use.

Digitized School Report Card. The Gambian school report card (SRC) is a school-level information product intended to promote community participation and increase accountability and transparency. The tool highlights priority areas for the coming year and informs the preparation of school improvement plans. In 2008, the first version of the SRC was created. Although there have been challenges using the SRC, it has been widely recognized and embedded in the country's EMIS practice. A limitation of the initial version was that sub-national levels could not access the data directly and had to wait for distributed printouts from the central level. This hindered broad engagement from regional officers, head teachers, parents, and community representatives in a timely manner. Furthermore, despite the focus on simplicity and visual guidance in designing the SRC, evaluations revealed challenges associated with interpretation of results.

By taking advantage of DHIS2's API, MoBSE, in collaboration with HISP WCA, and three informatics master students from UiO, developed a new web-application of the SRC – a DHIS2 addon – which could be integrated into the Gambian DHIS2-EMIS instance. Consequently, SRC data access can be granted to DHIS2-EMIS users and has allowed for decentralized access and improved availability and use. To support local use of the SRC, the web-application features a printer friendly version that can be printed at schools or nearby printing facilities. Figure 4 shows the remodeled SRC in DHIS2-EMIS.

5 Discussion

5.1 Granularity Levels

Volkoff and Strong [25, p. 241] argue the importance of selecting "an appropriate level(s) of granularity for the affordances". They point out that Strong et al.'s [16] widely accepted definition of IT affordances does not say anything about which granularity level is appropriate. Affordances can be decomposed to lower-level affordances and aggregated to higher-level affordances. To examine how DHIS2-EMIS affords informed decision-making that puts the Gambian education system on track to improve learning outcomes and social inclusion, it follows that the most relevant granularity level is at the level of the organization.

A problem with studying affordances at the organizational level (mid- or higher-level affordance), however, is the difficulty of distinguishing the affordance itself from its outcome, when the affordance is actualized. Volkoff and Strong give an example of *visibility,* which several researchers have identified as

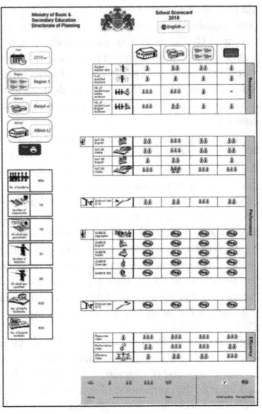

Fig. 4. The digitized school report card in the Gambian DHIS2-EMIS instance

an affordance (e.g., [34–37]). Visibility, in itself, is not an affordance but "a state, and masks the associated actions – and even the actor" [25, p. 242]. In the following we address this concern and argue that an organizational affordance, or action possibility, emerges from the actualization of an array of lower-level affordances. This view is consistent with IS researchers' prior arguments regarding the decomposability of affordances (e.g., [23, 25]).

5.2 DHIS2-EMIS Affordances

The DHIS2 platform, implemented in The Gambia as an EMIS backbone, affords action possibilities to education sector stakeholders. The most "hands-on" affordances, such as *configuring* the readily installed instance, *developing* and *integrating* an addon application, or *rewriting* the source code are readily perceived. However, in the following subsections we argue that, at a higher level of granularity, *decentralizing data access, educational decision-making,* and *ensuring equal access to quality education* are three affordances that emerge in the relation between DHIS2 and goal-oriented education sector stakeholders in The Gambia. The following subsections relate to the case descriptions in Subsect. 4.2.

Educational Decision-Making. Extant IS literature points out how affordances are interdependent and that the actualization of one affordance can cause other affordances to emerge (e.g., [3, 16, 19]). Data-driven decision-making depends on the actualization of lower- and mid-level affordances. DHIS2 affords the possibility of *configuring dashboards and analysis tools*. A user can thus have a personalized dashboard layout presenting the data, indicators, and analysis of most interest and relevance. The configured dashboards and analysis tools afford the user the possibility of *visualizing and inspecting educational data* from the user's own level and related sublevels. The user can – usually in collaboration with others – *take informed decisions* regarding a school, a school cluster, a region, or the entire country. Figure 5 illustrates how the actualization of the lower-level affordance *configuring dashboards and analysis tools* leads to the emergence of the subsequent mid-level affordance *visualizing and inspecting education data* and the higher-level, more abstract, affordance *informed decision-making*. The arrows in the figure indicate causal-temporal dependencies. For instance, it is a prerequisite for the *informed decision-making* affordance that the two preceding affordances have been actualized.

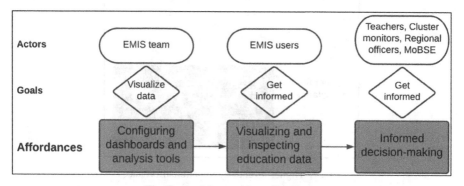

Fig. 5. Decision-making affordances

Decomposing Goals. Use of the DHIS2 Tracker module affords the possibility of *recording data on individuals*. When the EMIS contains individual data, teachers are afforded the possibility of *intervening in individual learner trajectories*. By following up the learners individually they enhance the possibility of *ensuring equal access to quality* education. Figure 6 illustrates how the actualization of the lower-level *recording data on individuals* affordance enables the mid-level affordance *intervening in individual trajectories* and the higher-level affordance *ensuring equal access to quality education*.

The *ensuring equal access to quality education* affordance can also be considered an ensemble affordance, as it both is dependent on and consists of the two preceding

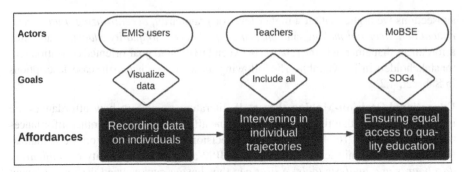

Fig. 6. Data disaggregation affordances

affordances of *recording data on individuals* and *intervening in individual trajectories* (Fig. 7). The affordance *ensuring equal access to quality education* cannot be actualized unless the two preceding affordances *recording data on individuals* and *intervening in individual trajectories* have been actualized. At the same time, *ensuring equal access to quality education* consists of the composite of the preceding affordances, as illustrated in Fig. 7.

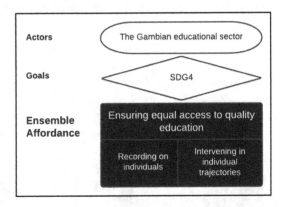

Fig. 7. Higher-level disaggregation affordance

Decentralizing Data Access – a Goal or an Affordance? Thapa and Sein [19] explain how multiple affordances can form an ensemble of affordances which together can be actualized in order to reach the ultimate goal. However, as pointed out by Volkoff and Strong [25], it can be difficult to distinguish an abstract affordance from the desired outcome (i.e., the goal). But does the goal necessarily have to be different from the affordance? Consider the digitized Gambian SRC. Figure 8 illustrates how the actualization of the *developing addon* affordance is a prerequisite for the *integrating addon* affordance. And once integrated, trained users can start *accessing the data* provided through the SRC app. There are of course other affordances at play, such as *quality data collecting* and *timely data inputting,* which are also necessary for the *accessing data* affordance to emerge. The underlying affordances that constitute a higher-level affordance may need to be identified and examined whenever there is a breakdown or failure to realize the higher-level IT affordance. This is for example the case when stakeholders at the school level provide feedback that the available data is erroneous or misrepresents local reality. In this case, it is necessary to consider the *collecting data* affordance.

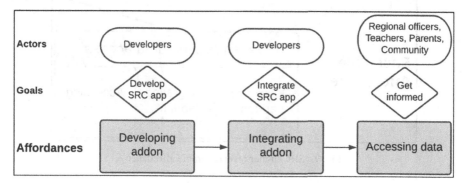

Fig. 8. SRC lower-level affordances

The three singular affordances illustrated in Fig. 8 form the composite affordance of *decentralizing data access* (Fig. 9). Just as Shaw and Bransford's [38, p. 42] example of the *eating* affordance being an ensemble of the biting, chewing and swallowing affordances, the *decentralizing data access* affordance is composed from the *developing addon*, *integrating addon* and *accessing data* affordances. While the singular affordances are lower-level technology use-affordances, the ensemble affordance is a mid-level affordance, which requires action from several actors to be actualized.

Through actualizing the three lower-level affordances, the *decentralizing data access* affordance is also actualized, and the "immediate concrete outcome" [16, p. 69] is decentralized data access, allowing local stakeholders to access data previously unavailable to them. In this case, the goal and outcome are somewhat indistinguishable from the affordance itself.

Extending the Conceptual Framework. In the framework derived from Gaver's [26] affordances, as illustrated in Fig. 2, sub-affordance n_1 and sub-affordance n_2 are actualized simultaneously (e.g., in Gaver's example, the human pulls the door while pulling the door handle). However, this is not necessarily the case. The findings in the preceding subsections show that a composite affordance can also consist of sequential sub-affordances, as indicated by Shaw and Bransford's eating affordance [38, p. 42]. For instance, the *ensuring equal access to quality education* affordance is a composite of the sequential affordances *recording on individuals* and *intervening in individual trajectories* (see Fig. 7). Thus, we have extended the conceptual framework we derived from Gaver's affordances to include sequential affordances in a composite affordance. In Fig. 10 the affordance *m* consists of three other affordances, one of which is also a composite affordance (n).

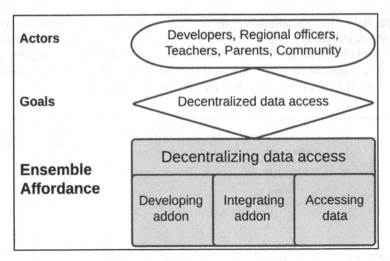

Fig. 9. SRC higher-level ensemble affordance

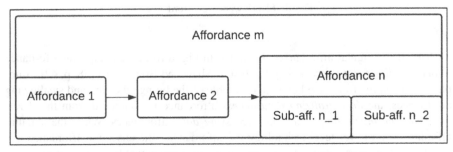

Fig. 10. Our extended conceptual framework

5.3 Choosing the Appropriate Level of Granularity

As seen from the Gambian examples, the design and use flexibility of the DHIS2 platform, matched with local capacity strengthening in both software configuration and data analysis, opens an array of action possibilities. However, it is not the direct technology use, exemplified by the lower-level affordances in this paper (e.g., developing and integrating addons, accessing data, recording data on individuals), that are the key affordances to understand. These lower-level affordances resemble the technology functionalities themselves and might appear indistinguishable from the functionalities. However, just as a knife affords humans the very basic cutting affordance [22, pp. 133, 137], developing addon, integrating addon, and accessing data should also be considered affordances. What we should be concerned with, is what use of technology in context affords, that is, what mid- and higher-level affordances emerge from the actualization of lower-level affordances to address real world problems. The mid- and higher-level affordances identified in our case are *decentralizing data access, intervening in individual trajectories, ensuring equal access to quality education, visualizing and inspecting education data,* and *informed decision-making.*

5.4 Defining Granularity Levels

While technology certainly offers an opportunity for development, it is not a panacea for development [7, p. 12]. Our intention is not to say that technology drives development outcomes at a societal level, such as equitable access to education. Rather, our analysis highlights how mid- and higher-level affordances are composed from lower-level affordances. Hence, an understanding of affordances as action possibilities that are interdependent both temporally (sequence of affordances) and spatially (composite affordances) [3, 16, 19, 26] is necessary to understand when, in what way and for whom higher-level affordances become actualized, or not. Scholars studying IT affordances tend to distinguish between lower-level affordances (typically basic technology use) and abstract higher-level affordances emerging from lower-level affordances. However, in many cases, such as in the cases presented here, it is more revealing to identify and study the actualization of *mid-level* affordances.

5.5 Mid-level Affordances

Mid-level affordances are affordances on a granularity level between lower-level technology use affordances and abstract higher-level affordances. Similar to higher-level affordances, mid-level affordances do not denote direct technology use. However, we argue that they are more directly related to organizations' technology use than the abstract

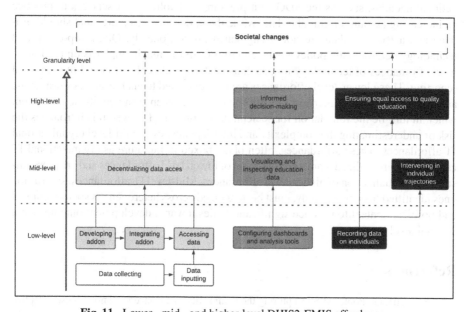

Fig. 11. Lower-, mid-, and higher-level DHIS2-EMIS affordances

higher-level affordances. Mid-level affordances emerge directly as a result of actualization of lower-level affordances in organizational contexts. Figure 11 illustrates how the affordances identified through the Gambian DHIS2-EMIS case study relate to the three granularity levels we have outlined. Mid-level IT affordances can be thought of as the perceived and realized action possibilities of what is often associated with organizational "IT capabilities" (e.g., [39, 40]) and in many studies are left as a black box.

6 Conclusion

EMIS stakeholders strive to identify and scale (desirable) action possibilities that may be actualized to produce value in local context. The actualization of the action possibilities in any local setting relies on a conducive interplay between technology, the capability of the enacting actor, and goal-oriented action. Both the affordance and the actor can be composites, in the sense that an affordance can emerge from an ensemble of lower-level affordances (e.g., the affordances *developing addon*, *integrating addon*, and *accessing data* constitute the *decentralizing data access* affordance), while enacting actors can be an individual, a group of individuals, an organization or a social movement with a shared aspiration. For practitioners, this means that higher-level shared goals (outcomes), such as the SDG4, needs to be aligned with contextual conditions as well as affordances that can be actualized in those contexts. When desirable affordances are not actualized, we can start to unpack the ensemble affordance to identify constitutive affordances that need to be actualized.

We believe a composite affordance perspective, which recognizes temporal and spatial interdependencies of IT affordances, is useful in bridging what we perceive to be a growing policy-practice divide in the education sector in low-income countries. International agendas, such as the SDGs put pressure on public sector services to produce an increasing amount of granular data, while the underlying structures that should produce and act on the data are not strengthened proportionately. Often, top-down and technology deterministic policy goals tend to inform too much emphasis on the lower-level affordances of technology use, such as enabling data collection and international reporting. These lower-level affordances are then expected to enable strides towards the actualization of lofty higher-level IT affordances such as ensuring equitable education, which in turn lie the foundation for societal development. However, this introduces the risk of underestimating the complexity and interdependency of mid-level organizational IT affordances. These affordances, often black-boxed in literature as organizational IT capabilities, are realized from a combination of lower-level affordances and are prerequisite to the actualization of higher-level affordances. Mid-level IT affordances, such as the ones identified in our case study, must be actualized across heterogenous socio-technical and political context to produce significant strides towards development outcomes at a societal level.

References

1. DeSanctis, G., Poole, M.S.: Capturing the complexity in advanced technology use: adaptive structuration theory. Organ. Sci. 5(2), 121–147 (1994)

2. Alam, S.L., Campbell, J.: Temporal motivations of volunteers to participate in cultural crowdsourcing work. Inf. Syst. Res. **28**(4), 744–759 (2017). https://doi.org/10.1287/isre.2017.0719

3. Burton-Jones, A., Volkoff, O.: How can we develop contextualized theories of effective use? A demonstration in the context of community-care electronic health records. Inf. Syst. Res. **28**(3), 468–489 (2017). https://doi.org/10.1287/isre.2017.0702

4. Bygstad, B., Munkvold, B.E., Volkoff, O.: Identifying generative mechanisms through affordances: a framework for critical realist data analysis. J. Inf. Technol. **31**(1), 83–96 (2016). https://doi.org/10.1057/jit.2015.13

5. Chatterjee, S., Moody, G., Lowry, P.B., Chakraborty, S., Hardin, A.: Strategic relevance of organizational virtues enabled by information technology in organizational innovation. J. Manag. Inf. Syst. **32**(3), 158–196 (2015). https://doi.org/10.1080/07421222.2015.1099180

6. Faik, I., Barrett, M., Oborn, E.: How information technology matters in societal change: an affordance-based institutional perspective. MIS Q. **44**(3), 1359–1390 (2020). https://doi.org/10.25300/misq/2020/14193

7. Von Braun, J.: ICT for the poor at large scale: innovative connections to markets and services. In: Picot, A., Lorenz, J. (eds.) ICT for the Next Five Billion People, pp. 3–14. Springer, Heidelberg (2010). https://doi.org/10.1007/978-3-642-12225-5_2

8. De´, R., Pal, A., Sethi, R., Reddy, S.K., Chitre, C.: ICT4D research: a call for a strong critical approach. Inf. Technol. Dev. **24**(1), 63–94 (2018). https://doi.org/10.1080/02681102.2017.1286284

9. Ministries of Basic and Secondary Education and Higher Education, "Education Sector Strategic Plan 2016–2030" (2017). https://www.globalpartnership.org/sites/default/files/2018-09-the-gambia-essp-2016-30.pdf. Accessed 06 Dec 2021

10. United Nations, "Goal 4". https://sdgs.un.org/goals/goal4. Accessed 14 Dec 2021

11. UNICEF East Asia & Pacific, Review of Education Management Information Systems (EMIS) that Track Individual Student Data (2020). https://www.unicef.org/eap/media/6031/file/EMISsummary.pdf. Accessed 06 Dec 2021

12. Valbø, B.: The IS-notion of affordances: a mapping of the application of affordance theory in information systems research. In: Selected Papers of the IRIS, Issue Nr 12, no. 12 (2021). https://aisel.aisnet.org/iris2021/2/. Accessed 26 Nov 2021

13. Chatterjee, S., Moody, G., Lowry, P.B., Chakraborty, S., Hardin, A.: Information technology and organizational innovation: harmonious information technology affordance and courage-based actualization. J. Strateg. Inf. Syst. **29**(1), 101596 (2020). https://doi.org/10.1016/j.jsis.2020.101596

14. Leidner, D.E., Gonzalez, E., Koch, H.: An affordance perspective of enterprise social media and organizational socialization. J. Strateg. Inf. Syst. **27**(2), 117–138 (2018). https://doi.org/10.1016/j.jsis.2018.03.003

15. Leonardi, P.M.: When flexible routines meet flexible technologies: affordance, constraint, and the imbrication of human and material agencies. MIS Q. **35**(1), 147–167 (2011). https://doi.org/10.2307/23043493

16. Strong, D.M., et al.: A theory of organization-EHR affordance actualization. J. Assoc. Inf. Syst. **15**(2), 53–85 (2014)

17. Volkoff, O., Strong, D.M.: Critical realism and affordances: theorizing it-associated organizational change processes. MIS Q. **37**(3), 819–834 (2013)

18. Li, X., Rai, A., Ganapathy, K.: Designing cost-effective telemedicine camps for underprivileged individuals in less developed countries: a decomposed affordance-effectivity framework. J. Assoc. Inf. Syst. **21**(5), 1279–1312 (2020). https://doi.org/10.17705/1jais.00637

19. Thapa, D., Sein, M.K.: Trajectory of affordances: insights from a case of telemedicine in Nepal. Inf. Syst. J. **28**(5), 796–817 (2018). https://doi.org/10.1111/isj.12160

20. Zheng, Y., Yu, A.: Affordances of social media in collective action: the case of free lunch for children in China. Inf. Syst. J. **26**(3), 289–313 (2016). https://doi.org/10.1111/isj.12096

21. Gibson, J.J.: Gibson_James_J_1977_The_Theory_of_Affordances.pdf. In: Shaw, R., Bransford, J. (eds.) Perceiving, Acting, and Knowing: Toward an Ecological Psychology, pp. 67–82. Lawrence Erlbaum, Hillsdale (1977)

22. Gibson, J.J.: The theory of affordances. In: The Ecological Approach to Visual Perception, pp. 127–137. Houghton Mifflin (1979)

23. Markus, M.L., Silver, M.S.: A foundation for the study of IT effects: a new look at desanctis and poole's concepts of structural features and spirit. J. Assoc. Inf. Syst. **9**(10/11), 609–632 (2008)

24. Gutek, B.A., Bikson, T.K., Mankin, D.: Individual and organizational consequences of computer-based office information technology. Appl. Soc. Psychol. Annu. **5**, 231–254 (1984)

25. Volkoff, O., Strong, D.: Affordance theory and how to use it in IS research. In: Galliers, R.D., Stein, M.-K. (eds.) The Routledge Companion to Management Information Systems, pp. 232–245. Routledge, London/New York (2017)

26. Gaver, W.W.: Technology affordances. In: Conference on Human Factors in Computing Systems - Proceedings, pp. 79–84 (1991). https://doi.org/10.1145/108844.108856

27. Bernardi, R.: How Do Online Communities of Patients Aggregate on Twitter? An Affordance Perspective (2016)

28. Valbø, B.: Introducing a complex health information system in a developing country. Case: The Gambia. University of Oslo, Oslo (2010). http://urn.nb.no/URN:NBN:no-26992

29. Masiero, S., Amuha, M., Jallow, S.A., Sanner, T.A., Valbø, B.: Meeting the global learning crisis with data: a research agenda on digital platforms for education management, Manuscript Preparation (2022)

30. Jallow, S.A., Sanner, T.A.: Information system centralization and decentralization: the introduction of digital learner records in The Gambia, Manuscript Preparation (2022)

31. University of Oslo, "About DHIS2". https://dhis2.org/about/. Accessed 14 Mar 2022

32. University of Oslo, "DHIS2 In Action". https://dhis2.org/in-action/. Accessed 08 Apr 2022

33. University of Oslo, "Impact Stories". https://dhis2.org/category/impact-stories/. Accessed 06 Dec 2021

34. Arazy, O., Daxenberger, J., Lifshitz-Assaf, H., Nov, O., Gurevych, I.: Turbulent stability of emergent roles: the dualistic nature of self-organizing knowledge coproduction. Inf. Syst. Res. **27**(4), 792–812 (2016). https://doi.org/10.1287/isre.2016.0647

35. Argyris, Y.A., Ransbotham, S.: Knowledge entrepreneurship: institutionalising wiki-based knowledge-management processes in competitive and hierarchical organisations. J. Inf. Technol. **31**(2), 226–239 (2016). https://doi.org/10.1057/jit.2016.11

36. Porter, A.J., van den Hooff, B.: The complementarity of autonomy and control in mobile work. Eur. J. Inf. Syst. **29**(2), 172–189 (2020). https://doi.org/10.1080/0960085X.2020.1728200

37. Van Osch, W., Steinfield, C.W.: Team boundary spanning: strategic implications for the implementation and use of enterprise social media. J. Inf. Technol. **31**(2), 207–225 (2016). https://doi.org/10.1057/jit.2016.12

38. Shaw, R., Bransford, J.: Introduction: psychological approaches to the problem of knowledge. In: Shaw, R., Bransford, J. (eds.) Perceiving, Acting, and Knowing: Toward an Ecological Psychology, pp. 1–42. Lawrence Erlbaum, Hillsdale (1977). https://www.routledge.com/Perceiving-Acting-and-Knowing-Toward-an-Ecological-Psychology/Shaw-Bransford/p/book/9781138205055

39. Bharadwaj, A.S., Sambamurthy, V., Zmud, R.: IT Capabilities: theoretical perspectives and empirical operationalization. In: ICIS 1999 Proceedings, vol. 35, pp. 378–385 (1999). http://aisel.aisnet.org/icis1999/35. Accessed 17 Jan 2022
40. Kim, G., Shin, B., Kim, K.K., Lee, H.G.: IT capabilities, process-oriented dynamic capabilities, and firm financial performance* IT capabilities, process-oriented dynamic capabilities, and firm financial performance. J. Assoc. Inf. Syst. **12**(7), 487–517 (2011)

Connecting the Unconnected in the Global South: Bridging the Digital Divide from a Critical Perspective

Ana Paula dos Santos Tavares[1]([✉]) [iD], Sundeep Sahay[2] [iD], Luiz Antonio Joia[1] [iD], and Marcelo Fornazin[3] [iD]

[1] Getulio Vargas Foundation, Rio de Janeiro, Brazil
anapaula.dstavares@gmail.com, luiz.joia@fgv.br
[2] University of Oslo, Oslo, Norway
sundeeps@ifi.uio.no
[3] Oswaldo Cruz Foundation and Fluminense Federal University, Rio de Janeiro, Brazil

Abstract. Extant literature on information and communication technology for development (ICT4D) has increased the understanding of specific aspects of digital inclusion and development. However, theoretical questions regarding local social issues discussed by locally based researchers remain underrepresented in the ICT4D realm. Through a narrative review of the digital inclusion studies in IS literature and applying as the theoretical lenses the capability approach, network society and critical consciousness, this study proposes a Digital Inclusion for Emancipation (DI4E) conceptual model. This model recognizes the digital inclusion dimensions, as well as the underlying assumptions and limitations in the context of low- and middle-income countries (LMICs). Grounded on a critical interpretive approach, the main objective of the study is to shed light on the different aspects and viewpoints of digital inclusion from a local perspective to unveil potential challenges and opportunities to promote emancipation for the most marginalized groups.

Keywords: Digital inclusion · Digital divide · Development · Network society · Critical consciousness · Information and communication technology for development · Emancipation

1 Introduction

In a hyperconnected society, how to study a truly emancipatory digital inclusion? The Covid-19 pandemic unveiled wicked inequalities in global digital access, with nearly half of the world population – 3,6 billion people – outside the connected world [1] which reveals major challenges associated with the digital society. While digital technologies provided some relief during days of social isolation during the pandemic, enabling the working and studying from home [2] they also carried challenges of cyber threats, misinformation and human rights violations [3]. Indeed, the Covid-19 pandemic "hit

© IFIP International Federation for Information Processing 2022
Published by Springer Nature Switzerland AG 2022
Y. Zheng et al. (Eds.): ICT4D 2022, IFIP AICT 657, pp. 490–503, 2022.
https://doi.org/10.1007/978-3-031-19429-0_29

hardest those countries which were lagging behind in digital development and, by 2020, had not managed to build a reliable digital infrastructure, provide digital public services (including healthcare and education), build people's digital skills, or introduce digital technologies in the economy" [1] (p. 3).

The World Bank [1] describes the digital divide as the disparity between those who have access and skills to use the Internet and those who do not. These skills are important in engaging with complex social problems, in particular for marginalized communities [4–8]. Miscione et al. [9] (p. 281) writes that "over the last 20 years, practitioners and academics alike are becoming increasingly interested in the area of information technology and development". Consequently, theorizing ICT4D has gained increasing attention of researchers [10] and significant advancements are seen in this arena [7, 11]. Aiming at contributing to theoretical advancement, this paper focuses on the issue of digital inclusion, pursuing implications for research and practice [12].

That way, the specific research question addressed is: how to build a conceptualization of digital inclusion that emphasizes the emancipation of the marginalized groups in LMIC settings? We approache this question primarily through an analysis of existing theoretical frameworks from ICT4D research and build upon that through the incorporation of perspectives of emancipation and critical studies within local contexts. Next, we intend to apply this framework to digital inclusion projects in Brazil.

The rest of the study is organized in the following manner. After this introduction, Sect. 2 presents the research method, followed by a review of the scientific literature that has emerged from digital inclusion in the Information Systems field. Section 4 proposes a conceptual framework based on the review and interpretation of the selected theoretical lenses. Finally, in the Sect. 5, concluding remarks and future research avenues are set forth.

2 Research Method

This research is based on qualitative methodology [13], being designed as a structured narrative literature review [14] and grounded in a critical interpretive approach [15–17]. The critical interpretive method of research in IS is "aimed at producing an understanding of the context of the information system, and the process whereby the information system influences and is influenced by the context" [15]. Thus, the study is aimed at advancing the theoretical foundations of ICT4D research on the understanding of digital inclusion, drawing upon a dialectical engagement with key assumptions and beliefs related to this concept discussed in the literature [13]. Hence, review, interpretation and synthesis of a broad range of digital inclusion research is herein developed from three theoretical lenses, namely: the capability approach [18], the network society [19], and the critical consciousness [20], which provides the basis for an expanded framework. The three theoretical lenses emerged from the hermeneutic circle analysis to interpret and map the literature based on the main concept and discourses presented in this study.

The methodological approach involved a survey in relevant scientific libraries and databases (e.g., AIS library, Web of Science) and discussion with experienced research colleagues. As a result, the study comprises a dataset of 30 articles that were analyzed from three dimensions: level of analysis [19, 21, 22], critical approach [23, 24], and focus on marginalized groups [25, 26]. This analysis helped identify five key dimensions: type of digital technology, level of analysis (individual and collective), capabilities (well-being and agency freedom), use of ICTs (practical or strategic), and components of emancipation, as presented later. The five key dimensions emerged from the perusal of principles to conduct critical interpretive studies, namely: social and historical contextualization, critical interaction between the researchers and the subject, abstraction and generalization, and dialogical reasoning [15].

3   Digital Inclusion in Information Systems Research

Historically, Information Systems (IS) research has focused on issues associated with the development and diffusion of systems [27]. However, studies have identified that changes in the human condition and societal disparities together with the evolution of ICT usage have provided intended and unintended consequences, affecting mainly the marginalized groups [28]. Such analysis has highlighted debates around the so-called digital divide phenomena and the impacts of ICTs in LMICs (Low- and Middle-Income Countries) towards a better world "where people from less advantaged backgrounds can be enabled to enhance their capabilities and increase their participation in matters which affect their lives" [7] (p. 37).

The phenomenon of digital divide is not just related to the unavailability of ICT but also to "the social, political, institutional and cultural contexts which shape people's lack of access to ICTs, or their inability to use them effectively" [28] (p. 1). This finding shows the need to go beyond simplistic discourses of aligning technological diffusion with economic development and recognizing the differing roles that ICT can play in society [25], with contradictory implications on social exclusion [27].

Beyond issues of access to digital tools, digital inclusion encompasses people's ability to access and make use of those technologies to add value to their relevant social practices [29]. Furthermore, Warschauer [29] asserts that "those who are already marginalized will have fewer opportunities to access and use computers and the Internet" (p. 7). Given the entanglement of technology and society, it becomes important for research to focus on understanding how marginalized groups use ICT not just "to overcome a digital divide but rather to further a process of social inclusion" [28].

Indeed, questions of digital divide are always shaped in local contexts [5, 30], which "feature a wide range of theoretical and methodological perspectives when studying ICTs in LMICs" [31] (p. 2). This understanding is built around the study of processes of participation [32, 33] and how local processes shape development [34]. This was illustrated by Hayes and Westrup [35] in their analysis of M-PESA, now widely recognized as an innovative mobile banking application from Kenya. In the same vein, Avgerou et al. [36] present lessons from electronic voting in Brazil, and Walsham and Sahay [37] investigate the implementation of geographical information systems in India. Additionally, various other studies, for example, have helped highlighting a research agenda to promote sustainability, inclusion and growth [6, 28, 29, 38–41] to name just a few.

In such a context, one summarized the analysis of ICT4D literature identifying three important frameworks around digital inclusion: (i) Zheng and Walsham's [25] social exclusion as capability deprivation; (ii) Joia's [42] dynamic digital inclusion model;

(iii) Madon et al.'s [28] digital inclusion and the dynamics of institutional stability and change. Zheng and Walsham [25] (p. 223) drew on the capability approach as a "theoretical lens to help conceptualise the complexity and multiplicity of social exclusion in e-society". They assert that inequalities encompass material inequalities but also broader issues such as lack of opportunities, freedoms and choices. Joia's [42] digital inclusion model also built upon the logic of capability approach (CA) offering a basic structure for researchers to define the grid of actors that can influence the process of social inclusion through ICT. Finally, Madon et al. [28] analyze four key processes of Institutional Theory, considered relevant to digital inclusion projects: getting symbolic acceptance by the community; stimulating valuable social activity in relevant social groups; generating linkage to viable revenue streams; and enrolling government support.

While these frameworks have contributed to analyze key factors shaping an inclusive digital economy and society, we believe they can be strengthened in three directions: i) building a more critical perspective to understand local social issues and foster processes of freedom and empowerment, ii) understanding emancipation from the citizen's standpoint; and iii) focusing on the most vulnerable population historically left behind by digital transformation (UN, 2021).

In trying to build those extensions, we draw upon three theoretical perspectives: i) Sen's capability approach [18]; Castells network society [19]; and iii) Freire's critical consciousness [20]. Key concepts from these theories are put together to develop an integrated framework which is discussed below. That way, we bring a postcolonial critical approach to extend the current knowledge in the ICT4D field.

4   An Extended Theoretical Framework for Studying Digital Inclusion

Theorizing digital inclusion for development encompasses the understanding of political dimensions, cultural aspects and normative worldviews [44], situated within local social contexts. Current research in ICT4D suggests an inadequate "engagement in a plural dialogue between different systems of knowledge and between different epistemologies, without pre-established hierarchies" [44] (p. 184). These epistemologies underline the importance of individuals as part of a collective, the logic of shared interests (common well-being), the relevance of diversity and intercultural understanding from a critical lens [44].

The current study intends to advance the knowledge on ICT4D literature shedding light on the importance of citizens' perspective, the critical consciousness and the focus on the marginalized groups to foster digital inclusion and, by consequence, emancipation. As such, we concentrate on the role of humans, informational capabilities and power relations to promote technological projects for inclusion.

4.1 Capability Approach: The Human Development Perspective

According to Sen [18], development is a process of expansion of real freedoms that people appreciate, associated with freedom of choice in personal, social, political, and economic extent. The Capability Approach (CA) is, thus, defined as "a process of expanding the real freedoms of individuals" [18] (p. 3) to "lead the lives they have reason to value" [18] (p. 293). This theoretical view has been recognized and applied among scholars in diverse research fields, encouraging debates on inequality, digital inclusion, capital and savings, and non-market institutions [7].

In fact, the framework proposed by Sen on development improve the aspects of inter-action and articulation among social actors towards a more cooperative action logic, underlining the importance of building social networks [45]. In this regard, existing conceptualizations of digital inclusion in IS field applied Sen's framework [4, 24, 25, 32, 42], considering the social context, relations and interactions among actors sharing resources and obligations built on trust. Despite the relevance, some critics have been raised: lack of methodological clarity on how to apply the main concepts; too individ-ualistic approach; absence of attention to power relations; overreliance on the ability of human beings to make reasoned choices; and lack of attention on how to overcome adaptive preferences and their constraining effects on the individual's development [24, 32, 46–49].

Notwithstanding, Sen's approach provides a non-utilitarian perspective to investigate development concerns bringing forth important analytical and philosophical foundations to be explored [18]. Besides, Sen focuses on the deprivation of capabilities such as access to healthcare and education [18]. Such a viewpoint is scrutinized by the present study, which intends to investigate the contribution that technologies may have to increase freedoms and opportunities of individuals in societies. Thus, we intend to understand individual critical agency while addressing collective mobilization that will be explored from the Network Society lens [19] presented below. Table 1 summarize the key concepts drawn upon for building the expanded framework presented later.

Table 1. Capability approach key concepts to understand digital inclusion

Concepts	Components	Description
Commodities	Digital technology	The type of technology used and its main characteristics at the local level
Capabilities	Well-being freedom	Assess what capabilities are provided from a well-being perspective (e.g., health, internet access, education)
Capabilities	Agency freedom	Assess what capabilities are provided from an agency freedom perspective (e.g., social and political participation, religious freedom)

4.2 Network Society: Globalization, and Social Development Perspective

Throughout history, technology has been deeply implicated in the development process [50]. From industrialization and colonization to modernization and neoliberal paradigms, technology has played different roles in fostering development and economic growth [51]. The spread of Internet services in the 1990s provoked a transition from technology as a tool to a more holistic force to promote economic, social and cultural development [52]. According to Castells [19], the ongoing transformation of ICT in the digital age extends the reach to all domains of social life in a network that is simultaneously local and global. As such, power relations have become increasingly shaped by digital technologies and networks that are also influenced by a historical process of domination and counter-domination which frames the social interactions within the networking logic.

The power is thereby located in the networks and if one is not present/represented (s)he might be excluded and systematically marginalized. To contrast with such a view-point, Castells presents the counter-power movement consisting of the social actor's capacity to challenge and eventually change the power relations institutionalized in society (e.g., Black Lives Matter). Therefore, the network logic both connects and disconnects. It exacerbates the unintended effects of the new information-technology paradigm putting a lens on the double sword aspect of ICT [53, 54].

Despite the relevance of Castells' work to digital inclusion studies, some criticism has been raised [55]. The author's view of the power and identity of social movements have been already explored by other scholars [53] and networks are treated on a high level of abstraction. However, this approach is unique as it takes a historical and local perspective. Castells unveils the way formal network structures float to the surface and how such structures turn into vital causal powers [51]. Indeed, the network society is interconnected, which raises some important concerns about surveillance, regulation and free speech to name a few. Table 2 presents the main concepts of power and counter-power at both individual and collective levels derived from the abovementioned theoretical lens.

Table 2. Network society key concepts to understand digital inclusion

Concepts	Components	Description
Agents	Individual	Identify what agent has/doesn't have access to capabilities at an individual level (e.g., users, students)
Agents	Collective	Identify what group of agents have/ don't have access to capabilities at a collective level (e.g., local community, school, hospital)

In order to take a step further and advance the critical understanding of the dynamics of power, politics and inequalities that impact human development in poor countries [49, 56], we present below the literature on critical consciousness [20].

4.3 Emancipatory Pedagogy: Postcolonial Critical Consciousness Perspective

Emancipation is a central concept in critical theories yet underresearched by IS scholars [23]. It is a complex and multidimensional concept, including the freedoms to act, express, belong and think [23]. Critical theory asserts that dominant narratives confer "structural disadvantage as justified, normal and immutable, and that, as a result, people who are persistently subject to dominant narratives often internalize those values uncritically as if they represented their reasoned interests" [49] (p. 4). Such an argument complements both the CA and the network society as it yields guidance on how to overcome adaptive preferences and power relations [49].

Paulo Freire's theory of emancipatory pedagogy [20] introduces a critical perspective [23, 56] to understand how oppressed groups can achieve emancipation by promoting awareness of their reality and taking ownership of their struggle [57]. Critical consciousness provides the ability to read the world critically and agency makes possible to act for changing the world [20]. Freire articulates an epistemology to empower marginalized people to read critically about their world in a method called 'conscientization'. This approach allows members to critically investigate their own conditions, moving from passive objects to active and critical agents of their self-development [58]. Thus, questions such as why does this inequality exist? or who benefits from it? "challenge agents to reflect on the root causes of the disadvantage that they experience" [49] (p. 5). In IS, some studies have drawn upon Freire's tenets, such as Poveda and Roberts [49], who analyzed critical agency and development in Zambia and Brazil and Tygel and Kirsh [33], who investigated critical data literacy inspired by Freire's method.

Some critics highlight the absence of androcentric bias and gender inequalities in Freire's work [58], as well as an inadequate consideration of the dark side of empowerment and emancipation. First, if the implementation of emancipation requires political power and resources that the oppressed do not possess, can they achieve their emancipation on their own? Secondly, how does digital inclusion and emancipation at the individual level affect collective outcomes? Freire [20] suggests that when education is not liberating, the dream of the oppressed is to become the oppressor. The proposed framework examines the role of digital technologies to foster inclusion taking the Freire's key concepts presented in Table 3.

Table 3. Critical consciousness key concepts to understand digital inclusion

Concepts	Components	Description
Pedagogical approach	Practical	Identify if technology is being reproduced by those in power, choosing to use ICTs in ways that benefit the individual in a practical way
Pedagogical approach	Strategic	Identify if the use of technology reveals critical thinking abilities, which recognize the root causes of their problems, using ICT in more strategic ways
Emancipation	Freedom to act, express, belong, and think	Assess agents' freedom to act (e.g., surveillance, control, trust), freedom to express (e.g., voice-giving), freedom to belong (e.g., inclusion) and freedom to think (e.g., manipulation, bias)

4.4   The Proposed Theoretical Framework

Against this backdrop and based on the review and interpretation of the selected theoretical lenses, this paper proposed a framework to understand more deeply the phenomenon of digital inclusion. Through this framework, the study intends to deepen the extant conceptualizations of digital inclusion, as summarized in the Fig. 1 below.

The conceptual model is proposed by articulating five main dimensions: type of digital technology, level of analysis (individual and collective), capabilities (well-being and agency freedom), use of ICT (practical or strategic), and components of emancipation.

The component 'digital technology' addresses the use and the main characteristics of digital technologies applied at the local level. The 'agents' are those with or without access to capabilities at both the individual level (e.g., students, patients, consumers, etc.) and collective level (e.g., local community, hospital, school, etc.). The 'capability' is the ability to achieve your purpose and it has two main perspectives: the well-being freedom and the agency freedom. The agency freedom is the freedom to set and pursue your goals and interests (e.g., social participation, religious freedom), and the well-being freedom is one of the goals you wish to pursue as an individual (e.g., internet access, healthcare access) – "what real opportunities you have regarding the life you may lead" [18]. The 'use of ICT', in contrast, set forth a critical lens to identify if the digital technology is reproduced by those in power to benefit the individual (practical approach) or if the use of technology reveals critical thinking abilities, which recognize the root causes of their problems, using digital technologies in more strategic ways (a strategic approach).

Finally, the multidimensional framework presents the components of emancipation derived from the literature which encompasses the freedom to act, express, belong, and think. Around the system, we identify the context and its historical, cultural, social, and political dimensions. According to Avgerou [5] it is important to consider the social embeddedness perspective of ICT innovation to contribute toward improving living conditions through locally situated action.

The DI4E model is an integrated approach to studying digital inclusion for emancipation. The framework has been developed to advance the understanding of the dynamics of digital inclusion and untangle the paradox of inequalities from a critical consciousness perspective. Thereby, we intend to ascertain if:

(i)   technology reinforces domination or promotes transformation mediated by emancipation for the most marginalized groups;

(ii) inclusion at the individual level affects collective outcomes;

The framework illuminates the debate on digital inclusion by proposing a new approach that combines different yet complementary strands of literature. Building on Sen's capability approach [18], Castells' network society [19] and Freire's critical consciousness [20], we seek to understand the boundaries between participation, collaboration and negotiation among different agencies and communities of practices to promote digital inclusion in ICT4D projects. Thereby, the model intends to advance the extant knowledge addressing a critical viewpoint while focusing on the most marginalized groups. The combination of the three theoretical lenses allowed the unique perusal of the dynamics of digital inclusion combining an interdisciplinary perspective with a critical reflection.

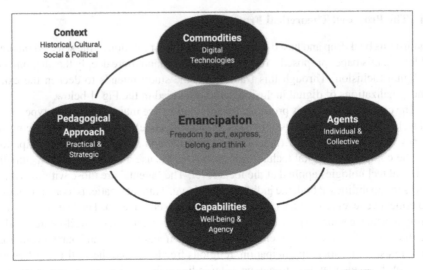

Fig. 1. The framework of Digital Inclusion for Emancipation (DI4E)

It intends to investigate (i) the contribution that technologies may have to increase the freedoms and opportunities of individuals in societies [18], (ii) combined with the analysis of power and counter-power at both individual and collective levels [19], aligned with (iii) the context of dynamics of power, politics, and inequalities that impact human development in poor countries [20, 66].

Furthermore, ICT4D research addresses crucial issues intricately tied up to practice, which supports the challenges for IS research in building a social agenda such as poverty alleviation and climate change [26]. In such a context, the ubiquity of digital technologies intertwined in human life raised important concerns about the unintended effects of ICT initiatives in LMICs (Low- and Middle-Income Countries). As suggested by some scholars [21, 26, 59], little is known about the dark side of digital technologies, so that a framework for digital inclusion for emancipation (DI4E) can be definitely proposed. In fact, the unintended effects of digital inclusion initiatives driven by economic and commercial interests have been little addressed by academia so far [54], which sheds light on the importance of addressing these gaps.

5 The Way Forward: A Research Agenda

The present study intends to explore the interplay between digital inclusion, emancipation and development providing evidence from the academic literature on how to strengthen human social capacity to achieve freedom, inclusiveness and growth [61]. To do that, the study discusses the main challenges and opportunities for future research related to the components of emancipation accrued from the theoretical lenses.

From a critical perspective, Escobar [62] argues that development is a contradictory process that might generate intended and unintended effects, giving rise to the postcolonial and post-development theories [24]. In order to unveil "the power structure and the ideological biases" behind development discourses [63], it is important to apply critical theories to expand critical awareness and sensitivity to the assumptions, discourses and power structures beneath ICT4D endeavors. Furthermore, it is fundamental to develop a plural dialogue between distinct systems of knowledge and epistemologies without hierarchies "understanding that reality is constituted not only by many worlds, but by many kinds of worlds, many ontologies, many ways of being in the world, many ways of knowing reality, and experimenting those many worlds" [44] (p. 185).

That way, we propose to investigate the emancipation dimensions of digital inclusion by analyzing two longitudinal case studies in Brazil. The first case study will analyze the project developed by "Lab Coco" - a training and development laboratory that operates in Recife, being one of the national references in digital inclusion. The project has been sponsored by Porto Digital, a major initiative in Recife, which aims to foster technological innovation in the Northeast region of Brazil. During the Covid-19 pandemic, Porto Digital provided free internet access to poor communities in the region to encourage social and economic activities. The second case study aims to investigate an initiative entitled "Vai na Web", a high-tech and human values program located in Rio de Janeiro that prepares talent from favelas for the new digital economy. The program democratizes access to technology, encourages autonomy and strengthens the plurality of labor in the IT market. The main challenge is, however, to teach programming languages combined with socio-emotional skills to digitally excluded young people.

Thus, by applying the theoretical framework grounded on the emancipatory critical view, the research aims at providing a critical analysis of digital inclusion initiatives, explaining the unintended consequences of the digital divide from a local social context. Essentially, one intends to provide normative guidance for how to promote inclusion and emancipation, by answering relevant questions such as:

- How does inclusion at the individual level affect collective outcomes?
- What roles should government, NGOs and platforms play in promoting inclusion and emancipation?
- Can ICT oppress?
- How does the digital divide hinder women's and girls' empowerment?

6   Conclusion

The digital technology has become increasingly embedded in the lives of individuals, communities and countries, being more critical than ever to ensure universal access and digital skills to promote development and emancipation [49]. In this context, digital inclusion has a key role to play by addressing the readiness and the critical consciousness of communities to fully embrace the digital age.

The current study offers several contributions to the ICT4D field. First, it contributes to the academic research on the discussion about ICT in LMICs [30, 64]. As already mentioned, it is paramount to address critical perspectives to understand development from a local social context and Freire's approach can fill this gap. According to Davison and Martinsons [65], ICT4D research requires deliberate attention to the conditions in the field. Thus, context cannot be ignored. Furthermore, contextual conditions combined with a close examination of socio-technical dimensions are conducive to understanding the local meaning of development [26].

Besides, the study proposes a strong ethical agenda stating that ICT is a necessary but not sufficient condition to empower vulnerable people [29]. Therefore, a local perspective can improve the understanding of successes and failures in ICT endeavours vis-à-vis the evolution of the digital society. Also, from a managerial perspective, this study aims to present a set of reflections that can help managers and policymakers to identify the consequences accrued from the digital divide, which can be a learning opportunity for them to be better prepared for the digital society. As stated by the United Nations [43], governments, in cooperation with relevant stakeholders, need to develop a commonly agreed framework for closing the digital divide. In fact, "rapid technological change without an inclusive and sustainable development strategic orientation risks entrenching existing inequalities while introducing new ones" [43] (p. 5).

Arguably, understanding the relevance of technologies along with individual's critical skills to improve human capacity and foster digital inclusion is paramount to improving the lives of vulnerable people in LMICs. As stated by Zheng et al. [54], perceiving ICT4D as part of a wider process combining social transformation, policies and development initiatives is needed to foster a more sustainable and less unequal world.

References

1. World Bank: Closing the Digital Divide: A Time to Stay Connected. Feature Story (2020). https://www.worldbank.org/en/news/feature/2020/10/26/closing-the-digital-divide-a-time-to-stay-connected. Accessed 26 Oct 2020
2. Venkatesh, V.: Impacts of COVID-19: a research agenda to support people in their fight. Int. J. Inf. Manag. **55**, 102197 (2020)
3. United Nations: High-level Panel on Digital Cooperation. The UN Secretary-General's Roadmap on Digital Cooperation (2020). https://www.un.org/en/sg-digital-cooperation-panel
4. Kleine, D.: ICT4WHAT? Using the choice framework to operationalise the capability approach to development. J. Int. Dev. **22**(5), 674–692 (2009)
5. Avgerou, C.: Discourses on ICT and development. Inf. Technol. Int. Dev. **6**(3), 1–18 (2010)
6. Teles, A., Joia, L.A.: Assessment of digital inclusion via the actor-network theory: the case of the Brazilian municipality of Piraí. Telematics Inform. **28**(3), 191–203 (2011)
7. Walsham, G.: ICT4D research: reflections on history and future agenda. Inf. Technol. Dev. **23**, 18–41 (2017)
8. Heeks, R.: ICT4D 3.0? Part 1—The components of an emerging "digital-for-development" paradigm. *The* Electron. J. Inf. Syst. Dev. Ctries. **86**(3), e12124 (2019)
9. Miscione, G., Hayes, N., Westrup, C.: Theorising development and technological change. Info Syst. J. **23**, 281–285 (2013)
10. Heeks, R.: Theorizing ICT4D research. Inf. Technol. Int. Dev. **3**(3), 1 (2006)
11. Sein, M.K., Thapa, D., Hatakka, M., Sæbø, Ø.: A holistic perspective on the theoretical foundations for ICT4D research. Inf. Technol. Dev. **25**(1), 7–25 (2019)
12. Harris, R.W.: How ICT4D research fails the poor. Inf. Technol. Dev. **22**(1), 177–192 (2016)
13. Alvesson, M., Sandberg, J.: Generating research questions through problematization. Acad. Manag. Rev. **36**(2), 247–271 (2011)
14. Paré, G., Trudel, M.C., Jaana, M., Kitsiou, S.: Synthesizing information systems knowledge: a typology of literature reviews. Inf. Manag. **52**(2), 183–199 (2015)

15. Klein, H.K., Myers, M.D.: A set of principles for conducting and evaluating interpretive field studies in information systems. MIS Q. 67–93 (1999)
16. Pozzebon, M.: Conducting and evaluating critical interpretive research: examining criteria as a key component in building a research tradition. In: Kaplan, B., Truex, D.P., Wastell, D., Wood-Harper, A.T., DeGross, J.I. (eds.) Information Systems Research, vol. 143, pp. 275–292. Springer, Cham (2004). https://doi.org/10.1007/1-4020-8095-6_16
17. Walsham, G.: Interpretive case studies in IS research: nature and method. Eur. J. Inf. Syst. 4, 74–81 (1995)
18. Sen, A.K.: Development as Freedom. Oxford University Press, Oxford (2001)
19. Castells, M.: Communication, power and counter-power in the network society. Int. J. Commun. 1(1), 29 (2007)
20. Freire, P.: Escola primária para o Brasil. Revista brasileira de estudos pedagógicos 86(212) (2005)
21. Viale Pereira, G., et al.: South American expert roundtable: increasing adaptive governance capacity for coping with unintended side effects of digital transformation. Sustainability 12(2), 718 (2020)
22. Gigler, B.S.: Development as freedom in a digital age: experiences from the rural poor in Bolivia. The World Bank (2015)
23. Young, A., Zhu, Y., Venkatesh, V.: Emancipation research in information systems: integrating agency, dialogue, inclusion, and rationality research. In: Proceedings of the 54th Hawaii International Conference on System Sciences (2021)
24. Thapa, D., Sæbø, Ø.: Exploring the link between ICT and development in the context of developing countries: a literature review. Electron. J. Inf. Syst. Dev. Ctries. 64(1), 1–15 (2014)
25. Zheng, Y., Walsham, G.: Inequality of what? Social exclusion in the e-society as capability deprivation. Inf. Technol. People 21, 222–243 (2008)
26. Sahay, S., Sein, M.K., Urquhart, C.: Flipping the context: ICT4D, the next grand challenge for IS research and practice. J. Assoc. Inf. Syst. 18(12), 5 (2017)
27. Trauth, E.M., Howcroft, D.: Social inclusion and the information systems field: why now? In: Trauth, E.M., Howcroft, D., Butler, T., Fitzgerald, B., DeGross, J.I. (eds.) Social Inclusion: Societal and Organizational Implications for Information Systems, vol. 208, pp. 347–364. Springer, Boston (2006). https://doi.org/10.1007/0-387-34588-4_1
28. Madon, S., Reinhard, N., Roode, D., Walsham, G.: Digital inclusion projects in developing countries: processes of institutionalization. Inf. Technol. Dev. 15(2), 95–107 (2009)
29. Warschauer, M.: Technology and Social Inclusion: Rethinking the Digital Divide. MIT Press, Boston (2003)
30. Walsham, G., Sahay, S.: Research on information systems in developing countries: current landscape and future prospects. Inf. Technol. Dev. 12(1), 7–24 (2006)
31. Fornazin, M., Joia, L.A.: Health information systems and democracy: contributions from the Brazilian sanitary movement. Electron. J. Inf. Syst. Dev. Ctries. 62(1), 1–18 (2014)
32. Poveda, S.C.: How can digital inclusion promote social change? Exploring two Brazilian case studies. In: Proceedings of the Eighth International Conference on Information and Communication Technologies and Development, pp. 1–11 (2016)
33. Tygel, A.F., Kirsch, R.: Contributions of Paulo Freire for a critical data literacy: a popular education approach. J. Community Inform. 12(3) (2016)
34. Unwin, P.T.H., Unwin, T. (eds.) ICT4D: Information and Communication Technology for Development. Cambridge University Press, Cambridge (2009)
35. Hayes, N., Westrup, C.: Context and the processes of ICT for development. Inf. Organ. 22(1), 23–36 (2012)
36. Avgerou, C., Ganzaroli, A., Poulymenakou, A., Reinhard, N.: Interpreting the trustworthiness of government mediated by information and communication technology: lessons from electronic voting in Brazil. Inf. Technol. Dev. 15(2), 133–148 (2009)

37. Walsham, G., Sahay, S.: GIS for district-level administration in India: problems and opportunities. MIS Q. **23**(1), 39–56 (1999)
38. Adachi, T.: Comitê gestor da internet no Brasil (CGI. br): uma evolução do sistema de informação nacional moldada socialmente (Doctoral dissertation, Universidade de São Paulo) (2011)
39. Pozzebon, M., Diniz, E.H.: Theorizing ICT and society in the Brazilian context: a multilevel, pluralistic and remixable framework. BAR-Braz. Adm. Rev. **9**(3), 287–307 (2012)
40. Wanderley, S., Faria, A.: The Chandler-Furtado case: a de-colonial re-framing of a North/South (dis) encounter. Manag. Organ. Hist. **7**(3), 219–236 (2012)
41. Santos, B.D.S., Meneses, M.P.: Epistemologias do sul, p. 637 (2010)
42. Joia, L.A.: Bridging the digital divide: some initiatives in Brazil. Electron. Gov. Int. J. **1**, 300–315 (2004)
43. United Nations: Leveraging digital technologies for social inclusion. Decade of Action. Policy Brief 92. United Nations Department of Economics and Social Affairs (2021). https://www.un.org/development/desa/dspd/2021/02/digital-technologies-for-social-inclusion/
44. Jimenez, A., Roberts, T.: Decolonising neo-liberal innovation: using the Andean philosophy of 'Buen Vivir' to reimagine innovation hubs. In: Nielsen, P., Kimaro, H. (eds.) Information and Communication Technologies for Development. Strengthening Southern-Driven Cooperation as a Catalyst for ICT4D, vol. 552, pp. 180–191. Springer, Cham (2019). https://doi.org/10.1007/978-3-030-19115-3_15
45. Coelho, T.R., Segatto, A.P., Frega, J.R.: Analysing ICT and development from the perspective of the capabilities approach: a study in South Brazil. Electron. J. Inf. Syst. Dev. Ctries. **67**(1), 1–14 (2015)
46. Navarro, V.: Development and quality of life: a critique of Amartya Sen's development as freedom. Int. J. Health Serv. **30**(4), 661–674 (2000)
47. Devereux, S.: Sen's entitlement approach: critiques and counter-critiques. Oxf. Dev. Stud. **29**(3), 245–263 (2001)
48. Corbridge, S.: Development as freedom: the spaces of Amartya Sen. Prog. Dev. Stud. **2**(3), 183–217 (2002)
49. Poveda, S., Roberts, T.: Critical agency and development: applying Freire and Sen to ICT4D in Zambia and Brazil. Inf. Technol. Dev. **24**(1), 119–137 (2018)
50. Pieterse, J.N.: Globalization and collective action. In: Globalization and Social Movements, pp. 21–40. Palgrave Macmillan, London (2001)
51. Castells, M.: Toward a sociology of the network society. Contemp. Sociol. **29**(5), 693–699 (2000)
52. Sein, M.K., Harindranath, G.: Conceptualizing the ICT artifact: toward understanding the role of ICT in national development. Inf. Soc. **20**(1), 15–24 (2004)
53. Van Dijk, J.A.: The one-dimensional network society of Manuel Castells. New Media Soc. **1**(1), 127–138 (1999)
54. Zheng, Y., Hatakka, M., Sahay, S., Andersson, A.: Conceptualizing development in information and communication technology for development (ICT4D). Inf. Technol. Dev. **24**(1), 1–14 (2018)
55. Dordick, H.S., Wang, G.: Information Society: A Retrospective View. Sage Publications Inc., Thousand Oaks (1993)
56. Mitev, N., De Vaujany, F.X.: Seizing the opportunity: towards a historiography of information systems. J. Inf. Technol. **27**(2), 110–124 (2012). https://doi.org/10.1057/jit.2012.1
57. Young, A.G.: Using ICT for social good: cultural identity restoration through emancipatory pedagogy. Inf. Syst. J. **28**(2), 340–358 (2018)
58. Ledwith, M.: Personal narratives/political lives: personal reflection as a tool for collective change. Reflective Pract. **6**(2), 255–262 (2005)

59. Avgerou, C.: Theoretical framing of ICT4D research. In: Choudrie, J., Islam, M., Wahid, F., Bass, J., Priyatma, J. (eds.) Information and Communication Technologies for Development, vol. 504, pp. 10–23. Springer, Cham (2017). https://doi.org/10.1007/978-3-319-59111-7_2

60. Leidner, D.E.: Review and theory symbiosis: an introspective retrospective. J. Assoc. Inf. Syst. **19**(6), 552–567 (2018)

61. Zheng, Y.: Different spaces for e-development: What can we learn from the capability approach? Inf. Technol. Dev. **15**(2), 66–82 (2009)

62. Escobar, A.: Encountering Development. Princeton University Press, Princeton (2011)

63. Díaz Andrade, A., Urquhart, C.: Unveiling the modernity bias: a critical examination of the politics of ICT4D. Inf. Technol. Dev. **18**(4), 281–292 (2012)

64. Avgerou, C.: Information systems in developing countries: a critical research review. J. Inf. Technol. **23**(3), 133–146 (2008)

65. Davison, R.M., Martinsons, M.G.: Context is king! Considering particularism in research design and reporting. J. Inf. Technol. **31**(3), 241–249 (2016)

66. Heeks, R.: From digital divide to digital justice in the global south: conceptualising adverse digital incorporation. arXiv preprint https://arxiv.org/abs/2108.09783 (2021)

Data Use as Liberation: A Case from an Education Management Information System in Uganda

Monica Grace Amuha and Silvia Masiero[✉]

University of Oslo, Oslo, Norway
{amuhamg,silvima}@ifi.uio.no

Abstract. The Information Systems (IS) literature explores multiple consequences of data use practices, including the role of such practices in achieving empowerment. Limited knowledge is, however, available on the role of data use in fighting political bias, a phenomenon through which an individual or a group's political influence diverts resources away from their optimal purposes. In this paper we rely on Freire's concept of *liberation* to study a pilot project of an Education Management Information System (EMIS), conducted in two districts in Uganda, to illuminate the links between EMIS data use and the delinking of education managers from political bias. Our field data enable us to theorise EMIS data use as a practice of liberation, aimed at strengthening decision making processes crucial to development policy.

Keywords: Data use · Education management information systems · Empowerment · Liberation · ICT4D

1 Introduction

Data use, especially when referred to public sector domains such as health and education, is a prominent topic in the Information Systems (IS) literature [6–8, 19, 35]. Among many strands of discussion, one centred on information and communication technologies for development (ICT4D) depicts health and education data use as a practice of empowerment, through which people are endowed with the ability to pursue the life they want [32]. Empowerment is multifaceted in ICT4D [3, 4], with Senian views of empowerment framing this concept in terms of people's ability to achieve the life they want, ultimately resulting in the pursuit of freedom in the face of constraints [30].

Limited knowledge is, however, available on the role of data use in fighting political bias, a substantial constraint to human empowerment which limits people's ability to pursue their freedoms. Political bias is presented as a phenomenon in which an individual or group's political influence diverts resources away from their optimal purposes, hampering development policy across many sectors [10]. Political bias results in resource

Research in Progress

distributions that follow politically determined preferences rather than the needs of the people, substantially preventing socio-economic development efforts from proceeding optimally and allocating resources in ways that maximise human freedoms [32].

In this paper we draw on the pilot implementation of a decentralised Education Management Information System (EMIS) in Uganda to begin outlining a theory of education data use as *liberation* from political bias. Drawing on data from the EMIS pilot project, conducted in two districts of Uganda in February and March 2020, we use concepts from Freire [16] to show a process in which education managers built critical consciousness and, on this basis, developed the agency needed to reappropriate technology towards liberation. This adds to existing conceptualisations of empowerment by showing how liberation from political bias, achieved through data use, participates in empowerment.

The purpose of this research-in-progress paper is to set the basis to theorise EMIS data use as a practice of liberation, defined in Freirian terms as the freeing of the oppressed through illumination of the root causes of disadvantage [28]. The concept of *liberation* adds to existing data use research by showing the potential of data use to free human beings from external sources of subjugation.

This paper is structured as follows. We first map the literature on data use and empowerment, focusing on the dimensions of empowerment that such a literature has contemplated. We then introduce the case of the EMIS pilot project in the districts of Gulu and Mayuge, Uganda, to illuminate EMIS data use as a practice of liberation. The discussion positions such a practice in the existing literature, introducing liberation as a core component of empowerment achievable by collectives through data use. Implications are drawn for the literature on data use in ICT4D.

2 Data Use: From Empowerment to Liberation

Data use has emerged as a prominent research topic in the IS field. Such a prominence is, somewhat paradoxically, countered by the paucity of scoping exercises on it, which are mostly focused on health data use [8, 19, 35]. As noted by Byrne and Sæbø [8], data use does not refer to the quality of data or access to them by individuals, but to effectively utilising them for diverse purposes. Multiple branches of IS have dealt with public sector data use, considered in its diverse manifestations.

Research shows how data use can empower individuals to better perform critical tasks in the health sector [19, 35]. Against this backdrop, the link between data use and empowerment offers the core perspective through which data use is depicted in IS.

2.1 The Core Perspective: Data Use as Empowerment

Byrne and Sæbø [8] note the breadth of the literature on data use. They do, at the same time, note the primary focus taken by this literature: it is a focus on data use as empowerment, framed, with Sen [32], as the possibility for people to pursue the life they want. Wide presence of an empowerment lens in data use literature has an important implication: data use, beyond quality and access, is leveraged in the pursuit of freedoms that lead to people's empowerment [30]. Studies in the data use landscape focus on multiple dimensions of empowerment: two examples are sub-national *districts*, empowered by greater awareness of data on their populations [11], and *digital platforms*, which are converted into tools for bottom-up decision making [5, 26].

In a recent literature review, Pandey and Zheng [27] map the core dimensions of empowerment used in ICT4D research. They present six dimensions: *community*; *psychological*; *gender*; *cultural*; *economic*; *political and structural* [27]. While varied, these dimensions have a common matrix, found in the view of development as "freedom" from the constraints that prevent individuals from living the life they want [30, 32]. As noted by Sæbø et al. [31], over time the ICT4D field has moved towards a collective vision of empowerment, where the good of the community overcomes the good of the individual in achieving goals such as public health, education or emergency relief.

While data use features strongly in discussions of empowerment, it does not feature as strongly in terms of *political bias*, a phenomenon in which the political influence of an individual or group diverts resources away from purposes that would be optimal for the community [10]. On the one hand, the literature review by Byrne and Sæbø [8] shows that there are many ways for data use to foster human empowerment. On the other hand, none of these ways contemplates political bias as a phenomenon that conditions people's ability to achieve empowerment. A multidimensional framework of data use for development still needs a proper theoretical understanding of political bias, one that, further developing the *political and structural* dimension of empowerment outlined by Pandey and Zheng [27], unpacks how liberation from political bias can act as a route to empowerment.

2.2 A Novel Dimension: Data Use as Liberation

In this paper we set the basis to theorise data use as a practice of *liberation*, which allows conceptualising freedom from political bias within the ICT4D field. On the one hand, Sen [32] argues that development is fundamentally predicated on people's agency, as a route to expose unfair social norms and foster social change. On the other, researchers have criticised the capabilities approach due to its limited engagement with praxis, a critique that, featured in seminal ICT4D work on this approach [36, 37], leaves subjects uncertain on the actionability of such an approach.

The concept of liberation, theorised in Freire's [16] Pedagogy of the Oppressed as a route to freedom from injustice, lays the conceptual basis for such an engagement with praxis. Liberation is conceived, in Freire [16], as a process in which oppressed communities acquire awareness of the roots of structural disadvantage, and are then enabled to use such an awareness to challenge the sources of their subjugation [28]. Theoretically, the two building blocks of Freire's notion of liberation are the concepts of *critical consciousness* and *agency*, which Freire [16] engages as follows:

- *Critical consciousness* refers to the human ability to read the world critically, identifying oppressive and alienating conditions in the status quo. Freire frames critical consciousness as achieved by laying bare the roots of structural inequality, engaging the structural factors that make people systemically prone to abuse and injustice. Central in the Pedagogy of the Oppressed, his educational method consists of a problem posing methodology [28] to enable participants make sense of the bases of their oppression:

this may involve, for example, inducing people to interrogate themselves on the roots of the injustice they suffer, and on the power dynamics behind them [33]. Development of critical consciousness in the oppressed is, in Freire, the epistemological basis of liberation.

- *Agency*, conceptually predicated on the development of critical consciousness, refers to "the ability to act in the world to change it" [28]. In Freire's theorisation, individuals who, based on the pedagogical method, develop critical consciousness, are enabled to convert such a consciousness into action that concurs to the achievement of freedom. While fundamentally based on the theoretical components of the pedagogical process, agency embodies the praxis at the core of the pedagogy of the oppressed, through which subjects of systemic injustice act against the sources of oppression. Though action is not a necessary consequence of the development of critical consciousness, agency, as the ability for individuals to choose which action to take, is fundamentally based on it.

Poveda [29] notes that lack of actionability of Sen's capabilities approach is filled by the coexistence of theory and praxis in Freire's pedagogy. The actionability of Freire's approach explains how it has inspired the work of multiple organisations, aimed at liberating people from the constraints of injustice through a pedagogy that brings to light the causes of structural unfairness [29, 33]. Unpacking the political and structural dimensions of empowerment in Pandey and Zheng [27] requires an approach to blend theory with liberating action: it is, with Myers [25], a critical approach that blends theorisation of reality with its transformation, to change an oppressive status quo.

Based on Freire [16], we hence propose a vision of data use as potentially connected to liberation from the political bias that poses a constraint to development. In what follows, we present the results of a study of a pilot project of EMIS conducted in two districts in Uganda, where education data use was related to liberation of education managers from the political biases implicit in the system.

3   Case Study: EMIS Pilot Project in Uganda

EMIS are core tools for data use in the education sector. An EMIS is "a system of people, technology, models, methods, processes, procedures, rules and regulations that function together to provide education leaders, decision makers and managers at all levels with a comprehensive, integrated set of relevant, reliable, unambiguous, timely data and information to support them in completion of their responsibilities" [9]. UNESCO [34] defines EMIS as an "ensemble of operational processes, increasingly supported by digital technology, that enable the collection, aggregation, analysis, and use of data and information in education, including for management and administration, planning, policy formulation, and monitoring and evaluation." Both these definitions highlight the systemic nature of EMIS, which is currently being used in Uganda to map education data at the district level.

3.1   EMIS in Uganda: A Three-Phase Timeline

EMIS in Uganda has evolved over three major phases. In the initial phase (2000–2005), the Ministry of Education and Sports (MoES) adopted a computer-based automated solution heavily biased towards the education statistics module, which lacked an interface with the Uganda National Examination Board (UNEB) in charge of examination results from primary and secondary schools. In addition, the personnel module was never operationalised and the system was limited in its single-year design, unable to provide multi-year reporting and longitudinal analysis of key indicators. Funders of the software had exclusive rights to the system, which limited MoES' ability to modify and use it.

During the second phase (2006–2008), another system was designed to be accessed via the MoES intranet and used for management and planning at the central level. However, the system presented problems of usability and lacked a reports module for easy access and visualisation of data.

A third phase (2008–2014) focused on addressing decentralisation needs of education data management and led to the design of a new EMIS, as an integrated solution to enable all stakeholders at MoES to access information via the Local Area Network (LAN) and link data between MoES and districts. At the district level, a Decentralised Education Management Information System (DEMIS) was designed and installed in 134 districts and municipalities, however, with the withdrawal of donor funding, the system was never operationalised nor linked to the central level. This left the MoES planning unit with the option of a centralised EMIS where data is collected using the annual statistical form from schools and entered into EMIS at MoES headquarters [14].

The Annual Schools Census (ASC) is a collection of basic (i.e. enrolment, learner characteristics, teacher details, infrastructure, etc.) educational data from mainly pre-primary, primary and secondary levels of the education system. A copy of the filled form is left at the school, another at the district and the final copy taken to the national MoES headquarters where data is entered in the standalone system and analysed using SQL and Excel. Annual statistical abstracts on data from the census are published on the MoES website and a few copies distributed to schools. This centralised management of data created challenges of work overload due to entry of large volumes of data, limited capacity to conduct data verification and validation from the source and failure to follow up non-reporting schools.

In 2017, a task force to oversee the realisation of a new robust and reliable EMIS capable of addressing the sector's information needs was initiated. In its EMIS review report, a task force highlighted the challenges above and proposed short and medium-term recommendations to revamp the current EMIS. These included redevelopment of EMIS to address current system challenges, operationalisation of dormant modules, strengthening of EMIS legal and policy framework, development of a communication and dissemination strategy, review of the current budget to incorporate EMIS activities and development of a sustainable financing strategy [1, 2, 13]. Following these recommendations, the MoES has, for the last five years, been in the process of redeveloping the EMIS into a robust system, albeit with limited success so far.

3.2 Pilot of DHIS2 for Education

In January 2019 the Health Information Systems Programme (HISP) Uganda initiated engagements with the MoES Basic Education department to pilot the District Health Information Software 2 (DHIS2) as an EMIS in the districts of Gulu and Mayuge. DHIS2 is an open source software used for managing health information in over 73 low-

and middle-income countries, currently used in Uganda by the Ministry of Health for reporting on health management data from 140 districts in the country.

During the pilot, several stakeholder engagements, to foster buy-in and support, were conducted for both the central and district level leadership. A requirements gathering process was conducted at the district level and selected schools to further understand the data management processes and data needs at those levels. DHIS2 was configured and deployed in three administrative units in the two districts to support collection, capture, validation and analysis of key education data from primary and pre-primary schools.

End user trainings on data entry, data validation, analysis, presentation and use for MoES central level staff, district education teams, district planners and biostatisticians, and support supervisions were conducted. The pilot districts entered EMIS data, collected on the annual statistical forms for three consecutive years 2016, 2017, 2018 into the DHIS2-EMIS. District dashboards were created as part of the EMIS to present education indicators like gross enrollment, teacher to pupil ratios, reporting rates, performance index, pass rates in visualised tools like charts, pivot tables, graphs and maps to support district education teams and the leadership in planning and decision making.

After a year of pilot implementation, an assessment of the DHIS2-EMIS pilot was made in partnership with Health Information Systems Program (HISP) Uganda, MoES and Save the Children Uganda. The team conducted the assessment in all the three implementation sites between February and March 2020. The overall objective of the assessment was to assess both the MoES and district capacity and readiness to utilise and maintain the DHIS2-EMIS and document lessons learnt to inform national scale.

The assessment methodology included a total of 22 key informant interviews with the MoES central level team (5), the district education team (6), district leadership (4) and school administrators (7). Two focus group discussions with school administrators and members of the school management committee were also conducted to understand the process and challenges of data management, reporting and data use practices at the school level. Primary sources of EMIS data (data collection tools) at the school level were reviewed to validate data collected in the annual statistical forms and entered into DHIS2-EMIS.

3.3 Findings: The DHIS2-EMIS Pilot Evaluation

Findings from the assessment indicate that overall, the DHIS2-EMIS pilot has had a positive outcome with buy-in from the MoES central level and improved management and use of education data in the pilot districts. The MoES leadership was committed to support the implementation of DHIS2-EMIS, which is in line with the Education Sector Strategic Plan FY 2017/2020 "To Strengthen the Education Management and Information System (EMIS) to collect and process more accurate and timely data for use by decision-makers."

Through training and support supervision conducted during the pilot, the districts were enabled to collect, enter, validate, present and use data from DHIS2-EMIS to inform district level plans, resource allocation and support supervision activities. The synergy between the health and education department eased implementation of DHIS2-EMIS, with district education teams continuously supported by the district biostatisticians who have longer experience using the DHIS2. Data from DHIS2-EMIS has been used by the districts as a basis for decision making: this affected the distribution of desks, allocation of teachers, building new latrine stances and classroom blocks. In addition, data from DHIS2-EMIS was used to guide planning and budgeting, allocation of resources for vaccination and other health programs in schools.

Most importantly, respondents interviewed through the pilot assessment have noted how the project has acted as a "game changer" in resource allocation [12]. District planners and education managers outlined two different scenaria: in a pre-EMIS era, resource allocation was influenced by local politicians, who exerted their influence to allocate resources in ways that did not reflect the real needs of the districts. In the pre-EMIS scenario, resource misallocation resulted in systematic constraints to empowerment, since a dashboard-centred source of data was not available to counter central decisions.

Transformation of such a scenario was, however, one of the main outcomes in the districts that piloted the EMIS. As powerfully synthesised by one of the district managers interviewed, "you cannot argue with the data": data use influenced district managers' ability to combat extant sources of political bias, using EMIS to illustrate the effective needs of the different districts and schools. Becoming aware of political bias, and hence using EMIS data to counter it, was a core process in plying data use to a purpose that goes beyond the dimension of community empowerment [18] that data use is normally adapted for. What was observed in the Uganda pilot project was a proper construction of awareness by district managers, who reappropriated EMIS data use from a tool for empowerment generically conceived to a tool for liberation from political bias, adapted and reappropriated on a daily basis from its own users.

4   The EMIS Pilot Project: An Ongoing Freirian Analysis

Research on EMIS in Uganda is part of an ongoing doctoral project centred on the shift to a decentralised EMIS, a shift of which the pilot project studied in this paper is an integral part. In this section, we map the current status of our research-in-progress work, setting the conceptual basis for theorisation of data use that the work is pursuing.

Such a theorisation starts from how, positioning EMIS within data use research, our study raises several known points in terms of empowerment. The DHIS2 software, a long-term endeavour of digital health in developing countries [6], has recently diversified into education, seeking to project the same empowerment goals that Byrne and Sæbø [8] described for the health sector. Mapping DHIS2 in terms of Pandey and Zheng's [27] dimensions of empowerment means touching upon several of them: community empowerment, to start with, is achieved by endowing local communities with the ability to manage their own data [11]. Psychological empowerment is also noted in DHIS2 research [21] and, while studies of gender and culture in relation to the software are yet to be conducted, research in the broader ICT4D space shows gendered effects that software changes can have on community empowerment [3, 4, 15, 18, 22].

What needs unpacking is Pandey and Zheng's [27] *political and structural* dimension of empowerment. Poveda and Roberts [28] illustrate the issue: Sen [32] lacks, as noted above, the praxis component found in Freire [16]. Where empowerment alone runs the risk of depoliticising injustice, overlooking its root causes, Freire's notion of liberation, based on development of critical consciousness, shows how freedom is based on learning the structural causes of disadvantage. Such a process affords individuals to enact agency, entering a process of resistance which builds the structural roots of liberation.

This is the process that is unfolding with EMIS in Uganda. All resembles a classic DHIS2 project: data are put in the hands of district managers, allowing them to take informed decisions on important topics. But the pilot has shown an unknown dimension, for which it is not so much community empowerment, but liberation from political bias that interviewees have clearly articulated. Interviews have outlined clear differences in the two scenaria: a pre-EMIS one in which political bias was present, and a post-pilot which allowed district managers to develop critical consciousness of such a bias and use EMIS to counter it. While anti-bias agency is predicated on many factors, and surely not only on the availability of a technology that puts data in the hands of education managers, data from the pilot project show the strong instrumentality of such a technology in countering political bias.

These raw observations, conducted in this initial phase of our research, led us to see Freire's concept of liberation as a guiding light through the phenomenon we are observing. While other candidate theories are being considered, two more tasks can be pursued through Freire [16]. First, a vision of disempowerment that instead of remaining superficial (for example, single instantiations of misallocation of resources in a given district) analyses the deep structural reasons for such occurrences, individuating structural patterns that repeat themselves over time. Through Freire we can analyse the self-perpetuation of injustice [24], enabling not only and not so much the external observer, but *the oppressed* community experiencing injustice to make sense of it.

Secondly, we can link these to broader theorisations of injustice in ICT4D. The field's turn to issues of power and justice [17, 20, 21, 23] specifically invites us to do so. In an ICT4D landscape whose core matter is not anymore development, but *justice* defined as fairness in the way people are dealt with [11, 20], understanding the structural roots of injustice has a crucial importance that it did not have before. Equipped with Freire's pedagogy of the oppressed, applied to an open source software for a long time framed in terms of non-political empowerment, we seek to produce a theory in which data use is openly and clearly linked to the possibility of liberation.

5 Conclusion

This paper has reported on an ongoing research project on EMIS, in which we seek to theorise data use as a practice of liberation from political bias. In doing so, we unpacked the political and structural dimension of empowerment from Pandey and Zheng [27], showing that the purpose of data use is not only, and not so much in terms of community empowerment, but in terms of the freedom from political bias achieved through the engagement of education managers with EMIS data sources.

Two main directions are to be pursued across future stages of this research. First, as an ongoing doctoral project, the research will involve further data collection on EMIS Uganda, to monitor the further developments of the project and the meaning of these for education managers through the state. As the EMIS is scaled across the country, the questions of liberation from political bias posed here become of relevance at a national scale, with important implications for the making of any initiative that aims to put data at the service of better education outcomes.

Second, the theory-building potential of this project is strongly tied to ideas of justice. The fact that data management systems like DHIS2 enable community empowerment has been noted across multiple works, but the possibilities of such software for the countering of political bias are much less well understood. In the context of today's ICT4D research, increasingly tied to visions of justice as the heart of development, understanding the root causes of structural advantage is a strongly needed component of theory-building efforts. We hope, with this work, to have offered a conceptualisation that can contribute to such efforts.

References

1. Abdul-Hamid, H.: What matters most for education management information systems: a framework paper. SABER Working Paper Series, no. 7 (2014)
2. ADEA: Report of the 2nd African Ministerial Forum on ICT integration in Education and Training Forum, Abidjan, 7–9 June 2016 (2016). https://www.adeanet.org/en/publications/report-2nd-african-ministerial-forum-ict-integration-education-training-forum-abidjan-7
3. Bailur, S., Masiero, S., Tacchi, J.: Gender, mobile, and mobile internetl gender, mobile, and development: the theory and practice of empowerment. Inf. Technol. Int. Dev. **14**(2), 96–104 (2018)
4. Bailur, S., Masiero, S.: Women's income generation through mobile Internet: a study of focus group data from Ghana, Kenya, and Uganda. Gend. Technol. Dev. **21**(1–2), 77–98 (2017)
5. Bonina, C., Koskinen, K., Eaton, B., Gawer, A.: Digital platforms for development: foundations and research agenda. Inf. Syst. J. **31**(6), 869–902 (2021)
6. Braa, J., Sahay, S.: Health information systems programme: Participatory design within the HISP network. In: Routledge International Handbook of Participatory Design, pp. 255–276. Routledge, London (2012)
7. Braa, J., Monteiro, E., Sahay, S.: Networks of action: sustainable health information systems across developing countries. MIS Q. **28**(3), 337–362 (2004)
8. Byrne, E., Saebø, J.I.: Routine Use of DHIS2 Data: A Scoping Review. Working Paper, University of Oslo (2021)
9. Cassidy, T.: Education management information systems (EMIS) in Latin America and the Caribbean: Lessons and challenges. Inter-American Development Bank (2006)
10. Chattopadhyay, R., Duflo, E.: Women as policy makers: Evidence from a randomized policy experiment in India. Econometrica **72**(5), 1409–1443 (2004)
11. Chrysantina, A., Sæbø, J.I.: Assessing user-designed dashboards: A case for developing data visualization competency. In: Nielsen, P., Kimaro, H.C. (eds.) Information and Communication Technologies for Development. Strengthening Southern-Driven Cooperation as a Catalyst for ICT4D, vol. 551, pp. 448–459. Springer, Cham (2019). https://doi.org/10.1007/978-3-030-18400-1_37
12. EMIS Pilot Project Report: Assessment of the Uganda DHIS2-EMIS Pilot in Gulu and Mayuge District. HISP Uganda, pilot project report, June 2020 (2020)
13. EMIS Review Taskforce Report: Concepts, Issues & Recommendations for Re-Engineering and Re-Development of Education Management Information System (EMIS) (2017). https://www.education.go.ug/wp-content/uploads/2019/08/EMIS-REVIEW-TASKFORCE-REPORT.pdf

14. EMIS Uganda Peer Review Report: Uganda Education Management Information Systems (2016). https://www.education.go.ug/wp-content/uploads/2019/08/Uganda-EMIS-PEER-REVIEW-REPORT.pdf
15. Faith, B.: Maintenance affordances and structural inequalities: mobile phone use by low-income women in the United Kingdom. Inf. Technol. Int. Dev. **14**(2), 66–80 (2018)
16. Freire, P.: Pedagogy of the Oppressed (Revised). Continuum, New York (1982)
17. Heeks, R., Wall, P.J.: Critical realism and ICT4D research. In: Choudrie, J., Islam, M., Wahid, F., Bass, J., Priyatma, J. (eds.) Information and Communication Technologies for Development, pp. 159–170. Springer, Cham (2017). https://doi.org/10.1007/978-3-319-59111-7_14
18. Kleine, D.: Technologies of Choice? ICTs, Development, and the Capabilities Approach. MIT Press, London (2013)
19. Lemma, S., Janson, A., Persson, L.Å., Wickremasinghe, D., Källestål, C.: Improving quality and use of routine health information system data in low-and middle-income countries: a scoping review. PLoS ONE **15**(10), e0239683 (2020)
20. Masiero, S.: Should we still be doing ICT4D research? Electron. J. Inf. Syst. Dev. Ctries. (2022)
21. Masiero, S., Arvidsson, V.: Degenerative outcomes of digital identity platforms for development. Inf. Syst. J. **31**(6), 903–928 (2021)
22. Masiero, S., Bailur, S.: Digital identity for development: the quest for justice and a research agenda. Inf. Technol. Dev. **27**(1), 1–12 (2021)
23. Masiero, S., Nielsen, P.: Resilient ICT4D: building and sustaining our community in pandemic times. In: Proceedings of the 1st IFIP 9.4 Virtual Conference on the Implications of Information and Digital Technologies for Development, 26–28 May 2021 (2021)
24. Masiero, S., Das, S.: Datafying anti-poverty programmes: implications for data justice. Inf. Commun. Soc. **22**(7), 916–933 (2019)
25. Myers, M.D.: Critical ethnography in information systems. In: Lee, A.S., Liebenau, J., DeGross, J.I. (eds.) Information Systems and Qualitative Research, pp. 276–300. Springer, Boston (1997). https://doi.org/10.1007/978-0-387-35309-8_15
26. Nicholson, B., Nielsen, P., Saebo, J., Sahay, S.: Exploring tensions of global public good platforms for development: the case of DHIS2. In: Nielsen, P., Kimaro, H.C. (eds.) Information and Communication Technologies for Development. Strengthening Southern-Driven Cooperation as a Catalyst for ICT4D, vol. 551, pp. 207–217. Springer, Cham (2019). https://doi.org/10.1007/978-3-030-18400-1_17
27. Pandey, P., Zheng, Y.: Unpacking empowerment in ICT4D research. In: Nielsen, P., Kimaro, H. (eds.) Information and Communication Technologies for Development. Strengthening Southern-Driven Cooperation as a Catalyst for ICT4D, vol. 552, pp. 83–94. Springer, Cham (2019). https://doi.org/10.1007/978-3-030-19115-3_8
28. Poveda, S., Roberts, T.: Critical agency and development: applying Freire and Sen to ICT4D in Zambia and Brazil. Inf. Technol. Dev. **24**(1), 119–137 (2018)
29. Poveda, S.C.: How can digital inclusion promote social change? Exploring two Brazilian case studies. In: Proceedings of the Eighth International Conference on Information and Communication Technologies and Development, pp. 1–11 (2016)
30. Robeyns, I.: Wellbeing, Freedom and Social Justice: The Capability Approach Re-examined. Open Book Publishers, London (2016)
31. Sæbø, Ø., Sein, M.K., Thapa, D.: Nepal wireless networking project: building infrastructure in the mountains from ground up. Commun. Assoc. Inf. Syst. **34**(1), 11–21 (2014)
32. Sen, A.: Development as Freedom. Routledge, London (2001)
33. Tygel, A.F., Kirsch, R.: Contributions of Paulo Freire for a critical data literacy: a popular education approach. J. Community Inf. **12**(3), 108–121 (2016)

34. UNESCO: Inclusion and education: all means all. Global education monitoring report 2020 (2020)
35. Wickremasinghe, D., Hashmi, I.E., Schellenberg, J., Avan, B.I.: District decision-making for health in low-income settings: a systematic literature review. Health Policy Plann. **31**(suppl_2), ii12–ii24 (2016)
36. Zheng, Y.: Different spaces for e-development: what can we learn from the capability approach? Inf. Technol. Dev. **15**(2), 66–82 (2009)
37. Zheng, Y., Walsham, G.: Inequality of what? Social exclusion in the e-society as capability deprivation. Inf. Technol. People **21**(3), 222–243 (2008)

Competing Logics in an ICT4D Partnership: Case Evidence from Indonesia

Aprisa Chrysantina[1] (✉) ⓘ, Brian Nicholson[2] ⓘ, and Johan Ivar Sæbø[1] ⓘ

[1] HISP Center, University of Oslo, Oslo, Norway
{aprisac,johansa}@ifi.uio.no
[2] University of Manchester, Manchester, UK
brian.nicholson@manchester.ac.uk

Abstract. The importance of partnerships is established in the ICT4D academic and practitioner literature as a success factor contributing towards achievement of development outcomes. However, it is also recognised that the failure of partnerships is a common occurrence and there is limited knowledge about the reasons for these failures. International development projects often include partnerships between international organizations and public sector implementers and little is understood about how and why such partnerships may succeed or flounder. This paper aims to improve our understanding of ICT4D project failure by exploring the interplay of logics within an international organization-local public sector partnership. The empirical basis is a longitudinal case study of a health-related ICT4D project in Indonesia. Three vignettes are presented, highlighting the dynamics between local public sector logic and international organization logic. The results show that the "accountability logic"of the international organization (WHO) conflicted with the "hierarchical" public sector logic of the ministry. The paper contributes work in progress towards an improved understanding of partnership failures in ICT4D.

Keywords: ICT4D partnership · Institutional logics · Public sector · International organization

1 Introduction

Information and communication technology for development (ICT4D) projects often feature an international partnership consisting of international organization partners and local implementers, often from the public sector. Within the health sector, such international-national collaboration, known as North-South global health partnerships (GHP) has become a dominant mechanism for reaching the Sustainable Development Goals (SDGs) [1]. Such mechanisms are incentivized by funding practices of global health actors, including private, public, and philanthropic institutions[2]. Naturally, the rise of GHP as dominant over the last couple of decades has spurred some critique, albeit the focus tends to center on success stories [1]. Already in 2007 it was pointed out that this global aid architecture in health was increasing complexity [3].

© IFIP International Federation for Information Processing 2022
Published by Springer Nature Switzerland AG 2022
Y. Zheng et al. (Eds.): ICT4D 2022, IFIP AICT 657, pp. 515–530, 2022.
https://doi.org/10.1007/978-3-031-19429-0_31

Prior work has shown that partnership involving different types of organizations is prone to competing logics [4, 5]. Research has investigated competing logics within partnerships such as public private partnership [5], government-professional partnership [6–8]. Tensions and conflicts, disappointments and misunderstandings are almost inherent to most ICT4D PPPs (public–private partnerships)[9].

This paper addresses Ismail, et al. [5] call to investigate patterns of logics in ICT4D partnerships. Although the most common form of partnerships in the ICT4D projects involves international organization partners and local public sector implementers to date there is no in-depth case research that has examined this form of partnership. We investigate a GHP project in Indonesia involving a global agency, the nation's ministry of health, and both local and foreign universities. To improve our understanding on this issue, this paper follows Reay and Hinings' [6] approach to logics to examine an international development partnership in Indonesia examining how logics can compete to the detriment of the partnership. This research in progress aims to answer the following research question:

- How do different institutional logics in ICT-enabled global health partnerships manifest themselves to the detriment of partnership?

The paper is organized as follows: In the next section we outline relevant research and the conceptual framework. We then proceed to the methods section followed by a case description. This paper presents early findings and analysis of the research through 3 vignettes to illustrate the types of interactions of the logics and how they affected the partnership. Finally we conclude and offer some future actions in this research in progress.

2 Conceptual Frame: Competing Institutional Logics

Institutional logics are "the belief systems and related practices that predominate in an organizational field" [6], although the use and manifestation of institutional logics are not limited to the organizational field but also present themselves at the societal or organizational level. Institutional logics consist of symbolic (ideas, values, discourses) and material elements (organization, tech, work process) [10]. In ICT4D partnerships, this can translate as: "goals and motivations, culture, and working practices" [5]. Table 1 outlines a preliminary review of some prior papers that are relevant to this inquiry in GHPs, HIS, and ICT4D.

ICT4D partnerships as well as GHPs are often composed of organizations from different domains such as public, private, non-government, or professional domains [1, 9, 11, 15, 16]. This combination of diverse organizational backgrounds is often problematic and institutional logics have been used to examine the dynamics in such partnerships from the perspectives of each group of actors [5, 6, 12, 14, 16]. Institutional logics offers a way to explain actors imposing practices from logics that are carried from their field to another [20].

Ismail, et al. (*ibid.*) demonstrated how the clash between a dominant private logic towards a public logic, Sah, Skel, Stra. These logics turned out to hinder the achievement of the development and partnership goals.

Table 1. Key literature focus and gap

Authors and year	Main findings and gaps
World Health Organization Maximizing Positive Synergies Collaborative Group (2009). [11]	The failures in GHPs have been debated to be a result or to be a consequence of the already fragile health systems in the countries
Reay & Hinings (2009) [6]	This paper examines how competing logics between medical professionals and government can be managed to achieve an institutional change
Sahay, S., Sæbø, J. I., Mekonnen, S. M., & Gizaw, A. A. (2010)[12]	The deep rooted logic from the historically embedded system that clashes with the proposed HIS logic hinders the HIS implementation in Tajikistan
Mizrachi, Y., & Ben-Attar, D. (2011) [9]	This paper is one among the earliest investigations on PPP in ICT4D, highlighting its challenges and opportunities, as well as the inherence of conflicts within this partnership
Dodson, Sterling, & Bennett (2012) [13]	This paper reviews ICT4D research and demonstrates how ICT4D potentially contributed to unsatisfactory development results. The paper calls for assessment to other development initiatives
Sanner, T. A., & Sæbø, J. I. (2014)[14]	This paper highlights how two seemingly incongruent logics from the different actors in a GHP reinforce each other to reach the project goals
Skelcher & Smith (2015) [15]	This paper introduces the categorization of organizational hybrids consisting of a public sector and a nonprofit using institutional logic
Stratton, C., Sholler, D., Bailey, D., Leonardi, P., & Rodríguez-Lluesma, C. (2016) [16]	Design-reality gap is presented through a study in South America where competing professional logics between the education and technology sectors hinder the participatory approach within the ICT4D project
Sligo, Gauld, Roberts, Villa (2017) [17]	Evaluating a large-scale HIS is a challenge and the quality of these evaluations varied. These evaluations show that the success of HIS implementation highly depends on the structural, contextual, and organizational factors

(*continued*)

Table 1. (*continued*)

Authors and year	Main findings and gaps
Ismail, Heeks, Nicholson, & Aman (2018). [5]	This paper analyzes interaction within a public private partnership in Malaysia as an example of common public private partnership in ICT4D setting. The lens of institutional logic is used to analyze how public and private logics interplay
Burton-Jones, Akhlaghpour, Ayre, Barde, Staib, & Sullivan, (2020) [18]	Addressing Sligo, et al. [n], Burton-Jones, et al.[n] introduces the use of institutional theory for evaluation research of digital transformation in healthcare and how it can provide a language to articulate and make sense of the complex nature of HIS
Plamondon, K. M., Brisbois, B., Dubent, L., & Larson, C. P. (2021) [1]	GHPs that are predominantly in the form of north-south partnership are portrayed as beneficial to the south counterparts without critically reflecting on the power imbalance. Due to the methods used in this paper, it failed to understand the depth of the actual dynamic in the field
Ramadani, L., Breidbach, C. F., & Kurnia, S. (2022). [19]	Using Indonesia as a backdrop, this paper observes ICT4D as a multi-level social process where top-down policies are translated from micro to macro level, therefore creating outcome bottom-up. This paper addresses the vertical relationship more than horizontal relationship in the central level

Reay and Hinings [6] also present classic conflicting logics between a medical professional association and the government. Boonstra et al. [7] use the same lens to analyze three rivaling logics in a hospital. Although the study does not represent an ICT4D partnership setting, this paper showed a typical professional mix in ICT4D in the health sector, the management, medical and IT professionalism. Each of the individuals in the study presented at least an additional logic that is different from their domain. For instance, a manager might exhibit a medical and/or IT professionalism logic in addition to their managerial logic.

3   Methods and Empirical Setting

Following Walsham [21, 22] this paper is an interpretive longitudinal qualitative case study of an ICT4D project in the public health sector in Indonesia. The method allows the author to understand the complex phenomenon being examined in its natural setting [16, 23]. The first author joined the project in August 2017 as a member of the core implementation team, attached first to the local and later the foreign university taking part in the project. Data was obtained through participant observation and interviews, both remotely and in-person. The project involved a range of activities such as attending meetings, training sessions, field visits, coworking and social activities.

The first author was actively involved in most of the core team activities, including remote meetings and field visits. Other members of the team were aware that the project was a part of a research project and the team members of both UGM and UiO were actively collecting data while participating. The participant observation included but not limited to the following: observations of conversations, behaviors, actions, decisions, and reactions of different actors, interactions, and documents. After each visit, the first author compiled field notes and discussed the emerging findings with fellow members from WHO, UGM and UiO in unstructured and unrecorded conversation to clarify the observations.

These conversations spanned from a few minutes to hours of conversations during for instance a shared plane ride or during dinner. These first-hand experiences were the main means to collect the data.

Nineteen scheduled formal semi structured interviews (shown in following table) were also used mostly to gather additional data on the logics and to clarify or make sense of observations of the logics as they were identified. The interviews and conversations explored their views on the roles of each stakeholder, the interaction among stakeholders, the rules and regulations that guide the implementation, and the implementation practices in the project. These interviews ranged from 32 to 64 min and most of them were recorded, transcribed, and translated into English.

Remote interviews were conducted via Whatsapp or Zoom calls. Meetings, observations, and interviews were carried out in either Indonesian and/or English. Field notes, meeting minutes, and interview transcriptions in Indonesian were summarized by the first author into a research documentation in English (Table 2).

Data was analyzed as follows: First, we produced a timeline of events. We then divided the timeline into 3 main phases. From these three phases we chose vignettes that illustrate pivotal episodes in the partnership where divergent opinions represented from different actors played out in a harmony (vignette 1) leading to breakdowns (vignette 2 and 3). These events were related to institutional logics concepts for sensemaking of the vignettes.

We follow a pattern inducing method to identifying logics, that is we were engaged in a process of working from the observations and interview data up to identify logics that can then be compared with extant literature [24]. This approach was chosen because it allowed the researchers to capture context-specific information, explain values and beliefs, and represent rich context (*ibid.*) A starting point set of categories to identify logics provided by Jay [25] and Sligo et al. [17] was chosen to inspire sense-making baseline situations and problematic incidents in the vignettes, as well as to guide the discussion among the authors and to theorize the events, as no formal coding is involved in the analysis (Table 3).

We followed the methods used by Ismail, et al. [5] in choosing the vignettes. Throughout the project, we selected snapshots of events that meet the following criteria: 1) it involves all four main stakeholders in the core team, 2) reflects different types of interactions between logics. The data used in vignette construction were triangulated from

Table 2. Semi-structured interviews

Organization	Number of interviews informing this paper	Description
Ministry	1 management level 2 data managers	Data Center and Subdirectorate
Provinces	3 data managers	Bali, West Java, and the Special Region of Yogyakarta Province
Districts	1 program manager 3 district consultant 3 data managers	Districts in North Sumatra, Capital Region of Jakarta, Special Region of Yogyakarta, Maluku, and Western Nusa Tenggara Province
UGM	3 project team members	1 involved in vignette 1 and 2 2 involved in vignette 2 and 3
UiO	1 online course team member	
WHO	1 national and 1 international consultant	
Total interviews		18

Table 3. Institutional logics categories

Logic category	Explanation
Normativity/strategic imperatives	Normative and strategic functions
Source of agency/capacity to act	The agent/source of agency of the agents
Basis of order	Regulative rules, binding expectations, constitutive schema
Indicators	Performance metrics
Tensions within logic	Tensions within each logic due to internal and external powers, different domains or disciplines

multiple respondents, and from a combination of interview transcripts, meeting observations and participation notes, and digitization of other documentary materials. The vignettes were also reviewed by the other authors of this paper to reduce dangers of participatory bias.

3.1 Empirical Setting

The research followed a multiyear health information systems strengthening project in Indonesia. The project is funded by Global Fund and run under the aegis of the Ministry of Health (MoH) as the principal recipient, with technical and administrative support from UGM, WHO and UiO. The project mission was to develop and implement an integrated health data dashboard system using a web-based platform developed by UiO (Table 4).

Table 4. Timeline of key events

Vignette	Date	Event
1	16 Feb 2017	Basic training for implementation for core team (MoH, WHO, UGM)
1	Feb-Mar 2017	Roll out to 10 pilot districts
3	Aug 2017	MoH, WHO, UGM agreed to adopt the online course
1	Nov 2017–Feb 2018	First round of supervisory visit to 10 pilot districts
1	19 Feb 2018	Refresher training to 10 pilot districts (new features, data visualization skills, sustainability and scalability > district developing new plans)
3	23 Feb 2018	Kick off of the online course development
3	16 Mar 2018	Beta test the the online course to university partners of MoH in April
	14 Mar 2018	Roadmap development
2	24–27 Apr 2018	Training for Trainers for 50 expansion districts
2	6–10 June 201	Requesting feedback for the online course from the training participants
2	May 2018	Second round of supervisory visit to pilot districts
2	Jun 2018	Planning for semi advanced training
2	2–6 Jul 2018	Semi advanced training and beta testing the Online Course
2	1–5 Aug 2018	Roll out to several new districts
3	3 Aug 2018	The online course was tested for bigger audience (260 onsite participants)
3	27 Aug 2018	The online course was officially launched with main purpose for training of 50 expansion districts
3	31 Dec 2018	The online course was temporarily closed and evaluated
3	Jan 2019	The online course reopened
3	2019	MoH, UGM, WHO go to the field to train expansion districts
3	Dec 2019	The online course discontinued

The project is characterized by an international partnership, involving actors in the Ministry of Health, World Health Organization (WHO), national university (Universitas Gadjah Mada/UGM) and a foreign university (University of Oslo/UiO).

4   Findings and Analysis

The findings are presented below in the form of 3 vignettes followed by the analysis using the institutional logics frame.

4.1   Vignette 1: The Roll Out of the Health Platform

In this first vignette of the roll out process, we set the scene of an initial harmonious relationship between the ministry, the international organization, and the universities. The web-based platform was introduced in Indonesia in 2010 through the collaboration between a national university and a foreign university. Since then, various activities were conducted to initiate the implementation of the platform to improve health data quality through data integration and visualization.

A core team consisting of the Ministry of Health, national university, foreign university, WHO was developed in 2016. The team underwent a series of training and carried out assessment and other activities necessary to kickstart the implementation of the platform in the country. After these preparation activities, the team went on to the roll out phase to 10 pilot districts.

Roll out involves a set of predefined activities that were repeated across all districts. Although the team members who went to each district varied, it always consisted of the following: at least 1 representative of MoH, local university, foreign university, and WHO. The activities also remained the same: 3 days visit with the first day getting formal buy-in from the province.

"Although our implementation is top-down, we also need to visit the province to acknowledge that they are the host in the area" - MoH

This visit is a "door knocking" gesture to acknowledge the autonomy and power of the province despite the top-down implementation, as well as to introduce the team to the province [26]. The second day would be to the district. The team gets to know the responsible person in the district (the key person who will get the implementation going is usually from the district level), the last day is the training in the health care facilities. On the other hand, the provinces and districts assumed their role as the host with pride by introducing the visiting team to their traditional food and scenic places.

The core team members are based in different places in the world and for a roll out would fly in to gather in the first district and from there moving from one district to another together. They traveled together with different modalities, plane, car, boat sharing hotels, dining tables, weekends in numerous districts, and a bond was created along the way, both among the team members and with the local authorities.

Analysis. At the beginning of the project, different logics did not play out due to mutual understanding among the involved stakeholders. This vignette serves as an example of how the interaction dynamic met the requirements from each logic. First, MoH got to play their role as the host and their view of other stakeholders such as WHO, UGM, and UiO as the supporting team persisted. Second, WHO got to play their role as the quality controller and extension of MoH and they mitigated any possible pitfalls. They can maintain their agency through the following tools: monitoring, performance, initiatives, and moving the needles. Any failing perceptions towards each other were managed through communication within the close coordination and trust, thus mitigating things from getting too bad. Table 5 above shows the identification of main logics that characterize the two main actors groups as "hierarchy logic" and "accountability logic", where these two logics were obtained inductively through a grounded approach from the data.

Table 5. Institutional logics of MoH and WHO

Institutional logic	Ministry of health	WHO
Logic employed	Local public sector hierarchy logic	Accountability logic
Normativity/strategic imperatives	Public service, policy implementation, serving constituents - MoH view of themselves: host, ruler, owner - MoH view of WHO: supporting team (source of funding and/or technical and/or administrative assistance)	Public service, mission for health status and national - WHO view of MoH: ("clueless governor") - WHO view of themselves: quality controller, extension of the (MoH) hand, initiator, mover who keeps the ball rolling
Source of agency/capacity to act	Coordination of public resources, rule making, enforcement power - Primary actors in MoH: management officials	Monitoring, performance, excellence, initiatives, innovation, risk management - Primary actors in WHO: national professional officer, international officer
Basis of order	Regulative: law, rules, hierarchy, budget spent - MoH embodying constraint: budget and KPIs from donor, higher officials (president, general secretary), promotion	Normative expectations of stakeholders - WHO embodying constraint: acceptance from MoH, accountability from Evaluation Office & donors
Indicators	Donor rating, public perception	Results report, program budget
Tensions within logic	Tensions due to internal and external powers	Tensions due to global and local demands

4.2 Vignette 2: The Evaluation of Training

This vignette involves a story about the breakdown of the partnership originating from the competing "hierarchical logic" in the public sector and an "evaluation logic" from the WHO.

A decision was made to expand the implementation of the web-based platform to 50 more districts in 25 provinces while maintaining the implementation in the existing 10 pilot districts. With the size of expansion, it was not feasible for the core team to utilize the same roll out approach where they went to all the new districts. The team also wished that each province would take responsibility to scale and sustain the web-based platform implementation in their districts. For this, the provinces would need support. Therefore, the core team engaged 9 national universities called Center of Excellence Universities (CoEs).

Having all of these requirements in consideration, the team planned a series of cascade training to prepare a pool of trainers for the expansion. First, the core team, which only consisted of less than 10 people, trained a trainer team consisting of MoH staff. Second training was aimed for 25 new provinces. The rationale was that the province staff as the authority will take the responsibility. This second training would also involve 9 national universities. These universities would be the extending hand of the core team, responsible to assist the provinces and districts, with troubleshooting etc.

MoH took the responsibility as both organizer and trainers for the training. The training was mostly done by the MoH, with support from UiO and UGM, and WHO was not in the trainer list.

"We are competent to train. After this project is finished, we will be the contact for the field staff." - MoH

However, WHO perceived that the first training did not meet the quality needed to move forward with the implementation.

"We are frustrated because they (MoH) are not serious about that and because that this project is not for clinical use so they can get away with it" - WHO

In the previous phases of the implementation, MoH staff rarely fully attended training from beginning to end. Having this experience at hand, WHO considered that MoH was not competent enough to take the lead in the training.

"This project is not as good as it should be, is (mentioning one MoH staff) a trainer? Does he know how to train? Some people are skillful but they're not trained to train." - WHO

On this ground, UGM proposed that MoH staff join both training as trainees to ensure that they have the necessary skills both as trainers and implementers. However, MoH refused this proposal and insisted on conducting the training, whereas WHO, UGM, UiO as the support. WHO and UGM decided to provide a proof to the MoH. So they ran an evaluation of the training without asking input or opinion from the MoH. MoH perceived this behavior as disrespectful and as a consequence, MoH stopped involving UGM and WHO in several activities. Eventually, this conflict resided. As MoH communicated *"we are the host of this project, don't evaluate us behind our back"*. This situation eventually resolved and the team members started working together again.

Table 6. Analysis of vignette 2

Local public sector hierarchy logic	How hierarchy logic organizes MoH behavior in the field	Accountability logic	How accountability logic organizes MoH behavior in the field
Vignette 2: The evaluation of training of trainers			
MoH decided that they would lead and conduct the follow up training. The background: some districts worried that once the project is no longer funded, the project will be abandoned again and the districts will suffer	MoH uses the training to gain trust from the districts, that this is MoH owned project, where MoH as the governing body has a total control towards the project, to get the buy in from the districts	WHO proposed WHO, UGM, and UiO to be the trainers, and MoH to join as trainees	To maintain training quality, trainers for trainers should be highly competent, both technically and pedagogically
MoH flipped out. They stopped involving UGM in various planning and implementation events, and stopped responding to several communication attempts from UGM	MoH perceived the evaluation as disrespectful. This is an attempt to gain back control of the behavior of WHO, UGM, and UiO as the supporting team	Involving UGM, carrying an evaluation towards the training of trainers mainly led by MoH to provide evidence to support their proposal	Using evaluation as it's objective and measurable to represent performance

Analysis. This breakdown can be explained using the competing logics frame in Table 6. WHO employed "accountability logic" that relies on monitoring and evaluation principles. In this case, this translates as follows: skillful field staff (output) means quality training (process) delivered by quality trainers (input) organized in a quality manner (input) [27]. Although WHO approach to evidence-based policy is a common practice, it clashes with public sector logic where hierarchy and rapport are considered higher priority. MoH perceived this as a double crossing to MoH as the governor, when according to MoH WHO should support MoH.

In addition to the competency of the field staff, MoH finds the training as a valuable opportunity for the ministry in following ways. One, to obtain trust from the districts and provinces. During the roll out, we observed some hesitation from several districts to implement the system due to past history of *pilotitis*, introducing a new system or technology and then failing to maintain it. This left the districts having to deal with the system themselves without support from the ministry. It was critical for the ministry to get all the involved provinces and districts to be on board with this mission. A way to do that is by showing the provinces and districts that MoH is in control of the project, application. This can be achieved by showing that MoH is competent enough to run the training without major involvement from WHO or universities.

Second, this performance will also affect the portfolio of the MoH managers when it is time for promotion. Lastly, MoH viewed the backstage evaluation conducted by WHO as disrespect to MoH as the host of this project.

This vignette highlights the conflict between WHO's data logic and MoH's hierarchy logic. WHO used their logic of evaluation which was essentially to remove the Ministry from the leading position. This openly criticizing behavior was badly received by MoH. MoH employs public sector logic in which relationships are prioritized over data. This includes managing relationships, avoiding conflict, not openly criticizing. Public sector relationships are governed by rank, mentoring, age vs supremacy of data.

4.3   Vignette 3: The Introduction of Online Course

This third vignette highlights the rivalry between the logic of onsite training from the ministry and the logic of an online course from the international organization and universities. All the stakeholders were enthusiastic with the idea of using an online course for project expansion. The online course was planned to be a part of the capacity building framework, complementary to the training plan described in vignette 2. The rationale was the online course could save the project a significant amount of resources (money, time, and human resources). The idea started in August 2017 when the core team attended the annual conference where an online course was presented as a supplement to the implementation package. The team was supposed to localize and launch the online course so field staff are able to learn at their own pace independently [28].

> *"If we want to massively expand, the online course can save time and money. MoH develops the regulations from the top, we train with this course in the middle, and the field staff implement, simultaneously."* - WHO

The implementation faced several challenges. Firstly, one by one stakeholders dropped out from the development. MoH referred to the course as *"UGM's"* project, showing that they do not feel the ownership of the online course. WHO withdrew themselves from the online course development for a similar reason.

> *"Everyone thinks this is UiO and UGM's idea when we were the one who proposed in the report. They did not include us, maybe it's about money for a research project?"* - WHO

When the online course was ready to launch in August 2018, only UGM actively worked on the course. The timing was at the same time as MoH was about to conduct onsite training to 50 districts. Although they bought in the idea of developing an online course as part of the expansion plan, the onsite training budget was not changed at all. MoH remained having the budget for onsite training to 50 districts that had to be spent for the exact activity.

> *"How would I endorse the field staff to use the online course if the data in the application is still messy, or when we use the app and our data is wrong? That is disappointing"* - MoH

However, UiO requested MoH for the online course to be used as a means for project expansion. As the core team went once again to the field for expansion, approximately 1–2 h were allocated for either UGM or UiO to introduce the online course to each new district. In these one or two hours, the field staff usually managed to at least sign up to the online course and learn to navigate the online course. However, as this online course is self-paced, these staff who signed up were not followed up and the completion rate was very low [28]. The online course did not meet the development objectives and as no system was put in place to ensure the maintenance of the online course, the online course was neglected until UGM and UiO stopped the maintenance in December 2019.

Table 7. Analysis of vignette 3

Local public sector hierarchy logic	How hierarchy logic organizes MoH behavior in the field	Accountability logic	How accountability logic organizes WHO behavior in the field
Vignette 3: The introduction of online course			
Valuing hierarchy and collaboration especially with international stakeholders	Accepting an invitation to innovate for the country's benefit, regardless of the operational and management of the innovation at the later stage. The project can be delegated to lower level staff	Highly valuing innovation, resource efficiency, and project performance	Proposing the adoption of the online course in the expansion plan
Among the KPIs, budget expense rate is one of the most important. Capacity building activities within the expansion plan have been budgeted as onsite training	Onsite training must be completed for the budget to be spent, although an online course has been developed	Procedures to manage risk related to failure to fully implement the planned improvement agenda	WHO realized that in order to successfully implement an online course, a more fundamental institutional change must take place. However, the online course was ready for launch, therefore the online course was endorsed to be introduced during the onsite training

Analysis. The non adoption of the online course can be explained using the logics frame in Table 7. Introducing an online course within a capacity building institution presents an interaction between logics of online course and onsite training. Online courses rely on the learners as the active pursuant of the knowledge [29] while onsite training are traditionally instructor-led [30]. The logic of an online course is contested with the practice of onsite training established within the public sector logic. Onsite training is not about travel but it has representation of it being a social event [31] as well as space for career and financial progression (e.g. per diem[14]). Indonesia is a vast country with a lot of countries and islands of which is not easy to travel around. However, this provides the opportunity to network, to explore. The meeting is part of the institutionalized networking, mentorship and entertainment. There are businesses other than learning the skills and knowledge the training is delivering. The logic of onsite training is resistant to change.

When the core team agreed to innovate the capacity building model with an online course, they were all employing the onsite training logic. The assumption was that the online course would help the country train more people with less resources (time, human power, and money). The realization that there are changes within the fundamental institutional elements to implement this initiative successfully came later when the online course was in the development and implementation stage.

5   Conclusion

Interagency logics are relatively unexplored in the literature and are recognised as involved in significant failure of ICT4D projects. To date all of the literature has indicated that partnerships are significantly important but failure is commonplace, this paper contributes novel insight into institutional logics derived explanations for partnership failure between donors, international organizations and public sector implementers which are very important pieces for solving the jigsaw puzzle. This in depth longitudinal study initiates the exploration of the reality of partners working together. It builds on prior work [5] by adding novel forms of partnership and logics contributing to the failure of the partnership. The logics examined in this paper were limited to those of the ministry and international organization as they are pivotal in this partnership. Other logics visible on the practices of the other groups (foreign and national university), are outside the scope of this paper and can be addressed in future. Future work will continue to refine this conceptualisation.

References

1. Plamondon, K.M., Brisbois, B., Dubent, L., Larson, C.P.: Assessing how global health partnerships function: an equity-informed critical interpretive synthesis (2021). https://doi.org/10.1186/s12992-021-00726-z
2. Herrick, C., Brooks, A.: The binds of global health partnership: working out working together in Sierra Leone. Med. Anthropol. Q. 32(4), 520–538 (2018). https://doi.org/10.1111/maq.12462
3. Dodd, R., Schieber, G., Cassels, A., Fleisher, L., Gottret, P.: Aid effectiveness and health. In: Aid Effectiveness and Health (2007)
4. Pache, A.C., Santos, F.: Inside the hybrid organization: selective coupling as a response to competing institutional logics. Acad. Manag. J. 56(4), 972–1001 (2013). https://doi.org/10.5465/amj.2011.0405

5. Ismail, S.A., Heeks, R., Nicholson, B., Aman, A.: Analyzing conflict and its management within ICT4D partnerships: an institutional logics perspective. Inf. Technol. Dev. **24**(1), 165–187 (2018). https://doi.org/10.1080/02681102.2017.1320962

6. Reay, T., Hinings, C.R.: Managing the rivalry of competing institutional logics. Organ. Stud. **30**(6), 629–652 (2009). https://doi.org/10.1177/0170840609104803

7. Boonstra, A., Eseryel, U.Y., van Offenbeek, M.A.: Stakeholders' enactment of competing logics in IT governance: polarization, compromise or synthesis? Eur. J. Inf. Syst. 1–20 (2017). https://doi.org/10.1057/s41303-017-0055-0

8. Currie, W.L., Guah, M.W.: Conflicting institutional logics: a national programme for IT in the organisational field of healthcare. J. Inf. Technol. **22**(3), 235–247 (2007). https://doi.org/10.1057/palgrave.jit.2000102

9. Mizrachi, Y., Ben-Attar, D.: "Downtown" and "suburbia" public-private partnerships (PPP) in the application of information and communication technologies for development (ICT4D). In: Desivilya, H.S., Palgi, M. (eds.) The Paradox in Partnership: The Role of Conflict in Partnership Building, pp. 36–48. Bentham Science, Sharjah (2011). https://doi.org/10.2174/978160805211011101010036

10. Thornton, P.H., Ocasio, W.: Institutional logics. In: The Sage Handbook of Organizational Institutionalism, vol. 840, no. 2008, pp. 99–28 (2008)

11. World Health Organization Maximizing Positive Synergies Collaborative Group: An assessment of interactions between global health initiatives and country health systems. The Lancet **373**(9681), 2137–2169 (2009)

12. Sahay, S., Sæbø, J.I., Mekonnen, S.M., Gizaw, A.A.: Interplay of institutional logics and implications for deinstitutionalization: case study of HMIS implementation in Tajikistan. Inf. Technol. Int. Dev. **6**(3), 19 (2010)

13. Dodson, L.L., Sterling, S., Bennett, J.K.: Considering failure: eight years of ITID research. In: Proceedings of the 5th International Conference on Information and Communication Technologies and Development, pp. 56–64 (2012)

14. Sanner, T.A., Sæbø, J.I.: Paying per diems for ICT4D project participation: a sustainability challenge. Inf. Technol. Int. Dev. **10**(2), 33 (2014)

15. Skelcher, C., Smith, S.R.: Theorizing hybridity: Institutional logics, complex organizations, and actor identities: the case of nonprofits. Public Adm. **93**(2), 433–448 (2015). https://doi.org/10.1111/padm.12105

16. Stratton, C., Sholler, D., Bailey, D., Leonardi, P., Rodríguez-Lluesma, C.: Competing institutional logics in ICT4D education projects: a South American study. In: Proceedings of the Eighth International Conference on Information and Communication Technologies and Development, pp. 1–11 (2016). https://doi.org/10.1145/2909609.2909665

17. Sligo, J., Gauld, R., Roberts, V., Villa, L.: A literature review for large-scale health information system project planning, implementation and evaluation. Int. J. Med. Inform. **97**, 86–97 (2017). https://doi.org/10.1016/j.ijmedinf.2016.09.007

18. Burton-Jones, A., Akhlaghpour, S., Ayre, S., Barde, P., Staib, A., Sullivan, C.: Changing the conversation on evaluating digital transformation in healthcare: insights from an institutional analysis. Inf. Organ. **30**(1), 100255 (2020). https://doi.org/10.1016/j.infoandorg.2019.100255

19. Ramadani, L., Breidbach, C.F., Kurnia, S.: Investigating information and communication technology-enabled national development as a multi-level social process. Inf. Syst. J. (2022). https://doi.org/10.1111/isj.12381

20. Perkmann, M., Phillips, N., Greenwood, R.: Institutional arbitrage: how actors exploit institutional difference. Organ. Theory **3**(2) (2022). https://doi.org/10.1177/26317877221090313

21. Walsham, G.: Interpretive case studies in IS research: nature and method. Eur. J. Inf. Syst. **4**(2), 74–81 (1995). https://doi.org/10.1057/ejis.1995.9

22. Walsham, G.: Doing interpretive research. Eur. J. Inf. Syst. **15**(3), 320–330 (2006). https://doi.org/10.1057/palgrave.ejis.3000589

23. Benbasat, I., Goldstein, D.K., Mead, M.: The case research strategy in studies of information systems. MIS Q. 369–386 (1987)

24. Reay, T., Jones, C.: Qualitatively capturing institutional logics. Strateg. Organ. **14**(4), 441–454 (2016)

25. Jay, J.: Navigating paradox as a mechanism of change and innovation in hybrid organizations. Acad. Manag. J. **56**(1), 137–159 (2013). https://doi.org/10.5465/amj.2010.0772

26. Braa, J., Sahay, S., Lewis, J., Senyoni, W.: Health information systems in indonesia: understanding and addressing complexity. In: Choudrie, J., Islam, M., Wahid, F., Bass, J., Priyatma, J. (eds.) Information and Communication Technologies for Development, vol. 504, pp. 59–70. Springer, Cham (2017). https://doi.org/10.1007/978-3-319-59111-7_6

27. WHO, GAVI, the Global Fund and the World Bank. Monitoring and evaluation of health systems strengthening: an operational framework. Geneva, World Health Organization (2010). http://www.who.int/healthinfo/HSS_MandE_framework_Oct_2010.pdf

28. Chrysantina, A., Sanjaya, G., Pinard, M., Hanifah, N.: Improving health information management capacity with digital learning platform: the case of DHIS2 online academy. Procedia Comput. Sci. **161**, 195–203 (2019). https://doi.org/10.1016/j.procs.2019.11.115

29. Joosten, T., Cusatis, R.: Online learning readiness. Am. J. Distance Educ. **34**(3), 180–193 (2020). https://doi.org/10.1080/08923647.2020.1726167

30. Paul, T.V.: An evaluation of the effectiveness of e-learning, mobile learning, and instructor-led training in organizational training and development. Hampton University (2014)

31. Schaefer, T., Rahn, J., Kopp, T., Fabian, C.M., Brown, A.: Fostering online learning at the workplace: a scheme to identify and analyse collaboration processes in asynchronous discussions. Br. J. Edu. Technol. **50**(3), 1354–1367 (2019). https://doi.org/10.1111/bjet.12617

Reimagining Digital Technology for the "New Normal": A Feminist Approach to Freedom and Social Inclusion

Leaving No-One Behind? A Research Agenda for Queer Issues in ICT4D

Katherine Wyers[✉][iD]

University of Oslo, Oslo, Norway
katherwy@ifi.uio.no

Abstract. The ICT4D community, and the IFIP Working Group 9.4, is bound by a shared interest in social emancipation through digital technologies. The Sustainable Development Goals (SDG) are often evoked to highlight the many social, economic, and environmental arenas where we are active. However, a perspective centring on queer issues is notably absent from our various mission statements. In this paper, I present a research agenda for queer issues in ICT4D to address this absence. I examine the literature that presents such a perspective in information systems and ICT4D, exploring the challenges that the invisibility of queer issues leads to. For LGBTQ+ people, this absence causes barriers and hesitancy in engaging with public services, and worse, the perpetuation and amplification of systematic discrimination. As researchers, developers, and practitioners, we can and should adopt a more inclusive approach, building on past experiences with ICT to address the plights of marginalized groups.

Keywords: LGBTQ+ · Transgender · Queer · Information systems · ICT4D · Queering scholarship

1 Introduction

1.1 Overview

In this paper, I propose a research agenda to introduce a queer, trans-feminist, intersectional perspective in ICT4D research and practice. I aim to highlight the gaps in literature, discuss the issues that these gaps are having on a vulnerable population, and present a research agenda that the ICT4D community can use to approach these topics. I introduce some of the issues that emerge as information systems and ICT4D interventions continue to impact on the lives of LGBTQ+ populations, leading to challenges in accessing vital services, healthcare, housing, social protection and employment. I describe research streams conducted in related fields of technology, data-systems and data justice, and use these to highlight possible avenues to begin exploring this topic in ICT4D research. Finally, based on this I present a research agenda for queer information systems research within ICT4D.

What We Talk About When We Talk About LGBTQ+ People. There are certain challenges that arise when attempting to define communities that do not conform to socially-constructed norms of sexual orientation and/or gender identity and expression. There is no unequivocally agreed-upon term to describe such communities in a way that is sufficiently inclusive whilst recognising and respecting that western terms such as LGBTQ+ may not be universally accepted. The Fa'afafine people of Samoa do not have the same experiences as the Hijra populations in India, or the Two-spirit people of native America, or people across the Global North and beyond who identify as transgender men or transgender women. The communities of self-identified non-homosexual men who have sex with men (MSM) have different experiences than gay men. Likewise, intersex people have distinct experiences, separate from the experience of other LGBTQ+ communities. While many people within these communities do not identify with LGBTQ+, there are shared experiences across all these communities that are connected to cisnormativity and heteronormativity. Judith Butler shows us that language influences society, literature and philosophy since "its dimensions of dynamism enable humans to establish themselves as gendered subjects" [1]. Therefore, in presenting this paper, I spent significant time considering the use of language, and how to refer to a broad, diverse, globally-distributed population. To this effect, I have chosen the term "sexual orientation, gender identity and expression" (SOGIE) as a broad term to refer to the source of the violence and discrimination experienced by these communities, and "lesbian, gay, bisexual, transgender, queer, other" (LGBTQ+) as the broad term to refer to members of these communities. LGBTQ+ here includes populations such as the Hijra in India, men who have sex with men (MSM), Fa'afafine in Samoa, Two-spirit people in native American culture, and all other groups who do not identify with identities that in western countries are referred to as cisgender and/or heterosexual. While there are drawbacks to using such a term, not least that LGBTQ+ is a term originating from the global North and many communities do not identify as LGBTQ+, I have chosen this acronym because it is widely recognised in the research community and is broadly inclusive with the intent to highlight the issues that affect many of the people in these diverse, globally-distributed communities.

Terminology. In this paper, there are several terms that are commonly used within the LGBTQ+ community. For readers unfamiliar with these terms, Table 1 describes how I use these terms. While the issues raised are often broadly applicable to all members of the LGBTQ+ communities, at times throughout this paper, specific communities are highlighted to illuminate individual cases where issues are felt most acutely.

The Intersectional Lens. Intersectionality is a tool for analysing how our complex identities and group memberships overlap to form our whole selves. The term was coined by Kimberlé Crenshaw in 1990 [4], when she found that women of colour had fewer opportunities because of the combined disadvantages of their gender identity and race. Everyone has multiple identities, be it their race, gender identity, poverty-status, sexual orientation or another identity, and each identity has a positive or negative impact on the person's experiences and opportunities in life. An intersectional lens allows the researcher to analyse each identity individually, and helps us to see how the combined effects of these identities interlock. The lens can help when discussing the diversity,

Table 1. Definitions of key terms used within the LGBTQ+ community

Cisgender	A person who is not transgender. A person who identifies with the gender assigned to them at birth
Cisnormative	The assumption that all human beings are cisgender
Intersectional (research perspective)	A research perspective that takes into account how people's social identities can overlap, creating different modes of discrimination and privilege [2]
LGBTQ+	Lesbian, Gay, Bisexual, Transgender, Queer, and others - Broad umbrella term used to describe a large population of people. The plus symbol is intended to be more inclusive, denotes people who are not heterosexual or cisgender but who do not identify as one of the labels of LGBTQ. For example, asexual or pansexual. As discussed earlier, the acronym LGBTQ+ is used in this paper to refers to Hijra, Two-spirited people, Fa'afafine, MSM and other communities who are not heterosexual and/or cisgender
Non-binary people	People assigned either male or female at birth who do not identify with either male or female
Queer (identity)	A term that was formerly considered a slur. It has been reclaimed and refers now to a way of living in which people consciously challenge cisgender heterosexual norms
Queer (research perspective)	A term that has broadly been associated with the study and theorisation of gender and sexual practices that exist outside of heterosexuality, and which challenge the notion that heterosexuality and cisgender is "normal". Queer theorists are often critical of essentialist views of sexuality and gender. Instead, they view these as socially constructed
SOGIE	Sexual orientation, gender identity and expression
Trans-feminist (research perspective)	This is a perspective that emerged from queer theory. It critiques queer theory and feminist theory for its focus on sexuality and lack of representation of transgender identities
Transgender	An umbrella term used to describe people whose gender identity or expression does not conform to that typically associated with the sex they were born as or assigned to at birth [3]
Transgender men	People assigned female at birth who identify as male
Transgender women	People assigned male at birth who identify as female

equality and inclusion within a group, and to build an equitable space where everyone has equal opportunities. Here, the intersectional lens is used to consider how LGBTQ+ identities interlock with other identities such as race, poverty-status and social status to create layers of oppression that lead to inequities. Within ICT4D, identities can be additionally complex as LGBTQ+ people have roles in technology development [5], international aid [6], and direct and indirect users of technology [7–9], often bringing people from different contexts together, across geographical and cultural borders.

Queering Scholarship. The "queering" of scholarship is a process of adjusting research methodologies to make queer identities visible. This approach, emerging from queer theory and feminist theory, seeks to subvert the taken-for-granted assumptions in society that invisibilise people with queer identities [10]. It assumes that sex, sexuality and gender identity are fluid, and it questions the societal assumptions that are based on stable, cisgender, heterosexual identities [11]. This fluidity of sex, sexuality and gender identity has implications for research, indicating that there is a greater degree of diversity than understood in the past. With this research agenda, I present how this understanding of gender identity, sex and sexuality can guide ICT4D research to reveal insights that, until now, have been rendered invisible.

1.2 SDGs and LGBTQ+ Communities

The Sustainable Development Goals (SDGs) are a major benchmark for development organisations and a framework often referred to in ICT4D literature. Their core mission is to "leave no-one behind". However, seven areas within the SDGs have been identified where the lack of explicit inclusion of LGBTQ+ people risk their exclusion from development projects. These seven areas are (1) poverty, (2) health, (3) education, (4) gender equality and women's empowerment, (5) economic growth and opportunity, (6) safe resilient sustainable cities and human settlements and (7) justice and accountability [12].

   With regards to the poverty-related SDGs (SDG1 and SDG3), same-sex families are more likely to be poor than heterosexual families, and social protections are created around the heterosexual family structure, often excluding people who have different sexual orientations or gender expressions [13]. Within healthcare, there is a need to raise awareness about the health rights of people who are not cisgender or not heterosexual, beyond the scope of HIV-programmes and men who have sex with men [14]. There is a need for greater inclusion of LGBTQ+ relationships in sex education programmes, highlighting absences and active avoidance of these topics [12]. The gender-equality issues raised by SDG5 treat gender through the lens of cisnormativity and heteronormativity, and this should be broadened to incorporate transgender people in gender equality discourse [15]. Vandeskog et al. [16] have further critiqued the SDG5 for its failure to define gender, and for conflating the concept of gender with the term "woman". To promote economic growth and opportunities for LGBTQ+ people, and to ensure safe access to accommodation, the SDGs should be expanded to promote workplace anti-discrimination laws for people who are not heterosexual and people who are not cisgender. This promotes stability and reduces the risk of poverty [12, 17, 18]. By promoting the abolition of discriminatory laws that actively cause emotional, physical and economic harm to LGBTQ+ people, development organisations following the SDGs will be proactively helping LGBTQ+ people build better, safer and more dignified lives [12].

1.3 ICT4D and LGBTQ+ Communities: The Queer Divide

The ICT4D field aims to protect vulnerable people. Since early ICT4D studies in the 1980s, the field has been motivated by the interest in "developing countries", and since 2001 the field has been increasingly concerned with the ethical motivations of engaging ICTs for socio-economic development [19, 20]. The SDGs, and the SDG agenda, have been used as benchmarks for many studies in the field. The lack of reference to LGBTQ+ communities in the SDGs should be cause for concern, as the SDGs are a major benchmark motivating research in ICT4D [21], and risks the "leaving behind" of a substantial population. If ICT4D is to understand the adoption, use and subsequent impact of ICTs in developing societies [22], the field needs a more thorough understanding of the vulnerable communities it engages, and an assessment of vulnerability that transcends the binaristic focus that the field has adopted so far.

Raftree [5] discusses how, within the global South, there is an emergence of the "queer divide", where a divide appears to be emerging between LGBTQ+ people and people who are both cisgender and heterosexual. She suggests that this is as a result of people being forced to disengage from "normal" society so as to lead their authentic lives in safety.

Van Zyl and McLean [9] take a queer-feminist perspective in ICT4D, raising concerns about the impact of contact tracing on the privacy of LGBTQ+ communities, recommending that further research be conducted in ICT4D using "a critical intersectional feminist approach which account for the lived experiences of the most vulnerable, while critically considering the concentration of power over access to personal data".

If ICT4D really is to "leave no one behind" it needs, in the first place, to deal with the binary and, arguably cisnormative assumptions that underpin its literature. Such assumptions are found even in the most recent landscape papers of the field: Walsham [20] poses the question of gender in terms of the advantages ICTs can bring for women. This binaristic understanding of the problem unfortunately silences queer perspectives, confining the analysis of socio-economic development advantages to traditional and crystallised gender roles. While recent works [9] and calls for papers [23] take such perspectives as the center of their attention, ICT4D lexicon still tends to be framed in binary terms that preclude the discussions made in this paper from happening, and LGBTQ+ communities to have a voice in the global agenda on "leaving no one behind".

While there has been little discussion of LGBTQ+ issues in peer-reviewed ICT4D academic discourse, these issues have been discussed in other outlets. In 2015, the Technology Salon in New York held a conference on ICTs and LGBTQ+ rights to discuss the challenges and possibilities. Central to this discussion was the role of the Internet and mobile devices for building communities, and the concerns of surveillance and privacy that this increased connectedness creates. When LGBTQ+ issues are discussed in ICT4D, the focus tends to be on LGBQ people, omitting transgender and intersex people. Concerns were also raised at the conference by LGBTQ+ practitioners who gave a voice to the LGBTQ+ communities. This decision lead to them "outing" themselves, which they discovered was a trade-off that compromised the opportunities they had in their future careers. Therefore, there exists a paradox in ICT4D whereby LGBTQ+ practitioners are crucial to the ICT4D field to identify the issues, while at the same time their LGBTQ+ identities place them as personal risk, sometimes with grave consequences, due to the cultural and legal contexts of many countries where ICT4D work is conducted [5].

2 Motivation for Including Queer Issues in ICT4D

I have discussed the absence of a queer-feminist perspective in peer-reviewed ICT4D outlets. I now introduce my motivations in presenting a new research agenda to include queer issues in ICT4D. The section opens with an outline of discriminations experienced by LGBTQ+ communities, and how information systems influence this discrimination.

2.1 Discrimination of LGBTQ+ Populations

LGBTQ+ people account for a large percentage of the world's population, and a recent survey in the US indicates that the number of people identifying as LGBTQ+ is growing. The study revealed that 9.1% of those born between 1981 and 1996 identify as LGBTQ+, with the number increasing to 15.9% for those born between 1997 and 2002 [24].

Despite the growing number of LGBTQ+ -identifying people, these populations continue to experience discrimination, with high levels of social, legal, political and employment hostility, violent assault and healthcare discrimination [25]. This is a global problem, affecting people in the Global North and the Global South.

In the US, 41% of transgender people experience discrimination related to healthcare [26], with similar discrimination documented in Brazil [27]. In Indonesia, transgender populations experience rejection, misidentification, harassment, correction and bureaucratic discrimination [28]. In 2021, two transgender women in Cameroon were arrested and sentenced to five years in prison for "public indecency" simply for visiting a restaurant [29]. In India, transgender people are deemed "deviants" and are subject to victimisation and discrimination that manifests in name-calling, exclusion, rejection, outright harassment, and violence. This leads to physical and mental distress [30]. Despite Ireland's progressive LGBTQ+ rights, transgender discrimination leads a huge percentage (78%) of the transgender population considering suicide [31]. Despite the systematic discrimination of many transgender people [32], Shon Faye notes that the public debate on these issues has remained shallow, distracting from the core concerns experienced by LGBTQ+ people:

> As trans people face a broken healthcare system – which in turn leaves them with a desperate lack of support both with their gender and the mental health impacts of the all-too-commonly associated problems of family rejection, bullying, homelessness and unemployment – trans people with any kind of platform or access have tried to focus media reporting on these issues, to no avail. Instead, we are invited on television to debate whether trans people should be allowed to use public toilets. [33]

2.2 Information Systems and LGBTQ+ Populations

Information systems risk the perpetuation of transgender discrimination and create challenges for LGBTQ+ communities. I have identified three sources where these challenges emerge from:

(1) Digital Representation: the data models used to represent people,
(2) Data-processing Systems: the technical systems used to collect, update, aggregate and analyse data,
(3) Visibility: the impact of the inclusion of LGBTQ people in the data-sets.

One of the lenses used in the literature to examine our topic is that of data justice. Data justice is defined as "fairness in the way people are made visible, represented and treated as a result of their production of digital data" [34]. Taylor [34] argues that, for establishing the rule of law, a world in which people are datafied – meaning, converted into digital data – requires a concept of "data justice" beyond ordinary justice [35]. Data injustice can occur, as illustrated below, in ways that result in LGBTQ+ discrimination.

Digital Representation: Data Models Used to Represent People. Data is not just a set of facts for satisfying curiosity; it is the fundamental basis for decision making in modern organizations. The way data is represented has long been known to have impact on inclusion and exclusion [36]. Rendering gender non-conforming people illegible, thus invisible, and finally non-existent in data systems undermines their representation in data-driven processes. Johnson [8] noted that "as data-driven decisions become increasingly the norm, attention to values, building for pluralist rather than unitary purposes, and inclusivity in the design process will become critical elements of information systems design". Milan et al. [37] similarly note how data injustice can result by omitting non-legible people from the provisions resulting from relevant systems, such as social protection and humanitarian aid.

The approach to representing gender within an information system can have serious implications for individual civil rights protection for people whose reality is shaped by the socio-technical systems that "manage and create what [transgender people] will be understood to deserve" [38]. This representation of gender as a binary is not just an issue of self-actualisation. It has practical consequences related to justice and access to services, with ramifications for the access of transgender people to healthcare services such as HIV testing [39]. Despite the pressing need to resolve these issues, the design of information systems has proved to be inadequate for dealing with gender-variance. Despite the social changes taking place in many countries, "information technology systems [...] remain inflexible for the purposes of recording multifactor gender information" [40].

The representation of gender and gender-diversity in an information system leads to several other manifestations of discrimination or ignorance. A study by Kirkland [38] reviewing complaints to healthcare providers highlighted how complaints that had arisen from transgender discrimination were miscategorised and silenced. Public health advertisements based on traditional gender representations create barriers for transgender men for cervical cancer screening [41] and breast-cancer screening [42]. These issues of binary gender representation are difficult to resolve. Even the most progressive information system designers are bound to the wider institutions of gender representation. In

2014, Facebook expanded its list of gender representation to 52. However, it received harsh criticism when it was discovered that they were aggregating this data to a binary representation in order to remain interoperable with marketing platforms [43].

Data-Processing Systems: Technical Systems Used to Collect, Update, Aggregate and Analyse Data. The design of a data-processing system impacts on LGBTQ+ people. Information systems are sites for political contestation and should be viewed as important loci for efforts to promote social justice. The technical systems embody political values and have the potential to be significant contributors to social injustices affecting groups of LGBTQ+ people [8]. For example, restricting the ease with which a gender-field can be updated in an information system leads to many barriers for the ability of transgender people to exist in public spaces and access vital services. In one recent example from 2020, the mismatches between identification documentation and personal gender presentation meant that 5 million transgender people in India could not access the funds and food rations made available as a response to the pandemic lockdown [44].

ICTs and digital identities impact on the ability of an LGBTQ+ person to access employment. Mismatches between gender presentation and digital identities create barriers to employment. In a case from Vietnam, a transgender person reported that they experienced discrimination when applying for employment. The gender indicated on their identity documents did not match with their gender presentation, and it was not possible to update the identity documents. As a result, the person could not access employment [45]. This reflects Heeks and Renken's [46] notion of structural data injustice, reflecting how structural injustices present in society tend to be crystallised and reflected in a datafied world.

The increased reliance of ICTs on facial recognition algorithms leads to issues for transgender and non-binary people, such as classification of images and their potential to reinforce binary gender structures. A recent study showed that a commonly used gender recognition algorithm was unable to correctly label non-binary people [47].

Visibility - Impact of the Inclusion of LGBTQ+ People in Data-Sets. SOGIE-related violence affects people's ability to access employment [45], healthcare [39] and other vital services [44]. As noted by Milan et al. [37], there is a strong thread of continuity between invisibilisation of people and data injustices perpetrated on them [48, 49]. LGBTQ+ people must be visible in national statistics so that governments can include them in planning decision for healthcare and public services. However, in most countries in the world, it is unsafe for an individual to be identifiable as being LGBTQ+. This leads to a paradox, whereby the population must be both visible for national statistics and invisible for the safety of the individual and the population. If population-based surveys do not include items that identify LGBTQ+ people, this limits public health surveillance and the ability to provide healthcare services [50].

If an information system exposes a person as being a member of the LGBTQ+ community, this can lead to discrimination and harassment. For example, within the healthcare domain, there is a move to include gender identity in electronic health records. However, many transgender and gender non-conforming people do not feel safe with this as they are concerned that it will lead to discrimination and harassment at the point of care, or if the information is shared or the data exposed [51]. There are concerns in other areas, such as digital identity systems, where the status of a person's gender identity or sexual orientation can become exposed and lead to issues in employment, education or other services. While the increased visibility can lead to greater public awareness about the existence of LGBTQ+ populations, there are examples of how this visibility fuels a backlash and increased political opposition [33].

3 Approaches Being Explored in Related Fields

I have outlined key terminology, presented an overview of the sources of discrimination, and discussed how these issues relate to ICT4D. I now present some promising research being conducted in related fields that explore potential approaches for addressing some of the issues raised.

3.1 LGBTQ+ Inclusion in the SDGs

In the Mills [12] report described earlier, the SDGs were critiqued for their lack of explicit inclusion of LGBTQ+ people. She makes several recommendations for how international development actors can develop a more inclusive understanding of the SDGs and implement them in a way that is more inclusive. She recommends that actors involve members of the LGBTQ+ communities when developing programmes, and that they should explicitly include LGBTQ+ communities in all programmes. Awareness should be raised among delivery partners and staff of the need to include LGBTQ+ communities to maintain the "leave no one behind" promise. When reporting on outcomes, report on SOGIE-related success stories and link the successes to the SDGs. International actors should use their influence to lobby for greater inclusion of LGBTQ+ communities in international development frameworks [12]. Vandeskog et al. [16] caution against the limited use of the term "gender" in the SDG agenda, arguing that the concept of gender is too often conflated with "woman". They recommend a broader understanding of the term when applying the SDG framework.

3.2 Embodiment of Prejudice in Information Systems

Queer bodies have traditionally been sites of both regulation and resistance in information systems. By adopting the use of queer theory, we can explore embodiment and affect beyond physical practices, pointing research practices to become better attuned to embodied and affective power dynamics. It allows researchers to "draw connections between bodies and feelings that necessarily factor into any information interaction" [52]. Studies in human-computer interaction are exploring how prejudices become embodied within systems. The inscription of LGBTQ+ prejudice within information systems often occurs unintentionally through a lack of awareness rather than through malicious intent. Despite the lack of an intent, this embodiment of prejudice leads to many challenges for LGBTQ+ people, perpetuating oppressions for many years and amplifying existing inequalities, reinforcing stereotypes and exposing vulnerable populations to discrimination [53].

3.3 Participatory Design

Several studies are exploring the role that queer, transgender and other LGBTQ+ communities can play in the design of ICTs. Haimson et al. [7] conducted studies to assess the effect of involving transgender people in the design process for ICTs. The study found that a number of novel solutions emerged during the design process, and concluded that there was a need for a community-based intersectional approach when developing technologies that affect transgender people. A recent study by Brulé and Spiel [54] explored how children with queer and disabled identities can be involved in the participatory design process. They find that participatory design allows participants to explore roles and identities and leads to solutions that better meet their needs. They also bring insight to the challenges for LGBTQ+ people who are conducting research. LGBTQ+ researchers are under heightened scrutiny when conducting research, and they are under pressure to reflect on their own convictions and how this could impact the participatory approach. Cisgender heterosexual people are not expected to reflect on their beliefs about gender identity or sexual orientation. This is despite the fact that cisgender heterosexual people also bring their individual normative identities and this can impact on the participatory process, such as assuming a participant is heterosexual and cisgender [54].

3.4 Algorithmic Bias

Algorithmic bias, a form of data injustice perpetrated by computer systems that create unfair outcomes, emerges across the studies reviewed here. In a study of transgender people in the UK who sought to correct the gender on their ID cards, Hicks [55] found explicit attempts to make it impossible to conduct such an operation through the UK government's computer systems. Beyond instances of transphobic algorithmic bias, the paper looks at people's resistance against them, resulting in the exposure and rediscussion of the system in point. By inscribing users into categories and targeting specific ones, algorithmic bias generates situations of systemic injustice for the affected people [56].

In their study of gender classification in commercial facial analysis and image labelling services, Scheuerman et al. [47] unpack algorithmic biases implicit in automated gender recognition. In studying how gender is encoded into such services, they find systemic worse performance on recognition of transgender individuals and universal inability to recognise non-binary genders. Their problematisation pertains to both classifiers and data standards: classification, they find, is systemically predetermined on binary terms, resulting into inability of systems to conceive non-traditional gender roles and account for them through data. This results again in the perpetuation of bias, with significant impacts on the lives of the affected individuals.

Spiel et al. [57] introduce a non-binary perspective in the field of human-computer interaction (HCI). Through the narration of "stylised slice-of-life" reports, they narrate encounters with technology that, ranging from software for university application to face recognition systems, can be marginalising and, to the extreme, violent and risky to non-binary people. Narrated instantiations span the fields of lived life (from visiting a shop to crossing an international border) to encounters occurred as non-binary researchers in the academic space. Proposing to "patch the gender bugs" of the HCI field, Spiel et al. [57]

illustrate how elements of contextualised technology, common to ICT4D, can represent risks for non-binary people that HCI research needs to tackle.

Relatedly, DeVito et al. [58] discuss routes to support LGBTQ+ researchers and research across different disciplines. Their work starts from the point that many disciplines, similarly to ICT4D, do not clearly tackle or give sufficient space to perspectives beyond the binary and cisnormative. They note how, differently from that, Queer HCI is becoming a substantial part of the broader field, and devise routes for other fields to openly embrace LGBTQ+ perspectives. In doing so, they focus on the creation of a Special Interest Group (SIG) in the core HCI conference, a proposal that other communities, including the ICT4D one, have the elements and ability to undertake.

3.5 Designing for Marginalised Populations

While illuminating the forms of data injustice detailed above, research also shows how technology can be designed for inclusive and, particularly, intersectional purposes, tackling diverse forms of oppression. This idea is reflected in Costanza-Chock's [59] notion of design justice, which conceives technology design as built towards collective liberation of oppressed community. Advocated, in Costanza-Chock's book "design justice", is a form of justice where design is oriented to challenging intersectional sources of domination.

One operationalisation of the notion of design justice is found in the work of Erete et al. [60]. Looking at established research on participatory design, they note how marginalised groups have historically not been taken into specific account in design processes. To explicitly engage communities at the margins, they propose a reflection on design for underserved communities, illustrating ways in which technology – rather than just producing injustice – can increase people's ability to challenge such sources of oppression. Resonating with these ideas, Rohm and Martins [61] devise routes through which technology can be adapted to voice LGBTQ+ communities during the COVID-19 pandemic.

3.6 Health Information Use Within LGBTQ+ Communities

Wagner et al. [53] explores the approaches to data use that transgender communities take. The study seeks to highlight the need for healthcare providers to work more closely with transgender people when designing information systems. These communities have data practices that have emerged from decades of oppression and persecution; practices that maintain privacy and anonymity and seek to protect members of the community. The study concluded that closer engagement with transgender people will lead health information system designers to create more inclusive systems that better serve the population.

3.7 Representation of Gender Variance in Digital Identities

In recent years, researchers have come to understand both gender and sex as a continuum rather than binary states of "male" and "female". While the concept of a gender continuum is not new, it has been increasingly normalized over the past decade [62]. This shift towards a pluralist understanding of gender creates challenges for information systems designers, where gender has traditionally been represented as a binary. The gender binary system is a social construct, created to classify the gender and sex continua [63]. This classification leads to inaccuracies in the way individuals are classified and, therefore, represented. 'There may not be gender categories available to adequately record the individual's [gender identity], and there are often no […] fields available to record gender information other than [gender identity]' [40].

4   Queering ICT4D Scholarship: What Does It Look like?

I propose the introduction of a critical, queer, trans-feminist, intersectional perspective into ICT4D and IS research. This perspective will have an impact on several key areas. The trans-feminist, queer perspective highlights new issues experienced by a marginalised group who are exposed to discrimination through the design and use of information systems. Introducing this perspective into the ICT4D discourse would serve to highlight the unique needs that these communities have, and how design decisions impact on their ability to lead lives with dignity.

4.1 Serving LGBTQ+ Populations

By studying ICTs using a critical, queer, trans-feminist, intersectional perspective, the research efforts highlight new issues experienced by a large population who have been historically silenced. The perspective highlights the pitfalls that are experienced by neglecting these issues; pitfalls whereby large populations are under-served with healthcare services and are exposed to discrimination. Using this lens, we can become more aware of the issues that exist. We can find solutions that lead to a reduction in the discrimination of this vulnerable population. This lens highlights unique socio-technical issues, exposing complex challenges and requiring novel approaches to the ethical and data-representation challenges faced by LGBTQ+ populations in ICT4D.

4.2 Serving Other Marginalised Populations

While many of the issues raised in this paper relate directly to the experiences of transgender and other LGBTQ+ communities, the challenges can also be broadly understood as issues related to serving other vulnerable, marginalised communities such as religious minorities and ethnic minorities. Many of the privacy and ethical issues experienced by LGBTQ+ people in relation to information systems are also experienced by other minorities. Groups such as ethnic minorities and religious minorities experience ongoing oppressions because of several of the challenges raised here. Using a queer, trans-feminist, intersectional perspective on research not only highlights issues experienced by queer populations. It also highlights issues experienced by other populations and has the potential to unearth novel solutions that are broadly applicable to other vulnerable populations.

4.3 Richer Understanding of Data

A queer, trans-feminist, intersectional perspective looks for the data that is absent as well as the data that is present. As Catherine Lord said of the analysis of historical records to identify LGBTQ+ people: 'we find our archive between the lines' [64]. The perspective assumes that LGBTQ+ people exist now and have existed in the past. By analysing historical data using this perspective, we can look for the people who we know existed, but who have been invisibilised through limitations in the design of data-collection systems, or through unintentional or malicious exclusion. By recognising queerness in historical data, these datasets can give richer insight into statistics, including healthcare analytics. For example, by recognising a patient as having been transgender, their diagnosis, treatment, healthcare service experience and health outcome can be better understood. This gives invaluable knowledge that can be used for treatment plans for other transgender patients.

5 Queer Issues in ICT4D: A Research Agenda

Despite the promise of the SDGs to "leave no one behind" [12], there is evidence to suggest that this promise is not being met for all populations on account of the absence of its reference to LGBTQ+ people and the impact this absence has. The field of ICT4D research is motivated by engagement with human socio-economic needs and should therefore be proactive in addressing the issues raised. The SDGs are a list of targets to achieve by 2030. The ICT4D field should not wait until the SDG time-period ends before it begins to address these issues. They are impacting people now, and the research should be conducted to determine how LGBTQ+ issues can be addressed within the field of ICT4D [16].

The research agenda outlined below proposes seven streams of research that ICT4D researchers can engage with to begin addressing these issues. It builds on the work taking place in related fields of research. It is informed by the SDG recommendations made by Mills [12], Matthyse [15] and Vandeskog et al. [16], encouraging ICT4D researchers and system designers to create strategies that are more inclusive of LGBTQ+ people, encouraging more research related to the unique needs of LGBTQ+ people and to tackle the experiences of populations who are being excluded based on SOGIE. While there are many areas of research that can and should be explored through a critical, queer, trans-feminist, intersectional lens, I proposed the following seven streams of research to begin exploring queer approaches to research in the field of ICT4D.

Stream 1 is concerned with the processes whereby prejudice manifests within ICT system design. Stream 2 explores the ethical and moral obligations that ICT developers have to limit the harm their systems cause to LGBTQ+ people. Stream 3 aims to ensure that queer voices are heard during ICT development. Stream 4 is concerned with how inequities created by ICTs affect LGBTQ+ people's sense of self. Stream 5 seeks to expand ICT development to be inclusive by design, and explores how this can be be achieved. Stream 6 aims to safely raise visibility of LGBTQ+ people. Stream 7 seeks to ensure that LGBTQ+ people working in ICT4D are safe from violence when carrying out their work.

Stream 1: How LGBTQ+ Prejudices Become Embodied Within Systems

> While many healthcare providers are not intentionally trans-exclusionary, the design of healthcare information systems rely on cis-normative values, thus excluding many [transgender and non-binary people] from accessing healthcare in comfortable and safe ways [53].

This area of research explores how LGBTQ+ prejudice becomes embodied within information systems. It investigates how cisnormativity and heteronormativity become established and maintained, and how these normativities influence the design decisions that are taken. It seeks to find approaches to information system design that limit the risk of embodiment of transgender prejudice and LGBTQ+ prejudice.

Stream 2: The Role of Information System Designers in Fighting Discrimination in the Global South

> Whatever our role, we are designers of information. Our choices alter the presentation and flow of human knowledge. We control how people find, understand, and use information in every facet of their lives. We must be very, very careful [65].

This topic explores the moral and ethical obligation that information system designers and developers have in ensuring that their systems do not perpetuate oppressions. It asks who should take the responsibility for resolving the issues that arise, and how these issues can be addressed. It investigates what role the system designers should take in affecting change, and what influence they should exert in the design and implementation of their systems to guide users towards a more equal information system and more equal society. It explores what role system designers have in ensuring that their systems are not used to embody prejudices and amplify inequalities. Within the ICT4D field, this topic deals with the ethics of knowledge-sharing between the global North and the global South. It explores the influence that system designers can and should have in pushing for better guidance in the use of their systems [66].

Stream 3: Involving LGBTQ+ People in ICT4D Participatory Design

> Nothing about us without us [67].

When designing information systems that will affect LGBTQ+ people, LGBTQ+ people should be involved in the design process. This stream of research explores the role that LGBTQ+ communities should play as value advocates in the design of information systems. It investigates what impact their involvement has on the system design and the wider impact that the system subsequently has on the perpetuation of discrimination and access to services. It explores the challenges of including LGBTQ+ populations in the design of systems within the ICT4D context, gathering their input while simultaneously ensuring that their identities remain private.

Stream 4: The Impact of ICTs on LGBQT+ People's Sense of Self and Sense of Capacity to Achieve

> As transgender people, we do not expect that we can have a long-term marriage (Transgender person in Vietnam, quoted by Oosterhoff [45]).

This stream of research investigates the role that ICTs have on the capability of LGBTQ+ people to envision a future where they lead lives with dignity. It explores how ICTs influence members of the LGBTQ+ communities in their vision for what they can achieve in their lives. People can only know what they can achieve if they are aware that it is achievable and available to them [68]. There are many countries where access to legal gender recognition is only available if a person has completed a set of medical interventions such as hormone replacement therapy or surgeries. People's sense of self becomes entangled in their ability to access these medical interventions, leaving people in limbo and "dehumanised" as the glacial process of access to these interventions proceeds [69]. In many countries, the access to legal gender recognition necessitates completing a set of these medical interventions. The barriers in healthcare and ongoing discrimination lead to people restricting what they allow themselves to believe they can achieve [68]. These processes disempower LGBTQ+ people, removing their agency and impacting negatively on their sense of self. This stream of research explores the role that ICTs play within this disempowerment. It explores how the design of an information system influences what an LGBTQ+ person believes their future can be and what they allow themselves to aspire to.

Stream 5: Seeking "Inclusion by Design"

Lack of standardised survey items on population-based surveys to identify transgender respondents limits existing public health surveillance [50].

This stream of research explores the implications of "inclusion by design" with regards to exposing individuals to discrimination. Exposing LGBTQ+ identities within an information system must be done with care to reduce the risk of exposing the individual to discrimination. We must find approaches that allow the information about LGBTQ+ people to be stored within information systems. We should seek "inclusion by design". However, subjective inclusiveness raises a host of challenges and ethical dilemmas, and there is a need for research and discussion of these dilemmas, and how the ICT4D community can include LGBTQ+ populations without exposing them to further discrimination. The inclusion of LGBTQ+ people should be the default within a system's design, and the decision to exclude this population should only be through a process of actively enabling the exclusion. Such an approach to design could involve taking active steps in the development of technology to be broadly inclusive. Within the context of gender representation, this could be achieved by incorporating predefined lists of gender identities. However, such an approach can lead to unintended consequences related to the inclusion of vulnerable populations in information systems.

Stream 6: Building better data-sets on LGBTQ+ People

To facilitate better programming for ICT4D projects, there is need for greater insight into the lives of LGBTQ+ people and how ICTs lead to inequities for these marginalised communities. By building these datasets, ICT4D projects can be better planned to accommodate their needs and the ensure that services are made available in an equitable manner. LGBTQ+ communities are marginalised and highly vulnerable. Members may be fearful of their safety as a direct result of their LGBTQ+ identities, living in countries where these identities are criminalised, and/or actively persecuted. Therefore, data about these populations must be ethically sourced, securely anonymised, and follow best practices to ensure that the members are not at risk of exposure to discrimination.

Stream 7: Reducing the risk of exposing LGBTQ+ people to violence when they conduct ICT4D work

LGBTQ+ researchers and practitioners are in a superior position to be inclusive and highlight the issues related to LGBTQ+ people due to their awareness, exposure and experience. At the same time, much ICT4D work takes place where LGBTQ+ people could be severely discriminated against and be in serious risk of violence. Measures and safeguards are needed to ensure members of the LGBTQ+ communities can conduct their work in ICT4D free of such risks. However, these are complex issues and they must be understood on a deep level to ensure the correct measures and safe-guards can be developed so that LGBTQ+ people are safe when conducting ICT4D work.

6 Conclusion

This paper stemmed from the recognition that, while the objectives of the ICT4D field are closely intertwined with the "Leaving No One Behind" agenda of the SDGs, the field is indeed leaving many people behind by silencing queer issues. This is not only a contradiction, but also a condition that makes the field unliveable for LGBTQ+ researchers [57] and makes us inadequate to elaborate recommendations for technologists, as these recommendations may end up producing binaristic, cisnormative, heteronormative systems that put LGBTQ+ people into precarious, vulnerable positions.

In response to this problem I have reviewed approaches to queer issues taken from other fields, cognate of ICT4D. With the purpose of learning from such fields, I have delineated a queer ICT4D agenda, exploring how biases are embedded in our systems and, vice versa, how technologies for socio-economic development can be designed towards inclusive, liberating purposes for LGBTQ+ people.

Firstly, I find that engagement of ICT4D with queer issues is a necessary step towards refocusing the field's agenda on the world it faces. While the field presents some attention to gender, the binaristic focus found in landscape papers up until recent days [20] is inadequate to represent the real world, and more dangerous given the enhanced vulnerabilities suffered by queer communities [9]. As a result, with this paper I want to openly incorporate queer issues in the field, delineating a path towards active measures for voicing queer issues in ICT4D forums. The track on "Feminist and Queer Approaches in ICT4D" in the IFIP 9.4 Virtual Conference, as well as the Queer HCI group created in HCI, are examples of such measures.

Secondly, I think it is crucial that a queer agenda inspires the engagements of ICT4D researchers with practice. This is important to avoid an absence of queer perspectives to be reflected in socio-economic development systems [57], resulting in technologies that deny queer identities and put LGBTQ+ users at risk of violence, threat or marginalisation. Producing technologies that caution against such bias is inevitably a concerted effort of researchers and practitioners, in which the researcher has the responsibility to formulate recommendations that caution against bias. It is in the light of this responsibility that this paper's agenda has been devised.

While a history of binarism, cisnormativity and heteronormativity affects ICT4D, other fields, such as STS [70] and HCI [58], demonstrate the urgency of incorporating a queer agenda into pre-existing fields. When such fields engage vulnerable people, as ICT4D intends to do since its early days, such an urgency is even more pronounced. LGBTQ+ issues in ICT4D have been raised in the past outside of the peer-reviewer ICT4D discourse. However, there has been little discussion of the issues within peer-reviewed ICT4D academic discourse. I hope, with this paper, to have made further steps towards a conversation the field must have, to devise an agenda that makes LGBTQ+ issues a priority topic of ICT4D research.

Acknowledgement. I would like to show my gratitude to Dr. Johan Ivar Sæbø, Assistant Professor at the Department of Informatics, University of Oslo, for his support and encouragement, and for his contributions to the structure of this paper. I would also like to thank Dr. Silvia Masiero, Assistant Professor at the Department of Informatics, University of Oslo, for her guidance through the literature on data justice, for her comments, and for the encouragement she gave me throughout the preparation of this research agenda.

References

1. Yaghoubi-Notash, M., Mohammad, V.N., Soufiani, M.: Language, gender and subjectivity from Judith Butler's perspective. Philos. Investig. **13**, 305–316 (2020)
2. Crenshaw, K.W.: On Intersectionality: Essential Writings. The New Press, New York (2017)
3. Mayer, K.H., Bradford, J.B., Makadon, H.J., Stall, R., Goldhammer, H., Landers, S.: Sexual and gender minority health: what we know and what needs to be done. Am. J. Public Health **98**, 989–995 (2008). https://doi.org/10.2105/AJPH.2007.127811
4. Crenshaw, K.: Mapping the margins: intersectionality, identity politics, and violence against women of color. Stanford Law Rev. **43**, 61 (1991)
5. Raftree, L., Kumar, M.: An Understanding of LGBTQI Rights and Technology for Development. Technology Salon Discussion at the Intersection of Technology Development (2015). https://technologysalon.org/an-understanding-of-lgbtqi-rights-and-technology-for-development/. Accessed 10 Apr 2022
6. Kumar, M.: Digital Security of LGBTQI Aid Workers: Awareness and Response. The European Interagency Security Forum, EISF 2020, 13 (2020)
7. Haimson, O.L., Gorrell, D., Starks, D.L., Weinger, Z.: Designing trans technology: defining challenges and envisioning community-centered solutions. In: Proceedings of 2020 CHI Conference on Human Factors in Computing Systems, pp. 1–13. ACM, Honolulu (2020). https://doi.org/10.1145/3313831.3376669
8. Johnson, J.A.: Information systems and the translation of transgender. TSQ Transgender Stud. Q. **2**, 160–165 (2015). https://doi.org/10.1215/23289252-2848940
9. van Zyl, I., McLean, N.: The Ethical Implications of Digital Contact Tracing for LGBTQIA+ Communities. (2021)
10. Browne, K., Nash, C.J., (eds.) Queer methods and methodologies: intersecting queer theories and social science research. Ashgate, Farnham (2010)
11. Thiel, M.: Queering scholarship? LGBT politics as an analytical challenge for political science and international relations. In: Bosia, M.J., McEvoy, S.M., Rahman, M. (eds). The Oxford Handbook of Global LGBT and Sexual Diversity Politics, pp. 119–135. Oxford University Press (2020). https://doi.org/10.1093/oxfordhb/9780190673741.013.5

12. Mills, E.: 'Leave No One Behind': Gender, Sexuality and the Sustainable Development Goals (2015). https://doi.org/10.1163/2210-7975_HRD-0148-2015071

13. Galang: How Filipino LBTs Cope with Economic Disadvantage. IDS, Brighton (2015)

14. Müller, A.: Teaching lesbian, gay, bisexual and transgender health in a South African health sciences faculty: addressing the gap. BMC Med. Educ. **13**, 174 (2013). https://doi.org/10.1186/1472-6920-13-174

15. Matthyse, L.: Achieving gender equality by 2030: transgender equality in relation to sustainable development goal 5. Agenda **34**, 124–132 (2020). https://doi.org/10.1080/10130950.2020.1744336

16. Vandeskog, H.O., Heggen, K.M., Engebretsen, E.: Gendered vulnerabilities and the blind spots of the 2030 Agenda's 'leave no one behind' pledge. Crit. Policy Stud. 1–17 (2021). https://doi.org/10.1080/19460171.2021.2014342

17. Swank, E., Fahs, B., Frost, D.M.: Region, social identities, and disclosure practices as predictors of heterosexist discrimination against sexual minorities in the United States. Sociol. Inq. **83**, 238–258 (2013). https://doi.org/10.1111/soin.12004

18. Botti, F., D'Ippoliti, C.: Don't ask don't tell (that you're poor). Sexual orientation and social exclusion in Italy. J. Behav. Exp. Econ. **49**, 8–25 (2014). https://doi.org/10.1016/j.socec.2014.02.002

19. Avgerou, C.: Theoretical framing of ICT4D research. In: Choudrie, J., Islam, M., Wahid, F., Bass, J., Priyatma, J. (eds.) Information and Communication Technologies for Development, vol. 504, pp. 10–23. Springer, Cham (2017). https://doi.org/10.1007/978-3-319-59111-7_2

20. Walsham, G.: ICT4D research: reflections on history and future agenda. Inf. Technol. Dev. **23**, 18–41 (2017). https://doi.org/10.1080/02681102.2016.1246406

21. Heeks, R.: Future priorities for development informatics research from the post-2015 development agenda. SSRN Electron. J. (2014). https://doi.org/10.2139/ssrn.3438434

22. Dey, B., Sorour, K., Filieri, R., (eds.): ICTs in Developing Countries. Palgrave Macmillan UK, London (2016). https://doi.org/10.1057/9781137469502

23. Vannini, S., Masiero, S., Tandon, A., Wellington, C., Wyers, K., Braa, K.: Feminist and queer approaches to ICT4D. Inf. Technol. Dev. (2021). Special Issue Call for Papers

24. Gallop: LGBT Identification Rises to 5.6% in Latest US Estimate. Gallop Poll (2021)

25. Reed, R.: Dignity in transgender lives: a capabilities approach. J. Hum. Dev. Capab. **21**, 36–48 (2020). https://doi.org/10.1080/19452829.2019.1661982

26. Bradford, J., Reisner, S.L., Honnold, J.A., Xavier, J.: Experiences of transgender-related discrimination and implications for health: results from the Virginia transgender health initiative study. Am. J. Public Health **103**, 1820–1829 (2013). https://doi.org/10.2105/AJPH.2012.300796

27. Costa, A.B., et al.: Healthcare needs of and access barriers for brazilian transgender and gender diverse people. J. Immigr. Minor. Health **20**(1), 115–123 (2016). https://doi.org/10.1007/s10903-016-0527-7

28. Gordon, D., Pratama, M.P.: Mapping discrimination experienced by Indonesian trans* FtM persons. J. Homosex **64**, 1283–1303 (2017). https://doi.org/10.1080/00918369.2016.1244446

29. Peltier, E.: Cameroon Sentences Transgender Women to 5 Years in Prison. N Y Times (2021)

30. Rani, N., Samuel, A.A.: Reducing transphobia: comparing the efficacy of direct and indirect contact. Ind. Commer. Train **51**, 445–460 (2019). https://doi.org/10.1108/ICT-12-2018-0102

31. Mcneil, J., Bailey, L., Ellis, S., Regan, M.: Speaking from the margins: trans mental health and well-being in Ireland (2013)

32. Murib, Z.: Administering biology: how "bathroom bills" criminalize and stigmatize trans and gender nonconforming people in public space. Adm. Theory Prax **42**, 153–171 (2020). https://doi.org/10.1080/10841806.2019.1659048

33. Faye, S.: The Transgender Issue: An Argument for Justice. Allen Lane, London (2021)

34. Taylor, L.: What is data justice? The case for connecting digital rights and freedoms globally. Big Data Soc. **4** (2017). https://doi.org/10.1177/2053951717736335

35. Mayer-Schönberger, V., Cukier, K.: Big data : a revolution that will transform how we live, work, and think (2013)

36. Bowker, G.C., Star, S.L.: Sorting things out : classification and its consequences (1999)

37. Milan, S., Treré, E., Masiero, S.: Introduction: COVID-19 seen from the land of otherwise. Covid-19 Margins Pandemic Invisibilities Policies Resist. Datafied Society, pp. 14–23. Institue of Network Cultures, Amsterdam, NL (2021)

38. Kirkland, A.: Dropdown rights: categorizing transgender discrimination in healthcare technologies. Soc. Sci. Med. **289**, 114348 (2021). https://doi.org/10.1016/j.socscimed.2021.114348

39. Saraswathi, A., Praveen, P.A.: To analyse the problems of transgender in India/study using new triangular combined block fuzzy cognitive maps. Int. J. Sci. Eng. Res. **6**, 186–195 (2015)

40. Costelloe, S.J., Hepburn, S.: Management of transgender patients in laboratory information management systems – moving on from binary and ternary logic. Ann. Clin. Biochem. Int. J. Lab. Med. **58**, 264–266 (2021). https://doi.org/10.1177/0004563220984825

41. Dhillon, N., Oliffe, J.L., Kelly, M.T., Krist, J.: Bridging barriers to cervical cancer screening in transgender men: a scoping review. Am. J. Men's Health **14** (2020). https://doi.org/10.1177/1557988320925691

42. Roznovjak, D., Petroll, A., Cortina, C.S.: Breast cancer risk and screening in transgender individuals. Curr. Breast Cancer Rep. **13**(1), 56–61 (2021). https://doi.org/10.1007/s12609-020-00403-x

43. D'Ignazio, C., Klein, L.F.: Data Feminism. MIT Press, Cambridge (2020)

44. Pandya, A.K., Redcay, A.: Access to health services: barriers faced by the transgender population in India. J. Gay Lesbian Ment. Health **25**, 132–54 (2021). https://doi.org/10.1080/19359705.2020.1850592

45. Oosterhoff, P., Hoang, T.-A., Trang, Q.: Negotiating Public and Legal Spaces: The Emergence of an LGBT Movement in Vietnam (2014). https://doi.org/10.13140/RG.2.1.3463.9129

46. Heeks, R., Renken, J.: Data justice for development: what would it mean? Inf. Dev. **34**, 90–102 (2018). https://doi.org/10.1177/0266666916678282

47. Scheuerman, M.K., Paul, J.M., Brubaker, J.R.: How computers see gender: an evaluation of gender classification in commercial facial analysis services. Proc. ACM Hum.-Comput. Interact. **3**, 1–33 (2019). https://doi.org/10.1145/3359246

48. Taylor, L., Sharma, G., Martin, A., Jameson, S.: What does the COVID-19 Response Mean for Global Data Justice? Data Justice COVID-19 Global Perspectives. Meatspace Press, Manchester (2020)

49. Weitzberg, K., Cheesman, M., Martin, A., Schoemaker, E.: Between surveillance and recognition: rethinking digital identity in aid. Big Data Soc. **8** (2021). https://doi.org/10.1177/20539517211006744

50. Reisner, S.L., Poteat, T., Keatley, J., Cabral, M., Mothopeng, T., Dunham, E., et al.: Global health burden and needs of transgender populations: a review. The Lancet **388**, 412–436 (2016). https://doi.org/10.1016/S0140-6736(16)00684-X

51. Dunne, M.J., Raynor, L.A., Cottrell, E.K., Pinnock, W.J.A.: Interviews with patients and providers on transgender and gender nonconforming health data collection in the electronic health record. Transgender Health **2**, 1–7 (2017). https://doi.org/10.1089/trgh.2016.0041

52. Floegel, D., Wagner, T.L., Delmonaco, D., Watson, B.M.: Expanding our conceptions of embodied and affective information interactions with queer theory. Proc. Assoc. Inf. Sci. Technol. **58**, 582–586 (2021). https://doi.org/10.1002/pra2.503

53. Wagner, T.L., Kitzie, V.L., Lookingbill, V.: Transgender and nonbinary individuals and ICT-driven information practices in response to transexclusionary healthcare systems: a qualitative study. J. Am. Med. Inform. Assoc. (2021). https://doi.org/10.1093/jamia/ocab234

54. Brulé, E., Spiel, K.: Negotiating gender and disability identities in participatory design. In: Proceedings of 9th International Conference on Communities and Technologies - Transforming Communities, New York, NY, USA, pp. 218–227. Association for Computing Machinery (2019). https://doi.org/10.1145/3328320.3328369

55. Hicks, M.: Hacking the Cis-tem. IEEE Ann. Hist. Comput. **41**, 20–33 (2019). https://doi.org/10.1109/MAHC.2019.2897667

56. Noble, S.U.: Algorithms of oppression : how search engines reinforce racism (2018)

57. Spiel, K., Keyes, O., Barlas, P.: Patching gender: non-binary utopias in HCI. In: Extended Abstracts of the 2019 CHI Conference on Human Factors Computer System, Glasgow, Scotland, UK, pp. 1–11. ACM (2019). https://doi.org/10.1145/3290607.3310425

58. DeVito, M.A., Walker, A.M., Lustig, C., Ko, A.J., Spiel, K., Ahmed, A.A., et al.: Queer in HCI: supporting LGBTQIA+ researchers and research across domains. In: Extended Abstracts of the 2020 CHI Conference Human Factors Computer System, Honolulu, HI, USA, pp. 1–4. ACM (2020). https://doi.org/10.1145/3334480.3381058

59. Costanza-Chock, S.: Design Justice : Community-Led Practices to Build the Worlds We Need. The MIT Press, Cambridge (2020)

60. Erete, S., Israni, A., Dillahunt, T.: An intersectional approach to designing in the margins. Interactions **25**, 66–69 (2018). https://doi.org/10.1145/3194349

61. Rohm, R., Martins, J.: The LGBTQ+ community during the COVID-19 Pandemic in Brazil. COVID-19 Margins Pandemic Invisibilities Policies Resist. Datafied Society, pp. 65–69. Institue of Network Cultures, Amsterdam, NL (2021)

62. Castleberry, J.: Addressing the gender continuum: a concept analysis. J. Transcult. Nurs. **30**, 403–409 (2019). https://doi.org/10.1177/1043659618818722

63. Butler, J.: Gender Trouble. Routledge, London (1990)

64. Lord, C.: Medium: ink on paper. GLQ J. Lesbian Gay Stud. **17**, 639–647 (2011). https://doi.org/10.1215/10642684-1302442

65. Martin, L.M.: Everyday Information Architecture, 1st edn. A Book Apart, New York (2019)

66. Connell, R.: Southern Theory. Polity Press, Cambridge (2007)

67. Scheim, A.I., Appenroth, M.N., Beckham, S.W., Goldstein, Z., Grinspan, M.C., Keatley, J.G., et al.: Transgender HIV research: nothing about us without us. Lancet HIV **6**, e566–e567 (2019). https://doi.org/10.1016/S2352-3018(19)30269-3

68. Nussbaum, M.: Creating Capabilities: The Human Development Approach. Harvard University Press, Cambridge (2011)

69. Pitts-Taylor, V.: A slow and unrewarding and miserable pause in your life": waiting in medicalized gender transition. Health Interdiscip. J. Soc. Study Health Illn. Med. **24**, 646–664 (2020). https://doi.org/10.1177/1363459319831330

70. Hofstätter, B., Thaler, A., Jauk, D., En, B., Klaura, I.M.: Irritating, Intervening, Interacting: Doing Queer Science and Technology Studies, vol. 1, p. 35 (2016)

Digital Rights and Activism

Digital Communication to Tackle Invisibility: A Project to Enhance Communication Capacities of Transmale Organizations in Peru and Central America

Juan Bossio[✉] [ID] and Illari Diez[ID]

Communications Department, Pontificia Universidad Católica del Perú, Lima, Peru
jfbossio@pucp.pe, illari.diez@pucp.edu.pe

Abstract. Transmale/Female to Male (FTM) people and their problems are mostly invisible for public policies, the media and academia around the world and in Peru. To help address those issues, we conducted a social responsibility project to develop digital communication capacities of FTM groups in Peru and Central America in 2021. This paper highlights the issues surrounding the FTM community and its use of digital media. Then, it presents the findings from the project's experience.

Keywords: Transmasculine · FTM · Community organizations · Social media · Capacity building

1 Introduction

We present the experience of a university social responsibility project, developed during 2021, that sought to develop digital communication capacities of organizations of youth trans male people from Peru and Central America. The reconstruction of the experience is a reflective effort in order to identify the learnings of the project to provide insight that can help other similar initiatives. To accomplish this, the main question to be addressed is how the project's methodology was useful to promote the capacity building of transmale activists? The second question we seek to answer is which new research topics arise from this experience?

First of all, we want to describe the project. It was built with transmasculine organization leaders, who talked with us about the problems and necessities of transmasculine people and validated our proposal taking into account its usefulness. On that basis, the project main objective was to contribute with the visibility of transmasculine population and the respect of their rights through:

- Identifying communication abilities and capacities
- Developing digital organizations' capacities for campaigns design
- Accompanying the design of a digital campaign

© IFIP International Federation for Information Processing 2022
Published by Springer Nature Switzerland AG 2022
Y. Zheng et al. (Eds.): ICT4D 2022, IFIP AICT 657, pp. 555–565, 2022.
https://doi.org/10.1007/978-3-031-19429-0_33

Then, we have divided the paper in 5 sections: (i) literature review, there we establish some practical concepts to understand trans phenomena, then present how big and important is the trans male invisibility in Peru, and lastly present other concepts related to the use and appropriation of social media by transmale people and organizations.; (ii) methodology of the systematization; (iii) the project, where we narrate its development in 3 phases; (iv) results, learnings and reflections, where we present the project achievements, what we learnt from it and present the research in project as an outcome of the project; finally, (v) we summarize our learnings in the conclusions.

2   Literature Review

This systematization is nourished by concepts of appropriation of technologies and identity. Firstly, it is necessary to describe trans male problematic.

The concept of trans gender can be used as an umbrella term which considers different variants, stages or embodiments to realize a transit impulse, intention or action [1, 2]. Trans male or Female to Male (FTM) people are subjects considered as women at birth, based on biologizing considerations of sexuality [1, 3].

The transition for them implies an intervention on the body. The importance - real and symbolic - of hormonal and surgical interventions is highlighted, but also social practices—such as dressing or behaving—and reflexivity about the body [4–7]. This transition is seen as a rebirth [8], which also includes a change of name. What those trans men want is to be recognized as men [7], therefore they behave and act as men.

2.1   Invisibility of the Trans Masculine

For trans men it is necessary to make their existence explicit since they are an underrepresented and invisible community in public policies, in the media and in academia. Regarding public policies in Peru, there isn't a Gender Identity Law, which means that changing name and/or sex in the ID must be done judicially, which takes time and money, and is not always successful [9, 10]. The lack of a proper legal identity produces violations of the right to vote, access to public services and generates violence from various sectors including police; as well as limitations in procedures for reporting discrimination and/or violence [11], as far as access to education and health [12]. Furthermore, during the pandemic some government actions that not considered trans people directly affected their rights, as when there were days to get out by sex.

Regarding the media, it can be said that when "trans" is heard or read, what is being thought or what is being talked about is trans women. Moreover, the quantity of films including transmale as characters or participants (in documentaries) is scarce according to Peruvian LGTB annual film festival (R. Salazar, personal communication, January, 12th 2022). As stated by the LGBT Human Rights Observatory (H. Amat y León, personal communication, November, 13th 2021), news about trans men are just a small part of those which report on human rights violations.

Additionally, trans men or trans-masculine are almost invisible to academia. What has been found in Peru regarding trans is recent and most of it focuses on trans women.

A psychology thesis [13] is the first study in Peru on "women who perform as men", this because, following Lamas [1], it is about "transgender" people and not transsexuals since they only modify their appearance according to how the "other sex" is socially conceived. The visibility of trans men in Peru began with a study by a LGBTI organization [14], for this, trans men would be the smallest sex-generic group among those considered (2.8%) and in which there are higher percentages of depression and victimization in general. It relates with findings by Gallegos Dextre who states that the corporality and identity of transmasculine people is built against discourses of power coming from the family, school or medicine [15]. These discourses of pathologizing and imposing 'normality' lead trans men to suffer torture, rape and murder.

Additionally, "Existimos" ("We exist") is the title of the first diagnosis on the situation of the male trans population in Peru published in 2018, which analyzes the process of identity construction, among other topics [2]. It underlines that isolation and the lack of information affect FTM youth people, while the Internet is identified as a resilient tool.

The most recent report on the situation of the transmasculine and non-binary population [11] finds that the negative impact on the rights of this population begins at home and the prejudices against them are supported or explained by the virtual absence of information and almost zero visibility. They report that only in 28% of cases the families support or accept gender identity, as well as that this population suffers discrimination at health and education services, and in the workplace. For this reason, they find the existence of meeting spaces with peers and support networks important; in the same way, they identify the relevance of political participation and collective action.

There are also studies related to legal issues and the exercise of rights [16–22], others related to health [12, 23–25] or related to communication issues [26–28].

The aforementioned invisibility and the scarcity of information about being trans make it difficult for adolescents and young people to identify themselves as such. As a consequence, in Peru the majority come to recognize themselves as trans and start transition processes as young adults [11, 26]. For this reason, many times the social networks publications of trans young people try to ease the way for adolescents due to the same identity crises and lack of references that they went through years before [26]. It is important to highlight that this situation has been observed in another Latin American country [5].

2.2 Transmasculine Community and Social Media

The Internet is identified as a space for affirmation to carry out multiple activities related to the construction of transmasculine identity and its dissemination [29–34].

In the first place, it is a space to find peers: young people who go through similar situations [5, 35]. Young male trans men select profiles to follow and authors to establish ties [30]. They also use different social media services for different purposes, often with different pseudonyms [36].

Thus, the Internet is seen as a potentially safe space that might help to escape street violence and the construction of support networks that contribute to resilience [29, 37, 38]. However, the Internet is also a terrain in which they can experience bullying [18, 38, 39]. For this reason, self-care strategies such as anonymity or the use of various accounts on social networks are analyzed [40].

The Internet is preferred for searching and accessing various information —legal, health, etc.- required by trans people or in the process of becoming trans [40–42]. Some seek public support for their transition medical procedures through fundraising campaigns [43].

There are also studies on the characteristics that a social medium should have for trans people, such as anonymity, security, privacy settings, community rules and warning or content filters [40, 44] or a health information service [45].

Communication, connection, information search and the disclosure of personal information related to the transition allow to produce feelings of collective identity and community [29, 30, 38, 40, 41, 46]. This is seen as something that develops empowerment among these young people [29, 38] and that also encourages them to organize and develop collective actions, developing tactics and using appropriate repertoires for that environment [47].

In addition to showing that they exist and should be visible, the action of posting on social media by these young people also seeks to generate community [28, 48–52]. We can see this in the use of identity hashtags such as #FTM or #Transmasculine with which they seek to develop ties with others [5, 26]. This is also reflected in the profiles of male trans organizations on networks such as Facebook, Twitter or Instagram. At this point, a connection can be found between the individual political action of young people publishing on networks and the collective action of a contentious political nature of their organizations and collectives.

Those organizations, as other various civil society organizations, have tried to empower traditionally excluded groups through the use of ICT [53]. The use of ICTs would help to strengthen the capacities of grassroots social organizations [54] considering technologies as amplifiers -not producers- of capacities [55]. The capacity building has been recognized by many institutions as an important strategy to promote sustainable development inside the organizations and to help them solve their problems [56]. Some of the capacities related to the project we are presenting are: capacity to use electronic media, plan projects, evaluate project's results, diagnose problems, access to information, recognize the necessity of using ITC, communicate (access to communication networks), use effective ways of communication and communicate their needs and achievements externally.

Finally, it is important to consider that, going further from its designer's purposes, technologies' usages and functions change over time following users´ lead improvisation and adaptation [57].

As it has been mentioned before, the literature about transmasculine people is scarce in Latin America and Peru. Thereupon we have identified that this lack of studies include the ones related to the experience of transmale and the utility of online spaces to build capacities that can help them to fight against the discrimination and violence they daily live. In consequence, this paper tries to fill that gap.

3   Methodology

In order to systematize our experience to get some learnings we started by analyzing our first diagnostic and data baseline, and the partial and final reports sent to the University.

Then we reviewed the plans and materials we produced for every workshop session. Lately we visualize the workshop videos. Furthermore, we share our findings with the other two members of the project team and the leaders of participating organizations to get their feedback.

4   The Project

We worked with trans guys and LGBTIQ organizations from Peru, Honduras, Costa Rica, Dominican Republic, Nicaragua, Guatemala, Mexico and El Salvador. The project had 3 phases.

During the first one, we made a diagnosis focused on how they use social networks as organizations and individuals, what they share, which information they look for, which negative experiences they had on the Internet and how do they deal with them. We did that research using social networks profiles analysis and a survey ($n = 23$) between members and contacts of the organizations.

We found that, although the organizations had practical knowledge about how to create content, construct communities and manage social media profiles, there were many aspects to improve. First of all, they needed to elaborate a plan (strategy) and define objectives for the content they wanted to publish, taking into account their public (s) and each social media characteristics. Secondly, the graphic style wasn't uniform throughout their different posts. Thirdly, they need to create strategies to generate more interaction and connection with their public. Furthermore, this social networks profiles analysis allowed us to identify that they use social media to provide support, information and make themselves visible.

Additionally, we explore the abilities, capabilities and experiences of the organizations' members or people of interest about social media and other technologies. About the people surveyed, half of them were between the ages of 24 and 31, they worked and studied, 17 were members of LGTBIQ organizations and 6 just participated in their activities, 17 are transmasculine and 3 transfeminine.

We found that the most used social media were Facebook, Instagram, Youtube, LinkedIn and Tik Tok. Also, we observed that they approach each one for different purposes: to look for information, they prefer Facebook, Youtube and Instagram; for entertainment, they use Instagram and Youtube; to learn something new, Youtube and Tik Tok; to connect with friends, Facebook and Instagram; and for activism, Twitter.

Related to their abilities to manage social media, the most known tools were video and picture edition, creation of a content grid and creation of digital campaigns. Also, the programs or apps most used to create content for social media were Zoom, Photoshop, Illustrator and Canva; and the least used were ProCreate, Premiere and Color Adobe.

Related to the contents they consume, the most preferred content of the trans organizations they follow were information, life stories, meetings, fight for their rights and interviews. Additionally, more than 70% of surveyed people always or almost always share the content they like.

Moreover, they would like to see content about collective action (dialogue between organizations and struggle stories), capacity building (guides, psychological and hormonal treatment information, collective workshops) and different kinds of content (videos and more interaction). In addition, they recommend to the organizations to post more frequently, have a graphic line, use better pictures and more or better use of hashtags.

Finally, the 60% of surveyed people said that they had been victims of online violence related to their identity or sexual orientation. And, all of them showed interest in knowing more about security in social media.

Then, for the second phase of the project, such information led us to plan a scheme of 8 workshops which included carrying out a diagnosis, definition and measurement of objectives, profile of target audiences, digital communication strategies, care in social networks, importance of having a graphic line and tools to create one, creation and content grid testing, how to take better advantage of the tools of each social media and devices, and generate a process of creation of content from non-digital tools: crafts, corporality exercises, photography, etc.

We had 23 people enrolled for the workshop, but on average just 7 participated in a synchronic way. During the workshop, the dynamics were oriented to create a secure sharing space, so the participants were able to talk about their experiences with digital media and tools. It is important to highlight that in the first workshop we made a compromise of participation, which included aspects such as security, punctuality and respect to each other.

The third phase was conceived as an accompaniment process, focused on helping the organization's members to design and develop their own digital campaign. However, due to time, we were just able to create a campaign brief.

The project ended with a participative evaluation which provided participants' perception of workshop contents, quality of learning, level of usefulness of the tools and learnings, among others. It also helped to identify different ways in which learning has already been used in digital communication by the organizations and what they were planning to do. In general, they mentioned that it helped them to change their perspective and find opportunities to improve their communication in social media. For example, the content grid helped them to organize and plan their content.

Also, as this project was part of a university social responsibility initiative, we disseminated the project results with the university community in spaces like a student's colloquium, general studies class and a funders' meeting.

5   Results, Learning and Reflections

This project had many results. Firstly, it was an achievement to have the participation of trans guys from 3 Peruvians organizations and many others from Central America and Caribbean countries. Secondly, with the participants of the workshops, we made a campaign brief, which consisted in establishing who was going to boost the digital campaign, the digital campaign main objectives, the public and the call to action phrase. Thirdly, there were cases or situations in which the learnings of the workshops were useful for the participants. For example, one of the organizations applied the knowledge about how to plan a communication campaign (define an objective, how to construct messages, among others) when promoting a health campaign in their region. Another organization member from El Salvador used the content grid and created a plan for the following year.

From all the experience, we learned more about the reality of trans people and the difficulties they face; how to bond with them and getting used to using the appropriate pronouns. Moreover, we strengthen our previous knowledge about the use of digital media from other contexts and problems, which implies enriching our field of action and learning. In addition to that, we test the usefulness of combining tools from various disciplines (relaxation exercises, movement, performing arts and visual creative processes) at workshops. And, we learn not to plan activities during the important dates for the community. This highlights the importance of the co-creation and participation of the organization members for the success of this kind of project.

This project helped us to reflect on the importance of building capacity in the use of digital media for transmasculine people, as it can be really helpful to cope with their different problems and meet their needs in many life dimensions (respect of their rights, visibility, support, among others). Furthermore, to take into account the times and priorities of the organizations and participants prove to be fundamental to achieve their involvement and the goals of the project.

Based on those findings and taking advantage of the contacts developed we submit a research proposal to study how Peruvian and Central American transmale organizations accompany or support the process of identity construction of youth transmale people by means of digital media. This research started in January 2022. After completing the theoretical framework and state of the art we were producing the tools and defining the corpus of publications to analyze and the sample for interviewing, following a mostly online design. However, from March 31th -the Trans Visibility Day- to April 14th there were two very interesting transmale events at which we decided to participate and that allowed us to talk with some activists. The first one was a fundraising event, with the objective of financing the second encounter of transmale and non-binary people in Peru. The second one was a documentary projection and discussion, focused on experiences of trans children. In both events we identified that the term 'trans' is actually used as an 'umbrella' to describe all the spectrum of trans and non-binary people. In addition, this exploratory approach already allows us to mention some findings, such as the awareness of many activists of the strong political content of their struggle and demands, the centrality of the demand for a Gender Identity Law, the potential role of 'influencers' within the community and the strong discursive weight of the concept of the body in relation to issues such as the experience of discrimination and the struggle against it, self-identification, enjoyment, among others.

6 Conclusions

In conclusion, we'd like to reinforce the importance of going against the invisibility of transmale people and how this kind of project can be helpful to it. The internet is useful to enhance the capacities of organization members in the creation of digital campaigns. However, to accomplish this, it is mandatory to engage them in the co-creation process. In other words, knowing their necessities and having their participation is the key. Moreover, we were able to see how the concepts of the literature review are applied in daily life. For example, the appropriation of technology, supports networks, the use of the word 'trans' as an umbrella term which identifies the spectrum of trans and non-binary people, among others.

References

1. Lamas M.: El fenómeno trans. Debate Fem **39**(39), 3–13 (2009). https://doi.org/10.22201/cieg.2594066xe.2009.39.1414, http://debatefeminista.cieg.unam.mx/df_ojs/index.php/debate_feminista/article/view/1414
2. Silva Santisteban A., Salazar, X.: Existimos: vivencias, experiencias y necesidades sociales de los hombres trans de Lima: un estudio exploratorio. Proyecto Unicxs, editor. Lima, 55 p. (2018)
3. Fausto-Sterling, A.: Cuerpos sexuados: la política de género y la construcción de la sexualidad. Barcelona, Editorial Melusina, 526 p. (2006)
4. Aboim, S., Vasconcelos, P.: What does it mean to be a man? Trans. Masculinities, Bodily Practices, and Reflexive Embodiment. Men Masc. https://doi.org/10.1177/1097184X211008519, https://journals.sagepub.com/doi/abs/10.1177/1097184X211008519. Accessed 26 Sept 2021
5. Campbell, B.: El "archivo del yo": activismo trans y redes sociales en Santiago de Chile. In: Kummels, I., Cánepa, G. (eds.) Antropología y Archivos en la era digital: usos emergentes de lo audiovisual, pp. 207–230. PUCP, Lima (2021)
6. Raun, T.: Video blogging as a vehicle of transformation: exploring the intersection between trans identity and information technology. Int. J. Cult. Stud. **18**(3), 365–378 (2014). https://doi.org/10.1177/1367877913513696. Accessed 11 Mar 2021
7. Green, J.: Part of the package. Men Masc. **7**(3), 291–299 (2005). http://journals.sagepub.com/doi/10.1177/1097184X04272116. Accessed 26 Sept 2021
8. Raun, T.: Screen-births: exploring the transformative potential in trans video blogs on YouTube. Grad. J. Soc. Sci. **7**(2), 113–130 (2010). https://www.gjss.org/sites/default/files/issues/chapters/papers/Journal-07-02--07-Raun.pdf. Accessed 6 Nov 2021
9. Atay, F., Ancí, N., Sotomayor, J.E.: Informe sobre la situación de la Identidad de género de las personas Trans en el Perú. Lima, Peru (2019). https://cdn.www.gob.pe/uploads/document/file/297521/Informe_CONACOD_Identidad_de_G%C3%A9nero.pdf
10. Centro de Investigación Interdisciplinaria en Sexualidad Sida y Sociedad, Proyecto Unicxs – Personas Trans por Inclusión Social, Observatorio de Derechos Humanos LGBT. Informe anual del observatorio de Derechos LGBT 2019 (2019). http://cvcdiversidadsexual.org/wp-content/uploads/2013/12/Informe_observatorio_2020.pdf
11. Instituto Internacional sobre Raza Igualdad y Derechos Humanos. Cuerpos y resistencias que transgreden la pandemia: trasmasculinidades y personas de género no binario AMAN en Perú. IIRIDH, Washington, DC, p. 215 (2021). https://raceandequality.org/wp-content/uploads/2021/09/FINAL_Cuerpos-y-resistencias-que-TRANSgreden_V4_240921.pdf?fbclid=IwAR0ywY6PcU58BlTGXdtjpspqehQLFIJBe0kko7c1JikefmHH8G0Ekm1oMEI
12. Romani, L., Ladera-Porta, K., Quiñones-Laveriano, D.M., Rios-Garcia, W, Juarez-Ubillus, A., Vilchez-Cornejo, J.: Factores asociados a la no utilización de servicios de salud en personas LGBTI de Perú. Rev. Peru. Med. Exp. Salud Publica **38**(2), 240–247 (2021). https://rpmesp.ins.gob.pe/rpmesp/article/view/6149 http://dx.doi.org/10.17843/rpmesp.2021.382.6149
13. Gallegos Dextre, A.: Características de la identidad de género en un grupo de 'mujeres masculinas' recluidas en un establecimiento penitenciario (E.P.) de Lima. Pontificia Universidad Católica del Perú. Pontificia Universidad Católica del Perú, Lima (2014). http://tesis.pucp.edu.pe/repositorio/handle/20.500.12404/5602. Accessed 26 July 2020
14. No tengo Miedo: Nuestra voz persiste: diagnóstico de situación de personas lesbianas, gays, bisexuales, transgénero, intersexuales y queer en el Perú. Lima: Tránsito, 266 p. (2016). https://www.idea.int/sites/default/files/publications/nuestra-vos-persiste.pdf
15. Gallegos Dextre, A.: 'Transcorporalidades': experiencias corporales e identitarias de un grupo de personas transmasculinas en la ciudad de Lima. Pontificia Universidad Católica del Perú. Pontificia Universidad Católica del Perú, Lima (2019). http://tesis.pucp.edu.pe/repositorio/handle/20.500.12404/14766 Accessed 26 July 2020

16. Bavio, P.S.: Propuesta para una ley de identidad de género peruana Bill for a gender identity peruvian law. Derecho & Sociedad (2016). http://revistas.pucp.edu.pe/index.php/derechoysociedad/article/view/18887. Accessed 26 July 2020
17. Díaz Díaz, M.-P.G.: Los nuevos retos del derecho a la identidad en el Perú: desde la heteroasignación hacia la autodeterminación. Pers. Fam. 5(9), 221–242 (2020). https://doi.org/10.33539/peryfa.2020.n9.2340, https://revistas.unife.edu.pe/index.php/personayfamilia/article/view/2340
18. Fraser, B.: Peru's transgender community: the battle for rights. Lance 388(10042), 324–350 (2016). https://doi.org/10.1016/S0140-6736(16)31146-1. Accessed 26 July 2020
19. Gutiérrez Arroyo, X.O.: El transexualismo y la necesidad de regular la identidad de género en el Código Civil Peruano. Universidad Nacional de Trujillo, Trujillo (2019). http://www.dspace.unitru.edu.pe/handle/UNITRU/15256. Accessed 26 July 2020
20. Mirez La Rosa, R.: Derecho a la Identidad y Cambio de Sexo. Universidad Nacional Pedro Ruiz Gallo (2017). https://hdl.handle.net/20.500.12893/7573
21. Sánchez Yaringaño, G.M.: Trabajando en el cis-tema: vínculos entre el ejercicio del derecho al acceso al empleo y el reconocimiento legal de la identidad de género para el colectivo trans. PUCP (2020). http://hdl.handle.net/20.500.12404/17151
22. Zelada, C.J., Neyra-Sevilla, C.: Trans* legalities: preliminary study of files on the recognition of trans* identities in Peru. In: The Asian Yearbook of Human Rights and Humanitarian Law [Internet]. Brill—Nijhoff, pp. 396–426 (2019). https://doi.org/10.1163/9789004401716_017. Accessed 26 July 2020
23. Castillo Soto, A.L., Cornejo Rojas, D.A.: Factores asociados al autoreporte de depresión y ansiedad en los últimos doce meses en personas LGTBI vía una encuesta virtual en Perú, 2017. Universidad Peruana de Ciencias Aplicadas (UPC) (2020). https://repositorioacademico.upc.edu.pe/bitstream/handle/10757/654732/Castillo_SA.pdf?sequence=3&isAllowed. Accessed 26 July 2020
24. Jaime, M.: La salud imperfecta: cuerpos y subjetividades en la medicina peruana: las personas TLGBI frente a la salud pública, la discriminación y la pobreza en el contexto [Internet]. Universidad Andina Simón Bolívar (2016). http://repositorio.uasb.edu.ec/handle/10644/4957
25. Vilchez Calderón, A.L.: Asociación entre identidad de género y discriminación en Perú, a partir de la primera encuesta virtual LGBTI 201. Universidad Nacional Mayor de San Marcos. Universidad Nacional Mayor de San Marcos (2019). https://cybertesis.unmsm.edu.pe/handle/20.500.12672/10347. Accessed 26 July 2020
26. Bossio, J.F.: Transition stories: analysis of Peruvian FTM Instagram posts. In: Iberian Conference on Information Systems and Technologies, CISTI. IEEE, Chaves, pp. 1–6 (2021). https://ieeexplore.ieee.org/document/9476372/ https://doi.org/10.23919/cisti52073.2021.9476372. Accessed 21 Sept 2021
27. Carbajal Palacios, L.: #Transformar: campaña periodística de visibilización a la comunidad trans de Lima Metropolitana. Universidad de Lima, Lima (2019). https://repositorio.ulima.edu.pe/bitstream/handle/20.500.12724/10055/Carbajal_Palacios_Lorena_Roxana.pdf. Accessed 26 July 2020
28. Espinoza, A.: Reforma Trans PUCP: Comunicación estratégica e incidencia política en la primera iniciativa por el reconocimiento de la identidad de género en una universidad peruana. Pontificia Universidad Católica del perú (2020). http://hdl.handle.net/20.500.12404/16774
29. Austin, A., Craig, S.L., Navega, N., McInroy, L.B.: It's my safe space: the life-saving role of the internet in the lives of transgender and gender diverse youth. Int. J. Transgender 21(1), 33 (2020). https://doi.org/10.1080/15532739.2019.1700202
30. Buss, J., Le, H., Haimson, O.: Transgender identity management across social media platforms. Media Cult. Soc. 1–17 (2021). https://journals.sagepub.com/doi/abs/10.1177/01634437211027106?journalCode=mcsa

31. Gauthier, D.K., Chaudoir, N.K.: tranny boyz: cyber community support in negotiating sex and gender mobility among female to male transsexuals. Deviant Behav. 25(4), 375–398 (2004). https://doi.org/10.1080/01639620490441272. http://www.tandfonline.com/doi/abs/10.1080/01639620490441272. Accessed 11 Mar 2021

32. Haimson, O.: The social complexities of transgender identity disclosure on social media. University of California Irvine (2018). https://escholarship.org/uc/item/19c235q0

33. Haimson, O.L., Brubaker, J.R., Dombrowski, L., Hayes, G.R.: Disclosure, stress, and support during gender transition on Facebook. In: Proceedings of the 18th ACM Conference on Computer Supported Cooperative Work & Social Computing. ACM, New York (2015), pp. 1176–1190. https://doi.org/10.1145/2675133.2675152, https://dl.acm.org/doi/10.1145/2675133.2675152

34. Horak, L.: Trans on YouTube: intimacy, visibility, temporality. TSQ Transgender Stud. Q. 1(4), 572–585 (2014).https://doi.org/10.1215/23289252-2815255, https://read.dukeupress.edu/tsq/article/1/4/572-585/91708. Accessed 11 Mar 2021

35. Simms, S., Nicolazzo, Z., Jones, A.: Don't say sorry, do better: trans students of color, disidentification, and internet futures. J. Divers High Educ. (2021). http://doi.apa.org/getdoi.cfm?doi=10.1037/dhe0000337

36. Haimson, O.: Social media as social transition machinery. Proc. ACM Hum.-Comput. Interact. 2(CSCW) (2018). https://doi.org/10.1145/3274332. Accessed 25 Oct 2021

37. Craig, S.L., McInroy, L., Mccready, L.T., Alaggia, R.: Media: a catalyst for resilience in lesbian, gay, bisexual, transgender, and queer youth. J. LGBT Youth 12(3), 254–275 (2015). https://doi.org/10.1080/19361653.2015.1040193

38. Etengoff, C.: Transvlogs: online communication tools for transformative agency and development. Mind, Cult. Act 26(2), 138–155 (2019). https://www.tandfonline.com/doi/full/10.1080/10749039.2019.1612438. Accessed 11 Mar 2021

39. Green, M., Bobrowicz, A., Ang, C.S.: The lesbian, gay, bisexual and transgender community online: discussions of bullying and self-disclosure in YouTube videos. Behav. Inf. Technol. 34(7):704–712 (2015). https://doi.org/10.1080/0144929X.2015.1012649, https://www.tandfonline.com/doi/full/10.1080/0144929X.2015.1012649. Accessed 4 Dec 2019

40. Cannon, Y., Speedlin, S., Avera, J., Robertson, D., Ingram, M., Prado, A.: Transition, connection, disconnection, and social media: examining the digital lived experiences of transgender individuals. J. LGBT Issues Couns. 11(2), 68–87 (2017). https://doi.org/10.1080/15538605.2017.1310006

41. McInroy, L.B., Craig, S.L.: Transgender representation in offline and online media: LGBTQ youth perspectives. J. Hum. Behav. Soc. Environ. 25(6), 606–617 (2015). http://www.tandfonline.com/doi/full/10.1080/10911359.2014.995392

42. Torruco López, I.M., Domínguez Aguirre, G.Á., González Fócil, R.C.: ¿Cómo me descubrí trans? Vivencia de un grupo de chicos transexuales. In: Psicología integral, al servicio de la humanidad, pp. 923–931. XLIV Congreso Nacional CNEIP-UAN, Nayarit (2017). https://www.repositorionacionalcti.mx/recurso/oai:ri.ujat.mx:20.500.12107/3119

43. Barcelos CA. 'Bye-bye boobies': normativity, deservingness and medicalisation in transgender medical crowdfunding. Cult. Health Sex Dec. 21(12), 1394–408 (2019). https://www.tandfonline.com/doi/full/https://doi.org/10.1080/13691058.2019.1566971

44. Haimson, O., Buss, J., Weinger, Z., Starks, D.L., Gorrell, D., Baron, B.S.: Trans time. In: Proceedings of ACM Human-Computer Interact 4(CSCW2), 1–27 (2020). https://dl.acm.org/doi/abs/10.1145/3415195

45. Augustaitis, L., Merrill, L.A., Gamarel, K.E., Haimson, O.: Online transgender health information seeking: Facilitators, barriers, and future directions. In: Conference on Human Factors Computing System – Proceedings (2021). https://doi.org/10.1145/3411764.3445091. Accessed 25 Oct 2021

46. Jenzen, O.: Trans youth and social media: moving between counterpublics and the wider web. Gender Place Cult. **24**(11), 1626–1641 (2017). https://doi.org/10.1080/0966369X.2017.139 6204

47. Shapiro, E.: Transcending Barriers. J. Gay Lesbian Soc. Serv. **16**, 165–179 (2004). https://www.tandfonline.com/action/journalInformation?journalCode=wgls20

48. Daniel Castellanos, H.: Santo Domingo's LGBT social movement: at the crossroads of HIV and LGBT activism. Glob. Public Health **14**(6–7), 963–976 (2019). https://www.tandfonline.com/doi/full/10.1080/17441692.2019.1585467

49. Ferrer Araújo, N.: Los nuevos movimientos sociales y las ciudadanías emergentes: reflexiones desde el concepto de democracia radical y el movimiento LGBTI en Colombia. Estud Socio-Jurídicos **19**(1), 43 (2016). https://doi.org/10.12804/revistas.urosario.edu.co/sociojuridicos/a.4025, http://revistas.urosario.edu.co/index.php/sociojuridicos/article/view/4025

50. Lins, C., Mesquita, M.: A compreensão da política por militantes do movimento trans alagoano. Psicol teor prát. **22**(1), 251–269 (2020). https://doi.org/10.5935/1980-6906/psicologia.v22n1p251-269

51. Olmedo Neri, R.: Cartografías conectivas: un acercamiento a la construcción de redes sociodigitales del movimiento #LGBT. Chasqui Rev Latinoam Comun (2021) **1**(147), 123–142. https://revistachasqui.org/index.php/chasqui/article/view/4456

52. Sánchez Barrera EL. El movimiento LGBT (I) en Colombia: la voz de la diversidad de género. Logros, retos y desafíos. Reflexión Política 19(38), 116–131 (2017). https://doi.org/10.29375/01240781.2843, https://revistas.unab.edu.co/index.php/reflexion/article/view/2843

53. Kannengießer, S.: Translocal empowerment communication: mediated networks of civil society organizations for political empowerment. North Light Film Media Stud. Yearb. **15**(1), 51–67 (2017). http://www.ingentaconnect.com/content/10.1386/nl.15.1.51_1

54. Bossio, J., Bossio, J.F., León, L.: El poder de las TIC en el fortalecimiento de las capacidades: el caso de las organizaciones sociales de base en las áreas rurales de los andes peruanos. In: Tecnología y cambio social: el impacto del acceso público a las computadoras e Internet en Argentina, pp. 105–147. Chile y Perú. Instituto de Estudios Peruanos, Lima (2012). https://idl-bnc-idrc.dspacedirect.org/bitstream/handle/10625/51521/IDL-51521.pdf?sequence=1&isAllowed=y

55. Toyama, K.: Technology as amplifier in international development. In: Proceedings of the 2011 iConference, pp. 75–82. ACM, New York (2011). https://dl.acm.org/doi/10.1145/1940761.1940772

56. Lusthaus, C., Carden, F., Adrien, M., Anderson, G., Montalván, G.P.: Organizational assesment: a framework for improving performance. IDRC/BID, Washington (2002)

57. Walsham, G.: Making a World of Difference: IT in a Global Context. Wiley, Chichester (2001)

WhatsApp Affordances Through an Intersectional Lens: Constructing and Rehearsing Citizenship in Western Kenya

Anna Colom[✉] [iD]

The Open University, Milton Keynes, UK
`anna.colom@open.ac.uk`

Abstract. This paper draws on a digital ethnography with young activists in Western Kenya to explore how WhatsApp's affordances mediate citizenship. It applies an intersectional lens to highlight sites of oppression and invisibility. The paper makes two central arguments. Firstly, it finds that WhatsApp is not only important for participants because of its communicative and organisational affordances, but also for agentic and social affordances that relate to activists' sense of belonging and purpose, and the discursive affordances that enable the building of narratives, making it a space for constructing and rehearsing citizenship. Secondly, it finds that inequalities in meaningful online access hindered some participants from these spaces of belonging, interaction, and visibility. These inequalities intersect and risk amplifying existing sites of disadvantage, like those related to gender, class or location. An intersectional digital rights approach is needed in the design of communication strategies by activists or organisations in civic engagement processes.

Keywords: Citizenship · WhatsApp · Intersectionality · Digital rights · Instant messaging · Affordances

1 Introduction

An expanding body of work from political, media and internet studies has documented the role of the internet, and in particular social media, in citizen engagement and political activism. Social media platforms like Twitter or Facebook have been found to enable the creation of alternative public spheres where new groups and agendas can visibilize and amplify counter-narratives and shape public discussion (Bosch 2017; Nyabola 2018).

Although less available to scrutiny, instant messaging apps, also called the Dark Social, are the most accessed type of online platform in many contexts, more so than Twitter or Facebook. In Kenya, WhatsApp is the favourite social platform among Internet users (Global Web Index 2020) and permeates all activities, including political mobilization and discourse (Omanga 2018).

This paper explores the role of instant messaging app WhatsApp in processes of civic engagement in Western Kenya. It takes an intersectional feminist approach to

Y. Zheng et al. (Eds.): ICT4D 2022, IFIP AICT 657, pp. 566–580, 2022.
https://doi.org/10.1007/978-3-031-19429-0_34

shed light on inequalities and sites of oppression and invisibility. It does so through a digital ethnography based around a group of young people engaged in a process of civic education and engagement in Busia county supported by the local civil society organization Siasa Place.

This paper is structured as follows. First, it sets out the context of the study within processes of citizen engagement and Internet use in Kenya. It then covers the theoretical framework used in the study, followed by the study's research approach. It then presents the analysis findings by discussing the WhatsApp affordances that mediate citizenship and how this mediation affects those without meaningful access to mobile internet and existing structural inequalities.

2   Citizen Engagement and Digital Technologies in Western Kenya: Case Study Context

This paper is based on a case study in Busia county, situated in Western Kenya and at the border with Uganda. Its overall research question is to understand how digital technologies, and in particular instant messaging, mediate civic engagement for young people. I used a multi-method digital ethnography approach that followed a network of young activists, online and offline, across the seven electoral constituencies of the county.

2.1   Enabling 'Active Citizenship'

Participants included a group of 18 to 35 years old supported by the youth-led civil society organisation Siasa Place, which enables spaces and civic education training for youth to engage in governance processes. Siasa Place identified a lack of knowledge on existing constitutional rights as well as a context in which young people felt dismissed and therefore discouraged from engaging. This sense of dismissal and lack of information was strongly echoed across participants' accounts.

Through a series of meetings and seminars, the group was given a space for discussion and learning on Kenya's system of devolved governance and the rights and mechanisms for political participation included in the country's 2010 constitution. This core group would in turn mobilise and share this information and skills with other peers in their communities.

The core group of activists would meet monthly or bi-monthly in Busia town to attend trainings facilitated by the organisation and discuss their plans for mobilising. In between meetings, they interacted more frequently through WhatsApp, which was the main digital technology used by the core group of participants to communicate between them and with peers in their communities with Internet access.

2.2   Internet and WhatsApp Access

In 2021, Kenya was the country with the highest monthly use of WhatsApp (Bayhack 2021; Rollason 2021). WhatsApp is ubiquitous among Internet users in Kenya, taking the role of what Gómez-Cruz and Harindranath have called a "technology of life" (Gómez-Cruz and Harindranath 2020, 1), used for all sorts of personal and social interactions, including work and, as stated by Omanga, important in Kenya's "political talk" (Omanga 2018, 2).

However, this apparent omnipresence contrasts with the still pervasive gaps in Internet access. In 2020, Internet penetration in Kenya was forecasted to be at approximately 40% (Global Web Index 2020; Hootsuite and We Are Social 2020). These statistics flatten unequal and intermittent access. According to the Kenya 2019 census, only 11.3% of the female rural population accessed the Internet in the last three months compared to 45.3% of the male urban population (Kenya National Bureau of Statistics 2019, 432). These inequalities were apparent also within the group of participants and throughout the research period. Not only did not everyone own a smartphone, but it also became clear that internet access is not binary (Roberts and Hernandez 2019) and that some participants were able to connect only intermittently because they could not afford data bundles, because they used someone else's phone or because of network access, among other reasons.

3 Theoretical Framework

The study of technology in processes of social change has been criticised for either being overly deterministic about the role of technology or, by contrast, for overlooking it and turning it into a neutral artefact (Roberts 2017). The Theory of Affordance has been used by scholars in the Information and Communication Technologies for Development (ICT4D) field and beyond because it accounts for the materiality of a particular technology whilst acknowledging that what this materiality affords is contingent on the political and cultural context in which the technology is interpreted and used (Zheng and Yu 2016). This study therefore draws on this theory to explore the action possibilities that WhatsApp affords and how these relate to participants' civic engagement.

In addition, a review of the ICT4D literature suggests the need for an agenda that focuses on the most disadvantaged and oppressed groups and for evidence on how ICTs contribute to specific and transformational outcomes (Walsham 2017; Zheng et al. 2018). Research in Kenya has found that the use of mobile phones helped women in rural locations "assert their agency", create communities of support (Sanya 2013, 13) and engage in discussions on rights and the Constitution (Sanya and Odero 2017). It has also found that online platforms enabled the networking between and the visibilizing of narratives from otherwise marginalised groups in the public spheres (Mukhongo 2020; Nyabola 2018). Yet, this scholarship also warns that these same technologies can replicate or amplify existing structural inequalities (Kibere 2016; Nyabola 2018).

This study draws on feminist intersectional theory to allow for the exploration of sites of oppression and invisibility that single-axis analysis can overlook (Carastathis 2016; Crenshaw 1989). As stated by Yuval-Davis: "when we carry out intersectional analysis, we cannot homogenize the ways any political project or claimings affect people who are differentially located within the same boundaries of belonging" (Yuval-Davis 2011, 4).

4 Research Approach

This study understands reality as constructed and situated in historic and relational dynamics of meaning-making based on power and language and therefore takes an interpretivist ontological approach. The research was based on a digital ethnography that encompassed both online and offline spaces and the connections between them (Hine 2017; Postill and Pink 2012). It included the following methods: face-to-face semi-structured interviews with 25 participants, participant offline observation, non-participant online observation in three WhatsApp groups, an online focus group discussion on WhatsApp (Colom 2021), and a fieldwork diary. Digital ethnography allowed the research to travel across offline and online fields and to explore the connections between the two; online interactions take place not in a vacuum but in relation to offline realities (Hine 2017; Postill and Pink 2012; Sumiala and Tikka 2020). The value of digital ethnography in acknowledging that participants interactions are "multi-modal", "multi-sited" and "networked" (Hine 2017, 23) crystallised in many occasions during the research and analysis. For example, whilst observing participants attending an in-person public participation event on the county's budget and development plan, I was also able to observe what and how the participants communicated with others in the WhatsApp group who were attending other simultaneous events in other parts of the county, as well as observe what narratives and reactions this created that related to their aspirations as citizens mobilized in civic engagement processes. Similarly, this approach helped me to observe first-hand how accounts during in-person interviews in relation to exclusion from the Internet manifested in participants' online presence and the types of disadvantages this created or amplified across the online, offline, public, and private spheres.

The data was all entered in Nvivo and analysed using a thematic analysis approach. The intersectionality lens was embedded in the design of tools to account for a multi-layered understanding of citizenship (Pailey 2016; Yuval-Davis 1997) that encompassed intersecting positionings across the private and public spheres and across the community, county and state level. It was also embedded in the analysis approach by intentionally focusing on identifying sites of oppression, difference or resistance in the language and accounts of participants.

5 WhatsApp Affordances and Citizenship

Affordances are action possibilities facilitated by the materiality of a technological arte-fact but contingent on the historical and social context in which they are interpreted. However, affordances can be conceptualized differently depending on the extent to which they focus on the functionalities of the technologies vis-a-vis their relational potential consequences. For example, both Roberts and Zheng and Yu distinguish the functional affordances of a technology from the collective actions they enable, a distinction that emphasises their relational and practical aspect (Roberts 2017; Zheng and Yu 2016).

The affordances identified and covered in this section result from the analysis of the accounts from participants in relation to the role of WhatsApp in their civic engagement processes and are largely functional. Understanding the functional affordances on instant messaging as a dark social is relevant as distinct from those that more open social media platforms have been found to offer. However, these functional affordances can be grouped into five categories based on their relational use and the transformational potential in the context of this study: communicative, organizational, social, agentic, and discursive. A functional affordance can relate to more than one of these categories and may only become actualized in combination with other functional affordances as found by Sæbø, Federici and Braccini when exploring how social media enabled specific collective action processes (Sæbø, Federici, and Braccini 2020, 714).

The functional affordances are briefly discussed as a list in this section before then unpacking their transformational potential for citizenship.

Immediacy

The labelling of apps like WhatsApp as *instant messaging* applications conveys an obvious but important affordance identified in participants' accounts, who referred to its use making it quick and easy to receive and send information, including the ability to know when someone is active or when they were last online. This was important for participants to share information, keep up-to-date, and mobilise as part of their activism. For example, a participant referred to the value of communicating via WhatsApp to organize meetings with less notice and planning: *"You know, like [in a] church meeting, we'll have to tell people (…) you tell them before, even 2 days or one week… But if you use WhatsApp, a person will get information immediately* (Interview P6)".

Scale

Related to the descriptions of immediacy was the ability to communicate with more than one person at the same time no matter where they were. Participants referred to the benefits of this affordance compared not only to offline communication but also to texting or calling, which was more expensive, as this participant said: *"… actually, it's been easier to communicate than when you communicate manually, or, rather when you just use calls and SMS. It has been easy because we are together and everyone can speak… is a free space in that, anyone, you can type at the same time, you can deliver messages, a message, as the other person delivers. But, for SMS, the message will go from one person to the next and then, sometimes you can feel that maybe, if they send you the message, you don't have maybe credit to reply, so it's easier. (…) And it's faster* (Interview P19)".

Multimodality

The literature often mentions this as a characteristic of instant messaging apps like WhatsApp (Baxter 2018; Treré 2020). It refers to the possibility to share not only text but also photos, audio-visual content, or other files. A participant during the focus group wrote: *"Its even easier to give evidence using Action photos, videos and statistical data from genuine source even if its a heavy document it can be uploaded easily as opposed to carry bags of papers to the meeting where you may not get a chance to contribute. so a person who is not in WhatsApp misses a lot."*[1] It was common for participants to share photos of themselves or group members speaking in public or delivering petitions

---

[1] Quotes from the WhatsApp focus group are included as typed by participants unless typos need to be corrected for intelligibility.

to governments officials as well as to share PDFs of official documents, such as county budgets or the Constitution.

Information visibility

In instant messaging apps like WhatsApp, information and conversations remain in the platform's interface and are visible to other members of the group as shared by the senders and unless deleted. Content can also be forwarded and shared with other contacts or in other groups.

This affordance is closely related to scale and multimodality and it also relates to the possibilities for building spaces and narratives where young people can find their own voice and make connections, as it will be later discussed. For example, participants expressed the value of sharing with others in their contacts pictures of themselves doing work for the community: *"Yeah it's made a difference because you call [reach] people very fast. They know also very fast. For example, when we were in Busia at [venue] after doing that [meeting] then I post. People, many people knew very fast! Hey, they said, wow, you have done a good job.* (Interview P18)".

Group relevance

WhatsApp was seen by participants as a space for more intimate conversations with relevant groups of people close their personal or social spaces and interests, especially when compared to other social media platforms. For example, a participant said: *"through WhatsApp, you just share with the people that you want but with Facebook everyone will just see it on their wall* (Interview P17)" and another participant referred to WhatsApp being for interacting with *"those people who think the same idea (...) yeah come up with a group and people of the same, the likeminded people, they join you in that WhatsApp group"* (Interview P9).

Participants referred to interactions being more intimate and information being more targeted to relevant people. In the context of activism, this provides a specific discursive potential resulting from a combination of traits from personal exchanges with those from public group discussions (Milan and Barbosa, 2020: 8).

This resonates with literature that finds WhatsApp to relate to "a stronger sense of belonging rather than network-based Facebook" (Milan and Barbosa 2020, 8) or to "collective identity [and] internal solidarity" (Treré 2020, 1).

Perceived privacy

Participants did not refer to privacy in relation to its end-to-end encryption but in relation to the less open nature of the space, which felt less exposed when compared to other social media platforms: *"I cannot say that there isn't anything I don't like in WhatsApp because I feel it has a little bit of privacy* (Interview P14)." Another participant also referred to this sense of safety: *"WhatsApp is also a bit safe in terms of... it's not... you can't track it so easily* (Interview P25)".

Privacy was however relative, hence the labelling of the affordance as 'perceived'. During the break of one of the events I attended, a few participants gathered around a mobile phone to watch the video of a Citizen TV news piece in which the National Cohesion and Integration Commission (NCIC) of Kenya was warning WhatsApp group administrators against hate speech. This observation contrasts with the accounts of participants on privacy, a difference enabled by the digital ethnography approach of the study.

Although WhatsApp was referred to in the research as a more private safe space, a participant mentioned having left WhatsApp for a period of time after being harassed for their activism, which highlights the contingency of affordances in relation to people's positionalities and experiences. Overall, however, there was a sense of control in the groups that I observed of who was allowed to be a member and this explains this perception of WhatsApp as a private space when compared to more open social media platforms where the sense of privacy is not afforded or requires a more complex use of the platforms' settings.

The contingency of this affordance is also reflected in the lack of references in participants' accounts to the ways in which Big Tech corporations like WhatsApp's company, Meta, use data. An understanding of privacy based on the storage and use of Big Data for micro-profiling and in governance processes would contradict this affordance, which is beyond the scope of this paper but highlights the need for more information among activists on digital citizenship and data justice (Dencik, Hintz, and Cable 2016).

Perceived freedom

Participants referred to WhatsApp as a free space, where they could share their views without being dismissed: "*Everyone has the liberty to air their views and thoughts with no fear resulting from a one on one engagement.* (WhatsApp FGD)".

Treré refers to the "digital comfort spaces" enabled by WhatsApp interactions (Treré 2015, 911) and a systematic review on the use of WhatsApp for political and civic engagement found people valued the "informal and 'de-politicised' conversations" (Pang and Woo 2020, 1). Online spaces of interaction more broadly have also been found to offer a disembodied experience that affords a sense of freedom (Ndlela and Mulwo 2017), including my own perceptions of the extent to which women participated in WhatsApp discussions when compared to offline meetings (Colom 2021).

Diffuse hierarchies

Some participants referred to WhatsApp as a "flat" space: "*with WhatsApp someone can ask me a question in a WhatsApp group, and I must answer you, I must, because it's in an open forum. And so it allows for people to… to feel that they have the same voice. On WhatsApp… it's a flat….it's a flat playing field* (Interview P23)." This affordance has also been referred to in the literature on WhatsApp as a tool for activism. For example, Bowes-Catton et al., argue that voices in the authors' activist WhatsApp group were equally treated (Bowes-Catton et al. 2020, 384) and Milan and Barbosa refer to the "equal footing" of WhatsApp conversations (Milan and Barbosa 2020, 6) characterised by "diffuse leadership and experimental pluralism" (2020: 9).

Deliberation

Participants talked about WhatsApp as a space where they can have discussions and make decisions: "*We share some issues, maybe we see the problems that people come up with… we try to get people ask maybe questions concerning what happens [to] them so we decide to discuss there in the group (…) to see maybe if we can make solutions*

(Interview P5)". They also referred to the value of WhatsApp as a space for discussion in comparison to Facebook, which they saw as a place for accessing or sharing news.

These discussions often combine synchronous and asynchronous interactions, allowing participants to reply in their own time, and it was not uncommon for participants to take part in synchronous WhatsApp meetings: "*WhatsApping, we conduct meetings. Because engagement sometimes is distant we call each other and say when it reaches at nine we can have a meeting, everybody will need to be on* (Interview P11)".

However, I observed that moments of deliberation tended to be short-lived or left for offline meetings, which I partly related to the lack of an obvious leadership or facilitation, linked to the affordance of diffuse hierarchies. The deliberative potential of WhatsApp in Kenya in the context of political participation has been documented by Omanga in his study of the *Nakuru Analysts* WhatsApp group. Omanga argues that the group acted as a digital public but also highlights the importance of facilitation and the role of the convenor: "Digital publics do not simply emerge, but are a complex product of specific agencies, cumulative social capital and voice within a digital space" (Omanga 2018, 13).

Yet, this possibility for deliberation in WhatsApp was referred to and valued by participants with online access, and seen also as a way to meaningfully engage in decision-making processes. For example, a participant talked about the value of a WhatsApp group to bring young people and political representatives together and continue constructive conversations initiated and convened offline; and a political representative mentioned during an event I observed having created a WhatsApp group to directly engage in discussions with young people.

6   Relational Affordances for Constructing and Rehearsing Citizenship

The functional affordances discussed interact with each other and are processed in the context of a civic engagement and civic education programme facilitated by a civil society organisation that included offline meetings. This resonates with Sæbø, Federici and Braccini's suggestions that affordances act in combination and that studying the online platform alone is not enough to understand how they become transformational action possibilities (Sæbø, Federici, and Braccini 2020, 722).

For example, some of the functional affordances, like scale, multimodality and information visibility, are typical of social media platforms but offer relational affordances specific to instant messaging when combined with affordances such as group relevance, perceived privacy or perceived freedom. In turn, affordances like group relevance or the information visibility are closely connected to antecedents that took place offline, like face-to-face meetings that helped to establish bonds and membership boundaries, or actions taken in in-person public participation meetings that then could be framed, visibilized, and amplified in WhatsApp in multi-modal ways among trusted relevant groups.

Considering these contingencies, the functional affordances can be categorised as follows based on their relational transformational potential:

- Communicative. These are affordances often mentioned when discussing WhatsApp (Treré 2020) and are those that can change "communicative practices or habits"

(Schrock 2015, 1232), such as immediacy and multimodality. These made WhatsApp a convenient space for accessing information for those who were online to the extent that it was common in the groups to communicate not only in relation to their civic engagement plans but also to share information related to jobs, grants, and funding opportunities.

- Organizational. Alongside changing communicative practices, the affordances of popular ubiquitous instant messaging apps like WhatsApp can support collective organizing. For example, group relevance, scale, immediacy, and diffuse hierarchies helped participants discuss, question, or agree on arrangements for collective action, such as attending public participation meetings. WhatsApp has indeed been discussed in the literature as a "robust organizational device" (Treré 2020, 1).
- Social. These are affordances that influence the way individuals and groups interact and affiliate. For example, affordances like perceived privacy or group relevance enabled participants ways for affiliation and interaction that are different from other online spaces because related more directly to their interests and aspirations and felt safer than more open social media platforms. This also resonates with Raemdonck and Pierson's taxonomy of social network platform affordances which finds that "closed many-to-many interactions" fosters social identity and norm-building (Van Raemdonck and Pierson 2021).
- Agentic. These refer to affordances that can enable the voice and agency of an individual or group. For example, according to participants accounts, the affordances of perceived freedom, perceived privacy, or diffuse hierarchies, enabled participants to feel freer in expressing their views without concerns of being dismissed when compared to public spaces.
- Discursive. Affordances such as group relevance, information visibility, multimodality or scale, can enable the construction and amplification of narratives through "framing", which Sebø, Federici and Braccini define as "construction of shared meanings and building of a collective understanding"(Sæbø, Federici, and Braccini 2020, 704).

The discursive potential, especially when associated to the affordance of scale, is typical of social media platforms more broadly. Nyabola, for example, has argued that the openness and networked characteristics of Twitter are allowing counter-narratives to emerge and shape Kenya's public debate (Nyabola 2018). In "open many-to-many interactions", however, participants have less influence in establishing norms other than commenting (Van Raemdonck and Pierson 2021, 6). By contrast, this discursive potential, takes a different form in instant messaging apps like WhatsApp due to other affordances that can make it a more private, intimate, and less hierarchical space.

Information visibility can also help to build a sense of purpose, group solidarity and respect, particularly important in a context where young people and women feel dismissed, because of the reasons already alluded to in relation to the affordances of multimodality and scale. For example, during a training event, and in relation to photos that had been shared on WhatsApp showing members speaking up in a public discussion, I observed the training facilitator saying to a participant: "I saw you in WhatsApp" and, to another one, "I saw you standing". Similar interactions took place in the WhatsApp groups in other instances. In the following example, the WhatsApp interaction takes place after a participant shared a number of photos of a petition with a list of signatures being delivered to the administrator of a local ward:

13:21: Great work (...)

14:02:

👏✊👏✊👏✊👏✊👏✊👏✊👏✊👏✊👏✊👏✊👏✊👏✊👏✊👏✊👏✊
👏✊ *Leading from the Front👏✊ (...) Chairman*

15:00 : Good work (...)

15:07: Hapo ni sawa bro! [This is good bro!]

This information visibility also helped with mobilising: "*You know, if we use WhatsApp, I have learnt that many people they have seen our views and they've known their rights and some they have been coming in our group asking questions, getting them I can see it is helping others* (Interview P6)."

In the context of this study, then, the discursive potential of a dark social like WhatsApp is associated with the organizational and social potential or possibility to organise, build a collective identity, and amplify discourses that can enable a sense of belonging, purpose, and collective action. For example, some participants shared a view that Twitter was an important avenue for youth to influence the public debate but added that, by contrast, WhatsApp helped them get organised: "*But, also, WhatsApp, it's used to organise us a lot. We've managed to even organise a demonstration on WhatsApp (...) So that's how I see technology changing how we are organised, and even for me, it's much easier for me to keep tabs of what's happening in the country, I would say, without having to delay in terms of communication and its immediate effect* (Interview P23)".

Affordances can also be in tension with each other. For example, the affordance for deliberation might sometimes be in tension with other affordances, such as the affordance of diffuse leadership and perceived freedom which meant that discussions were sometimes messy without a clear lead to facilitate discussions towards a clear conclusion. Similarly, participants would sometimes be asked by other members not to share content that was not relevant to the group's organisational purpose (civic engagement), yet this contradicted the social affordance of the group as a space of belonging where young people and women could be free to be themselves. I interpreted this messiness, however, as part of the process of constructing and rehearsing citizenship. The WhatsApp groups provided an alternative avenue where young citizens with online access had a space of belonging and shared interests where their voice could be heard, relationships built and maintained, and narratives and claims on citizenship constructed, practiced and amplified inwards, similar to Treré's reference to WhatsApp as a space for "backstage" activism (Treré 2020).

7 Seeing Affordances Through an Intersectional Lens

A focus on the transformational potential of these affordances without a nuanced understanding of structural inequalities risks amplifying oppressive and exclusionary dynamics. An intersectional lens requires looking not only at the axes and consequences of exclusion from online use but also how online use interacts with existing structural inequalities.

In relation to exclusion from meaningful online access, some participants in the WhatsApp groups I observed would drop in and out due to intermittent access to smartphones and data and there were compounding reasons for this that were not solved by simply providing an allowance to buy data bundles. A participant, for example, was offline for up to seven months during the digital ethnography because her phone broke and could not afford to repair it. Others used their husbands' phones to check in or catch up with the group communication from time to time. Some participants mentioned having to prioritise school fees or supporting others in their community over getting a smartphone. Some lived in areas with limited electricity or network access and had limited time and resources to travel to a place to access wi-fi. This intermittency, and the importance of offline communication for them, manifested also in the conversations in WhatsApp groups, where in various instances some members reminded others of texting or calling those offline:

"20:14 –: 👏👏👏👏👏👏👏👏👏 *Good job chair*

20:15 -: 👏👏👏👏👏👏 *kindly madam chair text, there are some members who have gone analog..*" (Observation - WhatsApp Group 1)

A number of axes of exclusion in relation to access and use of Internet were identified in the analysis, including class or socio-economic background, location, education level, gender, infrastructure, (digital) literacy, language, and (dis)ability. These intersected: a participant who identified as a young woman, located in a rural village with secondary education, with care responsibilities and intermittently working in the informal sector interacted with WhatsApp and its affordances differently compared to a young woman based in the capital town with a higher education degree, a more stable job and more limited care responsibilities.

Intermittent access to WhatsApp meant some participants could not benefit from the affordance of immediacy and this had an impact on the opportunities for some participants to receive information related to civic engagement plans, jobs, and opportunities for interaction and affiliation: "[In WhatsApp] *You just follow up what's going on every sub-county but now even I can't even know what's going on because I am not in access of WhatsApp. Even like somebody is telling me, he can say, tomorrow I am going to somewhere, if you are willing you come and join me, you are going to visit a certain place, but it is on WhatsApp so (…) we add on (…) when we go. [Interview P17]*".

Similarly, relying on the WhatsApp affordance of multi-modality excluded some participants and their potential for transformational impact in the community. For example, some participants mentioned the need for hard copies of the constitution to share with peers in their communities as part of their mobilising. Yet, this was not always taken into account by trainers. After copies of the constitution were requested during a training I observed, a civic education facilitator said to a participant that a soft copy would be shared instead and added "Technology makes things easier, doesn't it?", yet the participant did not have a working smartphone. Others had access to WhatsApp but could not afford opening data-hungry files, like videos.

Even for those who could be online, the social affordances of using WhatsApp interacted with structural gendered oppressive dynamics. For example, some women talked about how access to a smartphone and the social interaction it afforded upset power dynamics and resulted in enduring violence from their husbands: "*Ah it makes us really beaten there at night because of the phones*".

An intersectional lens helps to understand inequalities not only in relation to digital divisions but also in relation to the structural inequalities and power relations in which people are positioned (Zheng and Walsham 2021). In this study, the intersectional lens and digital ethnography helped to explore interactions across different socio-demographic positionings and across the private and public spheres and how the structural inequalities behind these positionings limited or changed the relational and transformational affordances either because of limited access to functional affordances or because the way these interacted with existing structural inequalities.

8 Conclusions

This paper has presented a list of functional affordances related to WhatsApp in the context of a civic engagement programme in Western Kenya and their relational and transformational impact in processes of citizen engagement. It concludes with two main arguments.

Firstly, the use of WhatsApp among young activists in Western Kenya needs to be understood not only in the context of its more obvious communicative and organisational affordances that helped young people communicate and plan more easily. Rather, its social, agentic, and discursive affordances helped participants find a safe space where they belonged, their views mattered and where they could share, build, and amplify narratives. This helped participants construct and rehearse citizenship inwards, building a sense of agency and purpose that interacted with more outward acts of citizenship, such as taking part in public participation meetings or signing petitions.

Secondly, these affordances could not be enjoyed by everyone and their transformational impact was limited for those who did not have meaningful access to the Internet. Even for those who had online access, the affordances interacted with structural inequalities and power relations. A reliance on WhatsApp in civic engagement programmes and activist can amplify existing inequalities related to gender, class, or location among others. The ubiquity of WhatsApp in the social, work, and political life of Kenyan internet users can overlook sites of oppression and disadvantage.

Initiatives supporting processes of civic engagement or citizen activism should take a digital rights and justice approach, mindful of intersecting sites of oppression, when considering the use of online spaces for interaction, even when these spaces appear to be as ubiquitous and omnipresent as WhatsApp.

Acknowledgements. The author is thankful to the members of the Kenyan organisation Siasa Place for the support and access to youth networks in Busia county and to all the research participants who took part. The author also thanks the reviewers of the paper for the constructive feedback. The author is grateful to Prof. Rose Capdevila, Dr. Charlotte Cross and Dr. Agnes Czajka for overall support in the broader doctoral research study as the supervisory team.

References

Baxter, J.: Keep strong, remember everything you have learnt: constructing support and solidarity through online interaction within a UK cancer support group. Discourse Soc. **29**(4), 363–379 (2018)

Bayhack, J.: 97% of Internet Users in Kenya Use WhatsApp; Here's How Businesses Can Reach Them. Africanews (2021). https://www.africanews.com/2021/05/20/97-of-internet-users-in-kenya-use-whatsapp-here-s-how-businesses-can-reach-them-by-james-bayhack/

Bosch, T.: Twitter activism and youth in South Africa: the case of #RhodesMustFall. Inf. Commun. Soc. **20**(2), 221–232 (2017). https://doi.org/10.1080/1369118X.2016.1162829

Bowes-Catton, H., et al.: Talkin about revolution? from quiescence to resistance in the contemporary university. Manag. Learn. **51**(4), 378–397 (2020). https://doi.org/10.1177/135050762092 5633

Carastathis, A.: Intersectionality: Origins, Contestations, Horizons. Lincoln & London: University of Nebraska Press (2016)

Colom, A.: Using Whatsapp for focus group discussions: ecological validity, inclusion and deliberation. Qual. Res. 1–16 (2021)

Crenshaw, K.: Demarginalizing the intersection of race and sex: a black feminist critique of antidiscrimination doctrine, feminist theory and antiracist policies. Uni. Chicago Legal Forum **1989**(1), 139–67 (1989). http://chicagounbound.uchicago.edu/uclf%5Cn. http://chicag ounbound.uchicago.edu/uclf/vol1989/iss1/8

Dencik, L., Hintz, A., Cable, J.: Towards data justice? the ambiguity of anti-surveillance resistance in political activism. Big Data Soc. **3**(2), 1–12 (2016). https://doi.org/10.1177/205395171667 9678

Global Web Index: GlobalWebIndex's Flagship Report on the Latest Trends in Social Media, **38** (2020). https://www.globalwebindex.com/reports/social%0A. https://www.global webindex.com

Gómez-Cruz, E., Harindranath, R.: WhatsApp as 'technology of life': reframing research agendas. First Monday **25**(12), 1–15 (2020)

Hine, C.: Ethnographies of online communities and social media: modes, varieties, affordances. In: Fielding, N.G., Lee, R.M., Blank, G. (eds.) The SAGE Handbook of Online Research Methods, pp. 401–413. SAGE Publications Ltd, 1 Oliver's Yard, 55 City Road London EC1Y 1SP (2017). https://doi.org/10.4135/9781473957992.n23

Hootsuite, and We Are Social. Digital 2020: Kenya: 80 (2020). https://datareportal.com/reports/ digital-2020-kenya

Kenya National Bureau of Statistics. 2019. "2019 Kenya Population and Housing Census Volume 4: Distribution of Population by Socio-Economic Characteristics." https://www.knbs.or.ke/? wpdmpro=2019-kenya-population-and-housing-census-volume-iv-distribution-of-population-by-socio-economic-characteristics

Kibere, F.N.: The paradox of mobility in the Kenyan ICT ecosystem: an ethnographic case of how the youth in Kibera slum use and appropriate the mobile phone and the mobile internet. Inf. Technol. Dev. **22**(July), 47–67 (2016)

Milan, S., Barbosa, S.: Enter the WhatsApper: reinventing digital activism at the time of chat apps. First Monday (2020). https://doi.org/10.5210/fm.v25i12.10414

Mukhongo, L.L.: Participatory media cultures: virality, humour, and online political contestations in Kenya. Afr. Spectr. **55**(2), 148–169 (2020)

Ndlela, M.N., Mulwo, A.: Social media, youth and everyday life in Kenya. J. Afr. Media Stud. **9**(2), 277–288 (2017)

Nyabola, N.: Digital Democracy, Analogue Politics: How the Internet Era Is Transforming Politics in Kenya. Zed Books, London (2018)

Omanga, D.: WhatsApp as 'digital publics': the nakuru analysts and the evolution of participation in county governance in Kenya. J. Eastern Afr. Stud. **13**(1), 1–17 (2018). https://doi.org/10.1080/17531055.2018.1548211

Pailey, R.N.: Birthplace, bloodline and beyond: how 'Liberian citizenship' is currently constructed in Liberia and abroad. Citizsh. Stud. **20**(6–7), 811–829 (2016). https://doi.org/10.1080/13621025.2016.1204269

Pang, N., Woo, Y.T.: What about WhatsApp? a systematic review of Whatsapp and its role in civic and political engagement. First Monday **25**(12) (2020)

Postill, J., Pink, S.: Social media ethnography: the digital researcher in a messy web. Media Int. Aust. **145**, 123–134 (2012)

Van Raemdonck, N., Pierson, Jo:. Taxonomy of social network platform affordances for group interactions. In: 14th CMI International Conference - Critical ICT Infrastructures and Platforms, CMI 2021 – Proceedings, pp. 1–8 (2021)

Roberts, T.: Participatory technologies: affordances for development. IFIP Adv. Inf. Commun. Technol. **504**, 194–205 (2017)

Roberts, T., Hernandez, K.: Digital access is not binary: the 5'A's of technology access in the philippines. Electron. J. Inf. Syst. Dev. Countries**85**(4),e12084 (2019). http://doi.wiley.com/10.1002/isd2.12084

Rollason, Harry. 2021. What countries are the biggest whatsapp users? Conversocial. (2021). https://www.conversocial.com/blog/what-countries-are-the-biggest-whatsapp-users

Sæbø, Ø., Federici, T., Braccini, A.M.: Combining social media affordances for organising collective action. Inf. Syst. J. **30**(4), 699–732 (2020)

Sanya, B.N.: Disrupting patriarchy: an examination of the role of e-technologies in rural Kenya. Feminist Afr. **18**(18), 12–24 (2013)

Sanya, B.N., Odero, P.W.: Feminist articulations, social literacies, and ubiquitous mobile technology use in kenya. Policy Futures Educ. **15**(3), 309–326 (2017)

Schrock, Andrew Richard. 2015. "Communicative Affordances of Mobile Media: Portability, Availability, Locatability, and Multimediality." *International Journal of Communication*: 1229–46

Sumiala, J., Tikka, M.: Digital media ethnographers on the move – an unexpected proposal. J. Digit. Soc. Res. **2**(1), 39–55 (2020)

Treré, E.: Reclaiming, proclaiming, and maintaining collective identity in the #YoSoy132 movement in Mexico: an examination of digital frontstage and backstage activism through social media and instant messaging platforms. Inf. Commun. Soc. **18**(8), 901–915 (2015). https://doi.org/10.1080/1369118X.2015.1043744

Treré, E.: The banality of Whatsapp: on the everyday politics of backstage activism in Mexico and Spain. First Monday **25**(12) (2020)

Walsham, G.: ICT4D research: reflections on history and future agenda. Inf. Technol. Dev. **23**(1), 18–41 (2017)

Yuval-Davis, N.: Women, citizenship and difference. Fem. Rev. **57**(1), 4–27 (1997)

Yuval-Davis, N.: Power, intersectionality and the politics of belonging. In: Harcourt, W. (ed.) The Palgrave Handbook of Gender and Development, pp. 367–381. Palgrave Macmillan UK, London (2016). https://doi.org/10.1007/978-1-137-38273-3_25

Zheng, Y., Hatakka, M., Sahay, S., Andersson, A.: Conceptualizing development in information and communication technology for development (ICT4D). Inf. Technol. Dev. **24**(1), 1–14 (2018)

Zheng, Y., Walsham, G.: Inequality of what? an intersectional approach to digital inequality under Covid-19. Inf. Organ. **31**(1), 100341 (2021). https://doi.org/10.1016/j.infoandorg.2021.100341

Zheng, Y., Ai, Y.: Affordances of social media in collective action: the case of free lunch for children in China. Inf. Syst. J. **26**(3), 289–313 (2016)

ICT in Displacement and Conflict Zones: Ideas, Disconnects, and Innovations

Evaluating Mobility and Access of Disabled Refugees in Rohingya Camps in COX'S Bazar

Suzana Brown[1]([⊠]) [iD], Faheem Hussain[2] [iD], Emily Hacker[3], Maurice Bess[1],
and Achilles Vairis[4] [iD]

[1] SUNY Korea, Incheon, South Korea
suzana.brown@sunykorea.ac.kr, maurice.bess@stonybrook.edu
[2] Arizona State University, Tempe, USA
faheem.Hussain@asu.edu
[3] University of Utah, Salt Lake City, USA
emily.hacker@hsc.utah.edu
[4] Hellenic Mediterranean University, Heraklion, Greece
vairis@hmu.gr

Abstract. To better understand the mobility needs of Rohingya refugees with physical disabilities, specifically lower limb impairments, members of the Mobility Aid project team visited Rohingya refugee camps in Cox's Bazar, Bangladesh. Interviews and gait analyses with 14 participants were conducted over a three-week period in September 2021. Interviews covered topics such as the origin of disability, barriers and challenges associated with physical disability in refugee camps, and disability-related discrimination. Participants were also asked about ways in which they adapt and compensate for physical disabilities in challenging environments. An analysis of these findings is presented to highlight the need for emergency and humanitarian response planning to include persons with disabilities. In addition, the team conducted gait analysis from videos obtained using a simple inexpensive setup and remotely evaluated six disabled participants. The preliminary results of this gait analysis are promising and comparable to the patterns observed in the lab settings.

Keywords: Rohingya refugees · Disabilities · Mobility · Access · Gait analysis

1 Introduction

The Rohingya have faced decades-long persecution from the Myanmar government. A Muslim ethnic minority living in the western Rakhine State of Myanmar, the Rohingya are considered to be one of the most victimized populations in the world. The Rohingya have had their citizenship revoked, are not allowed to vote, and the Myanmar government has strict laws regulating the Rohingyas' ability to work, marry, and own property. Starting in 2017, the Myanmar army began a new violent campaign against the Rohingya population living in Rakhine State after clashes with alleged Rohingya militants. Fleeing

© IFIP International Federation for Information Processing 2022
Published by Springer Nature Switzerland AG 2022
Y. Zheng et al. (Eds.): ICT4D 2022, IFIP AICT 657, pp. 583–592, 2022.
https://doi.org/10.1007/978-3-031-19429-0_35

rape, torture, physical violence, and murder, over one million Rohingya refugees have relocated to neighboring Bangladesh [1].

Refugees under any circumstance face tremendous obstacles, but these challenges are amplified for refugees with disabilities. It is estimated that 15% of the world's population lives with some form of disability [2] and that people with a physical disability are two to four times more likely to be killed or injured in natural disasters [3]. Priddy [2] identifies persons with disabilities (PWDs) as "the forgotten victims of armed conflict." Sexual and gender-based violence (SGBV) also disproportionately impact those with disabilities [4].

Mobility concerns for Rohingya refugees with physical disabilities are especially pressing in refugee camps in Bangladesh – most notably the Cox's Bazar area. This area is prone to monsoons, cyclones, and flooding; all of which contribute to landslides. Muddy, steep, and unstable terrain in these camps makes movement between shelters and facilities near impossible for refugees with physical disabilities [5].

To address the mobility challenges faced by Rohingya refugees with physical disabilities, partners from SUNY Korea, Arizona State University – Tempe, Hellenic Mediterranean University, and Youth Power in Social Action (YPSA) Bangladesh have come together to design an alternate crutch/cane shoe/tip. With a wider surface area and more flexible material, the alternate crutch shoe is better suited to the terrain of refugee camps. The alternate crutch shoes are produced using a combination of 3D printing a mold and pouring silicon rubber into the mold to manufacture on-site shoes for the replacement of existing crutch shoes. Remote gait analysis using OpenPose software identifies unique joint movements to help evaluate the performance of the alternate crutch shoe [6].

Creating a better understanding of the intersections of physical disability and forced displacement, medical care, aid access, safety, and inclusion requires intense consultation with those directly impacted by physical disability. Through interviews with Rohingya refugees with physical disabilities, the Mobility Aid project team is able to better tailor their services to fit specific needs.

2   Research Method

In this paper we examine three related research questions:

RQ1 – In Cox's Bazar, what are the primary concerns around mobility for Rohingya refugees with physical disabilities?

RQ2 – What are the other challenges disabled Rohingya refugees face in Cox's Bazar camps?

RQ3 – Are the camps' healthcare services sufficiently inclusive and accessible for the Rohingya refugees?

In order to answer these three questions our methodology combines both qualitative and quantitative data from video analysis and interview data to better understand obstacles disabled and injured refugees face.

Data collection occurred in September 2021 when one of the main investigators from Mobility Aid team traveled to Cox's Bazar, Bangladesh to conduct interviews with Rohingya refugees with physical disabilities. These interviews were conducted with the assistance of YPSA over a period of three weeks. Fourteen Rohingya refugees, reported ages seven to 106 (self-reported), were asked questions about the origin of their disability, barriers, and challenges related to their disability, existence of possible disability-related discrimination, and ways in which they adapt and compensate for physical disability.

It is to be noted that, due to COVID-related restrictions, movement within the camp areas has been significantly restricted, which made things even more challenging for people with disabilities. In order to make things a bit easier for the interview respondents, the interviews were centrally conducted in two different community centers, where the local partner YPSA provides healthcare services for the refugees. Senior respondents were assisted by the YPSA volunteers to traverse through the hilly terrains to attend the interviews. YPSA volunteers also helped as interpreters. The Rohingya language does not have any official alphabet and none of the respondents had English or Bengali literacy. Hence at the start of each interview, the volunteers communicated to every respondent about the goal of the study and the ethical measures the research project is taking to ensure their privacy. Interviews commenced after the respondents provided their verbal consent.

One way to access mobility is evaluating gait, which is a manner or style of walking. In the case of people walking with crutches enhancing their gait stability is paramount for their survival in unhospitable terrains. Gait analysis is typically based on sophisticated instrumentation measuring body movements, body mechanics and activity of the muscles. Assorted studies have been carried out using different tools such as force platform, optical markers and 3D-cameras. These motion capture systems are expensive and must be installed in appropriate rooms containing expensive equipment. In addition, these systems require installation in areas with sufficient space and a specialized technician is also required to properly operate the system [7].

The Mobility Aid team developed a new approach recording video obtained using two simple mobile phone cameras from six participants who walked 3 times each. The cameras were positioned as to provide a stereoscopic view of the participant's walking with crutches, with one camera recording the side view of the walk and the second camera, at 90 degrees to the first camera, recording the participant from the front view. The two cameras were calibrated using a large checkerboard pattern to obtain the stereoscopic transformation matrix, which was used to obtain the 3D position data of an object in the covered area. This non-contact and low-cost data collection was then evaluated and subsequently used to calculate Signal-to-Noise-Ratio (SNR) of acceleration and jerk, which is the first derivative of acceleration, for the ankle of each participant. This approach is building upon previous work of the Mobility Aid team [6, 8] on evaluating and verifying the approach applied to the gait of disabled people who walk with crutches in the lab environment in South Korea where the principal investigator works.

This was the first attempt to collect data directly from the field with disabled or injured Rohingya refugees. To gain a better understanding of the challenging terrain of the refugee camps in Cox's Bazar, Mobility Aid team members toured camps, documented different paths frequently used by the respondents and other people with physical disabilities, and visited the homes of five respondents. The team furthermore talked with the relatives, neighbors, and aid workers, who are closely involved with some of the respondents' daily lives in order to develop a comprehensive understanding of the latter group's mobility challenges.

The IRB approval for this study has been obtained from the organization where the principal investigator of the Mobility Aid project works, and it follows the Declaration of Helsinki and its set of ethical principles.

3 Results

In this section qualitative results of interviews are presented separately from the quantitative results of gait analysis. The integration of those results is presented in the discussion section.

3.1 Qualitative Data Results

Interviews with Rohingya refugees with physical disabilities were conducted in keeping with Mobility Aid's mission to "improve the mobility of people with disabilities in navigating environmental obstacles in [these] limited-resource settings" [9]. Fourteen respondents were interviewed of which 13 were male and one was female. Nine of the 14 respondents reported their cause of injury or disability as violence from the Myanmar army. The Rohingya population in Rakhine State, Myanmar has been subjected to "generations of statelessness and marginalization, extreme violence" and forced displacement [10]. The nine respondents who reported their cause of disability as violence from the Myanmar army were shot or beaten. Delay of medical care necessitated lower limb amputations for some respondents as wounds had become infected without treatment. In the words of one of the respondents (male, 30 year old):

> "The Burmese Army shot me, but I could not stop running. We walked and ran for several days before crossing the border. By the time I reached Bangladesh, my leg was already in very bad shape from the bullet wound's infection. They (the doctors) had to cut it, but I survived!"

Two of the respondents reported their disability resulted from accidents – one respondent was hit by a vehicle in the refugee camp and another sustained significant injury to his back and legs in a landslide. An additional two respondents reported their cause of disability as an unspecified congenital abnormality or birth defect and the final respondent stated their mobility challenges stemmed from an exacerbation of secondary medical conditions.

Respondents detailed a variety of challenges regarding the intersection of their disability and navigating life within refugee camps - one of the most reported issues being difficulty with the surrounding terrain. The Rohingya refugee camps in Bangladesh are frequently located in areas with steep environments and landslides and flooding from rain are common [11]. One respondent reported specifically avoiding leaving his home when it was raining, and another reported complete avoidance of any area with inclined terrain. Difficult terrain acts not only as a physical barrier to refugees with disabilities but a social and resource barrier as well. As one respondent (male, 40 year old) mentioned:

> "During the rainy season, I just cannot go outside. Sometimes I am stuck at home without anything. But it's impossible to walk in such a muddy terrain with my physical condition."

Respondents described the difficulties encountered when accessing food and other resources and aid items. Many reported hiring other refugees (camp porters) within the camp to carry aid items for them or to assist them in moving about the camp. Some respondents pay for these services through selling their aid items or by trading items for service. Respondents reported experiencing both exploitation and theft – primarily through having their aid items or money stolen by camp porters. It is well-documented that people with disabilities are at increased risk of experiencing physical and sexual violence and that this risk is increased in humanitarian settings [12]. The exploitation of people with disabilities through theft is itself a form of violence. As one of the senior respondents (male, 62 year old) described:

"It happened with me several times. I trusted people who offered help to carry my food relief. As soon as they get my food packets, they disappear. With my condition, there is no way I could keep up with them. My family and I end up being hungry."

The lack of appropriate medical care or lack of accessible medical care in refugee camps was also reported to be a challenge by the respondents. Further medical issues have arisen from the lack of appropriate medical care and from broken or improperly used mobility devices. Several respondents reported developing sores and infections in their armpits from defective or mismatched crutches. One respondent received surgical intervention for a leg injury from an unspecified NGO. By the time the respondent was ready for follow-up surgery, the NGO was no longer working within the camp. Seemingly simple barriers such as replacing a missing screw for a crutch present significant obstacles as the whole crutch must be replaced. Vendors within the refugee camp do not sell the required replacement screws.

In addition to physical concerns surrounding their disabilities, respondents also relayed concerns regarding social issues. The two respondents under the age of 18 reported concerns around isolation from schooling and peers. The people with disabilities who are most impacted by isolation and loneliness are young adults who are "economically inactive, living in rented or other accommodation, and have low levels of access to environmental assets" [13]. This group is heavily represented in Cox's Bazar and among the entire Rohingya refugee population in Bangladesh.

Concerns regarding disability-related discrimination were reported by one participant. They reported what they described as "intense discrimination" from medical providers. It is unclear if there is a cultural difference in how discrimination is experienced, if respondents were reluctant to report discrimination, or if discrimination against refugees with physical disabilities is not as prevalent as predicted. It also must be considered that Western perceptions and assumptions about discrimination against people with disabilities are being wrongly imposed.

3.2 Results of Gait Analysis

The synchronized videos from the two phone cameras were combined into a 3D representation of the participant's walk. With the help of machine learning algorithms of Open Pose, the participant and points on their body were identified and the coordinates in space of their movement with time were calculated. From the spatial information, kinematic parameters, such as velocity which is the rate of change of displacement with time; acceleration which is the rate of change of velocity with time; and jerk which is the rate of change of acceleration with time, were calculated for the ankle of the disabled participant.

As the participants were dressed in loose clothing it was not possible to accurately estimate the movement of the Centre of Gravity of the body, as it is frequently done in gait analysis with multiple video cameras. In the present case, points on the body such as the ankle were followed, as they can be identified clearly by the software and their spatial position can be calculated with far smaller error than the Centre of Gravity.

In addition, in conventional gait analysis, the individual phases of each step are calculated, but in this work, the study focused on the overall walk of the participant, which consisted of several steps during the video. In this work, the stability of the walk is assessed from the complete movement of the participant, as it is assumed of being more representative of the abilities and performance of the disabled person.

For the gait analysis, the Rohingya participant group consisted of six disabled people, with one of them being an amputee, while all of them were long-term users of crutches. The gait analysis metrics calculated were the Signal-to-Noise-Ratio of the kinematics of their ankle for the duration of the video. The subset of five long-term Rohingya crutch users, where the amputee was excluded, showed a consistent SNR of acceleration and jerk with a difference of 2% between the calculated SNR of the acceleration and jerk of the walk of each participant. The amputee Rohingya participant showed a much larger difference of 5% between the SNR of acceleration and jerk, with that of the jerk being lower than that of the acceleration. This qualitative difference has been observed previously with an experienced long-term crutch user of the early study of gait performed in South Korea whose difference was far larger. In South Korea, participants included long-term crutch users who were disabled of poliomyelitis, inexperienced short-term crutch users with no disability, and experienced long-term (because of injury from an accident) crutch users with no permanent disability. Out of these, an experienced long-term crutch user stood out for his stability and confidence in his walk. These observations were obvious in his videos, were identified in the gait analysis performed on the walk and were also confirmed in the subjective questionnaire used as well. This reference South Korean participant showed a difference between the SNR of acceleration and jerk for each of his three videos taken, which was also the case for the three videos taken for the Rohingya amputee participant.

It should be emphasized that high SNR values correlate with a better performance, which in this case relate to smaller abrupt changes to acceleration, while lower SNR values relate to higher abrupt changes to the rate of change of acceleration, or jerk. Therefore, in this case, the two participants, the Rohingya amputee, and the South Korean long-term crutch user showed a consistent, in all three runs, high SNR of acceleration, with a confident and strong movement in their walk. At the same time, they showed a consistent, in all three runs, distinctly lower SNR of the rate of change of acceleration (i.e., jerk) as they had rapid changes in acceleration in order to move in space as they desired. They were, in effect, more in control of their movement even though it required abrupt changes in the movement of the ankle to walk confidently. This quantitative observation seems correlated with how confident and strong crutch users are. It appears that the other five Rohingya crutch users are less confident which could be a consequence of them using crutches for a shorter time.

Figure 1 shows the front view and Fig. 2 the side view for one of the disabled participants using customized crutch shoes produced by the Mobility Aid project team.

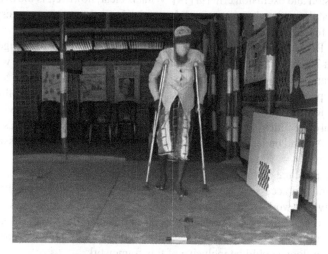

Fig. 1. Front view of participant's walk

Fig. 2. Side view of participant's walk

4   Discussion

Rohingya living in Myanmar have experienced decades of violence and dispossession. This violence does not always end once Rohingya refugees reach a host country or community. Refugees with disabilities are at increased risk of violence and exploitation and the lack of needs assessments based "on disability or specific vulnerability" leaves this population in a precarious situation [10]. Because of data disaggregation, a true understanding of the scope of disability among Rohingya refugees has not been obtained. Reports vary on the prevalence of disability, ranging from 3–14%, and reports have differing inclusion and exclusion criteria [14]. What is clear, however, is the overwhelming need for disability-related services in all humanitarian aid responses and especially for Rohingya refugees in Bangladesh.

A 2021 REACH report on age and disability in the Rohingya refugee response revealed that 76% of refugees with physical disabilities reported difficulty with mobility in refugee camps, 64% reported challenges accessing food and other aid services, and over 50% reported being unable to access medical services. For those able to access medical services, many did not get the appropriate care or there were no services for those with physical disabilities [15]. These reports mirror the responses of refugees interviewed by Mobility Aid and underscore the need for disability-inclusive and accessible medical services.

In lower resource settings, physical disabilities are often compounded by malnutrition, diminished access to WASH facilities, and the absence of rehabilitation facilities. Mobility Aid works to offset these factors by providing mobility assistive devices that adhere to concepts of usage such as physical availability, financial affordability, and acceptability [9]. Future research regarding refugees with physical disabilities and assistive technology should be inclusive of this framework.

Following a need for financial affordability, the current study is proposing a simple, inexpensive, non-contact, remote evaluation of stability in crutch users, something not done before. Typically, a standard gait evaluation measures body kinematics, muscle activity, and body mechanics using sophisticated instruments. All the studies that are measuring gait have been conducted using high-end tools including force platforms, 3D cameras, and optical markers. These advanced systems require installation in specialized spaces and are prohibitively expensive for limited-resource settings. In addition, a trained technician is necessary to properly operate the system [16]. To our knowledge, there has been only one exploratory study assessing stability by measuring the acceleration of the people who use crutches [17], and that study looked at periodic patterns while using sensors and optical motion capturing of participants.

The COVID-19 pandemic has suspended much on-the-ground research and continues to impact the ability of humanitarian actors to provide needed services. Therefore, remote assessment is a valuable addition accessing mobility of disabled refugees. Future and more elaborate study of mobility technology and Rohingya refugees with disabilities should be completed so Mobility Aid team members can continue to provide appropriately tailored services.

5   Conclusion

This paper presented a case study of Rohingya refugee camp and results of data collection by Mobility Aid team. Mobility Aid team works in collaboration with the local Bangladeshi NGO, YPSA, to support Rohingya refugees with physical disabilities, specifically lower limb impairments. The data collected during a visit during September

2021 by one of the investigators for Mobility Aid includes interviews with 14 Rohingya refugees with physical disabilities and video data of 6 participants. The data form the videos has been used to compare gait of the refugees who walk with crutches with the lab results and the conclusion was that is produced comparable results. This gives the team conformation that they can remotely monitor gait of disabled refugees. Qualitative data indicates that the difficult terrain is not only a physical barrier to refugees with disabilities but a social and resource barrier as well. Among many frustrations of this population are some simple barriers such as replacing a missing screw for a crutch since vendors in the camp do not sell the required replacement screws. Finally, very few respondents report discrimination, so it appears that the discrimination against refugees with physical disabilities is not as prevalent as expected.

References

1. BBC. Myanmar Rohingya: What you need to know about the crisis (2020). https://www.bbc.com/news/world-asia-41566561
2. Priddy, A.: Disability and armed conflict. Geneva Academy of International Humanitarian Law and Human Rights (2019). https://www.geneva-academy.ch/joomlatools-files/docman-files/Academy%20Briefing%2014-interactif.pdf
3. Quaill, J., Baker, R., West, C.: Experiences of individuals with physical impairments in natural disasters: an integrative review. Australian Institute for Disaster Resilience (2017). https://doi.org/10.3316/ielapa.793049280261310, https://search.informit.org/doi/epdf/
4. UNHCR. Working with persons with disabilities in forced displacement (2019). https://www.unhcr.org/en-us/publications/manuals/4ec3c81c9/working-persons-disabilities-forced-displacement.html
5. Human Rights Watch. Bangladesh: Rohingya endure floods, landslides (2018). https://www.hrw.org/news/2018/08/05/bangladesh-rohingya-endure-floods-landslides
6. Vairis, A., Boyak, J., Brown, S., Bess, M., Bae, K.: Gait analysis using non-contact meth-od for disabled people in marginalized communities. In: Proceedings, Part II, Singh, M., Kang, D.-K., Lee, J.-H., Tiwary, U.S., Singh, D., Chung, W.-Y. (Eds.) 12th International Conference, IHCI 2020, Daegu, South Korea, pp. 24–26 November 2020 (2020)
7. Nwanna, O.: Validation of an accelerometry based method of human gait analysis (2014). ETD Archive. 764. https://engagedscholarship.csuohio.edu/etdarchive/764
8. Vairis, A., Brown, S., Bess, M., Bae, K.H., Boyack, J.: Assessing stability of crutch users by non-contact methods. Int. J. Environ. Res. Public Health 18(6), 3001 (2021). https://doi.org/10.3390/ijerph18063001
9. Brown, S., Vairis, A., Masoumifar, A.M., Petousis, M.: Enhancing performance of crutches in challenging environments: proposing an alternative design and assessing the expected impact. In: TENCON 2019–2019 IEEE Region 10 Conference (TENCON), pp. 1717–1724. IEEE (2019)
10. Act Alliance. Emergency assistance to the Rohingya community in Cox's Bazar, Bangladesh (2017). https://actalliance.org/wp-content/uploads/2018/08/Bangladesh-Emergency-Assistance-to-the-Rohingya-Community-in-Coxs-Bazar-BGD172-Revision-1.pdf
11. Department for International Development. Inclusive access to services for persons with disabilities: Barriers and facilitators report, Jadimura camp, Teknaf (2019). https://data.humdata.org/dataset/inclusive-access-to-services-for-persons-with-disabilities/resource/be02365a-4037-4fa5-8269-6e88736030fd

12. Guglielmi, S., Jones, N., Muz, J., Baird, S, Mitu, K., Ala Uddin, M.: Age- and gender-based violence risks facing Rohingya and Bangladeshi adolescents in Cox's Bazar. Gender and Adolescence: Global Evidence, 2020 (2020). https://assets.publishing.service.gov.uk/media/5f3268d58fa8f57ac440fb1c/Age-and-gender-based-violence-risks-facing-Rohingya-and-Bangladeshi-adolescents-in-Cox_s-Bazar-1.pdf

13. Emerson, E., Fortune, N., Llewellyn, G., Stancliffe, R.: Loneliness, social support, social isolation and wellbeing among working-age adults with and without disability: cross-sectional study. Disabil. Health J. **14**(1), 100965 (2020). https://doi.org/10.1016/j.dhjo.2020.100965

14. ACAPS-NPM. Bangladesh: Considering age and disability in the Rohingya response (2021). https://www.acaps.org/special-report/bangladesh-considering-age-and-disability-rohingya-response?acaps_mode=slow&show_mode=1

15. REACH. Age and disability inclusion needs analysis: Rohingya refugee response (2021). https://www.impact-repository.org/document/reach/17afa088/REACH_BGD_Report_Age-and-Disability-Inclusion-Needs-Assessment_May-2021.pdf

16. Nwanna, O.: Validation of an Accelerometry Based Method of Human Gait Analysis (2014). https://engagedscholarship.csuohio.edu/etdarchive/764/?utm_source=engagedscholarship.csuohio.edu%2Fetdarchive%2F764&utm_medium=PDF&utm_campaign=PDFCoverPages

17. Tsuda, N.: Estimation model of body acceleration of crutch users based on body parts movement. In: Proceedings of the 2014 IEEE International Conference on Systems, Man, and Cybernetics (SMC), San Diego, CA, USA, 5–8 October 2014, pp. 3906–3911 (2014)

Research in Progress

The *Observatorio Metropolitano de Agua para Lima-Callao*: A Digital Platform for Water and Data Justice

Fenna Imara Hoefsloot[1]([✉]) [iD], Andrea Jiménez[2] [iD], Liliana Miranda Sara[3] [iD],
Lucio Estacio Flores[4] [iD], Javier Martinez[1] [iD], and Karin Pfeffer[1] [iD]

[1] University of Twente, Enschede, The Netherlands
{f.i.hoefsloot,j.a.martinez,k.pfeffer}@utwente.nl
[2] University of Sheffield, Sheffield, UK
a.jimenez@sheffield.ac.uk
[3] Foro Ciudades para la Vida, Lima, Peru
lmiranda@ciudad.org.pe
[4] Universidad Nacional de Ingeniería, Lima, Peru
lestaciof@uni.pe

Abstract. This paper details the development and design of the Observatorio Metropolitano de Agua para Lima-Callao (the metropolitan water observatory for Lima-Callao, MWO). The MWO is a digital, collaboratively developed observatory that aims to collect and share data about water access and infrastructuring practices within the metropolitan city of Lima-Callao, Peru. The purpose of developing the MWO has been to contribute to a fairer distribution of water resources amongst urban residents by creating an 'espacio de concertación' and collect and diffuse data on access to and quantity and quality of water for human consumption. By combining collaborative design approaches with the theory-informed data justice principles, we have been able to develop a prototype of the MWO. In general, this teaches us how to design digital platforms according to the principles of data justice in practice.

Keywords: Data justice · Urban development · Digital platforms · Water · Design · Lima

1 Introduction

In this paper, we detail the design of the Observatorio Metropolitano de Agua para Lima-Callao (the metropolitan water observatory for Lima-Callao), hereafter referred to as MWO. This is a digital, collaboratively developed observatory that aims to collect and share data about water access and infrastructuring practices within the metropolitan city of Lima-Callao in Peru. The purpose of developing the MWO has been to contribute to a fairer distribution of water resources amongst urban residents by exploring the potential of collecting and diffusing data on the access to, quantity, and quality of water for human consumption in the metropolitan area Lima-Callao.

Y. Zheng et al. (Eds.): ICT4D 2022, IFIP AICT 657, pp. 595–607, 2022.
https://doi.org/10.1007/978-3-031-19429-0_36

Over the past years, SEDAPAL, Lima's water company, has implemented a supervision, control, and data acquisition system (SCADA) to manage the water flows within the city. The use of digital technologies for water management, and the focus on data-driven decision-making, have been valued in Lima. With the help of this digital infrastructure, SEDAPAL has reduced non-revenue water significantly, improved the billing system for residents, and can respond faster to break-down or leakages in the system [1]. This is vital in a city of over 11 million people built in the desert.

However, previous research has shown how the datafication of Lima's water infrastructure, understood as the quantification of flows within the water distribution system, in Lima reproduces the structural inequalities within the water infrastructure, contributes to the further peripheralization of the non-digital city, and only partially accounts for other epistemologies, and water governance approaches [2, 3]. Within these conditions, an important portion of Lima's residents is not only structurally underserviced but also structurally underrepresented in the data about the water distribution in Lima due to a lack of registration or the absence of a water meter.

These gaps in the data have significant consequences for urban water consumers. Unregistered water consumers generally have less security over the quantity, quality, reliability, and continuity of the water service and, if registered but unmetered, are rationed by the water provider. While there are a number of tools that accommodate the data collection on unplanned urbanization and clandestine water infrastructures (e.g., drones and geo-radars) used by the water company [3], to date, there is no tool that facilitates the collection of data in collaboration with, and from the perspective of, the water consumers. Therefore, the central question explored in this research and the development of the MWO is: how can we design a platform that incorporates plural perspectives regarding water management to contribute data on water access, helps raise awareness of existing inequalities, and contributes to fairer policymaking? Specifically, if we consider water justice not only as the equitable socio-economic distribution of water but also the acknowledgment of plural perceptions, experiences, and normative approaches to water governance [4], it is vital to consider what knowledge we base water management decisions on.

2 Developing Citizens' Observatories

The MWO sits within a larger tradition of citizens' observatories and participatory urban dashboards, which aim to generate and exchange knowledge about cities or aspects of cities worldwide. These tools, which often take the shape of digital, geo-spatial information systems for collecting and sharing urban data, range in scope, levels of participation, interface, and contextualization. They can address place-specific issues unique to a particular urban context, such as the observatory for the Italo-Argentinian influence on architectural heritage in Buenos Aires [5]. Other urban observatories take a more comprehensive focus on urban governance and management or focus on particular infrastructures or urban phenomena (e.g., sound, air quality, housing stock) across cities [6–8]. Similarly, there is a wide range of ways to involve urban residents in the data practices of an urban observatory. Citizens can contribute passively through volunteered geographical information from sensors embedded in household appliances or mobile phone devices. In other cases, citizens take up a more active role by co-defining what needs to be observed and interpreting, validating, and using the data collected [9, 10]. Yet, most citizens' observatories and participatory dashboards share the common goals of wanting to increase transparency in policymaking by facilitating the exchange of information between stakeholders, mobilizing knowledge to tackle challenges in urban governance, and empowering citizens to voice their aspirations for their city [11].

Mattern [12] and Couldry and Mejias [13] explain how despite the fact that many digital technologies that have emerged during neoliberalism reproduce the long-term asymmetries in knowledge production along the lines of coloniality and capitalism, it can be fruitful to develop critical and experimental observatories or dashboards. The contribution of these platforms may not lie directly in the accuracy of the data generated, but rather in showing the messiness and complexity of the city, and visualizing a perspective on the city that is often unrepresented [12].

We do not deny – in fact, we emphasize – that creating a digital infrastructure to critically engage with digital infrastructure is paradoxical. Our research is inspired by experiments in 'statactivism,' which mobilize statistics' power for emancipation [14], and critical data sciences which specifically generate and reappropriate demographic data to visiblize and support feminist [15] and decolonial struggles [16]. These movements use data, indicators, and coded categories – compelling tools of the modernist state – to alter policy discourse and challenge the perceived neutrality of comparative statistics [14]. Making a platform teaches us about the limitations of the current data infrastructure. It is crucial to develop new socio-technological artifacts that can assist the act of imagining alternative narratives of data technology [13] and further theory about the role of datafication on water access.

There are many methods and approaches for designing citizens' observatories, usually following design science, collaborative design approaches, human-centered design, or emerging out of activism. This research adopted a collaborative process that follows similar principles as design science applied in action research and ICT4D. Originally stemming from engineering disciplines, design science research approaches the development of an artifact as the outcome of research, as well as the methodology to theorize about the environment in which the artifact is intervening [17]. Design science research departs from the premises that the process of design teaches us about the technological rules embedded in the artifact, how theoretical approaches are operationalized in practice, and in doing so, contributes to developing a more comprehensive body of knowledge and more useful design principles. While traditionally, design science research engages primarily with innovative solutions for business challenges, it has also been applied in cases that concern socio-economic problems and seek to contribute to technological interventions for human development [18, 19]. Sein et al. [18] and Islam and Grönlund [19] show that in aligning design science approaches with action research or ICT4D, the process of constructing an artifact is iterative. Rather than approaching the design process as a set of separated steps in sequence, the experience with design science research for action or development emphasized how the artifact developed is 'contextually situated and socio-technically enabled' [19, p. 140].

Our primary focus throughout all stages of the research is water and data justice. The reason we depart from these two central values is because water justice calls for a 're-politicization' of water governance in which not only the unequal distribution of water is made visible, but also the inequalities in political and economic power to influence water policies [20]. Hence, data on water should also be sensitive to and represent how people relate to water and participate in its governance. The current data technologies do not necessarily work towards increasing water justice but towards improving the efficiency of water distribution. It is too easily assumed that efficiency will eventually lead to water justice. Hence, while the goal of efficiency might be translated to more digital technologies and closing data gaps, the goal of water justice requires a different approach. One which acknowledges both the fair distribution of water as well as the plural ontologies of water [4].

We follow Taylor's [21, p. 1] definition of data justice as the "fairness in the way people are made visible, represented and treated as a result of their production of digital data." Specifically, Taylor [21] and Kitchin and Lauriault [22] emphasize that data need to be approached from a relational perspective, acknowledging how data infrastructures are part of the larger political, social and physical landscape and are inscribed by politics, power, and interests. In addition to explicitly paying attention to tensions and the lack of transparency in data practices [23], data justice requires fostering democratic dialogue and civic engagement [24]. It follows that the MWO does not strive towards 'objective knowledge' or a fully digital representation of the formal and informal water distribution system. Instead, it aims to engage critically with the current hegemonic representation of Lima's water infrastructure and establish itself as an 'espacio de concertación' [25] (space for concertation) or 'data subaltern' [26] to help communicate the experiences and views of residents currently overlooked. In doing so, the MWO builds on volunteered geographical information [27]. This work-in-progress paper will detail our collaborative design approach in developing the MWO and explain how the data justice design principles have been translated into the platform's design.

3 Methodology

In the development of the MWO, we bring together two knowledge bases. The first is from residents and experts in the field of water management through a collaborative design process. The second are data justice design principles formulated after a review of participatory urban dashboards and observatories in academic literature and practice. This review was conducted at an earlier stage of this research (manuscript under review). As seen in Table 1, the design principles depart from the three elements of Taylor's [21] data justice framework: (in)visibility, engagement, and non-discrimination. The design principles capture the generic characteristics the artifact should have through which the project objectives, in our case data justice, are met and dictate its technical features [28]. This offers several implications for the development of participatory observatories, their institutionalization, and the features they should contain.

The dimensions of the data justice referring to issue formulation, the embeddedness of the MWO in decision-making practices, the contestation of biases, and the pluralization of ontologies of the city, are not as much part of the design of the MWO as they are integral to the collaborative process of developing the platform. Therefore, the development of the MWO, guided by the aim to critically engage with and challenge the current representation of the water distribution system in data, has started with the collaborative formulation of the main issues and context of use that should be addressed. In the continuous conversation with the residents and civil society organizations we collaborate with, we aimed to create space to contest the biases in the development of the platform and the data collection practices. Additionally, with the current prototype of the MWO, we aim to establish further partnerships with government and non-governmental institutions in the field of water management in Lima to embed the platform within decision-making practices.

In line with the principles of design science as applied in action research and ICT4D, we structure the methodological approach into four stages: (i) problem formulation, (ii) building, intervention, and evaluation, (iii) reflection and learning, and (iv) formalization of learning [18]. As we are yet to launch the MWO in Lima and Callao, we can only describe the first two stages in this paper. The final two stages – both essential elements of design science [17] - focus on the evaluation of the adherence to the principles and contribution to theorizing about design principles for data justice and abstracting what we have learned for understanding water governance in Lima and Callao will be the focus of future work.

The collaborative design process took place between December 2019 and December 2021 (see Fig. 1). The first stage is primarily characterized by the exploration of the issues to be addressed in the MWO and the building of relationships (steps 1 and 2). The second stage (steps 3–6) focused on the formulation of the main needs and possible interventions from the perspective of the residents, translating these insights into the design and development of the digital platform, and moved towards evaluating the prototype and exploring the options to embed it institutionally within the water sector in Lima.

We formulated the functionalities of the MWO and the goal it should achieve in close cooperation with residents and civil society organizations in Lima. We work together with residents from three areas in Lima: José Carlos Mariátegui, Barrios Altos, and Miraflores. José Carlos Mariátegui is a largely organically built, peri-urban area characterized by high degrees of informality and poverty. Barrios Altos, part of the historical center of Lima, is a lower middle class to poor community in which the majority of the households are connected to basic utilities. Finally, Miraflores is the commercial and tourist center of the city with mainly middle to upper-class residents. Together, these three areas represent Lima's diversity regarding socio-economic living conditions and diverging degrees of geographical and political centrality. The suggestions from the focus groups from these three districts for the functionalities and design of the platform were systematized and categorized based on their priority to reach the aims of the MWO and their feasibility by the research team. This formed the input to the design of the MWO, implemented by the developer and the designer in step 4.

Additionally, we evaluated the MWO through interviews with experts in water management and urban development in Lima and experts in geo-information systems and application development. During these conversations, we mainly focused on evaluating the usefulness and utility of the MWO for policymakers and explored potential collaborations with relevant institutions in the field of water management in Lima-Callao. The outcome of these evaluations has iteratively been implemented in the design of the MWO.

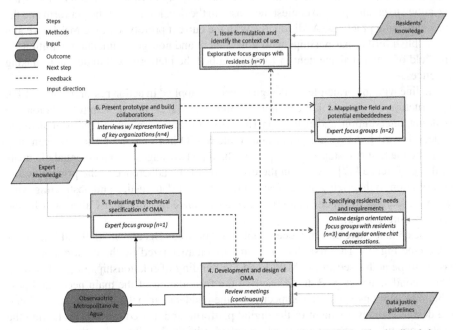

Fig. 1. Workflow and methods followed in the development of the MWO. The feedback loops indicate the various iterations of each of the steps taken.

4   The Design of the Observatorio de Agua Metropolitana

In this section, we mainly discuss how certain data justice design principles for Participatory Urban Observatories (PUO), specifically the right to invisibility, participation in and access to data practices, the contestation of biases, and the transparency about data practices, have been implemented in the collaborative design of the MWO. Table 1 summarises the data justice design principles and their implementation in the MWO. As indicated in Fig. 1, we are currently in the phase of presenting the prototype of the MWO to experts on water management or digital platforms and establishing routes for further collaborations with key actors in the field of water management in Lima.

The prototype of the MWO, i.e., a dedicated web application, includes an interactive map, layer management, a form for data input from residents, a forum for interaction between users, and social media integrations. Figure 2 shows the MWO interface layout where the interactive map with data from the 2017 census is the main component. Users can expand the map to cover the full-screen width, zoom in and out, (de)active or adjust

Table 1. Implementation of data justice design principles (derived from Taylor's data justice framework [21]) in the Observatorio Metropolitano de Agua.

Data justice dimensions		Design principles	Implementation in MWO	Example of implementation
1	Right to (in)visibility and to opt-in or opt-out of the data	PUOs should explicitly mention how residents can opt-out, be (in)visible, or only have some of their data shared. Specific attention should be granted to visibilizing the experiences and perspectives of marginalized communities	The MWO is designed to be accessible and usable for people without advanced digital skills and people living in informality	In addition to textual and numerical data, users can share pictures of the water infrastructure to diversify ways of visibilizing their experience. Users can send a request to have their submitted data removed or revised. We guarantee location privacy by adding 'noise' to the spatial data
2	Participation in and access to data practices	Citizens should be approached as expert observers within the city, stimulating their active participation in defining what needs to be observed and interpreting, using, or validating the information collected	Residents can share and download data and knowledge in multiple features and formats, allowing for diversity in ways knowledge can be shared, altered, or challenged	The MWO includes various data sharing methods, e.g., the data input form, the chat function, uploading photos, or using dedicated hashtags on social media platforms. Data can be downloaded in Geo-JSON, Excel, and PDF
3	Embedded in decision-making practices	PUO should foster relationships and communication between actors and feed into public planning and decision-making processes	The MWO is a collaborative project between civil society and research	We are currently in the process of formulating further partnerships with governmental institutions to embed the MWO in decision-making practices

(*continued*)

Table 1. (*continued*)

Data justice dimensions		Design principles	Implementation in MWO	Example of implementation
4	Issue formation	PUO should work towards empowering citizens to voice their aspirations for their city and mobilize knowledge to tackle challenges within their environment and urban governance	We have consulted residents in the early stages of development on what the main issues covered in the MWO should be. We are working towards supporting citizens' capacity to use the MWO data for development	Citizens' input has directly informed the questions in the data input form. We provide guidelines for using the data for advocacy and will organize a knowledge-sharing workshop
5	Contestation of biases	Participatory urban observatories should facilitate the contestation of internal and external biases	Externally, the MWO focuses on the biases and injustices in the water distribution system. Internally, we collaborate with various stakeholders to detect biases	Users can access and use the data for analysis or advocacy. The collaborative approach and features like the chat function allow discussing biases within the MWO
6	Transparency about data practices	In addition to contributing to administrative transparency, participatory urban observatories should be transparent concerning data generation, processing, and use. Ideally, this translated into opening the platforms' data, algorithms, and codes	The MWO is built on open-source software. The data collected is openly accessible. The source code of the MWO will be shared under a creative commons license after finishing the development	We use GeoServer, PostGis, Openlayers, and Open Street Maps as the main building blocks for the MWO

(*continued*)

Table 1. (*continued*)

Data justice dimensions		Design principles	Implementation in MWO	Example of implementation
7	Pluralization of ontologies of the city	PUO should facilitate the expression of plural ways of understanding and knowing the city	The MWO is developed to critically engage with the hegemonic datascape of the water distribution system in Lima	the MWO works towards diversifying the knowledge about water distribution by using indicators developed by citizens, focusing on representing the needs of people currently not represented in the data

the transparency of various data layers, switch between base maps, and click on data points for more information. A legend, scale bar, and information box have been included at the bottom of the map.

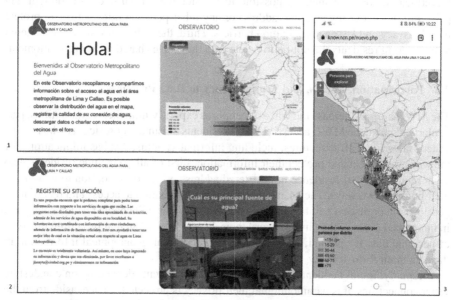

Fig. 2. Screenshot of the MWO prototype. Picture 1 shows the homepage with the map presenting data in a desktop browser. Picture 2 shows the data input form in a desktop browser. Picture 3 shows the homepage and map presenting data in a mobile phone browser.

4.1   Right to (In)visibility

In relation to the principle of the right to (in)visibility, there are some critical considerations in the data input form that we would like to highlight here and how we have tried
to translate that into the design of the MWO.

First of all, the right to (in)visibility refers to the ability of residents to determine what
data they would like to include in the MWO database. The MWO accommodates this by
offering various ways of sharing information. First, residents can start by filling in the
data input form. In addition to closed questions regarding, among others, the residents'
access to water, the continuity of the service, and its organization, the questionnaire
also includes an open question where residents can share any further information or
suggestions for improving the water distribution system and upload a photo of their water
infrastructure. The questions in the data input form were formulated in collaboration with
participants and reflect that people get water in various forms. To be able to get a more
diverse set of experiences, we developed different questions depending on where and
how respondents get water from. The list of questions automatically adjusts depending
on the answer selected.

Secondly, residents can share information and experiences more directly and openly
in the chat forum. This forum is accessible to all people who register with the MWO.
A registration function was necessary to block bots from taking over the chat function.
Nevertheless, we have made it possible to register with a name or pseudonym and
password, not requiring an email address or any other personal information, to protect
users' privacy and lessen participation barriers. Third, the right to invisibility is adhered
to by offering residents the option to delete data they have shared at any prior moment.

4.2   Participation, Access, and Transparency to Data Practices

The MWO aims to increase the voice of people as experts within their communities, particularly to make the MWO accessible to all residents of Lima. For residents who receive
water via various infrastructures, including informal systems, this has implications for
the ways we collect and protect their information. First of all, to include residents who
do not have a formal residence or registered address, we offer the option to geo-locate
their house in two ways. They can either allow the application to access and record their
geo-location or place a point on the map themselves. This will enable residents who live
in unmapped areas of the city to record their data as well. Note that providing this type
of personal data is optional; users have to volunteer their geographical information in
the data input form actively.

Secondly, for all residents, but in particular, for residents depending on clandestine
water connections, it is paramount that their privacy is protected. Hence, aside from the
location data, no personal data (data that can be traced to a natural person) is asked.
Additionally, the locational privacy of the people who share their data is guaranteed by
adding 'noise' to the geo-localization of the data points entered [29]. Each georeferenced
data point is randomly distributed within a buffer of 20–50 m wide around the original
location (see Fig. 3). Since this noise is added automatically while entering the data, and
the original location is never stored in the database, it is impossible to trace the exact
location of the respondent. Hence, the addition of noise entails increasing the inaccuracy

of the data to achieve a certain level of privacy. Nevertheless, a more accurate location is not needed to make visible the residential areas that are currently not yet officially mapped.

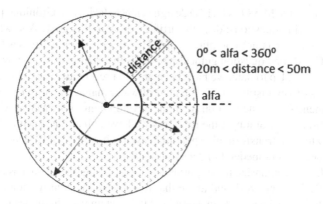

Fig. 3. Schematic representation of the 'noise' added to the coordinates of the data to protect the location privacy of residents via geo-indistinguishability [29]. The original geo-location is randomly distributed within the buffer zone. Figure developed by co-author.

Additionally, regarding access, we have designed the MWO, keeping in mind the requirements of residents who are not digital-savvy or who have limited access to the internet. The direct implications this had for the design are: (i) the MWO should be accessible via a browser rather than an app since this requires less storage on a device, (ii) the MWO should be responsive in order to be accessible via desktop as well as mobile phone, (iii) we have included guidelines and plain-text explanations on all tabs and pages of the MWO, guiding the users about the use and application of the observatory, and (iv) the data from the MWO can be downloaded in different formats (geo-JSON, excel, and PDF) along with the requirements of a specific user.

In line with the ambition to increase transparency and openness in the collection and use of data about water distribution in Lima, the MWO has been designed to adhere to the principles of open science. In addition to the open data practices, this entails that the MWO is built on open-source products (including geo- and database servers), and the source code of the MWO will be made open after the launch of the platform.

5   Concluding Remarks and Next Steps

By combining a collaborative design approach following the principles of design science with the theory-informed data justice principles, we have been able to develop a prototype of the MWO that aims to challenge the hegemonic representation of Lima's water infrastructure and help communicate the experiences and views of residents currently overlooked. In addition, the project of the MWO teaches us how to design digital platforms according to the principles of data justice in practice.

The MWO, as an artifact, took shape out of the interaction between researchers, activists, residents, and governmental organizations. The reflection and learning phase (stage iii) will mainly concern the accordance of the MWO with the criteria set: does it incorporate plural perspectives regarding water management to contribute data on water access, helps raise awareness of existing inequalities, and contribute to fairer policymaking?

For evaluating the MWO as ICT4D design science, Islam and Grönlund [19] propose asking the following questions: does the artifact research this goal? And what points to the fact that this is or is not complied with? The first question addresses the utility of the artifact. The second question guides us towards theorizing about how we can design data just platforms. Up to date, we have been able to present and test the prototype with representatives of key institutions in the field of water management in Lima. Following these recommendations, the next phase in the development of the MWO will consist of testing the observatory amongst the residents we have collaborated with. Additionally, for the MWO to have transformative potential, even if incremental [23], it is key that the observatory becomes embedded in decision-making practices.

Sein et al. [18] emphasize the importance of considering the artifact as emergent out of the organizational network and argue that to evaluate the contribution and utility of the tool in relation to the already existing SCADA system used in the water distribution system of Lima-Callao, we need to pay attention to its institutionalization within the network. For this, we will need to seek long-term partnerships with the aim to institutionalize the MWO as a space for concertation (*espacio de concertación*) [25].

References

1. SEDAPAL: Plan Estratégico de Tecnologías de la Información y Telecomunicaciones de Sedepal. Lima (2015)
2. Hoefsloot, F.I., Martinez, J., Pfeffer, K.: An emerging knowledge system for future water governance: sowing water for Lima. Territ. Polit. Gov. 1–21 (2022)
3. Hoefsloot, F.I., Richter, C., Martinez, J., Pfeffer, K.: The datafication of water infrastructure and its implications for (il)legible water consumers. Urban Geogr. 1–23 (2022)
4. Zwarteveen, M.Z., Boelens, R.: Defining, researching and struggling for water justice: some conceptual building blocks for research and action. Water Int. **39**(2), 143–158 (2014)
5. Carbonari, F., Chiavoni, E., Porfiri, F.: Interactive digital observatory on the cultural identity of Italo-Argentine heritage. SCIRES-IT **9**(2), 105–114 (2019)
6. Brown-Luthango, M., Makanga, P., Smit, J.: Towards effective city planning—the case of cape town in identifying potential housing land. Urban Forum **24**(2), 189–203 (2013)
7. Botteldooren, D., et al.: The internet of sound observatories. Proc. Meetings Acoust. **19**, 040140 (2013)
8. Castell, N., et al.: Mobile technologies and services for environmental monitoring: the Citi-Sense-MOB approach. Urban Clim. **14**, 370–382 (2015)
9. Dickey, A., Acuto, M., Washbourne, C.-L.: Urban Observatories: A Comparative Review, Melbourne (2021)
10. Young, G.W., Kitchin, R.: Creating design guidelines for building city dashboards from a user's perspectives. Int. J. Hum. Comput. Stud. **140**, 102429 (2020)
11. De Mesquita, N.B., Cila, N., Groen, M., Meys, W.: Socio-technical systems for citizen empowerment: how to mediate between different expectations and levels of participation in the design of civic apps. Int. J. Electron. Gov. **10**(2), 172 (2018)
12. Mattern, S.: A City is Not a Computer: Other Urban Intelligences. Places Books - Princeton University Press (2021)

13. Couldry, N., Mejias, U.A.: The decolonial turn in data and technology research: what is at stake and where is it heading? Inf. Commun. Soc. 1–17 (2021)
14. Bruno, I., Didier, E., Vitale, T.: Statactivism: forms of action between disclosure and affirmation. Open J. Sociopolitical Stud. **2**(7), 198–220 (2014)
15. D'Ignazio, C., Klein, L.F.: Data Feminism. MIT Press, Cambridge (2020)
16. Ricaurte, P.: Data epistemologies, the coloniality of power, and resistance. Telev. New Media **20**(4), 350–365 (2019)
17. Gregor, S., Hevner, A.R.: Positioning and presenting design science research for maximum impact. MIS Q. **37**(2), 337–355 (2013)
18. Sein, M.K., Henfridsson, O., Purao, S., Rossi, M., Lindgren, R.: Action design research. MIS Q. **35**(1), 37–56 (2011)
19. Islam, M.S., Grönlund, Å.: Applying design science approach in ICT4D research. In: Helfert, M., Donnellan, B. (eds.) EDSS 2011. CCIS, vol. 286, pp. 132–143. Springer, Heidelberg (2012). https://doi.org/10.1007/978-3-642-33681-2_11
20. Hartwig, L.D., Jackson, S., Markham, F., Osborne, N.: Water colonialism and Indigenous water justice in south-eastern Australia. Int. J. Water Resour. Dev. **00**(00), 1–34 (2021)
21. Taylor, L.: What is data justice? The case for connecting digital rights and freedoms globally. Big Data Soc. **4**(2), 205395171773633 (2017)
22. Kitchin, R., Lauriault, T.P.: Toward critical data studies : charting and unpacking data assemblages and their work. In: Thinking Big Data in Geography: New Regimes, New Research (2018)
23. Heeks, R., Shekhar, S.: Datafication, development and marginalised urban communities: an applied data justice framework. Inf. Commun. Soc. **22**(7), 992–1011 (2019)
24. Baibarac-Duignan, C., de Lange, M.: Controversing the datafied smart city: conceptualising a 'making-controversial' approach to civic engagement. Big Data Soc. **8**(2), 205395172110255 (2021)
25. Miranda Sara, L., Baud, I.: Knowledge-building in adaptation management: concertación processes in transforming Lima water and climate change governance. Environ. Urban **26**(2), 505–524 (2014)
26. Heeks, R., Renken, J.: Data justice for development. Inf. Dev. **34**(1), 90–102 (2018)
27. Elwood, S.: Volunteered geographic information: future research directions motivated by critical, participatory, and feminist GIS. GeoJournal **72**(3–4), 173–183 (2008)
28. Chanson, M., Bogner, A., Bilgeri, D., Fleisch, E., Wortmann, F.: Privacy-preserving data certification in the Internet of Things: leveraging blockchain technology to protect sensor data. J. Assoc. Inf. Syst. **20**(9), 1274–1309 (2019)
29. Chatzikokolakis, K., Palamidessi, C., Stronati, M.: Location privacy via geo-indistinguishability. ACM Siglog News **2**(3), 28–38 (2015)

Data Collection in the Global South and Other Resource-Constrained Environments: Practical, Methodological and Ethical Challenges

Suzana Brown[1] , Deepak Saxena[2] , P.J. Wall[3(✉)] , Cathy Roche[3] ,
Faheem Hussain[4] , and Dave Lewis[3]

[1] State University of New York (SUNY), Incheon, Korea
suzana.brown@sunykorea.ac.kr
[2] Indian Institute of Technology Jodhpur, Karwar, India
saxenad@iitj.ac.in
[3] ADAPT Centre, Trinity College Dublin, Dublin, Ireland
pj.wall@tcd.ie, {cathy.roche,dave.lewis}@adaptcentre.ie
[4] Arizona State University, Tempe, USA
faheem.hussain@gmail.com

Abstract. Collecting relevant and appropriate data when conducting research in the Global South and other resource-constrained environments can be challenging. This is particularly true when the researcher originates from a different country and has different social, cultural, and political beliefs to the research participants. Data collection in such contexts can be challenging for a variety of ethical, philosophical, theoretical, and methodological reasons which may arise resulting from the use of research approaches designed in the Global North. There are also many practical and infrastructural issues which may be relevant in resource-constrained countries. This paper provides examples of challenges encountered by the authors in a variety of ongoing research projects in the Global South. We propose approaches to address the identified challenges, and we conclude by calling for additional work on this important topic.

Keywords: Data collection · Methodology · Global South · Ethics

1 Introduction

This paper presents early-stage work which results from an examination of the philosophical, methodological, ethical, and practical challenges associated with data collection in various different social, cultural and political contexts in the Global South and other resource-constrained contexts. The paper has been motivated by the authors' ongoing research on projects in Malawi, Bangladesh, India, Sierra Leone and various other countries throughout Europe and across the world. We start by proposing that there is no one universal methodology or practical approach which is appropriate for data collection in all contexts. This has been further highlighted by the COVID-19 global pandemic which

© IFIP International Federation for Information Processing 2022
Published by Springer Nature Switzerland AG 2022
Y. Zheng et al. (Eds.): ICT4D 2022, IFIP AICT 657, pp. 608–618, 2022.
https://doi.org/10.1007/978-3-031-19429-0_37

has seen much data being collected remotely online or by local research assistants. The research gap identified in this paper arises from both a lack of literature on this topic and from the work of the authors who have experienced these data collection challenges personally in many countries over many years. The aim of this paper is to highlight these issues and to act as a catalyst to promote this conversation within the broader Global Development and technology for development (ICT4D) communities.

2 Literature Review

According to the World Economic Forum, as of 2020 world data is expected to reach approximately 44 zettabytes, with that number doubling every 2 to 3 years[1]. However, data production and collection is unequal across the planet, and the global data landscape remains heavily concentrated on English-speaking, urban, and relatively prosperous locations within the Global North. This may be because of the particular difficulties associated with data collection in resource-constrained contexts in the Global South where a variety of different ethical, social, cultural and political contexts are highly likely to apply.

This literature review is divided into two main sections. We begin by examining the body of literature which looks at practical and methodological challenges associated with data collection and methodology in the Global South. We then conclude with a review of the body of work concerning Southern-based Theory and an examination of whether this is relevant to data collection and methodology in the Global South.

2.1 Practical and Methodological Challenges Associated with Data Collection

Our work has highlighted a huge dearth of literature on practical and methodological challenges of data collection in the Global South. Among those writing about this topic include Shatz (2015), Asher (2010), and Roberts (2020). These authors warn of the difficulties of collecting data in such environments, with Asher (2010) highlighting that such data collection is not for the faint of heart or weak of stomach. Others have written more about challenges to data collection in specific fields, for example Ismail (2018) writes about data collection in community health, while Louis-Charles (2020) discusses ethical considerations for post-disaster fieldwork in the Caribbean. In addition, there exists a body of work which proposed solutions to the many and varied challenges identified. One such study is by Young et al. (2021) which features the potential power of crowdsourcing as a tool for knowledge production in the Global South. The authors point out that the success of such a crowdsourcing approach should focus on topics of high interest to the global development community as opposed to more traditional topics which may be of interest to a Global North audience.

---

[1] https://www.weforum.org/agenda/2019/04/how-much-data-is-generated-each-day-cf4bdd f29f/.

2.2 Southern-Based Theory

We also completed an examination of the body of literature examining philosophical and theoretical approaches to conducting research in the Global South. This body of work is far more extensive and includes the work of Frantz Fanon (1961) who originally came up with the idea of 'Southern Theory' which Connell (2014) defines as a social thought from the societies of the Global South which does not necessarily have to be about the Global South (Connell, 2014). The notion of Southern Theory was further developed by Connell (2007), Jean and John Comaroff (2012) and de Sousa Santos (2014) who all highlighted the possibilities of a different way to view theory in a Southern (or Global South) context. These studies fit in Avgerou's theoretical dimension for ICT4D, namely a foundational theory that problematizes 'development' (Avgerou, 2016).

The main difference between theories in the Global North and Southern-based theories according to Connell (2014) is concerned with colonial attitudes where various notions of progress are in the material culture. Southern-based theories are less concerned with such progress and represent the concerns of a rural, village-centred world-view. The concept of theory for Connell (2014) is not any specific theory, but to a spectrum of social thought with a range of different theories. This is further developed by Kreps & Bass (2019) who discusses Southern theory in data collection. In the light of Southern theories they propose a specific focus on appropriate research questions and the data which is required for support. The emphasis should be on whether or not ICT4D researchers follow the same data quality requirements when collecting data in the Global South. Furthermore, do they conduct research with or along local researchers, and if so, how do they choose and collect data to answer research questions that align ethical, social, cultural and political perspectives and contexts in the Global South? These are highly relevant questions which should be carefully considered when designing research to be conducted in the Global South.

3 Case Descriptions

The authors have been involved with research in the Global South over many years and are currently involved with a variety of research projects based in Bangladesh, Malawi, Sierra Leone and other parts of the world. This section provides some detail on these projects and the associated data collection challenges which have been encountered.

3.1 Bangladesh

The research in Bangladesh involves a project called Mobility Aid which is financed by a humanitarian grant from Grand Challenges Canada. This project focuses on the needs of persons with physical disabilities that can be ameliorated with alteration to canes or crutches. In September 2021 one of the investigators for the Mobility Aid project travelled to Cox's Bazar, Bangladesh to conduct interviews with Rohingya refugees with physical disabilities. These interviews were conducted with the assistance of Young Power in Soucial Action NGO over a period of three weeks. Fourteen Rohingya refugees were asked questions about the origin of their disability, barriers, and challenges related to their disability, and ways in which they adapt to compensate for physical disability, and disability-related discrimination. In addition, for the purpose of gait analysis, multiple videos were obtained using simple mobile phone cameras from six participants who walked three times each. The cameras were positioned to provide a stereoscopic view of the participant's walking with crutches, with one camera recording the side view of the walk and the second camera, at 90 degrees to the first camera, recording the participant from the front view. The two cameras were calibrated using a large checkerboard pattern to obtain the stereoscopic transformation matrix, which was used to obtain the 3D position data of an object in the covered area.

3.2 Malawi

An ongoing research project based in the Dzaleka refugee camp in Malawi investigates the role of technology in enabling refugee entrepreneurial activity. Drawing on 25 structured interviews with refugee entrepreneurs, the multilevel and multidimensional nature of refugee entrepreneurship was examined in an attempt to explore the challenges refugee entrepreneurs face. Dzaleka refugee camp is located in Dowa District approximately 45 km from Lilongwe, the capital city of Malawi. The camp houses refugees from different countries such as the Democratic Republic of Congo, Burundi, Rwanda, Somalia, and Ethiopia. Dzaleka refugee camp can thus be seen as a large and multicultural African community as the refugees brought their own cultures and norms with them from their native countries.

Interviews were conducted on a face-to-face basis by a local research assistant who is also a refugee in the camp and has resided there since January 2015. The research assistant was a student at the Global Education Movement (GEM) that provides access to online degrees to refugee learners, an initiative by the Southern New Hampshire University (SNHU). The research assistant speaks multiple languages and was trained by the SNHU faculty to conduct qualitative research. The interviews were conducted in French, English, Kinyarwanda, Kirundi, and Kiswahili which are all native languages of the camp residents. Engaging with a native of the camp and conducting the interviews in the native language helped in keeping the natural atmosphere and ensured the interpretive validity of the research.

3.3 Sierra Leone

The ongoing research project in the Bonthe District of southern Sierra Leone involves the design, implementation and scaling of a mobile health (mHealth) initiative. Extensive field work and data collection commenced in 2015 and continues to take place throughout 2022 with many researchers collecting data from a variety of stakeholders including community health workers, mHealth project team members, NGOs involved with the project and Government officials from the Ministry of Health and Sanitation in Sierra Leone. Various challenges arose during data collection including Africa's biggest cholera outbreak in 2012 with 22,885 reported cases and 298 confirmed deaths (WHO 2013), a landslide in Freetown in 2017 which killed 1,141 people and left more than 3,000 homeless (World Bank 2017), and four major floods in the last 15 years which have affected over 220,000 people and caused severe economic damage (World Bank

2017). In addition, the most widespread Ebola virus outbreak in history occurred in West Africa between May 2014 and March 2016 affecting Guinea, Liberia and Sierra Leone. According to the World Health Organization (2016) the total death toll in Sierra Leone was 3,955 with 11,308 deaths in total attributed to Ebola across the affected countries in West Africa.

3.4 AI Ethics in the Global South

This research project commenced in 2020 and examines Artificial Intelligence (AI) ethics and AI ethical standards in the Global South. The research is inspired by huge interest and growth in technology and AI, is an increasing corresponding discourse on AI governance and ethics, leading to a proliferation of documentation, including policies, strategies and frameworks from a variety of different agencies. Detailing approaches and plans for dealing with the impact of AI in various sectors and fields, such documents articulate the many social, legal, ethical and policy implications of autonomous and intelligent systems. As of January 2022, more than 500 documents related to AI from a range of sources have been produced (Fjeld et al., 2020; Jobin et al., 2019; Schiff et al., 2021). Analysis of a corpus of largely 'grey literature' found blind spots in the literature regarding both representation from the Global South and women (Roche et al., 2021). A review of the role of underrepresented groups in the broader AI discourse reveals voices from the Global South and consideration of marginalised populations are largely absent from the conversation, with this suggesting careful consideration should be given to the context in which research is conducted.

The proposed ethical frameworks and governance models are also reflective of power structures within the society in which they are developed. As technology is *"ultimately influenced by the people who build it and the data that feeds it"* (Chowdhury & Mulani, 2018), it is influenced by the cultural and social context. Similarly, any ethical frames of reference are situated in their context, meaning there is a risk of ethnocentrism. It cannot be assumed that ethical guidelines developed and accepted in a Global North context can be applied directly in any other environment. As noted earlier, there are particular challenges in collecting data in resource-constrained environments which can further enhance the dominance of Western or Northern research paradigms. Ownership of data in these environments is also a difficulty with power shifting from traditional development actors to corporations and public-private partnerships. While Kwet (2019) characterised United States (US) dominance of the digital ecosystem in many African countries as an insidious form of *"digital colonialism"*, Taylor and Broeders (2015) observed how datafication is affecting power dynamics in the Global South. Concerned at the growth in data collection and processing by large corporations in these countries, they identify the risk of development interventions becoming a by-product of *"informational capitalism"*. Within this context, it is therefore imperative that consideration is given to not only the power structures at play but the ethical framework guiding the sourcing and collection of data and the methodology underpinning the research approach adopted.

4 Specific Challenges Associated with Data Collection in the Global South

As mentioned, the primary motivation for this paper is the authors' personal experiences of a wide variety of practical difficulties associated with collecting data in the Global South and the dearth of literature on this topic. Personal experiences in the aforementioned research projects have shown that it is both challenging and extremely ambitious for a researcher from the Global North to attempt any level of understanding of the social, cultural, political and ethical nuances at play in these research projects in any significantly way. Research in such contexts and settings is highly likely to involve multiple interactions of ethical, structural, cultural, agential, political, social and technological factors which the researcher may not fully understand and have little experience of. The task at hand is made even more difficult when the researcher comes from a significantly different social and cultural background and the research site is located thousands of kilometres away from the researcher's home and place of work. The following subsections discuss these ethical, philosophical, social, cultural, and practical challenges in more detail.

4.1 Finding and Accessing a Suitable Research Project

Those of us interested in conducting research in the Global South are likely to find it difficult to negotiate access to a suitable project at a stage where research is appropriate or even possible. There are currently many research projects at various stages of completion around the world, but these projects may not be suitable as research sites for a variety of reasons including: the project may be too small, the project may be at an inappropriate stage of development, the project is already the subject of research from other researchers and institutions, or the project may be based in a country that is not possible to access as a result of global politics, bureaucracy, war or disease epidemic. Additionally, many such projects in the Global South do not allow access to external researchers for many reasons including the disruption the researcher might potentially cause, the additional costs the project implementer may have to incur, or the additional resources that may need to be deployed or redeployed when the research visits the research site.

A further practical difficulty associated with research based in the Global South is the likelihood that there will be a significant amount of additional work involved for the researcher. This includes the work needed to establish the various networks and collaborations required to carry out the research. This task is made more challenging as many of these collaborations may be extensive and geographically dispersed. In particular, NGOs may require extensive information about the nature of the research and the research frameworks to be used, as well as the research questions and research methodologies to be applied. They may also require details of how specifically the research would be disseminated across partner NGOs and academic networks, and how the research would be fed back to their people at community level in the field.

4.2 Poor Infrastructure and Difficulty of Travel

A number of practical and infrastructural issues in terms of accessing research participants are also likely to exist when researching in the Global South. Normally researchers from the Global North do not face significant difficulty getting a tourist visa, but getting a research-specific visa may be troublesome requiring various documentation and delayed approval processes (Musasa, 2021). Moreover, if the research is funded by a time-critical grant, such delay may be costly in terms of fund utilisation. Once a visa is secured, poor infrastructure and difficulty of travel may pose challenges in some resource-poor countries. Issues such as water purity, food quality, and disease may pose a significant health risk to the researcher. Researchers working in Europe and North America have the opportunity to avail of public transport, power and light, security, and are somewhat assured of their own personal safety. Research in the Global South may be far more challenging when the researcher does not have a source of electricity to power their laptop or a source of light to write notes by. Other practical challenges include the difficulty of travel to the research sites, the vast size and unequal travel infrastructure, and possible communication difficulties. In addition, there may be frequent obstructions on the roads such as fallen trees and floods.

4.3 Remotely Managing Field Research Staff

An alternative to problems highlighted in the previous section might involve hiring a local research assistants or a research team based in country. Hiring such local resources could be beneficial since not only do they possess contextual knowledge, they may also increase the interpretive validity of the study by conducting interviews in the local language (Maxwell 2012). However, this comes with its own challenges. Firstly, it may be difficult to find research assistants with the appropriate level of skills required to assist with research at a satisfactory level. Any research assistant is required to have a good working knowledge of research practices and principles. In addition, they will be required to have good computer skills and an excellent knowledge of both English and various local languages and dialects. Some project-specific requirements may also be critical. For instance, the Bangladeshi project (Vairis et al., 2020) required the hiring of a local technically competent person who could operate a 3D printer.

Once a good research assistant is found, the data collection protocol would need to be clearly defined and to be clearly explained to the research assistant(s). While this ensures that consistent data is collected from all participants, it also runs the risk of missing on any important insights due to a lack of flexibility. For instance, in the Malawi project there seemed to be a strong gender dimension in refugee entrepreneurship (Brown et al., 2022) which could not be investigated further simply because gender-related aspects were not part of the original data collection protocol. There is also the issue of their positionality (Turner, 2010) in terms of how much of their interpretation is incorporated (or otherwise) in the data collection and analysis process.

Despite this however, there are also possible practical issues when hiring research assistants. In some cases, it may be difficult to hire research assistant due to visa regimes. In the Sierra Leone, Malawi and Bangladesh cases the research assistants could be only hired and paid unofficially via researchers' own funds. Moreover, the fund transfers often proved to be problematic since out of all researchers, fund transfer mechanisms of only one researcher allowed transfer to Malawi. Such administrative process are complex and frequently require time and creative solutions. Money transfers eventually succeed but there are still monetary losses because of currency exchanges and bank fees. Even when such hiring and compensation mechanisms are resolved, there still may be problems in working remotely with research field staff. Remote meetings depend on internet availability and bandwidth, therefore, audio and particularly video calls are often impossible. Furthermore, time zones require different team members to work unsocial hours, sometimes late into the night or very early morning.

4.4 Social and Cultural Challenges that Come with Working the Global South

Perhaps most important are the social, cultural, and political challenges that come with working in the Global South. Any researcher coming from an individualistic culture may find it difficult to frame the norms and practises in collectivist culture. For instance, as opposed to an individual reading the consent form and recording their consent, a participant from a collectivist culture may wish to discuss it with their peer groups of family (Roberts et al., 2017). The cultural difference may also reflect in the attribution for success or failure. Participants from collectivist cultures may attribute success more to a charismatic leader (Pillai, 1995) whereas failure will be considered to be due to a lack of group effort (Yan and Hunt, 2005).

Another issue may be in terms of recording the data being collected. Our own experience suggests that the participants from the Global North are not averse to their interviews being recorded, given all the relevant protocols of informed consents are being communicated with the participating individuals transparently. In other parts of the world, we found the concept of informed consents to be considered as strange and inappropriate. In many cases, there is the existence of mistrust towards what are perceived as outsiders due to previous negative experiences with research. Often, the respondents in Global South countries or any vulnerable population within any country in the Global North are hesitant to get their responses recorded due to possible repercussions from the authorities or anyone who is perceived as superior or in a position of power. For instance, we have experience of a research project in India (not described in this paper) where the participants did not wish to be recorded so that the recording could not be 'used against them', not necessarily by the researcher but by anyone else who gets access to those recordings. Similarly, in our research in Malawi participants were concerned about informing us of the circumstances that led to them being in the refugee camp for the fear that their governments may find out about their whereabouts based on the information provided as part of the research project. This may be why some countries restrict data collection on what they perceive to be sensitive topics or with sensitive groups. In such cases, the researcher simply loses access to such vulnerable groups, such as Rohingyas in Myanmar or Uyghurs in China.

4.5 Research Rigour and Ethical Challenges

In many cases, research entities from the Global North may have unrealistic and disconnected research standards which are assumed to be followed irrespective of the geolocations and socio-cultural-political-economic realities in the ground in other parts of the world. For example, the Rohingyas from Myanmar maintain a rich oral history tradition due to the absence of the official alphabets for their language. Hence, whenever a Rohingya researcher has tried to publish about the plights of her/his people in any western research venue using English or any other accepted western language, her/his sources were considered to be not trustworthy or rigorous enough. Similarly, while we were working with the Rohingyas, our research team from different Global North universities had to depend to multi-level translations and data collection process (English to Bengali in the written format, then Bengali to Rohingya in the verbal format). Such complex processes meant the risk of losing valuable information between several translated iterations.

Also of relevance is the requirement to obtain ethical university from the University and many other bodies such as the NGO, the Ministry of Health and partner universities in the host country in the Global South. This is made complex as many countries have widely different requirements, for example some are regulating medical research while others have strict requirements to be applied where data is to be collected from individuals at community level. Also, privacy protection requirements across countries are often different and diverse, and in some cases are in conflict with each other. This is all further complicated by research funding entities who have their own requirements regarding ethical approval and rules for such things as compensation to researchers in another country. Conducting the fieldwork on the ground also raises ethical questions in terms of the health and safety of the research assistants.

4.6 'BLACK SWAN' Events

Even fieldwork is meticulously and carefully planned, some black swan events may provide significant obstacles and cause significant delay to the work. A good example of this is the Sierra Leone mHealth project which was severely interrupted by the Ebola virus epidemic which occurred in West Africa between May 2014 and March 2016. Travel to Sierra Leone was severely restricted during that time, and researcher's university would not approve research trips to any part of West Africa affected by Ebola. It was also extremely difficult to contact any of the people involved in the mHealth project as communications were poorer than normal and many key staff were redeployed to work on Ebola projects and were thus unavailable and difficult to contact. The ongoing Covid-19 pandemic was another black swan event that significantly restricted data collection for both the Malawi and Bangladesh projects. This was not just in terms of data collection by the lead researchers, but also by local research assistants due to health risks and government restrictions. Beyond epidemics and pandemics, socio-political conditions may also be of relevance when planning and conducting fieldwork. This includes political unrest, elections and changes of government. There are also likely to be institutional rules from each university which may prohibit travel to what are perceived to be dangerous or unstable countries, for instance currently Ukraine, Palestine, Afghanistan, Syria and South Sudan.

5 Discussion and Conclusions

As we have discussed in the previous sections, the six authors involved with this paper have significant experience of data collection in the Global South with previous sections of the paper outlining the many and significant challenges we have experienced when conducting research in this context. Our experiences may serve to make any researcher aspiring to work in such contexts fearful and reluctant! Despite the challenges associated with data collection outlined in this paper however, we suggest that it is very rewarding to carry out research in resource-constrained environments in the Global South with different social, cultural, political and ethical contexts. This is particularly relevant when the research being carried out has the potential to directly improve and enhance the lives of the local population and thus is likely to help many of the poorest and most disadvantaged people on the planet.

Our objective with this early-stage paper is to describe our experiences in the field in order to highlight these data collection issues. The purpose of this work is not to provide a significant contribution to either theory or practice, but instead we propose to act as a catalyst to promote this conversation amongst researchers from the various disciplines working in such situations. We note that this research-in-progress is not specific to the ICT4D community, but we do see this work as having specific relevance to this community for many reasons and we suggest that future iterations of this work will have the potential to make a significant contribution to the ICT4D field. Thus, we call on researchers and practitioners to further develop and expand this initial work in significant and creative ways in order to make a contribution to both theory and practice. Any such iteration of this work is highly likely to encourage and guide both experienced and early-stage researchers in their work in the Global South.

References

Asher, J.: Collecting data in challenging settings: in the global south—say, east Timor—data collection is not for the faint of heart or weak of stomach. Chance **23**(2), 6–13 (2010)

Avgerou, C.: Growth in ICT uptake in developing countries: new users, new uses, new challenges. J. Inf. Technol. **31**(329–333), 330 (2016)

Brown, S., Saxena, D., Wall, P.J.: The role of information and communications technology in refugee entrepreneurship: a critical realist case study. Electron. J. Inf. Syst. Develop. Countries **88**(1), e12195 (2022)

Chowdhury, R., Mulani, N.: Auditing Algorithms for Bias. Harvard Business Review (2018). https://hbr.org/2018/10/auditing-algorithms-for-bias

Connell, R.: Using southern theory: decolonizing social thought in theory, research and application. Plan. Theory **13**(2), 210–223 (2014)

Connell, R.: Southern Theory. Polity Press, Cambridge, UK (2007)

Fanon, F.: The Wretched of the Earth. Grove Press, New York (1961)

Comaroff, J., Comaroff, J.L.: Theory from the South. Routledge, London (2012)

de Sousa Santos, B.: Epistemologies of the South: Justice Against Epistemicide Abingdon: Routledge (2014)

Fjeld, J., Achten, N., Hilligoss, H., Nagy, A., Srikumar, M.: Principled artificial intelligence: mapping consensus in ethical and rights-based approaches to principles for AI. SSRN Electron. J. (2020). https://doi.org/10.2139/ssrn.3518482

Ismail, A., Kumar, N.: Engaging solidarity in data collection practices for community health. Proc. ACM Hum.-Comput. Interact. **2**(cscw), 1–24 (2018)

Jobin, A., Ienca, M., Vayena, E.: The global landscape of AI ethics guidelines. Nat. Mach. Intell. **1**(9), 389–399 (2019). https://doi.org/10.1038/s42256-019-0088-2

Kreps, D., Bass, J.M.: Southern theories in ICT4D. In International Conference on Social Implications of Computers in Developing Countries, pp. 3–13. Springer, Cham (2019)

Kwet, M.: Digital colonialism: US empire and the new imperialism in the global South. Race Class **60**(4), 3–26 (2019). https://doi.org/10.1177/0306396818823172

Lebel, J., McLean, R.: A better measure of research from the global south (2018)

Maxwell, J.: Understanding and validity in qualitative research. Harv. Educ. Rev. **62**(3), 279–301 (1992)

Louis-Charles, H.M., Howard, R., Remy, L., Nibbs, F., Turner, G.: Ethical considerations for postdisaster fieldwork and data collection in the Caribbean. Am. Behav. Sci. **64**(8), 1129–1144 (2020)

Musasa, G.: Qualitative research in the politically hostile environment of zimbabwe: a practical guide. Qual. Rep. **26**(1), 115–124 (2021)

Pillai, R.: Context and charisma: the role of organic structure, collectivism, and crisis in the emergence of charismatic leadership. In: Academy of Management Proceedings, vol. 1995, no. 1, pp. 332–336. Briarcliff Manor, NY 10510: Academy of Management (1995).

Roberts, L.R., Jadalla, A., Jones-Oyefeso, V., Winslow, B., Taylor, E.J.: Researching in collectivist cultures: reflections and recommendations. J. Transcult. Nurs. **28**(2), 137–143 (2017)

Roberts, K., et al.: 'When you are a data collector you must expect anything'. Barriers, boundaries and breakthroughs: insights from the South African data-collection experience. Glob. Health Promot. **27**(2), 54–62 (2020)

Roche, C., Lewis, D., Wall, P.J.: Artificial Intelligence Ethics: An Inclusive Global Discourse? (2021). *arXiv preprint* arXiv:2108.09959

Schiff, D., Borenstein, J., Biddle, J., Laas, K.: AI Ethics in the public, private, and NGO sectors: a review of a global document collection. IEEE Trans. Technol. Soc. **2**(1), 31–42 (2021). https://doi.org/10.1109/TTS.2021.3052127

Schatz, E., et al.: Working with teams of "insiders" qualitative approaches to data collection in the global south. Demogr. Res. **32**, 369–396 (2015)

Taylor, L., Broeders, D.: In the name of development: power, profit and the datafication of the global South. Geoforum **64**, 229–237 (2015). https://doi.org/10.1016/j.geoforum.2015.07.002

Turner, S.: Research Note: The silenced assistant. Reflections of invisible interpreters and research assistants. Asia Pac. Viewpoint, **51**(2), 206–219 (2010)

WHO (2013). https://www.who.int/cholera/countries/SierraLeoneCountryProfile2013.pdf

World Health Organization (WHO): Ebola Situation Report. World Health Organization, Geneva (2016)

World Bank (2017). https://data.worldbank.org/indicator/SP.POP.TOTL?locations=SL

Yan, J., Hunt, J.G.J.: A cross cultural perspective on perceived leadership effectiveness. Int. J. Cross Cult. Manage. **5**(1), 49–66 (2005)

Young, J.C., Lynch, R., Boakye-Achampong, S., Jowaisas, C., Sam, J., Norlander, B.: Volunteer geographic information in the Global South: Barriers to local imp (2021)

Seeking for a Framework to Advance Fintech-Mediated Digital Financial Inclusion for Brazilian Small Business Companies

Rogerio de Castro Melo[1]([⊠]) [iD], Elaine Tavares[1] [iD], and Eduardo H. Diniz[2] [iD]

[1] UFRJ/COPPEAD School of Business, Rio de Janeiro, Brazil
{rogerio.melo,elaine.tavares}@coppead.ufrj.br
[2] FGV/EAESP, São Paulo, Brazil
eduardo.diniz@fgv.br

Abstract. This research-in-progress aims to study digital financial inclusion, mediated by fintech, of Brazil's micro and small business companies. Digital financial inclusion is a critical factor in helping reduce social inequalities and promote economic growth, acting as a shortcut to achieve sustainable development goals (SDGs). Digital technologies in the financial market bring the promise of digital financial inclusion induced by fintech. However, the complexity of financial systems leads us to explain better the business environment and the social context of this phenomenon. Thus, we will conduct a case study on Brazilian Development Bank (BNDES), the leading Development Finance Institution (DFI) and a key actor in the financial inclusion agenda in Brazil that uses a digital platform to partner with fintech and give credit loans to small businesses. We aim to produce a framework to explain better the business environment of the digital financial inclusion induced by fintech for micro and small business companies.

Keywords: Digital financial inclusion · Fintech · Business environment · Micro and small businesses · SDG

1 Introduction

This research-in-progress aims to study how to advance digital financial inclusion, mediated by fintech, for small business companies in Brazil, given the business environment and the social context encompassing technology, the financial market, and the policy regulations.

Digital financial inclusion can be defined as the digital access to and use of formal financial services by the underserved segments of society [9]. Also, it is a key factor in achieving sustainable development and reducing social inequalities [38].

Digital technologies disrupt financial markets [13] and bring the promise of financial inclusion mediated by fintech, as suggested by several studies. Gomber *et al.* [16], Milian *et al.* [26], Lagna & Ravishankar [23], Gálvez-Sánchez *et al.* [14], Arner *et al.* [3], and Sahay *et al.* [33] point to an increasing interest of the scientific community to research

© IFIP International Federation for Information Processing 2022
Published by Springer Nature Switzerland AG 2022
Y. Zheng et al. (Eds.): ICT4D 2022, IFIP AICT 657, pp. 619–628, 2022.
https://doi.org/10.1007/978-3-031-19429-0_38

not only on fintech and financial inclusion but also on its effects on small businesses and its relationships with sustainability.

One purpose of those new technologies is to offer better financial services [30], especially for poor individuals and small businesses companies, thus helping to advance financial inclusion in terms of access, use, and quality [32] for those underserved segments of the society.

Digital financial inclusion also has a relationship with sustainability. Sustainable Development Goals (SDGs) are a part of the 2030 Agenda for Sustainable Development that includes environmental, social, and economic dimensions and were adopted in 2015 by 195 countries, members of the United Nations, including Brazil. Relationships have been identified between digital financial inclusion and all the 17 SDGs [38]. At least five SDGs are directly linked with fintech for financial inclusion: SDG 5- Gender Equality, SDG 8- Decent Work and Economic Growth, SDG 9- Industry, Innovation, and Infrastructure, SDG 10- Reduced inequalities, and SDG 17 – Partnerships for the Goals [3].

According to the MSME finance gap study [22], USD 5,2 trillion is the estimated credit gap for the millions of formal and informal Small and Medium Enterprises (SMEs) in developing countries. It is around 19% of the Gross Domestic Product (GDP) of the 128 economies comprised by the study.

Brazil has about 17,3 million small businesses, classified as individual microentrepreneurs (MEI) and micro, small and medium companies. Those small companies contribute approximately 30% of the Brazilian Gross Domestic Product (GDP), representing USD 430 billion on average [35].

Credit is an important tool of financial inclusion for small business companies. However, especially in Brazil, small entrepreneurs have difficulties accessing credit and quality banking services [29]. A study of the credit for the small businesses in Brazil [15] pointed out that the credit demand overtakes the offers up to USD 33 billion, and the credit gap for those small enterprises, considering the first quarter of 2021, is USD 10 billion, on average.

Beyond that, several innovations in financial systems are occurring worldwide and in Brazil [25]. The Brazilian Central Bank (Banco Central do Brasil – BCB) is Brazil's leading bank system regulation of the National Financial System (Sistema Financeiro Nacional – SFN). It has initiated on the year 2016 a series of procedures and rules, revisited in 2019 at *Agenda BC#*, focused on five key aspects: inclusion, competition, transparency, education, and sustainability. The Brazilian instant payment system (PIX) and the open financial system, known as Open Banking, are being implemented as innovations of this agenda [25].

This scenario brings opportunities but also poses challenges for governments, businesses, and civil society [38] and risks in terms of financial stability [17], cyber security and hacking [30], network actors' growth and service scale, as well as unexpected effects of digital innovations [12].

This research aims to help to face these challenges using a qualitative approach with a case study on the Brazilian Development Bank (Banco Nacional de Desenvolvimento Econômico e Social - BNDES), the foremost Development Finance Institution (DFI) of

Brazil, a government-owned bank, one of the major DFIs in the world and one of the key actors on the financial inclusion agenda in Brazil [36].

The bank uses a digital platform, Canal MPME (which stands for Micro, Pequenas e Médias Empresas, or Micro, Small and Medium Enterprises - MSMEs), to partner with financial agents including fintech, which is the main tool to give credit loans to MSMEs [4, 25].

Recent studies have proposed literature reviews on the thematic covered by this study. Still, a gap remains in the body of knowledge on Management Information Systems (MIS), as explained in the next section.

2 Formulating the Research Question: Initial Findings from the Literature Review

Digital financial inclusion in the context of a digital revolution in financial services is a complex phenomenon that allows for a qualitative approach where reality is socially constructed [39].

We have found recent illustrative literature review studies on fintech [26], fintech for financial inclusion [23], financial inclusion itself [14], and digital finance and SME [31, 44]. However, those initial results reveal a gap regarding the social context and business environment related to digital financial inclusion, mediated by fintech, for micro and small business companies and its impacts on SDGs.

The systematic literature review to be conducted in our study intends to use the structured concept-driven approach proposed by Webster & Watson [41] to identify new thematic areas and possibilities of research, thus contributing to the Information Systems (IS) field.

Lagna & Ravishankar [23] argue that IS research on fintech for financial inclusion should be more engaged and needs to consider the principles of making a responsible IS research [19] and a better world with ICTs [40]. The authors have presented a literature review that uses the "IS research on fintech" and the "ICT4D research on financial inclusion" thematic to propose a new research agenda, "Fintech and the promise of financial inclusion."

One of the research opportunities identified in the Lagna & Ravishankar study [23] is the "*Business environment of fintech-led financial inclusion.*" The authors agree that the financial inclusion business environment is a complex phenomenon. This complexity is also cited in studies such as Leonardi *et al.* [24] that illustrate the Corresponding banking system implementation in Brazil, where technology is just one piece of a broader network of financial inclusion with several actors like banks, retail stores, policymakers, and customers.

Gomber *et al.* [18] also point to the complexity of the business environment, which comprises the technology, the financial market, and the regulations involving financial services: "*Financial services are created and delivered through complex systems in business with processes, organizational and operational structures, human capital and talent, and a variety of choice behaviors, subject to ethical, regulatory, and legal restrictions*" (p. 227).

Joia & Cordeiro [20], studying fintech and financial inclusion, shed light on the importance of public policies and a regulatory environment for fintech. The research also points out that one of the drivers of fintech-induced financial inclusion should be to assist in managing formal and informal micro and small businesses.

Following the financial inclusion thematic, Gálvez-Sánchez *et al.* [14] conducted a literature review study showing a growing interest of the scientific community in fintech research to advance financial inclusion and encourage further research investigation between financial inclusion, the 2030 Agenda, and the SDGs.

These implementations need to come up way responsible and sustainably as a short-cut to achieving Sustainable Development Goals (SDGs). Evidence shows gaps related to digital financial inclusion and SMEs. On SDG 5- Gender Equality the small business owned by women, faces an estimated credit gap of USD 1,7 trillion globally. Considering SDG 8- Decent Work and Economic Growth, projections show that, by 2030, 470 million employments are needed. Also, the unmet SME credit gap, until 2015, was around USD 5 trillion. At SDG 9- Industry, Innovation and Infrastructure, SMEs have constrained access to finance, especially in emerging economies [38].

Zhiqiang *et al.* [44] presented a study on digital financial inclusion and SMEs' finance constraints, revealing that digital finance technologies influence the relationship between SMEs and traditional banks. They also point out that local bank branches and fintech can be game changers to reduce the effects of financial constraints for those small businesses.

Zalan & Toufaily [43] also suggest that SMEs can benefit from the innovative technologies brought by fintech to reduce the side effects from risk-averse banks and do not offer quality credit lending to these small businesses.

Regarding the business environment and social context of digital financial inclusion mediated by fintech, Zalan & Toufaily [43] argue that fintech in the emerging markets does not always disrupt the whole financial market but aims to partner with traditional financial institutions, such as banks.

Toward this direction, Zalan & Toufaily [43] have proposed a framework based on a qualitative approach that comprises a hybrid platform into a broader ecosystem. It allows for partnership between banks and fintech (Fig. 1).

Although the framework was not designed to address the financial inclusion phenomenon, Zalan & Toufaily [43] cite that the opportunity to promote financial inclusion mediated by fintech was mentioned by several respondents during their research.

We believe Zalan & Toufaily model [43] can be used as a starting point for the framework that will be constructed during our research for a number of reasons.

First, Application Programming Interfaces (APIs), located at the center of the hybrid platform model, allow data exchange and communications between different organizations. As Zalan & Toufaily [43] point out, a collaboration between banks and fintech is necessary to enable innovative solutions, and APIs are a key element in this scenario.

Open APIs are a Digital Financial Services (DFS) model that has emerged to facilitate the integration between traditional banks and those new digital financial actors, mostly fintech. The most recent innovations in the financial sector, like Open Banking, also use APIs to exchange data between its participants [25, 42]. Moreover, OpenAPIs have shown the potential to foster financial inclusion [30] as they can reveal new business models [8].

Second, the broader ecosystem proposed by Zalan & Toufaily model [43] surrounds the hybrid platform and includes financial services' actors in the social context that encompasses technology, the financial market and the policy regulators. However, considering that DFIs are key actors in the financial inclusion agenda [25, 35], we propose that development finance institutions must be considered in the framework that will be developed during our research.

Third, considering the known challenge of digital financial inclusion and the business environment of fintech mediated digital financial inclusion, we believe Zalan & Toufaily model [43] can be a starting point to help answer the research question, "What is the business environment and social context that encompasses the technology, the financial market and the policy regulations that amplifies the digital financial inclusion, induced by fintech, of Brazilian micro and small business companies?".

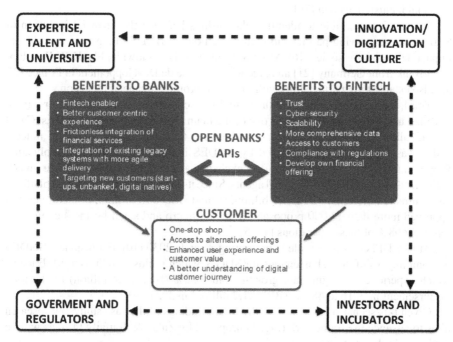

Fig. 1. Zalan & Toufaily model intends to be used as a starting point for our research. Source: Zalan & Toufaily [43]

In the next section, the proposed case study chosen to help find insights from the research question will be explained.

3   Case Study

To understand the phenomenon of Brazilian small business companies' digital financial inclusion, mediated by fintech, we intend to use an abductive approach [11] and the case study methodology proposed by Pan & Tan [28].

The case study proposed in this research is the Brazilian Development Bank (BNDES). This government-owned bank institution acts as a second-tier credit loan for micro and small business companies and entrepreneurs. In this indirect model of operation, the development bank passes along its money resources to financial agents, which then deal loans with SMEs and entrepreneurs' customers [7].

There is a number of reasons to choose BNDES as a case study. First, the bank is the leading Development Finance Institution (DFI) in Brazil, founded in 1952, and one of the major DFIs in the world. It has a significant role in helping SMEs and disbursed in 2020 more than 34 billion Brazilian Reais (BRL) (around USD 6 billion) for more than 460.000 Brazilian SMEs [5]. Also, BNDES is one of the key actors in the Brazilian financial inclusion agenda [36].

Second, it is possible to identify relationships between the financial inclusion of SMEs and the growing partnership with fintech on the BNDES long-term agenda and impact deliveries for society [6]. Moreover, other DFIs worldwide, like KfW Development Bank from Germany [21] and Agence Française de Développement in France [2], are also establishing partnerships with fintech to promote financial inclusion.

Third, the bank participates in the digital financial inclusion business environment in Brazil using a digital platform as one of the main tools to give credit to SMEs. Canal MPME allows for business partnerships between financial agents, including fintech, and it was conceived and developed by BNDES internal teams. It uses Application Programming Interfaces (APIs) for data exchange and communication with the fintech authorized to act as BNDES financial agents. Since its launch in 2017, the digital platform has contracted more than BRL 1,9 billion, around USD 350 million, in credit and has approved more than 13.000 proposals. Brazilian micro and small business companies represent 98% of these operations [4, 25].

At last, DFIs play a key role in promoting Agenda 2030 [10]. For instance, BNDES is promoting a shift in disbursements for SDG 8, which is closely related to SME loans, which experienced a significant growth from 32,2% (BRL 28,4 billion) of the total disbursement in 2016 to 48,0% (BRL 31,2 billion) in 2021 [10].

Given this scenario and based on the future findings of the case study, our research aims to advance the framework (Fig. 1) proposed by Zalan & Toufaily [43], as will be explained in the next section.

4   Proposed Research Design and Expected Contributions to the IS Field

The complexity of the financial information systems business environment phenomenon leads us to consider those three dimensions of our research design: the technology, the financial market, and the regulation.

Taking Zalan & Toufaily's [43] framework as a starting point, our study will consist of three phases to encompass those three dimensions in our future framework proposal.

In the first phase, we aim to conduct a systematic literature review to advance theoretical contributions in IS field. Topics include the advances on the financial inclusion agenda in Brazil, considering the digital financial inclusion induced by fintech, financial inclusion and SMEs, and the relationships with SDGs. The findings of the systematic literature review will also help to choose the theoretical models that will be used in our study.

The second phase of the study will be data gathering and analysis. Primary data will be collected by semi-structured interviews conducted with the following actors: employees from several organizational levels, ranging from technology to business areas, from operational to managerial levels, and that deal with fintech partnerships and SME credit lending from BNDES. CEOs and CTOs from different sizes of Canal MPME partner fintech companies, as well as representatives of ABFINTECHS [1], the primary fintech hub association in Brazil will also be interviewed. Our research plans to interview small business entrepreneurs that have and have not used Canal MPME to get loans from fintechs and, at last, employees of BCB that deal with the policy regulation of fintech and financial inclusion.

These data will be codified using the approach suggested by Saldaña [34]. A qualitative data analysis software tool will also be considered [37].

Then, the data will be complemented by researcher observations and financial inclusion workshops conducted with the study participants. Also, we plan to confront those data with secondary data analysis such as internal organizational reports from BNDES, partner fintech companies, and BCB. At last, we intend to use news related to the research on the media and the social networks as another source of secondary data.

The coding categories will come from the framework Zalan & Toufaily [43] that will be used as a starting point for our research and from the literature review. Other categories will arise from the case study.

In the third phase of the study, we will adjust and validate the proposed framework using a round of specialists, as indicated by the Delphi method approach [27].

In our research, we aim to produce a framework that contributes to IS field and helps to explain better the business environment of the digital financial inclusion induced by fintech for micro and small business companies. We believe this future framework can be used as a tool to advance digital financial inclusion and to guide scholars, practitioners, policy regulators, development finance organizations, fintech companies, and their associations.

References

1. ABFINTECHS: Associação Brasileira de Fintechs (2022). https://www.abfintechs.com.br/. Accessed 04 Jan 2022
2. AFD: Agence Française de Dévelopment. Fintech helps African entrepreneurs grow. AFD, Paris (2018). https://www.afd.fr/en/ressources/fintech-helps-african-entrepreneurs-grow. Accessed 04 Jan 2022
3. Arner, D.W., Buckley, R.P., Zetzsche, D.A., Veidt, R.: Sustainability, FinTech and financial inclusion. Eur. Bus. Organiz. Law Rev. **21**(1), 7–35 (2020)

4. BNDES: Banco Nacional de Desenvolvimento Econômico e Social. Canal MPME. BNDES, Rio de Janeiro (2022a). https://ws.bndes.gov.br/canal-mpme/#/home. Accessed 04 Jan 2022

5. BNDES: Banco Nacional de Desenvolvimento Econômico e Social. Resultados financeiros em destaque 2020 - 4° Trimestre. BNDES, Rio de Janeiro (2022b). https://www.bndes.gov.br/wps/portal/site/home/transparencia/prestacao-de-contas/informacoes-financeiras/resultados-financeiros-destaque/bndes/resultado-financeiro-em-destaque-2020-4-trimestre. Accessed 29 Oct 2022

6. BNDES: Banco Nacional de Desenvolvimento Econômico e Social. Conheça a agenda de longo prazo do BNDES. BNDES, Rio de Janeiro (2022c). https://www.bndes.gov.br/wps/portal/site/home/quem-somos/planejamento-estrategico/agenda-de-longo-prazo-do-bndes. Accessed 03 Jan 2022

7. Borça Júnior, G.R., Faleiros, J.P.M., Zylberberg, R.S.: O modelo indireto do BNDES: benefícios, diagnóstico e perspectivas = The indirect model of BNDES: advantages, diagnosis and perspectives. Revista do BNDES, Rio de Janeiro 27(53), 53–88 (2020)

8. CGAP: Open APIs for digital finance (2022a). https://www.cgap.org/topics/collections/open-apis. Accessed 04 Jan 2022

9. CGAP: What Is Digital Financial Inclusion and Why Does It Matter? (2022b). http://www.cgap.org/blog/what-digital-financial-inclusion-and-why-does-it-matter. Accessed 05 Jan 2022

10. Chan, I.Y.R.K., Freitas, M.B.D.: O papel dos bancos de desenvolvimento na Agenda 2030: o caso do BNDES = The role of development banks in the 2030 Agenda: the case of the BNDES. Revista do BNDES, Rio de Janeiro 28(56), 11–54 (2021)

11. Dubois, A., Gadde, L.: Systematic combining: an abductive approach to case research. J. Bus. Res. 55(7), 553–560 (2002). https://doi.org/10.1016/S0148-2963(00)00195-8. ISSN 0148-2963

12. Foster, C., Heeks, R.: Innovation and scaling of ICT for the bottom-of-the-pyramid. J. Inf. Technol. 28(4), 296–315 (2013)

13. Gabor, D., Brooks, S.: The digital revolution in financial inclusion: international development in the fintech era. New Polit. Econ. 22(4), 423–436 (2017). https://doi.org/10.1080/13563467.2017.1259298

14. Gálvez-Sánchez, F.J., Lara-Rubio, J., Verdú-Jóver, A.J., Meseguer-Sánchez, V.: Research advances on financial inclusion: a bibliometric analysis. Sustainability 13, 3156 (2021). https://doi.org/10.3390/su13063156

15. Gonzalez, L., Barreira, B., Ridolfo, A.: Crédito para os pequenos em tempos de pandemia. São Paulo: [FGV EAESP, 2021]. In: Working Paper - GVcemif - Centro de Estudos de Microfinanças e Inclusão Financeira (2021)

16. Gomber, P., Koch, J.-A., Siering, M.: Digital Finance and FinTech: current research and future research directions. J. Bus. Econ. 87(5), 537–580 (2017). https://doi.org/10.1007/s11573-017-0852-x

17. Gomber, P., Kauffman, R., Parker, C., Weber, B.: On the fintech revolution: Interpreting the forces of innovation, disruption, and transformation in financial services. J. Manag. Inf. Syst. 35(1), 220–265 (2018)

18. Gomber, P., Kauffman, R., Parker, C., Weber, B.: Special issue: financial information systems and the fintech revolution. J. Manag. Inf. Syst. 35(1), 12–18 (2018)

19. ISJ: Call for papers: Special issue on responsible IS research for a better world. Inf. Syst. J. (2019). https://onlinelibrary.wiley.com/page/journal/13652575/homepage/special_issues.htm. Accessed 03 Jan 2022

20. Joia, L.A., Cordeiro, J.P.V.: Unlocking the potential of fintechs for financial inclusion: a Delphi-based approach. Sustainability 13(21), 11675 (2021)

21. KFW: KfW Development Bank. Facilitating access to SME finance. KfW Development Bank, Frankfurt am Main, 1 March 2017 (2017). https://www.kfw-entwicklungsbank.de/Internati onal-financing/KfW-Development-Bank/News/News-Details_401856.html. Accessed 03 Jan 2022
22. Khanna, M., et al.: MSME finance gap: assessment of the shortfalls and opportunities in financing micro, small, and medium enterprises in emerging markets. The World Bank Group, Washington, D.C. (2017). http://documents.worldbank.org/curated/en/653831510 568517947/MSME-finance-gap-assessment-of-the-shortfalls-and-opportunities-in-financ ing-micro-small-and-medium-enterprises-in-emerging-markets. Accessed 03 Jan 2022
23. Lagna, A., Ravishankar, M.N.: Making the world a better place with fintech research. Inf. Syst. J. 1–42 (2021). https://doi.org/10.1111/isj.12333
24. Leonardi, P., Bailey, D., Diniz, E., Sholler, D., Nardi, B.: Multiplex appropriation in complex systems implementation: the case of Brazil's correspondent banking system. MIS Q. **40**(2), 461–473 (2016)
25. Melo, R.D.C., Almeida, H.T.V.D., Braga, H.V., Moscon, L.M., Alvim, R.B., Silva, T.M.D.D.: As inovações dos serviços financeiros e o open banking: um caminho possível para acelerar a inclusão financeira de micro e pequenas empresas no Brasil? = Innovations on the financial sector and open banking: a possible pathway to accelerate financial inclusion of micro and small enterprises in Brazil? Revista do BNDES, Rio de Janeiro **28**(56), 519–572 (2021)
26. Milian, E.Z., Spinola, M.D.M., de Carvalho, M.M.: Fintechs: a literature review and research agenda. Electron. Commer. Res. Appl. **34**, 100833 (2019)
27. Mullen, P.: Delphi: myths and reality. J. Health Organ. Manag. **17**(1), 37–52 (2003). https://doi.org/10.1108/14777260310469319
28. Pan, S., Tan, B.: Demystifying case research: a structured–pragmatic–situational (SPS) approach to conducting case studies. Inf. Organiz. **21**(3), 161–176 (2011). https://doi.org/10.1016/j.infoandorg.2011.07.001. ISSN 1471-7727
29. Paula, G.M.: Inclusão financeira de pequenas e médias empresas no Brasil. CEPAL, Santiago. (Documentos de projetos) (2017). https://repositorio.cepal.org/bitstream/handle/11362/43229/1/S1701094_pt.pdf. Accessed 03 Jan 2022
30. Pazarbasioglu, C., Mora, A.G., Uttamchandani, M., Natarajan, H., Feyen, E., Saal, M.: Digital financial services. World Bank Group, Washington (2020). http://pubdocs.worldbank.org/en/230281588169110691/Digital-Financial-Services.pdf. Accessed 03 Jan 2022
31. Rasheed, R., Siddiqui, S.H., Mahmood, I., Khan, S.N.: Financial inclusion for SMEs: role of digital micro-financial services. Rev. Econ. Dev. Stud. **5**(3), 571–580 (2019)
32. Roa, M.J.: Financial inclusion in Latin America and the Caribbean: access, usage and quality, vol. 10. CEMLA, Mexico, DF (2015)
33. Sahay, R., et al.: The Promise of Fintech: Financial Inclusion in the Post COVID-19 Era. IMF PFFIEA no. 20/09, July (2020). https://doi.org/10.5089/9781513512242.087
34. Saldaña, J.: The Coding Manual for Qualitative Researchers. Sage Publications, Thousand Oaks (2015)
35. SEBRAE: Atualização de estudo sobre participação de micro e pequenas empresas na economia nacional. FGV Projetos, Brasília, D.F. (2020). https://datasebrae.com.br/wp-content/upl oads/2020/04/Relat%C3%B3rio-Participa%C3%A7%C3%A3o-mpe-pib-Na.pdf. Accessed 03 Jan 2022
36. Sela, V.M., Gonzalez, L., Christopoulos, T.P.: Construction of the financial inclusion agenda in light of the actor-network theory. Revista de Administração Pública **54**, 162–180 (2020)
37. Sinkovics, R.R., Penz, E., Ghauri, P.N.: Enhancing the trustworthiness of qualitative research in international business. Manag. Int. Rev. **48**(6), 689–714 (2008)
38. UNSGSA: Igniting SDG progress through digital financial inclusion. United Nations Secretary-General's Special Advocate for Inclusive Finance for Development (UNSGSA)

(2018). https://www.unsgsa.org/files/1615/3738/5820/SDG_Compendium_Digital_Financ ial_Inclusion_September_2018.pdf. Accessed 03 Jan 2022

39. Walsham, G.: Interpretive case studies in IS research: nature and method. Eur. J Inf. Syst. **4**, 74–81 (1995). https://doi.org/10.1057/ejis.1995.9
40. Walsham, G.: Are we making a better world with ICTs? Reflections on a future agenda for the IS field. J. Inf. Technol. **27**(2), 87–93 (2012)
41. Webster, J., Watson, R.: Analyze the past to prepare for the future: writing a literature review. MIS Q. **26**(2), xiii–xxiii (2002)
42. Zachariadis, M., Ozcan, P.: The API economy and digital transformation in financial services: the case of Open Banking. SWIFT Institute Working Paper, London, n. 2016001 (2017). https://papers.ssrn.com/sol3/papers.cfm?abstract_id=2975199. Accessed 03 Jan 2022
43. Zalan, T., Toufaily, E.: The promise of fintech in emerging markets: not as disruptive. Contemp. Econ. **11**(4), 415–431 (2017)
44. Zhiqiang, L., Junjie, W., Hongyu, L., Duc, K.N.: Local bank, digital financial inclusion and SME financing constraints: empirical evidence from China. Emerg. Mark. Finance Trade (2021). https://doi.org/10.1080/1540496X.2021.1923477

Author Index